ISBN: 9781290632461

Published by:
HardPress Publishing
8345 NW 66TH ST #2561
MIAMI FL 33166-2626

Email: info@hardpress.net
Web: http://www.hardpress.net

ENCYCLOPEDIA

of

VIRGINIA BIOGRAPHY

UNDER THE EDITORIAL SUPERVISION OF

LYON GARDINER TYLER, LL. D.

President of William and Mary College, Williamsburg; Author of "Parties and Patronage in the United States," "The Cradle of the Republic," "Williamsburg, the Old Colonial Capital," "England in America," "The Letters and Times of the Tylers," etc.; Vice-President of the Virginia Historical Society, Member of the Maryland Historical Society, and various other societies.

VOLUME I

NEW YORK
LEWIS HISTORICAL PUBLISHING COMPANY
1915

Copyright, 1915
Lewis Historical Publishing Company

VIRGINIA BIOGRAPHY

PREFACE

The successful planting of an English Colony at Jamestown in 1607 had the effect that England had become the world power in the place of Spain.

One hundred years previous, Spain became the head of the dominant religious influence and military power of Europe. She had the monopoly of America, and her treasury was filled with the gold and silver of Mexico and Peru. Her title to the whole of the new continent was based upon the great discovery of Columbus in 1492. The conscious rivalry of England with this colossal power did not begin till Elizabeth ascended the throne in 1558. Then it was the rising of a nation instinct with enthusiasm, daring, and activity. For the negation of the exclusive right of Spain to the American continent, the almost forgotten voyage to North America of John Cabot in 1497, under the auspices of Henry VII., an English King, was revived by Richard Hakluyt. The next fifty years were replete with deeds of splendor and glory. First, Sir John Hawkins threw down the barriers which for so long had withheld English ships from the Western continent by sailing to the West Indies and selling negroes to the Spanish planters. Then Drake and Cavendish hurled themselves upon the Spanish settlements on the west coast of South America and plundered them of their gold and circumnavigated the globe. Next, in their eager desire to outdo even Columbus in search for the East Indies, Frobisher and Davis performed their glorious voyages to the Northwest and wrote their names upon the icy waters of Labrador and British America. The grand Armada was overthrown in 1588, and the maritime power of Spain was utterly crushed by another great naval victory won by the English eight years later in the harbor of Cadiz.

Among the schemes to cut into the power of Spain was one contemplating the establishment of an English colony in North America. This noble design was conceived by Sir Humphrey Gilbert and promoted by his half brother Sir Walter Raleigh, and they are the glorious twin spirits that stand on the threshold of American history. Newfoundland and Roanoke are dedicated to their memories. Though the times were not yet ripe for success, their faith soared above all reverses. "We are as near Heaven by sea as by land," said the one as he yielded up his life in the stormy waters. "I shall yet live to see Virginia an English nation," said the other, as he went to confinement in the Tower of London, and eventually also to his death. In 1605, Spain, humbled and shorn of power, made peace with England; and now in the place of private enterprise like Gilbert's and Raleigh's, organized capital, under influences of noble spirits, like Sir Thomas Smythe, Richard Hakluyt, Sir

Edwin Sandys, Nichols Ferrar and the Earl of Southampton—worthy successors of Gilbert and Raleigh—undertook the solution of the problem. Raleigh, confined in the Tower, could not take an active part at this time, but his friends and relations were the chief actors and workers in the new colonization schemes.

Two large associations were formed—one composed of lords, knights and merchants of the city of London, and the other of residents in the cities of Bristol, Exeter and Plymouth, and they obtained from King James I., April 10, 1606, a joint charter which defined Virginia as the portion of North America lying between the 34th and 45th parallel of north latitude, practically the present United States. In this vast extent of territory the first Company, called the Virginia Company of London, was permitted to establish a settlement anywhere between 34 and 41 degrees; and the second, called the Plymouth Company, anywhere between 38 and 45 degrees. The actual jurisdiction of each Company was represented by a rectangle extending fifty miles north of the settlement and fifty miles south, and east and west 100 miles from the coast seaward, and 100 miles from the coast inland. The Plymouth Company was singularly unfortunate in its attempts, but the efforts of the Virginia Company were crowned with success; and by two new charters, 1609 and 1612, its jurisdiction was extended over the entire limit of its original sphere of possible settlement, and from sea to sea.

The subsequent history of Virginia affairs under the Company for nearly twenty years is one of stupendous selfsacrifice both in England and America. The men in England who had the supreme control gave freely of their money and time, and received no return except the satisfaction of having founded in America a fifth kingdom under the Crown. The men in Virginia incurred hardships without parallel in the world's history, and most of them went to the martyrdom of cruel death by climatic disease, starvation and Indian attack. It was but natural that, in those unprecedented conditions, those in England should try to shield themselves from the blame and throw upon the settlers the responsibility. But discriminating history has seen the light at last, and while the motives of the directors of the enterprise were always high and honorable, it is now recognized that in the government of the colony they made many and serious blunders. For fear of making the enterprise unpopular they refused to tell the English public the real truth as to the dangerous climate and the other natural conditions making for evil. Virginia, as a country, had to be "boomed," at all events. Thus the poor settlers, who, for the most part, consisted of the best materials in England—old sailors under Hawkins and Drake, or old soldiers of the Netherlands—were abused and shamelessly villified. The appalling mortality which overwhelmed them for a great number of years is itself a pathetic and passionate vindication. Never did any martyr suffer so patiently, so patriotically, as these devoted settlers did—a prey to Indian attack, martial law, and climatic diseases—influences which, as the records show, left but one settler alive at the end of a single year of residence, out of every five that came over.

Indeed, how can the body of the settlers be made responsible for the calamities that ensued when they lived under a form of government made for them by others, productive from the first of discord and faction; when they were not permitted to work for themselves, but for a present return of profit to the Company, had to give their time and labor to loading ships with sassafras, cedar, and other salable commodities; when they had no choice of the place of settlement, and which was selected in accordance with orders of the council in England; when they had no chance to till the fields, but were required to hunt for gold and silver mines and make tedious discoveries by land and water? Deprived of the opportunity to make their own living, they had to depend upon food sent from England, which, when it reached America, was often unfit for hogs to eat, and introduced all manner of disease. Above all, they had to deal with a climate which was singularly fatal to new comers, and to fight off numerous bands of fierce and ferocious Indians who surrounded them on all sides.

Thus, the conditions were in every respect the reverse of those of the Plymouth settlement in 1620 on Cape Cod Bay; for there the Pilgrim Fathers had the control of their own government, the advantage of a dry and healthful situation, a sparkling stream of fresh water at their doors, open fields deserted by the Indians, whose nearest town was forty miles distant, a bay teeming with fish and a country abounding in animals whose skins brought a large profit in England. And yet, favored as they were, had they not been succored by Virginia ships, the settlers there might have all perished of famine.

Nevertheless, the settlers in Virginia held grimly to their duty, and, the dying being constantly succeeded by fresh bands doomed also to early death, but as determined as themselves, prosperity at last succeeded to misfortune, and plenty and happiness to poverty and despair. When the civil wars in England broke out in 1642, the tone of society in Virginia was raised by the great influx of cavaliers and other persons of means who sought safety in Virginia. The clearing away of the woods improved the health conditions, and men came no longer over to make tobacco, but to make homes for themselves and their families. Virginia continued to grow and improve until, at the beginning of the American Revolution, she was the leading and most powerful of all the colonies.

The priorities of Virginia may be briefly stated. As the first permanent British Colony, she may claim as her product not only the present Virginia and Southland, but all the other English colonies in America, and indeed all the colonies of the present widespreading British Empire. She was the eldest of all, and the inspiration of all. Because her governors kept the New England coast clear of the French, and two ships sailing from Jamestown succored founder at Jamestown, and when, in 1622, they were at the point of starvation, she can lay claim to being the mother of New England. She had the first English institutions—trial by jury, law courts, representative lawmaking body, and free school. She was the first to proclaim the principle of the indissolubility of taxation and representation. She led in all events pointing to the American Revolution—that is to say—struck the first blow in the French and Indian war, out of which war sprung the idea of taxing America; rallied the opposition against the Stamp Act; and under the Revenue Act solved the four different problems that arose, proposing as a remedy for the first the policy of non-importation; for the second a system of intercolonial committees; for the third a general congress; and for the fourth—Independence!

The life of a State is seen best in the lives of the citizens. The aim of this book will be to give the biographies of all those who had any important connection with the founding of Virginia down to the American Revolution. Thus the book will be divided into four parts under the following headings:

I. The Founders; II. The Presidents and Governors; III. The Council of State; IV. The Burgesses and Other Prominent Citizens.

THE AUTHOR.

VIRGINIA BIOGRAPHY

I—THE FOUNDERS

Henry VII., King of England, was the son of Edward Tudor, Earl of Richmond, by his marriage with Margaret Beaufort, only daughter of John Duke of Beaufort. The deaths of Henry VI. and of his son Prince Edward made Henry the head of the House of Lancaster. He remained in Brittainy during the whole of the reign of Edward IV. But Edward's death in 1483, and the murder of his two sons by the usurper Richard, removed almost every rival belonging to the house of York that could dispute his pretensions. He made war against Richard and defeated him at Bosworth in Leicestershire, and became King in his place. In his administration of the government he was politic and prudent. He encouraged men of letters and was a great patron of commerce. He came very nearly anticipating Ferdinand and Isabella in sending out Columbus; and under his encouragement the Cabots discovered North America in 1497. Henry VII. was the father of Henry VIII., and grandfather of Queen Elizabeth. He died at Richmond, April 2, 1509.

Cabot, John, a Venetian navigator, and first discoverer of North America. He visited Arabia, and in 1491 was employed by some merchants in Bristol, England, in hunting for the mythical island of the seven cities and Brazil. In 1495, in one of these private voyages, he saw land. Encouraged accordingly, he petitioned Henry VII., King of England, to grant unto him and his three sons Lewis, Sebastian and Sanctius, a charter to discover and possess new lands. The letters about passed the seals on March 5, 1496, and on May 2, 1497. John Cabot sailed from Bristol with a small ship and 18 persons. Having reached the continent of North America, somewhere about Cape Breton Island, he coasted down 300 miles. He was three months on the voyage, and on his return received much honor, and the people, we are told, "ran after him like mad," for enlistment in his voyages. To show where he landed he made a chart and globe with the place designated. The King gave him presents and a pension out of the customs of the port of Bristol. Aided by Henry, Cabot sailed on a second voyage in the beginning of summer, 1498, with five ships, but it is probable that he died on the voyage, as the expedition seems to have returned under the charge of his son, Sebastian Cabot. Columbus never saw any part of the territory of the United States, and as a nation we trace back to the discoveries of John Cabot.

Cabot, Sebastian, second son of John Cabot, was probably born in Bristol, about 1477, and probably sailed with his father in many of his voyages. His name appears in the petition to Henry VII. and in the charter granted by the King, March 5, 1496. He probably went with his father in his voyage to America, May 2, 1497, and the voyage of 1498 which sailed under the father was probably, on account of the latter's death, under the son's charge on its return. Later under the auspices of Thomas Pert, vice-admiral of England, he paid a visit to South America and the West India Islands. Not finding much encouragement in England, which was not yet a maritime nation, he entered the service of the King of Spain and was appointed "pilot major." In 1526 he sailed to Brazil and spent four years in exploring the country, but was imprisoned a year on his return, on the charge of mismanagement. He was, however, soon reinstated in his former position, and remained for many years examiner of pilots at Seville, during which time he made his famous "mappe monde," which was first engraved in 1544. He returned to England on the death of Henry VIII., and Edward VI. gave him a pension and made him grand pilot of England. Under his leadership a Company of Discoverers, of which he was made governor for life, was formed. They sent out in 1553 an expedition under Sir Hugh Willoughby and Richard Chancellor, which reached the White Sea and discovered Russia. This ancient company, which still exists, has a direct connection with the settlement of Virginia. Sir Thomas Smythe, treasurer of the Virginia Company of London, was a successor of Cabot as governor of this company in 1607, and its ships were employed in taking emigrants to Virginia. Sebastian Cabot died about 1557.

Hawkins, William, son of John Hawkins, Esq., of Tavistock, Devonshire, and Joan, daughter of William Amidas, Esq., of Lancaster, Cornwall. He made several voyages to the coast of Africa and carried slaves from thence to Brazil in 1530, and after. He married Joan, daughter of William Trelawney, Esq., of Cornwall. He was the father of Sir John Hawkins.

Elizabeth, Queen of England, daughter of Henry VIII by Anne Boleyn, was born at Greenwich, September 7, 1533. She was educated by Grindall and Ascham, who made her a great scholar and an expert linguist. She succeeded to the throne on the death of her sister Mary, November 17, 1558. Her reign lasted 45 years, and it is sufficient to say that she held with honor and glory the central figure of a period that has hardly a parallel in history for the outburst of activity along all lines—literary, political, maritime and military. She encouraged especially Sir Humphrey Gilbert and Sir Walter Raleigh in their plans of colonizing Virginia, and when Sir Richard Grenville returned with his accounts of the new found land she gave it the name of "Virginia" in memory of herself as the Virgin Queen. She died March 24, 1603.

Cecil, William, Lord Burleigh, the great minister of State to Queen Elizabeth. He was born at Bourne, Lincolnshire, September 13, 1520. His biography would be almost a history of the times in which he lived. He patronized Sir Humphrey Gilbert and Sir Walter Raleigh, and all the other English voyagers for discovery. He was a man of immense capacity for business, and held the full confidence of the Queen. He died May 4, 1598.

Walsingham, Sir Francis, third and youngest son of William Walsingham, of Scadbury, parish of Chislehurst; principal Secretary of State of Queen Elizabeth in 1573, and "one of the pillars of her throne." He was a promoter of all the great expeditions during his time, and staunch friend of Gilbert's and Raleigh's plans to colonize America. He was born in 1536, died April 6, 1590, and was buried in St. Paul's Cathedral, London.

Hawkins, Sir John, a great navigator, son of William Hawkins, was born at Plymouth,

England, about 1532, entered the naval service in 1551, and went on various voyages into Spain, Portugal and the Canaries; he invented the chain pump for ships, 1558-59, following in the track of his father he visited Guinea in 1562, and sailed to the West Indies with a cargo of 300 negroes, whom he sold to the Spaniards residing there. He returned to England with a rich cargo of ginger, hides and pearls. In 1564 Hawkins repeated the experiment with greater success, and on his way home stopped in Florida and relieved the struggling colony of Huguenots planted there by Admiral Coligny and barbarously destroyed by the Spaniards soon after Hawkins' departure. The Queen rewarded him with a crest, consisting of "a demi moor in his proper colors, his hands behind him bound with a cord." In 1567 Hawkins went on a third expedition from Africa to the West Indies, but was attacked by the Spanish fleet in the harbor of San Juan de Ulloa, and most of his ships and men were destroyed; two ships escaped, commanded respectively by Hawkins and Drake. Pretending to be a traitor, he was made a grandee of Spain and he received large sums of money from Philip II., and in 1572 equipped a fleet and sailed to the Azores to lie in wait for Philip's Mexican fleet; appointed treasurer of the navy in 1573; as rear-admiral he had a great part in preparing England to resist the Spaniards, and commanded the left wing of the English fleet in the great battle with the Armada in 1588. For his gallantry and efficiency at this time he was knighted by the Queen. In 1590 he had the command of a squadron, which, in conjunction with another under Sir Martin Frobisher, was sent to infest the coast of Spain. In 1595 he joined with Drake in an expedition against the Spanish West Indies, but the two commanders disagreed and he was unsuccessful in an attack on the Canaries; and at Porto Rico he fell sick and died and was buried in the sea. He sat twice in Parliament for Plymouth, and founded and endowed St. John's Hospital there for decayed mariners and shipwrights of the royal navy. He married Katherine, daughter of Benjamin Golson, and his son, Sir Richard Hawkins, an able and distinguished seaman, was member of the council for Virginia in 1607.

Frobisher, Sir Martin, son of Bernard Frobisher by his wife Margaret, daughter of Sir Richard Yorke, a great seaman and discoverer, was born at Altofts, Normanton, Yorkshire, about 1535; made a voyage to Guinea and other places; served with Gilbert in Ireland; stimulated by reading Gilbert's "Discourse to Prove a Passage by the Northwest to Cathaia and the East Indies," he began his glorious voyages to the northwest coast of North America. Before Frobisher's departure on his first voyage Queen Elizabeth sent for him, commended him for his enterprise, and when he sailed July 1, 1576, she waved her hand to him from her palace window. He explored Frobisher's strait and took possession of the land called Meta Incognita in the Queen's name. The vain hope of a gold mine inspired two other voyages to the same region (1577-78). On his third voyage he discovered Hudson strait; vice-admiral in the Drake Sidney voyage, 1585-86; served against the Armada and was knighted in 1588; commanded vessels against the Spanish commerce 1589-92; in 1594 he commanded the squadron sent to aid Henry IV. of France; wounded at the attack on Brest, November 7; died at Plymouth, and was interred in St. Giles Church, Cripple Gate, February, 1595.

Davis, John, a great navigator, born at Sandridge, England, near Dartmouth, not far iron, the Gilberts and Raleighs, about 1555. He was early inured to a seafaring life and distinguished himself by three voyages which he undertook for the discovery of a northwest passage between 1585-87. He discovered the great strait which bears his name, and sailed along the coast of Greenland. In 1571 he went as second in command with Cavendish on an unfortunate journey to the South Sea. He afterwards made five voyages to the East Indies, and was killed in the battle with the Japanese pirates in the straits of Malacca, December 27, 1605. He published several books on maritime subjects, and invented the quadrant which was invariably used for taking the sun's altitude at sea until it was superseded by Hadley's sextant.

Drake, Sir Francis, circumnavigator of the globe, and the most famous seaman of his age. His parentage is not certain, but he was probably a son of Robert Drake of Otterton, by his wife Agnes Kelloway. The date and place of his birth are equally uncertain, but he was probably born at Crowndale, near Tavistock, Devonshire, in 1539, and was named for his godfather, Francis Russell, afterward second earl of Bedford. His father suffered persecution and was forced to fly from his home at Tavistock, and inhabit in the hull of a ship, where most of his younger sons were born; he had twelve in all. Francis was at an early age apprenticed to the master of a small coasting vessel, who dying without heirs, left the bark to him. He seems to have followed this petty trade for a short time, but in 1565 he was engaged in one or two voyages to Guinea, the Spanish Main, and South America. Influenced by the accounts he heard of the exploits of Hawkins, who was his kinsman, he commanded the Judith in the fleet fitted out by that great commander, which sailed from Plymouth, October 2, 1667, and which, with the exception of the Minion and the Judith conveying Hawkins and Drake, were destroyed in the harbor of San Juan d'Ulloa by a treacherous attack of the Spaniards. In 1570 he went on his own account to the West Indies and in 1571 went again, the chief fruit of which voyages was the intelligence he gained of men and places which were useful for his future movements. In 1572 he sailed with two small ships, having on board the parts of three "dainty pinnaces," and being reinforced on the way by another English ship arrived at the Isle of Pines in Cuba, where they captured two Spanish vessels. This adventure was followed by numberless others which involved the surrender of Nombre de Dios, the burning of Porto Bello, the sacking of Vera Cruz, the destruction of many Spanish ships, and the capture of a caravan of mules loaded with thirty tons of silver. On this voyage, in one of his journeys into the country of Panama, Drake, from a tree on the ridge, had a view of both oceans, and, transported at the sight, prayed fervently that he might live to sail the one he now first saw but had never visited. At length returning homeward, he arrived in Plymouth, Sunday, August 9, 1587, when, at the news, leaving the preacher in the midst of his sermon, everybody ran out of church to see the famous seaman.

This was the most famous voyage ever made by an Englishman, but Drake contemplated greater things. After some service in Ireland, Drake got together a squadron of five vessels and sailed again to America. He determined to visit that great wide spreading sea of the west, which he had seen from the ridge of Panama. He left Falmouth, December 13,

1577, and sailed to Brazil, and thence coasting southward passed through the straits of Magellan. All of his ships but the Pelican, in which he sailed, were either abandoned, destroyed in the storm or returned to England. But Drake was undismayed. Changing the name of his vessel to Golden Hind, he swept up the western coast of South America, plundering towns and shipping as he went. He then coasted California and North America, as far as 48° north latitude. Returning again southward, he anchored in a little harbor near the Bay of San Francisco and took possession of the country in the name of Queen Elizabeth, calling it New Albion. Having overhauled and reprovisioned his ship, he struck boldly across the Pacific and after an absence of nearly three years at last reached Plymouth, England, on Sunday, September 26, 1580—being the first Englishman and the next person after Magellan to circumnavigate the globe. He arrived very richly freighted with gold, silver, silk, pearls and precious stones, amounting in value to one million and a half sterling, represented perhaps in modern values about $40,000,000. Queen Elizabeth visited Drake's ship at Deptford, and knighted him and bestowed upon him a coat of arms and a crest. And the King of Spain issued a proclamation offering 20,000 ducats for Drake's head. Soon after these events he served as mayor of Plymouth and as member of Parliament.

Queen Elizabeth having come to an open breach with the King of Spain, Drake was sent in 1585 with a fleet of twenty-six sail to attack the Spanish settlements in the West Indies. He took St. Jago in Cuba, St. Domingo, Carthegena and St. Augustine, and carried away booty to the amount of £60,000 sterling. Sailing northward he visited Lane's colony at Roanoke, and finding them disheartened took them all on board and carried them back to Portsmouth, England, which he reached July 28, 1586.

Drake was not long left idle. In 1581 he was sent with a strong fleet against the Spanish coast and created much havoc in sinking and burning 100 Spanish vessels, and destroying four castles on the shore; and off the Azores captured a Portugese East Indiaman loaded with wealth estimated at £10,000. This was what Drake called "singing the King's beard." He liberally employed some of the wealth he had acquired in bringing water from a distant spring to the town of Plymouth. Drake was active in preparing England against the attack of the Spanish Armada. It was his urgent advice to the Queen not to wait the attack, but to carry the war to the Spanish coast and thereby break up the proposed movement. In the battle with the Armada he was vice-admiral under Lord Charles Howard, and his squadron had the principal share in the discomfiture of the Spanish fleet as it fled before the storms and foe.

The next year Drake was sent with a body of land forces under Sir John Norris for the purpose of restoring Don Antonio to the throne of Portugal, but the expedition was attended with a large loss of life and was not successful in its primary objects, though Drake had the good fortune to capture a large fleet laden with naval stores, thus putting an end to all proposals of an invasion from Spain. For the next few years Drake was actively but peacefully employed on shore, and in 1593 sat in parliament for Plymouth. In 1594 he was admiral of a fleet to make another attack on the West Indies, and Sir John Hawkins was vice-admiral. The expedition seems to have been unfortunate from the beginning.

The enemy were forewarned, and everywhere they met with determined opposition. Various towns, including Nombre de Dios, were burned and sacked, but they obtained no booty. Hawkins died when off Porto Rico, and Drake fell sick of dysentery. His disease was aggravated by his disappointment and exertions, and it finally took a bad turn. On the return he also died off Porto Rico, the date being January 28, 1595-96. His body, encased in a leaden coffin, was committed to the deep next day. He was twice married; first to Mary Newman, and secondly to Elizabeth, daughter of Sir George Sydenham, who survived him and afterwards married Sir William Courtenay, of Powderham, in Devonshire. He left no children nor did any of his eleven brothers, except one Captain Thomas Drake, who left a daughter Elizabeth, wife of John Bamfield, Esq.; and a son Francis, who was created baronet August 2, 1622.

Hakluyt, Rev. Richard, a celebrated naval historian, born about 1555, brought up at Westminster School, and graduated A. B. at Christ Church College, Oxford, February 19, 1573; M. A. June 27, 1577. His interest in navigation was early excited by the example and teaching of his cousin Richard Hakluyt, Sr., and he devoted himself to the study of geography and collecting and publishing the accounts of travels and discoveries. In 1582 appeared his "Divers Voyages;" in 1584 he wrote his "Discourse on Western Planting" for Raleigh, in which he pictured the advantage of an English settlement in America; in 1586 he caused the journals of Ribault and others to be published; in 1587 he published an improved edition of Peter Martyr's work, "De Orbe Novo," afterwards translated in English and published under the title of "The Historie of the West Indies;" in 1588 he applied himself to his greatest work, "Principal Navigations," which he published in 1589; and shortly after he issued a second edition. In 1601 he published a translation of Antonio Galvano's "History of Discoveries," and in 1609 a translation of Ferdinand De Soto's "Description of Florida." During this time he filled many offices. He was appointed at a very early age to read public lectures at Oxford upon cosmography; in 1582-83 he was chaplain of the English embassy at Paris, where he remained five years; during his absence he was made a prebendary of Bristol; in 1605 he was appointed rector of Wetheringset in Suffolk. He took great interest in the colonization of Virginia, and was one of the four incorporators mentioned by name in the patent granted to the Virginia Company of London in 1606. On the recommendation of Dr. Richard Bancroft, Archbishop of Canterbury, the post of minister at Jamestown was offered to him, but he declined in favor of Robert Hunt. Hackluyt died at Eton in Hertfordshire in November, 1606, and was buried among the illustrious dead in Westminster Abbey. No man did more for the English occupation of America, since by his numerous works he fired the imagination of the nation and inspired the navigators with the zeal of crusaders to whom no sea or enterprise, however hazardous, had any terrors.

Gilbert, Sir Humphrey, son of Otho Gilbert and his wife Katherine Champernoun, was born in Devonshire, at his father's house called Greenway, upon Dart river, about 1639; educated at Eton and Oxford; devoted himself to the study of navigation and the art of war; was wounded at Havre in fighting against the French, and afterwards saw much military experience in Ireland, where after defeating the celebrated McCarthy More he was made governor of Munster in October, 1569; knighted at Drogheda by the lord lieutenant of Ireland, Sir Henry Sidney, January 1, 1570, and the same year returned to England and married Joan, only daughter and heiress of John Ancher, of Otterden, by his wife Ann, daughter of Sir William Kellaway; M. P. from Plymouth in 1571; commanded the squadron sent to reinforce Flushing in the autumn of 1572; returned to England in the fall of 1573, and was living at Limehouse in 1575-78. He became greatly interested in making discoveries, and in 1566 petitioned the Queen for the privilege of making northeast discoveries, and in 1567 of making northwest discoveries. He wrote a "Discourse of a Discovery for a new passage to Cataia," and conceived the design of planting an English settlement in the New World to countervail the power of Spain. Accordingly, he obtained a patent from Queen Elizabeth for this purpose, dated June 11, 1578; sailed in the fall of that year with seven ships and 387 men, but was soon forced to return; in 1579 he sent Simon Ferdinando and in 1580 John Walker to make preliminary explorations, and on June 11, 1583, sailed himself a second time with five ships bearing 260 men; August 3, 1583, he reached Newfoundland, of which he took possession in the name of Queen Elizabeth. From here he sailed southward, but the desertion and loss of several of his vessels forced him to abandon the expedition and to attempt to return home with the two that remained. On the way a terrible storm on September 10, 1583, swallowed up one of them bearing Gilbert himself. Throughout the whole expedition he showed an invincible spirit, and his last words will be kept in precious remembrance: "We are as near Heaven by sea as by land." He is justly considered the founder of American colonization. He was the father of a number of children, among whom were John, Bartholomew and Raleigh Gilbert, all of whom were interested in the settlement of America.

Gilbert, Adrian, of Sandridge, son of Otho Gilbert, of Compton, and brother of Sir Humphrey Gilbert, made a voyage to the northwest prior to 1583; interested in the voyages of his brother Sir Humphrey, in the voyages of John Davis 1586-87, and in the voyage of Cavendish, 1591; was constable of Sherborne Castle, 1596-1603; member of parliament for Bridgeport, 1597-98.

Gilbert, Sir John, of Greenway, eldest son of Otho Gilbert and Katherine Champernoun, his wife, and brother of Sir Humphrey Gilbert; knighted by Queen Elizabeth at Westminster, 1571; vice-admiral of Devon, 1585; mayor of Plymouth, 1589; married Elizabeth, daughter of Sir Richard Chudleigh, and was buried in St. Peter's Cathedral, Exeter, where an elegant monument remains to his memory. Interested in the expeditions of his brother Sir Humphrey.

Gilbert, Sir John, eldest son of Sir Humphrey Gilbert, went with Raleigh to Guiana in 1595; showed gallantry at the battle of Cadiz in 1596 and was knighted by Essex; governor of the fort at Plymouth, 1597; member of the council for Virginia, 1607; was a brave officer; married a daughter of Sir Richard Molyneux, of Sefton, but died without issue, July 5, 1608, of smallpox, and was buried at Marldon Church. His brother Raleigh Gilbert was his heir.

Ferdinando, Simon, a Portugese pilot, sailed with Drake on his celebrated voyage to the

West Indies in 1577, and in 1579 Gilbert sent him to America to explore the way for his colony; he was a pilot in Fenton's voyage in 1582-83, and in the exploring voyage to North Carolina of Amidas and Barlow in 1584; subsequently he went with the colonies of Lane and John White to Roanoke. He was probably one of those who disappeared with the last.

Walker, John, was employed by Sir Humphrey Gilbert to make an exploring voyage in 1580 to America. He visited the Penobscot river and reported to Sir Humphrey the discovery of a silver mine within the river. This induced Gilbert to direct his voyage to Newfoundland in 1583, and probably prompted the plans which he appears to have formed on the return voyage of sending out two new expeditions the following spring.

Raleigh, Sir Walter, son of Walter Raleigh, Esq., of Fardel, near Plymouth, and Katharine Champernoun, daughter of Sir Philip Champernoun, of Modbury, in Devonshire, and widow of Otho Gilbert, Esq., of Compton. He was born at Hayes Barton, in Devonshire, 1552; educated at Oriel College, Oxford, about 1568; served in France five years to assist the French Huguenots, returned to London in 1576; in 1578 went to the Netherlands under Sir John Norris to help the Dutch against the Spaniards; the following year engaged with his brother Sir Humphrey Gilbert in his American schemes and sailed in the Falcon, but the expedition was unfortunate and he soon returned; in 1580 he raised troops and took part in suppressing an insurrection in Ireland and received a grant there from Queen Elizabeth of 12,000 acres; furnished a ship to Sir Humphrey's second colonization expedition in 1583; interested in Adrian Gilbert's patent of the Northwest passage; obtained patent March 25, 1584, for planting a colony in America; sends Amidas and Barlow to America, April 27, 1584, who explored the coast of North Carolina; on their return the Queen named the country Virginia, in honor of herself; member of parliament for Devon, November 23, 1584, to September 14, 1585; his patent of colonization confirmed by parliament in December, 1584; grows in favor of the Queen and is knighted at Greenwich, January 1, 1585. About the same time he received the grant of a monopoly for the selling of wine throughout the kingdom, was made seneschal of the duchies of Cornwall and Exeter and lord warden of the Stannaries; pleased at the success of Amidas and Barlow, Raleigh sent seven ships under Sir Richard Grenville and 200 settlers under Capt. Ralph Lane, who occupied Roanoke Island, in Pamlico Sound, North Carolina, August 17, 1585, but the colonists returned to England the following year in the fleet of Sir Francis Drake; member of parliament for Devon in 1586-87; during this time he was made captain of the Queen's Guard and member of the council of war; May 8, 1587, he sent another colony to Roanoke under Governor John White; in 1588 he was one of the captains of the English fleet who fought the Armada; assigned his interests in America to Thomas Smith and others in 1589, but aided in sending an expedition in 1591 to the relief of the colonists at Roanoke, who were never found; planned a voyage against Panama in 1592; married Elizabeth Throckmorton, and thereby incurred the anger of Queen Elizabeth, who imprisoned him in the tower of London; 1593, member of parliament for St. Michaels; went on a voyage to Guiana in 1595; took a prominent part in the taking of Cadiz in June, 1596; published an account of his voyage of 1595 to Guiana in 1596, and sent a voyage there under Captain Keymis, and another under Berry, 1596-97; in 1597 he sailed on the celebrated voyage to the Azores; member of parliament for Dorset 1597-98; governor and captain of Jersey, August 26, 1600; member of parliament for Cornwall, 1600-1601; sends Mace on a voyage to America and his nephew Bartholomew Gilbert, 1602; gives permission to Martin Pring to make a voyage in 1603; upon the accession of King James he lost his influence at Court, was stripped of his preferments, and accused, tried and condemned for high treason, as a participator in Lord Cobham's plot for placing Lady Arabella Stuart on the throne; was confined in the Tower from 1603 to January 30, 1616, during which time he wrote "The History of the World," down to the end of the Macedonian war, B. C. 167; in 1616 he was temporarily released by the King and sent to find a gold mine in Guiana; when he returned empty handed he was arrested on the complaint of the Spanish ambassador and sentenced to death, and executed October 29, 1619, on the verdict of the jury seventeen years before, now recognized to have been based on charges trumped up by political enemies. He was buried in St. Margaret's, Westminster. He was the most accomplished gentleman of his age, and to him is due more than any other man the popularizing of colonization. He introduced into general use the potato, which he planted on his estate in Ireland, and tobacco, which he taught the courtiers to smoke. He left an only surviving son, Carew Raleigh, who was a member of the Virginia Company of London, April 2, 1623.

Amidas, Philip, said to have been born at Hull, England, 1550; was sent by Raleigh with Arthur Barlow to explore the coast of North Carolina or Virginia. He left the west of England, April 27, 1584, visited North Carolina and explored Pamlico Sound, which he found dotted with many islands, the largest of which was Roanoke. When he returned and reported his new discovery, the Queen called the country in honor of herself, Virginia. He died in 1618.

Barlow, Arthur, employed by Sir Walter Raleigh with Philip Amidas to lead an exploring expedition to North Carolina in 1584.

Grenville, Sir Richard, son of Sir Roger Grenville, and his wife Thomasine, daughter of Thomas Cole, Esq., of Slade, in Devonshire, was born in 1540, and at an early age acquired much distinction in fighting the Turks; member of parliament for Cornwall, 1571, and for Launceston, 1572-83; knighted at "Windesore," in 1577; sheriff of Cornwall, 1578; became greatly interested in foreign discoveries; aided Raleigh in sending out Amidas and Barlow to America, 1584; member of parliament for Cornwall, 1584-85, and served on committee for conferring Raleigh's patent of colonization; took the first colony to Virginia, April to October, 1585; went on a second voyage bringing supplies, April to December, 1586; took Spanish prizes on each voyage; member of council of war to resist the Spanish Armada, 1587, and fought in the great sea fight 1588; 1591, vice-admiral of the fleet under Sir Thomas Howard, and lost his life in a sea fight near the Azores, in which his single ship withstood for many hours five Spanish galleons supported at intervals by ten others. An old chronicler asserts that it was "the stoutest sea fight ever waged." He married Mary, daughter of Sir John St. Leger, and their eldest son was Bernard Grenville.

Cavendish, Sir Thomas, an adventurous seaman, the second Englishman to circumnavigate the globe, was born at Grimston Hall, Trimley, St. Martin Parish, Suffolk county, England, 1564; he equipped a ship at his own expense and sailed with Sir Richard Grenville on the voyage to Roanoke Island in 1585; afterwards mortgaged his estates and fitted out a fleet to prey on Spanish commerce, and embarking from Plymouth, July 21, 1586, crossed the Atlantic, ran down the coast of South America, cleared the straits of Magellan and heading northward ravaged the seaboard of Chili, Peru and New Spain. He captured a galleon laden with valuable merchandise and 122,000 Spanish dollars. He went as far as Cape Lucas, on the coast of California, and then sailed for England by the way of the Cape of Good Hope, reaching Plymouth, September 9, 1588, after an absence of two years, one month and nineteen days. On his return home Queen Elizabeth knighted him. His share of the spoils was "rich enough to purchase a fair earldom." In three years he planned another voyage of the same scope, but his good genius deserted him. His plans were rendered abortive by tempestuous weather, sickness, hunger and desertion, and being compelled to turn homeward died at sea in the summer of 1592, heartbroken from want, anguish and fatigue.

Lane, Captain Ralph, second son of Sir Ralph Lane, of Orlinbury, and his wife Maud, daughter of William Lord Parr, uncle of Queen Katherine Parr, was born in Northamptonshire, about 1630; entered the Queen's service in 1563; distinguished himself in the rebellion of 1569, and was made governor of Kerry and Clan Morris; he is described by Stow as "a great projector in these times," and proposed to the crown many schemes of all kinds; was selected by Raleigh as governor of the colony to be sent to Roanoke Island in 1585; finding that there were no gold mines in North Carolina he returned home with the settlers in 1586; afterwards was a member of the commission to provide for the defence of England against the Spanish Armada; and in 1589 was a colonel in the expedition of Drake and Norris to Portugal; he was made muster-master-general in Ireland, where he was dangerously wounded; was knighted by Lord Fitzwilliam, deputy lord lieutenant of Ireland, in 1593, and died in 1604 or 1605.

Hariot, Thomas, an eminent English mathematician, born at Oxford, in 1560, studied at St. Mary's Hall, Oxford University, where he took the degree of Bachelor of Arts, February 12, 1580. Soon after he was entertained by Sir Walter Raleigh as his instructor in mathematics, and granted by him an annual pension. He was sent with Ralph Lane and his colony to Roanoke in 1585, and upon his return he published the results of his labors in "A Brief and True Report of the newfoundland of Virginia, etc., London, 1588." He was the constant companion of Sir Walter Raleigh when he was confined in the Tower of London. He made a sun dial for the Earl of Northumberland, which is still to be seen in the south face of St. Martin's tower. In 1607 he drew up observations on the comet known as "Halley's Comet." He was the first to detect the spots on the sun, and is said to have observed the satellites of Jupiter a few days after Galileo first discovered them. He arrived at a complete theory of the genesis of equations in algebra, which Cardan and Vieta had but partially conceived. He preserved a keen interest in the colonization of Virginia till his death, at London, July 2, 1621.

White, Captain John, was one of the settlers who went with Captain Ralph Lane and his colonists to Roanoke in 1586. He was an artist, and made maps of the country and drawings of the Indian life. Many of his paintings are now in the Sloane collection and in the Grenville Library in the British Museum. He was one of those to whom Raleigh assigned his patent in January, 1587, and went in charge of a second colony to Roanoke in May that year. In November he went to England for supplies, but his return to Roanoke was delayed on account of the invasion of England by the Spanish Armada. At length after three years he returned to Roanoke, but found no trace of the colony which he had left behind. Some of his maps and drawings were engraved in 1590 by De Bry in Hariot's report of the New found land of Virginia. He was living in 1594, when he wrote a letter to Raleigh. One of the lost colonists was his own daughter, wife of Annanias Dare, to whom was born a daughter, Virginia, August 18, 1578, the first child of English parents to be born in America.

Mace, Samuel, a mariner in the employment of Sir Walter Raleigh, was sent by him three times to Virginia to search for the "Lost Colony of Roanoke;" the third voyage was in 1602; he departed from Waymouth in March, and reaching the American coast forty leagues south of Cape Hatteras, spent a month searching the coast and trading with the Indians; he returned with a cargo of sassafras and roots of different kinds, but brought no news of the "Lost Colony."

James I. of England and VI. of Scotland, only child of Mary Queen of Scots, daughter of James V., by her cousin Henry Stuart, Lord Darnley, was born in the Castle of Edinburgh, June 19, 1566. He married Anne of Denmark, November 24, 1589, and was proclaimed King of England on the death of Queen Elizabeth, March 24, 1603. His reign lasted till March 27, 1625, when he died. In estimating his career, while we must condemn his subserviency to favorites like Somerset and Buckingham, and his exhorbitant ideas of his prerogative, we must praise his actions in other respects. He loved peace, and was fond of books and literary men. He had patriotic views on extending the trade and power of the nation by favoring merchants, discoveries and colonization. He enlarged the privileges of the East India, the Muscovy, the Turkey and the Merchant Adventurers Companies, and granted three charters to the Virginia Company, successively increasing its powers. While he has been condemned for having the company dissolved, it cannot be said that he acted without some good reasons. The company had fallen into factions, and the terrible mortality in Virginia gave the appearance of careless administration. Of course Sandys and Southampton were not responsible for this, but subsequent events justified King James' action. As a matter of fact the colony had outgrown the care of a distant corporation. Jamestown, James river and James City county in Virginia still remind us of his name and reign.

Cecil, Sir Robert, Earl of Salisbury, born June 1, 1560, son of William Cecil, Lord Burleigh, whom he succeeded as secretary of state on his death in 1598. In that office he was in fact prime minister during the next five years of his life. He was sole secretary of state to James I. from 1603 to his death in 1612. He was one of the earliest and constant friends of the Virginia enterprise, and subscribed £333 6s. 8d. to its stock.

Gosnold, Bartholomew, (q. v.).

Gilbert, Bartholomew, son of Sir Humphrey Gilbert, sailed with Bartholomew Gosnold in the ship Concord, sent out by the Earl of Southampton to the New England coast, March 26, 1602; May 10, 1603, in a small bark of fifty tons, he sailed to Chesapeake Bay; when landing on the eastern shore he was attacked by Indians and killed in July of that year. The ship returned to England about the end of September.

Pring, Martin, sea captain, son of John Pring of Awliscomb, Devonshire, was in 1603 sent out by Richard Hakluyt and others of Bristol under license from Sir Walter Raleigh with two ships the Speedwell and Discovery to perform a voyage to the coast of New England. They arrived at Bristol on October 2, where they reported the land they had visited "full of God's blessings." He then went on a voyage to Guiana, and, afterwards in October, 1606, went out to New England in an expedition fitted out by Sir John Popham, and "brought back with him," wrote Sir Ferdinand Gorges, "the most exact discovery of that land that ever came to my hand since." Pring afterwards saw much service in the employment of the East India Company's ships. On his passage home in 1621, in the Royal James, the officers and men made a subscription towards building a free school in Virginia, amounting to £70 8s. 6d., of which Pring contributed £6 13s. 4d. On July 3 he was made a freeman of the Virginia Company of London and was granted two shares of land in Virginia. The East India Company, however, censured him for engaging in private trade, and for being too complacent to the Dutch. He died in 1626, and was buried at St. Stephen's Church, Bristol, where there is a monument to his memory. His daughter Alice married Andrews, son of William Burwell, a commissioner of the navy.

Weymouth, George, voyager, was employed by the East India Company in 1601, to make a voyage for the discovery of a northwest passage to India. He penetrated some distance into Hudson Strait, and thus "lit the light" which guided Hudson to the great waters in British America which bear his name. In 1605 Weymouth was put in command of the Archangel, a vessel fitted out by the Earl of Southampton and his brother-in-law, Lord Thomas Arundell, of Wardour. He sailed from Ratcliffe in the beginning of March and visited Nantucket, Monhegan Island, and discovered a large river which has never been definitely identified. He traded with the Indians and returned to England with a very valuable cargo of furs. He arrived at Dartmouth, July 18, 1605. The last mention of him is on October 27, 1607, when he was granted a pension of 3s. 4d. per diem.

Gilbert, Raleigh, a son of Sir Humphrey Gilbert, brother of Sir John Gilbert, and nephew of Sir Walter Raleigh; very active in the settlement of America; an incorporator in the first Virginia charter April 10, 1606; May 31, 1607, sailed from Plymouth, England, in the expedition sent out by the Plymouth Company to the Kennebec river in Maine; was member of the local council, and after the death of George Popham was president; after a winter of much suffering he returned with the settlers to England; married Elizabeth, daughter of John Kelley, Esq., of Devon; member of the council for New England in 1620; he died in 1626, leaving seven children, many of whose descendants are living in Cornwall, England.

Smith or Smythe, Sir Thomas, a great merchant and first treasurer of the Virginia Company of London, born about 1558, son of Sir Thomas Smythe, of Ostenhanger in Kent, a merchant of large wealth, who at the coming of the Armada lent Queen Elizabeth £1000, and who, as collector of the customs, was generally known as "Mr. Customer Smith." The son was probably the most important merchant of his day, being at one time head of all the leading merchant companies of London. He was educated at Oxford, and went early into business. He was an incorporator of the Turkey Company in 1581, a principal member of the Russia Company in 1587, and the first on the list of those persons to whom Raleigh assigned (March 7, 1589) his interest in Virginia. He formed a friendship with the Earl of Essex and accompanied him to Cadiz in 1596, where he was knighted by him for gallantry. In 1599 he was sheriff of London, and in 1600 was first governor of the East India Company. In 1601 he was captain of the trained bands of London, and was arrested about this time for suspected complicity in the insurrection of Essex. He was confined a short time and was released from the Tower of London in September, 1602. King James regarded Essex's friends as his friends, and on May 13 knighted him at the Tower. In 1604 he was appointed, on account of his concern in the Muscovy Company, special ambassador to Russia. He visited the Czar at Jaroslav and obtained from him new privileges for the Muscovy Company. In 1603 he was reëlected governor of the East India Company and held the office till 1621; M. P. for Dunwich, 1604-11, and for Saltash, 1621-22.

In 1606 he was active in forming the Virginia Company and was appointed member of the Virginia Council in England, and treasurer of the company. He continued treasurer for twelve years. In 1618 he was appointed one of the commissioners of the navy and held that office till his death in 1625. In 1618 the Virginia Company divided into three parties—one composed of the lords and many gentlemen under the lead of Robert Rich, Earl of Warwick, and the Earl of Southampton; another consisting principally of merchants under the lead of Sir Thomas Smythe; and a third, "the faction of the auditors," under Sir Edwin Sandys. Smythe had been alienated from Rich on account of the marriage of his son John, a mere youth of 18, to a sister of the Earl, without the privity of the father. So the first and third factions united, and elected Sir Edwin Sandys as treasurer in 1619. Smythe, doubtless knowing his defeat to be certain, declined to stand. He continued, however, governor of the East India Company and the Bermuda Islands Company. The factional disturbances in the Virginia Company continued to grow, and the Smythe faction, now reinforced by the Earl of Warwick, assailed the government of the Virginia Colony as conducted by their adversaries, with such violence that King James finally had the charter abrogated in the courts in June, 1624. After this abrogation Smith was a member of the royal commission for Virginia affairs till his death, September 4, 1625. He was buried at Hone Church, Kent, where is to be seen a superb monument to his memory.

In estimating the services of Smythe to Virginia, while there is no doubt that he had its interest clearly to heart and gave largely of his time and money to the enterprise, his policy of ruling the settlers like a military camp and establishing martial law cannot be approved. On the general subject of explorations he had noble and enlarged views. Besides performing the main part in establishing an English colony in Virginia, he aided and promoted many voyages to find a northwest passage to India—Henry Hudson's in 1610, Jonas Poole's in 1611, Captain Button's in 1612, Robert Fotherbie's in 1615, Robert Bileth and William Baffin's in 1616, when "Smith's Sound" was discovered and named for him. Indeed, his name was engrafted everywhere upon land and water beyond perhaps that of any other Englishman. He was besides the patron of many men of science, and his gifts and bequests were very numerous. He married three times, his third wife being Sarah, daughter of William Blount, Esq., by whom he had two sons —Thomas and John Smythe. The line of the former ended with the accomplished geographer the Eighth Viscount Strangford, who died in 1869, and the line of the latter expired with Sir Sidney Stafford Smythe, chief baron of the exchequer in 1772. The family always wrote the name Smythe, though it is generally rendered Smith. A portrait belonging to the Skinner's Company has been identified with Sir Thomas Smythe.

Newport, Capt. Christopher. A Founder. (q. v.).

Wingfield, Edward Maria. A Founder. (q. v.).

Ratcliffe, John. A Founder. (q. v.).

Smith, Captain John. A Founder. (q. v.).

Percey, George. A Founder. (q. v.).

Gates, Sir Thomas. A Founder. (q. v.).

Somers, Sir George. A Founder. (q. v.).

Dale, Sir Thomas. A Founder. (q. v.).

West, Sir Thomas, Lord Delaware. A Founder. (q. v.).

Argall, Sir Samuel. A Founder. (q. v.).

Yardley, Sir George. A Founder. (q. v.).

Symonds, Rev. William, born in Oxfordshire about 1557, educated at Magdalene College, Oxford, and in 1579 a fellow thereof. About this time he received a curacy, the gift of Captain John Smith's friend, Lord Willoughby, at Hatton Holgate, in the Diocese of Lincoln. He preached the first sermon before the Virginia Company of London, April 25, 1609. He revised Smith's "Map of Virginia and Annexed Relation," which was published at Oxford in 1612.

Crashaw, Rev. William, a member of the Virginia Company, an eloquent preacher sometimes classed as a Puritan divine and poet; was baptized at Handsworth, October 26, 1572, educated at Cambridge; prebend of the church of Ripon, 1604; preacher at the Inner Temple, London; at church of St. Mary Matfellon, of White Chapel, London, November 13, 1618; died in 1626. He was father of the poet, Richard Crashaw, a Roman Catholic. In February, 1610, he preached before Lord Delaware and the London Company an eloquent sermon defending the character of the settlers against malicious imputations, and praising the objects of the Virginia enterprise.

Sandys, Sir Edwin, second treasurer of the Virginia Company, second son of Dr. Edwin Sandys, Archbishop of York, by Ciceley, sister of Sir Thomas Wilford, was born December 9, 1561; educated at Corpus Christi College; B. A. October 16, 1579, and M. A. June 5, 1583. He was collated to the prebend of Wetwang in the Cathedral of York, and in 1589 was admitted a student of the Middle Temple.

On October 13, 1586, Sandys entered parliament as a member for Andover. From the first he took an active part in its proceedings and repeatedly served on committees. In the parliament for 1588-89 he sat for Plymton, Devonshire, for which he was reëlected in 1592-93. Soon after the dissolution of parliament in 1593 he traveled abroad and was at Paris in 1599, when he prepared an account of the state of religion in Europe which he entitled "Europae Speculum," which is remarkably tolerant for the times. Sandys returned to England the same year, and in 1602 resigned his prebend at Wetwang. He was knighted by King James at the Charter House, May 11, 1603, and was returned March 12, 1604, to James I.'s first parliament as member for Stockbridge, Hampshire. Sandys had imbibed from Richard Hooker, who had been his tutor and afterwards his intimate friend, the ideas of a liberal government, and in parliament he assumed a leading part in opposing all exactions and monopolies. He attempted to have abolished all the royal tenures and to throw trade open, instead of confining it to the great trading companies. In the parliament of 1607 he urged that all prisoners should be allowed the benefit of counsel, and in the same session he carried a resolution for the regular keeping of the journals of the House of Commons, which had not been done before. With a view to placating him, Sandys was granted by the King a moiety of the manor of Northbourne, Kent, but when parliament met on April 5, 1614, Sandys maintained his old attitude. He opposed Winwood's demand for a supply and was the moving spirit on a committee appointed to consider taxes. In a remarkable speech on May 21 he declared that the King's authority rested on the consent of the people, and that any King who ruled by any other title ought to be dethroned. All this exasperated James against him, and on the adjournment of parliament he was summoned before the council and punished by being ordered not to leave London without permission, and to give bonds for his appearance whenever he was called upon.

No parliament was summoned for more than six years after this, and meanwhile Sandys turned his attention to colonial affairs. He was a member of the Somers Island Company and of the East India Company, and in both he took an active part. But his energies were especially devoted to the Virginia Company, of which he had been appointed a member of the superior council in 1607, and he had the greater part in drafting the charters of 1609 and 1612, which vested the power of government in the company instead of the King as hitherto. Then in 1617 he was chosen by the company to assist Sir Thomas Smythe in his management of Virginia affairs. In this capacity he warmly supported the request of the Leyden exiles to be allowed to settle in the company's domains, and it was largely owing to him that a patent was granted them. On April 28, 1619, a combination of parties in the company resulted in the almost unanimous election of Sandys as the successor of Sir Thomas Smythe in the office of treasurer. He made a complete departure from the old method of government, and each colonist was given a dividend of land and invited to share in the government. Acting on the company's instructions, Yardley was sent over as governor and summoned an assembly of burgesses to meet in the church at Jamestown, July 30, 1619. It was the first representative body assembled in America. On June 6, 1619, Sandys obtained the company's sanction to a college at Henrico, and during the same year procured the transshipment of a number of women to the c[olo]ny to serve as wives to the tenants on the public lands. He also secured the exclusion from England of foreign tobacco in the interest of the Virginia trade. When his year as treasurer expired, Sandys was not reelected, because of the violent interference of the King, who sent word to the company "to choose the devil if you will, but not Sir Edwin Sandys." The company would not, however, take any of the nominees of the King, but elected Henry Wriothesley, Earl of Southampton, and John Ferrar was elected his deputy. Both were staunch adherents of the Sandys party, and during the frequent absences of Southampton, Sandys still took the leading part in the company's business. He opposed the movement to dissolve the charter with all his might, and had the question brought up in parliament, where he charged the commissioners appointed by the King to investigate Virginia affairs with extreme partiality, and ascribed the intrigues against the company to the influence of the Spanish ambassador, Gondomar. Despite his efforts, judgment was rendered against the charter June 24, 1624, and the company was dissolved. Sandys did not very long survive this action, but continued as the leader of the popular party in parliament till his death in October, 1629. He was interred in the church of Northbourne, in Kent. He was married four times, and by the last wife, Catherine, daughter of Sir Richard Bulkley, he had with other issue, five sons, all of whom, save one, adhered in the civil war to the popular side. Sir Edwin Sandys had an elder brother, Sir Samuel Sandys, who served in parliament, was knighted, etc., and had two daughters by his wife Mercy, daughter of Martin Culpeper, Esq., one who married Sir Francis Wyatt, governor of Virginia, and another who married Sir Fernando Weyman, who died in Virginia. Another brother was George Sandys, the poet, who resided in Virginia, where he acted as treasurer of the colony and was a member of the local council there.

Wriothesley, Henry, third Earl of Southampton and third treasurer of the Virginia Company, was the second and only surviving son of Henry Wriothesley, the second earl, by his wife Mary Browne, daughter of the last Viscount Montague. He was born October 6, 1573, and succeeded to the earldom at the death of his father in 1581. He attended St. John's College, Cambridge, and in 1589 at the age of 16 graduated as Master of Arts. In the autumn of 1592 he was accounted the most handsome and accomplished of all the young lords who accompanied Elizabeth to Oxford that year. On November 17, 1595, he distinguished himself in the lists set up in the Queen's presence in honor of the thirty-seventh anniversary of her accession, and was likened by George Poe in his account of the same to Bevis of Southampton, the ancient type of chivalry. His martial ardor was encouraged by his association with Essex, whom he accompanied in 1596 in the military and naval expedition to Cadiz. Next year he again accompanied Essex in the expedition to the Azores, but he alienated the Queen by marrying without her consent one of the Queen's waiting women, Elizabeth Vernon, a cousin of Essex. He was thrown into the Tower, but soon released. He went with Essex on the military expedition to Ireland, and on his return was drawn into the conspiracy, whereby Essex and his friends desired to regain by violence their influence at court. The rising failed completely, and Essex and Southampton were tried for treason and condemned to death.

While Essex was executed, the sentence of Southampton, owing to his youth, was commuted by the influence of Sir Robert Cecil to imprisonment for life. On the death of Queen Elizabeth in 1603, the first act of King James was to set Southampton free. He was given high honors; made knight of the garter, appointed captain of the Isle of Wight and Carisbrook Castle, as well as steward, receiver and bailiff of the royal manors on the Island. In 1604 he was fully restored in blood by an act of parliament, and recreated Earl of Southampton. He became Keeper of the King's game in the divisions of Andover, Sawley and Kingsclere, Hampshire, and lord lieutenant of Hampshire, jointly with the Earl of Devonshire. He was sworn of the King's council, April 19, 1619.

In three aspects especially he shone with surpassing lustre. Literature was from his early manhood a chief interest of Southampton's life. He was the Maecenas of his age, and loved to surround himself with poets and men of letters, whom he encouraged with word and money. Among these were Gervas Markham, Barnabe Barnes, Thomas Nash, Florio and Shakespeare, who celebrated his name in prose and verse. Then his impetuous spirit begat a love of freedom which showed itself in his opposition at court and in the house of lords to the arbitrary orders of King James and his favorite Buckingham, whom he thoroughly disliked. He was a strong friend of the Protestant interest, and opposed the Spanish match proposed for Prince Charles, and on account of his too great familiarity with the popular party he was arrested and temporarily confined.

But especially was he the friend of colonization, acting the part of another Sir Walter Raleigh, and his dream was to extend the power of England throughout the world. To this object he devoted his leisure and ample wealth without stint. He sent Gosnold and Gilbert to Virginia in 1602 and Weymouth in 1605, had a great share in forming the Virginia Company of London in 1606 and was a member of the Virginia Company's council in England in 1609. The same year he was admitted a member of the East India Company's council. In 1610 he helped to dispatch Henry Hudson to North America, and was a member of the Northwest Passage Company 1612, and of the Somers Island Company in 1615. He was chosen treasurer of the Virginia Company, 1620, and devoted much energy to championing its interests, to which Gondomar, the Spanish ambassador, was resolutely hostile, but was unable to prevent the withdrawal of the company's charter in June, 1624. He had a copy of the record of the company made of the period of his administration, and when the King's commissioners demanded its delivery, the Earl made the brave answer that he would as soon part with the title deeds of his land as part with these manuscripts, since he regarded them as the evidence of his honor in the Virginia service. The maps of New England, Virginia and Bermuda commemorate Southampton's labors as a colonial pioneer. In his honor Southampton Hundred, Hampton river and Hampton roads in Virginia were named.

When in 1624 a defensive treaty of alliance was made between England and Holland against the Emperor of Germany, Southampton, accompanied by his son, James, left England and took command of a troop of English volunteers. But not long after reaching Holland both were attacked with fever and soon died. Southampton's death occurred November 10, 1624.

Ferrar, Nicholas, Sr., skinner, a member

of the Virginia Company, ranked high among the merchants of London, and traded very extensively with the East and West Indies. He was interested in the adventures of Hawkins, Drake and Raleigh. He died in April, 1620, and was buried in the church of St. Bennet, Sherhog, London. He gave by will £300 to the college in Virginia, to be paid when there shall be ten of the Indian children placed in it, and in the meantime £24 by the year for the instruction of three Indian children in the Christian religion. His son Nicholas finally transferred his bequest to the Bermuda Islands. He married Mary, daughter of Lawrence Wodenoth, Esq., a woman of fervent piety and a model mother, and had issue: (1) Susan, married John Collett, of Bourne Bridge, Cambridgeshire; (2) John; (3) Erasmus, a barrister-of-law; (4) Nicholas; (5) William, who was a member of the council in Virginia; (6) Richard.

Ferrar, John, a member of the Virginia Company, which he joined in 1612. He was afterwards added to his Majesty's council for Virginia, and was deputy treasurer from April 28, 1619, to May 22, 1622. He was a member of parliament for Tamworth in 1621-22. Like his brother Nicholas, he was devoted to the interest of the Virginia Company, and contributed all his power to the success of the colony. When his brother retired to Little Giddings in Huntingdonshire, he soon joined him with his family, and shared in the religious life established there. After the death of his brother Nicholas, he continued to live according to the same rule. In 1629 Charles I., who was always friendly to the Ferrars, visited the settlement and was greatly pleased with what he saw. In 1647 the home and church of Little Giddings were spoiled by some adherents of the parliament, and the little community was broken up. He wrote the life of his brother Nicholas, which was published by Rev. Peter Peckard, Master of Magdalene College, Cambridge, in 1790, and of his own son Nicholas, who died in 1640. John Ferrar married twice: First Anne, daughter of William Shepherd, Esq., of Oxfordshire, who died without issue; and secondly, Bathsheba, daughter of Israel Owen, of London, and had issue by her: Nicholas, John and Virginia. The last who never married inherited the family interest in Virginia and kept up a great correspondence with her cousins there and other planters, and was especially interested in the silk culture.

Ferrar, Nicholas, Jr., one of the greatest friends of the Virginia Colony, was third son of Nicholas Ferrar, of London, merchant, by his wife Mary, daughter of Laurence Wodenoth, of Savington Hall, Cheshire. Under the excellent care of his father and mother he soon developed a character which united a great aptitude for management with a singularly pious and gentle disposition. From his earliest years he was regarded by his family as a prodigy. In 1610 he took the degree of Bachelor of Arts at Clare Hall, Cambridge University, and in 1613 was Master of Arts. He travelled extensively on the continent and visited Holland, Germany, Italy and Spain. He returned in 1618, and joined the Virginia Company, buying two shares from Sir William Smith. He became greatly interested in its affairs, and devoted himself heart and soul to its work, being made member of the company's council in 1619. In 1622 he succeeded his brother John as deputy treasurer, and for the next two years was the chief adviser of the Earl of Southampton and Sir Edwin Sandys in withstanding the assaults of the King and the privy council upon the charter. During this time he caused to be made the copies of the Virginia records which are now preserved in the Library of Congress and were recently published. Despite all his efforts the company was deprived of its patent in 1624.

Ferrar was a well known man in political circles. In 1624 he was elected to parliament for Lymington, and took part in the impeachment of the lord treasurer, the Earl of Middlesex, who had been foremost in the dissolution of the Virginia Company. But this was the last act of Ferrar's political life. Disgusted with the world of business and politics, he wound up his business concerns and retired to Little Giddings, in Huntingdonshire, and established there a settlement of a religious nature. He was joined by the families of his brother John, and his brother-in-law, John Collet. The entire household comprised 30 persons. He himself acted as chaplain of the community. There was a definite occupation for every hour of the day, and vigils were kept during the night. Little Giddings was the school, the infirmary and the dispensary of the region round about. Thus engaged and removed from the turmoil of the world, Nicholas Ferrar yielded up his pure soul December 4, 1637. He never married.

Rich, Sir Robert, eldest son of Robert Rich, third Lord Rich, born in May or June, 1587; made a knight of the Bath at the coronation of James I., July 25, 1603, and succeeded his father as second Earl of Warwick in April, 1619. He played an important though not always enviable part in the affairs of Virginia and New England. In 1616, when the Duke of Savoy was at war with Spain, he sent out several ships under the commission of the Duke to prey upon Spanish commerce. One of these ships, the Treasurer, under Captain Daniel Elfrith, roved about in the West Indies, where she took certain negroes from the Spaniards, and in consort with a man-of-war of Flushing brought them to Virginia in 1619. These were the first negroes imported. Rich was added to the council for Virginia in 1619. Having quarrelled with Sir Thomas Smythe, the treasurer of the company, because of bad feeling created by the marriage of his sister Isabel to Smythe's son, Sir John Smythe, he united with the popular party in the Virginia Company and elected Sir Edwin Sandys as treasurer. He soon repented of this act, and was afterwards a bitter opponent of Southampton and Sandys, and contributed to the abrogation of the charter in 1624. After the dissolution he was a member of the council for Virginia appointed by the King. Warwick River county, founded in 1634, was named for him, which in 1643 received its present name, Warwick county.

He was active in the affairs of New England, was member of the New England council in 1620, signed the first Plymouth patent, June 1, 1621, and was president of the New England council, 1630-32. He was also interested in the Bermudas, the Bahamas and in Guiana. He espoused the Puritan side in the civil wars, and parliament in 1643 made him admiral of the islands and coasts of America, but he was deprived of this office in 1645. In May, 1648, he was made lord high admiral by parliament, but his commission was revoked the following year. When Cromwell succeeded to power, Lord Rich made friends with him, and on his death April 18, 1658, left his estate more improved and repaired than any man who figured in the rebellion.

Rich, Sir Nathaniel, eldest son of Richard, illegitimate son of Robert, second Lord Rich; member of parliament at different times; interested in the Bermudas in 1616; knighted at Hutton House, November 8, 1617. He was a leading member of the Warwick party in the factions of the Virginia Company, 1622, and wrote many of the papers and documents emanating from his side. After the dissolution of the company in 1624, he was one of the commissioners for Virginia appointed by the King. He was also member of the council for New England in 1620, and deputy governor of the Bahamas Company in 1635. He died in 1636.

Danvers, Sir John, regicide, born about 1588, third and youngest son of Sir John Danvers, of Dauntsey, Wiltshire, by Elizabeth, fourth daughter and coheiress of John Neville, last Lord Latimer. He was a very handsome man, and it is said people would run to see him on the streets. In 1608 he married Magdalene Herbert, widow of Richard Herbert and mother of ten children, including George Herbert, the poet, and Edward, Lord Herbert of Cherbury. He was knighted by King James, and under Charles I. became a gentleman of the privy chamber. He was a member of the Virginia council, 1612-20, and was one of the Sandys faction in the Virginia Company, 1620-25. He acquired an intense jealousy of the crown and sided with the parliament against the King. He was a member of the commission nominated to try the King in January, 1649, and signed the death warrant. In February of the same year he was given a seat in the council of state, which he retained till the council's dissolution in 1653. He died at his home in Chelsea in April, 1655, and was buried at Dauntsey. His name was in the act of attainder passed at the restoration. He had two brothers—Sir Charles Danvers, who was beheaded for participation in Essex's Rebellion of 1601; and Sir Henry Danvers, Earl of Danby, and afterwards a friend of Charles I., who died in 1644.

Wroth, Sir Thomas, prominent member of the Virginia Company, was brother-in-law of Sir Nathaniel Rich, and sided with him against Southampton and Sandys. He was a subscriber to the Virginia Company in 1609, and after the dissolution of the charter was one of the commissioners appointed to take charge of the colony July 15, 1624. On November 3, 1620, he became a member of the council in New England, and June 25, 1653, he was made a commissioner for the government of the Bermudas. In domestic politics Wroth joined the opposition to the King and was a member of the Long Parliament. He adopted the views of the independents, and on June 3, 1647-48, moved the famous resolution that Charles I. be impeached and the kingdom settled without him. He was appointed one of the judges to try the King, but attended only one session. After the restoration he petitioned for pardon, which was apparently granted, and Wroth lived in retirement until his death, aged 88, at Petherton Park, July 11, 1672.

Wolstenholme, Sir John, merchant, was second son of Sir John Wolstenholme, of London, of an ancient Derbyshire family. He was a leading man in the East India Company and the Virginia Company. On April 28, 1619, he was one of the candidates for treasurer of the Virginia Company, and in May, 1622, was recommended by the King as a person most suited to the office, but he was not elected. He was a member of the commission appointed July 15, 1624, to take charge of the company's affairs after its dissolution in May, and in 1631 held place on the commission requested to suggest to the King a form of government for Virginia. He aided Capt. William Clayborne in settling Kent Island, and in 1634 he was one of the tobacco commissioners. He had a strong faith in the Northwest Passage, and contributed liberally to all the different expeditions sent out while he was living—Henry Hudson's, Button's, etc. He died aged 77, November 25, 1639, and was buried in Magna Church, where there is a handsome monument to his memory.

Smith, or Smyth, John, a great antiquary, son of Thomas Smyth, of Hoby, Leicestershire, and grandson of William Smyth, of Humberton, in Leicestershire; was born in 1567, and educated at Magdalene College, Oxford. He is generally known as John Smyth of Nibley. After completing his studies he returned to the Berkeley family as household steward, a post which he exchanged in 1597 for the more lucrative and dignified office of steward of the hundred and liberty of Berkeley. As keeper of the archives at Berkeley Castle, he had rich material for his "Lives" of the first twenty-one Lords Berkeley from the Conquest down, which after remaining in manuscript for a long time has been published. He left also in MSS. a "History of the Borough and Manor of Tetbury," "Tenure by Knights Service Under the Berkeleys," and several other works. He was an active member of the Virginia Company and regularly attended its meetings, and in 1618 determined to make a plantation of his own in that country. For this purpose he formed a partnership with Sir William Throckmorton, Sir George Yeardley, Richard Berkeley and George Thorpe, and obtained a special charter from the parent company. They established a settlement at James river, which was called "Berkeley Hundred," and which was afterwards the birthplace of President William Henry Harrison. He was a member of parliament in 1621, but took little part in the politics of the stormy times in which he lived. He died at Nibley in the autumn of 1640.

Martin, Richard, a noted lawyer, born at Otterton in Devonshire; student at Oxford, and afterwards at the Middle Temple. His learning, politeness and wit were the delight and admiration of all his acquaintances. He was frequently a member of parliament, and in 1601 spoke most eloquently against the monopolists. In 1612 he was a member of the council for the Virginia Company, and in 1614 he made a vigorous speech in behalf of the colony in parliament. In 1617 he was head of a private company which obtained from the Virginia Company a grant of 80,000 acres of land about seven miles below Jamestown. The estate called "Carter's Grove" is situated in this region in James City county. In 1618 he was made recorder of the city of London, but died a month later of the smallpox, and was buried in Temple Church, London. His grant of land in Virginia was known as "Martin's Hundred."

Cranfield, Lionel, Earl of Middlesex, was the younger son of Thomas Cranfield, Mercer of London, by Martha, daughter of Vincent Randolph, was baptized March 13, 1575; was an active and successful man of affairs, and rose rapidly to all the honors of the kingdom; was knighted July 4, 1613, and a few days later made surveyor-general of the customs; was master of the court of requests; master of the wardrobe; master of the wards; and commissioner of the navy; privy councillor; lord treasurer; Baron Cranfield, and Earl of Middlesex. He was a member of the council for the Virginia Company, and the Sandys-Ferrar faction attributed to him more than any other man the abrogation of the charter—by urging the company into dissensions over the tobacco contract. Having incurred the enmity of Buckingham, King James' favorite, he was impeached and fined £50,000, but a year later Charles I. released him from the fine, and August 20, 1626, he was granted a formal pardon. He retired to his splendid seat, Copt Hall in Essex, where he died August 6, 1645. He was buried in Westminster Abbey.

Digges, Sir Dudley, eldest son of Thomas Digges by his wife Anne St. Leger, was born in 1583, and educated at University College, Oxford. He studied law, and after being knighted at Whitehall, April 29, 1607, travelled to improve himself on the continent. He was sent in 1618 as ambassador to Russia by James I.; two years after, he went to Holland as commissioner, with Sir Maurice Abbott, to settle differences between the English and Dutch East India Company. He served in parliament during the reigns of James I. and Charles I., and his conduct was very independent and often hostile to the measures of the court. He was one of the commissioners to conduct the impeachment of the King's favorite, the Duke of Buckingham, and the King arrested him and sent him a prisoner to the Tower of London, but he was released in a few days on complaint of parliament. After this, measures were taken to win him over to the King's side, and he was granted the reversion of master of the rolls, November 17, 1630. He died March 18, 1639, and was buried at Chilham Manor near Canterbury.

He was greatly interested in explorations and colonization. In 1610 he aided in sending Henry Hudson to the northwest, and wrote a little tract on the Northwest Passage. For the same end he aided in 1612 in sending out Capt. Thomas Button and Master Francis Nelson, and was one of the directors of the Northwest Passage Company. He was member of the Bermuda Islands Company, and of the East India Company. In addition he was constantly interested in the Virginia Company, of which he was also a member. He was member of the royal council for Virginia in 1609, and in 1619 was one of the committee of the Virginia Company to codify the rules. He was also one of the committee regarding the establishment of the college at Henrico. In 1631 he was appointed one of the commissioners to advise concerning Virginia. He married Mary, youngest daughter and coheir of Sir Thomas Kemp, of Olantigh. Edward, one of his sons, settled in Virginia, and was governor of the colony in 1656.

Copeland, Rev. Patrick, was a Puritan minister, who was first employed in the service of the East India Company. In 1614 he was chaplain on one of the company's ships. In 1616 he returned to England accompanied by a native whom he had taught chiefly by signs to speak, read and write the English language correctly in less than a year. At his suggestion this lad was publicly baptized on December 22, in St. Dennis Church, London, "as the first fruits of India." Not long after, in 1617, Copeland, with his pupil, sailed for the Indian ocean in the Royal James, one of the fleet which Sir Thomas Dale, late governor of Virginia, assumed the command of on September 19, 1618. In the presence of Dale, in view of an impending naval conflict with the Dutch on December 2, Copeland preached on the Royal James. On August 9, 1619, Dale died, and his old associate, Sir Thomas Gates, died in the same service the next year. Copeland on the Royal James went to Java. Leaving Java in February, 1621, the ship slowly returned to England, and Copeland having become interested in Virginia by conversing with Dale and Gates, collected on the homeward voyage from his fellow passengers the sum of £70, to be employed for the use of a church or school in Virginia. This sum, when he arrived in London, he delivered to the authorities of the Virginia Company, who made him a free member. They decided that there was more need of a school than a church, and designed the money, increased to £100 by a gift of £30 from another source, for the establishment of a free school at Charles City, now City Point, which should hold a due dependence on the proposed university at Henrico and be called the "East India School," after its East India benefactors. In recognition of his zeal for the colony and his experience as a missionary, the company on July 3, 1622, appointed Mr. Copeland rector of the intended college for the Indians, a part of the university, as well as a member of the council for Virginia.

On Wednesday, April 17, 1622, Copeland, at the invitation of the London Company, preached a thanksgiving sermon in London for the happy success of affairs in Virginia the previous year. But about the middle of July it was learned from Capt. Daniel Gookin, who came from Newport News, that on Good Friday, March 22, the Indians, whose children were so largely in the proposed scheme of instruction, had risen and barbarously destroyed George Thorpe, the noble superintendent in charge of the college lands, and 346 more of the unsuspecting settlers. The university, college and free school were all three abandoned, and Copeland did not go to Virginia. He afterwards went to the Bermuda Islands, where he was living in 1638 and later. About 1645 he left the Bermudas and went to a small island in the Bahama group, to form a Puritan church which should have no connection with the state. The isle, which was called "Eluthera," proved a dreary place, and friends of the religion in Boston were obliged to send the settlers supplies, and in 1651 many of them returned to Bermuda, where Copeland, then more than four score years of age, must soon have died.

Sackvill, Sir Edward, Earl of Dorset, born in 1590, educated at Christ Church, Oxford, 1605-09; made a knight of the Bath, November 3, 1618; commanded troops sent to the Elector Palatine, and fought at Prague in 1620; member of parliament; sent on an embassy to France; member of the privy council. He was an active member of the Virginia Company, and took sides with Southampton and Sandys in the factions from 1620 to 1625. After his brother Richard's death in March, 1624, he succeeded him as fourth Earl of Dorset. He was on the commission of 1631 for the management of Virginia affairs, and constantly tried to influence Charles to reestablish the Virginia Company of London. He was a distinguished cavalier in the civil war, and died at Withiam, Sussex, July 27, 1625.

Purchas, Rev. Samuel, a divine known as an early collector of voyages and travels, born in 1574, at Thaxted in Essex, and educated at St. John's College, Cambridge; he was curate of Purleigh, in Essex, the parish of which Rev. Lawrence Washington was rector, 1633-43. He was afterwards vicar of Eastwood in Essex, 1604-13. In 1614 he was collated to the rectory of St. Martin's Ludgate, London, where he continued till his death, and appointed chaplain to George Abbott, archbishop of Canterbury. His "Pilgrimage" was published soon after November 5, 1612. The second edition appeared in 1614. After Hakluyt's death he had access to his papers, and published a third edition of his work much enlarged in 1617. "Purchas his Pilgrim— Microcosmos, or the Historie of Man," was published in 1619. In December, 1621, "Purchas his Pilgrims" was entered at Stationers Hall for publication. May 22, 1622, he was admitted into the Virginia Company of London. His last work appears to have been "The King's Tower and Triumphant Arch of London." He died in 1626, aged 51 years.

COLONIAL PRESIDENTS AND GOVERNORS

II—COLONIAL PRESIDENTS AND GOVERNORS

Wingfield, Edward Maria, first president of the council of Virginia, of "Stoneley Priorye" in Huntingdonshire, was born about 1560, of a very distinguished family and was a soldier in Ireland and the Netherlands. He was active in procuring the charter of 1606, and his name is one of the first of the incorporators, which appear in that paper. He was appointed by the Council in England one of the local Council in Virginia and on May 14, 1607, he was elected at Jamestown by this body their first president. His experience was unfortunate. The colony was at once assailed by the Indians, and the president was among the foremost in repelling the attacks, "having an arrow shot clean through his beard." Then followed a pestilential sickness which prostrated everybody in the fort. Added to this the constitution of the Council under the charter offered a premium to wranglings and dissensions, for a mere majority controlled everything and could remove the president or any of the members. Wingfield was blamed by the others for what could not be prevented, by any president, and the most trivial objections were made against him to justify his deposition from the presidency. It was charged that he was a Catholic, because he did not bring a Bible with him, that he monopolized the liquors and other provisions, etc., all of which Wingfield vigorously denies in his statement, and shows that he made many sacrifices out of his own private stores for the good of the colony. He was, nevertheless, removed both from the Council and his office as president, September 10, 1607. He was kept a prisoner on shipboard till Newport's arrival in January, 1608, and April 10, 1608, he returned with Newport to England. He afterwards wrote an account of his stay in Virginia, which was discovered and published not many years ago, and it gives us a very different idea of the man from that so long current on the authority of John Smith, who was his bitter personal enemy. He never returned to Virginia.

Ratcliffe, John, alias Sicklemore, second president of the local council at Jamestown, had seen service as a seaman before coming to Virginia. He was also, it is believed, a soldier in the Low Countries, and is supposed to have been the Captain Ratcliffe who was taken prisoner with Sir Henry Cary and Captain Pigott at Mulheim in October, 1605. He commanded the Discovery, the smallest of the three ships that brought the emigrants to Jamestown. When the names of the councillors were read, April 26, 1607, Ratcliffe's name was one of them. On the deposition of Wingfield, Ratcliffe became president, but the summer of 1608 proving as unhealthy as that of 1607, Ratcliffe suffered an experience similar to Wingfield's, was removed from the government in July, 1608, and succeeded by Mathew Scrivener. One subject of complaint against him was that he enlisted the men in building a governor's house. When Captain Newport sailed from Virginia, December, 1608, Captain Ratcliffe accompanied him. Owing to his complaints and Wingfield's, a new charter was obtained by the London Company, and Ratcliffe commanded the

Diamond, one of the ships in the great fleet of Sir Thomas Gates, who bore the commission of governor. During the temporary administration of George Percy, he was sent in October, 1609, to build a fort at Old Point Comfort, which was named "Algernourne Fort" in honor of President Percy's ancestor. The following December, going to trade with the Indians, he was led into an ambush and killed with fourteen others under his command, at Werowocomoco on York river. Smith calls him "a poor counterfeit imposter," because he used an alias, but there was no imposition. Ratcliffe made no secret of his double name, signing himself "John Ratcliffe commonly called." Very frequently in his time men wrote their names with an alias on account of a second marriage of their mother. Ratcliffe's mother probably first married Sicklemore and afterwards Ratcliffe, and Ratcliffe's real name was probably John Sicklemore.

Scrivener, Mathew, third president of the Virginia council under the first charter. He subscribed largely to the stock of the company. He arrived in Virginia with Newport in the "First Supply," which came in January, 1608, a member of the council in Virginia; participated in the expedition up York river in February, 1608; on the authority of Smith acting president of the council from July to September 10, 1608, and in January, 1609, at which time he was drowned in James river. Rev. Richard Hakluyt mentions in his will "Rev. John Scrivener, late of Barbican in the suburbs of the Cittie of London;" and as Scrivener is not a very common name, the aforesaid Matthew and John were probably members of the same family and doubtless relatives of Richard Hakluyt.

Smith, John, fourth president of the Virginia council, was the eldest son of George and Alice Smith, tenants of Peregrine Bertie, Lord Willoughby; was baptized at Willoughby, January 9, 1580; travelled extensively abroad, where he encountered many perils by sea and land; distinguished himself by killing three Turks one after another, for which astonishing prowess he received from Prince Sigismund of Transylvania, a coat-of-arms charged with three Turks heads. That he was a man of distinction in England is proved by the fact of his selection by the king as a member of the first Virginia council. He sailed to America with the first colonists, but was charged by Wingfield and others as an instigator of Galthorpe's mutiny in the West Indies, and was kept under arrest till June 10, 1607, some three weeks after the landing at Jamestown. After the deposition of Wingfield from the presidency and the election of Ratcliffe, Smith acted as cape merchant, and was quite successful in procuring corn from the Indians. In one of these expeditions up the Chickahominy river he was taken prisoner by the Indians. He remained a prisoner about three weeks, during which time he was taken from town to town and finally conducted to Werowocomoco on York river to be put to death. From this peril he was rescued by Pocahontas, one of the daughters of Powhatan, head chief of the Powhatan confederacy, and soon after was suffered to return unharmed to Jamestown. Here he ran into a new danger, when the council, under lead of Gabriel Archer, condemned him to be hanged as responsible for the death of Emry and Robinson, who accompanied him to the Chickahominy; but Captain Newport arriving the same night (January 2, 1608) with the "First Supply," and inter-

JOHN SMITH

fering in his behalf, Smith was released. Smith continued his explorations and in the summer of 1608 made a full discovery of Chesapeake Bay, and its tributary rivers. On September 10, 1608, he assumed the presidency, and among the first things he did was to enlarge the area of the fort by the addition of about three acres, changing the plan from a triangle to a pentagon. After the "Second Supply" of men and provisions arrived, in October, 1608, there occurred two months later the first marriage of English people in America, that of John Laydon and Ann Burras. Smith started an extensive system of improvements at Jamestown, in which he kept the men engaged for several months, but a remarkable disclosure of carelessness on his part rendered the work of little value. It was suddenly discovered that the corn in the storehouse on which the colonists depended was nearly all consumed by rats and the remainder was unfit to eat. To save the colonists from starvation he had to break them up in small parties, and station them at different points, sending some to live with the Indians and others to the oyster banks down the river. While the colony was in this desperate condition, the "Third Supply" arrived, bringing news of a new charter and the appointment of Sir Thomas Gates as governor. As Sir Thomas' ship, the Sea Venture, had been wrecked and given up for lost, the crowd of settlers who landed had no recognized leader and Smith declined to surrender his authority. Violent quarrels took place. Smith was arrested, and in October, 1609, he returned to England. Smith, in contrasting the results of his administration with the "starving time," which followed, claims credit rather unjustly for what the new arrivals accomplished. In reviewing his connection with Virginia, the evidence is reached that while he was a strong and masterful spirit, he was contentious, boastful and illiberal in his treatment of others. So long as he stayed, the colony was rent by factions of which he was certainly an active promoter.

Smith was in England from 1609 to 1614, when he was taken into the employment of the North Virginia Company, created admiral of New England, and sent on several voyages thither. He remained in this service two years, after which till his death, June 21, 1631, he lived in England devoting himself to writing. During his stay in Virginia he had sent home in 1608 a report which was soon after published as "A Trewe Relation." In 1612 he published his "Map of Virginia," in 1616 his "Description of New England," in 1620 "New England's Trials," and in 1624 the "General Historie of Virginia, New England and the Summer Islands," and in 1630 "The True Travels." These works have all the same general style, suggestive of the character of Smith, being involved, hasty, inaccurate and illiberal, but sincere, open and fearless. While his narratives must not be taken without qualifications, and not much weight is to be attached to his opinions of others, there is no real reason to reject his authority on the main issues.

Percy, George, fifth president of the council, was the eighth son of Henry, eighth Earl of Northumberland, by his wife Catherine, eldest daughter and co-heir of John Neville, Lord Latimer, was born September 4, 1580, served for a time in the Low countries, and sailed for Virginia in the first expedition, December, 1606. Here he was very useful in obtaining corn from the Indians and assisting in the explorations. When the settlers, who came over under the second charter, appeared at Jamestown without their governor or their charter. Percy was persuaded to accept the presidency on the expiration of Smith's term of office. Probably no ability as a leader could have accomplished anything, and Percy was soon incapacitated by illness. The period of his administration is known as the starving time. The new settlers had landed sick and without adequate supplies, and they soon consumed the provisions that the old settlers had at Jamestown. The consequence was that they nearly all died, and there were only sixty settlers remaining, when the governor under the new commission, Sir Thomas Gates arrived from Bermuda where he had been wrecked and compelled to remain for forty weeks. When Lord Delaware left Virginia in March, 1611, Percy was appointed deputy governor, which shows the confidence entertained in him, despite his unfortunate experiences. He was a brave soldier, and in punishment for treachery attacked and destroyed the towns of the Paspaheghs and of the Appomattox people. He left Virginia, April 22, 1612, and reached England in the following summer. He never returned to Virginia, but about 1625, when war was declared against Spain, he went again to the Netherlands where as captain of a company he distinguished himself, losing a finger in battle. He died unmarried in 1632.

He kept a journal of the original Virginia voyage, an abridgement of which was published for the first time in 1625 by Samuel Purchas. Mutilated as it was, it presents the fullest account we have of the voyage and of the first events of the settlement to Newport's departure June 12, 1607. After the appearance of Smith's "General Historie" with his very prejudiced account of the affairs during the time of Percy's government, Captain Percy wrote "A Trewe Relacyon" of the occurrences in Virginia from the time of the shipwreck of Sir Thomas Gates in 1609 until his own departure from the country in 1612. In a letter to his brother Henry, Earl of Northumberland, he declared that his account was induced by the many untruths formerly published. This interesting narrative still remains in manuscript owing to the narrow conceptions of its present possessor, although he has suffered some few extracts to be published by Dr. E. D. Neill and Mr. G. C. Eggleston.

Gates, Sir Thomas, appointed the first and absolute governor of Virginia under the second charter to the Virginia Company of London, is said to have been born at Colyford, in Colyton parish, Devonshire; was a lieutenant of Captain Christopher Carleill's own company in the celebrated Drake-Sidney voyage to America 1585-86; published the Brigges Croftes account of this voyage in 1589, which he dedicated to the Earl of Essex; served gallantly at the capture of Cadiz and was knighted by Essex in June, 1596. He also served in the island voyage August-October, 1597; entered Gray's Inn March 14, 1598. About 1603 he enlisted in the service of the Netherlands, but when King James granted the first charter to the Virginia Company of London, he "had the honor to all posterity" of being first named in that celebrated document. He was in the garrison at Oudwater in South Holland with Dale in November, 1606; and in 1608 he received leave of absence to go to Virginia. The Virginia Company selected him as first governor under the new charter (1609), and in June he took passage with about 500 settlers. This expedition is known as the "Third Supply," and the emigration was the largest that ever left England up to that time. But the voyage over was very unfortunate, for an epidemic broke out among the passengers and there followed a great storm which scattered the fleet and wrecked upon the Bermuda Islands the Sea Venture which bore the governor and one hundred and fifty passengers; and though the rest of the fleet reached Jamestown in safety, their arrival only added to the trouble already existing there. The new settlers brought with them the yellow fever and the London plague, and, as their provisions were all ruined by sea water, the next nine months were a season of disease and starvation.

In the meantime, Gates and his fellow passengers on the Sea Venture were comfortably housed on the Bermuda Islands, and out of the cedar that grew there they constructed two vessels in which they at length got away. On May 23, 1610, they arrived at Jamestown to find all but sixty of the settlers dead. Gates relieved the immediate distress by the prompt distribution of provisions, and then asserted order by the publication of a code of martial law drawn up in England. Deeming the conditions desperate, Gates, with the advice of his council, determined to abandon Jamestown, and on June 7, 1610, embarked with all the surviving settlers. On the way down the river he learned of the arrival of Lord Delaware at Point Comfort as governor for life, and in obedience to instructions took his fleet back to Jamestown. Under Delaware's commission Gates became lieutenant-governor and commanded an expedition against the Indians, whom he drove from Kecoughtan. In July, however, of the same year, he was sent to England for supplies. He returned to Jamestown August 1, 1611, when finding that Lord Delaware had departed he again assumed direction of affairs. He remained in Virginia nearly three years, and returned to England in April, 1614. Soon after, he resumed his service in Holland and was paid by the states all past dues. He appears to have retained his interest in Virginia, and in 1620 we find him as one of "the Ancient Adventurers" petitioning to have some man of quality sent over as governor. During his administration new settlements were established at Henrico, Bermuda Hundred, City Point and other places; the French were driven from New England; and Pocahontas, daughter to the Emperor Powhatan, was captured and soon after married to John Rolfe. He left a son of the same name, who distinguished himself in 1626 in the expedition against Cadiz and in 1627 at the Isle of Ré and Rochelle, when he was killed by a cannon shot.

Dale, Sir Thomas, high marshal of Virginia, and deputy governor from May 21, to August 1, 1611, and from March, 1614, till May, 1616. He entered the service of the Low Countries with the Earl of Essex in 1588. In 1595 he was sent by the Provinces into Scotland, where he became one of the retinue of the infant Prince Henry, who had a great affection for him. He remained in Scotland some years, but returned to the Netherlands probably in 1603. In 1604 Lord Cecil wrote to the English ambassador at the Hague to inform him of the king's gracious interest in the military advancement of Dale. On June 19, 1606, while on a visit to England, he was knighted at Richmond by King James as "Sir Thomas Dale of Surrey." He remained in the service of the Low Countries till February 1611, when he came to England and entered into the service of the Virginia Company of London. Dale was selected to head the expedition then preparing, and on March 27, 1611, he left Land's End with three ships carrying 300 people and also horses, cows, goats, fowl, etc. He reached Point Comfort or Algernourne Fort on May 22, 1611, and succeeded Captain George Percy in command of the colony. He found forts Charles and Henry, at the mouth of Hampton river, deserted, and his first labor was to restore them. Constituting James Davis as captain of all three forts, he sailed up the river and arrived at Jamestown May 29, 1611, where he landed and heard a sermon from Rev. Mr. Poole. After consulting his council, Dale set about many extensive improvements at Jamestown and determined to build a new town at Henrico, near the Indian town of Arrohatec. Fears of the intervention of the Spaniards had long disturbed the colonists and there was a great excitement in the colony when some Spaniards from ships sent to find out about the English settlement, landing at Point Comfort, were captured and sent to Jamestown, where they were detained in captivity for a long time. He began the work of building the settlement at Henrico under the severest code of martial law, introduced by Gates, and which he ruthlessly enforced. Gates, who arrived August 1 and became Dale's superior officer, endorsed his policy. After Gates' departure for England in 1614, Dale was again chief magistrate in Virginia. While he has received praise for his administration of affairs it appears to have been in large measure undeserved. The men were given food not fit for hogs, and mutinies repeatedly occurred, which were suppressed by the most atrocious cruelties. When Dale left Virginia in 1616, there were only 300 settlers living in the colony, and the frail habitations at Henrico, which he had built in blood, were decayed and ready to fall. He took with him to England Pocahontas and several other Indians, who attracted much attention and lent a glamour to his return.

The states general of the Low Countries paid him £1,000 for the period when he was in Virginia, though during that time he rendered no service. A voyage was intended for the East Indies, and Dale was selected to head it. His fleet arrived near Java on December 23, 1618, and in conjunction with Captain Martin Pring he made an attack on the Dutch fleet. It was "a cruel bloody fight" and both sides claimed the victory. He arrived with his fleet at Masulipitan July 19 and he died there August 9, 1619, after twenty days of languishing sickness. Sir Thomas Dale married, in January, 1611, Elizabeth, daughter of Sir Thomas Throckmorton and his wife Elizabeth, daughter of Sir Richard Berkeley.

West, Thomas, Lord Delaware, second governor of Virginia, was the son of Sir Thomas West, second Lord Delaware, and Annie his wife, daughter of Sir Francis Knollys and Katherine Cary, his wife. He was one of thirteen children, and was born July 9, 1577; educated at Oxford, and was a Master of Arts at that university. He early saw military service and was a great friend of the Earl of Essex, who knighted him at Dublin, July 12, 1599. He was implicated in the Essex rebellion and was imprisoned. Essex, however, asked pardon of his father, the second Lord Delaware, for bringing his son into danger. After the father's death, March 24, 1602, he succeeded as third Lord Delaware, and was a member of the privy council of Queen Elizabeth, and on her death became a privy councillor to King James. He took a most active interest in the American enterprise, and in 1609 was a member of the superior council of Virginia in England. The experience with the first charter left the impression with the public, that only a supreme and abso-

LORD DE LA WARE

lute governor could obviate the dissensions and faction that characterized the history of the colony. A help to order lay, it was believed, in the selection of a man whose rank would inspire respect, and when the second charter was obtained the Virginia Company turned to Lord Delaware. As he was, however, unable to go at once, they conferred the office of governor temporarily upon Sir Thomas Gates. On February 28, 1610, Delaware was commissioned governor of the Virginia colony for life, and was sent with 150 emigrants, chiefly workmen, to the assistance of Jamestown. He arrived at Point Comfort, June 7, 1610, just in time to save the colony from abandonment by Gates. Delaware sent the pinnace *Virginia* up the river to meet the departing settlers, and under the orders of the new governor they were all taken back again to Jamestown. Sunday, June 10, Lord Delaware himself arrived. He had the town cleaned and rehabilitated the frail houses. The settlement of four acres was defended by new palisades and everything was made safe and comfortable for the time being. He next proceeded to settle matters with the Indians, and after driving Pochins and his tribe from Kecoughtan he erected two forts at the mouth of Hampton river, called Charles and Henry, about three miles from Point Comfort. In the interim he sent out an expedition to search for mines above the falls, but the Indians were very troublesome and no mines were found. It was the fashion of the times to boost the country at the expense of the poor colonists, who were traduced and villified. Delaware, in a letter to the London Company, pursued the example, but retribution followed fast. The great trouble was the unhealthiness of the country and the rotten supplies sent over, which introduced sickness and death, and Delaware was literally bombarded out of the country by a combined attack of ague, flux, cramp and gout. To save his life he went first to the West Indies, whence he sailed to England, where he arrived rather crestfallen about a year after his departure. He remained in the latter country till 1618, and in his absence the government of Virginia was administered by Deputy Governors Gates, Dale, Yardley and Argall. In the latter year he was sent again to Virginia to rescue the government from the hands of Samuel Argall, who had incurred the strong resentment of the Virginia Company of London, but on the way over he died June 7, 1618, aged forty-one. He married Cecily, daughter of Sir Thomas Sherley. His son and successor was Henry, fourth Lord Delaware, who married Isabella, daughter of Sir Thomas Edmunds. Governor Delaware had three brothers—Francis West, John West and Nathaniel West, who all lived in Virginia, and the first two of whom were deputy governors at different times; William West, a nephew, was killed by Indians at the Falls of James river, Virginia, in 1611. Through Captain John West, the noble family of the Delawares is widely represented in Virginia and the south and west.

Yardley, George, deputy governor of Virginia, from May, 1616, to May, 1617 and governor and captain-general of Virginia from April, 1619 to November 18, 1621, and from May 17, 1626 to November 13, 1627, was son of Ralph Yardley, citizen and merchant tailor of Bionshaw Lane, London, who married (1) Agnes Abbot and (2) Rhoda ———. He was one of four brothers: Ralph; George, the subject of the present sketch; John and Thomas; and a sister Anne, who married Edward Irby. He served like many other of the early settlers as a soldier in the Low Countries, that "university of war." He sailed to Virginia in 1609, with Sir Thomas Gates, as captain of his company; was wrecked with his superior officer on the Bermuda Islands, but finally arrived in Virginia in May, 1610. When Gates embarked the colonists to return to England, the company, commanded by Captain Yardley, was the last to get aboard, thereby preventing the town from being burned. When Lord Delaware turned the departing settlers back and resumed the work of colonization, Yardley was made commandant of Forts Charles and Henry, at the mouth of Hampton river. Subsequently under orders he abandoned these forts in order to lead an expedition to discover a gold mine beyond the Falls of James river. The Queen of Appomattox invited some of his companions to a feast, and while they were eating, treacherously massacred fourteen of them, including "all the chief men skillful in finding out mines." The colonists retorted by burning her town and killing some of her people. The expedition got no farther than the falls of the river, where they built a fort and remained six months. When Sir Thomas Dale began to build at Bermuda City, Yardley was commandant of the town. When Dale left Virginia in 1616, Yardley, who acted as deputy-governor resided at Bermuda City for the most part. He encouraged the planting of tobacco, with the result that emigration, which had almost entirely ceased, set in again with strong force. Private stock companies were formed, which sent colonies on their own account to Virginia. Yardley also taught the Indians a punitive lesson. The Chickahominy tribe declined to pay the corn tax, which they had promised Sir Thomas Dale, and about Christmas, 1616, Yardley with 84 men promptly attacked them and in a very short time brought them to terms. In May, 1617, Captain Argall came in, with a commission as deputy governor, and with orders to portion out lands, as the joint stock period of the charter had expired. This he did not do, and he is charged not only with continuing the common slavery, but plundering the "common garden" belonging to the company. Then the company tried to send back the Lord Governor Delaware, but he died on the way, and in January, 1619, Captain Yardley was commissioned as governor and captain-general under an order abolishing martial law and establishing a free government. Yardley arrived at Jamestown April 10, and immediately called the first legislative assembly that ever convened in America. Other events render the year memorable such as the introduction in August of the first negro slaves, and the arrival from England of a ship with twenty young maidens "pure and undefiled" to furnish wives to the tenants of the public lands. Despite the terrible mortality of the climate the colony increased in population and property. Dale in 1616 left 351 persons in the colony, but there were about 1200 at the close of Yardley's administration in 1621, all of them "seasoned" settlers. Sir Francis Wyatt came in as governor in November of that year, and Yardley was then a member of the council until May, 1626. He was very efficient in punishing the Indians after the massacre of 1622. When Wyatt wished to leave Virginia for a time on business, the king commissioned Yardley to be governor of Virginia a second time. He entered into that office in May, 1626, but did not serve much more than a year. He died November 13, 1627, and was interred in the church at Jamestown. He married, about 1618, Temperance West, and had issue two sons, Argall and Francis, the first of whom has numerous descendants in the United States. Yardley made a great deal of money out of tobacco, and was as popular with the Indians as with the whites. The Indian King of Weyanoke gave him a fertile tract of land in Charles City county between Mapsico creek and Queen's creek, known as Weyanoke. This good man was one of the greatest benefactors of Virginia, and with Sir Edwyn Sandys deserves a monument at the hands of the people of the United States. If Sandys instituted the move which freed the people of Virginia from martial law and gave them representative government, Yardley executed the orders and proved himself always the sympathetic friend of liberty.

Argall, Samuel, deputy governor and admiral of Virginia from May, 1617, to April 10, 1619, was born about 1580. Little is known of his early life, but as he was selected to discover a shorter way to Virginia in 1609, he must have been very early regarded as a mariner of tact and ability. He brought to Smith and the colony of Jamestown the first news of the second charter and the appointment of Sir Thomas Gates as governor. Finding the colony in great need, he furnished them with some provisions, and after making a successful trial of sturgeon fishing he returned to England. When Lord Delaware sailed on March, 1610, as governor, Captain Argall conducted him by way of the Canary and Azores Islands—the shorter route discovered by him. June 18, 1610, he was made a member of the governor's council and next day sailed with Somers to the Bermuda Islands, but missed them and sailed to Cape Cod, where he engaged in successful fishing. On his voyage homewards he explored the coast and discovered Delaware Bay. September 1 he reached Algernourne Fort on Point Comfort. During the autumn and winter he explored the waters of Chesapeake Bay, and sailed from Virginia with Lord Delaware March 28, reaching England in June, 1611. On July 23, 1612, he made another trip to Virginia, and for a year remained in the service of the colony, voyaging about the bay and the rivers exploring and securing corn from the Indians, in which business he was remarkably successful. In one of these voyages he captured Pocahontas, daughter of King Powhatan, and brought her to Jamestown. Soon after June 28, 1613, he sailed from Virginia under orders from Sir Thomas Gates, and drove away the French from New England, thus keeping that country open to the Pilgrim Fathers, who came seven years later. He is said to have visited on this voyage the Dutch settlement on the Hudson, and compelled the governor, Hendrick Christiansen, to submit to the king of England. After that he was variously employed in Virginia from December, 1613, to June 18, 1614, when he sailed for England. In February, 1615, he again sailed to Virginia and returned to England with Dale in May, 1616. Early in 1617 he was appointed deputy governor and admiral of Virginia. He continued in this office two years, and he is generally represented as an unscrupulous chief magistrate, but party feeling was very high at this time, and the evidence cannot be relied on. He appears to have been a partner with the Earl of Warwick in bringing the first negroes to Jamestown in 1619. After Lord Delaware's death he quarrelled with Captain Edward Brewster, who had care of Delaware's estate, and wanted to put him to death for mutiny. The company became incensed with him and sent orders by Captain Yardley, appointed to succeed him, to arrest him and to examine into his acts. But the Earl of Warwick took means to rescue his friend and dispatched a small vessel to fetch him and his goods away before Yardley could arrive. This vessel arrived in Virginia, April 6, and Argall sailed away on her about the 10th, leaving Captain Nathaniel Powell as deputy governor. On his arrival from Virginia he answered the different charges brought again him, satisfactorily to some, but not to others. His activity as a seaman still continued. In 1620-21 he commanded a ship in the fleet of Sir Robert Mansell in the Mediterranean Sea. About 1621 he urged that an English settlement be made in New Netherlands, afterwards New York. In 1624 his friends wished to make him governor again of Virginia, but Sir Francis Wyatt was preferred. He was admiral in September, 1625, of 28 ships, and during his cruise captured from the Spaniards seven vessels valued at £100,000. In the attack on Cadiz in 1625 he commanded the flagship. He was still alive in 1633, but was dead before 1641, as in that year his daughter Ann, widow of Alexander Bolling, and her second husband, Samuel Percivall, complained to the House of Commons that they had been deprived by John Woodhall of property in Virginia left to the petitioner Anne by her late father, Sir Samuel Argall, sometime governor of Virginia. From this account it is seen that Argall was one of the most active and remarkable men of his age.

Powell, Nathaniel, deputy governor of Virginia, in 1619, was one of the first planters; left England in December, 1606, and arrived in Virginia in April, 1607. He went with Captain Newport in the winter of 1608 to explore the York river, and in the summer of 1608 he went with John Smith to explore Chesapeake Bay. In 1617 Governor Argall gave him a commission to be sergeant-major general to Francis West, master of the ordinance during life. When Governor Argall suddenly left Virginia about April 10, 1619, he turned over the government to Captain Powell, which was held by him for a week, until Sir George Yardley arrived with a full commission as governor. The only matter of public interest that happened during Powell's brief administration was the coming of Captain John Ward, with fifty emigrants, including Rev. Thomas Bargrave, nephew of Dr. Bargrave, dean of Canterbury. They made a settlement above Martin's Brandon, on what is still known as Ward's creek. Captain Powell's plantation of 600 acres was known as "Powell Brook," afterwards "Merchant's Hope." There March 12, 1622, he and his wife, who was a daughter of William Tracy, one of the partners in the settlement of Berkeley Hundred, were murdered by the Indians. He left no descendants, and his plantation was sold by his brother and heir, Thomas Powell, of Howellton, county Suffolk, England. Near Powell's plantation in Virginia is still standing a very old brick church known as Merchant's Hope Church. The creek bounding his place still bears Captain Powell's name.

Wyatt, Sir Francis, governor and captain general of Virginia from 1621 to 1626 and from 1639 to 1642, was the son of George Wyatt, Esq., and Jane his wife, a daughter of Sir Thomas Finch. Francis married, in 1618, Margaret, daughter of Sir Samuel Sandys, of Outersbury, Worcester, brother of Sir Edwin Sandys. He arrived in Virginia in October, 1621, with an appointment to relieve Governor Yardley (whose term expired November 18). Sir Francis was accompanied by his brother, Rev. Hawte Wyatt; Dr. John Pott, physician general, afterwards deputy governor; William

Claiborne, surveyor-general; and George Sandys, uncle of his wife, who acted as treasurer of the colony. He brought with him also an ordinance of the London Company, confirming the government and freedom granted under Yardley in 1619. Wyatt had not long arrived before a great calamity befell the colony. Powhatan had died in 1618, and the real head of the Indians in Virginia was his brother, the ferocious Opechancanough. He arranged a massacre of the whites, and the blow fell March 22, 1622. One-fourth of the settlers were destroyed, and the number would have been much larger had not Governor Wyatt received news through a Christian Indian named Chanco of the impending massacre in time to save Jamestown and put the neighboring settlements on their guard. After the massacre the colonists concentrated for some time the surviving population in five or six well fortified places. Jamestown Peninsula was one of these, and as the old quarters were overcrowded, Claiborne, the surveyor, laid out in 1623 a new section for habitation on the river side, eastward of the old stockade. The additions were called "New Town," where already stood, it is believed, the governor's house, built by Gates in 1614, enlarged by Argall in 1617, and granted by the London Company in 1618 to the use of Governor Yardley and his successors forever. "New Town" never became a town of much size, for the settlers soon drove the Indians into the forests, and it was not long before the abandoned plantations were reestablished.

The Indian massacre was speedily followed by the revocation of the charter of the London Company, which Wyatt and other leaders in Virginia regarded as a dire calamity, though time proved the contrary. In January, 1624, they signed a protest called the "Tragicall Relation," denouncing the administration of the London Company by Sir Thomas Smythe and extolling that of Sandys and Southampton and asking for the old charter. The father of Governor Wyatt died in September, 1625, and he asked permission of the king to return to England, which was granted, and Sir George Yardley became governor in May, 1626. Wyatt remained in England till 1639, when he returned once more as governor. His appointment seems to have been due to the efforts of the leaders of the old London Company, who had never ceased their work for restoration of the charter. His administration was a reaction against that of Sir John Harvey. He reversed the edit of banishment against Rev. Anthony Panton, and Harvey himself was broken with suits in the courts. George Sandys, his wife's uncle, was sent to England to voice the wishes of the governor and assembly for the restoration of the old London Company charter. He could get no direct promise from the king, and so he had recourse to parliament, which did in fact reissue the old charter of 1609, though it never went into effect in Virginia. Before that time Wyatt was recalled, and Sir William Berkeley arrived as governor in 1642.

The Wyatt family to which Sir Francis belonged was one of great antiquity and of much renown. His great-great-grandfather, Sir Henry Wyatt, had taken a leading part in favor of Henry VII. against Richard III., and his grandfather, Sir Thomas, had been executed for raising a rebellion against Queen Mary. Sir Francis died in 1644, at Boxley, the home of the Wyatts, in county Kent, England. His brother, Rev. Hawte Wyatt, has many descendants in Virginia.

West, Francis, deputy governor of Virginia from November 14, 1627, on the death of Governor Yardley, to March 5, 1629, when Dr. John Pott was elected by the council to take his place. West having been selected to go to England to represent the interest of the colony, which was still in an unsettled condition by the revocation of the charter in 1624. He was born October 28, 1586, and was a brother of Thomas Lord Delaware. When Captain Newport came over with the "Second Supply" in October, 1608, he was accompanied by Francis West, who was elected a member of the council there in August, 1609, after the arrival of the "Third Supply" sent out under the new charter. During the "starving time" which soon followed, West attempted to get provisions from the Indians, but being unsuccessful he left the colony to its fate and sailed away to England. After a few months he returned again to Virginia, and after Percy left in 1612 he succeeded him as commandant at Jamestown in which office he continued till 1617, when he was succeeded by Captain William Powell. He was a member of the council again from April, 1619, to February, 1633. In connection with his brothers, Lord Delaware, and John and Nathaniel West, he owned lands at Westover and Shirley. In November, 1622, he was appointed admiral of New England, and went there to suppress illicit fishing, but he found the New Englanders difficult persons to deal with. In 1624 Captain West was living on his estate at Westover in Virginia, and soon after succeeded Sir George Yardley as deputy governor. His administration is distinguished for the assembling at Jamestown on March 26, 1628, after an interval of four years, of the regular law making body—an event second only in importance to the original meeting in 1619: for its restoration was proof that despite the revocation of her charter Virginia was to continue in the enjoyment of political liberty. After Pott took charge in 1629, West went to England, but he was in Virginia again prior to December, 1631, when he attended a meeting of the council, again in February and September, 1632, and in February, 1633. After the last date he drops out of Virginia records, and there is a tradition in Earl Delaware's family that he was drowned.

Pott, John, governor of Virginia from March 5, 1629, to March 24, 1630, came to Virginia with Governor Wyatt in 1621 to fill the position of physician general, vacant by the death of Lawrence Bohun, slain in a naval battle between the Spanish and the English in the West Indies. He was a Master of Arts, and was recommended to the London Company by Theodore Gulstone, founder of the Gulstonian lectureship in the London College of Physicians. He was made a member of the council in 1621, and on the departure of Francis West to England in 1629, Dr. John Pott was chosen by the council temporary governor. He figured as such little more than a year, and the leading event of this time was the arrival at Jamestown of the first Lord Baltimore—the proprietor of Avalon in Newfoundland. Pott tendered to him the oath of allegiance and supremacy, which Baltimore as a Catholic refused to take. Sir John Harvey, who was a friend of Baltimore, on his arrival arrested Dr. Pott, and a jury convicted him of felony, for stealing cattle, but politics was doubtless at the bottom, and the king pardoned him. Sometime later, however, Pott had his revenge by taking part with the other councillors in Harvey's arrest and deposition from the government. Dr. Pott was the first to locate land at the present site of Williamsburg, and he called his place Harrop, after the place of his family in Cheshire. He had a brother, Francis Pott, who was a prominent member of the assembly. His nephew, John Pott, moved to Patuxent in Maryland, where he was one of the justices in 1657.

Harvey, Sir John, governor from March 24, 1630, to April 28, 1635, was a native of Lyme Regis, Dorsetshire; had been a captain of a ship in the East Indies. In 1624 he was one of the commissioners appointed to report to the king upon the conditions of the colony. He was appointed a member of the council in August, 1624, and in the commission to Sir George Yardley, March 4, 1625-26, Harvey was named his successor. He left Virginia, and commanded a ship in the expedition against Cadiz in 1625. He did not return till March 24, 1630. During his administration the first settlements were made on the York river and on Kent Island. In the dispute with Lord Baltimore he took sides against Claiborne, deposed him in 1634 from his position as secretary of state, and on April 28, 1635, was himself deposed from the government by the council, which action was confirmed by the assembly. Sent prisoner to England in the custody of two of the assembly, Francis Pott and Thomas Harwood, he had his guards arrested on their arrival, and brought the matter of his deposition up before the privy council. The king declared the transaction "an act of regal authority," and fearing the example, kept the two daring burgesses in prison, and sent orders for the arrest of the councillors who took part in Harvey's deposition. Meanwhile, to rebuke the dangerous precedent set in Virginia, he restored Harvey to his government. This second administration began with Harvey's arrival in the colony January 18, 1637, and was marked by measures taken by Harvey to build up Jamestown. Some twelve brick houses were erected, and steps taken to build a brick church and brick state house. But Harvey resumed his arbitrary behavior, and raised so many quarrels that the king in August, 1639, commissioned Sir Francis Wyatt, who had already figured once before as governor, to be his successor. On Wyatt's arrival, Harvey's property at York and Jamestown was seized to repay his numerous creditors, and the ex-governor died a bankrupt not long after.

West, Captain John, deputy governor from April 28, 1635, to January 18, 1637, was the brother of Lord Delaware, and was born December 14, 1590. He came to Virginia about 1620, and after the massacre in 1622 commanded a company of men against the Indians. He was a member of the council, and when in 1630 the council resolved to plant a settlement on the York, Captain West was one of the two first settlers to patent lands on King's creek. There at his residence afterwards known as Bellfield was born, in 1632, the first child of English parents born on York river. When Sir John Harvey was deposed April 28, 1635, Captain West was prevailed upon by the council to accept the office of governor, which he held for eighteen months; and though he and the other leading men were arrested for their presumption, nothing was done to him. So far from that, Wyatt was sent over governor in 1639, John West's name appeared in the new commission as "Marshall and Muster Master General," in King Charles' own handwriting. He remained a member of the council for many years later. In 1650 he sold his plantation on York river to Edward Digges, Esq., and removed to West Point, which was named for him. In March, 1660, a resolution of good will was passed by the general assembly, when in recognition of the many important favors and services rendered Virginia by "the noble family of the Wests," Captain West, now in his old age, and his family, were exempted from taxation during his life. Captain West left an only son Lieutenant Col. John West, who resided at West Point and took an important part in the affairs of the colony during his lifetime.

Berkeley, Sir William, governor and captain general of Virginia from 1642 to 1652 and from 1660 to 1677, was son of Sir Maurice Berkeley, and brother of Lord John Berkeley of Stratton. He was born at Bruton, in Somersetshire, England, about 1610; graduated Master of Arts at Oxford in 1629, and travelled extensively in Europe. He was commissioned by King Charles governor of Virginia, August 9, 1641, and arrived in the colony in February, 1642, bearing with him the assurance of the king that the charter would not be restored. On April 18, 1644, a second Indian massacre occurred, but this did not prevent his visiting England in June, 1644, where he remained at the king's camp till June, 1645. In his absence his place was filled by Richard Kemp, a member of the council, who had been its secretary. Another event of Berkeley's first administration was the expulsion of the Puritans from Norfolk and Nansemond counties. During the civil war in England many cavalier officers and other friends of the king emigrated to Virginia. The result was to give a strong royalist sympathy to the colony, so that the death of Charles I. was denounced by the assembly as murder, and to question the right of Charles II. was declared treason. At last, in 1651, parliament sent a fleet to subdue the country, but force was not used, and an accommodation was agreed to by both sides. April 30, 1652, Berkeley was superceded in the government by Richard Bennett; whereupon he retired to his country residence, "Greenspring," distant about five miles from Jamestown.

In January, 1660, Governor Samuel Matthews died and the general assembly, who had became disgusted with the chaotic state of affairs in England, recalled Governor Berkeley to the government in the March following. He was commissioned by Charles II. July 31, 1660, and Charles II. himself was proclaimed in Virginia, September 20, 1660. In April, 1661, Berkeley was sent by the colony to England to protest against the navigation act, Col. Francis Morryson acting as governor till Berkeley's return in the fall of 1662. The reaction of the restoration occasioning much extravagance among the government officials finally brought about a great feeling of unrest in Virginia. This discontent, increased by the lavish grants of land by King Charles to certain court favorites, was brought to a head, in 1676, by an Indian attack. The measures taken by Berkeley were deemed ineffective, and the authority of defending the people was assumed by Nathaniel Bacon, Jr., a recent arrival. Sir William Berkeley declared him a rebel, and the colony was torn with opposing factions of armed men for nearly a year. Bacon perished of camp fever, and Berkeley showed much severity in punishing the surviving leaders. He was finally recalled by the king and died at Twickenham, July 9, 1677. He wrote two plays, and is the author of a "Description of Virginia," folio, 1663. He was survived by his wife, Lady Frances Berkeley, who was a Culpeper, and married three times: 1. Samuel Stephens; 2. Sir William Berkeley; 3. Colonel Philip Ludwell. Her brother, Alexander Culpeper, was surveyor-general of the colony from 1672 to 1692.

Kemp, Richard, deputy governor from 1644 to 1645, was a son, it is believed, of Sir Robert Kemp, of Gissing, in Suffolk county, England. He succeeded William Claiborne as secretary of state in 1634. When in 1639 Harvey was supplanted as governor by Sir Francis Wyatt, Kemp, by the influence of Lord Baltimore and Secretary of State Windebank, retained his place as secretary. Incurring the enmity of Rev. Anthony Panton, whom Harvey and himself had treated with great severity, he returned to England in 1640 to defend his conduct, leaving his friend George Reade as deputy secretary. Richard Kemp staid in England about two years, and returned in 1642 to his old post, with Sir William Berkeley. He was deputy governor during the absence of the latter in England from June, 1644 to June, 1645. He made his will in 1649, and his widow Elizabeth (whose maiden name is not known) married (secondly) Sir Thomas Lunsford, and after his death (thirdly) Major-General Robert Smith. He left no children, but there is a numerous Virginia family of his name descended from his nephew, Edmund Kemp.

Bennett, Richard, governor of Virginia from April 30, 1652, until March 2, 1655, was of the same family as Henry Bennett Lord Arlington. His uncle Edward Bennett, an eminent London merchant, was a member of the London Company, and with other persons of means planted in 1621 a settlement in Wariscoyack, or Isle of Wight county, Virginia, which was known as Edward Bennett's plantation. At the time of the Indian uprising in March, 1622, more than fifty persons were killed at this settlement. In 1624 Robert Bennett, merchant, and Rev. William Bennett, minister, were living at Edward Bennett's plantation. They were probably his kinsmen. In 1629 Richard Bennett was a burgess from the Wariscoyack district, and in 1632 was one of the county court. In 1639 he was a councillor. He was a Puritan in sympathy, and joined in a petition, which was taken by his brother Philip to Boston, asking for three able ministers to occupy parishes in his neighborhood. When Sir William Berkeley in 1649 drove the Puritans out of Nansemond and Elizabeth City counties, Bennett went with them to Maryland, but only stayed a short time. In 1651 he was living on Bennett's creek in Nansemond county, and that year he was named by parliament as one of the commissioners for the reduction of Virginia. When Virginia submitted, he was elected by the general assembly governor of the colony. He held office from April 30, 1652, to March 30, 1655, when he was sent to England as agent. On November 30, 1657, he signed the agreement with Lord Baltimore by which the latter's claim to Maryland was finally recognized. After the restoration of Charles II., Bennett held the offices of councillor and major-general of the militia. In 1667 he went as a commissioner to Maryland to negotiate for a cessation in the cultivation of tobacco, the price having fallen very low. He was a member of the council as late as 1675, and his will was proved April 12, 1675. His daughter Anne married Theodorick Bland, of Virginia, and his son and grandson of the same name were members of the council of Maryland.

Digges, Edward, governor of Virginia from March 30, 1655, to March 13, 1658, son of

Sir Dudley Digges, of Chilham, county Kent, England, who was knight and baronet, and master of the rolls in the reign of Charles I., was born about 1620 and came to Virginia before 1650, when he purchased an estate on York river from Captain John West, subsequently known as Bellfield. On November 22, 1654, he was made a member of the council, and was elected March 30, 1655, to succeed Governor Bennett. He was therefore the second governor under the "Commonwealth of England." He served as governor till March 13, 1658, when he was sent to England to coöperate with Bennett and Mathews against the rival claims of Lord Baltimore. The articles of surrender in 1652 guaranteed to Virginia her ancient boundaries, and the effort of the assembly was to get the Maryland charter annulled, in which, however, they were not successful. After the restoration of Charles II., Digges served as a member of the council, and was greatly interested in the culture of silk and tobacco at his plantation on York river. In the silk culture he employed three Armenians, and the tobacco which he grew on his plantation became known as the E. D. Tobacco. More than a century after his death the tobacco grown at Bellfield had such a reputation that it brought one shilling per pound in the London market, when other tobaccos brought only three pence. Digges was auditor general from 1670 to 1675, and receiver general from 1672 to 1675. He died March 15, 1675, and his tombstone is still standing at Bellfield, his old home place on York river. His eldest son, Col. William Digges, settled in Maryland and was founder of a well known family in that state. His younger son, Colonel Dudley Digges, was a member of the council of Virginia. Cole Digges, a grandson, was also a councillor; and Dudley Digges, a great-grandson, was a member of the Virginia committee of safety, which in 1776 had really the executive power in its hands.

Mathews, Samuel, governor of Virginia from March 13, 1658, to his death in January, 1660, was born in England about 1600, and came to Virginia in 1622. In 1623 he led a force against the Tanx Powhatan Indians. In 1624 he was one of the commissioners appointed by the King to enquire into the condition of the colony. In 1630 he built a fort at Point Comfort. In 1635 he took a leading part in the deposition of Sir John Harvey. He was appointed to the council in 1623, and in 1652 was sent as one of the agents to England to obtain a confirmation of the agreement with the parliamentary commissioners, securing to Virginia her anicent bounds, and he remained there till 1657. He was unsuccessful in his mission to recover Maryland to Virginia, and at length signed articles of accommodation with Lord Baltimore. He became governor of the colony March 13, 1658, and soon became involved in a controversy with the house of burgesses regarding the power of the council to dissolve the assembly. The house would not admit the contention, and claimed that the supreme power lay in the house as the representatives of the people. Mathews and his council were by the burgesses deposed from authority, but on their submitting to the will of the house were reelected and took the oath recognizing its authority. He died before the expiration of his term, in January, 1660. He was a very active citizen during his lifetime. His residence was at "Denbigh," on Deep creek, Warwick county, where he had a fine house and employed many servants. He married, about 1629, Frances, daughter of Sir

Thomas Hinton, and widow successively of Captain Nathaniel West and of Abraham Piersey, the last of whom "left the best estate that ever was known in Virginia." He had issue, Samuel Mathews, who was a member of the council in 1655, and Francis, who was a justice of York county and captain of the militia, and died February 16, 1675.

Moryson, Francis, governor of Virginia from April 30, 1661, to the fall of 1662, was a son of Sir Richard Moryson, who was secretary of state to King James I. He served in King Charles' army with the rank of major and he embarked from London with his fellow loyalists, Colonel Henry Norwood, Major Richard Fox and Major Francis Cary, for Virginia, September 23, 1649, and arrived in Virginia the November following. Driven by a storm, their ship found itself on June 12, 1650, among the islands of Assateague Bay, on the Atlantic coast of Virginia. Upon one of these Colonel Moryson landed with several of his companions, and after various experiences in Accomac crossed over to the main shore and was kindly received by Sir William Berkeley, who gave him the command of the fort at Point Comfort. In 1655 he was speaker of the house of burgesses, and when Governor Berkeley visited England in 1662, Moryson acted as governor till sometime in the fall of the following year. The memory of his service as chief executive is marked by his gift of a splendid service of church plate to the church at Jamestown, which is preserved by the church in Williamsburg. After the return of Berkeley, Moryson was sent as agent to England at an annual salary of £200 to protest against a grant of the Northern Neck to several court favorites. He remained as agent in England till 1677, when he returned to Virginia as one of a commission to enquire into the disturbances known as Bacon's rebellion. The commissioners held court at Swann's Point, over against Jamestown, which had been destroyed. Their report was a very full account of this interesting episode in Virginia history, and the finding was very much against Governor Berkeley. Moryson soon after returned to England, and died there not long after. He left a widow Cecilia, sister of Giles Rawlins, and a son Henry, who in 1699 was colonel of the Colstream Foot Guards. Colonel Moryson was preceded to Virginia by his two brothers—Richard and Robert Moryson, who also commanded at Point Comfort, and after Major Moryson his nephew Charles, son of Richard Moryson, held commission about 1664. His sister, Letitia Moryson, was wife of the noble cavalier, Lucius Cary, Lord Falkland.

Jeffreys, Herbert, commissioned lieutenant-governor November 11, 1675, was an officer in the English army and commanded the regiment sent over to Virginia in 1676 to put down the rebellion of Bacon. He was also head of the commission to enquire into the causes of the troubles in Virginia, Major Francis Moryson, and Sir John Berry, admiral of the fleet, being the other members. He arrived in Virginia, February 2, 1677, and encamped his troops among the ruins of the brick buildings at Jamestown, which had been burned by Nathaniel Bacon. The commissioners made the residence of Colonel Thomas Swann, at Swann's Point, on the other side of the river, their headquarters, whence they issued a call to the different counties for a statement of their grievances. From the first their relations with Berkeley were far from sympathetic. Upon the departure of Berkeley from the colony. Jeffreys by virtue of his commission assumed the government, and marching his troops to Middle Plantation (now Williamsburg) concluded a treaty of friendship with the neighboring Indian tribes. His sympathies being with the popular side, by his influence the assembly in October, 1677, passed an act of amnesty, and threatened a heavy fine against anybody who would call another "a rebel or traitor." Those, therefore, who had been friends of Sir William Berkeley, received very little favor at his hands, and were denounced by him as the "Greenspring faction," whose tyranny had been one of the chief causes of the civil war. He incurred the special enmity of Philip Ludwell, who married Berkeley's widow, because he would not let him sue Walklett for damages done during that time. In this Jeffreys seemed to be right, as Berkeley had promised Walklett, a leader of the rebels after Bacon's death, indemnity on his surrendering West Point. In another matter in which Robert Beverley, the other leader of the Greenspring faction, was involved, Jeffreys' position was not as defensible. In order to make a full report he and the other commissioners demanded of Beverley, who was clerk of the assembly, the journals and papers of the house of burgesses, and when the latter declined to give them up they seized them out of his possession. As this appeared to the house an attack upon their privileges, they passed strong resolutions when they met protesting against the action of the commissioners. The growing importance of Middle Plantation was shown by a petition from some inhabitants of York county that the place be recommended to the king for the seat of government. But the commissioners, including Jeffreys, were not willing to abandon Jamestown, and on April 25, 1678, the general assembly resumed its sittings at the country's ancient capital, and steps were taken to rebuild the state house and church. Jeffreys, however, did not long survive this meeting of the assembly. He died in Virginia, December 30, 1678. The surviving commissioners made a voluminous report to the English government, in which, under the thin guise of a censure of Bacon, the entire blame of the civil war was really thrown upon Sir William Berkeley and his friends.

Chicheley, Sir Henry, lieutenant-governor of Virginia from December 30, 1678, to May 10, 1680, son of Sir Thomas Chicheley of Wimpole, in Cambridgeshire, was born in 1615, matriculated at University College, Oxford, April 27, 1632, and was Bachellor of Arts February 5, 1634-35. He served as an officer in the army of Charles I., and for a short time was imprisoned in the Tower of London. In 1649, after the execution of the king, he emigrated to Virginia with many other cavaliers. Here he married in 1652 the widow of Colonel Ralph Wormeley, and resided at Rosegill, in Middlesex county. On December 1, 1656, he took his seat in the house of burgesses, having been elected to fill a vacancy. In 1660 he was for a time in England, where he was probably a witness of King Charles II.'s restoration. On November 20, 1673, he was commissioned lieutenant-general of the Virginia militia, and on February 28, 1673-74, the king gave him a commission as deputy governor of the colony. In the beginning of 1676, when the Indians were ranging the frontier, Chicheley had command of the forces raised to subdue them, but his troops were disbanded by Governor Berkeley

LORD CULPEPER

before they could attack the invaders. This action occasioned much discontent and was the direct cause of Bacon's rebellion.

During this troublous time Chicheley adhered to the governor and suffered very much in consequence. His estate was greatly damaged and he endured a severe imprisonment. When the civil war subsided, he was appointed to the council November 16, 1676, and became its president, and on the death of Governor Jeffreys he produced his commission as deputy governor. He remained the colony executive till Lord Culpeper was sworn into office May 10, 1680, becoming, however, the chief executive again when Lord Culpeper left Virginia in August, three months later. He served till Culpeper's return in December, 1682, during which interval there was unusual distress on account of the low price of tobacco. On the petition of the suffering people, Chicheley called an assembly which met in April, 1682, but in obedience to orders from England to await Lord Culpeper's arrival he adjourned it before it could adopt a law for a cessation of planting, whereupon many planters in Gloucester, New Kent and Middlesex assembled together and going from place to place riotously cut up the tobacco plants. Chicheley called out the militia and promptly suppressed the disturbances, but issued a general pardon to all who would behave peaceably. Major Robert Beverley was deemed, however, the real sinner, as he was prominent in urging the cessation of planting. Therefore, Chicheley had him arrested, and confined him on shipboard and kept him a prisoner for seven months, finally releasing him under heavy bond to appear when summoned. Culpeper returned in December, 1682, and though he bore instructions to proceed rigorously against the plant cutters, whose action had entailed a heavy loss of English revenue, he imitated Chicheley's clemency by issuing a similar proclamation of amnesty. To placate his masters in England, however, he executed two of the most violent of the ringleaders and threw the blame of his not executing more upon Sir Henry Chicheley, who had forestalled him. Sir Henry had become at this time very old and feeble, and his death occurred not long after Culpeper's arrival. He died at Rosegill, on the Rappahannock, February 5, 1682, and was interred at old Christ Church, Middlesex county. He left no issue.

Culpeper, Thomas, Lord, governor of Virignia from May 10, 1680, to August 10, 1680, and from December 17, 1682, to May 28, 1683, was the eldest son of John Lord Culpeper, whom he succeeded as Baron of Thorseway on the death of the latter in 1660. Lord John Culpeper was one of the most eminent friends of Charles I. in the civil war in England, and one of the first acts of Charles II., after the execution of his father, was to grant to him and Henry Bennett, Earl of Arlington, and several other great favorites the Northern Neck of Virginia, lying between the Potomac and Rappahannock rivers. This grant, after lying dormant during the commonwealth, was revived on the restoration of the king and ultimately became vested by purchase in Sir Thomas Culpeper, who in 1674 received in company with Lord Arlington the benefit of another grant of all Virginia for thirty-one years. Though neither of these grants were intended to interfere with the political government of the colony as it then existed, their provisions, especially those of the latter grant, were so extensive that had they been completely executed little but the shadow of power would have been left to the central authority.

Eventually, by purchase Lord Thomas Culpeper possessed himself of both patents and all the privileges and benefits of each. Naturally these grants were very distasteful to the Virginians, and for a long time they paid no attention to the demands of the patentees and of Culpeper, and sent various agents to England to protest against them. In 1675 Culpeper obtained from the king a commission to succeed Sir William Berkeley, on his demise, as governor of Virginia, and in May, 1680, he came to Virginia, hoping doubtless to put some life into the privileges of his proprietor-ship. He brought instructions intended to put the government of Virginia on a more royal basis, but he succeeded in carrying out only a part of his policy. The clerk of the assembly, who had hitherto been elected by that body, became now the appointee of the governor, a permanent revenue was established rendering the salaries of the governor and council independent of the people; and instead of annual meetings of the assembly, the custom of calling it for special occasions and proroguing it from time to time, was begun. In August, not long after the adjournment of the assembly, Culpeper set out for England by way of New England, whereupon, Sir Henry Chicheley reassumed the government. Culpeper was absent for more than two years from Virginia, during which time, on account of the low price of tobacco, the Plant Cutters rebellion occurred. Culpeper was ordered by the king to return to his charge, and he arrived in Virginia December 17, 1682, but found the rebellion already suppressed by Sir Henry Chicheley. To serve as an example, he, however, executed two of the ring leaders, and continued under bond for his appearance Major Robert Beverley, clerk of the assembly, who had been arrested by Sir Henry Chicheley as the chief instigator. Before leaving England he had received fresh instructions aimed at the rights and liberties of the assembly, but Culpeper declined to oppose himself to the popular will on most of the questions. The assembly, however, lost its power as the court of appeals, and the council, by order of the crown, was made the court of last resort, except in cases of £300 value, when an appeal might be made to the privy council in England. Culpeper soon gave the king and his advisers an opportunity of punishing him and replacing him with a more efficient instrument of tyranny. Directly in face of an order of the council forbidding him to receive any presents, he accepted large sums of money from the assembly, and contrary to another express order forbidding any colonial governor from absenting himself from his government without special leave, he returned a second time to England after a stay in the colony of only about five months. He was at once deprived of his office, and Lord Howard of Effingham dispatched to succeed him. A year later he sold the larger share of his Virginia rights to the crown for an annuity of £600 for twenty years, retaining only the portion of the territory called the Northern Neck, which was now confirmed to him by a patent from the crown dated September 27, 1688. While governor, however, he made a little headway in bringing the residents of the Northern Neck to submit to him as proprietor, and for many years after his death, which occurred in 1690, the inhabitants continued indifferent. It was not till 1703, when Robert Carter became the managing agent, that the people began to patent lands in his office. The proprietor then was Thomas Lord Fairfax, who before 1692 married Katherine, Lord Culpeper's only daughter, and heiress by his wife, Lady Marguerite Hesse.

LORD HOWARD OF EFFINGHAM

Spencer, Nicholas, president of the council and acting governor after Lord Culpeper's departure from Virginia, May 28, 1683, to the incoming of Francis Lord Howard of Effingham in February, 1684. He was the son of Nicholas Spencer, Esq., of Cople, in Bedfordshire, England, by his wife Mary, daughter of Sir Edward Gostwick. He first engaged in merchandizing in London, and like many merchants became interested in Virginia, to which he emigrated in 1659. He settled in Westmoreland county, where the parish of Cople was named in honor of the home of his family; was a member of the house of burgesses from 1666 to 1676; and was secretary of state from 1679 till his death in 1689. Placed by Lord Culpeper, who was his cousin, at the head of the council, he succeeded him as acting governor, on his departure from Virginia, in September, 1683, according to an order issued shortly before by the privy council establishing the rule which was always afterwards followed that the president of the council should succeed to the executive duties in case of the absence or death of the incumbent. Spencer's administration was quiet, except for some inroads of the Seneca Indians, who were driven off with the aid of the tributary tribes. In February, 1684, Lord Howard arrived, and Spencer acted as one of his councillors till his death, September 23, 1689. He married Frances, daughter of Colonel John Mottrom, of Northumberland county, and left several children who have descendants in Virginia.

Howard, Francis, Baron of Effingham, governor of Virginia from February, 1684 to October 20, 1688, was a distant kinsman of Charles Lord Howard of Effingham, who commanded the English fleet in 1588 in its famous battle with the Spanish Armada. He was son of Sir William Howard of Lingfield, in Surrey county, England, by his wife Frances, daughter of Sir George Courthope, of Whiligh, county of Sussex, knight, and succeeded in 1681 to the title of Lord Howard of Effingham on the death of Lord Charles Howard, grandson of the hero of the battle of the Armada. He was commissioned governor of Virginia, September 28, 1683, and arrived in Virginia in February, 1684. Among his first proceedings was one to summon Robert Beverley before the council on the old charge of instigating the plant cutters. Found guilty, Beverley was released on his making an humble and abject apology, which doubtless, like Nathaniel Bacon, Jr., on a similar occasion, he regarded as a mere formality. It was far from making him submissive to the governor's will, and when the governor set to work to exalt his prerogatives at the expense of the liberties of the assembly, Beverley as clerk, and his friend Philip Ludwell, firmly resisted him. Hitherto the governors of Virginia had seldom, if ever, used their negative on the laws of the assembly. Lord Howard asserted this right, and was successful in making it a part of the constitution ever afterwards. He attempted to get the house to authorize himself and the council to lay taxes on urgent occasions, but failed. He exacted a fee for attaching the seal of the colony to land grants and, erecting a new court of chancery, made himself a petty lord chancellor. All who opposed him in any way were made to feel the effects of resentment. Robert Beverley was removed from his office as clerk and Ludwell was suspended from the council. In one measure, at least, Howard deserved the gratitude of the people. In the summer of 1684 he went to Albany, and there with the governor of New York made a treaty with the

Five Nations, which put an end to the raids of the Senecas on the frontiers. At length Howard departed for England, October 20, 1688, leaving Nathaniel Bacon, Sr., in charge of the government. The assembly sent Ludwell as their agent to urge complaints against him. He did not return, but he was allowed to retain his office of governor as an absentee with half his salary, while his duties were discharged by a lieutenant. He died March 30, 1694. While he lived in Virginia, he spent much of his time at Rosegill, the house of the Wormeleys, on the Rappahannock. On August 31, 1685, his wife Lady Philadelphia Howard (daughter of Sir Thomas Pelham), died in Virginia, aged thirty-one, and her remains were carried to England and interred at Lingfield. On the way over, his daughter Margaret Frances, who accompanied her mother's body, also died.

Bacon, Nathaniel, Sr., president of the council and acting governor of Virginia, was baptized at St. Mary, Bury St. Edmund's, August 29, 1620, and died in York county, Virginia, March 16, 1692. His father, Rev. James Bacon, was rector of Burgate, Suffolk, and died August 25, 1670, and his grandfather, Sir James Bacon, of Friston Hall, Suffolk, was first cousin of Francis Bacon, Lord Verulam. Nathaniel Bacon, the subject of this sketch, was first cousin once removed of Nathaniel Bacon, Jr., "the Rebel." He travelled in France in 1647, and was probably a graduate of Cambridge; came about 1650 to Virginia, where he settled first in Isle of Wight county, and then at "King's Creek," York county, on one of the first tracts of land patented on York river. He was chosen member of the council in 1657, but held the office for only a year; was burgess for York county in 1658-59, and was reappointed to the council in 1660; appointed auditor general March 12, 1675, resigning in December, 1687, was president of the council, and as such acting governor during the absence of Lord Howard in New York in the summer of 1684, during his absence on a visit to the southern part of the colony in December, 1687, and in the interval between his departure for England, October 28, 1688, and the arrival of Governor Francis Nicholson, May 16, 1690. He did not approve the course of his young kinsman Nathaniel Bacon, Jr., and it was at his house on King's creek that Sir William Berkeley first put foot to land after his return from the eastern shore in 1676.

Lord Howard had left the colony just before the abdication of James II., and the uncertainty attending affairs in England created something like a panic in Virginia. Rumors of terrible plots of Catholics and Indians were circulated, which President Bacon and his council allayed as far as possible. But the difficulties of maintaining order might have became insuperable, had not the news of the accession of the Prince and Princess of Orange arrived. Colonel Bacon's health was very feeble at this time, and he died March 16, 1692. As he had no children he bequeathed his estate to his niece Abigail Smith, who married Major Lewis Burwell, of Gloucester county, and has many descendants in Virginia and the south.

Nicholson, Sir Francis, lieutenant-governor from May 16, 1690, to January, 1694, and from 1698 to April, 1705, was born in 1660; obtained a commission in the English army as ensign January 9, 1678, and as lieutenant May 6, 1684. He was a strong Tory and churchman. When in 1686 the whole body of colonies north of Chesapeake Bay were formed into a single province under Sir Edmund Andros, Nicholson, was appointed lieutenant-governor, and remained at New York to represent his superior officer. When Andros was deposed by the men of Boston in 1689, Nicholson's hot temper betrayed him into violent language and conduct, which induced a rebellion headed by Jacob Leisler. Nicholson left the colony for England, which temporarily increased the anarchic conditions in New York, though they ended in the execution of Jacob Leisler and several of his rebel associates. In spite of his failure, Nicholson was appointed lieutenant-governor of Virginia in 1690, and for four years discharged the duties of his new office with ability and entire credit to himself. He instituted athletic games and offered prizes to those who should excel in riding, running, shooting, wrestling and fencing. He did all he could to promote the founding of William and Mary College, and contributed largely from his own private means for that purpose. In 1694 Lord Howard of Effingham, the titular governor of Virginia, under whom Nicholson served as deputy, died, and that post was conferred upon Sir Edmund Andros, while Nicholson was appointed in January, 1694, governor of Maryland. Here he proved himself, as in Virginia, the patron of learning, and laid out Annapolis and established King William's school, now St. John's College. His arrogant disposition precipitated him into quarrels with the commissary Thomas Bray and other leading men, and in 1698 he returned to Virginia as governor. His second term of office opened auspiciously. He caused a general census of the colony to be made in respect to schools, churches, and population, and as the state house had been accidentally burned at Jamestown, persuaded the English government to transfer the seat of government to Middle Plantation, which he named Williamsburg in honor of the reigning king, William, formerly Prince of Orange. But his peppery temper soon involved him into difficulties with his council and with James Blair, president of the college. He also displeased the assembly by trying to get them to contribute towards a fort on the northwest frontier of New York. Displeased in turn at their unwillingness, he advised the crown that all the American colonies should be placed under one governor and a standing army be maintained among them at their own expense, believing it to be the only means of preserving an effective unity against Canada and the French. But this recommendation was not approved by Queen Ann and her ministers, and in April, 1705, he was recalled. During the next fifteen years such public services as he discharged were of a military character, and he headed two expeditions against Canada, but for want of a fleet the expeditions proved failures. In 1713 Nicholson was appointed governor of Acadia, but here again he met difficulties owing to his imperious temper. When in 1719 the privy council decided that the proprietors of South Carolina had forfeited their charter, Nicholson was appointed governor, and speedily restored order to that distracted province. Here Nicholson showed the best side of his character, promoted the building of schools and churches, and succeeded in conciliating the Cherokees. In June, 1725, Nicholson returned to England on leave, and does not seem again to have visited America. He had been knighted in 1720 and was promoted to lieutenant-general. He retained the colonial governorship of South Carolina until his death, which took place in London, March 5, 1728. He never married and by his will left all his lands and property in New England, Maryland and Virginia to the Society for the Propagation of Christianity in Foreign Parts, and to educate in England young New England ministers to be sent back to their native country.

Andros, Sir Edmund, governor of Virginia from 1692 to 1698, was the second son of a Guernsey gentleman belonging to Charles I.'s household. He was born in London, December 6, 1637, appointed gentleman in ordinary to the Queen of Bohemia in 1660, served in the regiment of foot sent to America in 1666, was major in Rupert's dragoons in 1672, and succeeded his father as bailiff of Guernsey in 1674. The same year he was appointed by James, Duke of York, to be governor of the province of New York, which had been granted to the duke by Charles II. In 1678 he was knighted while governor from New York. He engaged in some disputes with the authorities of the neighboring colonies and in 1681 was recalled to England. The authorities in England had borne with great patience the oppressive governments of the New England oligarchies, and their conduct brought punishment not altogether undeserved. Their charters were confiscated, and Andros was appointed in 1686 governor of the various colonies consolidated to form the dominion of New England. In this position Andros made himself very unpopular by his energy in carrying out the instructions of James II. Acting under the king's directions he put restrictions on the freedom of the press, and appointed a general council by whose advice he laid taxes and carried on all government and legislation. This was a reversion to the Spanish type of colonial government, which could not be justified, but he performed a good part in proclaiming liberty of conscience, in subduing the Indians, and in repressing the pirates, who were the scourge of the New England coast. His unpopularity continued to increase, however, and when the news of the abdication of King James arrived, the people of Boston, on April 18, 1689, suddenly seized the governor and some of his subordinates and imprisoned them. Sir Edmund was sent over to England, where, to the disappointment of his enemies, he was released without a formal trial. King William seemed to think that he had only done his duty in carrying out the instructions sent him, and so returned him to America as governor of Virginia. Here he showed both his good and evil side. He promoted manufactures and agriculture, put in order the government records which were in a chaotic state, and by his affability made himself generally popular with the people, but he quarrelled with Commissary James Blair, and after helping him to establish the new college at Williamsburg, permitted his angry feelings against Dr. Blair to make him an enemy of the institution. The result was that, through the influence of the commissary and his relations and friends on the council, Andros was recalled in 1698. In 1704 Andros was appointed governor of Jersey, which office he held until 1706. The remainder of his life seems to have been passed in London, where he died February 22, 1713-14.

Hamilton, George, Earl of Orkney, governor-in-chief of Virginia from 1697 to his death in 1737, never residing in the colony, but enjoying his office as a pensionary sinecure for forty years; was fifth son of William, Earl of Selkirk, who became Duke of Hamilton. He was born at Hamilton Palace, Lanark, and was baptized there February 9, 1666.

He had a long and distinguished career in the British army, and was present at the battles of the Boyne, Anghrim, Steinkirk, Blenheim and Oudenard, and at the sieges of Limerick, Athlone, Namur, Stevensvaert, Menin and Tournay. He was made colonel of the Royal Foot, August 3, 1692, major-general March 9, 1702, and lieutenant-general June 1, 1704. On January 10, 1696, Hamilton was created Earl of Orkney, and in 1697 became titular governor of Virginia, drawing a salary, but not performing any duties. On February 12, 1707, he was elected one of the sixteen representative peers of Scotland to sit in the first parliament of Great Britain. In 1710 he was sworn of the privy council, and the same year was appointed general of the Foot in Flanders. He was likewise appointed afterwards constable, governor and captain of Edinburgh Castle, lord lieutenant of the county of Clydesdale, and on June 12, 1736, field marshal of "all of his majesty's forces." On November 25, 1695, he married his cousin, Elizabeth Villiers, the well known mistress of William III., and from this marriage the present Earl of Orkney is descended. Orkney was no military strategist, and was not very successful when first in command, but he was an admirable subordinate. He died at his residence in Albemarle street, London on January 29, 1737, and was buried at Taplow, and September 6 of that year was succeeded as governor-in-chief of Virginia by the Earl of Albemarle.

Nott, Edward, lieutenant-governor of Virginia under the Earl of Orkney, from August 18, 1705, to August 23, 1706, was born in England in 1657. He served very gallantly in the West Indies as major and colonel of a regiment. On August 15, 1705, he succeeded Colonel Francis Nicholson as governor of Virginia. Wiser than Nicholson, he took care not to offend the council, and was very popular with all classes, but he died only about a year after his arrival. Several important events, however, in the colonial annals are identified with his brief administration: The completion of the capitol building begun by Nicholson; the burning of the college, October, 1705; the founding by Mrs. Mary Whaley of Mattey's Free School near Williamsburg, and the adoption by the assembly of a revised code of laws—the fourth since the first settlement. In this code provision was made for building a governor's house, for completing the founding of Williamsburg, and for encouraging the French Protestant refugees whose settlement was above the falls of the river at "King William's parish in the county of Henrico." Some years after the sudden demise of Nott, August 23, 1706, a handsome box monument of marble was erected by the general assembly over his remains in Bruton parish churchyard. It is still standing. He was succeeded at the head of the government by the president of the council, Edmund Jennings.

Edmund, Jenings, president of the council and acting governor from June, 1706, to August, 1710, was son of Sir Edmund Jenings, of Ripon, Yorkshire, England, and his wife Margaret, daughter of Sir Edward Barkham, lord mayor of London, 1621-22. He was born in 1659, and died June 2, 1727. He came to Virginia at an early, age, and settled in York county. He was appointed attorney-general in 1680, and retained the office till after 1692. He was appointed to the council in 1701, and remained a member till his death. In 1704 he was appointed secretary of state, and from June, 1706, till August 23, 1710, he was acting governor. Later, after the death of Hugh Drysdale, he would have again become acting governor, but was set aside on account of his feeble health. He married, Frances, daughter of Henry Corbin, of Buckingham House, and had issue (1) Frances, married Charles Grymes, of Moratico, Richmond county, and was ancestress of General R. E. Lee; (2) Elizabeth, married Robert Porteus, of New Bottle, Gloucester county, who afterwards removed to England, where she became the mother of Beilby Porteus, Bishop of London; (3) Edmund, secretary of Maryland, married in 1728, Anna, widow of James Frisby and Thomas Bordley, and daughter of Matthias Vanderheyden, by which marriage he was father of Ariana (who married John Randolph of Virginia, father of Edmund Randolph, first attorney-general of Virginia and of the United States), and a son Edmund, who died unmarried in 1819.

Hunter, Col. Robert, an officer in the English army, was appointed governor of Virginia in 1706 to succeed Sir Francis Nicholson, but in his voyage was captured by a French privateer and remained prisoner until the end of 1709. In June, 1710, he became governor of New York, and held that office till 1719. In July, 1727, was appointed governor of Jamaica and died there March 11, 1734.

Spotswood, Alexander, lieutenant-governor under the Earl of Orkney (1710-1722) was a great-grandson of John Spotswood or Spotiswood, Scotland, who in 1635 became archbishop of Glasgow and one of the privy council. His grandfather, Sir Robert Spotswood, was an eminent lawyer, who was elected president of the court of sessions in Scotland. In the civil war, Sir Robert was a staunch supporter of Charles I, and was temporary secretary of state in 1643. Taken prisoner at the battle of Philiphaugh, he was tried by the Scotch parliament, sentenced to death, and executed. Alexander Spotswood's father was Dr. Robert Spotswood, who was a physician to the governor and garrison at Tangier. His mother was Catherine Elliott, a widow who had by her first husband a son, General Roger Elliott, whose portrait is now in the state library at Richmond, Virginia. Alexander was born at Tangier in 1676, educated for a military life, fought under Marlborough, was quartermaster-general with the rank of colonel, and was dangerously wounded in the breast at the battle of Blenheim. In 1710 he was appointed lieutenant-governor of Virginia, and showed himself a conspicuously energetic administrator. He bestowed much attention upon Williamsburg, leveled the streets, assisted in rebuilding the church, providing some of the brick, built a brick magazine for the safekeeping of the public arms, and aided in rebuilding the college, which had been burned in 1705; and in 1722, on the petition of the people of Williamsburg and the assembly, he granted a charter of incorporation to the city of Williamsburg. Against the enemies of the colony he took firm and decided steps. The coast of Virginia was harassed by piratical vessels. Spotswood sent an expedition against them under Captain Maynard, killed the pirate. Teach or Blackbeard, and hanged others. As to the Indians he blended humanity with policy. He established a school for the Sapies at Fort Christanna in Brunswick county, and paid the master, Mr. Griffin, out of his own pocket, and arranged a treaty by which the chiefs of the tributary tribes promised to send their sons to college. He sent soldiers against the Tuscaroras, who had attacked North Carolina, but laid force aside when he

ALEXANDER SPOTSWOOD

found them ready to negotiate a treaty of peace. Against the French and Indians he established two forts on the frontiers to guard the northern and southern passes. At the first of these he planted the German settlement and at the other he gathered the Sapony Indians. His idea was to extend the line of Virginia settlements so as to check the further extension of French influence on this continent. With this in view he explored the back country, and in 1716 crossed the Blue Ridge mountains and visited the Shenandoah river and the beautiful valley through which it runs. He urged upon the mother country the policy of establishing a chain of posts back of the mountains, from the great lakes to the Mississippi river. But Spotswood had his weak points like Nicholson, another capable man before him. He was overbearing and had great ideas of the royal prerogative. And so, though he encouraged the rights of the subject by bringing over with him a confirmation of the writ of habeas corpus, he did not like Nott attempt to conciliate the people. The result was that he got at cross purposes with the assembly, with the council, and with Dr. James Blair, the president of the college, which resulted in his removal September 27. 1722. He continued to reside in Virginia and led an active life. During his governorship he had established a postal system in Virginia, and in 1730-1739 was deputy postmaster-general for the American colonies, in which capacity he arranged the transfer of mails with great energy. It was he who made Benjamin Franklin postmaster for Pennsylvania. He had also called the legislature's attention to the iron ores of Virginia, though without effect; and now in a private capacity he established a furnace in Spotsylvania county, where he had patented 40,000 acres of land. In 1740 Spotswood was made general of an expedition against Carthagena. He visited Williamsburg, and then repaired to Annapolis with the intention of embarking with the troops, but he died June 7, just before the embarkation, and Colonel William Gooch was appointed chief in his place. He left his books and mathematical instruments to the college. Colonel Spotswood married, in 1724, Ann Butler Brain, daughter of Mr. Richard Brain, of London, and they had two sons, John and Robert Spotswood, and two daughters, Ann Catherine, who married Bernard Moore, and Dorothea, who married Captain Nathaniel West Dandridge. Robert, his younger son, was slain by the Indians in the French and Indian war. John, the elder son, married, in 1745, Mary, daughter of William Dandridge, and had issue two sons, General Alexander Spotswood and Captain John Spotswood, both of the army of the revolution, and two daughters, Mary and Ann. The descendants of Governor Spotswood are now represented in numerous families of distinction.

Drysdale, Hugh, lieutenant-governor of Virginia (1722-1726), succeeded Governor Spotswood in the administration of the colony, September 27, 1722, and remained in office till his death, July 22, 1726. Very little is known of his antecedents, but during his administration in Virginia he was very popular. There were two sessions of the assembly during this period, one beginning May 9, 1723, and the other beginning May 12, 1726. At the first, on the recommendation of Governor Drysdale, laws were passed to regulate the militia and for the more effectual prevention of negro insurrections. It appears that not long before a conspiracy had been planned by negroes. This conspiracy furnished additional reasons for the duty laid the same session on liquors and slaves.

At the next session a commission was issued by the governor constituting Philip Finch to be the first sergeant-at-arms and mace-bearer of the house of burgesses. Previous to this time an officer called the messenger had discharged these duties. Governor Drysdale announced to the house that "the interfering interest of the African Company" had obtained from the board of trade the repeal of the law of the previous session imposing a duty on liquors and slaves. He stated his belief that if a new duty be laid on liquors for the support of the college, then "in a languishing condition," the English government would not object, and this was done. Drysdale was a sick man during this session, and not long after its adjournment he died at Williamsburg, July 22, 1726.

Carter, Robert, president of the council and acting governor from the death of Drysdale, July 22, 1726, till the arrival of William Gooch about October, 1727, was born in Virginia in 1663, son of Colonel John and Sarah (Ludlow) Carter. His father had been prominent in the colony as lieutenant-colonel, burgess and councillor. His mother was a daughter of Gabriel Ludlow, a nephew of General Edmund Ludlow, one of Cromwell's generals. Robert Carter was for many years the agent of Lord Fairfax, the proprietor of the Northern Neck grant. He was treasurer of the colony, speaker of the house of burgesses 1694-99, and member of the council for twenty-seven years (1699-1726). He became president of the council, and as such succeeded as acting governor. His great possessions earned him the name of "King" Carter. His residence was in Lancaster county, at Corotoman, on the Rappahannock river, and there is still standing nearby a church that he built shortly before his death, which occurred August 4, 1732. His splendid tomb in a rather shattered condition is still to be seen in the yard of the church. He was twice married, first to Judith, eldest daughter of John Armistead, Esq., a member of the council, and (second) to Elizabeth Willis, daughter of Thomas Landon, of an ancient family in Hereford county, England. By these wives he had numerous children, who have many influential descendants in Virginia and the south.

Gooch, William, lieutenant-governor of Virginia (1727-1749), was born October 12, 1681, in Yarmouth, county Suffolk, England, and was descended from an ancient family. His grandfather was William Gooch, of Suffolk, and his father was Thomas Gooch, alderman of Yarmouth, who married Frances, daughter of Thomas Love, of Norfolk county. His uncle, William Gooch, had emigrated to Virginia at a very early date and become a major in the York county militia and a member of the Virginia council, dying in 1655. The subject of this sketch entered the English army at an early age and took part in all of Queen Anne's wars, being present at the battle of Blenheim. In October, 1727, he superseded Robert Carter as lieutenant-governor of Virginia, and for more than twenty years conducted the affairs of the colony in a manner which occasioned complaint neither in England nor in America. Indeed, it is said that in this respect he stands alone among colonial governors. Still his administration was a period of much activity in Virginia. In 1730 tobacco notes, a new form of currency, were devised which proved salutary. The frontier line was pushed to the Alleghanies, and the valley of Virginia was settled with hardy and

ROBERT (KING) CARTER

enterprising German and Scotch-Irish settlers. Norfolk was chartered a town, and Fredericksburg, Winchester, Richmond and Petersburg were founded. The first newspaper in the colony, the Virginia Gazette, was published in Williamsburg in 1736. The boundary line between Virginia and North Carolina was run. In 1740, on account of the unexpected death of Major-General Alexander Spotswood, Governor Gooch assumed command of the four colonial battalions transported to join the British troops under Admiral Vernon in an attack on Carthagena in New Granada. He was absent one year, during which time Rev. Dr. James Blair, president of the college, acted as governor. The campaign proved unsuccessful, Gooch was severely wounded, and contracted the fever from which many of the English troops died. Upon his return to Virginia in July, 1741, he resumed the government of the colony, and among other events which followed, the capitol accidentally caught on fire and was burned in 1746. On June 20, 1749, he embarked for England, to the great sorrow of all the people of his colony to whom he had endeared himself by his noble and disinterested conduct. He died in London, December 17, 1751. Governor Gooch was created a baronet November 4, 1746. His wife was Rebecca, daughter of William Stanton, Esq., of Hampshire, England. He had an only son, William Gooch, who died in Virginia. His wife survived him till 1775, and in her will left a beautiful silver gilt communion service to the college chapel. This memorial of this excellent woman, who was once the first lady of Virginia, is still preserved in Bruton Church in Williamsburg.

The family of the Gooch name in Virginia are descended from Lieutenant-Colonel Henry Gooch, who was living in York county in 1656, and was an adherent of Nathaniel Bacon, Jr., in 1676. He was probably a member of Governor Gooch's family.

Keppel, William Anne, second Earl of Albemarle and titular governor of Virginia from the death of George Hamilton, Earl of Orkney, 1737, to his own death in 1754, son of Arnold Joost Van Keppel, first earl, and his wife Geertruid Johanna Quirina vander Duyn, was born at Whitehall, June 5, 1702; was baptized at the Chapel Royal, Queen Anne being his godmother, (hence his name Anne); was educated in Holland and on his return to England (as Viscount Bury) was appointed August 25, 1717, captain and lieutenant of the grenadier company of the Coldstream Guards. In 1718 he succeeded to his father's title and estates, and in 1722, at his family seat in Guelderland, entertained the Bishop of Munster. In 1725 he was made Knight of the Bath; in 1727 aide-de-camp to the king; and November 22, 1731, was appointed to the colonecy of the 29th Foot, then at Gibraltar, which he held until May 7, 1733, when he was appointed colonel of the third troop of Horse Guards. He was made governor of Virginia in 1737, a brigadier-general July, 1739, major-general February, 1742, and was transferred to the colonelcy of the Coldstream Guards in October, 1744. He went to Flanders with Lord Stair in 1742, and was a general on the staff at Dettingen, where he had a horse shot under him, and at Fontenoy, where he was wounded. He commanded the first line of Cumberland's army at Culloden, and was again on the staff in Flanders and present at the battle of Val. At the peace of 1748 he was sent as ambassador extraordinary and minister plenipotentiary at Paris, and was appointed commander-in-chief in North Britain, and in

1749 was made Knight of the Garter. The year after he was made groom of the stole and a privy councillor, and in 1752 was one of the lords justices during the king's absence in Hanover. In 1754 he was sent back to Paris to demand the liberation of some British subjects detained by the French in America, and died in Paris suddenly December 22, 1754. His remains were brought over and buried in the chapel in South Audley street, London. Albemarle married, in 1723, Lady Anne Lennox, daughter of Charles, first duke of Richmond, and by her had eight sons and seven daughters.

Albemarle Sound in North Carolina, Albemarle parish in Sussex county, Virginia, and Albemarle county in the same state, were named in his honor.

Blair, James, D. D., president of the council, and acting governor during the absence of Governor Gooch on the expedition against Carthagena (June, 1740—July, 1741) and first president of William and Mary College (1693—1743), was born in Scotland in 1655. He attended the University of Edinburgh and became Master of Arts in 1673. After his graduation he was ordained as a minister of the Church of England, and having served as such for some time in his native country removed to London, where he was clerk in the office of the master of rolls. Dr. Compton, Bishop of London, being much impressed with his talents and piety, suggested to him to go as missionary to Virginia. This he did in 1685. It happened that in Virginia he was given the parish of Varina, in Henrico county, where the attempt to establish a college was made in 1618. Having been made commissary of the Bishop of London in 1689, and inspired by his surroundings at Varina, he persuaded the clergy at their meeting at Jamestown in 1690 to revive the project of the college. They did so, and their recommendations received the approval of both the council and the general assembly; and in June, 1691, Dr. Blair was sent to England by the legislature with full instructions to obtain a charter from the king and queen. He remained there more than a year, and at length returned in 1693 with the much coveted document. It contemplated six professors, 100 students more or less, and three grades of instruction—the grammar school, the philosophy school, and the divinity school. The college was erected at Williamsburg according to a design of Sir Christopher Wren. Till 1712 only the grammar school was in operation, but in that year the first professor of mathematics was elected. In 1729 all the schools had been established, and in that year a transfer of the management took place from the trustees to the faculty, the former retaining visitorial powers only. In 1694 Dr. Blair removed from Henrico to Jamestown and accepted the parish there so as to be nearer his intended college, and in 1710 he accepted the rectorship at Bruton parish at Williamsburg. He became a member of the council in 1689 and continued a member till his death in 1643. He assisted Henry Hartwell and Edward Chilton in compiling in 1697 "The State of his Majesty's Colony in Virginia," and 117 sermons and discourses, expository of the sermon on the mount, were published in four volumes 8vo. at London in 1742. Dr. Blair was an active factor in the politics of the country. When Governor Andros assumed superior authority in ecclesiastical matters, Dr. Blair opposed him, and so successfully that Andros was recalled. He was largely instrumental in the downfall of Nicholson and Spotswood. The two succeeding governors

COLONIAL PRESIDENTS AND GOVERNORS 63

took warning, and Dr. Blair had the hearty cooperation of Drysdale and Gooch in all measures for the advancement of the college. When Gooch went on the expedition against Carthagena, Blair, as the oldest member and president of the council, succeeded him. The end of a useful life of 89 years occurred April 18, 1743. He married Sarah Harrison, daughter of Benjamin Harrison, in 1687, but they left no issue. His nephew, John Blair, son of his brother Dr. Archibald Blair, succeeded him as heir to his property and honors.

Robinson, John, president of the council, became acting governor on the departure of Sir William Gooch for England, June 20, 1749. His grandfather was John Robinson, of Cleasby, Yorkshire, England, who married Elizabeth Potter, daughter of Christopher Potter of Cleasby. His uncle was Dr. John Robinson, Bishop of Bristol and London, who served as British envoy to Sweden, writing while there a history of Sweden, and was also British plenipotentiary at the treaty of Utrecht. His father was Christopher Robinson, a member of the Virginia council in 1691-93, and secretary of state in 1692-93, who married Judith, daughter of Colonel Christopher Wormeley. John Robinson was born in 1683 in Middlesex county, Virginia, at "Hewick," his father's residence on the Rappahannock river. He occupied many important positions in the colony, was member of the house of burgesses in 1711 and other years, member of the council in 1720, and when Governor Gooch left for England, June 20, 1749, became as president of the council, acting governor. In this capacity he served but a few months only, dying September 3, 1749. He married Katherine, daughter of Robert Beverley, author of a history of Virginia, and their son John was speaker of the house of burgesses and treasurer of the colony.

Lee, Thomas, president of the council, and acting governor from the death of John Robinson, September 3, 1749, to his own death, November 14, 1750, was born in Westmoreland county, 1693. He was son of Colonel Richard Lee, who was one of the council of Virginia, and grandson of Colonel Richard Lee, who came to Virginia about 1642 and was secretary of state. Thomas Lee received a common education, "yet having strong natural parts, long after he was a man he learned the languages without any assistance but his own genius, and became tolerably adept in the Greek and Latin." He was long a member of the house of burgesses and the council, and when John Robinson died became by seniority president of the council and as such acting governor. In 1744 he was appointed by Governor Gooch to serve as commissioner with William Beverley to treat with the Six Nations. At Lancaster, Pennsylvania, they made a treaty by which the Indians released their title to lands west of the Alleghanies. Thus having cleared the way, Lee became the leading factor in 1749 in the organization of the Ohio Company, which had as one of its objects the severing of the French settlements in Canada and Louisiana. The company obtained from the king a grant of 500,000 acres of land west of the Alleghanies, between the Kanawha and Ohio rivers. It established trading posts, which, being seized by the French, were the direct cause of the French and Indian war. It is said that the king appointed Lee lieutenant-governor in 1750, but he died before the commission reached him. He was married in 1721 to Hannah, daughter of Colonel Philip Ludwell, and had by her six sons, five of them eminently distinguished for their services during the American revolution—Thomas Ludwell Lee, Richard Henry Lee, Francis Lightfoot Lee, William Lee, and Dr. Arthur Lee and two daughters. His death occurred at Stratford House, in Westmoreland county, Virginia, November 14, 1750; and in the absence of a commissioned governor he was succeeded by Lewis Burwell, member of the council next in seniority.

Burwell, Lewis, president of the council, succeeded on Thomas Lee's death, November 14, 1750, as acting governor of Virginia, and remained such till the arrival of Governor Dinwiddie, November 20, 1751. He was born in 1710, and was son of Major Nathaniel Burwell, of Carter's Creek, Gloucester county, and Elizabeth Carter his wife, daughter of Colonel Robert Carter, acting governor in 1726. Nathaniel Burwell was the son of Major Lewis Burwell, member of the council in 1702, and of Abigail Smith, niece and heiress of Nathaniel Bacon, Esq., president of the council. Then Major Lewis Burwell was son of Lewis Burwell, sergeant-major of the colony in 1652, and Lucy Higginson his wife, daughter of Captain Robert Higginson, who commanded at Middle Plantation (now Williamsburg) in 1646. This last Major Burwell was the emigrant ancestor, who came to Virginia about 1642, and was son of Edward Burwell of Bedfordshire, England, and Dorothy, his wife, daughter of William Bedell, of Catsworth. President Burwell was educated at the University of Cambridge, England, and was distinguished for his remarkable learning and scholarship. On his return to Virginia from England he was called to fill many important offices; was a burgess from Gloucester county in 1742; a member of the council in 1743, and, as president of that body, succeeded Thomas Lee in the administration of affairs. During his magistracy a contract was made for the repair of the governor's house or palace, and for the incoming governor a building near by was purchased of Dr. Kenneth McKenzie. The capitol, which had been burned in 1746, was also nearly completed. Among other incidents of his administration was the visit of Gov. Ogle of Maryland to Williamsburg, and the coming of a company of tragedians who had been playing in New York and Philadelphia. On November 20, 1751, Colonel Robert Dinwiddie arrived at Yorktown with his lady and two daughters, and the next day was sworn into the office of governor. President Burwell appears to have been in feeble health during his administration, for there is a record of his visit which he paid in the spring of 1750 to the Warm Sulphur Springs, in Berkeley county. He survived, however, till May, 1756, when he died at his seat in Gloucester county, Virginia. He married, in October, 1736, Mary, daughter of Colonel Francis and Ann Willis.

Dinwiddie, Robert, governor of Virginia (November 20, 1751 to January, 1758), was born in 1693, at Germiston, near Glasgow. He came of an ancient Scottish family, and his immediate ancestors were denizens of Glasgow. His father was a reputable merchant of that city and bore the same name. His mother was Sarah Cumming, daughter of Matthew Cumming, who was bailie of Glasgow in 1691-96-99 and the owner of the lands of Carderock in the contiguous parish of Cadder. Robert Dinwiddie, their son was brought up in his father's countinghouse and was probably for a time merchant in Glasgow. He was appointed December 1, 1727, a collector of customs in the island of Bermuda, which position he held till 1738, when in recognition of his exposing a long practiced system of fraud in the collecting of the customs of the West India Islands, he received the appointment of "surveyor-general of customs in the southern parts of the continent of America." He was named as his predecessors had been a member of all the councils of the American colonies. Though his claim to sit in the Virginia council was resisted by the councillors, the board of trade in May, 1742, ordered that the royal purpose should be enforced. On August 17, 1746, he was specially commissioned inspector general to examine into the duties of the collector of customs of the Island of Barbadoes. In the discharge of his duties he exposed a great defalcation in the revenues there. In 1749 he appears to have resided in London as a merchant engaged in trade with the colonies. He was appointed lieutenant-governor of Virginia, July 29, 1751 and with his wife Rebecca née Affleck and two daughters, Elizabeth and Rebecca, arrived in the colony November 20, 1751. His administration began rather inauspicuously, as he almost immediately fell into altercation with the house of burgesses over the fee of a pistole which he required for issuing patents. A similar fee had been exacted by Lord Culpeper many years before, and the remonstrance of the assembly had caused the king to forbid its collection. The Virginians regarded the present fee as a tax, and they sent John Randolph to England to represent their cause. The board of trade, after hearing the argument on both sides, recommended a compromise, and the fee was only permitted to be charged for large grants of land, and for none whatever beyond the mountains, where nearly all the ungranted land lay at this time.

VIR—5

This altercation had an important influence upon the endeavors of Dinwiddie in another direction. Dinwiddie had become a member of the Ohio Company and he had a direct interest in the destinies of the western country. When, therefore, the French began to plant settlements on the Ohio and occupied Venango, an Indian trading post at the junction of the Alleghany river and French creek, Dinwiddie sent George Washington to protest to the French commandant at Fort Le Boeuf. When no satisfactory answer was brought back, he sent orders to Captain William Trent to build a log fort at the junction of the Alleghany and Monongahela, where Pittsburgh now stands. This position was considered on all hands as the key to the situation in the West. The French were not long in driving the Virginians out and occupying the post themselves. While this was occurring, Washington with some 300 troops was marching to the assistance of Trent, when meeting with a scouting party of the French he attacked and killed some twenty of them, with a loss of only one man. This was the beginning of a war which was to spread practically over the whole civilized world. Dinwiddie more than any one else realized the situation, and he displayed prodigious energy in his efforts to arouse the British government and the colonists to the importance of the crisis. The home government was slow to move and the other colonies generally were indifferent, as was the Virginia assembly itself, who distrusting the purposes of Dinwiddie and deeming him too precipitate would not grant the money asked for, except on conditions calculated to humble the pride of the governor. So during the time that Dinwiddie held the government of Virginia, the war with the French and Indians proved very disastrous. In the attempt to take Fort Duquesne, as the French called the captured post at the forks of the Monongahela and Alleghany, Braddock's army was destroyed, and in the north the French captured Oswego and Fort William Henry. For four years the evil days followed one another, but amid the most disheartening conditions, Robert Dinwiddie remained undismayed. The ardent task of raising unwilling troops and directing the defense of 350 miles of frontier fell to him, and while he did not escape the charge of improper interference at times, on the whole, he discharged his duties ably and nobly.

To the excitement in the colony produced by the French war more was added by the passage in 1755 of the first of the Two Penny Act by the assembly, making the tax for salaries of the ministers payable either in tobacco or in money at two pence per pound, at the option of the tax payer. The ministers tried to get Governor Dinwiddie to veto the bill, but he was beginning to learn the lesson of non-interference with the legislature, and he declined. Worn out at length with the harassing duties of his office, he solicited from the authorities in England permission to return, and so in January, 1758, he departed from the colony, bearing with him the commendations of the assembly and the people of Virginia in general. He marked his interest in the colony by contributing many books to the College Library. He survived his return to England by twelve years, and finally died at Clifton, Bristol, whither he had gone for the benefit of the baths, July 27, 1770, in the 78th year of his age. His brother John was a merchant on the Rappahannock river in Virginia. He married Rosa Enfield Mason, of Stafford county, and is numerously represented in the South.

Blair, John, president of the council, and as such acting governor of Virginia from the departure for England of Governor Dinwiddie, January, 1758, till the arrival of Governor Francis Fauquier, June 7, 1758, and from the time of Governor Fauquier's death, March 3, 1768, till the arrival of Lord Botetourt, October, 1768. He was son of Dr. Archibald Blair, brother of Dr. James Blair, president of the College of William and Mary, and was born in Virginia in 1687. He was educated at William and Mary College, and was a burgess from Williamsburg in 1736-1740, and in 1743 became a member of the council, an office which he held till his death. During his first administration, which happened during the French and Indian war, the assembly augmented the forces in the pay of the colony to 2,000 men and issued £32,000 in treasury notes to defray the expenses of the increased defences of the colony. In the troubles which led to the American Revolution, Blair was always on the popular side. As a judge of the general court in April, 1764, he upheld the Two Penny Act, and as president of the committee of correspondence he voted to condemn the Stamp Act in June, 1764. When he became acting governor the second time he promptly called the general assembly together to consider the new revenue measures passed by parliament. When the assembly convened, March 31, 1768, he concurred with the council and house of burgesses in the bold resolutions unanimously adopted that only the general assembly could make any laws regarding "the internal policy or taxation of the colony." Blair was the source through which they were transmitted to England, and Lord Hillsborough, the secretary of colonial affairs, expressed himself amazed especially at the action of the council and its president, who were appointed by the Crown. When Norborne Berkeley, Baron de Botetourt, died, October 15, 1770, the government devolved for a third time upon President Blair, but he immediately resigned on account of old age and infirmities and was succeeded by William Nelson. He died in Williamsburg, November 5, 1771, leaving by his wife Mary Monro, daughter of Rev. John Monro, a son John, member of the Federal convention of 1787 and one of the first judges of the Supreme Court of the United States.

Campbell, John, fourth Earl of Loudoun, and titular governor of Virginia (1756-1763), the only son of Hugh, third Earl of Loudoun, and Lady Margaret Dalrymple, only daughter of the first Earl of Stair, was born on 5 May, 1705. He succeeded his father as earl in 1731, and from 1734 till his death was a representative peer of Scotland. He entered the army in 1727, was appointed governor of Stirling Castle in April, 1741, and became aide-de-camp to the King in July, 1743. He performed an important part in suppressing the rebellion of 1745, and had nearly the whole of his regiment killed at the battle of Preston. On February 17, 1756, Loudoun was appointed captain-general and governor-in-chief of the province of Virginia, and on March 30, commander-in-chief of the British forces in America in the French and Indian war. He arrived at New York on July 23, 1756. Owing to his own tardiness and the incompetency of those at the head of the government he accomplished nothing, and was therefore recalled to England, General Amherst being named his successor. On the declaration of war with Spain in 1762 he was appointed second in command, under Lord Tyrawley, of the troops sent to Portugal. He died at Loudoun Castle, April 27, 1762. He was unmarried, and on his death his title passed to his cousin, James Mure Campbell. He did much to improve the grounds around Loudoun Castle, in Ayrshire, Scotland.

Fauquier, Francis, colonial governor of Virginia (1758-1768), was eldest son of Dr. John Francis Fauquier (one of the directors of the Bank of England, who died September 22, 1726), and Elizabeth Chamberlayne, his wife. He was born in 1704, and though little appears to be known of his early life, he was distinguished for his learning, especially in the natural sciences, and in 1753 was made a fellow of the Royal Society. Previous to this, in 1751, he was a director of the South Sea Company. In January, 1758, he was appointed lieutenant-governor of Virginia, and soon after his arrival on June 4, 1758, the clouds which had hitherto hung over the British fortunes in the French and Indian war passed away, and a tide of uninterrupted British success set in. The treaty of peace in 1763 left the British power supreme in America and in the world. There are in the British museum nine letters written by Fauquier between 1759 and 1764, chiefly respecting the military forces of Virginia during his administration. The local agitations which led to the American Revolution began in Fauquier's administration. In these he was, as far as his situation permitted, entirely on the popular side, the natural result of his devotion to scientific matters, which made him hostile to dogmas of all kinds. In the matter of the Two Penny Act he gave the parsons to understand, that, law or no law, he was unequivocally against them. In 1760 he expressed great apprehensions to William Pitt that the colonies would not submit to any stamp act. Fauquier was still governor when the stamp act passed, and though he was loyal to his superiors in England, he had no heart in the enforcement of this or of the Revenue act which followed. After the passage of the latter act he prorogued the legislature from time to time both on account of sickness and in order to avoid a quarrel. He was sick a long time, and March 3, 1768, he died, and was buried in the north aisle of the church in Williamsburg. According to his will, proved at Yorktown, he left a wife Catherine; a brother-in-law, Francis Wollaston; a brother, William Fauquier; and two sons, Francis and William Fauquier.

Fauquier was a very affable and agreeable man, though somewhat excitable. He was an excellent talker, and delighted in the company of Dr. William Small, the professor of natural philosophy at William and Mary College, and of George Wythe, the great Williamsburg lawyer; and at his table many rising young men of Virginia, like Jefferson and John Page, learned their lessons in the rights of man. As an indication of his interest in scientific matters it may be mentioned that his brother William read before the Royal Society in London an article prepared by him in Virginia on 'Hailstones observed in Virginia, July 9, 1758." His influence in another respect was not so fortunate. He diffused in the colony a passion for playing cards, which lasted till it was rebuked by the orders of the Revolutionary county committees in 1775.

Amherst, Jeffrey, titular governor of Virginia (1763-1768), was the second son of Jeffrey Amherst, of Riverhead, Kent county, England. His family had no influence, and the remarkable fact of the rise of Amherst from page to field marshal is a tribute to his own merit. He was page to the Duke of Dorset, who procured for him an ensigncy in the Guards in 1731. He next served on General Ligonier's staff, and afterwards on that of the Duke of Cumberland. In 1756 he was made lieutenant-colonel of the Fifteenth regiment. When Pitt became chancellor, and was fitting out an expedition to North America, he picked out Amherst as the man to lead. The expedition that sailed from Portsmouth in May, 1758, was 14,000 strong, and was embarked in fifteen ships under the command of Admiral Boscawen. On reaching the Island of Cape Breton he captured Louisburg, and in September, Amherst was as a reward appointed commander-in-chief of the forces in the place of James Abercrombie. In November, 1758, he captured Fort Duquesne from the French. He was even more successful in the different campaigns of the next year (1759). Ticonderoga fell before him, and his generals Sir William Johnson and Wolfe took Fort Niagara and Quebec, which in 1760 was followed by the surrender of Montreal, the capital of Canada. Amherst was at once appointed governor-general of North America, and in 1761 received the thanks of parliament and was made a knight of the Bath. The French sued for peace, but war still continued with the Indians. They were led by Pontiac, and Amherst proved unfit to deal with him. His failure no doubt was the chief cause of his return to England in 1763. There Pontiac's conspiracy was unknown, and Amherst was received as the conqueror of Canada and made governor of Virginia and colonel of the 60th or American regiment. His fame became very great. In 1770 he was made governor of Guernsey, and in 1772, a privy councillor and lieutenant-general of the ordinance. During the American war he served in the capacity of adviser to the government. His

steady support of the American war endeared him to the King, who made him in 1776 Lord Amherst, in 1778 a general, and in 1780 colonel of the 2nd Horse Grenadiers. After various other honors he was raised in 1796 to the rank of field marshal. He did not long survive this last honor, and died at Montreal, his seat in Kent, August 3, 1797.

Berkeley, Norborne, Baron de Botetourt, governor-in-chief of Virginia (1768-1770), was born in England, in 1718. He was the only son of John Symes Berkeley, Esq., of Stoke Gifford, county Gloucester, England, by his wife Elizabeth, daughter and coheir of Walter Norborne of Caline, county Wilts. Of this branch of the distinguished and ennobled family of Berkeley an extended pedigree appears in the Visitation of Gloucester of 1623. In 1764 Botetourt was raised to the peerage of England as Norborne, Baron de Botetourt. Previous to this he had been colonel of the North Gloucestershire militia and a member of parliament, and afterwards in 1767 became constable of the Tower of London. No governor-in-chief had resided in the colony of Virginia for three-quarters of a century, and, to appease the growing discontent there over the revenue law, the home authorities sent Botetourt over with the full title and dignity of "His Majesty's Lieutenant, Governor-General and Commander-in-Chief." He was appointed in July, 1768, and arrived in the colony October 28, 1769. His reception was enthusiastic, and his affable deportment made him immediately very popular, which was increased by his concurring shortly after his arrival with his council in declaring writs of assistance illegal. The quarrel over the revenue act had come to a crisis at this time. Parliament had sent an order over for the arrest of the patriot leaders in New England, who were to be transported to England for trial, and Virginia was the first colony to take action. When Botetourt convened the assembly, that body on May 26, 1769, passed stirring resolutions condemning parliament. Botetourt dissolved the assembly, and the members, with the speaker, Peyton Randolph, at their head, met immediately at the Raleigh tavern and adopted an extensive system of non-importation. They rallied all the other colonies to do the same, and parliament, yielding to the pressure, abolished all the taxes complained of except a small tax on tea. Botetourt had cherished the hope that all the taxes would be repealed, and relying upon the assurances of the English secretary of state had called an assembly in November following the May session in 1769 to convey to them the joyous information of this purpose of the British ministry. He was, therefore, greatly disappointed when only a partial repeal was made. It is said that he contemplated a resignation of his office and was only prevented from sending it on by his sickness and death, which occurred October 15, 1770. There are various contemporary notices of his social acts, his dinner companies at the palace, the distinction of his manner, and the urbanity of his address. Through his munificence two gold medals were established in the College of William and Mary, to be given annually one for excellence in classical learning, and the other for excellence in philosophy. Eight of these prizes were bestowed, and they are said to be the earliest of their kind in the United States. Lord Botetourt was honored by the people with a splendid funeral, and he was buried in a vault underneath the floor of the chapel of William and Mary, and subsequently a statue was erected to his memory. Close by his vault lie the remains of Peyton Randolph, who presided over the councils of the Virginia revolutionists, when Botetourt was living, and was afterwards first president of the Continental Congress. Botetourt was a bachelor, and so left no children.

Nelson, William, president of the council and acting governor (1770-1771), was born in Yorktown, Virginia, in 1711, son of Thomas Nelson (1667-1745), who came to America from Penrith in England, on the borders of Scotland, about 1690, and hence was called "Scotch Tom." This Thomas Nelson settled at Yorktown about 1705, where he became the leading merchant. He married Margaret Reade, daughter of Robert Reade, son of Colonel George Reade, who in 1660 owned the site of the place. Thomas Nelson, a son, became secretary of state. William Nelson, another son and subject of this sketch, inherited a great deal of wealth, which he managed largely to increase by his extensive business as a merchant at Yorktown. He married Elizabeth Burwell, daughter of Major Nathaniel Burwell. He represented the county of York in the house of burgesses in 1742-44, and in 1745 was promoted to the council of state. He supported the cause of the colony against the stamp act and the revenue act, and as president of the council acted as governor of the colony from the death of Lord Botetourt, October 15, 1770, to the coming of the Earl of Dunmore in August, 1771. During this interval the opposition to the revenue taxes, which had been shorn down to a slight duty on tea, very sensibly declined, and the agitation in the colonies might have died out altogether had not the British ministry raised new issues. Nelson died at Yorktown, November 19, 1772. He was father of General Thomas Nelson, who distinguished himself in the war of the Revolution and was also governor of the State.

Murray, John, fourth Earl of Dunmore, last colonial governor of Virginia (1771-1775), was born in 1732, eldest son of William Murray, third Earl of Dunmore, and Catherine Nairne his wife. He was descended on his mother's side from the royal house of Stuart, succeeded to the peerage, and during 1761-69 sat in the house of lords. In January, 1770, he was appointed governor of the colony of New York, and in July, 1771, governor of Virginia. He arrived in Williamsburg in October, 1771, where he was received with the usual courtesies and congratulations. The controversy with the mother country had lost its rancour after the repeal of all the taxes except that on tea, but the King, by instructions to his governors, managed to affront all the colonies on different issues. The public sentiment in Virginia particularly condemned the order which restrained the governors from approving any restriction of the slave trade, and when the assembly, pursuant to a summons from Dunmore met in February, 1772, a noble protest was adopted by that body. Dunmore prorogued the house, and he did not again convene it till March, 1773. In the meantime, a government revenue cutter called the Gaspée, which had been rigorously enforcing the navigation laws in Narragansett Bay, was boarded at night by some disguised men and set on fire. The King was much exasperated, and he created a board of enquiry, who were directed to find out the guilty parties and send them to England for trial. The issue was once more met by Virginia. The assembly adopted resolutions at its meeting in March, 1773, denouncing this attempt to ignore the right of a trial by a jury of the vicinage, and recommending a system of intercolonial committees, which proved the first direct step towards a general and permanent union. Immediately after this

act Lord Dunmore dissolved the assembly. The effect of the action of Virginia was to demoralize the court of enquiry, and in their report they conceded that the commander of the Gaspée, in detaining vessels indiscriminately, had exceeded the bounds of his duty, and no arrests were made. This affair not turning out to the satisfaction of the British government, another attempt was made to enforce the tax on tea in America by removing the tax in England. This occasioned the affair of the "tea party," which occurred in Boston on December 16, 1773, when a band of men disguised as Indians boarded the ships sent to Boston by the East India Company and threw the tea overboard. Parliament in resentment, passed an act to close the Port of Boston, on June 1, 1774—a measure which involved the innocent with the guilty. Virginia again showed her leadership, and was first of all of the colonies to declare her sympathy with Massachusetts. Dunmore prorogued the assembly May 27, 1774, and thereupon the burgesses, meeting in the Raleigh tavern, adopted resolutions calling for an annual congress and non-intercourse. Accordingly, on September 5, 1774, the first general congress met in Philadelphia and recommended a general continental plan of non-intercourse, and committees everywhere to see it enforced. About this time a war with the Shawnees on the Ohio broke out, and Andrew Lewis won the great battle of Point Pleasant. Dunmore gained applause from the Virginians for his willingness to head the troops, but he was afterwards charged, without much reason, with being the real author of the Indian war. The British government now placed the trade with most of the colonies under a boycott, and orders were sent over to the governors to seize all the ammunition and arms accessible to the colonists.

Governor Gage in Massachusetts sent troops to destroy the ammunition at Concord, and on the march thither they became engaged April 19, 1775, with the Massachusetts militia at Lexington, where the first blood was shed. In Virginia, by order of Governor Dunmore, the powder was removed from the magazine in Williamsburg on April 20. This created great alarm, and an armed body of men under Patrick Henry marched down to Williamsburg. They were quieted by the governor giving a bill of exchange for the value of the powder. Succeeding this, Dunmore called a meeting of the assembly to submit the overture known as Lord North's "Olive Branch." But before any answer could be returned from the assembly, Dunmore, fearing that he might be seized and detained as a hostage, fled from the palace to the protection of a British man-of-war in York river. Dunmore took up his headquarters near Norfolk, which was burned in the civil war that now began. Dunmore proclaimed freedom to all negroes and servants who would join his standard, and carried on a predatory maritime warfare, but after suffering various reverses at Great Bridge, Hampton and Gwynn's Island, he dismissed his ships, joined the British naval force in New York, and towards the end of the year 1776 sailed away to England. His furniture and books in the palace were confiscated by the State and sold at public outcry. He had been elected in January, 1776, to the house of lords, and on his return to England took his seat and served till 1784. In 1787 he was appointed governor of Barbadoes, and served till 1796. He died at Ramsgate, England, in May, 1809. He was a man of culture, and possessed a large and valuable library; and while he has been represented in America as rude in his deportment and treacherous in his conduct, his friends praise him for the noble and admirable traits of character, which they attribute to him. The Tories who had to fly from Virginia during the war, abandoning everything except loyalty to their King, found in him a real haven of refuge in London. His home and money were at their service. He married February 21, 1759, Lady Charlotte Stewart, sixth daughter of Alexander, sixth earl of Gallway. Late in April, 1774, he was joined at Williamsburg by his wife and her children, George Lord Fincastle, the Honorables Alexander and John Murray, and Ladies Catherine, Augusta and Susan Murray. To these were added another daughter born in the colony, and named in its honor Virginia. The three young noblemen were put to school at the College. In 1834 Charles Murray, a grandson of Lord Dunmore, visited Virginia, and afterwards published an account of his travels.

COLONIAL COUNCILLORS OF STATE

III—COLONIAL COUNCILLORS OF STATE

Newport, Christopher. There can be no doubt that King James displayed great wisdom in choosing so experienced and able a seaman as Christopher Newport to command the colonizing expedition of 1607 to Virginia, and in sealing the box which contained his list of councillors during the voyage, in order that there might be no conflict of authority with his. He had sailed the Spanish Main and taken an active part in the privateering exploits against the Spanish in the New World. In 1592 he sailed in command of four ships when he "took and Spoyled Yaguana and Ocoa and Hispaniola and Truxillo, besides other prizes." After the brilliant capture of the "Madre de Dios" by the ships of Sir Walter Raleigh and the Earl of Cumberland, Capt. Newport, who played an important part in the fight, was given command of her and took her to Dartmouth.

When the expedition of 1607 arrived at Jamestown, Newport's name was found on the list of councillors, though he was not expected to become a planter but to serve as admiral in the voyages between England and the colony. In pursuance of his orders to remain two months in the New World exploring, he started May 21 on a voyage up the James river, which he followed as far as the "falls," the present site of the city of Richmond. Here, finding that he could go no further without great danger, he set up a cross with the inscription "Jacobus Rex, 1607," and his own name underneath. Upon inquiry by the Indians as to the meaning of this cross and ceremony, the wily captain told them that the two arms of the cross signified Powhatan and himself, and their juncture the league they had entered into. On June 22 of the same year he returned to England with a cargo of "sasafrax rootes" instead of the gold which the Virginia Company had so ardently hoped for.

Newport's second arrival in Virginia (Jan. 2, 1608) was a timely one. The death of Gosnold had left Wingfield open to attacks of his opponents—Archer, Smith, Ratcliffe and Martin, who had first deposed him from the presidency and finally imprisoned him, Capt. Smith, too, who had just returned from captivity with the Indians, was in chains under sentence of hanging. Newport at once set these men at liberty and restored some measure of peace in the colony and council. A few days later, however, a fire broke out and destroyed the whole of the little settlement, thus exposing its occupants to the severity of the winter's weather. Newport again came to the rescue and employed his mariners in helping to rebuild the church, storehouse and other houses. Capt. Newport later made a third voyage to Virginia, and brought on this occasion (Oct., 1608) the first gentlewoman, Mrs. Forrest, and Anne Buras, her maid. As was to have been expected, there occurred, shortly after, the first marriage in the colony which was of this same Anne Buras and John Laydon, a carpenter; and to them was born a year later a girl, Virginia Laydon—the first child of English parentage born in the first permanent English colony.

Newport's fourth voyage was in command

of the expedition sent out under the second charter, which left Falmouth June 8, 1609. There were nine ships carrying Sir Thomas Gates as governor, and about 500 persons, some of them women. Two of the vessels were wrecked and Newport himself was cast away on the Bermudas with Gov. Gates and 150 other passengers and a large portion of the stores for the colony. He finally got away from the islands, and made his way to Virginia just in time to save the colony from starvation. The casting away of Newport's ship, the "Sea Venture," was the occasion of Shakespeare's great play, "The Tempest," interest in the subject having most probably been communicated to him by Southampton. After one more voyage to Virginia, Capt. Newport's connection with the colony ceased. He resigned his position with the Virginia Company and was appointed one of the six masters of the Royal Navy, and performed several voyages for the East India Company. On the third of these his death occurred about August 15, 1617, while his fleet lay at anchor in a Javan port. The stalwart captain died thus as he had lived, in command of his ship, in the midst of new lands and untried seas.

Wingfield, Edward Maria, first president of the council (q. v.).

Largely instrumental in bringing about the successful expedition of 1607, was

Gosnold, Bartholomew, a seasoned mariner who had been associated with Raleigh in his attempts to colonize Virginia, and not less was he the leaven of peace among the discordant elements in the first Jamestown council, of which he was a member. Respected by all the diverse factions as no one else was, he was able to effect something like a concert of purpose and action among his fellows, and stave off, in a measure, the dissensions which broke out so violently after his death. Upon the failure of Raleigh's expeditions, Gosnold had returned to England still hopeful, and in 1602 he took command of a vessel fitted out by the Earl of Southampton, the friend and patron of Shakespeare. Gosnold's intended destination was Virginia, but, the ship being driven from her course by adverse winds, they touched upon the New England coast, where they were the first Englishmen to land and where they named Cape Cod and Martha's Vineyard. Those who had proposed remaining as colonists lost heart, however, and returned to England, but Gosnold, undisheartened, continued his efforts and finally beheld his hopes' fruition in Jamestown. His voice, indeed, was raised against the site chosen, on the ground of its obvious unhealthfulness, but, being overruled, he turned to with heart and soul to give success to the enterprise. He was spared the pain of beholding the pains and horrors the colony was doomed to undergo, his death occurring before the close of the first summer, Aug. 22, 1607, when fate seemed still auspicious. All record unite in praising his singleness of purpose and hardihood, and Pres. Wingfield made him his sole confidant in matters of importance such as that of the diminishing supplies. It is possible, therefore, that, while it may have been a personal good fortune to have escaped the misfortunes of his fellows he might, had he lived, have done much to alleviate their sorrows by uniting them in a more harmonious effort.

Smith, John, councillor and president of the council (q. v.).

Ratcliffe, John, councillor and president of the council (q. v.).

Kendall, George, one of the original council. The record which has come down to us in regard to this man is not at all flattering, but it must be remembered that he stands convicted on the evidence of bitter enemies. In the days in which he lived there was no such thing as moderation of expression. He was a cousin of the Earl of Southampton, and the fact that he was appointed in England a member of the council in Virginia shows that he must have been well known in London as a man of experience and courage. Doubtless in Virginia under the terrible stress of circumstances during the first summer there was much to criticise, and the evidence, at least, shows that he was not a man afraid to speak out his mind. George Percy and Wingfield denounced him as a stirrer up of dissensions, and Capt. Smith also speaks of his being driven from the council, which he says was for "divers reasons" and occurred about June 22, 1607. He was afterwards released, though without the privilege of carrying arms, but was again arrested on the statement of one James Read, a smith, who had been condemned to death, and who accused Kendall of conspiring to cause a mutiny. Read was forthwith pardoned and Kendall condemned to be shot. The president at the time was John Ratcliffe, and Kendall, it is said, sought to prevent the execution by claiming that Sicklemore, and not Ratcliffe, was his true name, and that consequently he had no right to pronounce judgment. The practical gentlemen of the time refused, however, to delay justice on any such quibble, and, without attempting any controversy on the subject, merely caused John Martin, another councillor, to perform the president's office, which he promptly did, and Kendall quickly paid the penalty of his sins.

Martin, John, one of the councillors, was the son of Sir Richard Martin who "thrice filled the office of lord mayor, and was Master of the Mint in the reigns of Elizabeth and James I." The profession of the law had been chosen for him, but when he was about twenty-one years old he went to sea in obedience to a longing for the then most romantic life of the mariner. He commanded the "Benjamin" in Sir Francis Drake's fleet in that commander's marauding expedition among the West Indies in 1585. On Drake's homeward voyage Martin touched at Virginia, whither the fleet had repaired in aid of Raleigh's colonists on Roanoke Island.

Martin was bitterly opposed to Pres. Wingfield, and after the death of Gosnold, the return to England of Capt. Newport and the deposing of Kendall from the council, he was one of the three remaining councillors who forced Wingfield from the presidency. Martin's health was poor, and besides his other afflictions he was badly smitten with the "gold fever," which gave his enemies afterwards a chance to ridicule him, amongst whom was Capt. John Smith, who gave him the name of "refining Captain Martin," and helped to make him unpopular. He returned to England in June, 1608, but the following year he came again to Virginia, where he was very coldly welcomed but admitted to the council. Upon Capt. Smith's absence from Jamestown in the summer of 1609, he appointed Martin in his place, but for this office, according to Smith, the latter gentleman had no relish and he resigned after three hours. But that Martin was no weakling is proved by the fact that he was the only person who protested against the abandonment of Jamestown in 1610, and unlike Smith he stuck to Virginia to the end. He made a second trip to England in 1616, and again returned to Virginia the year following. This trip was the cause of further friction between Martin and the colonists, as the Virginia Company in London had granted him a patent for ten shares of land in Virginia with unusual rights to its enjoyment, which the others did not approve. Despite the representations of the Virginia Company that Martin had been a "long and faithful servant to the Colony of Virginia," the colonial council remained firm and his privileges were curtailed. The breach between Martin and the council was finally healed, and he located his patent at Brandon on James river.

The date of Martin's death is unknown, though it must have taken place subsequently to March 8, 1626, as there is a letter of this date from him to his brother-in-law, Sir Julius Caesar. He is supposed to have died and been buried at Brandon. His daughter Dorcas married Capt. George Bargrave, son of Robert Bargrave, of Bridge in Kent. George Bargrave came to Virginia, and was largely interested with his brother, John Bargrave, in the trade of the colony. His son, Robert Bargrave, sold Brandon to Richard Quiney and John Sadler, from whom it came by descent to Robert Richardson, who sold it in 1720 to Nathaniel Harrison, in whose family Brandon still remains. The original patent for Brandon, granted to Capt. John Martin from the Virginia Company of London, is still preserved at the place. It bears date 1617, and is by long odds the most ancient official record relating to the American soil to be found in the United States.

Archer, Gabriel, was a man of talent and courage. He is described as of Mountnessing, Essex county, England. He entered Gray's Inn as a student of law Mar. 15, 1593. In 1602 he went with Bartholomew Gosnold to New England and wrote an interesting account of the discovery and naming of Cape Cod and Martha's Vineyard. On his return he was active in arousing interest in an attempt to locate a colony in Virginia, and came with the first settlers. He was among the first to put foot to land at Cape Henry, Apr. 26, 1606, and was one of the two first settlers to Virginia to be wounded by the savages. He was appointed recorder of the colony, and on May 21, he went with Newport from Jamestown on a voyage of discovery up James river, and afterwards "wrote a Relatyon of the Voyage." The charter permitted a majority of the council to elect the president or turn him out, to turn out any member of the council and elect a substitute. It was, therefore, a veritable hothouse of faction. Archer seems to have furnished his full share to the quarrels of Jamestown, though probably no more than his share. He joined with Smith, Martin and Ratcliffe in displacing Wingfield as president, and afterwards when Ratcliffe admitted him to the council in Dec., 1607, caused Smith to be indicted "upon a chapter in Leviticus" for the death of two of his men on his trip up Chickahominy, and Ratcliffe, the president, approved the sentence of execution. And Smith would have been hanged the next day, had not Capt. Newport arrived the evening before (Jan. 2, 1608) and interferred to save his life.

When Newport set out April 10, 1608, to return to England, he carried with him both Wingfield and Archer, whose complaints on their arrival were directed with such good effect against the charter that a petition for a new one creating a more suitable form of government was soon presented to the King, and granted. Under this second charter dated (May 23, 1609) Sir Thomas Gates was made governor, and had the selection of his council, and Archer, flattering himself that he was rid of the dominance of John Smith, returned to the colony. Of the voyage he wrote an interesting account. But the unexpected happened, and Gates was wrecked on the Bermuda Islands. Then to the disappointment of all the gentlemen of the rest of the expedition which got to Jamestown, Smith would not give up his commission, in which he was only technically right. Fresh brawls ensued, and after a few months Smith returned to England, while Archer remained and died at Jamestown during the Starving Time of 1609-1610.

Scrivener, Matthew, councillor and president of the council (q. v.).

Wynne, Peter, was one of the gentlemen who came to Virginia with Capt. Newport on that officer's second voyage of relief to the colony. He arrived there in Sept., 1608, and was immediately admitted to the council. The advent of such men as Wynne and Scrivener, with their sincere wishes for the welfare of the enterprise and their sense of responsibility, must have acted like ballast in a storm-driven ship upon the faction-rent council, but it must have been a thankless task which devolved upon them for the next few months during the starving time. Wynne, himself, was one of those who succumbed to the conditions and he died in the spring of 1609, while Sir Thomas Gates, the representative of Lord De la Warr, or Delaware, and Christopher Newport were in the Bermudas, seeking some means of escape therefrom. He thus did not live to see the relief which these and Lord Delaware were soon to bring. He enjoys the unique distinction of having been appointed deputy governor of Virginia after his death, for Gates, who reposed especial confidence in him, and had not heard of the event, selected him to act as governor while he was absent in the Bermudas, and sent him a particular commission.

Another gentleman who came to Virginia with Capt. Newport on the second expedition of 1608, arriving in September, was

Waldo, Richard, who, with Capt. Wynne, was at once admitted to the council. During his brief career in America, he seems to have been chiefly occupied in the trips of exploration undertaken by Newport and Smith. He was one of the commanders of the expedition which the former officer made into the Monacan country and very probably witnessed the ceremony of Powhatan's coronation in the European style, which must altogether have been a most delightful comedy, the great Indian "Emperor" understanding the significance of neither crown nor the act of kneeling to receive it. He also formed one of Smith's party which set out from Jamestown to visit that same dignitary. On this occasion, however, he seems not to have gone the whole way, but to have returned to Jamestown before Smith, for on Jan. 7, 1609, while crossing from that place to Hog Island in a boat with Councillor Scrivener and others, he was drowned.

Percy, George, councillor and president (q. v.).

West, Francis, councillor and governor (q. v.).

Somers, Sir George, was born at Lyme Regis, Dorsetshire, in 1554, and is supposed to have been related to the Somers family of White Ladies, Worcestershire. Although his name was second in the royal patent of Apr. 10, 1606, he took no active part in colonial affairs until 1609, when he sailed with Sir Thomas Gates and Capt. Newport in the expedition of that year. He was fifty-odd years of age at the time of his sailing and had already distinguished himself in the military and naval service, having commanded several expeditions and, in 1595, accompanied Capt. Amias Preston to the West Indies. He was knighted at Whitehall, July 23, 1603, in reward for his services, and represented Lyme Regis in parliament for a number of years. He was appointed admiral for the colony, and was on the "Sea Adventure" on the way to take command, when she was cast away. Sir George Somers was the first on the shipwrecked vessel to sight land, but strange to say, his discovery was not hailed with the joy that men in such straits are prone to feel. The reason for this is explained by the fact that the shores he had seen were those of a Bermudan island, supposed by mariners to be inhabited by fairies and devils. However, in a choice between them and the deep sea, the party, with more prudence than religion, chose the former and were soon comfortably landed, where, to their further comfort, they found the fairies to be flocks of birds upon the shore and the devils, herds of wild swine running in the wood. After sojourning there until they had completed the construction of two vessels to be their transport, they set sail therein for Virginia. But Somers was not destined to more than reach the promised land, for, finding the colonists in the sorriest of plights, and well nigh starving to death, he volunteered to return at once to the fruitful Bermudas for supplies. He started at once, but adverse winds drove him as far North as New England before he finally reached his destination.

His death occurred on the 9th of Nov., 1610, shortly after his arrival in Bermuda, and it is stated that it was occasioned by a too hearty repast on one of the Bermuda "devils," with which he had intended lading his ships for the colony. Feeling the approach of death, he exhorted his followers to perform the task they had undertaken without him. This, however, they did not do. They buried his heart in the island and his cedar ship with his dead body at last arrived at Whitechurch, in Dorsetshire, about Feb. 26, 1611, where it was buried with military honors.

Gates, Sir Thomas, governor, 1609 (q. v.).

Weyman, Sir Ferdinando, had every reason to regard the Virginia colony as the appropriate scene for his endeavors. It might almost be called a family matter, related, as he was, on all sides to the prominent figures in the enterprise. He was a cousin of Thomas Lord Delaware, governor of Virginia, and of Francis and John West who played distinguished parts there, the latter being also governor. His wife was a sister-in-law of Sir Francis Wyatt, governor of Virginia, and a niece of Sir George Sandys, the poet, and treasurer of the colony. Another cousin, Penelope West, married Herbert Pelham and of their sixteen children, one was the first treasurer of Harvard College, and another the wife of Gov. Bellingham of Massachusetts. Weyman was born in Caswell, Oxfordshire, the son of Thomas Weyman, Esq., of that place, and came to the colony in 1610. On June 12, of that year, he was appointed admiral and master of the horse. But Weyman was not destined to enjoy his honors long, for, as was the case with so many of his fellows, he died shortly after his arrival in the colony, leaving a young daughter. Of this young lady's life in that inauspicious environment but little is known, but it can scarcely have been a very happy one under the circumstances. However, she must have had powerful friends who would alleviate, in so far as it lay in their power, the discomforts of her position. In 1620 it was reported to the Virginia Company that Sir Ferdinando Weyman, who "adventured one hundred pounds with Lord La Warr, besides the adventure of his person to Virginia," had died there, leaving an only child, a daughter, who had received a letter from Lady La Warr expressing a willingness to have the above amount deducted from his Lordship's account and given to her. This the company "well allowed" and agreed besides to give the little orphan four shares of land in Virginia for the adventure of her father's person, he "being a man of worth."

Strachey, William; there appears to be some confusion as to his identity, the question being whether the person prominent in the Virginia colonization was the elder or younger of the two men of that name, father and son, who flourished at the time. Brown, in his "Genesis of the United States," inclines to the opinion that it was the former, but Sir Edward Strachey, of Sutton Court, the present representative of the family, believes it to have been the younger man whose death did not occur until 1634. However this may be, the Strachey with whom history is concerned was something of an author and scholar, and in the dedication to Lord Bacon of his "Historie of Travaile into Virginia Brittania," he claims membership in Gray's Inn, though his name does not appear in the index to Foster's "Gray's Inn Admissions." Before his adventure to Virginia, he seems to have done some travelling in the Mediterranean, as he mentions visits to the "Coast of Barbary and Algiers, in the Levant." He was a member of the notable expedition of 1609, of Sir Thomas Gates, and was one of those cast away in the Bermudas with the chiefs of the party. He has written an account of the experience entitled "A True Repertory of the Wracke and Redemption of Sir Thomas Gates upon and from the Islands of Bermudas." This work was published in the fourth volume of Purchas' "Pilgrims." He also compiled for the colony of Virginia "Laws Devine, Morall, and Marshall" (London, 1612). His most important work, the "Historie of Travaile into Virginia Brittania," has already been mentioned. It was written about 1618 and published by the Hakluyt Society in 1849. Strachey arrived in Virginia in May, 1610, with the rest of the castaways, and was shortly after appointed to the council, and on June 12, of the same year, recorder general of Virginia. He went to England after about a year's stay in the colony. He was either father or grandfather of William Strachey, who came to Virginia and died in 1686, leaving a daughter Arabella, who married Henry Cox, of Essex county. Another son or grandson, John Strachey, had a grandson, Dr. John Strachey, who came to Virginia and has now descendants of the name of Mastin living in Alabama.

Dale, Sir Thomas, councillor and deputy governor (q. v.).

Argall, Sir Samuel, councillor and deputy governor.

Hamor, Ralph, was a son of "Ralph Hamor the elder, of London, merchant tailor." Both father and son were members of the Virginia Company in 1609, the father paying £133.6.8. The elder Hamor was also an incorporator, and for a time, a director, of the East India Company. He died in 1615, leaving two sons, Ralph and Thomas, who both came to Virginia. Ralph came over in 1609 and remained until June 8, 1614, when he sailed for England. In the next year he published "A true discourse of the present estate of Virginia until the 18th of June 1614." Hamor stayed in England until 1617, in which year, upon the 8th of January, the company gave him eight shares in Virginia, and he soon afterwards sailed once more for the colony, arriving there in May. He seems to have returned to England again in a few years, for we find a grant to some one who is said to have, in 1621, "paid her own costs to Virginia," in the ship "Sea Flower," "with Captain Ralph Hamor." It was in the last named year that he was appointed a member of the council, an office which he retained until his death. In the massacre of 1622, Capt. Hamor was attacked by the Indians near a new house he was having built, but with the help of a few other persons, drove them off with bricks, spades, picks, etc. His brother, Thomas Hamor, who lived nearby, also escaped but was wounded. Soon after the massacre, Capt. Ralph wrote a letter to the Virginia Company, which was received in England October 22, 1622, giving an account of what had happened since that event, and saying that it was the governor's intention to attack the Indians with 500 men at the end of August. A letter from the governor and council, written Jan. 20, 1622-23, told how Capt. Hamor, "being sent to the Patomacs to trade for corn, slew divers of the Nechonicos who sought to circumvent him by treachery." On Apr. 2, 1623, George Sandys wrote to England in regard to the character and capacity of the various councillors. He said that Hamor's extreme poverty forced him "to shifts." Capt. Hamor married a widow, Mrs. Elizabeth Clements. In 1625 his "muster" included himself, Mrs. Elizabeth Hamor, and her children, Jeremy and Elizabeth Clements. In 1626 he owned 250 acres at Hog Island, and 500 at Blunt Point, but lived at Jamestown. On March 4, 1626, and again on March 22, 1627-28, he was commissioned a councillor. He probably died soon after the latter date. In addition to his seat in the council, he held for a time, the place of recorder of the colony from 1611 to 1614.

Rolfe, John, belonged to a family well known in the county of Norfolk, England, for centuries. The names of Rolfe's immediate ancestors, the Rolfes of Heacham Hall, appear on the register of Heacham Church as early as May 27, 1560. John Rolfe, himself, was baptized there May 6, 1585. Rolfe was an energetic and enterprising man and one of the type most needed in the Virginia colony, a man ready for any adventure. The elder Hamor wrote that "during the time of his abode there no man hath labored more than he hath done." He had been educated in an English university and was married to an English girl, when, in 1619, he embarked for Virginia on board the "Sea Venture," which was cast away in the Bermudas with Sir Thomas Gates and other leaders of the expedition. During their ten months' stay in the islands, a little daughter was born to the Rolfes and named for her birthplace, Bermuda. The child did not live, however, nor did Mrs. Rolfe more than a short time after her arrival in Virginia. Rolfe speedily became prominent in the colony and to him belongs the credit of introducing tobacco in 1612, which afterwards became the source of such large revenue to Virginia and was long used as currency. He was made a member of

COLONIAL COUNCILLORS OF STATE 83

the council in 1614, and at this time succeeded Ralph Hamor, recorder of the colony, an office which he held till the office of secretary of state was created in 1619. But in spite of Rolfe's virtues, his fame rests largely upon his romantic marriage with Pocahontas, the Indian maiden, whose story has justly gained so wide a fame. The account of Capt. John Smith's deliverance by this "Guardian Angel of Virginia" was for long accepted without question and has grown to be a part of the nation's treasured lore. Of recent years, however, there has been an effort on the part of some eminent historians to discredit the tale and set it down as a mere invention of Smith. They point out that in a published letter of Smith to a friend in England, written shortly after his release by Powhatan, nothing was said of his fair rescuer, nor, indeed, is she mentioned in his first historical accounts. It is answered, however, by the no less eminent opponents of those idol breakers, that the publisher of the letter explicitly states that he has omitted a portion as being of a private nature, that his first history is admittedly incomplete, and that Smith told the tale unrefuted at the time of Pocahontas' visit to London, when there were many there besides herself who were familiar with the facts and might have exposed the gallant captain had his account not tallied with them. However this may be, there is no doubt that, even excluding this episode, the story of Pocahontas is a most romantic one or that she rendered the colony a great service by means of her friendship. At the age of fifteen she was apparently married to an Indian chief called Kocoum, with whose people she was found by Gov. Argall, who bribed an Indian to deliver her a captive to him for the gift of a copper kettle. Argall's purpose in holding Pocahontas prisoner was that she might act as hostage for her father Powhatan's good behavior. An entirely new turn was given the matter by an attachment which grew up between her and John Rolfe. Rolfe hesitated for some time both on account of the effect on his fellow colonists and because he shrank from marrying a heathen princess unless he could make it the occasion of saving her soul. The latter scruple was soon removed by the conversion of Pocahontas, and the favor of Sir Thomas Dale being secured, the picturesque marriage was celebrated in the little church at Jamestown in Apr., 1614. The great Powhatan also smiled on the union and two of the bride's brothers were present. There can be little doubt that it served as Sir Thomas hoped it would to cement more closely the friendship of the English and Indians and postpone violence for a time. A year later Rolfe and Pocahontas sailed for England with Sir Thomas Dale, who took with him also, a number of young Indians, both men and maidens. Pocahontas was royally received and feted, entertained by the great, both secular, who treated her as a princess, and the clergy, who regarded her as the first fruit of the church in the New World. While in London, she saw Ben Jonson's "Christmas his Mask" played at court, had her portrait painted and was altogether the center of attention. But while Pocahontas thus found favor, poor Rolfe's experience was not so pleasant. It is said that King James was envious of his marriage to a foreign princess and feared that he might attempt to establish himself King of America. The council of the company in England, when news of his marriage first reached them, actually considered, it is said, whether Rolfe might not be guilty of high treason in marrying a foreign king's daughter, and if other matter had not pressed for attention, he might even have been hanged. A good deal of this was doubtless gossip. Rolfe occupied himself during his stay in England in writing a "relation" of affairs in Virginia which he dedicated to the King. It was arranged that the couple should return to the colony with Capt. Argall in 1617, but the little Indian princess was never again to see her native woods. She died and was buried at Gravesend and her husband proceeded on his way, leaving their son, Thomas Rolfe, in charge of Sir William Stukeley at Plymouth. Rolfe married a third wife in 1620, Jane, a daughter of William Pierce, of Virginia, by whom he had a daughter Elizabeth. He retained his seat in the council until his death in 1622.

Yeardley, Sir George, governor of Virginia, 1619 (q. v.).

Powell, Nathaniel, councillor and deputy governor (q. v.).

Pory, John, was already a man of wide travel and experience and an author and geographer of note, when he first became associated with the Virginia colony. Born about 1570, he possessed a naturally quick intelligence and entered Cambridge University at the age of seventeen. He later became a disciple of Hakluyt, the distinguished geographer and ardent advocate of American colonization, and it is possible that he gained his first knowledge of and interest in the subject from his master, with whom he studied "cosmographie and foreign histories." Pory won considerable distinction in 1600 by the publication of "A Geographical History of Africa written in Arabicke and Italian by John Leo, a More, born in Granada and brought up in Barbarie; Translated and Collected by John Pory, London."

The work was later incorporated by old Purchas in his "Pilgrims." Its method seems to have been a "link between the narratives of the Arabian geographers and the discoveries of modern travellers and navigators." Besides the translation he added a considerable amount of original matter to the work. In recognition of the service he had rendered science, he was given the degree of Master of Arts of Cambridge. He represented Bridgewater in parliament from 1605 to 1611. Pory's knowledge of geography was not to remain merely hearsay. In 1611 he obtained a license to travel and went to Paris, where he remained a considerable period. On his way thither he was the bearer of important state documents to Cardinal Perron. He was also able to provide the French historian, De Thou, with material for his life of Mary, Queen of Scotts. After his sojourn in Paris, he travelled extensively and made a long stay in Constantinople. Pory enjoyed a wide acquaintance and knew many of the most distinguished men of his time. The first appearance of his name in connection with the Virginia colony was in 1609, in the second royal charter, but it was not until January 19, 1619, that he actually set foot in the New World. He was the first secretary of state that "ever was chosen and appointed by commission from the counsell and company in England, under their hand and common seal." Upon his arrival he was promptly made a member of the council, and on July 30, 1619, he had the honor of being the first speaker of the first free assembly in America. He was a valuable addition to the colony during the three years he remained in Virginia, embarking upon many trips of discovery and research and writing descriptive letters which are now very valuable to the historian and antiquary. On one of these trips, begun with the intention of exploring the coast line, he was driven out of his course by storms and wrecked on the Azores, where he was seized, tried for piracy and in danger of being hung. He escaped in some unknown manner and return to England, but was chosen in 1623 to carry to Virginia and there publish throughout the country three royal proclamations. He was also appointed one of the commissioners to inquire into the condition of the colony. After his return to London from this second American voyage, he became a member of the home council for Virginia, but never again crossed the water. He lived in London until about 1631, writing news letters. In this year he withdrew from active life to the retirement of his home at Sutton Saint Edmunds, where he lived until his death in 1635-36.

Tucker, Daniel, was a native of Milton, in Kent, and was the son of George Tucker, of that place. As was the case of so many young gentlemen of that age, he came under the influence of the romantic west and the new discoveries, and took to a seafaring life in consequence. In 1606 he sailed with Challoner to North Virginia, and was prominent in the South Virginia Colony from 1608 to 1613. He became a member of the Virginia Company under the charter of 1609, and the following year was appointed by Lord Delaware to be "clerk in the store" in Virginia. There is an interesting record in the proceedings of the Virginia Company of the request made by Tucker that the company confer upon him twenty shares for his five years service, in consideration of the several eminent offices he had held in the colony. He then enumerates these to have been cape merchant, provost master, one of the council, truck master and vice-admiral. It seems to have been conceded that Tucker was a very capable as well as industrious and energetic member of the community, but he never attained a higher office in the Jamestown colony than that of councillor. It is probable that it was well for Virginia that this was so, as the subsequent chapter in his life does not redound so much to his credit. In 1615-16 Tucker was commissioned governor of Bermuda, the first man to hold the office. It may have been that his was a nature that could not resist the temptations of power, but certain it is that after a three years tenure of office, he was accused of severe oppression of the commonalty and was obliged to return to England to defend himself, and leave one Miles Kendall as his deputy. Evidently the charges were well sustained as Tucker was never reinstated in spite of the fact that he was admitted to have exercised "great pains and industry" in his government. He returned to the islands, nevertheless, sometime prior to 1623 and lived there until his death about a year later at Port Royal. He was buried Feb. 10, 1624-25. Governor Tucker has many descendants living in Bermuda, the United States, England and India.

Newce, Thomas, came from a family seated at Much Hadham, Hertfordshire. The pedigree of this family in the "Visitation" of 1634, begins with Clement Newce of London, Mercer, whose great grandson, William Newce of Much Hadham, married Mary, daughter of Sir John Fanshawe, and had issue: 1. Thomas, councillor of Virginia; 2. William, councillor of Virginia; 3. Henry; 4. Clement. At a meeting of the Virginia Company, May 17, 1620, Mr. Treasurer signified to the court the company's former resolve for the entertainment of two new officers by them, namely, deputies to govern two parts of the public land in Virginia." Mr. George Thorpe had already been chosen for one of these places, and the treasurer now anounced that the other was to be filled by a gentleman of the same worth, now present, called Mr. Thomas Newce, touching whom it was agreed that he should take charge of the company's land and tenants in Virginia whatsoever, and that they for his entertainment have ordered that he and such as shall succeed him shall have 1200 acres belonging to that office, 600 at Kiquotan, now called Elizabeth City, 400 at Charles City, 100 at Henrico, and 100 at James City; and, for the managing of this land, (they) have further agreed that he shall have forty tenants to be placed thereon, whereof twenty (are) to be sent presently, and the other twenty in the spring ensuing, all which now being put to the question received a general approbation." On June 28, 1620, Newce was further honored by appointment to the Virginia council, and he arrived in the colony the following winter. On April 30, 1621, the company adopted a resolution "concerning Capt. Thos. Newce, the company's deputy in Virginia, as well in the discharge of a former promise made unto him, to the end that his reward might be no less than of others whose persons and deserts they doubted not but he could equal, they therefore agreed to add ten persons more when the company shall be able to make the former number 50." Newce's name appears signed to several letters from the governor and council in Virginia, but he did not live long in the land of his adoption. The governor and council, writing to the Earl of Southampton April 3, 1623, mention "Captain" Newce as "lately dead," and George Sandys wrote of him on April 8, that he died "very poor" and that an allowance had been made for his wife and child.

Thorpe, George, was a native of Gloucestershire and the son of Nicholas Thorpe of Wanswell Court. He was related both in blood and by marriage with some of the distinguished men of the Jamestown colony, and among others with Sir Thomas Dale. The Thorpe family was a prominent one and our subject became a gentleman pensioner, a gentleman of the privy chamber of the king and a member of parliament from Portsmouth. He was a man of strong religious feeling and became greatly interested in the problem of the conversion of the savages with which his countrymen were newly coming into contact in the new world. He formed a partnership with Sir William Throckmorton, John Smith of Nibley, Richard Berkeley and others for the ownership and conduct of a private plantation in Virginia, and selling his English property, he set sail for Virginia, where he arrived March, 1620. He was appointed deputy to govern the college land and to have three hundred acres and ten tenants, and on June 28, 1620, he was made a member of the council. The advent of this friend of the Indians in Virginia was coincident with the formation of the great Indian plot against the English of 1621-22, and there are some who hold that his disinterested friendship for the red man was an aid to them in their undertaking. Thorpe certainly displayed the most complete faith in his dusky charges and visited them in the forest, discussing religion with Opochankano, from which he derived great encouragement for the hope of their final conversion. Thorpe's interests were not confined to the Indians, however, as the following letter received by him from the company in 1621 will show: "And to you, Mr. Thorpe, we will freely confesse that both your letter and endeavors are most acceptable to us; the entering upon the staple comodoties of wine and silk we highly commend, and assure you it is the Companie's care to reward your merit. * * * In the meantime they desire you to proceed in these noble courses assuring you of all love and respect." In spite of this, however, it would seem that his attention was chiefly given to the colony's relations with the savages, especially in regard to the conversion of the latter. His manner of winning their friendship was certainly worthy of his professions and even went to the length of building a handsome house in the English style for Opochankano and putting to death a number of English mastiffs of which the Indians had expressed fear. It was certainly one of the blackest stains on the Indian character, to be found in all the white man's dealings with him that, when, on March 22, 1621-22, the colonists were surprised in the great massacre, George Thorpe was not spared, but was murdered with every circumstance of remorseless cruelty. Thorpe was twice married, first to Margaret, a daughter of Sir Thomas Porter and after her death to Margaret, a daughter of David Harris, who survived him.

Upon the next two names in the list of councillors, the records have but little to say, they are those of

Middleton, David, councillor, 1620, and

Blewitt, Mr., councillor, 1620, whose Christian name is not given.

Tracy, William, was one of those who formed with Thorpe, Berkeley and others a company to conduct a private plantation in Virginia. He is believed by Alexander Brown, author of "The Genesis of the United States," to have been the son of Sir John Tracy. It is probable that he came to Virginia at the same time that Thorpe did, the latter arrived in March, 1620, as on June 28, of the same year he was, along with Thorpe, appointed a member of the colonial council. The following September he sailed in the ship "Supply," with emigrants for Berkeley Hundred, now Berkeley, Charles City county. There is no direct record of his death, but it is evident that he did not even live to witness the terrible massacre by the Indians which brought death, in 1622, to his friend and partner, Thorpe, and to so many of the colonists, as the records of the company state, under date of July, 1621, that the news of his death had been received in England. But although Tracy himself escaped the horror, one of his daughters, who had married Capt. Nathaniel Powell, was not so fortunate, but was killed with her husband in that dreadful affair.

Harwood, William, came to Virginia about 1620, and on June 28, of that year, the Virginia Company appointed him, as "Mr. Harwood the chief of Martin's Hundred," a member of the council, along with George Thorpe, William Tracy and others. In a letter dated Aug. 21, 1621, the company again speaks of him as "governor of Martin's Hundred," and in another letter of Jan. 10, 1622, the authorities of Virginia are informed by the company that the adventurers of Martin's Hundred desired that Mr. Harwood might be spared from the office of councillor, their business requiring his presence continually. He was probably a relative of Sir Edward Harwood, a distinguished soldier, who was a member of the Virginia Company and in 1619 presented a petition to that body in behalf of the proprietors of Martin's Hundred. An examination of Sir Edward's will, however, shows no reference to him.

Pountis, John, was appointed councillor

on June 28, 1620, and again, in the instructions to Governor Wyatt, July 24, 1621, his name was included among those upon whom that honor was to be conferred. At a meeting of the Virginia Company on July 10, 1621, it was moved that some "place of command" should be bestowed upon Mr. John Pountis, "as well in respect of his own worth and sufficiency, as also in reward of his pains and endeavors in the company's service," and "for so much as there was a great use of a vice-admiral in Virginia to take care of the company's ships that came thither, and other matters thereunto appertaining," it was recommended that he be "therefore appointed Vice Admiral, which was done." Under date Nov. 14, 1621, the minutes of the Virginia Company say, that "in regard to the worth and services of Mr. John Pountis, it had pleased the Company to confer upon him the place of Vice Admiral, provisionally, as by his Commission dated the 21st of July last might appear, the said appointment is now confirmed, and a competant proportion of land for that office is to be allotted him." Upon Nov. 21, the length of his term of office was fixed at three years. In March, 1623-24, Pountis was present, as a councillor, at a meeting of the assembly. The Virginia assembly having prepared replies to certain defamatory petitions circulated by the commissioners whom the King had sent over, and also a petition to his majesty, and some other papers all of which they wished to have safely transmitted to England, entrusted them to "Mr. John Pountis, Councillor of state, going to England (being willing by our intreatie to accept that employment) to solicite the general cause of the country to his Majesty and Counsell." It was ordered that, to defray the expenses of the worthy councillor's voyage, he should be paid four pounds of tobacco per capita for every male resident in Virginia, above the age of sixteen years. Mr. Pountis died on board ship before reaching his journey's end. His executor was his cousin, Sir Thomas Merry.

Bohun, Laurence, "long time brought up amongst the most learned Surgeons and Physicians in the Netherlands," came to Virginia with Lord Delaware in 1610. His lordship, writing from Jamestown on July 7, of that year, says "Dr. Boone whose care and industrie for the preservation of our lives (assaulted with strange fluxes and agues) we have just cause to commend to your favors * * * * since we have true experience how many mens lives these phisicks helpes have preserved since coming in, God so blessed the practice and diligence of the Doctor." On March 28, of the next year, Dr. Bohun left Virginia with Lord Delaware for the "Western Isles" and thence accompanied him home to England. Prior to Feb. 2, 1620, the doctor with James Swift and others, was granted a patent in consideration of transporting 300 persons to Virginia, and on Dec. 3, of the same year, he was appointed "Phisitian General for the Colony," and was allotted 500 acres and twenty tenants. It seems to have been at this time also that Bohun, who was then in Virginia, was appointed councillor. Towards the end of March, 1621, he sailed for England in the ship "Margaret and John" and was mortally wounded by a Spanish man-of-war with which his vessel had a severe combat in the West Indies. Seeing him fall, Capt. Chester, commander of the "Margaret and John," embraced him and said, "O Dr. Bohun, what a disaster is this." The "Noble Doctor, no whit exanimated replyed, 'fight it out brave men, the cause is good, and the Lord receive my soule.'"

This fight caused great excitement and reports of it were published in London and Amsterdam. Upon July 16, 1621, the Virginia Company had received news of the death of "Dr. Bohun of the Counsel in Virginia," and on Oct. 3, of that year, his widow, Mrs. Alice Bohun, petitioned the company that, "as her husband in his lifetime was at great charge, as she supposes for the providing and transporting of servants into Virginia," she might be allowed some annual contribution, and also that her son, Edward Barnes, who was bound to serve the company for seven years, might be released. Both applications were rejected, the company stating that it, and not Dr. Bohun was at the said costs and charges, and that Edward Barnes was the company's servant and could not be set free.

Smith, Capt. Roger, who "served for twelve or thirteen years in the wars in the Low Countries," is first known to us as commanding a company of infantry under Sir Francis Vere, in 1592. His earliest voyage to Virginia was in the year 1616. In November, 1619, when he had been in the colony "about some three years" he sailed thence for England again, and while there made complaint to the Virginia Company of Sir George Yeardley's treatment of him. At a meeting of the company Dec 13, 1620, an entry was made that Capt. Roger Smith being desirous to go this present voyage to Virginia, moved that he might have the charge of some of those people now sent to the company's tenants, and further, that the company would be pleased to bestow upon him some means to make him the better fit for the said voyage; for as much therefore as the said Captain Smith is recommended to be a gentleman very fitting for that employment, and in regard to his good experience already (having been heretofore in Virginia about three years) might thereby do the company great service, the court was pleased for his better encouragement to give him £30 freely, to furnish him with necessarys, and ordered that he should have the command of fifty persons now transported to Virginia to be tenants upon the Company's land." Captain Smith sailed for the colony in Feb., 1621, and on July 24, of the same year, he was appointed a member of the council there. On March 22, 1623, the Indians killed five men near his plantation in Charles City county, and in April he was engaged in building a block house. Smith married Jane Pierce the widow of John Rolfe and, with his wife, was living in James City in 1625. The last mention of him is on Nov. 30, 1629, where he was still a member of the council.

Sandys, George, was the youngest son of Dr. Edwin Sandys, Archbishop of York, and was born in the archiepiscopal palace of Bishopsthorpe, near York. His godfathers were George, Earl of Cumberland and William, Lord Ewer, and his godmother, Catherine, Countess of Huntington. In England, Sandys was one of the most distinguished men of letters of his time, and he has the honor of having produced the first book ever written on American soil, a translation of parts of Ovid and Vergil. He was an unusually precocious student and entered Oxford University at the age of twelve. In 1610 he started on a two years' journey through the East, visiting Italy, Turkey, Greece, Egypt and the Holy Land. Upon his return to England, he published an account of his travels which he dedicated to "The Prince" as he always called Charles I. who had then been reigning about a year. This work became very popular and in 1673 reached a seventh edition. Sandys and members of his family were connected with the Virginia Company in the capacity of stockholders during the whole of its existence. He was a friend of Southampton, who, upon his resignation as treasurer of Virginia in 1621, recommended his election to fill the vacant office. He was forthwith elected and later, in April of the same year, his election was confirmed. He shortly after went to the colony where there was granted him 1500 acres with fifty tenants for the maintenance of his office. Shortly after his arrival, he received a rhymed letter from his friend, Michael Drayton, the poet, urging him to continue his poetic and literary efforts, but truly Virginia at the time seemed hardly a fit dwelling for the muse. It was unable to raise enough food for its own subsistence and had to depend upon a disappointed and unwilling mother country. Education was also in a most rudimentary state, but in the autumn of 1621, £100 were subscribed by members of the ship's company of the "Royal James," an East Indianman, to be expended for a church or free school. The latter was erected accordingly with a thousand acres for its maintenance and called the East India School after its donors. It was the first free school in the country. In the early part of the following year there was established, on account of the scattered population, which rendered it difficult for persons in the outlying districts to reach easily a court of law, a system of precinct courts, which afterwards took the form of county courts. It was in 1621 that the great dispute in England between King and commons began which threw the country into a ferment which led eventually to civil war. It happened that many prominent members of the Virginia Company took sides in this dispute with the people so that the ill will of the King became directed against the whole company to a degree most prejudicial to the colony. In addition to this the relations with the Indians were daily becoming more strained, and altogether the period was a stormy one for the colony. The Indian trouble culminated in the dreadful massacre of March 22, 1622, an account of which Sandys sent home to England. He also took an active part in the operations which the English set on foot against the red neighbors for the purpose of revenge and chastisement. The reputation of the treasurer seems to have been unassailed. In none of the old records is there to be found an adverse criticism of him and he unquestionably enjoyed the respect of all. He spent some time in the colony but eventually returned to England, though the precise date is unknown, and was made a "Gentleman of the King's Privy Chamber." In 1636 he published a "Paraphrase upon the Psalms of David and upon the Hymns dispersed throughout the Old and New Testaments." Sandys was a fruitful author and after his return published a considerable volume of work which met with the hearty approval of the critics and literateurs of the day. Among others, Pope declared in his notes to the "Iliad" that "English poetry owed much of its present beauty" to Sandys' translations. He was very popular and enjoyed the friendship of the great authors of his time, and seems to have been noted as much for the sweetness of his character as for his scholarship. He spent the last years of his life at Boxley Abbey in Kent, the home of Gov. Wyatt, whose wife was Sandys' niece. Here he died in March, 1643.

Paulett, Robert, came to Virginia in January, 1621, as preacher, physician and surgeon to the "adventurers" at Berkeley Hundred, and on July 16, of the same year, the Virginia Company elected him a member of the council. Governor Wyatt and the councillors, writing Jan., 1621-22, say that they have not sworn "Mr. Pawlett," and add "of whom we are doubtful, there being two of that name." Their hesitation was the occasion of no inconvenience, however, as Paulett, finding that the adventurers by whom he was employed felt that their business required his constant presence, declined the honor of a seat in the council of state. He probably died before the month of April, 1623. He was doubtless a near kinsman of Capt. Thomas Paulett (q. v.)

Newce, Sir William, a brother of Capt. Thomas Newce, of the council, is first mentioned in the records of the Virginia Company on April 12, 1621, under which date they declare that "out of a generous disposition" towards the "general plantation in Virginia," and "being induced thereto by reason of a good success he had in Ireland upon a like worthy action," Capt. William Newce "hath freely offered to the company to transport at his own cost and charges 1,000 persons into Virginia, betwixt this and midsummer 1625— to be planted and employed upon a certain plantation, and intendeth to go over himself in person, the better to direct and govern his own people, over whom he prays he may be appointed as General ; and to that end desireth a patent with the portion of land and with such large and complete privilege as are usually granted to others in the like kind, and also desires the company would grant him the place of marshall of Virginia, which office he effected the rather because he hath ever been exercised in military affairs and arms, as may appear by his many worthy services performed in Ireland well known to divers honorable persons in this Kingdom, who have testified the same upon their own knowledge to his exceeding great commendation." He also asked to be allowed fifty men as tenants upon the land attached to said office, and offered to transport them to Virginia and furnish them with clothing and necessary implements for £8 per man. His various requests were granted by the company, and he was elected to the office of marshall on May 2, 1621. On June 11, of the same year, it was reported to the Virginia Company that the king had conferred the honor of knighthood upon Newce, whom his majesty was pleased to style his "Knight Marshall of Virginia, and hopeth to have a better account of his doings than he hath had of others hitherto." The knight had served in Ireland at the siege of Kinsale in May, 1605, and afterwards led a company of Irish to join the Spanish service. In May, 1609, he was accused of being in a scheme to deliver Sluys, Flushing and other towns, held by the Dutch, to the archduke. He seems to have been cleared of these charges, however, and was soon again in Ireland, where he became the first mayor of the town of Bandon, and laid out Newce's Town, opposite Bandon. He was knighted at Theobalds, May 31, 1621, was appointed a member of the Virginia council on June 13, of the same year, and came over with Sir Francis Wyatt in October. George Sandys wrote that Sir William Newce brought with him "a very few weak and unserviceable people, ragged, and not above a fortnight's provisions, some bound for three years, and most upon wages." The "Knight Marshall" died within two months after his arrival in the colony. William Capps, in a grumbling letter written in March, 1623, calls him "Sir William Naughtworth."

Pott, John, councillor and deputy governor (q. v.)

Percy or Piercy, Abraham, merchant came to Virginia in the ship "Susan" in 1616 and was for a number of years certainly between 1619 and 1623, cape-merchant and treasurer of the colony. At the time of Argall's suspension from the office of admiral of Virginia, he appointed Persey, "the Cape-merchant," his vice-admiral, but this the Virginia Company held he had no power to do and instructed the governor and council of Virginia to make the appointment. Persey was a member of the house of burgesses in 1622, and on October 24, 1623, was appointed by the king one of the commissioners to examine the affairs in Virginia. The following year he was appointed to the council and held his seat in that body until his death in 1628. Persey was undoubtedly one of the richest men in the colony and his estate was for some time a bone of contention between his heirs. Its seizure by Governor Harvey was one of the numerous acts of that gentleman which aroused the ire of the colonists and finally led to his deposing. He married Frances, widow of Capt. Nathaniel West, and she married thirdly Capt. Samuel Mathews. She was probably a daughter of Sir Thomas Hinton.

Lapworth, Michael. Nothing is known of Michael Lapworth further than that the Virginia Company appointed him a member of the council in 1621 and that he appears to have come to Virginia. The company, writing under date of July 25, 1621 to the colonial authorities, say "and here againe we renew our commendation of Mr. Lapworth and that in a very effective manner."

Madison, Isaac, came to Virginia in 1608, only a year after the founding of Jamestown, and was employed in exploring the country and probably in making maps, etc. He went to England in 1620 and while there, on July 10, 1621, the Virginia Company, in recognition of his services in the colony, presented him with two shares in the company. He seems to have returned to Virginia shortly, for immediately after the massacre of 1622, we find him actively employed against the Indians and becoming one of the best known soldiers of the colony. About the first of July, 1622, the governor sent Capt. Isaac Madison with thirty odd men to the Patomac, where it was thought corn could be purchased from the friendly Indians and a possible alliance with them be formed against the hostile tribes. Madison conducted the affair very badly, and, notwithstanding orders to the contrary was soon at odds with the well disposed savages. He was led into this by tales of a conspiracy on the part of the Indians which, though quite unfounded, moved him into an indefensible treachery against them whereby he captured the chief and his son and killed many of their unfortunate tribesmen. The captives were finally ransomed for a quantity of corn. Such perfidy did not pass altogether unnoticed by the better men among the colonists, and a complaint was taken to court which bitterly denounced Madison and his confederates. Proceedings were about to be instituted against them, but Madison left for England at about this time. But Madison's act was not as unpopular as it deserved to be. After the massacre of 1622, people felt that there was nothing too bad for the Indians and they lacked discrimination to except the tribes who were not responsible for the outrage. It thus happened that Madison became quite a hero with a large element of the populace. Madison's stay in England was a short one and he soon returned to Virginia and once more took part in the colony's affairs, being even employed again against the Indians. He was commissioned a member of the council, Aug. 26, 1624, but probably died before his commission reached him.

Farrar or Ferrar, William, was probably William Ferrar, who was a younger son of Nicholas Ferrar, an eminent merchant of London and a distinguished member of the Virginia Company, and a brother of John and Nicholas Ferrar, who were both deputy treasurers of the company, the latter being also M. P. In certain verses of John Ferrar, Jr., grandson of the elder Nicholas, "William Ferrar," of Virginia, is referred to as "honored kinsman." The infant colony had no more useful friend than the Ferrar family, and William Ferrar, who is said to have been a barrister, had come himself to Virginia in or before 1621, as in that year he was living there. On March 14, 1625, he was appointed a councillor and his commission was renewed in March, 1627-28. On April 29, 1635, he was one of the councillors who deposed Harvey. He died in or before 1637, leaving descendants.

Tucker, William, was born in 1589 and came to Virginia in the "Mary and James" in 1610. He became a member of the Virginia Company in 1620 and was elected to the house of burgesses in 1623-24. He became a councillor on March 4, 1625-26 and was again included in the commission to the council under Yeardley, March 22, 1627-28. He was appointed by the king one of the commissioners to supervise the government of Virginia in 1623. He was for long the principal man in Elizabeth City county and had taken an active part in the defense of the colony against the Indians. In August, 1633, Tucker, then in England, presented a memorial to the privy council, in which he endeavored to show that Dutch trade with Virginia, if allowed, would result in great loss to the king and prejudice to the plantation. It is not surprising that Tucker, as an English trader, should take this view since the Dutch offered a much larger price to the planters for their tobacco than what he had been in the habit of paying, and thus would cut the profits of its sale in Europe. Tucker must have died some time before Feb. 17, 1644, when his will was proved in London. He left three children: William, Thomas and Mary.

Utie, John, first appears in Virginia in Feb., 1623, when Ensign John Utie is returned in the census as living at Hog Island with his wife and son John, then an infant. In the year following, he had a grant of 100 acres on the south side of James river, and in 1629 was burgess for the plantations between Archer's Hope and Martin's Hundred and for Hog Island in 1629-30. On May 29, 1630, Governor Harvey writes that since his (Harvey's) arrival in Virginia, he had added Captain John Utie to the council, and on December 20, 1631, Utie was one of the signers of the accord between the governor and council. On Oct. 8, 1630, a resolution of the council stated that Capt. John West and John Utie had "seated" the first settlement on the York river, and ordered that they should each receive 600 acres there for so doing. Later Capt. Utie added largely to his estate in that region and named his whole property "Utiemaria." When Harvey's misgovernment became unbearable, Utie was one of the leaders of the opposition to him and took part in the final scene which ended in the governor's deposition. When the governor struck George

Menifie on the shoulder and told him he arrested him in the king's name for high treason. Utie, according to Harvey's own statement, struck him (the governor) "a very great and violent stroke upon the shoulder and said with a loud voice, 'I arrest you for treason,'" whereupon the rest of the councillors crowded about Harvey and laid hold of him. It seems likely that the cause of the councillors laying hold of Harvey was, as is stated in Mathews' account, because on Utie's rejoinder, the governor's rage became so violent that they were obliged to restrain him to prevent harm being wrought. An act so extreme on the part of the colonists did not, of course, pass unnoticed by the authorities in England and, on Dec. 22, 1635, the privy council recommended to the king that the persons who took the leading part in deposing Harvey, Mathews, Utie, etc., should be ordered sent to England "to answer their misdemeanors, they being the prime actors in the late mutiny in Virginia." Just what was done in the case does not appear, but apparently before their case came to actual trial, they were allowed to return to Virginia and their prosecution dropped. On May 25, 1637, West, Mathews, Utie and Peirce petition the English privy council, stating that they had been lately sent prisoners, and that they had heard by recent letters that divers of their goods, cattle and servants, had been seized by order of Governor Harvey and begged that a letter might be written commanding that the property be restored. The petition was granted and the required letter written, but, in case of Mathews at least, a second order from the privy council was needed before Harvey would disgorge. Capt. Utie probably died soon after his return to Virginia, that is, if he did return, of which there is no positive evidence.

Blaney, Edward, was in 1621, keeper of the "Colony Magazine," and in the same year was appointed factor and agent for the company organized to carry on a glass house, and was authorized to trade with the Indians. Blaney was a member of the house of burgesses in 1623, and was appointed to the council on March 4, 1626. He married the widow of William Powell, captain of Jamestown fort.

Macock, Samuel, was a "Cambridge scholar and a gentleman of birth, virtue and industry." In March, 1617, Governor Argall requested the authorities in England that Mr. Macock might be obtained. In June, 1619, Governor Yeardley appointed him a member of the council. The colony was not long to enjoy the benefit of his services, however, for upon March 21, 1622, he and four others were killed by the Indians on the estate on James river in Prince George county, now called "Maycox," then described as "Master Macock's Dividend in the Territory of Great Weyanoke." Councillor Macock probably left an only daughter, as in Jan., 1625, Sarah Macock, aged two years, and born in Virginia, was living in the family of Capt. Roger Smith. She married George Pace, of "Pace's Pains," whose father Richard Pace had saved Jamestown from the Indians at the massacre of 1622.

Ouldsworth, Mr., whose Christian name has not come down to us, enjoyed the distinction of membership in the council for a very brief season. Upon April 12, 1621, it was moved that since Mr. Ouldsworth, then in Virginia, had, when he was in England, "lived in that reputation and credit as befitted a gentleman in his rank and ability as justice of the peace, and of the quorum," he might be admitted to the Virginia council. This motion was "conceived to be very reasonable," and it was "therefore ordered that it be moved in quarter court, and besides some place should be thought upon" for the new councillor, "suitable to his merit and worth." On May 2, upon Mr. Smith's recommendation of his "worth and sufficiency," and as "having been a justice of the peace here in England for so many years, and of the quorum," he was formally "chose and confirmed of the council of state in Virginia," by the Virginia Company. On July 16, 1621, the company had received information of his death.

Leech, Mr., was appointed by a court of the Virginia Company a provisional member of the council of Virginia until he should receive confirmation by the next quarter court. This was on July 16, 1621. About August of that year, he went to Virginia in the ship "Marmaduke," but nothing more is known of him, except that the governor and council of Virginia, in a letter dated January, 1621, stated that they had administered the oaths to several new councillors, but not to Mr. Leech, "Who came not to us."

Wickham, William, a minister, though without Episcopal ordination, had charge of the church at Henrico. Rolfe, writing in 1610, speaks of "Mr. Wickham the minister there, who in his life and doctrines gives good instruction to the people." On June 19, 1617, Gov. Argall requested Sir Dudley Digges to procure from the Archbishop of Canterbury, permission for Mr. Wickham to administer the sacrament, as there was no other person to do it, and in the following March he desired "ordination for Mr. Wickham and Mr. Macock, a Cambridge scholar, and a person to read to (for?) Mr. Wickham, his eyes being weak." In 1621 the Rev. William Wickham was appointed a member of the council. Nothing further is known of him.

Davison, Christopher, son of William Davison, who was secretary of state to Queen Elizabeth, was elected secretary of Virginia by the Virginia Company on June 11, 1621, to succeed John Pory. He came to the colony and was a member of the council in Jan., 1621, and Jan., 1623. He died soon after the last named date.

Whitaker, Jabez, styled in the old records "Captain Whitaker," was probably a brother of the Rev. Alexander Whitaker, the early minister, as the father of that good divine had by his second wife, a posthumous son named Jabez. Capt. Whitaker was a member of the house of burgesses in Mar., 1623-24, and of the council in 1626. In the last named year he was living in Elizabeth City county. He married before 1619, a daughter of Sir John Bourchier, a member of the Virginia Company and uncle of the regicide of that name. Our councillor's name appears several times in the proceedings of the Virginia Company. On Jan. 23, 1620, "Mr. Treasurer signified (that) having received notice of the good carriage of some persons in Virginia (he) was especially to recommend unto them one Mr. Jabez Whitakers, Lieutenant of the Company's men, who had given good account of the trust reposed in him," and in July, 1621, it was reported that "Mr. Whitaker had obeyed the Company's orders in building a guest house (at Kicotan) and had also begun to plant vines, corn, etc.; it was therefore ordered as a reward, that two boys should be sent him, and that the reward of tobacco allowed by the Governor of Virginia should be confirmed."

Claiborne, William. The ancient family of Claiborne derives its name from the Manor of Claiborne or Cliborne, in Westmoreland county, England, near the river Eden, and which is named in the Domesday Book (A. D. 1086). William Claiborne was born about 1587 and came to Virginia with Gov. Wyatt in 1621, in the employ of the Virginia Company as surveyor-general of Virginia at a salary of thirty pounds a year, a house and, in all probability fees. He quickly became prominent in colonial affairs, and, in 1624, was commissioned by the King as first royal secretary of state, a position which he held off and on for eighteen years. In 1626 he became a member of the council. On July 22, 1629, he received a commission from Gov. Pott appointing him captain and commander of all the forces to be levied for a war against the Indians, and as a reward for the successful conduct of the campaign, was granted, in 1640, a tract of land on the Pamunkey river. In the latter year he petitioned the King to create an office which should have the keeping of the Virginia seal. The King referred the matter back to the governor and council of Virginia, who decided that such an office was appropriate and appointed Claiborne to fill it. In 1634 through the influence of Harvey he lost his place as secretary of state, but on Apr. 6, 1642, Charles I. appointed him treasurer of Virginia for life. He again commanded forces against the Indians in 1644, and again received a grant of land in reward. Claiborne was a great explorer and traded with the Indians as well as fought them. In 1627, the government of Virginia gave him permission to discover the source of Chesapeake Bay and explore any body of water between the thirty-fourth and forty-first parallels of latitude, and, on May 16, 1631, the King granted a license to "our trusty and well-beloved Wm. Claiborne" to trade in the colonies of New England and New Scotland, and commanded Gov. Harvey and the council to allow him to do so. Claiborne soon afterwards established a trading post on Kent Island near the present city of Annapolis, and this caused him to oppose with great persistence the efforts of the Baltimores to establish the colony of Maryland. When in 1632 that part of Virginia lying north of the Potomac was granted to Cecilius Calvert, Lord Baltimore, the Virginians including Claiborne protested against it on the ground that it was a territorial spoiliation. They brought the matter before the King and urged that in revoking the charter and assembling control over Virginia both his father James and himself had given assurances that the intention was to alter the form of government, not to dispute property rights. The political existence of the colony remained as much a fact as before, and if the King could grant away Maryland, he could grant away Jamestown itself. The King and his commissioners of foreign plantations were nevertheless adverse to this view, and the legality of Baltimore's charter was upheld.

The Virginians hoped, however, to except Kent Island from its operation on the ground that the Island was actually occupied by Virginia settlers. They argued that the assurances given at the revocation meant, at least, that actual occupation was to be respected. It made no difference whether Claiborne had any title to the soil or not, under his license to trade; the colony of Virginia had extended its laws over it, and the occupation was a legal one.

When, therefore, Leonard Calvert, Baltimore's governor, called upon Claiborne to recognize his authority in Kent Island, the council of Virginia, to whom Claiborne referred the request considered the claim and declared that the colony had as much right to Kent Island "as any other part of the country given by his Majesty's patent in 1609." This particular phase of the question came before the King like the more general phase and was referred by him as in the former case to the commissioners of foreign plantations. It pended before them for several years, and in the interim feeling grew warm. A miniature war developed and several persons were killed on both sides. Sir John Harvey interferred in behalf of Lord Baltimore, and this so incensed Claiborne's friends in Virginia that he was seized and sent back to England. At length, however, the commissioners in 1638 decided for Lord Baltimore and Kent Island, having been seized in Claiborne's absence in England by Capt. George Evelyn in behalf of Lord Baltimore, has remained ever since a part of Maryland.

While Claiborne never admitted the justice of the decision, it does not appear that he ever tried again to set up Kent Island as independent of Maryland. During the disturbances of Richard Ingle (1645-1647) he visited Kent Island, but appears to have come over to look after his property rights, which had been confiscated. Instead of posing as a friend of parliament, he showed a commission and letter from King Charles I., by whom he appears to have stood till the King's death in 1649.

After that time Claiborne went to England and espoused the parliament side, and Gov. Berkeley in 1650 declared the office of treasurer vacant on account of Claiborne's "delinquency."

In Sept., 1651, Claiborne was appointed with Capt. Robert Dennis, Mr. Richard Bennett and Mr. Thomas Stegg on a commission to reduce Virginia to obedience to the parliament of England, an office which they succeeded in performing in Mar., 1652. They then repaired to Maryland and reduced that province also. The ascendency of Claiborne in Maryland was complete, but beyond renewing this property claim to Kent Island he did not treat it politically different from the rest of Maryland. In Virginia the two surviving commissioners Bennett and Claiborne shared the chief offices between them. Bennett became governor and Claiborne secretary of state. Maryland was only temporarily pacified. Lord Baltimore encouraged his adherents to resist and a civil war ensued and much blood was shed. The design of the commissioners appears to have been to have brought about the union of Virginia and Maryland again, but Baltimore won such favor with Cromwell in England that the contest was given up and his authority finally recognized.

When the restoration of Charles II. took place, Claiborne was deprived of his office as secretary and removed from Elizabeth City, where he had formerly lived, to Romancoke, near West Point, the scene of one of his former victories over the Indians. Romancoke was then situated in the county of New Kent, which had been cut from York in 1654, when Claiborne was at the heighth of his power.

The county was evidently named by him after his beloved Kent Island. Here he lived many years, siding with the government in the disturbances of Bacon's rebellion, and dying about 1677, when he was upwards of ninety years of age. To the last he remained unconquered in spirit, and as late as 1675, he sent to parliament a long recital of his injuries suffered at the hands of the Baltimores, asking satisfaction and urging the union of Maryland with Virginia.

Berkeley, John. He was the son of Sir John Berkeley, of the castle and manor of Beverstone, in the county of Gloucester, England, an eminent branch of the noble family of the Berkeleys of Berkeley castle. He lived but eight months in Virginia, but in that time was well known as the "master and overseer" of America's first effort to manufacture iron. Iron ore was one of the first commodities carried back to England by the ships of the Virginia Company, which as early as 1619 considered the establishing of iron works in the colony. The following year 150 men were sent out to Virginia for this express purpose and, in 1621, Sir Edwin Sandis reports that a Mr. John Berkeley had been found to take up the work who was "very sufficient" in such service. The same year, Berkeley sailed to Virginia to take up the new task. The site chosen for the new works was on Falling creek which empties into the James river about sixty-six miles above Jamestown and some seven miles below the present city of Richmond. Berkeley sent an encouraging report of the conduct of the work and declared that by the following Whitsuntide the company might count on "good quantities of iron." The terrible Indian massacre of Mar. 22, 1622, intervened, however, and Berkeley was among those slain. John Berkeley had issue by Mary, daughter of John Snell, Esq.—Maurice, John, Henry, William, Edward, Thomas, Mary, Frances, Elizabeth and Anne. His son, Maurice, came to Virginia with his father and happily escaped the massacre. He married Barbara, daughter of Sir Walter Long, and had issue, "Edward and others." There is a prominent Berkeley family in Virginia which descend from Edmund Berkeley, living in 1674, who may have been a son of Edward last named.

Capps, William, came to Virginia before 1619, in which year he was burgess for Kicotan, as Hampton was then called. During many years Capps took an active part in the affairs of the colony. On Jan. 26, 1621, the company granted him a patent for land in consideration of his undertaking to transport 100 persons to Virginia, and on Feb. 22, upon his humble request, the court (of the Virginia Company) ordered a certificate to be drawn up by the secretary to testify to the good esteem in which he was held, "as well in the Colony of Virginia, and may appear by the rewards of his good service under them, as also of what ability he is reported to be there in respect of the great supplys he had sent there." On May 2, it was ordered that he should receive as a reward "five men's passage free at the Company's charge, in consideration of his many years service of the Company in Virginia, with the hazard of his life among the Indians." "Upon October 7, 1622," "Mr. William Capps, an ancient planter in Virginia," made the following requests of the company: (1), that Sir William Newce be required to deliver him the five men for whose transportation he had paid that gentleman thirty pounds here in town (London); (2), that Sir George Yeardley restore him a chest of goods he detained from him; (3), that he might have satisfaction for that land in Virginia taken from him by Yeardley. At a meeting of the company, Apr. 8, 1624, "Mr. William Capps openly declared, on the faith of an honest man, that with three boys only, which he said were not a man and a half, he had made 3,000 weight of tobacco, and sold 50 barrels of corn heaped measure, and kept beside 60 barrels for his own store, and all this he had performed by the labor of three boys only, himself having never done, as he termed it, one stroke of work." Two letters written by Capps in 1623, one to John Ferrar, and the other to Dr. Wynston, are preserved among the Duke of Manchester's manuscripts. The first of these letters has been published in full in "Virginia Vetusta." The writer seems to have been zealous for the welfare of the colony, but was evidently of a grumbling and fault-finding disposition. One fact connected with him should not be omitted. After the revocation of the charter in 1624 there was no regular general assembly of representatives of the people. The Virginia authorities sent over a memorial in 1627 on the subject, and by William Capps, who was in England, King Charles sent instructions allowing a general assembly and urging the cultivation of staple commodities, as heretofore they had depended too much "upon smoke." To Capps was given the privilege of erecting salt works. He arrived in Virginia Feb. 22, 1628 and on the 26th of the next month the colonial assembly met. He was a member of the council in 1627 and was alive in 1630.

Cowlinge, Christopher, is only known by the fact that Gov. Harvey wrote, on May 29, 1630, that since his arrival in Virginia, Apr., 1630, Christopher Cowlinge had been sworn a member of the council. No other mention of him occurs in the records.

Finch, Henry. Gov. Harvey, writing May 29, 1630, says that since his arrival in Virginia, a few weeks before, he has sworn as a member of the council, Henry Finch, "brother to Sir John Finch." Finch was present in council upon Dec. 20, 1631, Feb. 21, 1631-32, and Feb. 1, 1632-33, but there is no other notice of him. He probably died or left Virginia soon after the last named date. He was the son of Sir Henry Finch, sergeant-at-law, and brother of Sir John Finch, lord chief justice, speaker of the house of commons and lord keeper, who was knighted in 1626, and afterwards created Baron Finch of Ferdwick. The pedigrees given by Burke and Berry say that John Finch was the only son of Sir Henry, but this is certainly an error, for the "Dictionary of National Biography" gives a sketch of Edward Finch, a royalist devine, who was another son, stated, like our councillor, to have been "overlooked by the genealogists." Maj. Joseph Croshaw, of York county, Virginia, married a Widow Finch, who had a daughter Betty.

Stephens, Richard, came to Virginia in the year 1623, in the ship "George," and settled at Jamestown. In the same year he was granted sixty rods of land adjoining his dwelling house, in the "corporation of James Citty," in the hope that others might be "encouraged by his example to enclose some ground for gardens." In March of the year following he was a member of the house of burgesses. In the spring of 1624 Stephens awakened to find himself notorious as one of the principals in the first duel ever fought in Virginia. His antagonist, George Harrison, died fourteen days afterwards, and it has been generally stated that his death was caused by his wounds, but George Menifie, writing on April 28, 1624, to John Harrison, told him that post-mortem examination had shown that his brother George was in bad health, and that his death was not supposed to have been the result of being "hurt in the field," in the duel of fourteen days before, for that he had only received a slight wound in the leg between the garter and the knee. Early in 1630 Gov. Harvey added Stephens to the council, but some years later, probably in 1635, a quarrel arose between them and Harvey dashed out some of Stephens' teeth with a cudgel. This disgraceful act was one of the charges made against Harvey when he was sent to England for trial, but he sought to excuse himself by saying that it did not occur in the council, and that Stephens had assailed him with "ill language." Stephens does not seem to have lived many years after this. From the land patents it appears that the wife of Councillor Richard Stephens was Elizabeth, daughter of Abraham Piersey, formerly of the council. She took for a second husband, in or before 1642, Sir John Harvey, the same who had deprived her first consort of his teeth. In September of that year Captain De Vries, the Dutch trader, brought suit against the estate of Richard Stephens for £4.14, due "for goods sold Lady Harvey," who, it was explained, was at that time the wife of Stephens. Richard and Elizabeth Stephens had at least one child, a son Samuel. On Jan. 20, 1644-45, Dame Elizabeth Harvey petitioned the court to substitute Richard Kemp and Capt. William Pierce as trustees in place of Capt. Samuel Mathews, George Ludlow and Capt. Thomas Bernard, "former trustees under a feoffment made by the same Dame Elizabeth to Samuel Stephens, Gent., her son by a former marriage." The son, Samuel Stephens, of "Bolthorpe," Warwick county, was governor of Carolina, and died in 1670, leaving no children. His will was dated April 21, 1670. Gov. Samuel Stephens married Frances Culpeper, sister of Alexander Culpeper, afterwards surveyor-general of Virginia. In the diary of Mrs. Thornton, published by the Surtees Society, are several notices of the marriage in Virginia, about 1650, of the heir of the Danby family in Yorkshire to a Miss Culpeper. The editor states that she was a niece of Lord Culpeper, lord chancellor of England, and it seems highly probably that she was a sister of Frances Culpeper. Mrs. Frances Stephens married secondly, in June, 1670, Sir William Berkeley, governor of Virginia, whom she seems to have ruled with as high a hand as he showed the colony, and thirdly, sometime in 1680, Col. Philip Ludwell, of "Richneck," James City county, Virginia. She had no children by either marriage.

Basse, Nathaniel, with Sir Richard Worseley, John Hobson, gentleman, and others, associates of Capt. Christopher Lawne, deceased, presented a petition on June, 28, 1620, to the Virginia Company, and received a confirmation of an old patent and plantation, and that said plantation should be henceforth called the Isle of Wight's plantation. The tract was situated in the present Isle of Wight county, which took its name from the plantation, as did Lawne's creek from the first settler there. Sir Richard Worseley, and probably the other men interested in the enterprise also, lived in the Isle of Wight, England. On Jan. 30, 1621-22, Capt. Nathaniel Basse and his associates received a patent on condition that they would transport 100 persons to Virginia. Basse was a member of the house of burgesses for Worresqueiacke from 1623-24 to 1629, and was a councillor in Feb., 1631-32, at which time he was authorized to go to New England and offer the inhabitants a place of settlement on Delaware Bay. The name of his plantation was "Basse's Choice."

Purefoy, Thomas, Purfry, Purfee or Purfury, as the name is variously spelt, was born about 1582 and came to Virginia in the ship "George" in 1621. In 1625, when he is styled Lieut. Thomas Purefoy, he was living in Elizabeth City, and in 1628, was chief commander and one of the commissioners of that place. On July 4, 1627, the governor and council ordered him to make an attack upon the Indians. As "Captain Thomas Purefoy," he was a member of the house of burgesses for "the lower parts of Elizabeth City," at the session of March, 1629-30, and on Dec. 20, 1621, appears as a councillor. He was probably appointed by Harvey, whom he always faithfully supported during the long dispute between the governor and the council and burgesses. When this contest reached a climax and an address from the house of burgesses to the English government was being circulated for signatures, the people of the lower country went in such numbers to sign it that "Captain Purfry took an affright that caused him to write to the Governor of many incident dangers, insomuch that he durst not keep a court until he heard from him or had a letter from the King." Samuel Mathews says that in this letter Capt. Purefoy accused the people of being "in a near sense to rebellion, which since he denied, it being very usual with him to affirm and deny often the same things." This, of course, is the opinion of a member of the hostile party. The opinion of another contemporary is very different. "He is a soldier and a man of open heart, hating for aught I can see all kinds of dissimulation and baseness." In spite of his adherence to Harvey, Purefoy continued a member of the council after the governor's deposition, and was one of those whom the King thought fit to allow to retain their seats. He named, according to a land patent, one of his estates, a 1,000 acre track, "Drayton," doubtless after a place of that name mentioned by Burke as a seat of the Purefoys in England. He left a son Thomas who had an only daughter Frances who had many descendants in Virginia—Tabbs, Bookers, Lowrys, etc. Capt. Purefoy was alive in 1640.

Peirce, William, came from England in the "Sea Venture" in 1609 and was, for many years one of the foremost men of the colony. In May, 1623, Gov. Wyatt appointed him captain of the guard and commander of James City. In the same year, the governor ordered "Captain Wm. Peirce, Captain of his guard and lieutenant governor of James City," to lead an expedition against the Chickahominies. This Peirce did, falling upon them on July 23, "with no small slaughter." He had already made a very favorable impression upon George Sandys, the treasurer of Virginia, who wrote to England in 1623 that William Peirce, the governor of Jamestown, was inferior to none in experience, ability and capacity and recommended him for appointment to the council. In 1627, he was again commissioned to attack the Chickahominies with Thomas Harwood as his second in command. In 1629, he was in England and while there, prepared "A Relation of the Present State of the Colony of Virginia, by Capt. William Perse, an ancient planter of twenty years standing there." He states that there were in Virginia between four and five thousand English, generally well housed, besides much other valuable information in regard to those times. In 1631, Peirce was appointed a member of the council and, on December 20, signed the accord between that body and Governor Harvey. He was a strong opponent of Harvey's misgovernment and was one of the councillors who, on April 28, 1635, arrested and deposed him, himself leading thirty, or according to some accounts, fifty musketeers to beset Harvey's house. Early in the next month, when Claiborne complained to the new governor, West, and the council of his treatment in Maryland, Capts. Utie and Peirce were sent to that colony to protest, to the authorities there, against their violence towards him. Peirce was one of those who was ordered by the King to be sent to England to answer Harvey's charges but who were never actually prosecuted. He was also one of those to whom the privy council directed the reinstated governor to restore the property he had taken from them. Peirce returned to Virginia on a sort of parole and though once more summoned to England, never went there, as the civil war intervened. He was present in council in 1639 and it seems probable that some other influence had been brought to bear upon the King as he was included in the last royal commission of councillors before the war, dated Aug. 9, 1641. The last mention we have of the councillor is of his being present in council, Feb., 1644-45. His daughter Jane became the third wife of John Rolfe.

West, John, deputy governor of Virginia (q. v.).

Harvey, Sir John, governor of Virginia. (q. v.).

Bullock, Hugh, first appears as a councillor in Dec., 1631. He went to England in the following spring, but was back in Virginia and present in the council, in Feb., 1632-33, and in February and March of the next year. In 1637 he was one of the members of the council whom the King directed should be retained, but it is likely that he soon after removed finally to England, and never lived in Virginia again. On March 12, 1634, "Captain Hugh Bullocke" received a grant of 2,550 acres on the Pocosin river, in what is now York county. By deed dated July 8, 1637, and recorded in York, "Hugh Bullock of London, gentleman," conveyed to his son, "William Bullock of London, gentleman," his corn-mill, saw-mill and plantation in Virginia. His wife Mary joined in the deed. There can be no doubt that this William Bullock, son of the councillor, was the author of the rare pamphlet on Virginia. In it he states that his father owned land in the colony. In the general court records, under date of April, 1672, is to be found an entry list of a suit by Robert Bollock, son and heir of William Bullock, versus Col. Peter Jennings, guardian of John Mathews, orphan of Col. Mathews, deceased, in regard to a parcel of land in Warwick county, containing 5,500 acres.

Brewer, John, "citizen and grocer of London" was a son of Thomas Brewer, probably of the same city, and came to Virginia prior to the 1629. He was a member of the house of burgesses from Warwick county in 1629-30, and as "John Brewer, gent.," was appointed one of the commissioners (justices) for holding monthly courts in that county in Feb., 1631-32. He was a member of the council of state from 1632 until his death in 1635. All that is known of Brewer's wife is that her name was Mary, and that in 1636 she consoled herself for his death by becoming the wife of the Rev. Thomas Butler, "Pastor of Denby." The children of John and Mary Brewer were: John, Roger and Margaret. Councillor Brewer owned a plantation called "Stawley (or Stanley) Hundred, otherwise Bruer's Borough," in Warwick county, and not long before his death had obtained rights of 1,000 acres, which his wife and her second husband located and obtained a grant for, at what is still called "Brewer's Neck," between Brewer's and Chuckatuck Creeks, in Isle of Wight county. His will, dated Sept. 4, 1631, and proved in London, May 13, 1636, was published in "Waters' Gleanings."

Perry, William, came to Virginia in 1611.

In a list dated 1626, he is mentioned as owning 100 acres of land on the south side of the river below the falls, which it is probable were granted to him in the year of his coming over and at the time of Sir Thomas Dale's attempt to settle the upper region of the James. After the massacre of 1622, the settlements there were abandoned, and we find Perry living either at or near "Pace's Paines" on the south side of the river not far from Jamestown. He was in England in April, 1624, but was back in Virginia and, as "Lieutenant William Perry," was representing "Pace's Paines" in the house of burgesses in Oct., 1629, and in March of the year following. At this last session he was appointed one of a committee to manage the building of a fort at Point Comfort. In Feb., 1631-32, he was a burgess for the territory "From Capt. Perryes downwards to Hog Island." It was in the summer of 1632 that he was appointed to the council, and in September of the same year, that he appeared for the first time as a member. He was also present in Feb., 1632-33, and in March of the next year. Some years before his death he went to live in Charles City county, where he died in 1637, and was buried at the old "Westover" church. His tomb, which is doubtless the oldest in Virginia, may still be seen near "Westover" house, but the epitaph is entirely illegible. It was once examined by Charles Campbell, the historian, who says that there was engraved upon it a shield with armorial bearings which could not even then be made out, and also the following epitaph:

"Here lyeth the body of Captaine
Wm. Perry who lived neere
Westover in this Collony
Who departed this life the 6th day of
August, Anno Domini 1637."

Capt. Perry married prior to 1628, Isabella, widow of Richard Pace of "Pace's Paines." They had, as far as is known, only one child, Capt. Henry Perry, of whom a sketch will appear hereafter. In the general court records, under date of 1674, there is mention of a patent "long before" granted to Capt. Perry Sr., for 2,000 acres, and a later one to George Menifie of 1,500 acres, in behalf of Capt. Henry Perry the orphan. Both of these grants were situated in Charles City county.

Hinton, Thomas, first appears as a member of the council on Feb. 8, 1633-34. He did not enjoy the honor long as Harvey soon removed him on the charge that he had given the governor "ill words," which reason seems to have been accepted by the English privy council as a valid one, and there is no other mention of Thomas Hinton in our records. Neill, in "Virginia Carolorum," says that the councillor was Sir Thomas Hinton, whose daughter married Samuel Mathews, but this seems unlikely, for an account of Virginia written in 1649 asserts that Mathews married a daughter of Sir Thomas Hinton, while the notices of the Virginia councillors in 1634 and 1635 style him simply "Thomas Hinton, Esq." or "Mr. Thomas Hinton." He is "Mr. Thomas Hinton" in the account of the examination of Gov. Harvey before the English privy council on Dec. 11, 1635. Neill says that one William Hinton, a brother of Mrs. Mathews, was a gentleman of the King's privy chamber, and it seems probable that Thomas Hinton, the councillor, was another brother. Foster, in his "Oxford Matriculations," states that a Thomas Hinton was knighted July 1, 1619, and thinks he may have been the same as Thomas Hinton of Wiltshire, gent., who matriculated at Queen's College, Oct. 15, 1591, aged 17. Sir Thomas Hinton was of Chilton-Foliet, Wiltshire. The register of the parish gives the births of Thomas, April 8, 1600, and William, July 25, 1605, sons of Thomas Hinton Esq. and Katherine his wife; also the burials of Mrs. Katherine, wife of Mr. Thomas Hinton, Oct. 11, 1609, of Elizabeth, wife of Thomas Hinton (doubtless the son) Sept. 20, 1658, and of Thomas Hinton, Sept. 23, 1658.

Stoner, John. On Sept. 29, 1634, the King wrote to the governor of Virginia stating that the bearer of his letter, John Stoner, had been appointed one of the councillors of that colony, and his majesty's agent to treat for a yearly contract for tobacco. On Jan. 21, of the following year, Governor Harvey wrote that Mr. Stoner had died on his voyage to Virginia.

Browne, Henry, came to Virginia about 1634 and was evidently a man of property and influence. He had grants for several large 'tracts of land at various points in James City county, and was known as Col. Henry Browne of "Four Mile Tree,' his plantation locating in the ancient "Pace's Pains." He was also appointed to the council in the year of his arrival and is believed to have remained a member of that body until the surrender of the colony to the parliamentary forces in 1652. He was one of the strongest of Harvey's adherents and when the majority of the council proposed to depose the governor, Capt. Browne is said to have disliked the proceedings so greatly that he made an excuse of sickness and retired to his home. Before this time, Capt. Thomas Young in a letter of July 13, 1634, states that only two of the council were indifferent to Harvey's conduct as governor, Capt. Purefoy and another (Browne), who was "an honest and plain man, but of small capacity and less power." When Harvey was returned to power, Browne was one of the few councillors who acted with him and was present at meetings held in Jan. and Feb., 1636-37 and Jan., 1639, and was one of the few members of the council whom the King ordered retained. Upon the accession of Gov. Wyatt, the adherents of Harvey were in general disfavor in the colony and Browne was turned out of office, Oct., 1640. It amounted to only a suspension, however, for in the following March he was reinstated. He was included in the royal commission of 1641 under Berkeley, and after the temporary retirement of the royalist element at the time of the protectorate, was restored to the council when Berkeley was again made royal governor in 1660. In a deed of 1652, Browne is referred to as "Colonel Henry Browne." He died in 1661 or 1662, leaving a daughter Mary who married Lieut. Col. William Browne, who lived at "Four Mile Tree," and left many descendants.

Menifie, George, came to Virginia in July, 1623 and settled at Jamestown. He was for long one of the wealthiest and probably the leading merchant in the colony, and represented Jamestown in the house of burgesses in 1629. He made frequent voyages to England, probably beginning as early as 1625. In 1635, he was appointed a member of the council, and for a time was inclined to restrain the other councillors from their proposed arrest of Harvey, but after mature deliberation, became of a like mind with them. He it was that answered Harvey, when that violent officer asked the council what was the cause of the people's petition against him, and brought down the governor's wrath upon him. Harvery struck him violently upon the shoulder and said "I arrest you of suspicion and Treason to his Majestie." Upon this the other councillors, headed by Utie, arrested the governor. He was, with the other leaders of the council, ordered to England by the King to answer the charges preferred against them by Harvey. He petitioned the King to be allowed to return to Virginia and was given permission upon his furnishing a bond of £1,000 to appear before the star chamber at any time appointed. Menifie returned to Virginia almost at once, but was back in England shortly. He and Councillors Peirce, Mathews and West were at length ordered to return to answer the charges, but there is nothing to show that any of them went. Menifie's name was included by the King in his commission of councillors in 1641, so it appears probable that his majesty's feelings had changed towards the worthy councillors. In any event, the breaking out of the civil war must have suspended all the proceedings. He died in 1644, leaving a daughter who married Captain Henry Perry.

Hooke, Francis. Writing in 1635, Gov. Harvey informed Secretary Windebank that he knows no man so fit to command the fort at Point Comfort as Capt. Francis Hooke, who was an old servant of King James, and requested the King's approval of his appointment to that office. This was evidently received as the good captain was given the office and was also made a member of the council, Jan. 18, 1636-37. Little further is known of him save that prior to his residence in Virginia, he had been a naval officer and commanded a ship off the coast of Ireland.

Donne or Dunn, George, as his name was frequently spelt, was the second son of Dr. John Donne, the poet and Dean of St. Paul's. He was baptized, May 9, 1605, and led an eventful life. He was associated as sergeant major in the settlement of St. Christopher and, when the Spaniards captured the place, was carried as a hostage to Madrid, where he remained a long time a prisoner. He finally made his escape by bribing his jailors and got safely to England. He went to Virginia with Harvey and, in Jan., 1636-37, was a member of the council and marshall of Virginia. Early in 1640, he was in England in the interests of Harvey and presented the King with a treatise entitled "Virginia Reviewed" which is still extant and in the British Museum. He also petitioned the King to confirm his title to the various offices which he had held in the colony, and this was done. His death occurred in 1641.

Brocas, William, settled at an early date in Charles River, now York, and early in 1637 was called to the council on the order of the English government and was present at many meetings. He was again appointed in the royal commission of 1641, and once more by Charles II. in 1650. The house of burgesses failed to include him, however, in the council elected by them two years later. Capt. Brocas received numerous grants of land in York and on the Rappahannock, and about the year 1650, removed to what is now Middlesex county. The good captain appears to have married three times, but died without issue, as it is stated in the records that one John Jackson was his heir-at-law.

Thoroughgood, Adam, was the seventh son of William Thoroughgood of Grimston in Norfolk and brother of Sir John Thoroughgood, a pensioner of Charles I. He was born in 1602 and came to Virginia in 1621, settling in Kicotan, now Hampton. He acquired by patent large tracts of land in various localities, the latest being "granted to him at the especiall recommendation of him from their Lordshipps and others, his Ma'ties most Hon'ble privie Councell to the Governor and Councell of State for Virginia." Capt. Adam Thoroughgood was a commissioner and burgess for Elizabeth City in 1629 and 1630 and was appointed to the council in 1637 and the same year was presiding justice of the county court of Lower Norfolk. He died in the spring of 1640, leaving descendants in Virginia.

Townsend, Richard, was born in 1606 or 1607 and came to Virginia in 1620 as an apprentice to Dr. John Pott, afterward governor, who was to teach him the art of an apothecary. The doctor did not carry out his part of the contract satisfactorily to Townsend, who in 1626, complained to the authorities that Pott had neglected to do his duty in the matter. The student of drugs probably abandoned his intended profession when he came of age, and in course of time rose to be one of the leading men of the colony. He was burgess for the plantations between "Archer's Hope" and "Martin's Hundred," in Oct., 1628 and, removing in 1630, to what is now York county, became a commissioner or justice there in 1633, and presiding justice in 1646. Sometime in 1636-37, the secretary in England wrote to the governor and council in Virginia that Capt. Richard Townsend, having been recommended as "an able man for the execution of that service, in respect to his knowledge of the affairs of the Country," had been appointed a member of the council and that the King directed that he be forthwith sworn. He was probably turned out of office as some of the councillors were at the accession of Wyatt to the governorship, for he appears again as a burgess in 1642. He was again sworn to the council in that year, however, and probably retained his seat until his death, although his name does not appear in that connection later than Feb., 1645-46. Townsend was a prominent man in the colony and acquired considerable tracts of land there by grant. He seems to have made a number of trips to England.

Wormeley, Christopher, a son of Christopher Wormeley of Yorkshire and a descendant of Sir John de Wormeley, was governor of the island of Tortuga from 1632 to 1635, during which last year it was taken by the Spaniards, a loss said to have been due to the carelessness of the governor. He appears to have come directly to Virginia as he was a justice of Charles River county in 1636. In 1639 and 1640, he was commander-in-chief of Charles River and Elizabeth City counties. In 1636-37, he was appointed a member of the council, and, being a supporter of Harvey, received a share of the governor's unpopularity. When Secretary Kemp fled to England in 1640, Wormeley seems to have accompanied him. He and Kemp were accused of cruelty and oppression in the colony and had considerable difficulty in making their return to Virginia, being twice prevented from doing so by orders from the house of lords, the second order being served on them when they were already on shipboard and about to depart. These charges seem to have had a foundation in fact. Wormeley actually confessed later to having tried a case against one Taylor unjustly, when a commissioner of Elizabeth City. Moral standards seem to have been somewhat lax in Virginia in 1640 for, although the council directed Wormeley to make reparation to Tay-

COLONIAL COUNCILLORS OF STATE

lor, yet his sins do not seem to have debarred him from his office as councillor, and he was present at meetings of the council in 1642 and 1643. It seems probable that he died shortly after the latter date.

Evelyn, Robert, was a member of a family that had several representatives in Virginia and Maryland early in the seventeenth century. He was a relative of John Evelyn, the diarist and author of "Sylvia," and a brother of Capt. George Evelyn who emigrated from England to Maryland. Capt. Thomas Young, an uncle of Robert Evelyn, having obtained permission to trade in America and to explore there, sailed from England in 1634 with two ships, taking his nephew, Lieut. Robert Evelyn, as his second in command. They arrived at Point Comfort, in Virginia, on July 3, and on the first of September, Evelyn, in a small shallop, which Young had built, departed for the Delaware, whither he was soon followed by his uncle. Here they built a fort where Evelyn says he remained four years trading with the Indians. He doubtless means that he and his uncle retained an interest in the place for that length of time, for in 1634 Evelyn himself returned to England and was again there in 1637. In the latter year he made another trip to Virginia, carrying a recommendation from Secretary Windebanke to Gov. Harvey, who was "to let him passe without let or hinderance on this great and secret service of his Majesty's. What this great and secret service was does not appear, but it most probably relates to some rose colored accounts of profit in trade which Young and Evelyn had given. Immediately upon his arrival in Virginia, Gov. Harvey and Secretary Kemp chose Evelyn to be surveyor-general of the colony, in place of Gabriel Hawley, deceased. This appointment was ratified by the English government, which also appointed him a member of the council. In 1640, Evelyn again went to England and in the next year, published a pamphlet giving directions to emigrants to America. Before this time he appears to become a resident of Maryland and was a member of the assembly of that colony. He continued to play a prominent part in the affairs of Maryland for a time, but after 1642 he is not mentioned in the records. A nephew, Mountjoy Evelyn, son of Capt. George Evelyn resided in James City county, Virginia.

Hawley, Jerome. Burke's "Peerage and Baronetage" gives the pedigree of the present baronet of the name of Hawley, tracing to an ancestor in Somersetshire, from whose eldest son the extinct Lords Hawley were descended, and whose second son, Jeremy Hawley, of Boston, near Brentford, Middlesex, England, was the father of (1) James Hawley, Esq., of Brentford; (2) John, who married Amy, daughter of Thomas Studley, possibly the first "Cape Merchant" of Virginia; and (3) Capt. Henry Hawley. John and Amy (Studley) Hawley had issue: (1) Jerome, of Virginia and Maryland; (2) Capt. Henry, governor of Barbadoes; (3) Dr. Richard, of London, ancestor of the present baronet; (4) James, who was also interested in the colonies and perhaps lived in Northumberland county, Virginia; (5) William, who came from Barbadoes to Maryland after the death of his brother Jerome, and was a signer of the Protestant Declaration of 1650. There were two other sons, who were probably Gabriel, who died in Virginia while holding the office of surveyor-general, and John, who came to Virginia in 1619. Jerome Hawley was a councillor of Maryland in 1634, and returned to

England in the summer of 1635. On Jan. 5, 1637, the King appointed him treasurer of Virginia and a member of the council there. At this time he was "one of the gentlemen servers to Queen Henrietta Maria. He came to Virginia in March, but soon returned to Maryland, where he had large interests. He died about Aug., 1638, deeply in debt, and on the 14th of that month the Maryland authorities, who spoke of him as "late of St. Maries," appointed Thomas Cornwallis administrator of his estate.

Sibsey or Sipsey, John, is first mentioned on Sept. 2, 1624, when, as John Sipsey, of Kichoughtan, "yeoman," he was granted a tract of 250 acres on the "south side of the river over against Kiccoughtan," as Hampton was then called. He returned to England after this time, for in the winter of 1626-27, a ship going to Virginia carrying some planters and servants, chiefly Irish, ran aground in Barnstable Bay, the principal persons on board being Fell (Felgate?) and Sipsie. In Sept., 1632, and Feb., 1633, John Sibsey was a burgess for the upper parish of Elizabeth City, and in 1636-37, probably in January, he was made a councillor. He must have been one of the council for a very short time, however, for in 1639 he was burgess for Lower Norfolk, where he had acquired a considerable estate. On June 1, 1635, he had received two grants of 1500 acres each, one on the western branch of the Elizabeth river, and the other nearby, probably adjoining. In 1640 he was one of the residents of Lower Norfolk who subscribed to pay the salary of Thomas Harrison, the well known Puritan minister, and in 1641 he was again a burgess for that county. During a long period Capt. Sibsey was one of the leading men in this section of Virginia, and held all of the more important county offices. He was a justice from July, 1637, for many years succeeding, sheriff in 1642 and 1645, commander of Lower Norfolk in 1645 and 1646, and deputy lieutenant of the county in 1646. From an entry in the Lower Norfolk records, in 1646, it may be seen that Sibsey then had a son Thomas, and from another, dated June 22, 1647, that he was a co-partner in the ships "John and Barbary" and "America," and a freighter in the ships "Bellman" and "Blessing."

Hobson, John. On June 2, 1620, and Jan. 30, of the year following, Sir Richard Worseley, Bart., Capt. Nathaniel Basse, John Hobson, Gent., and Capt. Christopher Lawne agreed with the Virginia to transport 100 persons to Virginia and receive a "confirmation of their old patent." Their settlement was to be called "the Isle of Wight's plantation," and it is possible that all the patentees were, as Worseley certainly was, residents of the Isle of Wight, in England. Hobson came to Virginia about this time, but exactly when he arrived there or how long he remained is not known. In 1637, Capt. John Hobson, "who hath formerly been in Virginia and is now ready to return," was added to the council. He sailed from England soon after June 4, 1637, upon which day, at the request of "Captain John Hopsonn, one of his Majesty's Council in Virginia," the seamen of the ship in which he was about to take passage were exempted from empressment. He was present as a member of the council Feb. 20, 1637, and on the 4th of June following, and was included in the commission of councillors under Gov. Berkeley, Aug. 9, 1641. On March 16, 1635, "Captain John Hobson, Esq., one of the Council of State," received a grant of land extending from Pagan Point Creek, "hereafter to be called Hampstead Point," to Warruschisqueake river, "hereafter to be called New Town Haven," due him for "a share of his adventure." The grant was dated May 2, 1621, in the time of the Virginia Company, of which Hobson had been a member. When Capt. Hobson died is not known.

Willoughby, Thomas, was a nephew of Sir Percival Willoughby, of Wollaton, who was from Kent, married his relative, the heiress of the Willoughbys of Wollaton, and had several brothers. At least so runs the family tradition. Thomas was born in 1601, came to Virginia when he was nine years old, and lived first, in Elizabeth City county, and afterwards in Lower Norfolk. After reaching manhood, he was for many years one of the leading merchants of the colony. There is to be found in Sainsbury's "Calendar of Colonial State Papers" (vol. i.) a certificate, dated 1627, by Thomas Willoughby, of Rochester, aged twenty-seven years, in regard to a ship in which he was about to go to Virginia. There can hardly be a doubt that this was the Virginian returning from a visit to his old home. As soon as he arrived in Virginia, he was engaged in warfare with the Indians, for on July 4, 1627, Lieut. Pippet and Ensign Willoughby were ordered to attack the Chesapeakes. As "Lieutenant Thomas Willoughby," he was appointed a commissioner (justice) for Elizabeth City, on March 26, 1628-29, and again in Feb., 1631-32, and Sept., 1632. On March 11, 1639, "Capt. Thos. Willoughby, Esq.," was presiding justice of Lower Norfolk. He represented the "Upper Part of Elizabeth City," in the house of burgesses at the session of March, 1629-30, and was again a member for "Waters Creek and the Upper Part of Elizabeth City," in Feb., 1631-32. In Sept., 1632, he was a burgess, but was absent, at least at the beginning of the session, being in England about this time. On Jan. 6, 1639, Willoughby was present as a member of the council, and on Aug. 9, 1641, he was again commissioned as a councillor under Gov. Berkeley, and was present at the meetings of Feb., 1644-45, March, 1645-46, and Oct., 1646. In the last named year he was "high lieutenant" of Norfolk county. He was included in the commission of the council issued by Charles II. at Breda in 1650, but was not among the councillors elected by the house of burgesses in April, 1652. In Nov., 1654, the assembly made the following order: "It is ordered by the present Grand Assembly in the difference between Capt. Thos. Willoughby and Bartholomew Hodgskins (Hoskins) that Hodgskins the then sheriff is noway liable to make Willoughby any satisfaction, and the former proceedings against the said Willoughby were grounded upon very good reasons, because it appeareth that the said Willoughby was not sworn nor acted as a Councillor of this Country before the Levy was made which he refusing to pay, occasioned all the damage, which in this petition he doth pretend to." Thomas Willoughby patented large tracts of land in Lower Norfolk county which his descendants owned for several generations. Part of this estate, Willoughby Point, near Norfolk, known as the "manor plantation" was until lately the property of descendants through female lines. The name of Capt. Willoughby's wife is not known, unless, as seems probable, it appears under a patent to him in 1654, when Alice, Thomas and Elizabeth Willoughby are mentioned as head rights. In the old records of Lower Norfolk is the following: "At a Court held 16th August, 1658. Upon Peticon of Mr. Tho. Willoughby a commission of Adm'con is granted unto him on his father's estate, Capt. Tho. Willoughby who deceased in England, hee putting in Security according to law."

Wormeley, Ralph, was a son of Christopher Wormeley, Esq., and a descendant of Sir John de Wormeley, of Hadfield, county York, England (1312), and brother of Christopher Wormely, Esq., acting governor of the Tortuga Island, 1631-1635, who also settled in Virginia. He was born about 1620 and came to Virginia about 1635, and settled in York county. He was a justice of the county in 1648, with the rank of captain, and in 1650 was made a member of the council. He died in 1651. In 1646 he married Agatha Eltonhead, widow of Luke Stubbins, gentleman, of Northampton county, Virginia. She was the daughter of Richard Eltonhead, of Eltonhead, county Lancaster, England, and on the death of Wormeley she married Sir Henry Chicheley, a royalist who fled to Virginia in 1649 and was afterwards lieutenant governor. He was father of Ralph Wormeley, who became secretary of state of Virginia. He died in 1651.

Littleton, Nathaniel, was the sixth son of Sir Edward Littleton, of Henly, Shropshire, and brother of Sir Edward Littleton, lord keeper, served in the Low Countries, in the Earl of Southampton's company, in 1625, and emigrated in 1635 to Virginia, where he settled at Nadua Creek, Accomac county. In 1640, he was chief magistrate of that county, and on March 18, 1644, was appointed commander of Accomac, an office which he held for a number of years. On April 30, 1652, he was elected to the council, and was a member until his death about two years later.

Prior to March 1, 1652, Capt. Littleton, "Governor of Accomache," had married the widow of Charles Harmar. She was Ann, daughter of Henry Southey, Esq., of Rimpton, Somersetshire, to whom the company had issued a patent in reward of his undertaking to transport 100 persons to Virginia. Councillor Littleton's death occurred in or before 1654, and that of his wife in 1656. He has numerous descendants in Virginia.

Harmer, Ambrose, came to Virginia in about the year 1625. This much may be gathered from his petition to the King, asking to be given legal control over Benoni Buck, the first idiot who had ever lived in Virginia. The petition was dated 1637, and in it Mr. Harmer stated that he had had the tuition of Benoni and his brother, children of the well known Virginia clergyman, Rev. Richard Buck, for thirteen years past. Just when Harmer was appointed to the council does not appear, but he was present at meetings on Jan. 6, 1639, and March 5, 1640. He was left out of the commission of councillors of Aug. 9, 1641, but whatever the cause may have been, it was not unpopularity with the people, for he represented James City county in the house of burgesses at the sessions of Feb., 1644-45, Nov., 1645, March, 1645-46, and Oct., 1646, when his name appears for the last time in the records, and he was speaker of that honorable house. The land grants show a deed, dated April 18, 1642, from "William Taylor of Chisciacke, gent., to Ambrose Harmer, of Virginia, Esq., and Jane now his wife," reciting that on Nov. 9, 1638, a grant of 1200 acres was made to the said William Taylor, "the land lying on Chickahominy, in James City County, due him for the transportation of twenty-four persons, and said

Taylor now conveys the land to Harmer and wife." Elizabeth, wife of Taylor, also conveys her right of dower in the land. The wife of William Taylor, or Tayloe, was Elizabeth daughter of Richard Kingsmill, and it is possible that Mrs. Jane Harmer was her mother, as Richard Kingsmill's wife was named Jane.

Yardley, Argall, was a son of Sir George Yardley, governor and councillor of Virginia. The younger Yardley's name is first recorded among those present on Jan. 6, 1639, and on July 6, 1640. On Feb. 26, 1644, proceedings were instituted against "Col. Argall Yardley of the Council," for contempt. He was re-elected a councillor in April, 1652, and appointed justice for Northampton in 1653, and once more elected to the council March 31, 1654-55. Colonel Yardley married Sarah, eldest daughter of John Michael, merchant. Their marriage contract bears the date of Jan. 23, 1640. On March 28, 1656, the general assembly had ordered the "denization" of "John Michael, stranger," then a resident of Northampton county. A deed is recorded under date of Dec. 28, 1648, from "Argall Yardley, elder son and heir of Sir George Yardley, deceased," to his son Edmund, also a deed from Argall Yardley to Henry and Edmund Yardley, and a deed of gift recorded Aug., 1674, from John Michael, Sr., to his daughter Sarah and her husband, Argall Yardley, and to their children, Argall Yardley, Jr., John, Elizabeth and Frances Yardley. According to an inventory of the personal estate of Colonel Argall Yardley, Esq., dated Nov. 13, 1655, he had 41,269 pounds of tobacco, and a tobacco house and two servants in Barbadoes. He has numerous descendants in Virginia.

Bennett, Richard, governor of Virginia (q. v.).

Digges, Edward, governor of Virginia (q. v.).

Mathews, Samuel, governor of Virginia (q. v.).

Wingate, Roger, was a member of an old Bedfordshire family and the son of Roger Wingate, of Barnend, Bedfordshire. In the year 1637, he was living in London and two years later was appointed by the King treasurer of Virginia and a member of the council. He came to the colony at once and was present in council Jan., 1639-40, and subsequently. Wingate probably died in the beginning of the year 1641, as in February of that year, Richard Morrison was appointed to the council in his place. This may, however, have been in the following year as his name is included in the commission of Aug. 9, 1641.

Pettus, Thomas, first appears in the Virginia records as included in the commission to the councillors at the beginning of Berkeley's administration, Aug. 9, 1641. He probably came to the colony about that time. He was present at meetings as late as 1651, but in this year seems to have lost his seat on the arrival of the parliamentary commissioners. The house of burgesses, however, elected him a councillor in 1652 and reëlected him a number of times afterwards. Upon Berkeley's reappointment to the governorship at the time of the restoration, in 1660, the King again commissioned Pettus a councillor. Colonel Pettus made his home at "Littletown" on the James river, not far below Jamestown. The date of his death is not known.

Morrison or Moryson, Richard, together with two of his brothers, settled in Virginia during the first half of the seventeenth century, where they all became men of prominence, Francis Morrison serving as governor during Berkeley's absence in England, 1661 and 1662. They were sons of Sir Richard Morrison, M. P., of Tooley Park, Leicestershire, who had served long in the English army and was made lieutenant-general of ordnance. They were also brothers-in-law of Lucius Cary, Lord Falkland. Our subject, Maj. Richard Morrison, was appointed commander of the fort at Point Comfort in 1638 and in Feb., 1641, was appointed member of the council in the place of Roger Wingate, deceased. Maj. Morrison's death occurred in or prior to 1656, as in that year Mrs. Winifred Morrison is mentioned as his widow.

Higginson, Humphrey, born in 1607, sailed from London for Virginia in the ship "George," in 1635. On Feb. 6, 1637-38, as "Humphrey Higginson, Gentleman," he received a grant of 700 acres of land called "Tuttey's Neck," adjoining Harop, now Williamsburg, and lying on a branch of Archer's Hope Creek, "that partieth this land from Kingsmell's neck," said land being granted to Elizabeth, "his now wife," by order of the court dated October 4, 1637. Tuttey's Neck is still a well known place near Williamsburg, Virginia, and lies back of the "Kingsmill" estate. On Oct. 18, 1642, "Captain Humphrey Higginson, Esq.," received another grant of 320 acres adjoining Tuttey's Neck. Higginson's first official position of which there is any record was that of tobacco inspector in the section of James City county lying between the east side of Archer's Hope and Waram's ponds. On Aug. 9, 1641, he was appointed by the King a member of the council, and was present at the meetings held March, 1642-43, Oct., 1644, and Feb., 1644-45. On April 30, 1652, the burgesses elected him a member of the council, and he was present March 31, 1654-55, but he must have gone to England soon after, for in Dec., 1656, the house of burgesses made the following order: "Whereas Thos. Loving, high sheriff of James City County, by Petition Requested the Opinion of this house whether Coll. Higginson, having been so long absent out of the Country, should enjoy the Privilege of Counsellor by exempting certain persons out of the Levies, it is Resolved that in Respect of his long absence, he being upon no public employment, shall not have any Persons Belonging to him exempted." Besides the grants of land given above, Col. Higginson had two others, a partnership with Abraham Moone for 2,000 acres on the south side of the Potomac, Sept. 20, 1654, and one of "Colonel Humphrey Higginson, of the Council of State, and his son Thomas Higginson," for 800 acres on the south side of Pianketank, in Gloucester county, Sept. 20, 1654. The son probably died within a few years, for he is not mentioned in his father's will. Col. Higginson died at Ratcliffe, in Stepney parish, London, in 1665-1666. He left a brother, Capt. Christopher Higginson, Virginia, who has numerous descendants. See William and Mary Quarterly V, p. 186.

Pawlett or Paulett, Thomas, was born about 1585. In Aug., 1618, he came in the ship "Neptune" to Virginia, where he settled in the present Charles City county, and was a member of the first house of burgesses, assembled July 30, 1619. In 1623 he was living at "West Shirley Hundred." He was appointed a commissioner (justice) for Charles City and Henrico counties in Feb., 1631-32, and was a member of the house of burgesses for Westover and Flower de Hundred in February of the year following, and again for Charles City in Jan., 1639. He was commissioned member of the council Aug. 9, 1641, and retained his seat as a member of that body until his death in 1643. On Jan. 15, 1637, "Captain Thomas Pawlett" received a grant of 2,000 acres of land in Charles City county, at Westover, which was bounded on the south side by the river, east by the land of Capt. Perry, and west by Berkeley Hundred. This land was declared to be due to Capt. Pawlett for the "personal adventure" into the colony of himself and his brother, Chidock Pawlett, and for his transportation of thirty-eight other persons. By his will, dated Jan. 12, 1644, he left Westover to his brother, Sir John Lord Pawlett, then living in Manchester, county Southampton, England.

Wyatt, Sir Francis, governor of Virginia (q. v.).

Ludlow, George, was a descendant of the old and distinguished family of Ludlow of Wiltshire. He was baptized Sept. 15, 1596, and came to America about 1630. His first place of settlement was Massachusetts, where he was made a freeman, but about 1634, he removed to Virginia and settled in the upper county of New Norfolk, receiving there a grant of 500 acres of land. He appears to have been sworn as a member of the council in 1642 and on Aug. 1 of that year signed the "Declaration against the Company." He was present at the sessions of the council until the overthrow of the royal government in 1652, when he was at once elected to the same office by the house of burgesses, and by them re-elected a number of times. He held his office until his death in 1656. Though he was included in the commission issued to the council by Charles II. at Breda, in 1650, his sympathies were probably with parliament, and according to one authority declared openly in its favor at the time of the colony's surrender to the commissioners. Col. George Ludlow was for many years one of the wealthiest and most active merchants in Virginia and took up many thousand acres of land by patent and purchase. Like many of the prominent planters, he was much interested in the introduction of silk culture. Col. Ludlow's residence was at the place now known as "Temple Farm," a little below Yorktown and it is possible that the ancient house, still standing in part, in which Cornwallis signed his surrender, was built by Ludlow.

Freeman, Bridges, was a burgess for Pashbahay in 1629-30, before which date nothing is known of him. His lands lay on the east side of the Chickahominy river, and in Sept., 1632, he represented Chickahominy in the house of burgesses. In November, 1647, he was again a burgess, this time for James City. It was in the same month that the assembly appointed him collector of public levies at Chickahominy and Sandy Point. He was a member of the council, and present at the board, Sept. 30, 1650, and was reëlected a member, April 30, 1652, and again, as "Colonel Bridges Freeman," on March 31, 1654-55. It is probable that for a time he was adjutant-general of the colony, as "Adjutant Freeman" was present as a councillor, Nov. 6, 1651.

Davenant, Sir William, the famous English poet, and the successor to "Rare Ben Johnson" as poet laureate, was appointed to his Majesty's council in Virginia June 3, 1650. During the civil wars in England he had been prominent in the army of King Charles, who knighted him, but on the defeat of the Royalists, he took refuge in France and devoted himself to writing under the patronage of Queen Henrietta Maria, wife of the unfortunate King. When Sir William had completed two books of his heroic poem "Gondibert," upon which most of his reputation as a poet rests, the Queen ordered him to go to Virginia to convey to the colony some men skilled in various mechanical arts whom she thought would be useful there. Accompanied by the emigrants, and armed with a commission as councillor, the poet set sail for Jamestown, but he was destined never to fulfill his charge, for before he was out of sight of the French coast, he was captured by a parliament ship and carried a prisoner to Cowes Castle, where he was kept confined for two years. Here his life was spared partly through the influence of Milton, for whom, in true poetic justice, he was enabled to do a like service later in life. Sir William Davenant never made a second attempt to come to Virginia. After his release from prison he devoted himself to his literary work until his death, Sept. 7, 1658.

Stegg or Stagg, Thomas, merchant of London, came to the colony in or before 1636, when Gov. Harvey called him one of the "ablest merchants in Virginia." On Jan. 6, 1639, he received a grant of 1,000 acres between "Oldman's and Queen's Creeks," in Charles City county, which became his place of residence. In 1640 he aided Secretary Kemp to escape from the colony without the consent of the governor and council, and for this offence was fined fifty pounds and sentenced to be imprisoned during the governor's pleasure. It is probable that the imprisonment was not of long duration, as he was a burgess from Charles City county in March, 1642-43. At this session he was speaker of the house, and two years later was justice of the same county. He was included in the commission of 1650 to the councillors, issued by Charles II. at Breda, but was at that time in England a partisan of parliament. He was appointed one of the parliamentary commissioners to subdue Virginia, but the frigate "John," commanded by Capt. Dennis, himself a commissioner, was lost on its way to Virginia in 1652, and Stegg and Dennis perished.

Chiles, Walter, merchant, came to Virginia about 1638 and was granted 400 acres in Charles City county. As Lieut.-Col. Walter Chiles, he represented that county in 1642-43 in the house of burgesses. He subsequently removed to Jamestown Island and was burgess for James City county in 1645, 1645-46 and 1649. He is recorded to have sailed from Rotterdam in his own ship, the "Fame of Virginia," but, reaching Virginia waters, was captured by the "Hopeful Adventure," Capt. Richard Husband, upon pretext that he had no license. The Northampton court ordered Husband to release the vessel, but that bold captain, disregarding the order, calmly sailed away with it to the great anger of the worthy men of Northampton. It happened that when the dispute arising from this incident came up before the assembly for settlement, Walter Chiles himself was a candidate for the speakership of that body. Gov. Bennet thereupon sent a note to the burgesses in which, after stating that he did not wish to "intrench upon the right of Assemblies in the free choice of a speaker," pointed out that it would be highly inappropriate to appoint Chiles to any office in a body before which his own case must be tried. The assembly, however, with a sublime disregard of propriety and the interference of governors, promptly elected him to the post. Chiles himself, however, very much to his honor, declined the honor. He is recorded as being present at a session of the council in 1651. His death occurred about 1652. Through his son Walter, who was a member of the house of burgesses, he is numerously represented in Virginia.

Epes or Eppes, Francis, first styled captain and afterwards lieutenant-colonel, settled before 1625, in what soon became Charles City county. In the same year he was a member of the house of burgesses, and in Feb., 1631-32, represented in that house "Both Shirley Hundreds, the Farrar's and Chaplayne's." He was appointed a commissioner (justice) for Charles City and Henrico counties in 1631, and in 1639 and 1645, was a burgess from Charles City. It was on April 30, 1652, that Epes was elected a member of the council, and he probably died before 1655. On Aug. 26, 1635, he patented 1700 acres of land in Charles City county, on the south side of James river, bounded on the east by Bayly's creek, and on the west by Cosons (Cawson's) creek and the Appomattox river. Some of this land is believed to be owned by his descendants. Col. Francis Epes probably married in England, and the arms borne by his descendants in Virginia are the same as those ascribed in English heraldic works to "Epes, or Epps, of Canterbury, Kent."

Cheesman or Chisman, John, was born in 1595 and came to Virginia in the ship "Flying Hart" in 1621. At a later date, he lived in York county, where he was a justice in 1633, a captain in 1637 and a member of the house of burgesses in March, 1642-43. On April 30, 1652, as "Lieutenant-Colonel John Cheesman," he was elected councillor by the burgesses. Cheesman must have returned to England about 1661, as in that year he was mentioned in a power of attorney to Lawrence Smith as of the "parish of St. Mary Magdalene in Bermondsea, in the County of Surry, merchant." Under this power, Smith, in 1662, leased for twenty-one years, to Edmund Cheesman, or Chisman, of Poquoson parish, York county, Virginia, brother of said John Cheesman, the councillor, all of that gentleman's property in York county. Col. John Cheesman died before 1678, as in that year his widow Margaret gave a power of attorney to her "cozen," Thomas Cheesman, in Virginia. Councillor Cheesman's brother, Edmund Cheesman, was the father of the Edmund Cheesman, who took an active part in Bacon's rebellion and was sentenced to death by Gov. Berkeley, but died in prison. The family is numerously represented in Virginia.

Lunsford, Sir Thomas, son of Thomas Lunsford, of Wilegh, Sussex, England, was born about 1610. Though but little is known of his life in Virginia, and his only memorial there is a stone, his name was once a familiar one in every hamlet in England, and was the object of the most intense hatred and fear to a large part of the English people. He was, according to Clarendon, of a very old family, but of small fortune and without much education. His youth was wild and he was imprisoned and fined £9,000, for outrages of a violent kind. He made his escape into France, however, and a sentence of outlawry was pronounced against him in England. Upon his return to England, he was pardoned by the King and a large part of his fine remitted. In the following year, 1640, he was given a command against the Scots and distinguished himself at Newburn in spite of the English defeat. The King, who seems to have regarded him with favor from the start, now rewarded him by appointing him lieutenant of the Tower, an act which at once caused the most intense excitement all over the country. It was at the time when the struggle between the King and commons was rapidly drawing to a crises, and every royal act was scrutinized with hostile eyes. The placing of a man, whose youth had been anything but exemplary, was seized upon by the excited popular imagination and exaggerated beyond the bounds of reason. He was accused of every crime of oppression, of plotting against the people's and was even believed to be a cannibal who ate children. That Lunsford's sympathies were entirely royalist, that he was a resolute and dangerous enemy of the parliament in the civil wars, was later abundantly proven, and it seems quite possible that he was even violent towards those who opposed him; but the popular belief was undoubtedly quite without foundation, and merely one of those extravagances which the heated feelings of such a time give rise to. Lunsford took an active part in the wars which shook England, and was unusually successful in the field. He was thrice captured and twice released, though on each occasion he resolutely declared his allegiance to the King. The manner of his regaining his freedom for the third time is not known, but he was at liberty before June 29, 1648, for there is a letter of that date from him to the Prince of Wales. After the execution of the King, Lunsford, like so many of his fellow cavaliers, sought refuge in Virginia, which held out for the royal cause, and on Aug. 7, 1649, he received a pass for himself and family to the new home across the water. In Col. Norwood's account of his own voyage to Virginia, he relates finding at Capt. Wormley's, several friends and brother officers who, a short time before, had come from England. They were Cols. Philip Honeywood, Mainwaring Hammond, Sir Henry Chicheley and Sir Thomas Lunsford. In Oct., 1650, he received a patent for 3423 acres of land on the Rappahannock river. When Virginia was threatened with an invasion by the parliamentary forces from England, Gov. Berkeley did not overlook so distinguished a soldier as Lunsford, who accordingly appears in a list of councillors present on Nov. 6, 1651, as Sir Thomas Lunsford, lieutenant-general. He of course retired from the council on the colony's surrender to parliament. His death must have occurred about 1653, as there is, in that year, an order among the English records, appointing a guardian for his three daughters. By his third wife, whom he married in Virginia, he had a daughter Catherine, who married Hon. Ralph Wormeley, Esq., secretary of state, and from this marriage Sir Thomas has many descendants in Virginia.

Lee, Richard, who was honored in being the progenitor of the distinguished Lee family of Virginia, was descended from the Coton branch of the Shropshire Lees, one of the oldest families in England, their ancestry being traceable for some 750 years. "Colonel Richard Lee, Secretary of State in Virginia, anno 1659," was described by a descendant as "of good stature, comely visage, an enterprising genius, a sound head, vigorous spirit and generous nature." His first home in Virginia was in York county, where on Aug. 10, 1642, he was granted 1,000 acres of land. There is a tradition to the effect that Col. Lee was accompanied to Virginia by a brother Robert, who also settled in York, but whether or not this is true, or whether the other families of Lee in Virginia were in any way related to the councillor, cannot be proven. The first mention of Lee as holding a public place is in the official records under date of Feb., 1641, when he was appointed clerk of the council. On Oct. 12, 1643, he was made attorney-general, in 1646 he was a magistrate for York and the year following represented that county in the house of burgesses. He seems to have moved away from York in or before 1651, as in that year he was paid for services as a burgess of Northumberland. On Sept. 9, of the same year, he was present in the council as a member. He owned three plantations, one in York county, on the York river, and two in Northumberland on Dividing creeks, where necks of land afford such a good harbor that it is used to this day as a landing place for Baltimore steamers. In addition to these places grants of land in Lancaster, Westmoreland and Gloucester were made to him. He was a staunch Royalist and made many trips to England and on to Holland, the latter for the express purpose of seeing the exciled King, Charles II. According to John Gibbons, Lee intended to end his days in England, and with this in view, employed him, Gibbons, to oversee his estate in the colony. It happens, however, that his will arranges for the disposal of his English property and the settlement of his children in the colony, "all except Francis if he be pleased," so that it seems probable that Gibbons was in error. This will was executed in London on Feb. 6, 1663-64, while Col. Lee was in England. He must have returned to Virginia shortly after this and died almost upon arrival, as he is mentioned under date of April 20, 1664, as "Colonel Richard Lee Esq., who is now deceased."

Taylor or Tayloe, William, was an early settler in York county. In or before 1640, he purchased from John Utie the estate called "Utiemaria" in that county, but, it seems, did not long hold it. By a deed dated Dec. 25, 1640, "William Taylor of Utiemaria in the County of Charles River, in Virginia, merchant," sold to William Blackley, 100 acres of land which he had bought from John Utie, and on Jan. 7, 1641, he sold to Henry Corbell 1250 acres also purchased from Utie. Col. William Tayloe, as he ultimately became, was a burgess for York in March, 1642-43, and Nov., 1647. As Maj. William Taylor, he was present as a member of the council, Nov. 6, 1651, but lost his seat on the surrender of Virginia to the parliament. He was, however, again elected a councillor, April 30, 1652, and once more on March 31, 1654-55. He had been a justice of York since 1647. Col. Tayloe married Elizabeth, daughter of Richard Kingsmill, of Virginia, and died without issue. His widow married secondly Nathaniel Bacon. The tomb of Mrs. Elizabeth Bacon, now in St. Paul's Churchyard, Norfolk, bears the Kingsmill and Tayloe arms. Through his nephew, however, Col. William Tayloe, of Richmond county, he has numerous representatives in Virginia.

Bernard, William, was born about 1598, and came to the colony in 1625, in the ship "America." He was the son of Francis Bernard, Esq., of Kingsthorpe, Northamptonshire, and brother of Sir Robert Bernard, Bart., of Brampton, Huntingdonshire. He settled first in Isle of Wight county and probably continued to make his home there. He was certainly living there in 1639, when the assembly appointed him a tobacco inspector for the district extending from Laune's creek to Casstra (?) creek. The act styles him "Mr. William Barnett." Bernard first appears as a member of the council in March, 1642-43, and retained his seat until 1652. The house of burgesses again made him a councillor by successive elections in April, 1652; March, 1654-55; March, 1657-58 and April, 1658. He was also present as a member on March 13, 1659-60. He doubtless remained a councillor until his death, which occurred in or not long before 1662. Col. Bernard took part in the effort to make silk culture a success in Virginia, and in the "Reformed Virginia Silk Worm," published in 1652, John Ferrar Jr., who puts into rhyme the substance of letters lately received by his sister, Virginia Ferrar, says of him:

"Yea, worthy Bernard that stout Colonel
Informs the lady the work most facile
And of rich silken stuffs made shortly there
He hopes that he and others shall soon wear."

Only two grants of land to Bernard appear in the land books. The first, dated Aug. 10, 1642, was to "William Bernard, Esq., 1200 acres in Isle of Wight county, at the head of Laune's creek, and extending to the head of Pagan creek, due for his own adventure into the Colony four times, and for the transportation of 20 persons;" and the second to "Col. Bernard, Esq., 600 acres in Lancaster on Dividing Creek." Col. Bernard married in 1652 or the year following, Lucy, widow of Maj. Lewis Burwell, of "Carter's Creek," Gloucester county, and daughter of Capt. Robert Higginson. Several deeds in York prove this marriage, the earliest of them being from William Bernard, Esq., and his wife, Lucy, conveying to George Reade a tract of land which had been purchased by Capt. Robert Higginson on Jan. 9, 1648. Bernard died in or before 1662, in which year his widow had become the wife of Philip Ludwell. He left a daughter Elizabeth, who married Thomas Todd, of Toddsbury, Gloucester county, and has descendants.

Morrison, Francis, governor of Virginia (q. v.).

Harwood, Thomas, was a member of the house of burgesses for Mulberry Island in the years 1629, 1630, 1633 and 1642; speaker of the house 1648 and 1649, and chosen member of the council in 1652. He took a prominent part in the movement to depose Gov. Harvey, and when he was at length sent to England, Harwood and Francis Pott went with him, as representatives of the house of burgesses and the council. On their arrival in Plymouth, Harvey had them arrested by the mayor, and the letters carried by Harwood were sealed up. They appear to have been soon released, for in Aug., 1635, Harvey wrote to the English authorities that Harwood was in London, and asked that he be "restrained of his liberty." The English state papers give a glimpse of him on his way from Plymouth to London. One Browne gave information that on the 18th of July preceding he was in the house of one Ebbottson at the sign of the Valiant Soldier in Exeter, and Ebbottson spied the post that carried the packet to London, and a stranger with him riding post also, whom Ebbottson went into the street to meet, and they went into the house and drank a pint of wine together and parted, and Ebbottson then told Browne that the stranger was one Harwood new come from Virginia, who informed him that they have had great contentions, and have displaced Gov. Harvey, for he hath done great injuries to that country, and that Harwood was appointed by the country to carry letters to the King and that he would make great haste to be up before Sir John, that he might make friends and the case good against him. Sir John Harvey had so carried himself in Virginia that if he returned he would be pistolled or shot. Harwood appears, from a land grant to his son Humphrey, to have died in 1652. He patented large tracts of land in Warwick county, some portion of which is still owned by his descendants in the male line.

Mathews, Samuel Jr., was a son of Samuel Mathews, governor of Virginia. The younger Mathews was, like his father, a soldier, and is mentioned in the old records as "Lieutenant Colonel Mathews." He was a burgess for Warwick River county in April, 1652, and again in Nov., 1654, and was a justice for the same county in 1652. On March 31, 1654-55, he was elected a councillor. His death occurred in or before 1670, and was survived by a son John, then under age.

Perry, Henry, son of Capt. William Perry, of Charles City county, was a burgess for Charles City in Nov., 1652, and in Nov., 1654. In Jan., 1655, he was granted a commission allowing him to go with any volunteers who might offer themselves to discover the mountains. On March 31, of the year before, he had been elected a member of the council, and on April 1, 1658, he was elected again, and was present at meetings held in March, 1659-60, and on April 4, 1661. Perry married the daughter and heiress of George Menifie, Esq., of "Buckland," Charles City county, and acquired with her the estate which still bears that name that was late the property of Mr. Wilcox. He had two daughters and co-heiresses, Elizabeth, who married John Coggs, of Rainsliff, Middlesex, England, and Mary, who married Thomas Mercer, citizen and stationer of London.

Hill, Edward Sr., is supposed to have been the son of "Master Edward Hill," of Elizabeth City county, buried there in 1622, who distinguished himself by a brave and successful defense of his house against the Indians. Our first acquaintance with Col. Edward Hill, the subject of this sketch, is in 1639, when we find him living at the famous old Virginia home, "Shirley," and representing Charles City county in the house of burgesses. Mention is again made of him as a burgess for Charles City in 1642, as burgess for Charles City and speaker of the house in Oct., 1644, and in the following year. In March, 1645-46, the assembly ordered Capt. Hill and Capt. Thomas Willoughby to go Maryland and demand the return of certain Virginians who had remained there without permission. While in Maryland, Hill was chosen governor by the insurrectionist party, and stayed there in that office for some months. He held a commission from the council of Maryland, dated July 30, 1646, under the name of Gov. Calvert, but it cannot be proved that Calvert really signed it. On Jan. 18, 1646, Edward Hill wrote from Chicacone, Northumberland county, to Leonard Calvert, asking payment of his "sallary in that unhappy service." Gov. Thomas Green answered, promising that his demands should be satisfied. Near the end of the year, Gov. Calvert, in command of a small body of troops, entered the Maryland capital and reinstated himself in the government, whereupon Hill surrendered and returned to Virginia. In August of the following, Mr. Broadhurst was charged with saying that "there is now no governor in Maryland, for Captain Hill is governor, and him only he acknowledged." At a meeting of the Maryland council held June 10, 1648, Capt. Hill demanded from the governor and council "the arrears of what consideration was covenanted unto him by Leonard Calvert, Esq., for his services in the office of Governor of this province, being half of his Lordship's receipts for the year 1646, and half of the customs for the same year." It was ordered that he should be paid. On Aug. 26, 1649, Lord Baltimore issued a proclamation in which he declared that "Captain Edward Hill (the Governor in 1646)" was only his "pretended lieutenant of said province," but never fully authorized by or from him. After his return to Virginia, Hill resumed his seat in the assembly, as a burgess from Charles City. From that time until 1654, when he is mentioned as having been unanimously chosen speaker of the house of burgesses, nothing is known of him except that, in 1650, he was summoned before the council because, without obtaining the license required, he had "collected fifty men to accompany him on an expedition to the lands west of the falls, with the avowed intention of finding gold and silver in these parts." After his election as speaker, one William Hatcher "maliciously reported" him to be an atheist and blasphemer, to the great indignation of the "Honorable Governor and Council," who "cleared the said Colonel Hill, and certified the same unto the House." On March 31, 1654-55, Col. Hill was a member of the council, and in March of the year following, the council ordered that he should be given command of "100 men at least," and sent to remove "by force if necessary," 600 or 700 western and inland Indians who had "set down near the falls of James river and were a great danger." Hill, who was at that time commander-in-chief of Henrico and Charles City counties, at the head of a force consisting of colonists and friendly Pamunkey Indians, met the hostile savages on a small creek in Hanover county, as John Ledderer recites. His little army was put to confusion, and Tottopottomoy, the chief of the Pamunkeys was killed, whence since that day the creek has been known as Tottopottomoy Creek. The failure of the undertaking brought down upon Col. Hill, the censure of the assembly, which directed, in 1656, his suspension from all civil and military offices, that he should be "incapable of restitution but by an assembly," and charged to his account the expenses of procuring peace with the Indians. Col. Hill was successful, however, in regaining the favor of the assembly, for in April, 1658, he was again a member of the council, and in March, 1659, he was a burgess for Charles City and speaker of the house. His death occurred about the year 1663, and he was succeeded in his large landed estates by his son, Col. Edward Hill Jr., of Shirley, of whom a sketch will appear later.

Dew, Thomas, of Nansemond county, was, in Jan., 1639, appointed by the assembly an inspector of tobacco in Upper Norfolk county. He was a member of the house of burgesses in April, 1642 and again as "Captain Thos. Dew," in Nov., 1652, as "Lt. Col. Thos. Dew" in 1653, and as "Colonel Thos. Dew," in Nov., 1654. He was elected to the council on March 31, 1654-55, on March 13, 1657-58 and was present as a member in March 1659-60. In Dec., 1656, the assembly passed a resolution on the petition of Col. Thomas Dew, permitting that gentleman to make discoveries of the navigable rivers between Capes Hatteras and Fear, with such other gentlemen and planters as would, voluntarily and at their own charge, accompany him. Whether or not Col. Dew remained in the council after 1660, is not known. The following are the grants of land he received: (1) Thomas Dew, four hundred acres in the county of Norfolk on Nansemond river, Aug. 1, 1638; (2) 150 acres adjoining the preceding, Aug. 1, 1638; (3) 300 acres in the county of Upper Norfolk, Oct. 10, 1638; (4) 250 acres in the county of New Norfolk, adjoining a former patent of his, Nov. 7, 1640; (5) Thomas Dew, gentleman, 750 acres in Upper Norfolk on the east side of the southern branch of the Nansemond river; 300 acres of this a regrant, Jan. 8, 1643; (6) a regrant of No. 5, Oct. 10, 1670; (7) Col. Thomas Dew, 450 acres in the upper parish of Nansemond county, at the head of Craney creek, which was granted to Randall Crew in 1640, and had come by several surrenders and descents to Col. Thomas Dew. Perhaps this Col. Dew was not the councillor.

Gooch, William, probably came to Virginia about 1650, when he received a grant of land on the Potomac. He settled in York, where he was a justice in 1652, and represented the county in the house of burgesses in Nov., 1654. On March 31, 1654-55, the burgesses elected him a member of the council. William Gooch died Oct. 29, 1655, leaving an only daughter, Anne, who married Capt. Thomas Beale of "Chestnut Hill," in what is now called Richmond county, and later William Colston, also of Richmond county. Councillor Gooch's tomb bears his arms which are the same as those of the Gooch family of Norfolk, England. This tomb still remains at the site of the old York church on the "Temple Farm," and in addition to the arms bears the following epitaph:

"Major William Gooch of this Parish
    Dyed Octob. 29, 1655.
Within this tomb there doth interred lie
No shape, but substance, true nobility,
Itself, though young in years, just twenty-nine

Yet graced with virtues moral and devine
The Church from him did good participate
In Council rare, fit to adorn a state."

He was an uncle of Sir William Gooch, afterwards governor of Virginia.

Robins, Obedience, son of Thomas and (Bulkelay) Robins of Brackley, Northamptonshire, England, was born April 16, 1600, and at the age of twenty-one years, came with his brother, Edward Robins, to Virginia. He settled at first in Jamestown but, in 1628, removed to the eastern shore, where he bought lands in Accomac and made his home at Cherrystone. His house and lands were owned by the Robins family until the year 1855. Obedience Robins was a member of the house of burgesses for Accomac in March 1629-30 and was appointed commissioner, justice, in Feb., 1631-32, and commander of the county in 1632. He was again a burgess for Accomac in Jan., 1639, and for Northampton county in 1644 and 1652. Northampton county was formed in 1642 and is said to have been named in honor of Robins' native shire. In the year 1652, he is mentioned first as major, and later as Lieut. Col. Robins, and in March, 1654-55, he was first elected to the council. Three years later he was reelected, and is mentioned as being present at the meetings for a number of years. On March 12, 1656, the assembly appointed him to the office of colonel commanding the "Lower Precinct" of the eastern shore. Councillor Robins married in 1634, Grace O'Neil, widow of Edward Waters. His death occurred in 1662, leaving descendants in Virginia.

Bacon, Nathaniel Sr. President of the council and acting governor of Virginia (q. v.).

Wood, Abraham, was for many years one of the leading men of the colony. He came to Virginia as a little boy of ten years in 1620 in the "Margaret and John," commanded by Capt. Chester. This was the vessel that fought the famous sea fight with two Spanish men-of-war. Little Abraham escaped unharmed, and in 1625 was living at Jamestown in the employment of Capt. Samuel Mathews. He represented Henrico county in the house of burgesses from 1644 to 1646. He was placed in charge of Fort Henry at the falls of Appomatox, where, dwelling on the frontier wood, he became well acquainted with the Indians and their country. On Aug. 24, 1650, Wood, Edward Bland and a number of others set forth from Fort Henry, now the site of Petersburg, and made an exploration to the southwest, where they discovered a new river running west. Bland published an account of this journey in 1652. About the time of this trip, Wood changed his residence to the south side of the Appomatox river, in Charles City, and, as Major Abraham Wood, was burgess of that county from 1652 to 1656. In 1655, he was a justice of Charles City and the following year was made colonel of the regiment of Henrico and Charles City, in place of Col. Hill, suspended. In the same year, he was appointed on a committee to review the laws of Virginia. On March 13, 1657-58, he was elected to the council and remained a member of that body for many years, being present at the session of Sept., 1671. He appears to have held the office of major general until after Bacon's Rebellion, when, perhaps on account of opposition to the policy of the government, he seems to have lost his position and been reduced to the rank of colonel. In 1676, Gov. Berkeley wrote that Maj. Gen. Wood of the council kept to his house through infirmity, but he seems to have recovered as, in March, 1678-79, he was carrying on negotiations with the Indians and arranging for the chief men of the hostile tribes to meet in Jamestown. He died sometime between 1681 and 1686.

Carter, John Sr., was the first of the well known Virginia family of that name to come from England. He settled in Upper Norfolk which he represented in the house of burgesses in March, 1642-43. He was a burgess for Nansemond in Oct., 1649 and for Lancaster from 1654 to 1660. He was justice in Lancaster in 1653 and, at the division of the county on Dec. 13, 1656, he was appointed presiding justice and colonel commandant of Lancaster. In Nov., 1654, the assembly directed that an attack be made upon the Rappahanock Indians and that Maj. John Carter be appointed commander-in-chief. He was elected to the council on March 13, 1657-58, but was not sworn until the assembly adjourned. On March 8, 1659, Gov. Matthews issued an order to the sheriff of Lancaster to arrest Col. John Carter "for contempt of the late commission of Government sent out by his Highness (Cromwell) and the lords of the Council, to appear before the Governor and Council at Jamestown." He was one of the commissioners appointed in 1663, by the governor of Virginia to confer with the commissioners from Maryland as to a restriction of tobacco planting. He was a vestryman of Christ Church Parish in Lancaster and the original church there was built under his direction. The present edifice, one of the finest specimens of colonial architecture standing, was built by the councillor's son, Robert Carter. He died on the 10 of June, 1669, as stated on his tomb in Christ Church.

Horsmanden, Warham, was the son of the

Rev. Daniel Horsmanden D. D., who entered St. John's College, Cambridge, in 1596, and was rector of Ulcomb, Kent. Dr. Horsmanden, a learned and zealous churchman, was deprived of his living in 1643, and in other ways suffered much for the King's cause during the civil wars. He died in 1654, leaving a son, Warham St. Leger Horsmanden, who sailed for Virginia after being, it is said, an officer in the royal army. Col. Horsmanden settled in Charles City county, where he was a justice in 1655, and which he represented in the house of burgesses in March, 1657-58. On March 13, 1657-58, he was elected to the council, but it was ordered that he should not be sworn until the assembly adjourned. His service in the council was brief, for he was again a burgess for Charles City in March, 1658-59. He probably returned to England at the restoration, and in 1683, was living at Purleigh in Essex. His daughter Mary married Col. William Byrd, of Henrico county, Virginia, and has many descendants.

Reade, George, son of Robert Reade of Linkenholt, Southampton, England, came to Virginia in 1637, when a young man or youth. His brother Robert Reade, who was private secretary to Sir William Windebanke, secretary of state in England, seems to have secured for him the patronage of Gov. Harvey and Secretary Richard Kemp, in Virginia, and to have placed him under their care. On March 27, 1637, Jerome Hawley wrote Robert Reade that "at Christmas last," George Reade "had command of some forces sent upon a new plantation, but the design took no effect through the severity of the weather." Upon Nov. 17 of the same year, Gov. Harvey wrote to Robert Reade that his brother was well and was with him, but that he needed supplies that were to be sent to him in charge of Mr. Hawley. The governor added that he hoped to find a very good opportunity to employ young Reade upon a great business he had on hand against a neighboring Indian tribe, strong in people, in which he himself would appear in person. In a letter dated Feb. 26, 1638, from George Reade himself to his brother Robert, he acknowledges many favors from Gov. Harvey and Secretary Kemp, but complains of the conduct of Mr. Hawley towards him. Upon May 17, Jerome Hawley sent Robert Reade an account of "the whole business touching his brother," in which he said that since George Reade's arrival in the colony, he had lived in the governor's house and wanted for nothing. In a letter written on April 4, 1639, Secretary Kemp told Robert Reade that George wished some servants to be sent over to him, but the writer advised that they should await the result of the change of government in Virginia before young Reade should further engage himself in the affairs of the colony. In March of the next year, Kemp, wishing to go to England, requested Secretary Windebanke to get him permission to do so, and promised to make Windebanke's nephew, George Reade, his deputy while he was away, and accordingly, on Aug. 27, 1640, the King in council appointed Reade secretary of state for Virginia during the absence of Kemp. Grateful for the many favors he had received from them, Reade was an earnest adherent of Gov. Harvey and Secretary Kemp during the struggle with the people of Virginia which ended in the expulsion of Harvey, and was doubtless restored to grace when Harvey returned. In 1649, Reade represented James City county in the house of burgesses, and soon after removed to York county where he appears as a justice of the county court in 1652. He was a burgess for York, in Dec., 1656. Upon April 1, 1658, as "Colonel George Reade," the house of burgesses elected him a member of the council, and the same honor was conferred him in March, 1659-60. After the restoration, he was included in the royal commission of councillors and held office until his death. The last mention of his name as present at the council board was on Sept. 10, 1671. Col. George Reade married Elizabeth, daughter of Capt. Nicholas Martiau of York county, and died between Sep. 10 and Nov. 20, 1671. Upon the last named day, his will was proved in the general court, by the oaths of Thomas Reade and Henry Richardson. He was an ancestor of Gen. George Washington and other eminent Virginians. Mary Martiau, a sister of Col. George Reade's wife, married Capt. William Fuller, sometime governor of Maryland.

Warner, Augustine, came to Virginia about 1628, and was a justice of York county. He was burgess for York in 1652, and for Gloucester in 1655. After removing from York county he settled on the Pianketank in the territory of the Chiskiack Indians but afterwards removed to another part of Gloucester county, on the Severn river, where his estate became known as "Warner Hall." He served as member of the council from 1659 to 1667. He was born in 1611, married Mary ———, and died Dec. 24, 1674, leaving issue (1) Sarah, who married Lawrence Townley; (2) Augustine, speaker of the house of burgesses (q. v.).

Elliott, Anthony, first appears in the records in March, 1654-55, when the assembly contracted with him and Mr. Cornelius Lloyd to furnish beef and pork for certain troops which were to be raised for an Indian campaign. Elliott's earliest home was in Elizabeth City county, where on July 24, 1645, he received a grant of 300 acres near Point Comfort creek, which he had bought, Sept. 2, 1643, from Richard Kemp. He represented Elizabeth City in the house of burgesses in Nov., 1647, and was a justice of that county in Feb., 1649. He probably soon after removed to Gloucester, and was burgess from there in March, 1657-58. During that season, on March 13, he was elected a councillor, but it was ordered that he should not be sworn until after the adjournment of the house. Later he removed to that part of Lancaster county now called Middlesex, and was justice of the peace there in 1666. On March 20, 1650, "Mr. Anthony Ellyott" was granted 1,150 acres on North river in "Mojack Bay," Gloucester, and on Jan. 29, 1652, "Lieut. Col. Anthony Ellyott" was granted 200 more acres adjoining the first tract. It is believed that Councillor Anthony Elliott married Frances, sister of Col. John Armistead of Gloucester, and widow of the Rev. Justinian Aylmer. His will was proved in Jan., 1666, in Lancaster county and names sons William, Thomas and Robert.

Walker, John, was a member of the house of burgesses from Warwick county at various times between 1644 and 1656. On March 13, 1657-58, as Lieut. Col. John Walker, he was elected to the council, and again in March, 1659-60. He appears to have moved from Warwick to Gloucester about 1657, and from Gloucester to Rappahannock about 1662. He owned a considerable tract of land through various grants made to him. He died sometime between 1655 and 1658, leaving several daughters, who have descendants in Virginia.

Willis, Francis, was born in the city of Oxford, England, and was a near relative of several persons of his name, members and fellows of the colleges in the university there. He emigrated to Virginia when a young man and was soon appointed clerk of Charles River county. He appears to have been a friend of Sir John Harvey, and when that governor was succeeded by Sir Francis Wyatt, Willis severely denounced the new governor, the council and the house of burgesses for their hostility to Harvey. For this he was condemned in 1640 to lose his offices, to be disbarred from practicing as an attorney, to be fined and imprisoned during the governor's pleasure. His period of misfortune was brief, however, for in two years Wyatt was succeeded by Berkeley, and it is probable that Willis's disabilities were removed. Certain it is that in 1648 he was a justice of York county and in 1652 was one of the first representatives of Gloucester county. He was appointed to a committee for the review of the laws of Virginia in March, 1658-59, and a year later, he also became a councillor and held that office for many years, and even after he had returned to England in 1676. He never returned to Virginia, but died in Kent sometime between 1689 and 1691. He left all his large estates in Virginia to his nephew Francis Willis, son of Henry Willis, and from him descend our Virginia Willises.

Carter, Edward. Lieut. Col. Edward Carter was a burgess for Upper Norfolk in March 1657-58, and again in the following year. He was a councillor in 1659 and seems to have held his seat in the council until 1667, when his name appears as present at a session. He returned, however, to his home "Edmondton," Middlesex county, England, where he died in 1682.

Swann, Thomas, of Swann's Point, Surrey, county, son of William Swann of the same place, was a member of the house of burgesses from James City county, Nov., 1645, and Oct., 1649, and, as Lieut. Col. Thomas Swann, for Surrey, March, 1657-58. He was appointed to the council in 1659 and held that office until his death. He held many civil and military posts in Surry county and seems to have been a very prominent man there. During Bacon's rebellion and the preceding troubles, Col. Swann acted with great moderation. He was opposed to Berkeley's measures and signed the proclamation of April 11, 1676, calling for the election of burgesses to meet in September, but he did not follow Bacon in open opposition to the government, and when Gov. Berkeley refused to entertain the three commissioners sent from England to suppress the rebellion, Swann received them at his house at "Swann's Point," opposite Jamestown and all their meetings were held there. In Dec., 1677, the committee of trade and plantations of the English privy council, directed that Col. Swann be recommended to Gov. Jeffreys for some reward for his kindness and expense in receiving the commissioners at his house after Berkeley had refused. His tomb, with crest and epitaph is at Swann's Point and thereon is recorded the day of his death as the sixteenth of September, "in ye year of our Lord God 1680." The good councillor seems to have had an unusual number of wives even for that marrying day and generation, having been wed no less than five times. He had many descendants; some of them very distinguished.

Whitaker, William, of James City county, was a member of the house of burgesses at the session of Oct., 1649, April, 1652, Nov., 1652, July, 1653, Nov., 1654, Dec., 1656, and March, 1658-59. Soon after the last named session he was appointed to the council, and as "Major

William Whittaker," his name appears in a list of members present, Nov. 29, 1659. He died sometime between March 18, 1662, the date of the last grant of land to him, and Oct. 28, 1666, when "Mr. Richards Whittaker" was granted 135 acres in James City county, 100 acres of which had been given him by "Major William Whittaker, his deceased father." He was probably a near relative of Rev. Alexander Whitaker. He left numerous descendants.

Hammond, Mainwaring, who had been an officer in the royal army during the civil war, came to Virginia early in the year 1650. Col. Henry Norwood, also a cavalier officer, says in his "Voyage to Virginia," that when he landed in York county, Feb. 13, 1650, he found that Capt. Wormeley, of his majesty's council, had "guests at his house feasting and carousing that were lately come from England," and that most of them were of the writer's "intimate acquaintance." These guests were Sir Thomas Lunsford, Sir Henry Chicheley, Col. Philip Honeywood, afterward Sir Philip, and Col. Hammond. So far as the records show, Col. Hammond held no public office until Gov. Berkeley was restored to power in 1660. Soon after his arrival in Virginia, however, he acquired by patent a large tract of land. On March 15, 1649 (probably 1650) "Manwaring Hammond Esq.," was granted "3,760 acres on York River, on the south side called Fort Royall, 600 acres of which he purchased from Captain Marshall, and the remainder of which was due for the transportation of sixty persons to Virginia." On Nov. 11, 1659, as "Col. Mainwaring Hammond," he was granted 600 acres adjoining the above. As soon as Sir William Berkeley was reëlected governor, Hammond, who seems to have been one of his favorites, was brought into the public service. At the session of March, 1659-60, the assembly ordered that "Collonell Mannering Hammond, according to the desire of Sir William Berkeley, Kn't., Governor and Capt. Generall of Virginia, be constituted, authorized and made Major General of Virginia." In Oct., 1660, the governor and assembly employed Maj. Gen. Hammond and Col. Guy Molesworth, another distinguished cavalier officer, to go to England and procure from the King pardon for the Virginians for submitting to the parliamentary authority. In their lack of knowledge as to what might be the policy of the restored royal government, this was no act of mere sycophancy on the part of the colonists, but may have been necessary to secure them from fines or other legal penalties. It was ordered that the two agents should be paid 11,000 pounds of tobacco apiece out of the levies of that year and 11,000 more the next year. It was in 1660 also that Gen. Hammond was appointed to the council, but few references to his services as a member of that body have come down to us. On Feb. 3, 1661, he and Col. Edward Hill sat with the court of Charles City county as itinerant judges, and, on Nov. 6, of the same year, he was present as a councillor. It is likely that he soon after sailed for England and never returned to Virginia. He had a brother in Virginia named Francis Hammond.

Ludwell, Thomas, was son of Thomas Ludwell, of Bruton, in Somersetshire, England, and Jane Cottington, his wife, daughter of James Cottington and niece of Philip, Lord Cottington. His father was church warden of Bruton and steward of the Sexey Hospital in that town. He was born January 25, 1628-

1629, and probably came as a boy to Virginia with Sir William Berkeley, his kinsman, in 1642. He probably returned to England and served in the civil wars on the side of Charles I., as still later in a land grant he is styled "lieutenant."

After the deaths of Richard Kemp and Sir Thomas Lunsford, who married Kemp's widow, he acquired his (Kemp's) residence, near Williamsburg, called "Rich Neck," and on the restoration of Charles I., in 1660, was commissioned secretary of state and became a member of the colonial council. In this capacity he made frequent reports as to the condition of affairs in Virginia to the secretary of state in England, which speak much for his ability. In 1662 he served as escheator under the treasurer Major Henry Norwood, and in 1663 was one of the commissioners to arrange a cessation of tobacco planting with Maryland, which was, however, balked by Lord Baltimore. In 1673 he was appointed as the successor of Henry Randolph sole notary public for the colony and was authorized by the general assembly to appoint deputies in the different counties. In 1675 he was appointed one of three commissioners (Colonel Francis Moryson and Major-General Robert Smith being the other two) to proceed to London and seek an abrogation of the patents granted by Charles II. to Henry Bennett Lord Arlington, Thomas Lord Culpeper and other court favorites of proprietary rights in Virginia. On their arrival they opened negotiations for a charter incorporating the people of Virginia with a view to a purchase of the patents, the prevention of any new grants of the kind, and the assurance of the Virginians of all their liberties, among which was especially emphasized the sole right of taxing themselves. Ludwell probably drafted the papers which presented the views of the commissioners, and in which colonial rights were very fully and ably discussed. The commissioners were at first very successful; a complete charter was granted and passed most of the formalities, but was stopped in the Hamper office by the news of Bacon's rebellion. A new charter was prepared which, though not as full as the first, confirmed the political existence of Virginia as a colony and guaranteed the lands to the people residing in Virginia and to all actual immigrants. The more extensive of the two objectionable grants was surrendered by Lord Arlington to the King for an annual pension of £600. Ludwell was absent in England on this mission, when Bacon's rebellion broke out in Virginia, but returned soon after its close. He did not live long after his return, but died October 1, 1678, and was buried on his estate, "Rich Neck," near the graves of Richard Kemp and Sir Thomas Lunsford. As he never married, his property consisting of this estate and several houses at Jamestown went to his brother Philip, who survived him for many years. In 1674 the parishes of Middletown and Marston were united and named Bruton after the birthplace of Ludwell, the most prominent of the parishioners of Middletown. This parish included Williamsburg.

Beale, Thomas, was, when we first hear of him, a justice of York county and was styled by the records, "Major Thomas Beale." This was in 1652, and in the same year he deeded land in Gloucester to Robert Todd. He was justice of York again in 1661. On Aug. 25, 1662, Beale had become a member of the council and was present at its sessions in Sept., 1667 and April, 1670, on the latter occasion with the title of "Colonel." By letter of Sept. 30, 1668, his majesty recommended to the governor of Virginia, for the post of "Governor of the fort at Point Comfort." Thomas Beale, of whose "ability and prudence the King had had long experience." During Bacon's rebellion, Col. Beale was one of the signers of the proclamation, dated Aug. 11, 1676, calling the election of burgesses for an assembly to meet Sept. 4. York county records show a deed from "Lieut. Col. Thomas Beale" and "Alice his wife." He left a son Capt. Thomas Beale, from whom Gen. R. L. T. Beale, of the confederate army, was descended. This Capt. Beale married Anne Gooch, daughter of Councillor Major William Gooch.

Corbin, Henry, was a member of an ancient family in the counties of Stafford and Warwick in England, and the son of Thomas Corbin of Hall End, Warwickshire, and his wife Winifred, daughter of Gawin Grosvenor of Sutton Colfield in the same county. Henry Corbin was born, according to a deposition, about 1629, and came to Virginia in 1654. There is an old family tradition which his residence in England makes probable, that he assisted Charles II. in his escape after Worcester. Upon his arrival in Virginia, Corbin seems to have at once settled in that part of Lancaster county that is now Middlesex, and to have made his home there through life. Upon June 5, 1657, the governor and council directed that Henry Corbin should be of the quorum in the court of Lancaster. He remained a justice of Lancaster until the formation of Middlesex, and then became a member of the court of the new county. He was a burgess from Lancaster in 1659 and 1660, and at the same time was collector of customs for his district. He was a councillor in 1663, in which year he was appointed one of the commissioners on the part of Virginia to treat with Maryland with regard to the cessation of tobacco culture. He was frequently present at the meetings of the council until his death, Jan. 8, 1676. Col. Henry Corbin acquired a great landed estate, his chief residence being "Buckingham House" in Middlesex county. He married Alice, daughter of Richard Eltonhead, of Eltonhead, Lancashire, and widow of Rowland Burnham of Middlesex, Virginia. The date of this marriage has been given as July 5, 1645, but 1655 is evidently intended. He has many descendants in Virginia and the south.

Smith, Robert. If one may judge by the high military rank attained by Robert Smith in the colony, it seems probable that he had been an officer in the English army before coming to America. The first appearance of his name in the extant records, is as a member of the council in 1663, but it is quite possible that he may have been appointed to that body at the restoration. He soon became a man of prominence and was appointed one of the three major generals in the militia. As "Major General Robert Smith," he was present in council in March, 1666, and on July 10, of the same year, when an attack from a Dutch fleet was expected. The governor and council ordered Maj. Gen. Robert Smith to demand and seize all ammunition in the hands of any one in the colony. On July 12, he was appointed one of the commissioners on the part of Virginia to treat with Maryland concerning the culture of tobacco. He is recorded as being present at meetings of the council as late as 1671, and not long after this, must have been sent to England as the colony's agent, as on July 2, 1673, he is referred to as the agent of Virginia and authorized by the assembly to purchase as many shares as possible in the patent for the Northern Neck, which the King had granted. In 1674, he, together with Francis Moryson and Thomas Ludwell, was appointed an agent for Virginia to secure from the King a repeal of his grant of Virginia to Lords Arlington and Culpeper, and a new charter. The charter which they attempted to gain, and which embodied the ideas of the colonists as to their rights, was a splendid document and included among other provisions the prophetic stipulation that the Virginians, in common with all Englishmen, should not be taxed without their own consent. Unfortunately for the efforts of the agents, the news of Bacon's rebellion reached England just as the King seemed ready to sign the charter and served him as an excuse for withholding it. He withdrew his grant of the colony to the two noblemen, however, so that the colony were much beholden to their agents' efforts. After his return to the colony, he played a prominent part in the suppression of the "plant cutting" insurrection and continued to be present at the meetings of the council until 1683, after which he seems to have visited England. His only daughter Elizabeth married Harry Beverley.

Stegg, Thomas, Jr., was a son of the first Thomas Stegg, councillor, a sketch of whose life appears above. The earliest fact mentioned of the younger Stegg is that he was a justice of the peace of Charles City in 1661. On Nov. 24, 1664, a commission from the King confirming Thomas Stegg's appointment as auditor general was read in court. He was a member of the council in 1666 and died in 1670. His sister, Grace Stegg, was mother of the first William Byrd of Westover.

Bland, Theodorick, the ninth son of John Bland, an eminent merchant of London and member of the Virginia Company, was born on Jan. 16, 1629. He was a merchant at St. Lucar, Spain, in 1646, at the Canary Islands in 1647-48, and came to Virginia in 1654 as the representative of his father, who had large interests in the colony. He settled at Berkeley Hundred, Charles City county, and in 1659-60 he represented Henrico in the house of burgesses, of which he was the speaker. By instructions from England, dated Sept. 2, 1662, the act passed by the assembly, imposing two shillings per hogshead on all tobacco from Virginia, was confirmed and "Theodorick Bland, Esq." was appointed collector of the same. A few years later Bland was appointed a member of the council, and was present June 21, 1665, July 10, 1666, and March and April, 1670. On April 17, 1665, Theodorick Bland bought "Westover," Charles City county, an estate of 1,200 acres, for £170 sterling. His grandson, Richard Bland of "Jordan's," who says that his grandfather was "both in fortune and understanding, inferior to no person of his time in the country," also says that he built and gave to the county and parish the church at Westover, "with ten acres of land, a courthouse and prison." This may have been so, but it is more likely that he only gave the land. The worthy councillor died on April 23, 1671, and was buried in the chancel of Westover church. The church has long since disappeared but the tomb remains with his arms and the following epitaph:

S. M.
"Prudentis & Eruditi Theodorici
Bland Armig. qui obijt Aprilis
23d A. D. 1671 Aetatis 41
Cujus Vidua Maestissima Anna
Filia Richard Bennett Armig:
hoc Marmor Posuit."

Theodorick Bland married Anne, daughter of Gov. Richard Bennett. She married secondly, Col. St. Ledger Codd, and died Nov., 1687, at Wharton's Creek, Maryland. He was ancestor of Richard Bland, the great Virginia patriot of 1776.

Cary, Miles, son of John Cary, a merchant of Bristol, England, was born about 1620, and came to Virginia, it is believed, about 1645. He settled in Warwick county and lived at a place called "Magpie Swamp." His landed estate embraced about 2,000 acres, well stocked and having upon it numerous slaves, a store, mill etc. Cary was a collector of customs in March, 1658-59 and in 1663, and as "Col. Miles Cary," he was a member of the house of burgesses from Warwick county in March 1659-60. He was afterwards added to the council and was present at the meetings of that body June 21, 1665, and March 28 and July 10, 1666. He was doubtless still a councillor at the time of his death, June 11, 1667, when he is said to have been killed while defending the fort at Old Point against the Dutch. Lieut.-Col. Miles Cary married Anne, daughter of Thomas Taylor, a burgess from Warwick county. Many persons in Virginia and the south are descended from him.

Bridger, Joseph, the subject of this sketch, was born in 1628, and in March, 1657-58, he represented Isle of Wight in the house of burgesses, as also in 1663. The following year, he was one of the commissioners to decide upon the boundary line between Virginia and Maryland, and on July 12, 1666, he was one of the commissioners to treat with Maryland upon the subject of tobacco culture, and in the same year he is mentioned as a member of the general assembly with the title of adjutant general Bridger. In 1670, he was sworn a member of the council and was present at meetings in 1674. There seems to have been some question of his eligibility for membership, however, for in a list of the councillors made for the lord of trades and plantations, the name of Joseph Bridger is marked "query," and their lordships stated that they would inquire further into the ability and deserts of Col. Joseph Bridger to be of the council. The King, however, on March 14, 1678-79, directed that Joseph Bridger be continued in the council, and he is mentioned as a councillor as late as 1683. In 1675, Col. Bridger took part in the Indian wars, and in the year following, was described by Nat. Bacon, as one of Berkeley's "wicked and pernicious councillors." During Bacon's rebellion, Gov. Berkeley gave to Col. Bridger the command of "all the country south of James River." In 1680, he was commander-in-chief of the militia forces raised "so as to be ready for the Indians" in Isle of Wight, Surry, Nansemond and Lower Norfolk. In 1683, Lord Culpeper appointed him his deputy in the office of vice-admiral. Gen. Joseph Bridger died on April 15, 1686. He had acquired a very large landed estate in Isle of Wight county besides grants in Surry and James City counties and in Maryland. He has numerous descendants.

Ballard, Thomas, was born in 1630 and came to Virginia in or before 1652, at which date he was clerk of York county. In 1666, he represented James City in the house of burgesses and on July 12 of the same year was appointed one of the commissioners to treat with Maryland regarding tobacco culture. He was sworn a member of the council in 1670 and was present at sessions in 1670, 1672 and 1675. He was included among Berkeley's "wicked and pernicious councillors" in the proclamation of Nat. Bacon in 1676, which seems rather hard upon Ballard, as he was denounced by the opposite party as "a fellow of turbulent and mutinous speech and Bacon's chief trumpet, parasite &c.," and ultimately lost his seat in the council on account of his sympathy with and furtherance of the rebellion. In Aug., 1676, Col. Ballard issued warrants for pressing men and provisions for Bacon's service and on Aug. 11, he signed the petition calling for the election of burgesses for an assembly to meet Sept. 4, of that year. On June 11, 1677, Gov. Jeffreys wrote Secretary Williamson that he had suspended Ballard from the council and a collectorship, and on Feb. 10, 1678-79, the board of trade and plantations directed that Col. Ballard be put out of the council. Ballard continued to be a prominent figure in the colony, however, and in 1680, was speaker of the house of burgesses. His case as a creditor of "Bacon the Rebel" was represented to the King by the council in 1686. Ballard's wife, Anna ———, was one of the ladies of the council placed by Bacon upon the breastworks before Jamestown, to delay Berkeley's attack until he could complete his defences. He has many descendants.

Chicheley, Sir Henry. Governor of Virginia. (q. v.).

Jenings, Peter, represented Gloucester in the house of burgesses in March, 1659-60, prior to which date, nothing is known of him. He was again a burgess from Gloucester in 1663 and 1666, he was appointed one of the commissioners to treat with Maryland concerning the cessation of tobacco culture. He was sworn a member of the council on June 20, 1670, and on September 15 of the same year was commissioned attorney general of Virginia by the King and reappointed to the council. He died in or before 1671.

Spencer, Nicholas. President of the council and acting governor (q. v.).

Pate, John, of Gloucester county, was the nephew and administrator of Richard Pate who patented 1,154 acres of land on the north side of York river, and who represented Gloucester in the house of burgesses in 1653 and died in 1657. Col. John Pate was appointed a justice of Gloucester in the year of 1660 and took the oaths as a councillor, according to one account, in 1670, and according to another, on Sept. 27 of the year following. It is recorded that in 1672, "John Pate, Esq., dying possessed of a considerable estate in this country, and his wife being out of the country, Mr. Thomas Pate, his brother's son," had been appointed administrator. The Pate family is a well known one in Virginia.

Bray, James, of James City county, was living in Virginia as early as 1666, and, on April 15, 1670, was sworn a member of the council. He retained his seat until 1676, when during Bacon's rebellion, he seems to have been an active supporter of Gov. Berkeley. He signed the proclamation of Aug. 11, 1676, calling an assembly to meet in the following September. The commissioners sent to suppress the rebellion reported, on Dec. 6, 1677, that Mr. James Bray was a great loser in his estate by that uprising, but they were evidently not favorably disposed towards him, for the English board of trade and Plantations, on Dec. 6, 1677, pronounced him to be a "rash and fiery fellow," and, on Feb. 10, 1678-79, the same body directed that he be put out of the council. He was too friendly to Berkeley to suit the tastes of the royal commissioners. His wife, Mistress Angelica Bray, will always be remembered as one of the "guardian angels of the rebel camp," as the ladies whom Bacon stood in front of his men at Jamestown to protect them while they were throwing up fortifications, were called. Her maiden name is not known. Col. Bray was a wealthy merchant and ship owner in Virginia. He died Oct. 24, 1691. He had three sons who left issue and a grandson, Col. David Bray, who was also councillor for a few months.

Parke, Daniel, Sr., was descended from the Parke family of Essex, England, some account of which, tracing it back to 1486, is given in Morant's "History of Essex." The councillor's epitaph states that he was of the county of Essex, and his son, in his will, mentions certain plate bearing the arms of his family, "which is that of the county of Essex." Daniel Parke Sr. was born about 1629 and settled in York county, Virginia, in or before 1651. He was justice of York in 1655, sheriff in 1659, and a burgess from 1660 to 1670. On June 20, 1670, he was sworn as a member of the council and remained a member of that body until his death, nine years later. On Sept. 30, 1678, Gov. Jeffreys appointed him secretary of state and he held for a time the office of treasurer also. He married Rebecca, widow of "Bartholomew Knipe of Virginia, gentleman," as may be seen from a deed to his stepson, Christopher Knipe, dated 1658. This widow Knipe was a daughter of George Evelyn of Maryland and formerly of Godstone, Surrey, England. He left a son Daniel Parke Jr., who was also a member of the council.

Bacon, Nathaniel, known as "the Rebel," came to Virginia in 1673 and was made a member of the council in 1675. He was a cousin of Lord Francis Bacon and a cousin once removed of Nathaniel Bacon Sr., president of the council and acting governor (q. v.). His father was Thomas Bacon, a merchant of London, and he was born in England, January 2, 1647. In 1663 he went abroad with Sir Philip Skippon and others. He owned lands in England of the yearly value of £150 sterling, but on his marriage with Elizabeth Duke, daughter of Sir Edward Duke, of Benhill Lodge, near Saxmundham, he sold his lands to Sir Robert Jason for £1,200 and removed to Virginia. He purchased a plantation at "Curls," in Henrico county, called "Longfield," and had a quarter at the falls of the river where Richmond now stands. The colony was in a state of unrest, owing to high taxes and many corruptions in the public offices; and a sudden irruption on the frontiers of the Indians, which Governor Berkeley was slow in repressing, fanned the smouldering embers into flames. Urged by his neighbors, Bacon asked Berkeley for a commission to go out against the Indians, which he refused, and Bacon went out without one. Berkeley then proclaimed him a rebel, and out of this arose a civil war in which Bacon supported by the great majority of the people possessed himself of the main authority and drove Berkeley to seek refuge at "Arlington" on the eastern shore with Major-General John Custis. Jamestown was burned, and many estates were pillaged by both factions.

At length Bacon, through his exposures, contracted a dysentery, and the rebellion virtually came to an end through his death in Gloucester county at Major Pate's place, on Poropotank Creek, October 26, 1676. He left two daughters, one of whom Elizabeth, born April 12, 1674, married Hugh Chamberlain, physician to the King. Bacon's widow, Elizabeth Duke, married (second) Thomas Jarvis, a ship captain, who had 200 acres at Hampton, and after his death she married Edward Mole. In 1698 William Randolph patented "Longfield" and the slashes adjoining which had escheated to the King from Bacon because of his rebellion, and these lands descended to William Randolph's son, Richard Randolph, who was known as Richard Randolph, of "Curls." Bacon's rebellion is the most spectacular episode in all colonial history, and its leader will always be an interesting historical figure. He had good looks, a commanding manner, and remarkable eloquence, which made him the idol of his followers.

Bowler, Thomas, of Rappahannock county, was a merchant and appears in the records of Rappahannock county in 1663, and on Sept. 29, of the year following, "Mr. Thomas Bowler" was appointed a justice of Rappahannock county and took the usual oath. He was sworn a member of the council, Oct. 9, 1675 and died in 1679. He left many descendants in Virginia.

Cole, William, of "Bolthorpe," Warwick county, Virginia, was born in 1638. His first appearance in public life, so far as the records show, was on March 1, 1674-75, when he was appointed a member of the council, an office he held until his death. He was one of the persons denounced by Bacon in 1676, as one of Berkeley's evil advisers, and, of course, the commissioners sent to suppress Bacon's rebellion described him as "a very honest gentleman" and a member of the council who was all along constant to the governor and with him in all his troubles. In Oct., 1689, the president and council of Virginia wrote to England that on the death of the secretary, Spencer, in September, they had had appointed Col. William Cole to be secretary of the state of Virginia, and begged royal confirmation. This was given by commission, dated Jan. 17, 1690, and in it Cole is spoken of as a person of "known integrity and ability to execute the office." On Aug. 1, 1690, he wrote to Lord Nottingham, thanking him for the appointment. He did not hold the office long, however, for on April 15, 1692, he stated in a petition to Gov. Nicholson, that he had been one of the council of Virginia for about seventeen years, and had been appointed secretary of state; that lately he had become much "decayed" in body and strength, and by reason of a deep melancholy that had seized him, he found himself daily growing worse, and that he was "desirous to live a retired life and to serve God Almighty the small remainder of the time he had to live," and so prayed that a secretary might be appointed, and that he, the petitioner, might obtain his majesty's discharge. The request was granted. Councillor Cole died, March 4, 1694. His tomb, with his arms and an epitaph remains at his former seat, Bolthorpe, Warwick county. He is represented by many descendants in Virginia.

Place, Rowland, was living in Virginia as early as 1671, when he owned land in Charles City and near the falls of James river in Henrico county. It was on Oct. 9, 1675, that he was first sworn to the council and he continued to serve for several years. He was present as a member in March, 1678, but soon afterwards went to England, evidently with the intention of only making a visit there, though he afterwards seems to have changed his mind, for he never after returned to Virginia. William Sherwood, writing to Secretary Williamson, July 1, 1678, says that his letter will be carried by "Col. Rowland Place, a member of the council," who can give "an ample account of matters in Virginia," and, on July 10, 1678, Gov. Lord Culpeper wrote a letter which he stated he would confide to Col. Place, who had been an eye witness of many of the events of chief interest which had lately occurred in the colony. On Dec. 13, 1678, Francis Moryson wrote to William Blathwayt that he had "advice" that Col. Place had lately arrived in England from Virginia, and that the colonel was "one of the Council and a very honest gentleman." On March 14, 1678-79, the King directed that Place should be continued in the council, but on May 20 Capt. Rudge, of the ship "'Hopewell' just come from Virginia," appeared before the committee of trade and plantations, and stated, among other things, that the Indians had recently killed several people and totally ruined the plantation of Col. Place, who was in England. Perhaps it was this news that caused Place to linger abroad. He was included in the commission of councillors under Lord Culpeper, read on May 10, 1680, but still did not return to Virginia, and on Dec. 12, 1681, Gov. Culpeper wrote that he had appointed a councillor "in the room of Col. Rowland Place," who was "living in England." He was the son of Francis Place, the celebrated painter of York, and Ann Williamson, his wife. He married Priscilla, daughter of Sir John Brookes, of Norton, county York, baronet. He was born 1642 and died 1713 (see "Familiæ Minorum Gentium," vol. iii, p. 921).

Lee, Richard, Jr., was the second son of Richard Lee, the immigrant, and Anna, his wife, and the eldest son to leave male descendants in Virginia. He was born in 1647, probably at "Paradise," in Gloucester county, but afterwards went to Westmoreland and made his home at "Mount Pleasant," on the Potomac river. He was sent to England to be educated and became a student at Oxford. One of his grandsons wrote of him that "he was so clever that some great men offered to promote him to the highest dignities in the Church if his father would let him stay in England; but this offer was refused, as the old Gentleman was determined to fix all his children in Virginia. * * * Richard spent almost his whole life in study, and usually wrote his notes in Greek, Hebrew or Latin * * * so that he neither diminished nor improved his paternal estate. * * * He was of the Council in Virginia and also other offices of honor and profit, though they yielded little to him." In the proclamation made by "Nat Bacon," the rebel, concerning the grievances of "ye Commonality" against the royalist. Gov. Berkeley, Richard Lee is mentioned as one of the governor's "wicked and pernicious councell" who were commanded to surrender or be seized as "Trayters to ye King and Country." The official report to the English government regarding those who had suffered by Bacon's rebellion, made in March, 1677-78, described "Major Richard Lee" as "a Loyall, Discreet Person worthy of the Place to which hee was lately advanced of being one of his Majesties Council in Virginia." The second Richard Lee was a burgess in 1677 and perhaps earlier. He was a councillor in 1676, 1680-83, 1688, 1692-98 and possibly later. In 1691, out of a scruple of conscience arising from his attachment to the Stuarts and refusal to acknowledge the claim of William and Mary to the crown, Richard Lee, together with Isaac Allerton and John Armistead, refused to take the oaths, and he was therefore dropped from the council. In the following year, however, his name again appears on the records as a member of that body. According to a list of colonial officers, dated June 8, 1699, "Richard Lee, Esqr.," had been appointed by "Sir Edm.: Andros, Governor, &c., to be naval Officer and Receiver of Virginia Dutys for the River Potomac, in which is included Westmoreland, Northumberland and Stafford Counties." In 1680 he was spoken of as "Coll. Richard Lee, of the horse in ye Counties of Westmoreland, Northumberland and Stafford." It was probably sometime in the year 1674 that Col. Lee married Laetitia, eldest daughter of Henry and Alice (Eltonhead) Corbin. She was buried beside him in the family burying ground at "Mt. Pleasant," beneath a white marble tombstone bearing an elaborate Latin inscription. Col. Lee died on March 12, 1714.

Warner, Augustine, Jr., of Warner Hall, Gloucester county, son of Col. Augustine Warner, of the same place, and member of the council, was born, according to his epitaph, on July 3, 1642, but, according to the register of Merchant Taylor's School, London, on Oct. 20, 1643. His name appears on the books of that school as "eldest son of Agustine Warner of Virginia, gentleman." Warner was the speaker of the house of burgesses at the sessions of March, 1675-76, and Feb., 1776-77, and soon after the latter date must have been appointed to the council, for his name appears in a list of members presented to the lords of trade and plantations late in 1677, and was endorsed by them with the word "stet." On March 14, 1678-79, the King directed that he be continued a member of the council, and in a new commission, read May 10, 1680, his name appears as "Col. Augustine Warner." In this year he commanded the militia of Gloucester county. Col. Warner suffered great loss during Bacon's rebellion. The commissioners sent to suppress the uprising declared that "Col. Augustine Warner, Speaker of the House of Burgesses in the late Assembly, and now sworn as one of his Majesty's Council in Virginia," was "an honest, worthy person, and most loyal sufferer by the late rebels," that he was "plundered as much as any, and yet speaks as little of his losses, though they were very great." But the colonel did speak, and spoke with effect in regard to his losses. On June 27, 1678, he presented a petition to Thomas Ludwell, the president of the council, praying for a judgment against Capt. William Byrd, against whom he had brought his action in the general court for £1,000 sterling and costs of suit, for "forcibly entering his dwelling house in Abbington Parish, Gloucester, and taking goods and merchandise to the value of 845.2." Col. Augustine Warner Jr. married, about 1665, Mildred, daughter of Col. George Reade, of Gloucester, himself a councillor, and formerly deputy secretary of state. He died June 19, 1681, and his tomb may still be seen at "Warner Hall."

Leigh, Francis, as "Major Francis Leigh," was included under the great seal for a court of oyer and terminer in Virginia on Nov. 16, 1676, and on March 14, 1678-79, the King directed that he be continued in the council. Upon May 10, 1680, he was included in the commission of councillors under Culpeper. Nothing further is known of him, but he was doubtless ancestor of the family of Leigh in King and Queen county.

Custis, John, a son of John and Jeane Custis, of Accomac, Va., and formerly of Rotterdam, Holland, was born in 1630. He was sheriff of Accomac in 1664, and in 1676 he was appointed major-general of Virginia militia, and played an active part in the support of Gov. Berkeley during Bacon's rebellion. The commissioners, sent from England to suppress the rebellion, spoke in terms of the highest commendation of him. He was a member of the house of burgesses in 1677, but appears to have been immediately afterwards appointed to the council, as he was present at meetings of that body from 1677 to 1683. At this later date his health became very bad and he was unable to attend for sometime. His illness, indeed, was so serious and long continued that in England he was reported dead and his name left out of the commission to the councillors of 1685. He therefore prepared a petition setting forth his various services to the colony and praying to be restored to the council, which was forthwith done. He continued active up to 1690, but, his health again failing, he prepared, two years later, another petition asking to be relieved of all his public offices. This was also granted and the few remaining years of his life he spent in retirement at "Arlington," his house in the present Northampton county. He died on the 9th of Jan., 1696, according to the inscription on his tomb at "Arlington."

Meese, Henry, as "Colonel Henry Meese," received a grant of 2,000 acres of land in Stafford county on June 7, 1666, and, as "Lieut. Col. Henry Meese," he was, in the year following, a member of the Northern Neck committee. On March 14, 1678-79, the King ordered that Meese be added to the council, and his commission was dated May 10, 1680, but on Dec. 12, 1681, Lord Culpeper wrote that he had appointed a councillor in the place of Col. Henry Meese, who was living in England. It appears from the letters of William Fitzhugh that his wife survived him and made England her home. There is some reason to believe that he left a daughter Grace, who married Charles Ashton, of Northumberland county, Virginia, ancestor of the well-known family of that name.

Page, John, the progenitor of the Page family of Virginia, was a member of the English house of that name, a branch of "the Pages of Harrow on the Hill" of Middlesex, England. He was born in 1627 and came to Virginia about 1650. Of the earlier years of his life in Virginia, save that he acquired a considerable tract of land given in reward for services in transporting persons into the colony, very little is known, but 1657 he represented York county in the house of burgesses. The commissioners to suppress Bacon's rebellion reported that "Major John Page was a great loser in his estate by the rebellion." On Dec. 12, 1681, Lord Culpeper wrote to the authorities in England that he had appointed "Colonel John Page of the Assembly to be councillor." He was present at meetings of the council as late as 1689. In 1686 he was appointed, together with Nicholas Spencer and Philip Ludwell to revise and annotate the laws of the colony. On Oct. 15, 1691, the privy council in England ordered that Col. John Page, who had been thought to be dead, and for that reason omitted from the last nomination of members of the council, should be "restored to his place and presidency in the said Council of Virginia." Col. Page was a man of pious life and took a great interest in the welfare of his parish. It was he who gave the land and twenty pounds in money towards building the old Williamsburg church, which is still in a good state of preservation. A fine collection of portraits, representing members of this family, including Col. John Page, is to be seen in the library of William and Mary College.

Beverley, Robert, was a descendant of an old English family of Yorkshire, which had been staunch in its support of the King during the civil war. Robert Beverley himself growing up with strong royalist proclivities. He was probably a native of the town of Beverley and, coming to Virginia about 1663, settled in Middlesex county, of which he was a justice in 1673. He rapidly attained great prominence in colonial affairs and was one of the most popular men of his period with the rank and file of the colonists. The situation at the time was a peculiar one. In 1670 Beverley had been elected clerk of the house of burgesses and soon became the leader of the majority of that body, and it was they who, at the outbreak of Bacon's rebellion, were, with the Ludwells and Thomas Ballard in the council, the strongest supporters of Gov. Berkeley in his efforts to suppress the uprising. It seems surprising that the popular house with their chosen leader should have been so strong in support of the governor and that the only effective aid which the rebels received should have come from members of the aristocratic council. Beverley himself was very active in the field against Bacon's followers, and, in 1676, Berkeley appointed him commander of all his forces, and finally a member of the council. Upon the arrival of the commissioners, sent from England to suppress the rebellion, there was introduced another element into the dispute. Gov. Berkeley, resenting the intrusion of these strangers to the colony, was not disposed to yield any of his authority or prerogatives to them or to aid them in their task, and in this he was again strongly supported by the house of burgesses under Beverley's leadership, who, with the governor, were disposed to regard the commissioners as interlopers. Beverley thus incurred the enmity of those who were later to possess the authority in the colony, and especially of Jeffreys, soon to be the governor. Beverley was accused to the commissioners of plundering during his activities against Bacon, but Berkeley was able to save him from punishment for the time. During the governorship of Chicheley, however, Beverley was accused of inciting the rioting tobacco planters and was imprisoned on shipboard. He escaped a number of times, but was recommitted, while other charges were trumped up against him by his powerful enemies and carried to England. Gov. Culpeper, being at that time in England, the King directed him, upon returning to Virginia, to put Beverley out of all his public offices. He was finally released from prison upon his humbly asking pardon for his past offences and giving security for his future good behavior. His popularity had not waned in the meantime and the house of burgesses immediately elected him their clerk. But with Beverley's sturdy independence of spirit, position could only be the prelude of misfortune. The creatures of King James were now securely intrenched in their hold on the colony, and the only power with the inclination to resist them was the house of burgesses. The opportunity soon came, for at the session next following Beverley's reëlection the governor and council made the illegal request of the assembly to be empowered to levy a tax upon the colony. This the house at once and firmly refused, and, according to Gov. Effingham, even disputed the right of the King himself to use the veto. Beverley seems to have been a leader in this action and thus incurred the anger of the throne, which ordered him to be disabled from holding any public office and prosecuted to the full extent of the law as Effingham should deem advisable. It is illustrative of the fact that the political questions of that time were by no means simple, that the same man should have been at once a royalist and a champion of the people, and, furthermore, that the democratic Beverley should have so strongly opposed the popular uprising, and the loyal Beverley stood against the unjust usurpation of the King. It is also a high tribute to his courage and uprightness of purpose. He did not long survive his final political downfall, but died about March 16, 1687, leaving several sons of position and distinction, Robert Beverley, who wrote the history of Virginia, being one.

Kemp, Matthew, was a son of Edmund Kemp, of Lancaster county, a fact set forth in a grant to him of 1100 acres of land on Piankctank. He lived at first in Lancaster, then including Middlesex, and was justice and sheriff of that county in 1659. On Nov. 15, 1660, a certificate was granted by Lancaster county court to Matthew Kemp for the importation of certain head-rights, among whom were himself twice mentioned and his wife Dorothy. Later in life Col. Matthew Kemp removed to Gloucester county, which he represented in the house of burgesses. In 1676 Bacon, in his proclamation, included him among Gov. Berkeley's "wicked and pernicious councillors, aiders and assistants against the Commonality." The commissioners, sent to suppress the rebellion, however, regarding his character from their point of view, speak of him as a gentleman of an honest, loyal family, a very deserving person and a great sufferer at the hands of the rebels. In the years 1678 and 1679 Kemp was speaker of the house of burgesses, and on Dec. 12, 1681, he had recently been appointed by the governor a member of the council while still a burgess. He was county lieutenant of Gloucester, and on May 8, 1682, Gov. Chicheley wrote to the King that he had dispatched Col. Kemp, with orders, to raise horse and foot and suppress riotous "plant cutters." This he soon succeeded in doing, making a number of arrests. He died in 1683. There is hardly any doubt that Edmund Kemp was a grandson of Robert Kemp, of Gissing county, Norfolk, England, and nephew of Sir Robert Kemp, baronet.

Byrd, William, Sr., the founder of the distinguished Byrd family of "Westover," Virginia, was born about 1649, in London. He was the son of John Byrd, a London goldsmith and a descendant of an old Cheshire family. The date of his coming to Virginia is not known, but it must have been as very young man, as it is recorded that on Oct. 27, 1673, he was granted 1200 acres of land lying on the James river and Shokoe creek. He quickly assumed a prominent place in colonial affairs and was implicated in the matter of Bacon's rebellion. He was a near neighbor and adherent of Bacon in the early stages of his opposition, but it seems that he took no part in the actual rebellion and in all probability made his peace with Berkeley. He was accused by Col. Augustine Warner, after the rebellion, of having entered his house at the head of some of Bacon's men and plundered his estate to the value of £1,000 sterling, and Warner actually obtained judgment against him for the amount, but the end of the dispute is unknown and Byrd claimed that, at the time of the plundering, he was himself a prisoner in Bacon's hands. In a letter from his wife, written sometime before the rebellion to a friend in England, she speaks of the country as being well pleased with all that Bacon had done and remarks that she believed the council was, too, "so far as they durst show it." In the year 1695 Col. Byrd was alluded to as having been a member of the council for fifteen years, but the earliest record of him in this position, appearing in the official records, is in 1681, when he was appointed by Lord Culpeper. On Dec. 4, 1687, James II. ordered that he be sworn to the office of auditor-general of Virginia, in place of Col. Nathaniel Bacon, the elder. There was a dispute between him and one Robert Ayleway, who claimed to have been properly appointed to the place, but Col. Byrd is mentioned as holding the office as late as the year 1703. Col. Byrd was one of the gentlemen appointed by the general assembly to form the first board of trustees of the newly chartered William and Mary College, and he was one of the four councillors sent to England by Gov. Andros against the charges of Commissary Blair. Upon his return from a trip to England he brought with him the copy made for the Earl of Southampton of the minutes of the Virginia Company, which he placed in the famous Westover Library. This library, commenced by him, was added to by his son and grandson, until it became the largest in America at the time. The records of the Virginia Company furnished most of the material for William Smith's "History of Virginia." They are now in the Congressional Library at Washington. In April, 1679, the general assembly passed an act granting to Capt. William Byrd a tract of land extending five miles along the James river on both sides and three miles wide and which included nearly all the ground now occupied by the cities of Richmond and Manchester. The act was later vetoed by the King, but Byrd was still granted a large area, nearly 42,000 acres in all. He carried on an extensive trade with the Indians and at one time petitioned the exclusive right to the Indian trade in Virginia. He was sent on a number of occasions to treat with the Indians and on one of these trips went as far north as New York and Albany. He died at Westover, his residence on James river, Dec. 4, 1701.

Wormeley, Christopher, the second of that name to become councillor, was related to the Wormeleys of "Rosegill," Middlesex county, but the exact relationship is unknown. He is first mentioned in an order of court of Lancaster county, then including Middlesex, dated Nov. 9, 1666, which refers to Capt. Christopher Wormeley and his wife, who was the widow of Col. Anthony Elliott. In the next year he was a justice of Lancaster, in 1674 a justice of Middlesex, the colonel of the county militia in 1680, and sheriff of the county in 1681. It was in 1682 that he was appointed to the council, a member of which body he remained during the rest of his life. He held also the offices of collector and naval officer of the lower Potomac district, and deputy escheator. Col. Wormeley had taken the part of Gov. Berkeley in Bacon's rebellion, and was accordingly denounced in the proclamation of the rebel leader and commended by the commissioners appointed to suppress the same. He died in 1701.

Lear, John, probably came to Virginia about 1656, as in that year he had a grant of 100 acres of land on the "Oquiah River, in Westmoreland County." He soon removed to Nansemond county, which he represented in the house of burgesses from 1666 to 1676. During Bacon's rebellion, he was a staunch supporter of Gov. Berkeley, and remained with him until the rebellion was suppressed. He was the first to meet the commissioners, sent to suppress the rebellion, and give them an account of the condition of affairs, and by them was reported to have suffered heavily during the trouble. In 1676 a petition was sent the commissioners from some of the people of Nansemond county, complaining of the number of offices held by Col. John Lear and Mr. David Lear, probably his brother, the first of whom was county clerk, escheat master, notary public and surveyor, and the other "Sheriff superior." As relating to Col. Lear, remonstrance seems to have had no effect, for in 1680 he was presiding justice and colonel of militia. On May 23, 1683, Gov. Culpeper appointed him a member of the council, and the nomination was confirmed by the King. He continued in this office until his death. He was also one of the first trustees of William and Mary College in 1693, and, at the time of his death, was collector of the lower districts of James river. His death occurred in Nov. or Dec., 1695.

Allerton, Isaac, son of Isaac Allerton, one of the Puritan leaders of the "Mayflower" expedition, and his wife Fear, daughter of William Brewster, was born in Plymouth, Mass., in 1630, and graduated at Harvard College in 1650. He is said to have been, for a time, associated with his father in the business of trading between Plymouth, New Haven and New Amsterdam, but it is possible that during most of the time between his graduation and his father's death, in 1659, he was his representative in Virginia. As early as Feb. 6, 1650, there was recorded a dispute between the Indians and a Mr. Allerton, regarding a plantation which the latter had cleared, which reached the governor and council. It is believed that this refers to the elder Isaac Allerton, but it may be that immediately after leaving college the son established a plantation in Virginia. He appears to have made his first permanent residence in Virginia about 1660, and soon became a man of prominence. In 1663 he was sworn a justice of Northumberland. In 1675, with the rank of major, he was second in command to Col. John Washington, of the Virginia troops sent against the Indians. In the campaign which followed they allied themselves with the Maryland forces at the latter's invitation in the siege of an Indian fort, but before the opening of hostilities a horrible murder was committed by the Marylanders in the shooting of five Indian chiefs who had come to negotiate peace. This was done against the earnest opposition of Washington and Allerton, but caused such indignation on the part of the Virginia authorities that an investigation of their conduct was ordered, which, however, cleared them of all responsibility for the crime. Allerton was burgess for Westmoreland in 1676-77, and for Northumberland for a number of years between 1668 and 1677. In 1680 and 1688 he was escheator of Westmoreland with the rank of colonel, and prior to Sept. 25, 1683, he was appointed to the council. His occupation of the position at this time seems to have been only temporary, as in 1686-87 Secretary Spencer, acting governor, wrote, that he had called Col. Isaac Allerton to the council in Col. Ludwell's place. A little later King James wrote that Col. Allerton was to be sworn as a member of the council in Col. Ludwell's place, the royal favor being accounted for on the statement that Allerton was either a Catholic or inclined to that faith. He was present at sessions of the council regularly until 1691, when he refused, as did Armistead and Lee, to take the oath of allegiance to the new sovereigns, William and Mary. He was probably not formally dropped until 1693, when the governor wrote that Col. Allerton, of the council, was very old and had retired. His death occurred sometime in 1702.

Armistead, John, a son of William Armistead, of Elizabeth City county, and grandson of Anthony Armistead, of Kirk Deighton, in Yorkshire, England, settled in Gloucester county, of which he was sheriff in 1676, and a justice and lieutenant-colonel of horse in 1680. In 1685 he was a member of the house of burgesses, and on Feb. 14, 1687-88, Gov.

Effingham wrote to the English government that a vacancy had occurred in the council and that he had nominated Col. John Armistead as in every way qualified for the place. This nomination was confirmed on April 30, 1688, and Col. Armistead was sworn as member on Oct. 18 of the same year. He remained a councillor until 1691, when, feeling that he could not consistently with the allegiance he had sworn to James II., take the same oath to William and Mary, he declined and was accordingly removed from the council. It is probable that he later realized the hopelessness of the Stuart cause, and relented in his determination, for in 1693 Gov. Andros wrote that Col. John Armistead had retired from the council. He died soon after. He left two sons and two daughters and through them was the ancestor of many distinguished Virginians.

Hill, Edward, Jr., was the son of Edward Hill Sr., an account of whom appears above. He was probably born at "Shirley," Charles City county, on the banks of the James, in 1637, and upon the death of his father, about 1663, fell heir to that historic estate. Edward Hill Jr. held many offices in his time. He was commander-in-chief of Charles City and Surry counties, commissioned by Gov. Chicheley, Sept. 27, 1679; speaker of the house of burgesses, 1691; treasurer, elected 1691; collector of upper district of James river, 1692, and naval officer of Virginia duties. In 1697 Gov. Andros appointed him judge of the Admiralty for Virginia and North Carolina. It seems that upon the first day of Bacon's uprising there was an attempt made to pursuade Hill to join them, but he met the proposition with a scornful rebuff. He was an intimate friend of Gov. Berkeley and took an active part in quelling the rebellion. It naturally follows that he was cordially hated by the people in his county where the rebellion began. He was disfranchised by Bacon's house of burgesses in 1676, and after Bacon's death, when the counties capitulated to the King's commissioners, he was made a principal subject of their excuse for rebellion, and accused of oppression, misappropriation of public funds and other wrong doing. Col. Hill answered his accusers very effectively in a long and elaborate paper, but in the list of councillors made by the commissioners late in 1677 they recommended that he be left out, and on Feb. 19, 1678-79, the committee of trades and plantations recommended that Col. Hill, of "evil fame and behavior," be put out of all employment and declared unfit to serve his majesty, which recommendation the King saw fit to follow "until his Majesty's pleasure be further known." With the appointment of Lord Culpeper as governor there was, however, a turn in the tide of Virginia affairs, and Col. Hill's star was again in the ascendant. He was fully restored to both royal and popular favor and many of the offices which he held were bestowed upon him after this date. He died Nov. 30, 1700, at "Shirley," which is still owned by his descendants.

Whiting, Henry, of Gloucester county, was probably a son of the James Whiting, who patented 250 acres of land on York river and Timberneck creek, Gloucester, on Aug. 10, 1643. Henry Whiting was a physician and in 1681 was a justice of Gloucester. He seems to have been a sufferer at the hands of Bacon's rebels, but a few years later was treated as a rebel himself and accused before Gov. Culpeper and the council of having said in the assembly that if something were not done to bring about a cessation of tobacco planting the Virginians would have to "all go a plundering." Whiting was suspended from all offices, civil or military, until the King's pleasure were known, and obliged to give bond for his future good behavior. His political sympathies are borne witness to by the fact that in 1682 he was one of Robert Beverley's bondsmen. Dr. Whiting did not remain long in disfavor, however, for sometime prior to Oct. 9, 1690, he was appointed to the council, and was present at meetings in 1692 and 1693. On July 5 of the same year he was appointed treasurer of Virginia, but did not hold the office more than a few months. His descendants are numerous.

Nicholson, Sir Francis, governor of Virginia (q. v.).

Robinson, Christopher, son of John Robinson, of Cleasby, Yorkshire, England, and brother of John Robinson, bishop of London, was born in 1645. He came to Virginia about 1666 and settled on an estate in Middlesex county, near Urbanna, which was afterwards called "Hewick," and where he built a house which is still standing. Robinson was clerk of Middlesex county from 1675 to 1688, when he resigned. In 1691 he was a burgess, and on June 10 of that year Gov. Nicholson wrote that there were vacancies in the council and recommended "Christopher Robinson, a member of the House of Burgesses," to fill one of them. On Oct. 15 the privy council ordered that he be confirmed as a member of the Virginia council, and on Oct. 26 a letter to the same effect from the King was written. On July 5, 1692, he was furthered by the appointment of secretary of state for Virginia, and on the next day wrote to the lords of trades and plantations informing them that on the petition of Col. William Cole to be discharged from the position of secretary the lieutenant-governor, with the unanimous consent of the council, had given him, Robinson, the place until their majesties' pleasure might be known, and he begged their lordships' favorable consideration. On Oct. 25 the King in council granted him the wished-for secretaryship. Robinson was appointed one of the first trustees of William and Mary College in 1692. On March 3, 1692-93, Gov. Andros wrote that Secretary Robinson had died on the 13th of April preceding.

Scarborough, Charles, eldest son of Col. Edmund Scarborough, of Accomac county, is first mentioned in Nov., 1642, when he stated in a deposition that he was twenty-four years old. Col. Charles Scarborough seems to have been a man of bold temperament, which several times in his life got him into trouble. He took part in Bacon's rebellion, but was pardoned on the payment of a fine and, notwithstanding the offence, was, in 1680, presiding justice of Accomac and major of the militia. In 1687 he was prosecuted and removed from the court for saying that "King James would wear out the Church of England," for he was "constantly putting in those of another persuasion." In the next year, that of the revolution, such opinions became meritorious, and Maj. Scarborough was reappointed a justice and elected a member of the house of burgesses. On June 10, 1691, Gov. Nicholson wrote that there were vacancies in the council, and recommended as a fit person to fill one of them "Col. Charles Scarborough," a member of the house of burgesses, and Sir Charles Scarborough's nephew. On Oct. 15 of the same year the English privy council confirmed his appointment. He was at that time councillor, commander-in-chief of Accomac and president of the county court, and collector and naval officer of the eastern shore. For some reason, not now known, he was for a time left out of the council, but in 1697, was again sworn as a member. He died in or not long before 1703. The Scarborough family was for many generations one of the leading families in Virginia.

Pitt, Robert, son of William Pitt, merchant, (and Pary Pitt, his wife,) of Bristol, England, who made his will May 13, 1622, which was proved Feb. 4, 1624, in Bristol. Robert Pitt and his two brothers, Henry and Thomas, came to Virginia about 1640. Robert was a prominent merchant, burgess for Isle of Wight in 1649, 1652, 1654 (in which year he is mentioned as lieutenant-colonel) and 1659, 1660 (in which year he is mentioned as colonel). He was a member of the council in 1673. He married Martha Lear, sister of Col. John Lear, of the Virginia council. His will, dated June 6, 1672, was proved in Isle of Wight county, June 9, 1674.

Wormeley, Ralph, the second Ralph to be councillor, was a son of Ralph Wormeley, Esq., burgess and councillor, and of Agatha Eltonhead, who married (first) Luke Stubbins, of Northampton county, (second) Ralph Wormeley, and (third) Sir Henry Chicheley. He was born in 1650; matriculated, July 4, 1665, at Oriel College, Oxford; was a member of the house of burgesses in 1674; appointed member of the council in 1677; secretary of state in 1693, and became in the same year president of the council. He lived in such state at his residence, "Rosegill," on the Rappahannock river, and had such influence in affairs, that he was called the greatest man in "Virginia." He married (first) Catherine, widow of Colonel Peter Jenings and daughter of Sir Thomas Lunsford, by whom he had two daughters—Elizabeth, who married John Lomax, and Catherine, who married Gawin Corbin. He married (second) Elizabeth Armistead, daughter of Colonel John Armistead, of Gloucester county, and had several sons and daughters, one of whom was John Wormeley, who was grandfather of Ralph Wormeley, the third councillor of the name (q. v.). "Rosegill," his beautiful home on the Rappahannock, was the residence at different times of two of the governors of Virginia—Sir Henry Chicheley, who married his mother, and Lord Howard, of Effingham, who preferred living here to residing at Jamestown. Colonel Wormeley died December 5, 1703.

Parke, Daniel, Jr., was the only son of Councillor Daniel Parke I., and was born in 1669. He was probably educated in England, but was back in Virginia soon after reaching manhood, and in 1692 was appointed a member of the council. He was a favorite of Gov Andros, who gave him, besides the office of councillor, those of collector and naval officer of lower James river, escheator for the district between York and James and colonel of militia. Much of the record which has come to us of Col. Parke certainly presents him in a most unfavorable light, but it must be remembered that it is the product of pens bitterly opposed to him in the politics of the period. Commissary Blair has left us a picture of him anything but attractive, in which he is presented as a boaster and swaggerer who does not hesitate to take advantage over those who are defenceless, but who will not meet a formidable adversary face to face. Such was his behavior toward Gov. Nicholson, by Blair's account, and against his, the commissary's wife, the former of whom he insulted but contrived to avoid the duel, and the latter he bullied in church. Notwithstanding all this there can be no doubt that Parke was a man of courage and ability. He left Virginia in 1697, and in 1701 served a campaign in Flanders with Lord Arran, the Duke of Ormond's brother, and was in every action. For his efficiency he was made a colonel and "promised the first old regiment that shall fall." The Duke of Marlborough made him one of his aides and he behaved with such distinction at the battle of Blenheim that the Duke selected him to bear the news of the great victory to Queen Anne. It was at that time the custom in England to give the bearers of the first news of a victory a gratuity of £500, but Col. Parke begged that instead he might have the Queen's picture. His gallantry, fine appearance and handsome bearing pleased Queen Anne, and being patronized by the Duke he was in April 25, 1704, appointed governor of the Leeward Island. Here the government had been very lax and the settlers were many of them lawless and desperate characters, for the West Indies had been the stronghold of the pirates. Parke attempted to introduce some reforms and incurred the resentment of the people. He would not yield and placed his dependence upon a small military force at his command. A violent insurrection broke out at Antigua in 1710 and Parke made a gallant resistance, killing with his own hand Capt. John Piggott, one of the leaders of the insurrection. He was finally overpowered by numbers and the mob roused to fury dragged him through the streets till he was left expiring in the scorching sun. They broke open his storehouse and plundered his residence and other property to the amount of £5,000 sterling. Col. Daniel Parke married Jane, daughter of Col. Philip Ludwell, and left two daughters—Frances, who married Col. John Custis, of Arlington, Northampton county, and Lucy, who married Col. William Byrd, of Westover. He was certainly lacking in morality, but this was too often the characteristic of the men of fashion of his day. His portrait, showing Queen Anne's miniature hanging by a ribbon from his neck, is to be seen at Brandon, on James river.

Hartwell, Henry, was clerk of the council in 1677 and other years. On June 10, 1691, Gov. Nicholson wrote to England that there were vacancies in the council and recommended for one place Henry Hartwell, a member of the house of burgesses. The governor seems to have given him a pro tempore appointment at once, for he was present in council July 5, 1692. On March 2, 1693-94 the committee for trade and plantations agreed to move the King in council that Col. Henry Hartwell be added to the council in Virginia at the recommendation of the bishop of London, and on July 18, 1694, Gov. Andros wrote that Col. Hartwell had been accordingly sworn. He left Virginia for England in June, 1695, and never returned, but for some time his name was retained on the roll of the council. In 1699 he, with the Rev. James Blair and Edward Chilton, prepared an account of the colony which was published under the title of "The Present State of Virginia." Hartwell became a resident of London and died there in 1699. His brother, William Hartwell, was captain of Sir William Berkeley's body guard during Bacon's rebellion, and through him in female lines the family is still represented in Virginia.

Lightfoot, John, was a son of John Lightfoot, barrister-at-law, of Northampton county, England, and with his brother Philip, came to Virginia and settled in Gloucester county. On June 10, 1670, Lightfoot received the King's grant as auditor-general of Virginia, in place of Thomas Stegge, then lately deceased. On Dec. 17, 1671, his majesty, having learned that

Gov. Berkeley had appointed Digges to the place prior to his own letters patent to Lightfoot, and that Digges was "a person every way fit for said office," directed Berkeley to suspend Lightfoot and substitute Digges. Moryson in a letter to Lord Arlington said that Berkeley's commission to Digges "bore date long before Captain Lightfoot did so much as sue for his," and objects to Lightfoot on the grounds that at the time when he received his commission he was not a member of the council or a resident of Virginia, "so that if he hath the place he must be forced to execute it by deputy, which is contrary to law," and that he was reported to have "many great debts upon him, one no less than a statute of £700." In 1681 reference is made to Lightfoot as having married Anne, daughter of Thomas Goodrich, lieutenant-general in Bacon's rebellion, and in 1692 we are told that John Lightfoot, "lately come into the country," was a councillor. It is probable that he had lately returned from a visit to England. On Sept. 5, 1695, the lords justices, on recommendation of the committee of trades and plantations, directed that John Lightfoot be added to the Virginia council. In 1699 he was collector for the country between James and York rivers, and in 1701 voted with other councillors for the recall of Nicholson. He is also mentioned as having been commander-in-chief of King and Queen county. He died May 28, 1707, leaving issue.

Ludwell, Philip, was the son of Thomas Ludwell, of Bruton, in Somersetshire, England, who was church warden of the parish in 1636, and steward of Sexey Hospital in Bruton. Thomas Ludwell died at Discoe, in the parish of Bruton, and was buried July 7, 1637. Philip Ludwell's mother was Jane Cottington, a relative of Sir William Berkeley, and only daughter of James Cottington, of Discoe, a brother of Philip, Lord Cottington. Philip Ludwell, who belonged to a royalist family, was born about 1638, and probably came to Virginia about 1660 to join his brother Thomas, who was then secretary of state. He was captain of the James City county militia in 1667, and on March 5, 1675, took the oath as a councillor of state. During the absence of his brother Thomas in London, at this time, he was acting secretary of state for two years (1675-1677). During Bacon's rebellion (1676) he was one of the most efficient supporters of Gov. Berkeley. He showed distinguished courage and discretion in capturing an expedition under Giles Bland sent to Northampton county to siege the governor. After Berkeley's death, in 1677, Ludwell married his widow and became the head of the "Green Spring Faction," as it was called, comprised of friends of the late governor. From being the supporters of government Ludwell and Beverley became the champions of the rights of the general assembly and the people. Gov. Jeffreys had Ludwell excluded from the council. Jeffreys died and Lord Thomas Culpeper came over to Virginia in 1681. He was a cousin of Ludwell's wife, Lady Berkeley, whose maiden name was Frances Culpeper, and at the request of the whole council he restored Ludwell to his seat in that body. When Lord Howard, of Effingham, came as governor to Virginia in 1686 he tried to increase the power of the executive and instituted a fee for the use of the state seal to land grants. He was opposed by Ludwell and the fee was ordered to be discontinued, but he again lost his place in council. The dismissal only served to increase Ludwell's popularity, and the assembly sent him to England as their agent to petition for relief. While he was in attendance at the privy council King William came to the throne and Ludwell was successful in obtaining a favorable decision on most of the questions involved. He was again restored to the council and on May 7, 1691, the house of burgesses voted him the public thanks and presented him with £250. Before this, on Dec. 5, 1689, the lords proprietors of Carolina appointed him governor of North Carolina, and in 1693 of both North and South Carolina. He held office till 1694, when, tired of the quarrels of that turbulent country, he resigned. He continued in the council in Virginia and in 1690-92 was agent for the Culpepers in the Northern Neck. In 1693 he was one of the first board of visitors of William and Mary College. He heired from his brother Thomas, "Rich Neck," near Williamsburg, but his chief residence was at "Green Spring," which he obtained by his marriage with Lady Berkeley. About 1700, leaving his estates in the hands of his son Philip, he went to England, where he was living as late as 1711. Col. Philip Ludwell married, in or before 1667 (first) Lucy, widow of Col. William Bernard, and before that of Maj. Lewis Burwell, and daughter of Capt. Robert Higginson; (second) Lady Frances (Culpeper) Berkeley. His son Philip (by his first marriage) and his grandson Philip were both members of the council.

Johnson, Richard, lived in New Kent county in 1679, when he was styled "Captain Richard Johnson," and the following year was a justice and captain of horse there. On June 10, 1691, Gov. Nicholson wrote to England that there were vacancies in the council and recommended for one of the places Lieut.-Col. Richard Johnson, a member of the house of burgesses. He was not appointed, however, until 1696, when Andros gave him a seat in that body and he is recorded as being present on April 20 of that year. His death probably occurred in 1698, his will having been made then, on April 8. Col. Johnson came from Bilsby, county Lincoln, England. By a wife in England he had a daughter Judith, who married Sir Hardoff Wastnays. By a wife in Virginia he had several sons, one of whom was ancestor of the distinguished Virginia lawyer, Chapman Johnson.

Harrison, Benjamin, of "Wakefield," Surry county, a son of Benjamin Harrison, of the same place, was born Sept. 20, 1645. He was a minor at the time of his father's death, and in 1663, was under the guardianship of Capt. Thomas Flood, of Surry. On June 15, 1677, his name appears for the first time as a justice and he continued for many years to be a member of the county court. On June 16, 1679, he took the oath as sheriff. He was a member of the house of burgesses in 1681, 1692, 1696, 1697 and 1698, and in the latter year was promoted to the council, of which he was a regular attendant until his death. In the charter of William and Mary College, 1692, Benjamin Harrison was appointed one of the first trustees. Gov. Nicholson was not on friendly terms with Harrison and his friends and wrote to the lords of trades and plantations in 1703 that the family of Harrisons had endeavored to engross the major part of the land on the south side of Blackwater Swamp, but that, for his majesty's interest, he had put a stop to their proceedings. Col. Harrison died Jan. 30, 1712-13.

Jenings, Edmund, president of the council and acting governor (q. v.).

Digges, Dudley, of York county, son of Edward Digges, governor of Virginia, was born about 1665. Sometime in 1698 Gov.

Andros appointed him a member of the council, but for some reason he was not continued in office by Gov. Nicholson, and on Jan. 4, 1699-1700, the lords of trade and plantations wrote to Nicholson that they approved of his action in not admitting Col. Digges. Whatever the objection may have been it was removed in a few years, for on Feb. 23, 1703-04, the Queen appointed Col. Dudley Digges to the council, as had been recommended by Gov. Nicholson. He was also included in a new commission dated Feb. 23, 1709-10. In 1705 Digges was appointed auditor and surveyor-general of Virginia, offices which he held until his death, Jan. 18, 1710-11.

Carter, Robert, president of the council and acting governor of Virginia (q. v.).

Custis, John, son of Maj-Gen. John Custis, of "Arlington," Northampton county, was born in 1653. He was a justice of Northampton in 1680, a member of the house of burgesses from that county in 1685, 1692, 1696, and in 1699, when he is styled "Colonel John Custis," he was escheator, naval officer and receiver of Virginia for the eastern shore. He was appointed to the council Dec. 14, 1699, and later on Oct. 15, 1705. He was a constant attendant at the sessions during the remainder of his life, his name appearing for the last time on Oct. 15, 1712, just three months before his death. He died January 26, 1713, and was buried at "Wilsonia," Northampton county.

Page, Matthew, of "Rosewell," Gloucester county, was a son of Col. John Page, and was born in 1659. He was a member of the house of burgesses and a charter trustee of William and Mary College in 1692, and escheator for the district between the York and Rappahannock rivers from 1699 to 1702. He was appointed to the council in 1700, probably to fill a vacancy, and the appointment confirmed in 1702 by the Queen. He remained a member until his death in 1703. He married Mary Mann, of Gloucester county, Virginia.

Burwell, Lewis, of "Carter's Creek," Gloucester, and of "King's Creek," York, was a son of Maj. Lewis Burwell and Lucy Higginson, his wife. He was a justice of Gloucester in 1680 and a trustee of William and Mary College in 1692. He was probably appointed to the council by the governor in 1700. Such appointments were always provisional and had to be ratified by the English authorities and on Dec. 4, 1700, the lords of trade wrote to Gov. Nicholson that he had been appointed to the council. On Oct. 13, 1701, Maj. Burwell wrote to the lords of trade that he had received his majesty's command requiring his service as one of the council of the colony. It was his very great misfortune that upon this occasion it was not in his power to pay the respect of duty and obedience which he had always been ambitious to do, and therefore he prayed their lordships' intercession with his majesty not to insist upon his commands. Sickness and lameness, with which he was very often afflicted, made it impossible for him to attend. Accordingly, on May 7, 1702, the lords of trade recommended to the Queen that Lewis Burwell be discharged from the council, which was done. It was with one of this Maj. Burwell's daughters that Gov. Nicholson became infatuated, as Dr. Blair reports. He died Dec. 19, 1710. He married (first) Abigail Smith, niece of Hon. Nathaniel Bacon, Esq., and (second) Martha, widow of Col. William Cole, formerly secretary of state, and daughter of Councillor Col. John Lear.

Ludwell, Philip, Jr., of "Greenspring," James City county, was a son of the Philip Ludwell.

who was so long a prominent figure in the colony, and was born at "Carter's Creek," Gloucester county, Feb. 4, 1672. His father's influence and large estate brought the son into public life at an early age and he was chosen speaker of the house of burgesses in 1695, being probably the most youthful occupant of that chair. On May 14, 1702, on the recommendation of the governor, the Queen appointed him a member of the council. Though recommended by Nicholson, Ludwell was one of the party who opposed him and finally succeeded in having him removed from office. Ludwell's official life appears to have continued to run smoothly, he sat regularly at the meetings of the council, was appointed one of the trustees of the new college at Williamsburg in 1706, and 1709 was made a commissioner on the part of Virginia for establishing the boundary line with North Carolina. In 1711 he was appointed auditor of Virginia by Gov. Spotswood, who seems at first to have been favorably impressed with him. The good will between them did not last, however. The Ludwells, always on the side of the people, did not hesitate to oppose the governor in what they considered usurpations of the popular rights, and accordingly, when the clash between the house of burgesses and Spotswood occurred, the colonel sided with the former. So highly was the governor incensed that he suspended Ludwell from the office of auditor and accused him of mismanagement of the finances. There was a considerable dispute over this order, but the English authorities finally upheld Spotswood and appointed another in Ludwell's place. This did not, however, discourage that gentleman in his resistence to the governor, and in 1718 he sided with Commissary Blair in his dispute with Spotswood relative to the appointment of ministers to the Virginia churches. In this matter they were entirely successful in their opposition to him, though this and other disputes continued for sometime. These differences were finally composed in 1720, after which date there is scarcely any record of Ludwell's public life save the reports of his constant attendance at the council. He died Jan. 11, 1726-27.

Quarry, Robert, was appointed a member of the council in the commission of Oct. 16, 1702, and on Dec. 17, wrote the lords of trade that he had arrived in the colony about the middle of October. He made a visit to England the following year, but was again in Virginia in Sept., 1703, and in October of the same year was appointed surveyor-general of the customs in America, in which office he played an active part in the affairs of the colony. Like his predecessors in this office, he was so frequently absent in England that he can hardly be said to have been a citizen of Virginia at all. He sat as councillor in 1707 and 1709-10, and, under a new commission, was present and took the oaths as councillor, July 21, 1712. The colonial records contain no further information concerning him.

Duke, Henry, of James City county, was a justice of that county in 1680, sheriff in 1699 and member of the house of burgesses in 1692, 1696, 1699, 1700, and probably in the following year. In 1700 he was a member of the committee appointed to review the laws and, on May 14, 1702, was appointed by the Queen, a member of the council. He continued a member and a regular attendant at the sessions of that body until his death, the last record of his attendance being in 1713. It appears that he was also commander of the militia in James City county in 1710, for on Aug.

COLONIAL COUNCILLORS OF STATE

24 of that year, Gov. Spotswood made a memorandum, in the receipt of a letter from Col. Duke, giving an account of some negroes going away with arms, directing him, in case of a like happening, to raise the militia and go in pursuit. On Jan. 27, 1713, Spotswood wrote to the English authorities that there was a vacancy in the council on account of the death of Henry Duke, which had occurred during the winter.

Bassett, William, of "Eltham," New Kent county, was a son of Capt. William Bassett of the same county and was born in 1670. He was a member of the house of burgesses from New Kent in 1692, 1696, 1702 and probably in the intervening years. On May 22, 1702, Edmund Jenings and John Lightfoot certified that Col. William Bassett, who was elected burgess for New Kent, "was tendered the oaths for burgess and returned the following answer, 'I have already in several qualifications testified my allegiance to King William's government by taking the oaths &c.; but I am now informed, and fully satisfied that he is dead, and therefore I think myself obliged both in prudence and concience to decline taking ye oaths to him at this time.'" On May 14, 1702, the Queen appointed him a member of the council of Virginia and he was present at sessions of that body until April 15, 1708. Within a few years Bassett desired to retire from the council and wrote to England to that effect, stating that neither his health nor his private affairs would permit him to attend. This, after some delay, was granted, but Bassett seems to have made too high a record as an official to be allowed to remain long in retirement, and in 1711, he was returned to the council, but declined to accept as he was not restored to his former position in that body. On March 11, 1714-15, he was again included in a commission to the councillors and this time took his seat, attending regularly the sessions until his death in 1723.

Smith, John, of Gloucester county, a son of Col. Lawrence Smith of the same place, was appointed to the council in the spring of 1704 by Gov. Nicholson, but in the next commission to the council the names of Smith and John Lewis were omitted and they made application for restoration to the lords of trade. In Dec., 1705, the board ordered that Mr. Smith be reinstated, taking the place of William Byrd deceased, and the following year he took the oaths of office. He was among those councillors who opposed Gov. Spotswood and whom the latter petitioned the English authorities to have removed in 1718, a petition not granted. Besides being in the council, Smith was appointed by Nicholson to be quartermaster general of Virginia in 1704-05, and in 1707, he was made commander-in-chief of the militia in King and Queen county in place of Col. John Lightfoot deceased. His death occurred sometime prior to March, 1719-20. He married Arabella Cox, a descendant of William Strachey, secretary to Lord Delaware in 1611.

Lewis, John, Sr., of "Warner Hall," Gloucester county, was a son of John and Isabella Lewis of the same county and was born Nov. 30, 1699. Towards the close of Gov. Nicholson's administration, probably in the spring of 1704, he was appointed to the council, but in some way his name was omitted from the commission to that body under Nicholson's successor. Lewis and John Smith, who was in the same case, wrote to the lords of trade expressing surprise that they should have been left out as they were sensible of never having acted contrary to their duty to the Queen, her representatives or the welfare of the colony. The enemies of Nicholson strove to keep them excluded, but as nothing could be urged against them, they were successful in their efforts to be admitted and on June 26, 1707, they were finally sworn as members. Col. Lewis was a regular attendant at the sessions of the council until his death. On Sept. 2, 1707, he was appointed commander of King and Queen county. He died Nov. 14, 1725. He married Elizabeth Warner, daughter of Col. Augustine Warner and Mildred Reade, daughter of Col. George Reade, and left issue.

Churchill, William, of "Bushy Park" and "Wilton," Middlesex county, was born in Oxfordshire, England about 1650 and came to Virginia prior to 1687, when he was a justice of Middlesex. He became a man of large wealth and prominence in the colony and owned two estates in his county, entirely across which his lands were stated to extend. He was a member of the house of burgesses for Middlesex in 1704 and probably other years, and on April 20, 1705, was appointed by the English government a member of the council. He continued a regular attendant until his death in 1710. He married Elizabeth Armistead, daughter of Col. John Armistead, and widow of Ralph Wormeley, secretary of state, and left issue.

Cocke, Dr. William, a native of Suffolk, England, was born in 1671, matriculated in Queen's College, Cambridge, in 1688, and was elected fellow of the college in 1694. The exact date of his immigration to Virginia does not appear, but in the latter part of 1711 or early in 1712, upon the resignation of Edmund Jenings, he was appointed secretary of state of Virginia. There seems to have been some arrangement between Jenings and Cocke in regard to the profits of the office and there was some little delay before the latter came into full possession of the place. Gov. Spotswood wrote on Feb. 11, 1712-13 to the authorities in England that there was a vacancy in the council and recommended, as a fit person to fill it "the gentleman who was last year by her majesty's favor promoted to the office of Secretary, Mr. William Cocke." On July 23, 1713, the board of trade and plantations made a representation to the Queen recommending Secretary Cocke for the council, and on Aug. 18 the appointment was made. Dr. Cocke was present at the various sessions of the council until the spring of 1716, when he made a visit to England. He was a bearer on that occasion of a letter from Gov. Spotswood, in which he gives the highest praise to Cocke and recommends him to the Queen's favor. Dr. Cocke returned to Virginia prior to March 11, 1718, on which date he was present in council. He died Oct. 20, 1720. He married Elizabeth, sister of the celebrated naturalist Mark Catesby, and left descendants.

Berkeley, Edmund, of Middlesex county, was a son of Edmund and Mary Berkeley and was born sometime prior to 1674. On July 22, 1713, the board of trade and plantations made a representation to the Queen, recommending him for appointment to the council, and on Aug. 8 the appointment was made. There seems to have been a vigorous dispute between him and Gov. Spotswood regarding precedence in the council, Berkeley claiming that he should take precedence over the councillors appointed by the governor after the date of his letter from the Queen, but sworn before him. The dispute lasted for some time, Berkeley in the meantime refusing to take his seat, but at length a new commission

COL. WM. BYRD
Founder of Richmond

arrived in March, 1714-15, in which his name was again included and he seems after this to have been a regular attendant until his death in 1718, at his residence "Barn Elms" in Middlesex county. He married Lucy, daughter of Maj. Lewis Burwell and his wife Abigail Smith descended from the illustrious house of the Bacons in England.

Byrd, William, of Westover, a son of Councillor William Byrd, of the same place, was born March 28, 1674. He may truly be said to have been born under a lucky star, for his father had already made the name of Byrd distinguished in Virginia, and bequeathed to the son, besides worldly wealth and position, many admirable gifts of character and mind. He was sent to England as a mere lad for his education and placed under the direction of Sir Robert Southwell. Later he read law in the Middle Temple, and, in recognition of his gifts and scholarship, was made a fellow of the Royal Society of Great Britain. A trip to the continent and a visit to the court of France served as finishing touches to this education before his return to Virginia. Soon after reaching the colony, he was made a burgess and, in Oct., 1696, was sent as the official agent of that body to England, where he remained at least as late as 1702, though the date of his visit's termination is not definitely known. Upon his return, he entered eagerly into the affairs of the colony and soon came to be looked upon as the leading man of his time. In Sept., 1705, Gov. Nott, upon the advice of the council, appointed him receiver general of Virginia to fill the vacancy occasioned by the death of his father, and in December, of the same year, he succeeded to his father's place in the council. In the conflict that arose between the assembly and Gov. Spotswood, Col. Byrd took part with the former, and the governor's displeasure was further increased by a long visit Byrd made in England. He consequently wrote to England advising the authorities there to remove Byrd and a number of his other enemies from the council. In the case of Byrd there was a long dispute with varying success, but in the end he retained his seat. This quarrel was finally ended and Byrd and Spotswood became cordial friends after the latter's retirement from public life. In 1727, Byrd was appointed by Gov. Gooch, one of the commission to confer with North Carolina upon the boundary line between the two colonies. The Virginia commission consisted of Col. Byrd, Richard Fitzwilliam and William Dandridge. These gentlemen not only succeeded in fixing the position of the line but accompanied the engineers that drew it on their difficult and painful survey through the wilderness. Col. Byrd kept a diary of the expedition which has been preserved for us, and which, along with other similar writings by him, afford a vivid picture of colonial life in that period. Col. Byrd built the famous brick mansion which stands to this day at Westover, and collected the largest library of the day in America. This library boasted 3,625 volumes, among which was the "Records of the London Company," which the Earl of Southampton caused to be made, and which Byrd's father had purchased in London. Col. Byrd's death occurred Aug. 26, 1744, and he was buried in the garden at Westover.

It was fit that a man of his eminent character should have been founder of the city of Richmond, the present capital of Virginia.

Forteus, Robert, of "New Bottle," Gloucester county, was born in 1679. His father was Edward Porteus of the same county, who, in 1693, was recommended by the governor as one of the "gentlemen of estate and standing" suitable for appointment to the council. He was, however, never given the office. Robert Porteus was appointed sheriff of Gloucester in 1709, but declined the office. On March 1, 1713, he was sworn as member of the council and remained a member until 1719, when he went to England, dying at Ripon, Yorkshire, August 8, 1758. He was the father of Beilby Porteus, Bishop of London.

Harrison, Nathaniel, of "Wakefield," Surry county, was a son of Councillor Benjamin Harrison and was born in Surry county, Aug. 8, 1677. He was, for a number of years a very prominent and influential figure in the colony. Beginning his public life as a justice of Surry in 1698, he was later a member of the house of burgesses for that county from 1700 to 1706 inclusive. In 1702, he was naval officer for the upper district of James river; in 1704, he was appointed by the commissioners of the prize office in England, the agent for prizes in Virginia; in 1710, appointed by Spotswood, naval officer and receiver of Virginia duties; and on April 10 of the same year was made one of the commissioners on the part of Virginia to settle, with North Carolina, the question of their boundary. On Jan. 9, 1713-14, he became a councillor on Spotswood's appointment, this being confirmed by the English authorities the following year. On Dec. 8, 1715, he was appointed county lieutenant of Surry and Prince George, and appears at this time to have been receiver general of Virginia, the deputy in Virginia for the auditor and receiver general of all the colonies, who lived in England. He was a regular attendant at sessions of the council until his death, Nov. 30, 1727. He married Mary Cary, daughter of John Cary, merchant of London, by his wife Jane, daughter of Col. John Flood, of Surry county, Virginia, and had issue.

Page, Mann, of "Rosewell," Gloucester county, was a son of Matthew Page of the same place and was born in 1691. His grandson, Gov. Page, stated that he was educated at Eaton, and Foster's "Oxford Matriculations" shows that he was entered at St. John's College at that university in July, 1709. Early in 1714, a vacancy occurring in the council, Gov. Spotswood appointed him a member of that body, and on March 11, 1714-15, the English government confirmed his appointment. Page was a regular attendant at the sessions of the council until his death. Mann Page was the builder of the present house at "Rosewell," which was begun in 1725 and barely completed at the time of his death, Jan. 24, 1730. He married Judith, daughter of Secretary Ralph Wormeley, and had issue.

Digges, Cole, of "Bellfield," York county, was a son of Councillor Dudley Digges of the same place and was born in 1692. He was a member of the house of burgesses for York in 1718 and probably other years, and was first mentioned in 1718 as a candidate for the council, being recommended for that body by Gov. Spotswood in his letter of Sept. 17 of that year. There was some delay in the matter of his appointment due to politics but, in Sept., 1720, he finally received his commission and was sworn to office. He remained a member, and was a frequent attendant for many years, the last record of his appearance being on Sept. 4, 1744, in which year his death occurred. He married Elizabeth Power, daughter of Dr. Henry Power, son of John Power, "a Spanish merchant," and left issue.

Beverley, Peter, of Gloucester county, eldest son of Maj. Robert Beverley of Middlesex county, the councillor and patriot, was born probably about the year 1668. In 1691, soon after his coming of age, he was appointed clerk of the house of burgesses and held that office until the year 1700, when he was elected a member of the house from Gloucester county. He evidently soon attained prominence, for from 1702 to 1714, he was speaker of the assembly, and in the former year, the house, as a token of their esteem and gratitude voted him an annuity of 10,000 pounds of tobacco. From 1710 to 1723, he was treasurer of Virginia, elected by the house of burgesses. On May 23, 1716, Gov. Spotswood recommended for the position of auditor general, John Robinson or Peter Beverley, the latter of whom had been for several years speaker, and was then the country's treasurer. Writing again on July 3, Spotswood said that he intended to appoint as auditor pro tem Col. Peter Beverley. On April 9, 1719, the lords of trade recommended to the King that "Peter Beverley, a gentleman of good estate and abilities, of fair character and well affected to his majesty's person and government," should be appointed a member of the Virginia council. On June 20, 1720, the appointment was made. Col. Beverley remained a member until his death, his last appearance, as noted in the journal, being June 13, 1728, in which year he died. Besides the offices already mentioned as held by him, were those of visitor of William and Mary College and surveyor general of Virginia. He married Elizabeth, daughter of Maj. Robert Peyton, who was grandson of Sir Edward Peyton, of Isleham, county Kent, England, and left issue.

Robinson, John, president of the council and acting governor (q. v.).

Carter, John, was the eldest son of Robert Carter of "Corotoman," Lancaster county. He was a student at the Middle Temple and, in 1722, was a barrister at law at the Inns of Court. On June 23, 1722, Spotswood wrote to the lords of trade recommending "Mr. John Carter, eldest son of one of the council, and barrister at law in the Middle Temple, and a native of Virginia" for the position of solicitor of Virginia affairs in England. This position was obtained by Mr. Carter and held by him until the next year, when, being appointed to the office of secretary of state of Virginia, he returned there. On Nov. 1, 1723, Gov. Drysdale recommends the then secretary to fill a vacancy in the council. His father was already a councillor and if the affinity of father and son was too close to be allowed, he then recommended John Grymes, the King's receiver general, though his own inclinations were for Mr. Carter. On Jan. 17, 1723-24, Lord Orkney, governor of Virginia, recommended to the lords of trade that John Carter Esq. be appointed to the council to succeed Wm. Bassett, deceased. On Jan. 23, the King made the appointment and on April 25, 1724, Carter took his seat. Not long after this Carter obtained the position of secretary, for which, as was frequently done, he is said to have paid a large price. The great power attaching to this office came under discussion during Carter's incumbency and Gov. Drysdale laid before the lords of trade the fact that the secretary had the appointment of the several county clerks and, in virtue of their membership in the house of burgesses, the virtual appointment of one half of that body which would be thus largely devoted to his interests. He expressly stipulated that he was not reflecting upon the actions of the present secretary, but merely desired to lay before them this great change from the ancient constitution. In a letter dated Jan. 22, 1726-27, to the Duke of Newcastle, Carter defends his own actions in the matter. Carter seems to have been a regular attendant at the meetings of the council until 1741. His death occurred April 30, 1743.

Fitzwilliams, Richard, first appears in the Virginia records on Aug. 13, 1717, when he petitioned the council for the grant of a lot of land in Hampton. This was doubtless his residence, as in April of the next year he was described as collector of the lower district of the James river. Some years later, probably 1725, he was appointed surveyor general of the colonies in America, and on July 22 of that year, the lords justices, the King being then out of England, referred to the board of plantations and trade, a petition from Fitzwilliams in which he asks that he may be added to the councils of Virginia and South Carolina. On Dec. 15, 1725, took his seat in the Virginia council, and on Dec. 14, 1727, was appointed by the governor one of the commissioners to settle the dispute regarding the boundary with North Carolina. He appears to have been often absent from Virginia as his duties called him to the other colonies and to England, but the records show him to have been occasionally present in council and for the last time in 1730. He probably died in 1732 in England, when his successor was appointed, but nothing further appears regarding him in the records.

Grymes, John, of "Brandon," Middlesex county, was a son of John Grymes of "Grymesby," in the same county and was born in 1692. He was educated at William and Mary College and his first public office was that of justice of the peace for Middlesex, to which office he was appointed at an early age. On Nov. 22, 1716, the governor informed the council that Mr. John Grymes had presented him with a deputation from Wm. Blathwayt, auditor general of the American colonies, appointing him deputy auditor for Virginia, in the place of Philip Ludwell. This commission did not appear to the governor to be drawn in sufficiently legal form to entitle Mr. Grymes to act, but he stated that he would supply the defects as far as possible, and Grymes took the oath of office. He still held the position in 1719 and in 1721. In 1720, he was a member of the house of burgesses and in 1723, was receiver general. On Nov. 1, 1723, Gov. Drysdale recommended John Grymes, the King's receiver general, for appointment to the council, and two years later repeated it. Upon the latter occasion, the appointment was made and, on May 3, 1726, Grymes took his seat. He was a regular attendant until 1747. He died November 2, 1748. He married Lucy, daughter of Hon. Philip Ludwell, of "Greenspring," James City county, and left issue.

Blair, James, D. D., president of the council and acting governor (q. v.).

Dandridge, William, of "Elsing Green," King William county, and his brother, Col. John Dandridge, of New Kent, were the progenitors of the Dandridge family in Virginia. The first notice on record of Col. William Dandridge is under date of July 21, 1712, when he chartered his vessel to the governor of North Carolina to carry twenty soldiers to Charleston. At this time he seems to have been a merchant and ship owner at Hampton, Elizabeth City county, as on Jan. 23, 1713, he was allowed to build a wharf opposite to his lots in that town, and in 1717, he is said to have built a house and wharf there. On May 31, 1727, the King appointed William Dandridge a member of the council, in the place of Philip Ludwell, deceased, and on Dec. 4 of the same year, the governor appointed him one of the commissioners to settle the boundary line between Virginia and North Carolina. In 1738, Dandridge was given command of his majesty's sloop "Wolf," and in 1741, was transferred to the "South Sea," forty guns, in which he served in Oglethorpe's attack on St. Augustine, and Admiral Vernon's on Carthagena. In the last mentioned service he especially distinguished himself. Later he commanded the "Ludlow Castle," man-of-war. Dandridge died in 1743 in Hanover county. His brother, Col. John Dandridge, was the father of Mrs. Martha Washington.

Custis, John, the third of that name to hold the position of councillor, was the son of Col. John Custis of "Wilsonia," and the grandson of Maj. Gen. John Custis, both in their days councillors. He was born in 1678 and, his grandfather having bequeathed £100 per anum for his education, he went to England for that purpose. Upon returning to Virginia, he appears to have resided principally near Williamsburg, where he owned an estate. He was a member of the house of burgesses for the college in 1718 and probably other years. He was recommended for the council in 1727, by the Earl of Orkney, and appointed the same year. He married Frances, the eldest daughter of Col. Daniel Parke Jr., but being exceedingly eccentric, and his lady of a proud and haughty disposition, the union was a most unhappy one. His son, Daniel Parke Custis, later married Miss Martha Dandridge, who finally became the wife of Washington. He died November 2, 1749.

Randolph, William, of "Turkey Island," Henrico, was a son of Col. William Randolph of the same place, and was born in Nov., 1681. His first public office seems to have been assistant to his father as clerk of the house of burgesses, a position to which he finally succeeded, holding it until 1712. In 1720, and probably other years, he was a member of the house of burgesses for Henrico county, and in 1727, he was appointed to the council. In 1737, he made a voyage to England for his health, but returned the following year from which time he was a constant attendant at the sessions of the council until his death which occurred Oct. 19, 1742. He married Elizabeth Beverley, daughter of Hon. Peter Beverley, of Gloucester county, Virginia, and had issue.

Harrison, Henry, son of Benjamin Harrison of "Wakefield," Surry county, was born in 1692. He was a justice of Surry in 1710 and a burgess from that county in 1715, 1718 and perhaps other years. On Nov. 9, 1730, having been recommended as a "man in all respects equal and worthy to fill the vacant place," he was appointed by the King a member of the council and took his seat the following year. He did not live long to enjoy his honors, however, for his death occurred in 1732. He married, but had no issue.

Bray, David, of James City county, a son of Col. David Bray of the same place, and grandson of Councillor Bray, was born in 1699. He was a man of large estate and, in 1631, on the recommendation of Gov. Gooch, appointed a member of the council. He married Elizabeth, daughter of John Page, of Williamsburg, but died Oct. 5, 1731, without issue.

Phenny, George, was sworn a member of the council on June 4, 1734, pursuant to a warrant dated July 31, 1732, from the "Queen as Guardian of the Kingdom," directing that George Phenny Esq., surveyor general of the customs for the southern district of America, should become a member of the council. He seems never to have resided in Virginia.

Tayloe, John, of "Mt. Airy." Richmond county, a son of Col. William Tayloe, was born Feb. 15, 1687. From early manhood, he held a prominent place in the affairs of the county and the colony, becoming a justice of Richmond county in 1710, sheriff in 1712 and 1713, colonel of militia in 1713, and representing the county in 1728, 1730 and probably other years. In 1732, he was appointed by the King a member of the council. Col. Tayloe was a man of influence and large estate and took an active part in promoting the welfare of the colony. He was largely in iron mining and manufacture in Virginia and Maryland. He died in 1747. He married Elizabeth Fauntleroy, and had John Tayloe, second of that name.

Lee, Thomas, president of the council and acting governor (q. v.).

Lightfoot, Philip, of Yorktown and of "Sandy Point," Charles City county, was a son of Philip Lightfoot of the latter place, and was born in 1689. In 1707, he was appointed clerk of York county and held this office until 1733. During this period and later, he was extensively engaged in business as a merchant at Yorktown and acquired great wealth. On Jan. 10, 1732-33, the governor appointed him a councillor in the place of Robert Carter, deceased, and this appointment was confirmed by the King April 9, 1733. He appears to have been in constant attendance at the meetings until his death. Lightfoot was one of the wealthiest men of his day and owned a handsome town house in addition to his country seat. He died May 30, 1748. He married Mary, daughter of William Armistead, and widow of James Burwell, and had issue

Dinwiddie, Robert. Governor of Virginia (q. v.).

Dawson, Rev. William, son of William Dawson of Aspatria, Cumberland county, England, was born in 1704. When fifteen years of age, he entered Queen's College, Oxford, where he took the degree of bachelor of arts in his twenty-first year, and four years later, that of master of arts. Still later he was made a doctor of divinity. He was ordained to the ministry in 1728 and probably came to Virginia immediately, as in 1729 he was professor of moral philosophy at William and Mary College. During Blair's lifetime, he had Mr. Dawson read prayers for him, and when he was not well, to preach. Upon Blair's death in 1743, the visitors of the college, "by unanimous consent," chose Mr. Dawson president. At the same time he became a member of the council and was appointed commissary on the recommendation of Gov. Gooch. He died July 24, 1752, and was buried at Williamsburg.

Fairfax, William, was the second son of Henry Fairfax of Yorkshire, England and was baptized in that county in 1691. He served for a time in the navy under his kinsman, Capt. Fairfax, and afterwards in the army in Spain. His next public service was as chief justice of the Bahamas, but as the climate did not agree with him, he was given, in 1725, the appointment of collector of customs at Salem, Massachusetts. About 1734, he came to Virginia as agent for his cousin, Lord Fairfax, in the management of his great landed estate, the Northern Neck. He lived for a time in Westmoreland county, but upon receiving the appointment as collector of customs for South Potomac, removed to Fairfax county, where he built a mansion house. In 1742 he was a member of the house of burgesses, and in Nov., 1743, was appointed to the council. Col. Fairfax was a man of ability, and played a prominent part in the French and Indian war. He was an early friend of Washington, and by his introduction of him to Lord Fairfax, procured him his first position as surveyor. Died August 30, 1757.

Blair, John, president of the council and acting governor (q. v.).

Burwell, Lewis, president of the council and acting governor (q. v.).

Nelson, William, president of the council and acting governor (q. v.).

Lewis, John, Jr., of "Warner Hall," Gloucester county, son of the Hon. John Lewis of the same place, was born in 1694. He appears from the journals of the council, to have been a member of that body from Oct. 27, 1648, to Nov. 1, 1753, and perhaps later, as the records are incomplete. The date of his death is unknown.

Nelson, Thomas, of Yorktown, son of Thomas Nelson, Sr., of the same place, was born in 1716, and died in 1782. He was appointed secretary of state of Virginia in 1742, and was a member of the house of burgesses for York county in 1748 and 1749, and in all probability in preceding years. In 1749 he was appointed a member of the council, and the journals show him to have been a regular attendant at the board until the revolution. In 1775 he was president of the council, having perhaps acceded to that position on the death of his brother William in 1772. He was a firm adherent of the colonial side in the revolution, though he exerted himself to prevent any violence on the part of the people towards Lord Dunmore. The "Virginia Gazette" of May 6, 1775, has the following:

"The town of York being somewhat alarmed by a letter from Capt. Montague, commander of his majesty's ship, the "Fowey," addressed to the Hon. Thomas Nelson Esq., president of his majesty's honorable council in Virginia, threatening to fire upon the town of York in case a party sent from his ship to the support of Gov. Dunmore, was attacked, the York county committee, taking into consideration the time the letter was sent, which was too late to permit the president to use his influence had the people been disposed to molest or attack the detachment, and further considering that Col. Nelson, who, had the threat been carried into execution, would have been a principal sufferer, was at that very moment exerting his utmost endeavors in behalf of government and safety of his excellency's person, unanimously passed resolutions" denouncing Capt. Montague.

Though Thomas Nelson, from his long tenure of the office of secretary, was commonly styled Secretary Nelson, he was also the last president of the colonial council. Some idea of his great popularity may be gathered from the fact that when the convention, on June 29, 1776, ballotted for the first governor of the new state, he was nominated as a candidate for that office (probably by the conservative party) and received forty-five votes to the sixty for Patrick Henry. On the same day he was chosen one of the first privy council of the commonwealth, but declined the appointment "on account of his age and infirmities." He retired from public life at this time and lived quietly at his home in Yorktown, a retirement which was not interrupted until the occupation of that place by the British forces.

Campbell ("History of Virginia") says, "Upon the breaking out of the revolution the secretary had retired from public affairs. He lived at Yorktown, where he had erected a handsome house. Cornwallis made his headquarters in this house, which stood near the defensive works. It soon attracted the attention of the French artillery, and was almost entirely demolished. Secretary Nelson was in it when the first shot killed one of his negroes at a little distance from him. What increased his solicitude was that he had two sons in the American army; so that every shot, whether fired from the town or from the trenches, might prove equally fatal to him. When a flag was sent in to request that he might be conveyed within the American lines, one of his sons was observed gazing wistfully at the gate of the town by which his father, then disabled by the gout, was to come out. Cornwallis permitted his withdrawal, and he was taken to Washington's headquarters. Upon alighting, with a serene countenance, he related to the officers who stood around him what had been the effect of their batteries, and how much his mansion had suffered from the first shot."

Thomas Nelson was married to Lucy Armistead.

Corbin, Richard, of "Buckingham House," and "Corbin Hall," Middlesex county, and "Laneville," King and Queen county, was the son of Col. Gawin Corbin of the same place, and was for many years one of the most eminent and influential men of the colony of Virginia. He was educated in William and Mary College and probably also in England, and early in life was appointed a justice in Middlesex county. He represented this county in the house of burgesses in 1751 (and doubtless for several years before) and was, during that session of the assembly, appointed to the council, in which body he sat until the revolution. Col. Corbin was appointed receiver general of Virginia about 1754, an office which he also held until the close of the colonial regime. Through his influence George Washington received his first military commission. In 1754, young Washington wrote to Col. Corbin asking a commission in the military service of the colony. A major's commission was obtained and sent him with the following letter:

Dear George:
I enclose your commission. God prosper you with it.
Your Friend, RICHARD CORBIN.

Col. Corbin rendered efficient service in council during the French and Indian war, and received, along with Washington, William Fairfax, Gov. Dinwiddie and some others, a medal, as a sign of royal approbation. In April, 1775, Gov. Dinwiddie secretly removed the powder from the magazine in Williamsburg, and by so doing gave a great impetus to the revolutionary spirit in Virginia. Throughout the colony meetings were held, and armed volunteers offered their services to redress the indignity done to Virginia by the governor. The Hanover county committee of safety resolved to take immediate steps to recover the powder or to make reprisal for it. "Ensign Parke Goodall with sixteen men, was detached into King and Queen county to Laneville, on the Mattapony, the seat of Richard Corbin, the King's deputy receiver general, to demand of him the estimated value, and in case of refusal to make him a prisoner. The detachment reached Laneville about midnight and a guard was stationed around the house. At daybreak, Mrs. Corbin assurred Goodall that the King's money was never left there, but at Williamsburg and that Col. Corbin was then in that town. Henry, meanwhile, with 150 men, had marched on Williamsburg and halted at Doncastle's Ordinary to wait for Goodall. There was intense excitement at the capital. Dunmore made preparation for defence, and even the patriots there were alarmed at the approaching storm. Carter Braxton, Col. Corbin's son-in-law, interfered and obtained from the latter a bill of exchange for £330, the estimated value of the powder, which Henry promised to hold subject to the order for a general convention. In this way the disturbance in the country was temporarily allayed. It was subsequently ascertained that the powder was worth only about £112, and the residue of the money was returned to the receiver general. Though it was well known that Col. Corbin's sympathies and belief were with England in the contest, yet when he retired at the outbreak of the war, and lived quietly in the country, he received no molestation from the new government. Doubtless his high character and past services had much to do with this, but it may also have been due to his feeble health." There is an interesting reference to Col. Corbin in a letter written by his son, Francis P. Corbin, in 1813. In it is stated that the King actually sent a commission to Col. Corbin, appointing him governor of Virginia after the abdication of Lord Dunmore, but that it came too late and that Corbin prudently hid it in a secret drawer of his escretoire. No record has been found of the death of Richard Corbin, but it must have been in, or subsequent to, 1787.

Beverley, William, of "Blandfield," Essex county was the son of the historian, Robert Beverley of "Beverley Park," King and Queen county and was born about 1698. He was clerk of Essex county from 1716 to 1745, burgess from Orange county in 1736 and from Essex in 1741, 1744, 1748, 1751 and doubtless in intervening years. Having large landed interests in the western part of the colony, he was appointed county lieutenant of Orange and Augusta counties and, in 1751, was made a member of the council. Col. Beverley was one of the commissioners from Virginia to meet those from other colonies and treat with the six nations at Lancaster, Pennsylvania, in 1744. Beverley was also appointed by Lord Fairfax, one of the commissioners to settle in his behalf, the boundary of Northern Neck. He inherited large estates, including "Beverley Park," containing 7,600 acres, with "The Plains," of 1,200 acres adjoining, and "Blandfield" on the Rappahannock, in Essex, where he built the brick mansion which is one of the finest remaining examples of colonial architecture. He also became the possessor of immense tracts of land by patent. Besides several smaller grants of some thousand acres each, he obtained, Sept. 6, 1736, a grant of 118,420 acres lying around the present Staunton in Augusta county. This land, which he named "Beverley Manor," now the name of a magisterial district in Augusta, he patented in partnership with several persons, but on the day after the grant was made, they conveyed their interests to him. This estate he sold to settlers in smaller tracts. His death occurred about March 1, 1756.

Grymes, Philip, of "Brandon," Middlesex county, and son of Hon. John Grymes of the same place, was appointed justice of Middlesex in 1743, was a member of the house of burgesses in 1748, and, in 1749, was appointed receiver general of Virginia. In 1751, he was made a member of the council and was present at its sessions from that year until the close of 1761. His long will, disposing of a very large estate and dated 1756, is on record in Middlesex. He was the father of Philip Ludwell Grymes of "Brandon," burgess for Middlesex county 1769, member of the house of delegates 1778, and appointed to the state council in 1803; who died May 18, 1805.

Carter, Robert Jr., son of Robert Carter of "Nomini Hall," Westmoreland county, Virginia, and grandson of Col. Robert Carter, of "Corotoman," Lancaster county, Virginia, was born in 1728, and inherited large possessions of lands and houses in Virginia and Maryland. He removed in 1761 from Westmoreland to Williamsburg, where he had a fine residence. In 1764 he was made a member of the council, and in 1772 returned to his country seat at "Nomini Hall." Like a few of the other wealthy men of Virginia, he did not approve of separating from England, but when independence was declared he threw in his future with his native land. After the revolution, he freed many of his slaves, and changed his religion several times. On this account he has been referred to as the "Eccentric Robert Carter, of "Nomini Hall." But he was a man of great culture, possessed one of the finest libraries in America, and was the author of many noble deeds of kindness. He married Frances Anne Tasker, youngest daughter of Hon. Benjamin Tasker, of Maryland, and left issue.

Ludwell, Philip, the third of that name, of "Green Spring," James City county and son of Hon. Philip Ludwell of the same place, was born about the twenty-ninth of Dec., 1716. He was a member of the house of burgesses for Jamestown in 1748 and at that session was appointed one of the committee to make a general revision of the laws. He was a member of the house again in 1749 and probably in other years. The exact date of his appointment to the council does not appear, but the earliest mention of him as present was on March 26, 1752. From this time until 1761, he seems to have been a regular attendant. Soon after he probably went to England and spent the remaining years of his life there, though still retaining his position as councillor for the "Gazette" in speaking of his death calls him "one of his majesty's council in Virginia." He died on March 25, 1767, and was buried at Bow Church near London. With him became extinct, in the male line, the family of Ludwell, which for more than a hundred years had been possessed of large estate and great political influence in the colony, and whose members had so frequently defended the rights of the people and the legislature against the encroachments of the governors. For their own services and as ancestors of so many Virginians of fame, the Ludwells, though extinct, are held in honored memory.

Randolph, Peter, of Chatsworth, Henrico county, and son of Hon. William Randolph of "Turkey Island," was born about 1713. His first public office seems to have been clerk of Albemarle county, which he held only during the year 1749, and then only by deputy. In 1751, he was a member of the house of burgesses for Henrico, and in the next year, was appointed to the council, of which he remained a member until his death. Some years after he became a councillor, he was appointed by the King, surveyor general of the customs for the middle district of America. Col. Randolph strongly opposed the measures taken by the more advanced friends of American liberty, and Jefferson relates how, on the morning after Henry's famous resolutions were adopted by the house of burgesses, he came to the capitol before the session of the house began, and saw Col. Peter Randolph, of the council, sitting at the clerk's desk and examining the journals to find a precedent for expunging a vote of the house. He died, July 8, 1767, too early to see the result of the revolutionary spirit, which he opposed.

Dawson, Rev. Thomas, was a younger brother of the learned and good Commissary William Dawson, of whom a sketch is given above. He came to Virginia at an early age and was educated at William and Mary College. In 1738 he was master of the Indian school there and at the same time was studying divinity under the guidance of his brother, then a professor at the college. In May, 1740, he went to England to be ordained, carrying with him a letter of introduction to the bishop of London, written by Commissary Blair and describing him as "a young man of sober, regular life" and with "a very good character." Three years later Mr. Dawson was elected to succeed Dr. Blair as rector of Bruton parish. In 1752 he was appointed commissary and member of the council to succeed his brother. He enjoyed a high place in Gov. Dinwiddie's favor. The new commissary at first declined the seat in the council, forseeing trouble in regard to his brother's estate, but his objections were overruled and the records show him to have been a frequent attendant at the sessions as long as he held the office of commissary. Thomas Dawson presided and preached at the convention of the clergy of Virginia in 1754, and the following year succeeded Stith as president of William and Mary College. His administration fell upon years of religious and political strife, when the professors of the college and the board of visitors were divided into factions. Dawson became very unpopular with the faculty, but retained the friendship of Gov. Dinwiddie and his successor, Francis Fauquier. At the last he fell into habits of intemperance and confessed the fact before the whole board of the college managers, at which time he had the honor of having an excuse made for him by his friend, Gov. Fauquier, who said that it was no wonder that he had resorted to drink since he had been teased to desperation by persons of his own cloth. He did not long survive, dying Dec. 5, 1761, leaving issue.

Byrd, William, the third of that name, of Westover, Charles City county, was the son of Col. William Byrd, of the same place. His collegiate education is believed to have begun at William and Mary College, and to have been completed in England. When he reached manhood he inherited what was probably the greatest estate in Virginia, and the prestige attached to one of the most distinguished names. He at once entered public life, becoming a member of the house of burgesses in 1753 and 1754, and in the latter year a member of the council, an office he held until the end of the colonial government. In 1758 the exigencies of the French and Indian war required that another regiment be raised in Virginia, and William Byrd was appointed its colonel, going at once into service. Some thought that he showed even greater talents as a military man than Col. Washington. Although, so far as the records show, Col. Byrd filled his various public offices in a satisfactory manner, he was sadly imprudent in his private concerns and dissipated to a large extent the splendid estate he had inherited. He died Jan. 1, 1777. He married twice: (First) Elizabeth Hill, only daughter of John Carter, of "Shirley," and (second) Mary, daughter of

Charles Willing, of Philadelphia, first cousin of Peggy Shippen, the famous Philadelphia beauty, who married Benedict Arnold.

Thornton, Presley, son of Col. Anthony Thornton, who was descended from the Thorntons of Yorkshire, England, inherited almost all the large estates of the Presley family of Northumberland county, Virginia, through his mother, Winifred, daughter of Col. Peter Presley, of "Northumberland House." He was born in 1721, and at an early age he was elected to the house of burgesses for Northumberland and served continuously from 1748 to 1760, when he was appointed to the council. He married twice: (First) Elizabeth ———, (second) Charlotte Belson, an English lady, and left issue. He died Dec. 8, 1769. Washington spoke of him as "a man of great worth."

Robinson, Rev. William, son of Col. Christopher Robinson, of Middlesex county, Virginia, was born March 5, 1716, was sent to school in England at ten years of age and matriculated at Oriel College, Oxford, April 2, 1737. He took his B. A. degree in 1740. After enjoying for three years one of the "London exhibitions" established by his great-uncle, Dr. John Robinson, bishop of London, he was ordained priest by Dr. Gibson, the then bishop. In Oct., 1744, he returned to his native country and was made rector of Stratton Major Parish, King and Queen county, where he continued rector till his death. He was one of the leading clergymen in opposing the Two Penny Act, and incurred the enmity of Gov. Fauquier, who was in favor of it. Despite the latter's opposition he was appointed, in 1761, commissary of the bishop of London, and became, as usual in such cases, member of the colonial council. He died in 1767 or 1768, leaving issue several children by his wife Alice, daughter of Benjamin Needler, of King and Queen county, Virginia.

Fitzhugh, William, son of Col. William Fitzhugh, of Stafford county, Virginia, and grandson of Henry Fitzhugh, of Bedfordshire, England, inherited, under his father's will 18,723 acres in Stafford and Westmoreland counties, and was residuary legatee of all lands not bequeathed in Maryland, Virginia and England. He was appointed clerk of Stafford county July 18, 1701, and was a member of the house of burgesses for that county in 1700, 1701, 1702. He was appointed to the council on Dec. 19, 1712, and Fitzhugh took the oaths in Virginia Oct. 15, 1712. His tenure of office was short, for his last appearance in council was on Nov. 8, 1713, and on Jan. 27, 1714, there is an entry on the council journal that he was dead. He married Anne, daughter of Richard Lee, of Westmoreland county, and left issue: 1. Henry (q. v.). 2. Lettice, married George Turberville, of "Hickory Grove," Westmoreland county. 3. Sarah, married Edward Barradall, attorney-general of Virginia. His residence in Stafford county (now King George county) is known as "Eagle's Nest."

Lee, Philip Ludwell, was the eldest son of President Thomas Lee that survived him. He was born Feb. 24, 1726-27, and like many other young gentlemen of the day was sent to England to be educated, studying law in London at the Inner Temple. When Thomas Lee and William Beverley went to Pennsylvania to treat with the Iroquois in 1744, Philip Ludwell Lee, then a youth of eighteen, was one of the gallant party of gentlemen that accompanied them. He represented Westmoreland in the house of burgesses in 1756 and was present in council in 1758 and the year following. Upon the death of his father in 1750 Philip Ludwell fell heir to the larger part of his estate, and was also entrusted with the guardianship and education of his younger brothers. Perhaps it was these responsibilities that kept him a bachelor until he was about thirty-five years of age, when Elizabeth Steptoe, daughter of James Steptoe, of Westmoreland, became his wife. He seems to have been secretary of the council in 1770, as on the eighteenth of June of that year he made out a "list of Books necessary for the Council Chamber." Such books as reports of parliament, histories, philosophical transactions, the orations of Demosthenes, etc., were named in the list. Philip Ludwell Lee died Feb. 23, 1775, and was buried the next day, his forty-ninth birthday.

Horrocks, Rev. James, is chiefly known through his connection with William and Mary College. In 1764 Commissary Robinson wrote "Mr. Horrocks, a young clergyman, after having been master of the Grammar School two or three years, has found means of carrying the Presidentship of the college against Mr. Graham a clergyman of unexceptionable character and generally esteemed, who has been Professor of Mathematics in the college near twenty years." In the same letter Robinson charged that Horrocks had gained this promotion through time-serving. Besides being president of the college Horrocks, upon the death of Robinson a little later in the same year, was made commissary and was rector of Bruton Parish Church. His name is on record as present in the council in 1758 and 1759, and he remained a member until his death. He took an active part in the controversies which agitated Virginia while the revolution was brewing, especially in the disputes regarding the salaries of the clergy, the establishment of a bishopric in America and the stamp act. He expressed belief in the iniquity of the act of the house of burgesses providing that the clergy should be paid in paper money instead of tobacco, but opposed John Camm's plan of repeated appeal to England, believing it to be useless. His health failing in 1771 he sailed for England, accompanied by his wife, leaving Camm in his chair as president of William and Mary, the Rev. Mr. Willie as commissary and the Rev. Mr. Henley to fill the pulpit at Bruton. He died March 20, 1772. In spite of the stormy times Horrock's administration was a palmy time for William and Mary College. Harvard at the time was still under the charge of a president and tutors, with but two professors, while the younger sister in Virginia had for years enjoyed the advantages of a corps of professors, alumni of the great universities of England and Scotland.

Fairfax, George William, of "Belvoir," Fairfax county, Virginia, and of "Toulston," Yorkshire, England, was the son of Col. William Fairfax, of "Belvoir," and was born in the Bahamas in 1724. His education was obtained in England and, on his return to Virginia, in early manhood, he at once began to play an active part in the affairs of the colony. In his twenty-first year, he was appointed a justice in Fairfax county, and from 1748 to 1758 was a member of the house of burgesses. The companion of Washington on his first surveying expedition, he remained through life one of his most attached and valued friends. During the French and Indian war, as a colonel of militia, he actively assisted Washington in the defence of the frontier. He became a member of the council in April, 1768, and remained an active participant in its proceedings until 1773, when he went to England to take possession of Toulston, in Yorkshire, an estate which had descended to him through the death of his father's elder brother,

Henry Fairfax. He was also actuated in his return to England by the fact that Virginia had ceased to be an attractive place of residence for one so loyal as he. It is said that on his arrival, while sailing up the Thames, he actually passed the fateful tea, which was to prove the occasion of hostilities between the colonies and the mother country. Fairfax died at Bath, England, April 3, 1787, and appointed Washington one of his executors.

Burwell, Robert Carter, of Isle of Wight county, a son of Nathaniel Burwell, of Carter's Creek, Gloucester, was educated at William and Mary College. He settled in Isle of Wight county, on Burwell's Bay, and represented the county in the house of burgesses in 1752, and the same year was one of the first trustees of Smithfield. In 1764 he was elevated to the council, which he held till the revolution. His will, dated Jan. 10, 1777, was proved Oct. 13, 1777. He had a son Nathaniel, who was clerk of Isle of Wight court from 1772 to 1787, and a daughter Frances, who was first wife of Gov. John Page.

Tayloe, John, Jr., of "Mt. Airy," Richmond county, a son of Hon. John Tayloe, was born May 28, 1721. He is stated to have been educated in England at the University of Cambridge and to have inherited a very large estate from his father, who died when he was sixteen years of age. As soon as he reached his majority he was appointed a justice for Richmond county, and in a short time became one of the most influential, as he was probably the wealthiest man in the region. The exact date upon which he was commissioned a councillor does not appear from the extant records, but he sat as a member April 21, 1757, and held his office until the outbreak of the revolution. Though a supporter of American liberty and a friend of Gen. Washington, it seems probable that he was not in favor of an entire separation from Great Britain, for, though he was elected by the convention of 1776, a member of the first republican council of state, he declined to accept the office. In 1758 Col. Tayloe completed the fine house at "Mt. Airy," on the Rappahannock river, which, with its gardens and parks, remains such an interesting example of the home of the wealthy colonial planter. He had also a town house at Williamsburg for his winter residence, and "here and at Mt. Airy he was renowned for his hospitality." Col. Tayloe died April 18, 1779. He married Rebecca Plater, eldest daughter of George Plater, Esq., of St. Mary's county, Maryland, and had a son John and eight daughters who each married a man of distinction. "Mt. Airy" still remains in the Tayloe family.

Page, John, of "North End," on North river, Gloucester (now Matthews) county, was the son of Hon. Mann Page, of "Rosewell," Gloucester, and was born about 1720. According to the short autobiography of his nephew, Gov. Page, John Page, of "North End," was educated as a lawyer. The catalogue of William and Mary College shows that he was a student there. He was a member of the house of burgesses, representing Gloucester from 1754 to 1764, and was appointed to the council in 1768. The "Virginia Gazette" of June 16 in that year announces the appointment, and a later edition states that he was sworn and took his seat on June 30. He was also one of the visitors of William and Mary College. His tenure of office did not last long, for the "Gazette" of Oct. 6, 1774, records his death.

Wormeley, Ralph, the third of that name, of "Rosegill," Middlesex county, was the son of Ralph Wormeley, of the same place, and was born in 1744. He was educated at Eaton and the University of Cambridge, and became a finished scholar with tastes which ran rather to literature than to public life. From the great wealth and political influence of his family, however, it was almost a matter of course that he be called to a high office in the government of the colony, and accordingly we find him shortly before the revolution occupying a seat in the council to which he was appointed in June, 1771. Though apparently opposed to the measures of the English government in taxing Americans, he was yet steadfastly loyal, and throughout the revolutionary period suffered the consequences of his devotion to the crown. He wrote, unfortunately for himself a letter expressing disapproval of the steps which the patriots were taking and was obliged to give bond not to leave his father's estate until permitted. After the war, notwithstanding the strong feeling against British sympathizers existing in Virginia, the high character and large estate of Ralph Wormeley soon restored his influence. He was a member of the convention of 1788, was sheriff in 1794 and 1795 and a member of the house of delegates in 1787, 1789, 1790 and 1793. His death occurred Jan. 19, 1806.

Camm, John, the last colonial president of William and Mary College, was the son of Thomas Camm, of Hornsea, England, and was born there in 1718. When a boy he went to school in Beverley, Yorkshire, England, and at twenty years of age, matriculated at Trinity College, Cambridge. Eleven years later we find him in Virginia, professor of divinity in William and Mary College, upon which office he entered August 24, 1749. On Oct. 30, 1754, a convention of the clergy of Virginia met at William and Mary College and Camm took a leading part in it. He was appointed one of a committee to prepare "an humble address" from the convention to the bishop of London, and on several other committees. He took part in the controversy between the clergy and government of Virginia over the Two Penny Act, regarding the payment of salaries, and made a violent enemy of Gov. Fauquier. It was against the sentiment of the time for any member of the faculty of a college, except the president, to marry and Camm broke this convention at the age of fifty-seven and lost his professorship in consequence, but later, upon the death of Horrocks, in 1771, he was chosen president of the college and head of the church in Virginia as well. He became a member of the council in 1775, but in 1777 he was removed from the presidency of the college because, ardent tory that he was, he would not acknowledge the United States government. Two years later death ended the checkered career of "Old Parson," as he was familiarly called. He married Betsey Hansford, and has many descendants in Virginia.

Corbin, Gawin, Jr., of "Buckingham House," Middlesex county, eldest son of Hon. Richard Corbin, of "Laneville," was educated abroad and returned to Virginia about 1761. In Nov., 1758, ex-Gov. Dinwiddie, in a letter from London to Col. Richard Corbin, says: "Your son dined with me before he went to Cambridge. He is truly a sober well-bred young gentleman." After his return to Virginia, Corbin was a member of the house of burgesses for Middlesex and was appointed to the council in 1775, remaining a member until the end of the royal government. The "Virginia Gazette," March 6, 1775, says: "We are informed that Gawin Corbin, Esq., of Middlesex, is appointed one of his Majesty's honorable Council of this colony, in the room of the late John Page deceased."

BURGESSES AND OTHER PROMINENT PERSONS

IV—BURGESSES AND OTHER PROMINENT PERSONS

Abrahall, Robert, came to Virginia about 1650 and settled in New Kent county, which he represented in the house of burgesses in 1654 and 1660. In the first year he was captain in the New Kent militia, and in the last he was lieutenant-colonel. He used a seal having the arms of Abrahall of Herefordshire.

Abbott, Jeffrey, came to Virginia in the "Food Supply" in 1608; he had served as a soldier in Ireland and the Netherlands, and according to Smith was an excellent colonist. But rebelling against the tyranny of Sir Thomas Dale, he was executed in 1611.

Acrill, William, was a member of the house of burgesses from Charles City county in 1736, and died in November, 1738. He married Anne Cocke, of Surry, sister of Richard Cocke and Benjamin Cocke. He left a son, William Acrill, Jr.

Acrill, William, Jr., was a member of the house of burgesses for Charles City county from 1766 to 1775, and of the conventions of 1774, 1775 and 1776.

Ackiss, John, burgess for Princess Anne county in the assembly of May, 1769, and 1769-1771.

Adams, Richard, son of Ebenezer Adams, of New Kent county, Virginia, and grandson of Richard Adams, of Abridge, county Essex, England, citizen and merchant tailor of London, was born in New Kent county, May 17, 1726; member of the house of burgesses from New Kent and Henrico from 1752 to 1775; Henrico county committee, 1774-75; Virginia convention in 1775; house of delegates, 1776-1778; Virginia senate, 1779-1782. Died in Richmond, Aug. 2, 1800. He married Elizabeth, daughter of Leroy and Mary Anne Griffin.

Adams (Addams), Robert, was a member of the house of burgesses, 1623-24.

Aitchison, William, was burgess from Norfolk borough in the assembly of 1758-1761. He was a prominent merchant of Norfolk, and died Nov. 15, 1776. His tombstone, with a coat-of-arms upon it, is still standing. He left a son William.

Alexander, Gerard (Gerrard), was burgess from Fairfax county, session of 1752-1755. He was a great-grandson of John Alexander, the immigrant, and son of Robert Alexander, of Stafford county, and his wife, Anne Fowke, daughter of Col. Gerard Fowke, of Alexandria. At one time he resided at Holm's Island, Prince William county. In 1753 he docked the entail of a tract of 6,000 acres left him by his father, and settled other lands in Frederic and Fairfax counties to the same uses. His will was proved in Fairfax, Sept. 16, 1761. It names wife, Mary (Dent?), and six children, and disposes of houses and lots in Alexandria, chairs and horses, and land in Loudoun county.

Alexander, John, son of Capt. Philip Alexander, of King George county, was born Nov. 15, 1730, was burgess for Stafford county in the assemblies of Oct., 1765, 1766-1768, May, 1769, 1769-1772, 1772-1774. He married Lucy Thornton, daughter of William Thornton, and died about 1775.

Allen, Maj. Arthur, was the son and heir of Arthur Allen, of Surry county, and of his wife, Alice Tucker. Maj. Allen's father, in 1649, patented 200 acres between Lawne's creek and Lower Chippoakes creek. Maj. Allen was burgess from Surry county in 1682, in 1685-86 and in 1688. In the last-named session he was speaker of the assembly. He married Katherine, daughter and heiress of Capt. Laurence Baker, of Surry. On July 3, 1677, Mr. Arthur Allen sued Mr. Robert Burgess for that "during the late most Horrid Rebellion (Bacon's rebellion) he with others did seize and keep garrison in the plts' house neare fower months." This ancient brick mansion is still standing, one of the oldest houses in Virginia, and is known as "Bacon's Castle" (1914). Maj. Allen's will was proved in Surry court, Sept. 5, 1710.

Allen, Edmund, was burgess from Accomac in the session of Feb. 5, 1752. He resigned to accept the place of sheriff, and for the remainder of that assembly his place was srpplied by Ralph Justice. He also represented Accomac in the assemblies of 1756-1758 and 1758-1761.

Allen, Edward, was burgess from Accomac in the session of May 22, 1740, in the place of Henry Scarburgh, deceased. He also represented Accomac in the assembly of 1748-1749.

Allen, William, came in 1622; burgess for Henry Throckmorton's Plantation in 1629.

Allen, William, son of Joseph Allen and grandson of Maj. Arthur Allen, who was burgess and speaker, was educated at William and Mary College, was burgess for Surry county in the assemblies of 1758-1761, colonel of the militia, etc. He married (first) Clara Walker, and (second) Mary Lightfoot, daughter of William Lightfoot, of "Sandy Point," Charles City county, and by the last had Col. William Allen, of "Claremont," James river (1768-1831).

Allerton, Willoughby, son of Col. Isaac Allerton, of the council, and Elizabeth Willoughby, daughter of Capt. Thomas Willoughby, was a burgess for Westmoreland county in 1699, 1710, 1712 and 1712-1714; collector of customs for Potomac river in 1711. He married Hannah, daughter of William Keene, of Northumberland county, and widow of John Bushrod. He died in 1723-24, leaving issue—Elizabeth and Isaac.

Allington, Lieut. Giles, of Kecoughtan, gentleman; member of the London Company in 1620 and was probably of the family of Allington of Horsehester, Cambridgeshire; he was an "ancient planter," but the year in which he came to Virginia is not known.

Ambler, Edward, son of Richard Ambler, was born in 1733; was, like his brother John, schooled at Wakefield and Cambridge, and finished his education by making "the grand tour" of Europe. On his return to Virginia he was made collector of the port of Yorktown, and in 1766 succeeded his brother John as the representative for Jamestown in the assembly. He died Oct. 30, 1768. He married Mary, daughter of Col. Wilson Miles Cary.

Ambler, John, eldest son of Richard Ambler, merchant of Jamestown and Yorktown, was born at Yorktown, Dec. 31, 1765; educated at Leeds Academy, near Wakefield, in Yorktown, and at the University of Cambridge and the Middle Temple, from which last he graduated as barrister at law. He represented Jamestown in the house of burgesses in 1760, and was elected to that of 1766, but died before he took his seat, May 27, 1766.

Ambler, Richard, son of John Ambler, sheriff of Yorkshire, England, in 1721, and Elizabeth Bickadike, his wife. The son came to Virginia in the early part of the eighteenth century and settled at Yorktown. He married Elizabeth, daughter of Edward Jaquelin, and succeeded to the Jaquelin estates at Jamestown. He was also largely engaged as a merchant at Yorktown, at which place he died in 1766, leaving three sons—John, Edward and Jaquelin.

Anderson, Rev. Charles, was minister for twenty-four years of Westover parish, Charles City county. His tombstone at Westover states that he died April 7, 1718. He left a son Charles, and daughters—Frances, who married Thomas Pinkard; Elizabeth, who married John Stith; Charlotte, who married Henry Taylor, and Jane, who married Ellyson Armistead.

Anderson, Charles, was burgess from Prince Edward in the sessions of Feb. 14, 1754, Aug. 22, 1754, Oct. 17, 1754, May 1, 1755, Oct. 27, 1755, and in the assemblies of 1756-1758 and 1758-1761.

Anderson, David, a native of Scotland, was born in 1760, came to Petersburg, Va., was long a member of the Common Hall of the town, and chamberlain of the same. He founded the Anderson Seminary for the corporation of Petersburg. He died June 18, 1812.

Anderson, George, burgess for Stafford county in 1715.

Anderson, Matthew, succeeded, on the death of John Syme, as a burgess from Hanover county in 1732, and continued till the end of the assembly (1734).

Anderson, Richard, burgess for Louisa county in 1765, 1766-1768, 1769, 1769-1772 and 1772-1774. He was colonel of the county militia, and in 1780 married Catherine Fox.

Anderson, Robert, burgess for Louisa county in 1752-1755, in the place of Thomas Walker, who accepted the office of coroner. He was son of Robert Anderson, of "Gold Mine," and Mary Overton, his wife, was born Jan. 1, 1712, and died 1792. He was grandfather of Robert Anderson, who commanded at Fort Sumter in 1861.

Anderson, William, was a merchant of Accomac county, and served as burgess at the assembly of 1695-1696. His eldest daughter, Naomi, married Francis Makemie, the founder of the Presbyterian church in America. His will was proved Oct. 4, 1698. He was probably from the county of Sussex, England, as he left money due him there to his sister, Comfort Scott.

Andrews, Rev. Robert, was the son of Moses Andrews, of Pennsylvania, and great-grandson of John Andrews, who emigrated in 1654 from Leicestershire, England, to Maryland. He was educated at the College of Philadelphia, and was tutor for several years in the family of Mann Page, of "Rosewell," Va., and in 1772 went to England for ordination; professor of moral philosophy in William and Mary College, 1779; transferred to the mathematical chair in 1784; in 1781 was private secretary of Gen. Nelson; in 1788 represented Williamsburg in the state convention of 1788, and in 1798 was a member of the legislature and voted against the celebrated resolutions of Mr. Madison. He served with President James Madison, of William and Mary College, on a commission to define the Virginia and Pennsylvania line. He married (first) Elizabeth Ballard, (second) Mary Blair.

Andrews, William, an ancient planter, came before 1616, was living on the eastern shore in 1624; lieutenant-colonel of the militia of Northampton county; died in 1654 or 1655, leaving issue—William, John, Robert, Andrew and daughter Susanna, and grandchildren, Elisheba and Elizabeth Andrews.

Andrews, William, Jr., son of Lieut.-Col. William Andrews, was sheriff of Northampton county in 1655, and burgess in 1663. He married Dorothea, the widow of Mountjoy Evelyn and daughter of Col. Obedience Robins, of "Cherrystone." He was a justice, major of militia, etc.

Anne, Queen of the Pamunkey Indians in 1676, and widow of Tobopotomoi. She was a relative of Opechaucanough. Bacon attacked her tribe and she was forced to flee for her life. Sir Herbert Jefferyes completed a treaty of peace with her on May 29, 1677, at which time he gave her a coronet, or frontal, adorned with false jewels. By an English colonel she had a son Capt. John West, who was about twenty in 1676. Her coronet is preserved by the Virginia Historical Society.

Appleton, John, was born in 1640, and was probably from New England, where the name is prominent. He was burgess from Westmoreland in the session of March 7, 1675-76, and was a captain. He married Frances Gerrard (widow of Thomas Speke and Valentine Peyton). His widow married (fourthly) Col. John Washington, ancestor of George Washington. He had a "brother, Mr. Richard Colbourn, neare Spittlefields Gate, in London," in 1674. Capt. Appleton died in 1676.

Applewhaite, Capt. Henry, was a burgess for Isle of Wight county at the assembly of 1700-1702. He came from Barbadoes, and died in 1704, leaving issue—sons, Henry (q. v.), Thomas and William, and daughter Anne.

Applewhaite, Henry, son of Henry Applewhaite, was burgess for Isle of Wight county in 1723-1726.

Archer, Capt. James, ensign in the regiment of Col. Herbert Jefferyes, sent over in 1676 to subdue Bacon's rebellion; settled in Virginia and was justice of the peace for York county. His daughter Anne married Maj. William Barber (q. v.).

Armistead, Anthony, was son of the emigrant, William Armistead, who was son of Anthony Armistead and Frances Thompson, his wife, of Kirkdeighton, in Yorkshire, England, and resided in Elizabeth City county. He was one of Sir William Berkeley's courtmartial in 1676 to try the Bacon insurgents; justice of the peace and captain of horse in 1680; burgess from Elizabeth City county in 1693, 1696, 1697, 1699; and one of the committee in 1700 to report a revision of the laws which was approved by the general assembly in 1705. He married Hannah, daughter of Dr. Robert Ellyson, of James City county.

Armistead, Anthony, son of Anthony Armistead, son of William, the emigrant, was burgess from Elizabeth City county, in the assembly of 1720-1722. He was lieutenant-colonel of militia in 1724. He was justice and high sheriff of Elizabeth City county. He was called Anthony Armistead, Senior, to distinguish him from his nephew, Anthony Armistead, of Warwick county. He married, it is believed, twice: (First) Anne, who united with Anthony Armistead in a deed in 1717, (secondly) Elizabeth Westwood, sister of William Westwood. His will was probated Dec. 18, 1728.

Armistead, Gill, was the son and heir of Capt. John Armistead, of New Kent, and his wife, Elizabeth (Gill?). He lived in Blissland parish, New Kent. He was sheriff in 1751, and colonel in 1758. He married Betty Allen, of James City. He was burgess from New Kent in the sessions of Nov. 3, 1761, Jan. 14, 1762, March 30, 1762. In the sessions of Nov. 2, 1762, Burwell Bassett represented New Kent in place of Gill Armistead, deceased.

Armistead, Col. Henry, was son of Col. John Armistead, of the council, and lived first at "Hesse," at the mouth of Pianketank river, in Gloucester (now Mathews county). In 1733 he was sworn county lieutenant of Caroline, and must have lived, during the latter portion of his life, in Caroline county. He married Martha (baptized Nov. 16, 1685), daughter of Maj. Lewis Burwell. He had issue: 1. William, of Hesse. 2. Lucy, married Thomas Nelson, of Yorktown, secretary of state. 3. Martha, married Dudley Digges. 4. Robert.

Armistead, Robert, son of Anthony Armistead, and Hannah Ellyson, his wife, and grandson of the emigrant, William, was a burgess for Elizabeth City county in 1714, succeeding Nicholas Curle, who died; in 1715, agent for Row's warehouse on Poquosin river; justice and sheriff of York county; married (first) Miss Booth, (second) Katherine Nutting, and his will was proved in Elizabeth City county, May 9, 1742. He left issue—Ellyson Armistead and others.

Armistead, Robert, was burgess from Elizabeth City county in the session of May 12, 1726. He was son of Maj. William Armistead; married Ann, daughter of Rev. James Wallace, who came from Erroll, in Perthshire, Scotland. In 1737 the trustees for Eaton's Free School land rented him a portion of the land, for the natural lives of his sons, Robert, William and James, conditioned on his building two tobacco houses, planting and caring for an orchard of 200 winter apple trees and paying to the trustees the annual rent of six pounds current money. Robert Armistead was for many years church warden of his parish, and colonel of the militia. His will is dated July 28, 1771, and was proved Nov. 24, 1774.

Armistead, William, was son of Anthony Armistead (q. v.) and his wife, Hannah Ellyson. He resided in Elizabeth City county, and was major in the militia, high sheriff of Elizabeth City county (1695) and a justice. He was burgess from Elizabeth City county in the assembly of 1696-1697, and in the sessions of May 13 and June 18, 1702, Oct. 25, 1710, and Nov. 16, 1714. He married several times. His first wife was Hannah, born July 1, 1673, daughter of Thomas Hinde (or Hine) by his wife Hannah. Maj. Armistead's last wife was Rebecca, daughter of Edward Moss, J. P., of York county. Maj. Armistead's will is dated Jan. 5 (year blank), and probated Feb. 17, 1715-16.

Arundell or Erondelle, John, son of Peter Arundell, of Buckroe, was born in 1602. Appointed a commissioner of Elizabeth City in

Feb., 1632; member of the house of burgesses, Feb., 1633.

Arundell or Erondelle, Peter, gentleman, a native of Normandy; member of the London Company and a French teacher in London; published several books; came to Virginia in 1620; in 1624 he was living at Buckroe, in the corporation of Elizabeth City, with his children—John (q. v.), Elizabeth and Margaret.

Ashton, Charles, son of John Ashton, of Northumberland county, and Grace, his wife, was burgess for Westmoreland county in 1703-1705. He married (first) Miss Burdett, (second) in 1706, Margaret Hart, daughter of Edward Hart, and had issue—Burdett and Charles.

Ashton, Henry, was son of Capt. John Ashton and Grace (Meese?), his wife. He was born July 30, 1671. He was burgess from Westmoreland in the assemblies of 1702, 1703, 1705 and 1715. He was a colonel and a justice. He married (first) Elizabeth Hardidge (Hardwich), born 1678, died Feb., 1722, daughter and heiress of William Hardidge. Col. Ashton married (secondly) Mary Watts, daughter of Richard Watts. Col. Ashton was sheriff of Westmoreland county in 1717-18. He died Nov. 3, 1731.

Ashton, James, brother of Col. Peter Ashton was of Kirby Underwood, county Lincoln, England, came to Virginia after 1671; was a justice of Stafford county in 1680; died Aug., 1686.

Ashton, Peter, was descended from the Ashtons of Chatterton, in Lancashire, England. He came to Virginia about 1650, and was a member of the house of burgesses for Charles City county in 1656 and for Northumberland county, 1659, 1660; sheriff of Northumberland, 1658, and had the title of colonel. He gave his property in Virginia to his brothers, John Ashton, of Lowth, Lincolnshire, and James Ashton, of Kirby Underwood, in Lincolnshire, both of whom came to Virginia and died issueless.

Aston, Walter, son of Walter Aston, of Longden, Stafford county, England, gentleman, and great grandson of Sir Walter Aston, knighted in 1569, came to Virginia about 1628. In 1630 he represented Shirley Hundred as burgess. He patented in 1634, in Shirley Hundred 1,046 acres, endowing 200 acres known as "Cawsey's Cave." He was justice of the peace for Charles City county and lieutenant-colonel of the militia. He was born in 1607, and died April 6, 1656, leaving a son of the same name, who was also lieutenant-colonel.

Atkins, John, was burgess from Warrosqueake, in the assembly of 1629-30.

Atkinson, Roger, son of Roger and Jane Benson Atkinson, of Whitehaven, Cumberland county, England, was born June 25, 1725; came to Virginia about 1750, settled near Petersburg, and became a prosperous merchant. From 1760 to 1784 he was a member of the vestry of Bristol parish, dying shortly after 1784. He called his home "Mansfield," and used the arms of Atkinson of Newcastle. He married April 21, 1753, Ann, daughter of John Pleasants.

Aubrey, Henry, was burgess from Rappahannock in the assembly of 1688.

Aylett (Aylet), William, of "Fair Field," King William county, gentleman, son of Philip Aylett of "Fair Field," was burgess from King William county in the assembly of 1723-26. He bore arms which were to be seen pasted in a copy of Donne's "Poems," some time ago. He was a grandson of Capt. John Aylett or Ayloffe, a royalist officer who came to Virginia in 1656, son of Sir Benjamin Ayloffe, of county Essex, England. Issue, William and Philip.

Aylett (Aylet), William, son of Col. William Aylett, of "Fairfield" was burgess from Westmoreland in the assembly of 1736-1740. Capt. William Aylett, Jr., of Westmoreland, married (first) Anne Ashton, of Westmoreland, and (secondly) Elizabeth Eskridge, daughter of Maj. George Eskridge, of "Sandy Point." One of Capt. William Aylett's daughters married Richard Henry Lee, and another Augustine Washington.

Aylett, William, son of Philip Aylett, of "Fairfield," and grandson of Col. William Aylett, of "Fairfield" (q. v.), was born 1743; was burgess for King William county at the assemblies of 1772-1774 and of 1775-1776; member of the conventions of 1774, 1775 and 1776; resigned from the convention May 2, 1776, to accept commission as deputy commissary general in Virginia. He died at Yorktown, 1780. He married Elizabeth Macon, daughter of Col. James Macon and Elizabeth Moore, daughter of Augustine Moore, of "Chelsea."

Aylmer, Justinian, was born in 1635, matriculated at Trinity College, Oxford, 1656, and became A. M. in 1657. He was grandson of Theophilus Aylmer, archdeacon of London. In 1661 he was minister of Hampton parish, York county, Virginia, and a little later was minister of Jamestown. He died before 1671.

Bacon, Edmund, ancestor of the Bacon family in the south, patented land in New Kent county in 1687. He was captain of the militia. He probably married Anne Lyddall, daughter of Capt. George Lyddall. Edmund Bacon was, it is believed, a near kinsman of Nathaniel Bacon, Jr., the rebel.

Bacon, John, was son of Capt. Edmund Bacon, of New Kent, who patented land in 1687. John Bacon was vestryman of St. Peter's Church, sheriff in the county and burgess in 1727-1734. He married (first) Sarah Langston and (second) Susanna Parke.

Bagnall, James, burgess for Isle of Wight county in 1646 and for Lancaster county in 1654.

Bagnall, Roger, was a burgess for Isle of Wight county in 1641. His will dated October 19, 1647, is recorded in that county. He left a son James Bagnall.

Bagnell, Henry, was a member of the house of burgesses from Accomack, March, 1629-30, and Sept., 1632. His descendants have lived on the eastern shore to the present time. John Bagnell who was living in Accomac in 1679 was probably his son; Charles Bagnell was a vestryman of Accomack parish in 1772; Charles Bagnell was lieutenant-colonel of militia during the war of 1812; and Edmund R. Bagnell was brigadier-general of militia in 1870.

Bagwell, Thomas, an old settler, was burgess for Pasbehay, in James City corporation in 1629.

Bailey, Thomas, succeeded Henry Browne, deceased, as burgess for Surry county in Nov., 1762, and was burgess from that time till 1771.

Baker, Benjamin, of Nansemond, was a member of the convention of 1774.

Baker, Henry, of Nansemond, was son and heir of Lieut.-Col. Henry Baker, of Isle of Wight county. He was member of the house of burgesses for Nansemond in 1723-1726. He left a son Lawrence Baker.

Baker, Henry, of Isle of Wight county, was a merchant and planter living there as early as 1676. He was a justice of the peace and lieutenant-colonel of the militia; burgess for the county in 1692-93. His will dated June 10, 1707 was proved July 28, 1712. He was father of Henry Baker, of Nansemond, and of James, Lawrence and William Baker, of Isle of Wight county.

Baker, Capt. Lawrence, of Surry county, was a justice of Surry from 1652 to his death 1681. He was also a member of the house of burgesses from 1666 to 1676. His will was dated March 18, 1681 and was proved Sept. 6, 1681, and by it he left his whole estate to his wife Elizabeth, and to his daughter Catherine, wife of Arthur Allen of Surry county. He was a kinsman of Lieut.-Col. Henry Baker, of Isle of Wight county.

Baker, Richard, son of Lawrence Baker, of Isle of Wight county, and grandson of Lieut.-Col. Henry Baker, was vestryman of the upper parish, Isle of Wight county, in 1747, burgess in 1768 and 1769, and clerk of the county. He died in 1771, leaving a son Judge Richard H. Baker.

Baker, Thomas, burgess for a county not named, in 1702.

Baldry, Robert, was burgess from York county, in the session of 1659-1660. He was born in 1617, came to Virginia in 1635, was appointed justice of the peace for York county in 1661, was captain of the militia, and died in 1675; left his estate to the children of Capt. Thomas Ballard, of the council.

Baldridge, Thomas, represented Northumberland county in the house of burgesses in 1651. The Baldridges are a prominent Maryland family. The Westmoreland county (Virginia) records contain a "Deed of James Baldridge, administrator of my late brother, Major Thomas Baldridge, 1656." Grace Baldridge, widow of Maj. Thomas Baldridge, married John Tew, of Westmoreland.

Ball, George, son of Capt. George Ball, was burgess for Northumberland in the assembly of May, 1769. He was justice, vestryman, captain, married in 1736, Anne Taylor and died in 1770.

Ball, George, son of Capt. William Ball Jr., (born in England June 2, 1641; died in Lancaster county, Virginia, Sept. 30, 1694) was born about 1683; captain of militia; resided in Wicomico, Northumberland county, which he represented in the assembly of 1723-1726, 1727-1734, 1734-1740. He died in 1746, and names in his will sons George, John, David, Richard, Joseph, and daughter Harris Downman.

Ball, Henry, burgess for Elizabeth City in 1646. Richard Ball in 1627 leased six acres in Elizabeth City.

Ball, Col. James, Jr., commonly called "The Young Colonel" of "Bewdley," Lancaster county, was the son of Maj. James Ball and his second wife, Mary Conway Daingerfield. He was born Dec. 31, 1718. He married (first) —— (this marriage is recorded in the charts, but the name is not given); (second) Mildred ——, whose family name is not known; (third) in 1753, Lettice Lee, daughter of Richard Lee and his wife Miss Silk.

Col. Ball was burgess from Lancaster county, 1755, resigning that year to accept the office of sheriff. Col. Ball was a vestryman of St. Stephen's parish, Northumberland county, 1744-1789. In 1745 he was elected church warden when James Ball, Sr., was in the vestry. He was frequently church warden, and July 22, 1785, elected treasurer. He was with Col. Thomas Gaskins executor of Maj. Peter Conway's estate. For many years he was a delegate, and in 1788 a member of the Virginia convention.

Ball, Maj. James, of "Bewdley," Lancaster county, was son of Capt. William Ball and his second wife, Miss Harris, of Northumberland. He was born 1678. He was burgess from Lancaster county in the assemblies of 1715, 1718, 1720-22, in the session of May 18, 1732, and in the assembly of 1736-1740. He married (first) July 15, 1699, Eliza Howson, died Jan. 22, 1704-05, probably daughter of Leonard Howson. He married (secondly) April 16, 17—, Mary Conway Daingerfield, daughter of Col. Edwin Conway, and widow of John Daingerfield. She died Sept. 15, 1730. He married (thirdly) April 25, 1742, Mary Ann (Bertrand) Ballendine, daughter of Rev. John Bertrand, of Rappahannock county, and widow of Capt. William Ballendine. Maj. Ball was a vestryman of Christ Church, Lancaster county, and church warden 1743. In 1740 he and Mr. Joseph Ball were allowed to build a gallery in White Chapel Church for their families, provided that it be completed at the same time with the church and furnished in the same style as the west gallery. He died Oct. 13, 1754. His will was dated July 15, 1754, probated Lancaster county, Nov. 15, 1754.

Ball, Col. Joseph, of "Epping Forest," Lancaster, was son of Col. William Ball, of Lancaster, and his wife, Hannah Atherold. He was born in England, May 24, 1649, and came to Virginia in his infancy. He was burgess from Lancaster county in the assemblies of 1695 and 1698, and in the sessions of Aug. 6, 1701, and May 13 and June 18, 1702. He was lieutenant-colonel and a vestryman. He married (first), it is said, in England, Elizabeth Rogers, or Elizabeth Romney, daughter of William Romney, of London. He married (secondly) 1707-08, Mary Johnson, of Lancaster county, widow, born in England. Col. Ball's youngest daughter, Mary, married Augustine Washington, and was the mother of President George Washington. Col. Ball died at "Epping Forest," June, 1711. His will was dated June 25, probated Lancaster county July 11, 1711.

Ball, Col. Spencer, of Northumberland county, was born cir. 1700-05. He married Judith Jones. He was burgess from Northumberland county in 1748-1749, 1752-1755, 1756-1758, 1758-1761, 1761-1765 and 1766-1768. He was captain, justice and member Northumberland county court, 1735; inspector of tobacco, 1737; vestryman of St. Stephen's Parish, Northumberland county, 1738; qualified as lieutenant-colonel, 1753; was executor of Tunstall Hack, Nov., 1757; member of Westmoreland Association, Feb. 27, 1766, and signed the resolutions passed that day expressing in unmistakable language the purpose to resist the stamp act. He also signed the association of 1770. He died Feb. 11, 1767; his will was dated Jan. 21, 1767, probated Northumberland county, March 9, 1767. A daughter married William Roane of Essex, and was mother of Judge Spencer Roane, of the supreme court of Virginia.

Ball, Spencer Mottrom, son of Col. Spencer Ball, lived at "Coan." Northumberland county; was burgess in 1769-1771 and 1772-1774; resigned in 1773 to accept the office of sheriff. He was one of the signers of the Westmoreland Association against the stamp act. He married Elizabeth Waring, daughter of Col. Francis Waring, of "Goldsberry," Essex county. He died in Nov. or Dec., 1786.

Ball, Capt. William, Jr., was son of Col. William Ball, of Lancaster and his wife, Hannah Atherold. He was born in England, June 2, 1641. He was burgess from Lancaster county in the sessions of Sept. 17, 1668, Oct. 3, 1670, Sept. 21, 1674, in the assemblies of 1677, 1682, 1685-86 and 1688, and in the sessions of April 1, 1692. In 1687 Capt. William Ball, of Lancaster, was appointed to lay off the boundary between Lancaster and Northumberland counties. He was justice in 1680. He married (first) Mary Williamson, daughter of Dr. James Williamson, of Rappahannock, to whom John Hammond dedicated his tract "Leah and Rachel;" (secondly) Miss Harris, of "Bay View," Northumberland county; (thirdly) in 1675, Margaret Downman, daughter of Rawleigh Downman. Capt. Ball died in Lancaster county, Sept. 30, 1694. His will was dated Sept. 28, 1694, and probated Nov. 4, 1694.

Ball, Col. William, of Lancaster county, was the son of Capt. William Ball Jr. and his second wife, Miss Harris, of Northumberland county. He was a burgess from Lancaster county in the assembly of 1702-03-05, in the sessions of April 24, 1706, and Nov. 7, 1711, and in the assemblies of 1712-14, 1715 and 1723-26. He was the surveyor of Northumberland county in 1724. He was a vestryman of Christ Church, Lancaster county, in 1740-47. He married Hannah Heale. He died March, 1744-45. His will was dated Aug. 14, 1744, and probated March 8, 1744-45.

Ball, William, of "Millenbeck," St. Mary's White Chapel Parish, Lancaster county, was son of Capt. William Ball and Margaret Ball, his wife. He was burgess for Lancaster, 1757-58, and delegate, 1780. He married (first) ———, (second) in 1740 (?) Lettice Lee, who died in Lancaster county, Oct., 1788, daughter of Col. Henry Lee, of "Lee Hall," and his wife Mary. William Ball signed the Westmoreland address, 1766.

Ballard, Francis, son of Col. Thomas Ballard, of York county, moved to Elizabeth City county, where he was burgess in 1710-12. He married Mary Servant, daughter of Bertram Servant, and had sons, Francis and Servant Ballard, and daughters, Frances, Mary, Lucy and Anne Ballard.

Ballard, Robert, was son of Capt. John Ballard, of York county, who died in 1745, and a great-grandson of Thomas Ballard, of the governor's council; was clerk of Princess Anne from 1761 to 1765, and burgess in 1766-1768. He married Anne, daughter of Nathaniel Newton and Elizabeth, his wife, daughter of Charles Sayer (clerk of Princess Anne, 1716-1740).

Ballard, Thomas, son of Col. Thomas Ballard, of the council of state, was one of the justices of York county and colonel of the militia. He was burgess for the county in 1693, 1697, 1698, 1699, 1700-1702, 1703-1705 and 1710-1712. He married Catherine, daughter of John Hubard. His will was proved in York county, June 18, 1711. He left issue, and among them was Capt. John Ballard, of York county, who died in 1745.

BURGESSES AND OTHER PROMINENT PERSONS

Banister, John, was a minister of the Church of England, and lived in Charles City county as early as 1678. He had grants of land in Bristol parish in 1690. He was accidentally killed in Henrico county in 1692. He had travelled in the West Indies and was a naturalist and entomologist. He compiled a catalogue of Virginia plants, which is published in Ray's "Historia Plantarum." He published various papers in the "Philosophical Transactions." Among them were "Observations on the Natural Productions of Jamaica," "Insects of Virginia," "Curiosities in Virginia," "On Several Sorts of Snails," "Descriptions of the Snake Root," etc.

Banister, John, son of Rev. John Banister, lived at Petersburg and was collector for Upper James river in 1724, and vestryman of Bristol parish in 1735. He married Wilmette ———, and had issue: 1. Martha, who married Robert Bolling, of "Bollingbrook," Petersburg. 2. Col. John, of Battersea, Dinwiddie county.

Bankhead, James, was an early physician of Westmoreland county, and married Ellinor Monroe, aunt of President James Monroe, on Aug. 20, 1738. His son was James Bankhead, a lieutenant in the naval service of the American revolution. This lad was father of Gen. James Bankhead, of the United States army, and an attaché of Mr. Monroe when United States envoy in France and England.

Banks, Thomas, son of Thomas Banks and Dorothy, his wife, was born at Woodstock, Wiltshire, England, in 1642, and after serving an apprenticeship of seven years in Southampton came to Virginia and settled in Northumberland county. He married Elizabeth, relict of William Keene, and daughter of Maj. John Rogers. He was a prominent merchant. He died Sept. 20, 1697.

Barber, Charles, was burgess from Richmond in the assemblies of 1720-22 and of 1723-26. He qualified in 1713 as a lieutenant-colonel in the militia of Richmond county. He died on Nov. 24, 1726. He was son of William Barber, of Richmond county, and was born June 19, 1676.

Barber, Thomas, son of William Barber (q. v.), was born in 1653, lived in Hampton parish, York county; was burgess in 1680, 1693, 1696, 1700-1702, 1703-1705 and 1705-1706; justice of the peace from 1678, and in 1717 excused from further attendance on the court because of infirmities. He was captain of the militia and died in 1718, leaving issue by Elizabeth Petters—William Jr. (q. v.) and Thomas Barber.

Barber, William, Jr., son of Capt. Thomas Barber (q. v.), was born about 1675; was churchwarden of Hampton parish, York county; justice of the peace from 1705; major of the militia, and burgess from 1710 to 1718 inclusive. He married (first) Judith Cary, daughter of Henry Cary; (second) Anne Archer, daughter of Capt. James Archer, who came as ensign to Virginia in the regiment sent over to put down Bacon's rebellion; (third) Anna Maria Jones, widow of Capt. William Timson and daughter of Rev. Rowland Jones.

Barber, William, was born about 1642, came to Virginia before 1638, and carried on the trade of a cooper in York county; justice of the peace as early as 1652; burgess in 1663 and 1666, and lieutenant-colonel in 1655. He died in 1669, leaving issue—Thomas (q. v.), and Mary, who married John Baskerville, clerk of York county.

Barbour, James, third of the name in Virginia in descent, was burgess from Culpeper county, assembly of 1761-1765. He was an ensign in the Culpeper militia, 1756, under Col. Thomas Slaughter, and "marched on an expedition against the Indians above Winchester." In 1775 he was county lieutenant of the Culpeper militia, and was afterwards an officer in the American revolution.

Barbour, Thomas, son of James Barbour, was born in 1735; was justice of the peace of Orange county in 1768, and was continuously in the commission until his death; burgess for Orange county from 1769 to 1775, and member of the conventions of 1774 and 1775, and county lieutenant in the latter years of the revolutionary war. He was father of James Barbour, governor of Virginia, and of Philip P. Barbour, judge of the supreme court of the United States.

Barham, Anthony, was burgess from Mulberry Island in the session of 1629-30. In 1626 he patented 100 acres in what is now Isle of Wight county. He died in England in 1641, leaving a daughter Elizabeth. He married the sister of Maj.-Gen. Richard Bennett, of Nansemond county, Virginia.

Bargrave, George, brother of Rev. Thomas Bargrave (q. v.), was born about 1584. He was a sea captain employed in the trade between England, Bermuda and Virginia. He married Dorcas, daughter of Capt. John Martin. His son, Robert Bargrave, sold "Brandon," on James river, to certain merchants of London, William Barker, John Sadler and Richard Quiney. In 1616 he brought the first negro slave to the Bermuda Islands.

Bargrave, Capt. John, brother of Capt. George Bargrave (q. v.), was born about 1578. He became interested in Virginia, established the first private plantation on James river, and sent thither many servants. He had a long dispute with Sir Thomas Smythe regarding his interests in the colony, and all of his claims were denied.

Bargrave, Rev. Thomas, son of Robert Bargrave, of Bridge, in Kent, England, and his wife Joanna, daughter of John Gilbert, of Sandwich, England, came to Virginia about 1619, and died there in 1621, leaving his library, valued at 100 marks, to the proposed college at Henrico. He was brother of George Bargrave (q. v.).

Barker, William, was burgess from Charles City county in the assembly of 1645. He was a sea captain and patented large tracts of land on the south side of James river, in company with Richard Quiney and John Sadler, merchants of London. He left descendants in Virginia.

Barnes, Lancelot, resided in Elizabeth City, and was burgess for the lower parish in 1629-30. In 1632 he leased from Gov. Harvey 100 acres of the public lands, commonly known as the "Indian Thicket," believed to have been near the present Hampton Normal School.

Barradall, Edward, succeeded John Clayton as attorney-general in 1737, and was also judge of the admiralty court. He was born in 1704 and died in 1743. He married Sarah Fitzhugh, youngest daughter of William Fitzhugh, Esq. He compiled a report of the decisions of the general court which has been recently published.

Barret, Charles, was a burgess from Louisa, May, 1742 to 1748. He was son of Charles

Barret and Mary Chiswell, of Hanover county. His will, dated Sept. 10, 1770, was proved in Louisa county, June 10, 1771. He was brother of Rev. Robert Barret (q. v.).

Barret, Rev. Robert, son of Charles Barret and Mary, his wife, of Louisa county, was a student at William and Mary College; usher of the grammar school; qualified June 28, 1737, master of the Indian school; was ordained minister in England soon after, and on Dec. 25, 1737, received the royal funds to defray his return passage; was minister for many years of St. Martin's Parish, Hanover county. He married (first) Elizabeth, daughter of Col. Robert Lewis, and (second) Anne ———. He had a son, Rev. Lewis Barret, who married Elizabeth Anderson (1753-1773), by whom he had Anderson Barret, of Richmond.

Barret, Thomas, was one of the two first settlers, who when freed from service to the colony in 1614, went to work on his own account. Ensign William Spencer was the other.

Barrett, William, was a burgess from James City, Feb., 1644-45, Oct., 1646, Oct., 1646, Oct., 1649. He died before 1677, leaving a son James. In 1789 William E. Barrett was living on the "Ferry Plantation" in James City county. He was a descendant of William Barret, first named (see "William and Mary College Quarterly," vii, 202).

Barrington, Robert, was clerk of the council in 1632, and member of the house of burgesses for James City, 1629-30.

Barron, Samuel, commander of Fort George at Point Comfort in 1737. After the destruction of the fort by the hurricane of 1749 he removed with his family to the upper part of Mill creek. He was father of the naval officers, Samuel and James Barron, of the United States navy.

Baskervyle, John, son of John and Magdalene (Hope) Baskervyle, of Ould Withington, Cheshire, England, was born 1635, baptized at Gorsetry, settled in York county, Virginia, about 1662, and was clerk of York county from 1664 to 1679. He died in 1679. He married Mary, daughter of Lieut.-Col. William Barber, and left a daughter Mary and a son George.

Bassett, Burwell, son of William Bassett, of "Eltham," New Kent, was born in 1734; was member of the house of burgesses, 1762, 1763, 1764, 1765, 1766-68, 1769-1771, 1772, 1773, 1774, 1775, and of the conventions of 1774 and 1775. He married Anna Maria Dandridge, daughter of Col. John Dandridge, of New Kent, and died Jan. 4, 1793.

Bassett, William, son of William Bassett, "yeoman," of Newport, in Isle of Wight, England, had seen military service; came to Virginia prior to 1665, when he was made commander of the workmen employed in building a fort at Jamestown; was paid 10,000 pounds of tobacco for his services; acquired a large estate, and died in 1672, leaving a son, William Bassett, of "Eltham," New Kent county, member of the council, by Bridget Cary, daughter of Capt. Miles Cary.

Bassett, William, of "Eltham," New Kent county, Virginia, was son of Col. William Bassett and Joanna Burwell, his wife; was member of the assembly of 1742-1747, but died in 1744, before the termination thereof. He married Elizabeth Churchill, daughter of Col. William Churchill, and was father of Burwell Bassett (q. v.).

Baughan, Capt. James, was a burgess for Essex county in 1698, 1702-03, 1704. He was also justice and sheriff for the county. He married Mary, daughter of Richard Tyler.

Bates, John, was a burgess from Halifax county, Nov., 1753 to 1758. He was son of John Bates and Susannah Fleming, of York county, Quakers, and descended from John Bates (born 1600—died 1666), an early immigrant to Virginia. He died in Halifax county about 1777, leaving issue David, Elizabeth, John, James, Fleming and Susanna and a wife surviving named Chloe.

Bathurst, Lancelot, was son of Sir Edward Bathurst, of Sussex county, England, whose estates were sequestered on account of his loyalty to Charles I. Lancelot Bathurst lived in Essex county, and was a lawyer. He had four children: Mary, married Francis Meriwether; Lawrence, who died about 1705 without issue; Elizabeth, married (first) William Tomlin, and (second) in 1709, William Daingerfield; Susanna married Drury Stith.

Battaile, Capt. John, of Rappahannock, afterwards Essex county, was a captain of a company of rangers in service against the Indians in 1692, member of the house of burgesses from Essex the same year. He married Elizabeth, daughter of Col. Lawrence Smith, and his will dated Jan. 24, 1707-1708 was recorded Feb., 1707-1708.

Batte, Capt. Henry, son of Capt. John Batte, a royalist officer, was a resident of the Appomattox river, and it is said by Robert Beverley that sometime before Bacon's rebellion he led a company to explore the country to the west and passed the mountains. In 1685 he represented Charles City county in the house of burgesses. He left two sons, Henry and William.

Batte, John, was a royalist officer in the civil war in England. He was fined £364, and is said to have been a captain at the battle of Adwalton. He was of Okewell, county York, England. His wife was Martha Mallory, sister of Rev. Philip Mallory. He came with his sons John, William, Thomas and Henry to Virginia and brought over many others. He patented over 5,000 acres on Appomattox river. He died about 1668.

Batte, Thomas, son of Capt. John Batte, a royalist officer, settled with his brother Henry on Appomattox river. In 1671 he was with Robert Falland, Thomas Wood and several others sent out by Gen. Abraham Wood to explore the western country. He appears to have proceeded as far as the New river in Southwest Virginia.

Batte, William, patented in 1643 220 acres on Mobjack Bay and in 1649, 182 acres on Chipokes Creek in James City county. Soon after Surry county was formed from James City county, he represented it in 1654 in the house of burgesses. In 1658 he represented Elizabeth City county. He was a son of Robert Batte and Elizabeth Parry, his wife, of Okewell, county York, England, and a brother of Capt. John Batte. His father was fellow and vicar master of University College, Oxford.

Baugh, John, was a burgess from Henrico in the assembly that convened Jan. 12, 1641; and again from the same county in the assembly that convened Feb. 17, 1644-45. He was probably brother of Mr. William Baugh, of the same county, who was born in 1612 and died in 1687, leaving two sons John and James from, whom the present family in Virginia is descended.

Bayley, Arthur, was a burgess from Henrico county, 1642-43. He was a merchant of London and patented a lot in Jamestown Island, 1642. He appears to have returned to England and probably died there. In 1654 a warrant was issued to him and others, requiring the commissioners of customs to permit him and others, part owners of certain ships, "all bound on a voyage to Virginia" to transport thither in each ship 120 dozen of shoes, six barrels of gunpowder and one ton of shot, paying custom and other duties thereon. On Aug. 3, 1658, he signed with others, a "petition of the merchants and traders to Virginia and the rest of the English Plantations in America to His Highness' Privy council," praying for the enforcement of the laws "for suppressing the planting of English tobacco."

Bayley, Richard, was a burgess from Accomac in 1696-97. In a list of field officers of the Virginia militia in 1699, Charles Scarborough is named as colonel and commander-in-chief of Accomac, and Richard Bayley as major. He was descended from Richard Bayley, of Craddock, in England.

Bayley, William, was born in 1583 and came to Virginia in 1617. In 1624 he lived at West Shirley Hundred. He had a son Thomas, who patented 150 acres in Prince George county, on Bayley's Creek. In 1626 Temperance Bailey had 200 acres on this creek and she was probably the mother of Thomas Bailey.

Baylis, John, was a burgess from Prince William county, Nov., 1761, and continuously thenceforward to Sept., 1765. His service in the general assembly was cut short by his death Sept. 4, 1765, in a duel with Cuthbert Bullitt. He was colonel in the county militia. His will was dated Oct. 22, 1764, was proved Oct. 9, 1765, and recorded in Prince William county.

Baylor, John, son of John Baylor, was born in 1650 at Tiverton, Devonshire, England, came to Gloucester county, Virginia, in the latter part of the seventeenth century, and acquired a large estate by extensive trade as merchant. He was burgess for Gloucester in 1692, and King and Queen 1718. He married Lucy Todd O'Brien, of New Kent, in 1698, and at his death left a large estate appraised at £6,500.

Baylor, John, son of John Baylor and Lucy, his wife, was born in Gloucester county, Virginia, May 12, 1705. He moved in 1726 to "New Market," King and Queen county, and when Caroline county was formed in 1727, from King and Queen, "New Market" fell into that county. He was county lieutenant for Caroline in 1752, and represented it as burgess from 1742 to 1765. He married Frances Walker, daughter of Jacob Walker, of Elizabeth City county, and was father of Col. George Baylor, of the revolution.

Baynham, Alexander, was a burgess from Westmoreland county in 1654, and in 1655 was one of the justices and captain of the county militia. He died in 1662, leaving a daughter Anne.

Baytop, Thomas, merchant, emigrated from Staplehurst, Kent, England, in 1679, and by his wife Hanna had a son Thomas, who married a daughter of Dr. David Alexander, of York county. He has many descendants. (See "Descendants of John Stubbs," by W. C. Stubbs, Ph. D.).

Beazley, Robert, was a burgess from Isle of Wight in the assembly of 1655-1656.

Beckwith, Sir Marmaduke, son of Sir Roger Beckwith, knight baronet, in Aldborough, Yorkshire, England, came to Virginia about 1709, settled in Richmond county, and was clerk of the county till 1748. He married Elizabeth Brockenbrough, and was living in 1770 at a very advanced age. He left issue, Sir Jennings Beckwith and others.

Bell, Henry, was a burgess for Buckingham county from Feb. 10, 1772, to the end of the session May 5, 1774.

Bell, Rev. John, succeeded Andrew Jackson as minister of Lancaster county in 1710, and held office till 1743. He was a man of means, owning land in Lancaster and Prince William and forty-three slaves.

Bell, John, burgess for Prince William county in the assembly of 1756-1758.

Benn, Capt. James, was burgess for Isle of Wight county in 1696-1697, and died the latter year. His wife was Jane, daughter of Col. Arthur Smith. He left issue Arthur, James, George, Mary, Jane and Anne.

Bennett, Philip, was kinsman of Gov. Richard Bennett, member of the house of burgesses for Upper Norfolk (Nansemond) in 1644-45; he was a Puritan and was sent to New England in 1642 to procure ministers for the Puritan congregation in Nansemond and Lower Norfolk counties.

Bennett, Thomas, was a burgess for Mulberry Island in the assembly that convened Sept. 4, 1632.

Benskin, Henry, a royalist, son of Francis Benskin, Esq., of St. Martin's-in-the-Field, Middlesex, England, came to Virginia with Sir Thomas Lunsford, in 1649. He settled in New Kent and died about 1692, leaving issue, two daughters, Mary, who married William Harman, and Frances, who married William Marston, of James City county.

Bentley, Matthew, was a shoemaker, who was one of Bacon's leading officers in the Rappahannock Neck. He was a man of means and appears as defendant in many suits for damages after the rebellion. He married Mary Willis, a widow of Thomas Willis.

Bentley, William, came in 1624, "a new planter," member of the house of burgesses in Oct., 1629.

Berkeley, Edmund, of "Barn Elms," son of Col. Edmund Berkeley and Mary, daughter of Thomas Nelson, was burgess for Middlesex county at the third session of the assembly of 1769-1771. He was burgess again in 1772-1774, 1775-1776, and member of the convention of 1774, 1775, 1776. His will was proved and recorded in Middlesex July 26, 1802.

Berkeley, Capt. William, was a burgess from New Kent county in the assembly that convened Oct. 23, 1666.

Bernard, Richard, came from England to Virginia about 1647. He was born in Petsworth, Buckinghamshire in 1618, and married in 1634 Anne Corderoy (born 1620). He located afterward at "Purton" in Gloucester county, which has been identified with Powhatan's "Werowocomoco," where Pocahontas saved John Smith. He was ancestor of the Bernard family of Virginia.

Bernard, (Barnett) Capt. Thomas, was an early settler in the present Warwick county. He was burgess for Stanley Hundred in 1632 and for Warwick river in 1641, 1642, 1644 and 1645. His daughter, Behethland, married Maj. Francis Dade.

Bernard, William, was a son of Richard Bernard, of St. Paul's parish, Stafford county, and grandson of the immigrant. Richard Bernard, of Buckinghamshire, England; was born Sept. 6, 1730, and practiced law in Westmoreland county. He was an attorney-at-law and President Monroe studied law in his office. He married Winifred Thornton, daughter of Anthony Thornton and Winifred, his wife, daughter of Col. Peter Presley. William Bernard's will was proved in King George county May 1, 1783.

Berry, Sir John, second son of a clergyman of Knaston in Devonshire, England, who lost his life in the civil war in England between parliament and the King. Sir John entered the navy and served against the pirates and the French. He was promoted to the rank of captain and in 1672 took part in the battle of Solebay, where he rescued the Duke of York, whose ship was hard pressed. For this aid he was knighted by the King. In 1676 he was sent as admiral of the fleet, which brought a regiment over to Virginia to suppress Bacon's rebellion. He was joined in commission with Col. Herbert Jeffryes and Maj. Francis Moryson to enquire into and report upon the Virginia disturbances. On his return he served in the Mediterranean till 1680. In 1682 he commanded the "Gloucester," in which the Duke of York took passage to Scotland. The ship was wrecked and Berry was the last to leave the deck. In 1683 he was vice-admiral of the squadron under Lord Dartmouth sent to dismantle Tangier, and on his return he was appointed one of the commissioners of the navy. He died shortly before March 22, 1689-90. "Virginia Magazine" iii. p. 47.

Beverley, Capt. Harry, was son of Maj. Robert Beverley, was a justice of Middlesex in 1700 and surveyor of King and Queen and King William counties 1702-1714. In 1713 he helped the Virginia commissioners to survey the line between North Carolina and Virginia. In 1716 Spotswood sent him in command of a vessel to search for pirates, Spanish wrecks, etc. He was taken by a Spanish man-of-war and kept seven months in imprisonment without a trial. He escaped from Vera Cruz and reached Virginia before Aug., 1717. He removed to Spotsylvania county, about 1720 and was for a number of years presiding justice of that county. He died in 1730, having married about 1700 Elizabeth, daughter and heiress of Gen. Robert Smith, of Brandon, Middlesex county.

Beverley, Robert, of "Beverley Park," King and Queen county, the eldest son of Maj. Robert Beverley, was clerk of the council in 1697 and clerk of King and Queen county (1699-1702), member of the house of burgesses in 1699, 1700, 1702, 1706 for Jamestown, where he had a lot near the state house; was one of the knights of the horseshoe, who went with Spotswood across the Blue Ridge in 1718; presiding justice of King and Queen, 1718. His "History of Virginia" was published in London in 1705 and a second edition in 1722. He married Ursula, daughter of Col. William Byrd, of Westover.

Beverly, William, son of Robert Beverley, the historian, was born about 1698, lived at "Blandfield," Essex county, which he built and which still remains in the possession of the family. He was clerk of Essex county from 1716 to 1745, burgess for Orange county 1734-1740 and for Essex 1742-1747 and 1748-1749. With Sir John Randolph, Richard Randolph and John Robinson, he obtained on Sept. 6, 1636, a grant of 118,490 acres called "Beverley Manor," in Augusta county, though he had the chief interest. He married Elizabeth Bland, (born May 29, 1706) daughter of Richard Bland of "Jordan's," Prince George county, and died on or before 1766.

Bertrand, Rev. John, succeeded Rev. Benjamin Doggett as minister in Lancaster county and died in 1701.

Bibb, William, was a burgess for Prince Edward county, and a member of the conventions of July and Dec., 1775.

Bird, Abraham, came from Pennsylvania and settled in the valley of Virginia, was burgess for the county of Dunmore (later Shenandoah) at the last session under the regal government, and member of the convention of May 6, 1776. He was frequently a member of the state legislature and was a colonel of militia.

Bickley, Sir William, son of Joseph Bickley, of King and Queen county, Virginia, who came to Virginia about 1700. He resided in Hanover county, and in 1752 on the death in England of his uncle Sir Humphrey Bickley, baronet, succeeded to the baronetcy as sixth baronet. Sir William Bickley died in Hanover county, Sept. 3, 1771, leaving issue.

Bigge, Richard, was a burgess in the general assembly of 1623-24, which assembled March 5, 1623-24.

Bill, John, was a burgess from Prince William county in the assembly of 1756-58; and again was a burgess from Fauquier county in the assembly of 1760-1761.

Bird, William, was a burgess from King and Queen county, elected to succeed William Leigh, deceased, for the session of the general assembly beginning April 20, 1704. He was again a member of the session of Nov. 16, 1714.

Bishop, Henry, of Henfield, county Sussex, England, came to Virginia in 1640, when he patented 1,200 acres on Lower Chippokes creek, in what is now Surry county. He returned to England and was a colonel in the army of Charles I. He was in Virginia again before March 17, 1646, when the house of burgesses sent a letter by him to England. He was in the colony once more a few years later, but in 1660 he again went back, and was made by Charles II. postmaster general of England. He was charged, however, with consorting too freely with the Puritans during the days of the commonwealth, and in 1663 Daniel Neale was appointed his successor as postmaster general.

Bishop, John, was a burgess for Charles City county in 1644, 1652 and 1653. He was captain of the militia.

Blackheard, a celebrated pirate, whose real name was Edward Teach. He kept the coast in terror, till Alexander Spotswood sent an armed sloop against him under Capt. Henry Maynard, who surprised him in Pamlico Sound and killed him Nov. 21, 1718, in a hand to hand fight. The survivors of the pirate's crew were hanged at Williamsburg. A few years later Maynard himself suffered a sudden death at the hand of two negro slaves in Prince George county.

Blackburn, Richard, born in 1706 at Ripon in Yorkshire, England, settled in Prince William county, which he represented in the general assembly 1745, 1746 and 1747 He acquired a very large estate as planter and contractor. He married Mary Watts, and was father of Alice Blackburn, who married Col. Thomas Elzey of Loudoun county, and of Thomas Blackburn, lieutenant colonel of the Second Virginia Regiment in the war of the revolution. He died July 5, 1757, in the fifty-second year of his age, and was buried at his estate "Ripon Lodge," near Dumfries, Prince William county.

Blackburn, Thomas, son of Col. Richard Blackburn, of "Ripon Lodge," Prince William county, was born in 1740, was burgess for Prince William in the place of Foushee Tebbs at the third session of the assembly of 1772-1774 and in the assembly of 1775-1776, and was a member of the March and July conventions. He was afterwards lieutenant colonel of the Second Virginia Regiment and aide to Gen. Washington. He married Christian Scott, daughter of Rev. James Scott, and died about 1804.

Blackburn, Capt. William, was born at New Castle on Tyne in Great Britain, Sept. 17, 1653, resided in Abingdon parish, Gloucester county, Virginia, and died there Oct. 18, 1714 (tombstone). He was probably father of Capt. William Blackburn of the adjoining county of Middlesex, who was burgess in 1715. He died in 1738.

Blacke, William, was a burgess from New Kent county in the general assembly of March 1, 1658-59, being the sole representative of the county in that session.

Blackwell, Joseph, son of Samuel Blackwell of Northumberland county, was born July 9, 1715. He moved to Prince William county, which he represented in the house of burgesses from 1749 to 1755. He married Lucy Steptoe, daughter of Capt. John Steptoe, and left issue named in his will proved in Fauquier county, 1787. He was a grandson of Joseph Blackwell, a matriculate of Trinity College, Oxford, in 1658, who emigrated to Virginia.

Blackwell, Samuel, son of Samuel Blackwell, was born in Northumberland county Jan. 19, 1710, and was a member of the house of burgesses in 1742-1747. He was brother of Joseph Blackwell (q. v.).

Blacky, William, was a burgess from New Kent county in the general assembly of 1657-58, that convened March 13th. He is evidently the William Blacke, burgess from New Kent in the succeeding sessions of 1658-59.

Blagrave, Henry, was apparently a descendant of Dr. Henry Blagrave who appears in the York county, Virginia, records about 1660. The subject of this sketch was a burgess of Lunenberg county from 1761 to 1772.

Blair, Dr. Archibald, brother of Dr. James Blair, president of William and Mary College, was born in Scotland; at the University of Edinburgh in 1685; came to Virginia about 1690; was a burgess for Jamestown in 1718 and 1732-1734; and for James City county in 1720-1722, 1723-1726; major of the York county militia in 1728 and one of the justices; died about 1734. He married three times, and by a first wife was father of John Blair (1687-1771), president of the Virginia council.

Blake, Capt. John, appears as Capt. Blake on the list of the burgesses in the assembly of 1655-56 from Nansemond county. He was a burgess from that county in the session of Oct., 1666.

Blakiston, Nathaniel, grandson of John Blakiston, one of the regicide judges and belonging to a family, several of whom emigrated to Maryland, was governor of that colony 1698-1701. On his return to England he became agent for Maryland and in 1706 was appointed by the Virginia council agent for Virginia. See "Maryland Historical Magazine" ii. 54, 172, for a genealogy of the Blakiston family.

Bland, Edward, son of John Bland, an eminent merchant of London, emigrated to Virginia where he was agent for his brother John Bland, who had large estates in Virginia. In 1649 he took part in an exploring expedition to the westward. He married Jane, daughter of his uncle Gregory Bland, and died about 1653. His widow married (secondly) John Holmwood, of Charles City county. Edward Bland left issue a son Edward of "Kymages," in Charles City county, Virginia.

Bland, Giles, son of John Bland, an eminent merchant of London, went to Virginia to manage his father's plantations there in 1674; quarreled with the secretary of state, Thomas Ludwell, and was fined by the general assembly; appointed collector of the customs, took part with Nathaniel Bacon Jr., in 1676, was captured by Philip Ludwell in Accomac, and hanged.

Bland, Peregrine, was a burgess for Charles river (York) county in 1639.

Bland, Richard, son of Theodorick Bland of the council and Anna Bennett, his wife, was born at Berkeley, James river, Aug. 11, 1665. He resided at Jordan's Point and represented Charles City county, then including the present Prince George, in 1700-1702 and 1703-1705 and Prince George in 1706. He died at Jordan's April 6, 1729. He married (first) Mary, daughter of Col. Thomas Swan of the council, and (second) Elizabeth, daughter of Col. William Randolph, of Turkey Island. By the last wife he was father of the distinguished revolutionary patriot of the same name.

Bland, Theodorick, Sr., of Cawson's, Prince George county, was born Dec. 2, 1708, was colonel of the Prince George militia, and long clerk of the county. He married (first) in 1739, Frances, daughter and heiress of Drury Bolling of Prince George county; and (secondly) Elizabeth, widow of Rev. William Yates and daughter of Edward Randolph. By his first marriage he had Col. Theodorick Bland of the revolution.

Blayton, Thomas, was a very active promoter of the disturbances in Virginia known as "Bacon's Rebellion." He took a prominent part in the assembly called under Bacon's authority in June, 1676, and was also a member of Ingram's assembly called

ROBERT BOLLING
Husband of Jane Rolf

after Bacon's death in Oct., 1676. He is said to have written the stirring "Declaration," put forth by Bacon and was active in administering Bacon's oaths to the people. He was pardoned by Sir William Berkeley. He lived in Charles City county.

Blow, Michael, was burgess for Sussex county in the last assembly, 1775-1776. He was son of Richard Blow, whose will was proved Feb. 18, 1762.

Bolling, Alexander, was a burgess from Prince George county in the general assembly of 1756-58; and in those of 1758-61; 1765; 1766-68. Peter Poythress was a member of the session of March 31, 1768, from Prince George county, "in place of Alexander Bolling deceased." He was son of Stith Bolling, and grandson of Col. Robert Bolling, the immigrant.

Bolling, John, son of Col. Robert Bolling, (q. v.) and Jane Rolfe, his wife, was born Jan. 26, 1676, in Charles City county. He lived at "Cobbs" in Chesterfield county, formerly a part of Henrico. He was an active merchant and planter and took a large part in politics. He was a justice of Henrico in 1699 and other years. In 1707 he is styled captain and later was major. He was member of the house of burgesses for Henrico in the assemblies of 1710-1712, 1712-1714, 1718 and 1723-26. He died April 20, 1729, leaving issue by Mary Kennon, his wife, John Bolling Jr., (q. v.).

Bolling, John, son of Maj. John Bolling, of "Cobbs," was born Jan. 20, 1700, was burgess for Henrico county in the assemblies of 1727-1734, 1742-1748, 1748-1749 and for Chesterfield in the assemblies of 1752-1755 and 1756-1758, though he died Sept. 6, 1757. He was colonel commanding the Chesterfield militia, and justice of the peace. He added greatly to the estates inherited by him. He married (first) Elizabeth Lewis; (second) Elizabeth Blair.

Bolling, John, son of Col. John Bolling, of "Cobbs" (q. v.), lived first in Gloucester county from which he was a delegate in the house of burgesses in 1766-1769. Afterwards, in 1778, he was a member of the house of delegates from Chesterfield county. He married Mary, sister of Thomas Jefferson. He was born June 24, 1737, and died in 179—.

Bolling, Robert, a descendant of the Bollings of Bradford in Yorkshire, was son of John Bolling, of the parish of All-Hallows Barking, Tower street, London. He was born Dec. 26, 1646, and came to Virginia in 1660. He engaged in trade as a merchant and acquired large tracts of land. His residence was in Charles City county on the south side of James river in what is now Prince George county. The name of his residence was "Kippax." He was sheriff and lieutenant-colonel of the militia and in 1688, 1692 and 1699 he represented Charles City county in the house of burgesses, and in 1704, 1705-06 he represented Prince George county. He died July 17, 1709. His first wife was Jane Rolfe, daughter of Capt. Thomas Rolfe, son of Pocahontas, and his second was Anne Stith, daughter of Capt. John Stith, of Charles City county.

Bolling, Robert, son of Col. Robert Bolling (q. v.), was born Jan. 25, 1686, and was burgess for Prince George county in 1710-1712; 1712-1714, 1723-1726 and 1727-1734. He married Anne Meriwether and had issue: 1. Mary, married William Stark. 2. Elizabeth, married James Munford. 3. Anne, married John Hall. 4. Lucy, married Peter Randolph. 5. Jane, married Hugh Miller. 6. Martha, married Richard Eppes. 7. Susanna, married Alexander Bolling. 8. Robert, married Mary Tabb. He died 1749.

Bolling, Robert, son of Robert Bolling (q. v.), and grandson of Col. Robert Bolling, was born June 12, 1730, was burgess for Dinwiddie county from 1758 to 1774. He settled at Petersburg, where his residence was known as "Bollingbrook." He was colonel of the militia and had large estates. He married (first) Martha Bannister; and (second) Mary Marshall Tabb. He died Feb. 24, 1775.

Bolling, Robert, Jr., was son of Col. John Bolling, of "Cobbs," and lived at "Chellowe" in Buckingham county. He was born at Varina, Henrico county, Aug. 17, 1738, and was educated at Wakefield, Yorkshire, England. He was a man of learning, and wrote "The Bolling Memoir," besides two volumes of verse. He was a member of the house of burgesses for Cumberland from 1761 to 1765, and of the convention of July, 1775. He married (first) Mary Burton; (second) Susannah Watson. Died in 1775.

Bonall, James, vine dresser, was doubtless a near relative of John Bonall, or Bonnell, silkworm raised to the King at Oakland, England, who selected the vine dressers sent to Buckroe, Elizabeth City, Virginia, in 1620. James Bonall was one of these. In 1627 he leased fifty acres from the government at Buckroe, where the public lands lay. Bonnell may have been later anglicised into "Bonny," the name of a well known family of Princess Anne.

Bond, Maj. John, was burgess for Isle of Wight county in 1654, 1656, 1658, 1659 and 1660. He was a Puritan, and after the restoration in 1660 he was removed by the general assembly from his office as justice "because of factious and schismatical behavior." His will dated May 2, 1669, was proved June 9, 1669, and by it he left two sons William and John.

Booker, Edmund, son of Col. Edmund Booker and grandson of Capt. Richard Booker, of Gloucester county, was a burgess for Amelia county, 1758-1761. He married Edith Marot, daughter of Samuel Cobbs of Amelia, and his will, dated Sept. 26, 1792, was proved in Amelia Sept. 24, 1793.

Booker, Edward, son of Capt. Richard Booker and Rebecca, his wife, was baptized June 2, 1680. He removed from Gloucester to the part of Prince George county which is now Amelia county, and was appointed justice of Prince George in 1733, and was one of the first justices of Amelia county in 1736. The same year he represented Amelia in the house of burgesses, and continued a member till 1747. He was lieutenant colonel of the militia of Amelia. He died in 1750. His residence was called "Winterham."

Booker, Richard, son of Col. Edward Booker, of "Winterham," Amelia county, was colonel in the militia, and represented his county in the house of burgesses from 1756 to 1760. He married Rachel Marot, daughter of Jean Marot, of Williamsburg. He had sons Edward, Richard, Parham, John, and William Marshall Booker.

Booth, Robert, was clerk of York county from about 1640 till his death 1657; burgess for York county in 1653 and 1654, married Frances ———, and was father of (1) Robert, captain and justice of the peace for York county, who married Anne, daughter of James Bray, Esq., and Angelica, his wife; (2) Elizabeth, who married Dr. Patrick Napier; and (3) probably William, J. P. of York county.

Booth, Thomas, merchant, born in Lancashire, England, in 1663, came to Ware parish, Gloucester county, Virginia, about 1690, and died there Oct. 11, 1736. He was son of St. John Booth, of the same family as George Booth, first Lord Delamere. He married Mary Cooke, and left numerous issue.

Borden, (Burden) Benjamin, was a merchant of New Jersey, who came to Virginia and became an agent for Lord Fairfax. He procured a grant for 500,000 acres of land on the upper waters of the Shenandoah and James rivers, comprising the southern part of Augusta and the whole of the present Rockbridge county. His surveyor was Capt. John McDowell. He died in 1742 and left issue a son Benjamin, who died in 1753, leaving issue.

Boucher, Daniel, was a burgess for Isle of Wight county in 1653, and a justice in 1667. He died in 1667-1668, leaving a daughter Elizabeth and a kinsman Robert Boucher in Virginia. There is some reason to believe that he was connected with Henry Boucher, a royalist, who tried to secure the city of Bristol for Prince Rupert in 1643.

Bouldin, Thomas, yeoman, an ancient planter came in 1610, living in Elizabeth City in 1625, with his wife Mary, and William Bouldin.

Bourne (Borne), Capt. Robert, was a burgess for York county in 1658.

Boush, Maximillian, was a son of Maximillian Boush by his wife Mary, relict of Rev. Jonathan Saunders. He was Queen's counsel for the counties of Princess Anne, Norfolk and Nansemond and lieutenant colonel of the militia in the reign of Queen Anne, and King's council for Princess Anne and Norfolk counties in the reign of King George the First. From 1710 to 1727, he represented Princess Anne county in the house of burgesses. He died in 1728 leaving two sons Samuel and Maximillian.

Boush, Samuel, son of Maximillian Boush, was first mayor of Norfolk, and burgess for Norfolk county in 1734-1740.

Boush, Samuel Jr., son of Samuel Boush (q. v.), was burgess for Norfolk county in 1752-1755. He discharged the office of clerk of the county from 1742 to 1774.

Bowden, William, was attorney general of Virginia from 1743 to 1748. But little is known of him.

Bowdoin, Peter, was burgess for Northampton county in the assembly of 1727-1734, but vacated his office in 1732, by accepting the position of tobacco inspector. He was burgess again in 1736-1740.

Bowyer, John, was captain of the Augusta militia 1763, member of the first county court of Botetourt, 1771, and burgess for that county in the assemblies of 1769-1771, 1772-1774, 1775-1776, and member of the convention of 1774, 1775, 1776, signer of the Williamsburg association 1772.

Boyse, Cheney, born 1586, came to Virginia in 1617, and was member of the house of burgesses from Hog Island Oct., 1629, March, 1629-30, and Sept., 1632. His wife Sarah was carried off by the Indians, during the massacre of 1622, but was returned later apparreled as an Indian queen. Cheney Boyse was doubtless a brother of John Boyse (q. v.) and a son of Rev. John Boyse, deacon of Canterbury.

Boyse, John, was a member of the first house of burgesses in 1619 from Martin's Hundred. He returned to England died on his way back in 1649.

Boyse, Luke, born 1580, came to Virginia in 1619, was a member of the house of burgesses 1623-24 and died before 1635. He married Alice, who subsequently married Matthew Edloe and had one daughter, Hannah.

Bowker, Rev. James, was brother of Rev. Ralph Bowker, minister of St. Stephen's parish, in King and Queen county. He was elected by the vestry of St. Peter's Church, New Kent county, rector of the parish July 10, 1698, and continued minister till his death March 10, 1703.

Bowker, Rev. Ralph, came to Virginia before 1700, and was minister of St. Stephen's parish, King and Queen county. He was a member of the conventions of the clergy which assembled at Williamsburg in 1705 and 1719. His daughter Anne married John Smith, son of Rev. Guy Smith.

Bradley, Thomas, (born 1633) a merchant in Virginia in 1665, eldest son of Thomas Bradley D. D., chaplain to Charles I., prebend of York, and rector of Ackworth, a great royalist, and his wife Frances, daughter of John Lord Saville of Pontefract.

Bradley, William, burgess for Norfolk county, succeeding George Veale in 1759.

Branch, Christopher, emigrated to Virginia in 1620, and in 1625 he and his wife Mary Branch and son Thomas Branch, nine months old, were residents at the "College Land." In 1634 he patented 100 acres at "Arrowhattocks" in Henrico county, but the permanent home of Christopher Branch was a plantation almost immediately opposite "Arrowhattocks" on the south side of James river. He was descended from an ancient family of Abington, Berkshire, England. He was son of Lionel Branch, of that place, and grandson of William Branch, gent. (died 1602). He was a burgess for Henrico in 1639, and a justice of the peace in 1656. He died at a very advanced age about 1682, leaving issue.

Branch, John, owned land in Elizabeth City county as early as 1636. In 1639 he was a receiver of tobacco and in 1641 a burgess for the county.

Brasseur, John, son of Robert Brasseur, was a burgess for Nansemond county at the assemblies of 1685, 1695-1696, 1696-1697. He married Mary, daughter of Col. Robert Pitt, of the council and Martha Lear, his wife, sister of Col. John Lear.

Braxton, George, was born in 1677, and appears as a merchant in Virginia in 1703. Later he is styled Col. George Braxton. He was a member of the house of burgesses for King and Queen in 1718, 1720, 1723-1726, 1727-1728, 1742, 1744, 1745, 1746, 1747, 1748. He died July 1, 1748. He left issue one son George Braxton Jr., and two daughters.

Chinn, Joseph, son of Rawleigh Chinn, of Lancaster county, and Esther Ball, daughter of Colonel Joseph Ball, of "Epping Forest;" was burgess for Lancaster in 1748-1749 and 1752-1755.

Chisman, Edmund, son of Edmund Chisman (brother of Colonel John Chisman, of the council), qualified as justice of York county, Virginia, July 25, 1670, and in 1676 was one of Bacon's majors. After Bacon's death he was captured by Robert Beverley and sentenced to be hanged, but died in prison before execution. He married Lydia, niece of Captain George Farlow, who was also a friend of Bacon and is described as a "great mathematician."

Chisman, Lydia, daughter of Mrs. Elizabeth Bushrod, wife of Thomas Bushrod, by a former husband, and niece of Captain George Farlow. She was one of the early heroines of Virginia. When her husband, Major Edmund Chisman, was captured during Bacon's rebellion she threw herself at Sir William Berkeley's feet and begged to be executed in his stead. Her husband died in prison and she married Thomas Harwood. Later she was killed by lightning, March 16, 1694.

Chisman, Thomas, brother of Major Edmund Chisman, was born in 1652, qualified as justice of York county, August 24, 1680, and was a member of the house of burgesses in 1685. His will was proved July 18, 1715. He married Elizabeth Reade, daughter of Colonel George Reade, of the council, and left issue.

Chiswell, Charles, was clerk of the general court in 1706. He lived in Hanover county and died April, 1737, aged sixty, leaving a son John, who was a member of the house of burgesses, colonel, etc. (q. v.).

Chiswell, Colonel John, son of Charles Chiswell, was for a number of years one of the most prominent men in the colony. He was burgess from Hanover county from 1744 to 1755, when he removed to Williamsburg and represented the city in 1756, 1757 and 1758. He engaged actively in lead and iron mining, and in 1752 operated a furnace for the manufacture of iron five miles south of Fredericksburg. In 1757 he discovered the New river lead and zinc mines, about which time Fort Chiswell, a few miles distant, was erected and named for him. In 1766 he got into a quarrel at a tavern in New Kent with a Scotch gentleman named Robert Routledge, in the course of which Routledge was killed. He was arrested and sent by the examining justices to Williamsburg to await trial. But on his way thither he was released on bail, out of term time, by three of the judges of the general court. His prosecutor was chosen in the prevailing custom by lot, and it fell to John Blair Jr., an intimate friend, to conduct the case against him, but the suicide of Colonel Chiswell at his home on Francis street, in the city of Williamsburg, prevented any trial. His residence in the city is still standing. He married Elizabeth Randolph, daughter of William Randolph, of Turkey Island.

Christian, Israel, was a merchant who lived first at Staunton and afterward in that part of Augusta now Botetourt county; burgess for Augusta county in the assemblies of 1758-1761 and 1761-1765. He was the founder of the towns of Fincastle and Christiansburg. He was father of Colonel William Christian (q. v.).

Christian, Thomas, ancestor of the well known Christian family of East Virginia, is believed to have come from the Isle of Man to Virginia. He patented land in Charles City county in 1687.

Christian, William, son of Israel Christian, was born in Augusta county in 1743. He was a burgess for Fincastle county at its creation in 1773, and until 1775-1776, which saw the end of the house of burgesses; member for Fincastle in the convention of 1775; lieutenant-colonel of the First Virginia Regiment, raised by the state; commanded in 1776 and 1780 expeditions against the Cherokees; in 1785 removed to Kentucky and was killed, April 9, 1786, by Indians. He married a sister of Patrick Henry.

Christmas, Doctoris, of Elizabeth City, planter, leased from the governor fifty acres of the company's land in 1627. His will, dated December 20, 1754, is recorded in York county. He leaves all his estate to his wife and his friend, Peter Starkey.

Church, Richard, was a burgess from Lower Norfolk in the assembly of 1676 and from Norfolk in the sessions of May 13 and June 18, 1702.

Clack, Rev. James, son of William and Mary Clack, of Marsden, in Wiltshire, came to Virginia in 1678, and was minister of Ware parish from 1679 to December 20, 1723, when he died. James Clack, believed to be his son, resided in Brunswick county.

Clack, John, was a burgess from Brunswick county in the place of Edmund Goodrich, who had accepted the office of sheriff, in the sessions of November 1, 1759, and of 1760 and 1761. Married Mary Kennon, and left issue. He was brother of Sterling Clack (q. v.).

Clack, Sterling, was a burgess from Brunswick county in the assembly of 1748-1749. He was son of James Clack, of Brunswick county, who was son of Rev. James Clack (q. v.), of Ware parish, Gloucester county. He was clerk of Brunswick county from 1740 to 1751. He married Anne Eldridge, daughter of Thomas Eldridge, and died in 1757.

Claiborne, Colonel Augustine, of "Windsor," son of Captain Thomas Claiborne, of "Sweet Hall," was born in 1721; removed from King William county to Surry and was burgess for that county in 1748-1749 and 1752-1757, but resigned in 1754 to become clerk of Sussex. In 1780 he was a state senator. He married Mary Herbert, daughter of Buller Herbert, and died May 3, 1789. He was an eminent lawyer.

Claiborne, Major Buller, born October 27, 1755, second lieutenant of Second Virginia Regiment, October 2, 1775; captain from March 8, 1776, to July 27, 1777; brigade major and aide-de-camp to General Lincoln, 1779-1780; commanded a squadron of cavalry at the battle of the Cowpens; appointed justice of Dinwiddie in 1789; sheriff in 1802-04. He married Patsy, daughter of Edward Ruffin, of Sussex county.

Claiborne, Herbert, of "Chestnut Grove," New Kent county, son of Colonel Augustine Claiborne, born August 7, 1746; married (first) Mary Ruffin, daughter of Robert Ruffin, (second) Mary, daughter of William Burnett Browne, of Elsing Green, King William county, great-grandson of Gilbert Burnett, bishop of Salisbury, England.

Claiborne, Leonard, son of Captain Thomas Claiborne, of "Sweet Hall," King William county; was sheriff for the county in 1732 and burgess in 1734-1740. He married Martha, daughter of Major Francis Burnell, and had issue—Leonard Claiborne Jr., of Dinwiddie county (q. v.).

Claiborne, Leonard, Jr., of Dinwiddie county, son of Leonard Claiborne, of King William county, was burgess for Dinwiddie in 1758, 1759, 1761, 1762, 1763, 1764 and 1765. He is said to have removed to Georgia.

Claiborne, Colonel Nathaniel, son of Captain Thomas Claiborne, of "Sweet Hall," King William county, married Jane Cole, daughter of Colonel William Cole, of Warwick county. He was born about 1719, and died in his fortieth year. His widow married (second) Stephen Bingham and (third) Francis West, and was living in 1787.

Claiborne, Philip Whitehead, son of William Claiborne, of "Romancoke," King William county, lived at "Liberty Hall," King William county. In 1771 he was a member of the house of burgesses for King William and died in 1772. He married Elizabeth, daughter of William Dandridge, of King William county, and his wife Unity, daughter of Nathaniel West (a great-nephew of Lord Delaware, governor of Virginia).

Claiborne, Richard, of Lunenburg county, son of Colonel Nathaniel Claiborne, of King William county, was member of the house of burgesses for Lunenburg in 1772 and 1774, and member of the conventions of 1774 and 1775. He died in 1776, leaving issue—sons, John, Richard Henry, Leonard, and daughter, Molly, married William Warwick, of North Carolina.

Claiborne, Lieutenant-Colonel Thomas, son of Colonel William Claiborne, secretary of state, was born August 17, 1647; served against the Indians, and is said to have been killed by an arrow October 7, 1683. He was buried at Romancoke, in King William county, where his tomb remains. He married Sarah, daughter of Samuel and Dorothy Fenn, of Middle Plantation. His widow Sarah married (second) Thomas Bray. By her will Sarah established a scholarship at William and Mary College.

Claiborne, Captain Thomas, of "Sweet Hall," King William county, son of Lieutenant-Colonel Thomas Claiborne, was born December 16, 1680, and died August 10, 1732. He is said to have married three times and to have had twenty-seven children, which is probably an exaggeration. His last wife was Anne, daughter of Henry Fox, of King William county, by his wife Anne, daughter of Colonel John West (nephew of Lord Delaware).

Claiborne, Thomas, son of Captain Thomas Claiborne, of "Sweet Hall," King William county, was born January 9, 1704, and died December 1, 1735; clerk of Stafford county; buried at "Sweet Hall," where his tomb still stands.

Claiborne, Thomas, son of Colonel Nathaniel Claiborne, of "Sweet Hall," King William county, succeeded, on the death of Major Harry Gaines, as burgess for the county in 1768 and 1769.

Claiborne, William, of "Romancoke," son of Lieutenant-Colonel William Claiborne. He died in 1705, leaving a son William, who was sheriff of King William county in 1728 and 1729 and married a daughter of Philip Whitehead, of the same county.

Clapham, Josias, burgess for Loudoun county to succeed James Hamilton in 1774 at the last session of the assembly of 1772-1774; burgess in the assembly of 1775-1776, and in the conventions of 1774, 1775 and 1776.

Clarke, John, son of Sir John Clarke, of Wrotham, in Kent county, England, lived for a time at Middle Plantation, and died about 1644.

Clause (Close), Phettiplace, came to Virginia in 1608; in 1624 was living at Pace's Paines; in 1619 and in 1626 patented land on Warwicksqueak river (Pagan creek); was burgess for Mulberry Island, October, 1629, and for "From Denbigh to Waters' Creek" in 1632.

Clay, John, an ancient planter, came to Virginia in 1613 and his wife Ann in 1623. He patented lands in 1635 on Ward's creek, in what is now Prince George county.

Clayton, Rev. John, was minister at Jamestown from 1684 to 1686. He returned to England, and in May, 1688, was minister of Crofton, at Wakefield, in Yorkshire. He was a member of the Royal Society, and contributed some valuable papers on Virginia, which were published in the "Transactions."

Clayton, John, son of John Clayton, the attorney-general of Virginia, was born at Fulham, England, in 1685, and died in Gloucester county, Virginia, December 15, 1773. He came to Virginia with his father in 1705; was an eminent botanist; member of some of the most learned societies of Europe; president of the Virginia Society for Promoting Useful Knowledge, 1773, and author of "Flora Virginica." He was for fifty years clerk of Gloucester county, and had a botanical garden at his estate, "Windsor," in that county. He married, January 2, 1723, Elizabeth Whiting, of Gloucester. He had several sons—Captain Jasper Clayton, of Gloucester county; Arthur Clayton, clerk of one of the "upper counties," and it is believed Colonel William Clayton, of New Kent county.

Clayton, John, was son of Sir John Clayton, of London and Parson's Green, Fulham, Middlesex county, England, and of the Inner Temple, who was knighted 1664, and his wife Alice, daughter of Sir William Bowyer, of Denham, Bucks, baronet. He was brother of Lieutenant-General Jasper Clayton, of the British army, who was killed at Dettingen in 1743. His grandfather was Sir Jasper Clayton, of St. Edmunds, Lombard Manor, who was knighted at Guildhall, July 5, 1660. He was born in 1665; studied at one of the universities of England; was admitted to the Inner Temple, June 6, 1682; was called to the bar, and coming to Virginia in 1705, was appointed attorney-general of the colony in 1714. In 1724 he was also appointed judge of the admiralty court. He represented James City county in the house of burgesses in 1720-22, 1723-26, 1727-28; recorder of Williamsburg from 1723. He died November 18, 1737. He was father of John Clayton, the botanist.

Clayton, Jasper, son of John Clayton, the botanist, resided at "Windsor," on the Panketank river, and was clerk of the county committee of safety of Gloucester county in 1725. He married Courtney, daughter of Colonel John Baylor, of New Market, Caroline county.

Clayton, Thomas, M. D., son of John Clayton, the attorney-general of Virginia; educated at Pembroke College, Cambridge, and afterwards completed his medical studies in London; married Isabella Lewis, of Warner Hall, Gloucester county, Virginia, and died October 17, 1730, aged thirty-eight. He had an only child, who died in infancy. His armorial tomb is at "Warner Hall," Gloucester county.

Clayton, Thomas, was a lawyer; resided at Jamestown, which he represented in the house of burgesses in 1683.

Clayton, Colonel William, of New Kent county, was probably a son of John Clayton, the botanist. He was Jasper Clayton's executor in 1779. From 1766 to 1772 he was member of the house of burgesses for New Kent county, and was a member of the state conventions of 1776 and 1788. In 1774 he was member of the county committee of safety and subsequently served as clerk of New Kent. He died 1797.

Clements, Francis, son of Francis Clements, lived in Surry county, which he represented as a burgess in 1692-93. He was a justice, captain of militia, etc. He married Elizabeth, daughter of Nicholas Meriwether, and left issue.

Clinch, William, was a burgess from Surry county in March, 1756, and September, 1756. In the session of April 30, 1757, Benjamin Cocke represented Surry in place of William Clinch, expelled April 26. He was member of the county committee of safety in 1776.

Clopton, William, ancestor of the Virginia family of that name, was descended from the Cloptons of Warwick and Suffolk, England. He was born in 1655, emigrated to Virginia at an early age, settled in York county and married, about 1680, Ann Booth, widow of Thomas Dennett, and daughter of Robert Booth, clerk of York county. William Clopton moved after 1683 to New Kent county, where the Clopton family was resident for many years later. He died before 1733.

Cobbs, Samuel, was descended from Ambrose Cobbs, who on July 25, 1639, patented 350 acres upon the Appomattox river. He removed from York county to Amelia, which he represented in the house of burgesses during the general assemblies of 1742-1747 and 1748-1749. In 1717 he married Edith Marot, daughter of Jean Marot, a French Huguenot innkeeper of Williamsburg. He died in 1757, leaving issue.

Cocke, Colonel Allen, son of Benjamin Cocke, represented Surry county in the house of burgesses, 1772-1774, and in all the constitutional conventions of 1774, 1775 and 1776; member of the Surry county committee of safety in 1775. He married Nancy Kennon, daughter of Colonel Richard Kennon, of Charles City county. His will, recorded in Surry, is dated November 20, 1780.

Cocke, Benjamin, son of Richard Cocke, and great-grandson of Richard Cocke, of "Bremo," was born about 1710. He moved to Goochland county, which he represented in the house of burgesses in the assembly of 1742-1747. He married Catherine Allen, daughter of Arthur Allen, of "Bacon's Castle," in Surry county, and represented

Surry county in the house of burgesses in 1756 and 1758. He was father of Colonel Allen Cocke.

Cocke, Bowler, son of Richard Cocke, of "Bremo," and Ann Bowler, daughter of Colonel Thomas Bowler, of Rappahannock. He was brother of Benjamin and Richard Cocke, of Surry. He was member of the house of burgesses for Henrico from 1752 to 1763. He married (first) Sarah ———, (second) Elizabeth Hill, daughter of John Carter. After the last marriage he lived at "Shirley," in Charles City county. He died in 1771.

Cocke, Bowler, Jr., son of Bowler Cocke, was member of the house of burgesses for Henrico county from 1763 to 1769. He was born in 1726 and died in 1772, a few months after his father. He married Elizabeth, widow of Harry Turner, of King George county, and daughter of Colonel Nicholas Smith.

Cocke, Hartwell, was son of Richard Cocke and Elizabeth Hartwell, daughter of John Hartwell, of Surry. He lived at "Mount Pleasant," on James river, and represented Surry county in the house of burgesses from 1758 to 1773. He married Anne Ruffin, daughter of John Ruffin. His will, dated May 29, 1772, was proved in Surry, August 25, 1772. He was father of John Hartwell Cocke, of Surry, who was member of the state convention of 1788.

Cocke, James, son of Thomas Cocke, was born about 1666; married Elizabeth Pleasants, daughter of John and Jane Pleasants, by which marriage he acquired the estate of "Curls," on James river, in Henrico county; member of the house of burgesses in 1696 and 1699; clerk of Henrico county from 1692 to 1707. He died about 1721.

Cocke, Richard, son of Richard Cocke, and great-grandson of Richard Cocke, of "Bremo," in Henrico county, settled in Surry county, where he married (first) Elizabeth Hartwell, daughter of John Hartwell, (second) Elizabeth Ruffin. He represented the county in the house of burgesses in 1744, 1745, 1746 and 1747. His will, dated September 13, 1771, was proved in Surry, April 21, 1772.

Cocke, Richard, the emigrant settler, was born about 1600. He married twice. Name of first wife not known, but his second was Mary Aston, daughter of Lieutenant-Colonel Walter Aston. He obtained large grants of land, and settled at "Bremo," on James river, in Henrico county. He was lieutenant-colonel of his county, and was a member of the house of burgesses in 1632 from Weyanke, and in 1644 and 1654 from Henrico county. He died in 1665, leaving issue —five sons and one daughter—Thomas, Richard, John, William, Richard, "the younger," and Elizabeth.

Cocke, Captain Thomas, son of Thomas Cocke, and brother of James Cocke, was born about 1662. He married (first) Mary Brasier, (second) Frances ———. He represented Henrico in the house of burgesses in 1696, in 1698, 1699, 1700-1702; sheriff in 1699. He left six children: Thomas, James Powell, Henry, Brasier, Mary, Elizabeth. He died in 1707.

Cocke, Thomas, of "Malvern Hill," Henrico county, was son of Richard Cocke, of "Bremo." He was a justice of Henrico in 1678, 1680. He was also sheriff and coroner, and represented Henrico in the house of burgesses in 1677.

Cocke, William, was a burgess from Henrico in the assembly of 1646. He was son of Richard Cocke, the immigrant.

Cockeram, Captain William, was a burgess from Surry county in the session of September 10, 1663. Justice of the peace in 1660. He died in 1669, leaving issue—two sons—William and Thomas.

Codd, Colonel St. Leger, son of William Codd, of Pelicans, Kent, England, esquire, who married, in 1632, Mary, daughter of Sir Warham St. Leger, of Ulcombe, Kent. In 1671 he was one of the commissioners to superintend the building of a fort on Potomac river; presiding justice of Northumberland county, Virginia, in 1680; member of the house of burgesses, 1680, 1682. About 1688 he removed to Maryland and was a member of the legislature from Cecil county in 1694 and 1702. He was married twice. By his first marriage he had James and Berkeley Codd, and by his second, with Anna, widow of Theodorick Bland and daughter of Governor Richard Bennett, Captain St. Leger Codd, of Maryland.

Coke, John, goldsmith of Williamsburg, son of Richard Coke, of "Trusley," in Derbyshire, England, a descendant of Sir Francis Coke, was born April 6, 1704; emigrated to Virginia in 1724 and settled in Williamsburg. Ancestor of Richard Coke, United States Senator from Texas. He died in 1767.

Cole, Rev. Samuel, in 1657 served as minister of Lancaster county. He died before September 28, 1659.

Cole, William, was a burgess for Nutmeg Quarters (now in Warwick county) in 1629. He may have been father of Colonel William Cole, of the council.

Cole, William, was son of Colonel William Cole, of the council of state, and Martha Lear, his wife. He was born about 1692, and was a member of the house of burgesses for Warwick county in 1715, 1718, 1720, 1723, 1726. In 1721 he was deputy receiver-general and colonel of the militia. He married Mary Roscow, and made his will in 1729. In the latter part of his life he appears to have lived in Charles City county.

Coleman, Francis, burgess for Caroline county in May, 1769. His daughter Anne married Colonel William Green.

Coleman, Henry, came to Virginia, and in 1635 patented lands in Elizabeth City county, near Thomas Eaton. On October 7, 1634 he was excommunicated for forty days for "using scornful speeches and putting on his hat in church."

Collclough, George, was a burgess from Northumberland county in the assembly of 1658-59. He was brother of Thomas Collclough, a prominent merchant of London. He married (first) Ursula Bysshe, (second) Elizabeth Thorowgood. He died in 1662.

Colville, John, son of John Colville, of New Castle, England, baker and brewer, and first cousin of Camilla Colville, who married Henry Bennett, earl of Tankerville; was a burgess for Prince William county in 1744, 1745, 1746, 1747. He was colonel of the militia, and died in Fairfax county in 1756, leaving bequests to the earl's son and to his brother, Thomas Colville, of Fairfax county.

Coles, John, a native of Enniscorthy, Ireland, was a merchant of Henrico, Virginia, where he accumulated a large estate. His will was proved in Henrico, March, 1748, and his legatees were his wife Mary, sons Walter, Isaac and John, and brother William. Among his descendants were Edward Coles, governor of Illinois, and Isaac and Walter Coles, members of congress from Virginia.

Coles, Walter, son of John Coles, a merchant of Richmond, who emigrated from "Enniscorthy," Ireland, by his wife Mary, daughter of Isaac Winston, of Hanover county, Virginia, was born November 14, 1739, in Hanover county; was colonel of the militia and burgess for Halifax county in 1765, 1766-1769 and 1769-1771. He married, February 28, 1767, Mildred Lightfoot, daughter of William Lightfoot and his wife, Mildred Howell. He died in Halifax county, November 7, 1780.

Collier, Isaac, came to Virginia about 1660 and settled in York county. He married a sister of Edward and John Lockey, two London merchants, the former of whom settled in York county and died without issue. Isaac Collier died in 1671.

Collier, Samuel, was a boy who came in the First Supply in January, 1608. He was shortly after left by John Smith with the Warascoyack Indians to learn their language. He became useful as an interpreter. In 1622 he was living at Elizabeth, where he was killed accidentally by a sentinel.

Collier, William, citizen and weaver of London, came to York county in 1670, and finally settled in New Kent county, where in 1675 he was lieutenant-colonel of the militia. From him descended a numerous offspring in King William, New Kent and Charles City counties.

Colston, William, son of a great merchant and warm royalist, William Colston, sheriff of Bristol; came to Virginia about the middle of the seventeenth century. He had a son William who married Anne Gooch, widow of Captain Thomas Beale, and was a burgess in 1692 and 1699. The family is numerously represented.

Comrie, Dr. William, resided in Henrico county in 1739. His wife was Margaret Baintone, daughter of Josias Baintone, one of the six clerks in chancery in England, and niece of Thomas Pratt, one of the masters in chancery.

Coney, Henry, gentleman, lived at "Coney borough," and was a burgess for Archer's Hope and the Glebe Land in 1629-30, 1632 and 1632-33.

Conway, Edwin, son of Edwin Conway and Sarah Walker, daughter of Lieutenant-Colonel John Walker, was born in 1682, was lieutenant-colonel of the militia of Lancaster county and a burgess from 1710 to 1758; vestryman of Christ Church and St. Mary's White Chapel. He died October 3, 1763, leaving issue, Peter and other children.

Conway, Major Peter, was the son of Colonel Edwin Conway and his wife, Anne Ball. He married (first) Elizabeth Spann, of Northumberland; (second) Elizabeth Lee, of the same county. He was a justice of Lancaster county in 1742; burgess from Lancaster in the assembly of 1748-1749. He died in 1753.

Cooke, Giles, son of Mordecai Cooke, the

immigrant to Virginia, was tobacco agent in 1714, and was burgess for Gloucester county in the assembly of 1723-1726.

Cooke, John, came from Youghall in the county of Cork, Ireland, and settled in Overwharton parish, Stafford county, Virginia, early in the eighteenth century. He married Elizabeth Travers, daughter of Raleigh Travers and his wife, Hannah Ball, half sister of Mary Ball, mother of Washington. He had issue, a son, Traverse, and three daughters Ann, Hannah and Million.

Cooke, Mordecai, ancestor of a well-known family in Virginia, patented October 2, 1650, 1,174 acres in Mobjack Bay, which he called "Mordecai's Mount." He had issue Mordecai, Thomas, Giles, John, Mary married Thomas Booth; Frances married Gabriel Throckmorton, and Susannah married Henry Fitzhugh. He used the same arms as the Cookes of Whitefield, county Suffolk, England. (See Descendants of Mordecai Cooke of Mordecai's Mount," Gloucester county, Virginia, by Dr. William Carter Stubbs).

Cooke, Mordecai, Jr., son of Mordecai Cooke, patented land in 1703, was sheriff of Gloucester county in 1703 and burgess in 1696, 1699, 1700-1702 and 1712-1714.

Cooper, Sampson, of Ripon, Yorkshire, England, alderman, had extensive dealings with Virginia and Maryland, died in Northumberland county in 1659, and was buried at Colonel John Trussell's. He directed that his son Samuel should be sent back to England and bound out to Samuel Coke, silkman in London. To son Jonathan, meadow land at Maidstone in Kent; wife Bridget.

Copeland, John, a Quaker, who suffered much at the hands of the New England Puritans. When Thomas Story, the Quaker, visited him in Isle of Wight county in 1699, he showed him his right ear mutilated by the Puritans.

Cooper, George, a justice of Northumberland county, colonel of the militia, and burgess in 1692, 1699 and 1700-1702. His will dated November 13, 1708, was proved July 18, 1711. Made liberal gifts of land to the churches of his county and for the support of the aged and needful of St. Stephen's parish.

Corbin, Gawin, of Middlesex county, son of Henry Corbin, of the colonial council, was naval officer of the Rappahannock in 1705. He was burgess for Middlesex county in 1698, 1699, 1700-1702, 1703-1705, 1718-1720 and for King and Queen county in 1715. He was county lieutenant. He married three times: (first) Catherine Wormeley; (second) Jane Lane, widow of Willis Wilson of Elizabeth City county, and daughter of John Lane of King and Queen, and (third) Martha Bassett. He died January 1, 1745, and was father of: 1. Richard Corbin, of "Laneville." 2. John Corbin, of "Portobago," Essex county. 3. Gawin Corbin, of "Pecatone."

Corbin, Gawin, son of Gawin Corbin and Jane Lane, his wife, lived at "Pekatone," Westmoreland county, and at "Laneville," King and Queen county. He was burgess for King and Queen county in 1736-1740 and for Middlesex county in 1742-1747. He married Hannah Lee, daughter of Thomas Lee, of "Stratford," Westmoreland county, Virginia, and his will was proved in Westmoreland county January 29, 1760.

Corbin, John Tayloe, son of Colonel Richard Corbin, of "Laneville," King and Queen county, member of the council, was a burgess for King and Queen county 1769-1772, 1772-1774, 1775; did not approve of separation from Great Britain; he married Maria Waller, daughter of Judge Benjamin Waller, of Williamsburg; grandfather of General Richard Corbin, of the confederate army.

Corker, John, was burgess for Passbehay in the assembly of September 4, 1632, and for Passbehay, James City and Chickahominy in that of February, 1633. He was clerk of the house of burgesses in 1645 and was still clerk in 1653. He married Dorcas, born in 1601, and was father of William Corker (q. v.).

Corker, William, son of John Corker (q. v.) and Dorcas, his wife, was burgess for James City in 1655-1656, and captain of the militia. He married Lucy, daughter of Captain John White. He left three daughters, Susanna, who married George Branch, Judith who married ———— Clay, and Lucy who married ———— Jordan. His will was proved in Surry county September 4, 1677.

Corprew, Joshua, was a burgess from Norfolk in the assembly of 1756-1758.

Cotton, Anne, wife of John Cotton of Queen's Creek, York county, Virginia. She wrote an account of Bacon's rebellion entitled "Our Late Troubles in Virginia, written in 1676 by Mrs. An. Cotton of Q. Creeke" (Force's Tracts I. No. ix). Internal evidence shows that she was also the author of "A Narrative of the Indian and Civil Wars in Virginia in the years 1675 and 1676" (Force's Tracts I. No. xi).

Cotton, Rev. William, was minister of Accomac, and brother-in-law of William Stone, first Protestant governor of Maryland. His mother Joane Cotton in 1640 was living at Bunbury in Cheshire, England. He died in 1640.

Covington, Richard, was a burgess for Essex county in the assembly of 1703-1705, and was justice of the peace and lieutenant-colonel of the militia.

Cowles, Thomas, was burgess for James City county in 1698; sheriff in 1700. He was ancestor of a well-known family in James City county.

Coxe, Richard, was a burgess from Weyanoke in the assembly of 1632.

Crabb, John, settled in Westmoreland county, Virginia, was a successful merchant and married about 1673 Temperance, daughter of Dr. Thomas Gerrard, and widow of Daniel Hutt, of the same county. He left sons Osman and Thomas Crabb. His brother, Osman Crabb, of Brislington, alias Busselton, Somerset, England, died about 1695, leaving the bulk of his estate to his brother John, of Virginia.

Craddock, Lieutenant William, had charge in 1614 of the first salt works in Virginia on Smith's Island, near Cape Charles. In 1618 he was provost marshal of Bermuda City and of all the hundreds thereto belonging. He died before 1625.

Crashaw, Raleigh (Rawley), member of the Virginia Company of London, came to Virginia in 1608, was prominent in the early adventures, went on a trading expedition up the Potomac at the time of the massacre in 1622, and so escaped death; member of the house of burgesses in 1623; was probably a near relative of Rev. William and his son, the poet, Crashaw.

Crawford (Craford, Crafford), William, was a burgess from Lower Norfolk in the assembly of 1688, and from Norfolk in the assembly of 1696, and in the session of November 10, 1714, and in the assemblies of 1716, 1718, 1720-22, 1723-26, 1736-1740, and 1742-1747.

Crawley, Thomas, son of Robert and Margaret Crawley, was baptized in the parish of St. Margaret's, Bristol, August 27, 1637. He resided in Rappahannock county, Virginia, and left issue.

Crew, Randall, was a burgess from Upper Norfolk in the assemblies of 1639, and 1642-43, and from Warwick in the assemblies of 1645, and 1646.

Crews, Captain James, of Turkey Island, Henrico county, was one of Nathaniel Bacon's most active friends. He was captured by Sir William Berkeley, and hanged. As he never married, his property went to his nephew and niece in England, Matthew Crews, son of Francis Crews, deceased, and Sarah Whittingham, daughter of Edward Crews, deceased.

Cripps, Zachariah, came to Virginia in 1621, burgess for Warwick River, October, 1629, commissioned justice of Warwick River 1631; burgess for Stanley Hundred, 1632-33, and 1639; patented in 1628 100 acres at the end of Mulberry Island, adjoining the land of Gilbert Peppet, deceased.

Croshaw, Joseph, was justice of the peace of York county in 1655; and in subsequent years major of the militia; and burgess for York county in 1656, 1659, and 1660. His estate in York county was called "Poplar Neck." In 1687 Colonel John West and Unity his wife, daughter of Major Joseph Croshaw, sold "Poplar Neck" to Edmund Jennings, Esq., who called it "Ripon Hall," after Ripon in Yorkshire, whence he came.

Crump, Sergeant Thomas, was burgess for James City, February, 1631-32, for Neck of Land, September, 1632. It is probable that he married Elizabeth, a daughter of Rev. Richard Buck.

Culpeper, Captain Alexander, whose father lost "life, liberty and estate in the King's service" was appointed surveyor general of Virginia in 1672, and again in the first year of James II. He appears to have had an interest with Lord Culpeper in the lands in the Northern Neck. He was brother of Lady Frances Berkeley, wife of Sir William Berkeley.

Curle, Nicholas, was son of Pasco Curle, of Elizabeth City county, and nephew of Thomas Curle, which last was born in St. Michael's parish, Lewes, county Sussex, England, November 24, 1640 and died in Elizabeth City county May 30, 1700. Nicholas Curle was member of the house of burgesses in 1710-1712 and died August 15, 1714. He was grandfather of William Roscow Wilson Curle.

Currie, David, a native of Scotland, came to Virginia about 1743 and was minister of Lancaster county till his death in 1792. He came of a good family, and had doubtless received a university education. He married Elizabeth, daughter of Captain Ellyson Armistead, of York county, and Jane Anderson, his wife, and had issue, with other children, Ellyson Currie, a distinguished lawyer of Lancaster county, who died in 1829.

Curtis, John, was a burgess from Lancaster county in the assembly of 1659-1660. He was son of Major Thomas Curtis and Averilia, his wife.

Curtis, Rice, son of Rice Curtis, of Middlesex county, was a magistrate of Spottsylvania county, major in the militia, and burgess in the assemblies of 1736-1740, 1748-1749, 1752-1755, 1756-1758. He resigned in 1756 to accept the office of sheriff. His will dated August 8, 1763, names son Rice, and daughters Mary Vass, Martha Pendleton, Elizabeth Waller, Frances Carter and Jane Curtis.

Custis, Hancock, a burgess for Accomac county in 1710-1712.

Dade, Francis, son of William Dade, Esq., of Tannington, county Suffolk, England, came to Virginia about 1650. He was doubtless involved in some royalist plot, for he was for many years, known as John Smith. He married Behethland Bernard, daughter of Captain Thomas Bernard, burgess for Warwick county. He died at sea in 1662. He was a major in the militia of Westmoreland county. His widow married Major Andrew Gilson.

Daingerfield, William, son of John Daingerfield and Anne Walker, his wife, daughter of Colonel John Walker, of the council. he was burgess for Essex county in 1718, 1723-1726, and 1727-1734. He married Elizabeth Bathurst, daughter of Lancelot Bathurst, attorney-at-law (q. v.). His will was proved in Essex county, November 18, 1735.

Daingerfield, William, Jr., son of William Daingerfield and Elizabeth Bathurst, his wife, was burgess for Essex county in 1754, 1755 and 1756-1758. He married Apphia Fauntleroy, daughter of Colonel Griffin Fauntleroy, of Northumberland county. He died in Essex, April 29, 1769, "at an advanced age," and left issue.

Dalby, Thomas, was burgess from Northampton county in the assembly of 1761-1765.

Dale, Edward, a royalist, came to Virginia about 1650. His wife was Diana Skipwith, daughter of Sir Henry Skipwith, of Prestwould, in Lancashire, England. Dale was justice of the peace for Lancaster county, Virginia, from 1669 to 1684; sheriff in 1670, 1671, 1679 and 1680; burgess in 1677 and 1682; major of militia in 1680; and clerk of the county from 1655 to 1674. He died February 2, 1695. His daughter Katherine married Captain Thomas Carter, of Lancaster county.

Dandridge, Bartholomew, son of Colonel John Dandridge, of New Kent county, was born December 25, 1737, and died April 18, 1785. He represented New Kent county in the house of burgesses in 1772-1774 and 1775-1776, and in the conventions of 1775 and of 1776. He was a member of the house of delegates and in 1778 was made judge of the general court. Brother of Mrs. Washington.

Dandridge, Colonel John, brother of Colonel William Dandridge, of the council, was born in 1700, and came to Virginia about 1722, when he had a grant of a water-front lot in Hampton, Elizabeth City county; clerk of New Kent county in 1747; married

Frances Jones, daughter of Orlando Jones, on July 22, 1730; was father of Martha Dandridge, who married (first) Daniel Parke Custis; (second) George Washington. He died August 31, 1756, and was buried at Fredericksburg.

Dandridge, Martha, daughter of Colonel John Dandridge of New Kent and Frances Jones, daughter of Orlando Jones, of King William county, was born June 2, 1731. She married (first) Daniel Parke Custis in 1749 and had issue, one son surviving, John Parke Custis, who died in 1781, of campfever contracted at the siege of Yorktown, while serving on the staff of General Washington. She married (second) General George Washington. Died May 22, 1802.

Dandridge, Nathaniel West, was son of Colonel William Dandridge of the council, and Unity, his wife, only child of Colonel Nathaniel West, of West Point. He was a burgess from Hanover county from 1758 to 1764, when he was defeated for reelection by Colonel James Littlepage. He contested the election and his attorney, Patrick Henry, made a great speech, but he was not successful. He married Dorothea, daughter of Governor Alexander Spotswood, and died January 16, 1786, leaving issue.

Davenport, Joseph, first town clerk of Williamsburg. He died in 1761. His son Joseph studied at William and Mary, and in 1755, went to England to be ordained. On his return, the same year, he became minister of Charles parish, York county, and remained such till his death in 1788. His son, Matthew, was writing master in the college.

Davies, Samuel, an eminent Presbyterian divine, born in New Castle, Delaware, November 3, 1723, of Welsh extraction, educated under Rev. Samuel Blair at Fogg's Manor, came to Hanover county, Virginia, in 1746, and during his residence greatly increased the Presbyterian influence in Virginia; in 1753 Mr. Davies went to England to solicit funds for the establishment of a college in New Jersey and in 1758, was chosen to succeed Jonathan Edwards as president. He died at Princeton, New Jersey, February 4, 1761.

Davis, James, gentleman, came to Virginia before 1616, as did his wife Rachel; settled in Henrico county. Thomas Davis, his son and heir, patented land in Isle of Wight county in 1633.

Davis, Thomas, was burgess from Martin-Brandon (Captain John Martin's plantation) in the assembly of 1619. He was excluded from the assembly, because Captain Martin claimed an exclusive authority under his patent.

Davis, Thomas, was burgess for Warwick county in the assemblies of 1655-1656 and 1657-1658. In 1662 he was granted 500 acres, and is called "major."

Davis, William, was burgess from James City in the assemblies of 1642-43, and of 1647.

Dawkes, Henry, an ancient planter, came to Virginia in 1608, and in 1632 his "son and heir apparent." William Dawkes of Varina, patented lands due him for the personal adventure of his father, and for a subscription to the stock of the London Company, paid by his father.

Dawson, Rev. Musgrave, son of William

Dawson, of Aspatria, Cumberland county, England; born 1724, matriculated at Queen's College, Oxford, March 7, 1744; B. A., 1747; came to Virginia and was minister of Raleigh parish, Amelia county, in 1754, of St. Mary's, Caroline, 1758 etc. He married in 1757 Mary Waugh, daughter of Alexander Waugh. He was father of Hon. John Dawson, M. C., and brother of William Dawson, president of William and Mary College.

Day, John, member of the house of burgesses for Isle of Wight county in 1775. He was a descendant of James Day, who married Mary, daughter of Thomas Bland and Mary Bennett, daughter of Edward Bennett, a London merchant, who in cooperation with his brother, Robert Bennett, his nephew, Richard Bennett, and others established the plantation called "Warrascoyack" in Isle of Wight county.

Death, Richard, was burgess from Isle of Wight county in the assemblies of 1642-43 and 1644. His will was dated March 3, 1647.

Debedeavon, otherwise "Laughing King," head chief of the Accomac Indians, who was a friend of the English at the time of the massacres of 1622, 1644, and would take no part in the murder.

DeButts, Lawrence, came from England in 1721, and was rector of Washington parish, Westmoreland county. He also served in St. Stephen's parish in Northumberland, Farnham in Richmond, and Cople parish in Westmoreland county. In 1735 he removed to Maryland where he was minister of St. Mary's parish, in St. Mary's county. He died in 1752, leaving a brother Robert DeButts.

Delany, Henry, was a burgess for Mecklenburg county in the assemblies of 1765, 1766-68. He married Rebecca Brodnax, widow of Alexander Walker, and died in 1785, leaving issue Edward, Mary Persons, Lucy wife of Robert Brooking (son of Vivion Brooking), William, Lucy, Fanny.

Delke, Captain Clement, born in 1598, probably son of Sir Thomas Delke, of Maxtoke Castle, Warwickshire, and his wife, Ann, daughter of Sir Clement Fisher, of Packington; he and others contracted in 1623 with the London Company to bring over 100 emigrants; afterwards in 1627 he patented land on the eastern shore; in 1624 a member of the house of burgesses.

Delke (or Dilke), Roger, came to Virginia before 1625, when he was one of the servants of Mr. John Chew at Hog Island. He was burgess for Stanley Hundred in 1631-32. He died about 1635, leaving a widow Alice and son Roger.

Denson, William, was burgess from Upper Norfolk, in the assembly of 1659-60.

DeRichebourg, Claude Phillipe, came to Virginia in 1700 with the French Huguenots. He was minister of Manakintown, but, owing to disputes in the parish which were referred to the council of Virginia, he left Virginia in 1707, and with numerous followers, settled in the Carolinas.

Dewey, Stephen, a lawyer of distinction, was King's attorney for Charles City county in 1740, and burgess for Prince George county in 1752-1755. He married Elizabeth Walker, daughter of George

BURGESSES AND OTHER PROMINENT PERSONS

Walker, of Elizabeth City county, and Anne Keith, his wife, daughter of George Keith, the eminent preacher, of Pennsylvania. George Wythe, nephew to his wife, studied in his office.

Dick, Charles, one of the trustees of Alexandria, appointed major and commissary during the French and Indian War. During the American revolution he was appointed one of a board to carry on a powder factory at Fredericksburg. He had one son and two daughters: Alexander Dick, a major in the revolution, and Eleanor, who married Judge James Mercer, and Mary Dick, who married (first) Sir John Peyton, and (second) James Taliaferro. He died in 1779, at Fredericksburg.

Digges, Dudley, son of Dudley Digges Esq., and Susannah Cole, his wife, was justice of Goochland in 1735, burgess for the county in 1732, and in 1741 qualified as an attorney-at-law. He married Mary Hubard, daughter of James Hubard, of York county, and left several children, who died without issue. One of them Maria Digges, was stewardess of William and Mary College.

Digges, Edward, was eldest son of Colonel Cole Digges and Elizabeth Power, his wife, was sworn justice of the peace for Yorktown in 1734, commissioned lieutenant-colonel of horse and foot for York county, November 18, 1734, sworn county lieutenant, September 19, 1748. Member of the house of burgesses from 1736 to 1752. He died March 22, 1769. He lived at "Bellfield" York county, and his wife was Anne Harrison, daughter of Colonel Nathaniel Harrison, of the council.

Digges, William, eldest son of Governor Edward Digges, was justice of the peace for York county in 1671; captain of horse in 1674; cut off one of Thomas Hansford's fingers in a hand-to-hand fight during Bacon's rebellion; sheriff of York county in 1679; removed to Maryland soon after, and died in 1698. He was member of the Maryland council and lieutenant-colonel. He married Elizabeth Sewell, daughter of Henry Sewell, of Patuxent, Maryland, step-daughter of the third Lord Baltimore.

Digges, William, son of Lieutenant-Colonel Cole Digges, of the council, by Elizabeth Power, his wife, lived at "Denbigh," Warwick county. He was lieutenant-colonel of the Warwick militia, justice of the peace and from 1752 to 1772 was member of the house of burgesses. He married Frances Robinson, daughter of Major Anthony Robinson, of York county. He left issue.

Dipnall (Dipdall), Thomas, was a burgess from James City county in the assembly of 1654. He was son of Rev. John Dipdall, who patented lands on Powell's Creek, south side of James river in 1653.

Dixon, Adam, yeoman, came to Virginia in 1612 as master cawker of ships for three years at thirty-six shillings per month, but he was forcibly detained in service seven more years. He returned to England in 1622, when he made complaint of not being paid for his services and of being by Sir George Yardley turned out of his land; returning the same year with his wife and daughter, he received in 1672 200 acres on the south side of James river.

Dixon, Rev. John, son of John Dixon, of Bristol, Esquire, and Lucy, daughter of Thomas Reade, of Gloucester county, Virginia, was educated at William and Mary College; entered the ministry of the Church of England; appointed usher of William and Mary College, March 28, 1747; appointed rector of Kingston parish, Gloucester county, now Mathews county, 1754; professor of divinity of William and Mary, 1770; sympathized with England during the revolution; prominent Mason; buried in the new church of Kingston parish, May 4, 1777.

Dixon, John, was a printer, who married Susanna Hunter, daughter of William Hunter, second editor of the "Virginia Gazette." He formed a partnership with Alexander Purdie to carry on the paper after Hunter's death, which continued until 1774 when he took in William Hunter Jr., as his partner. In 1778 Hunter left Virginia, and Thomas Nicholson was substituted. This partnership continued in Richmond, when the editors moved their office in 1780. Dixon died in Richmond in 1791.

Dixon, John, a merchant of Bristol, England, came to Virginia in the early part of the eighteenth century and acquired large tracts of land in Hanover, Louisa, Albemarle and Culpeper counties. He was a vestryman of St. Paul's parish, Hanover county, 1744-1748. He removed to England with his second wife, Anne Lyde, and died in 1758 at Bristol. By his first wife, Lucy Reade, he was father of Rev. John Dixon, Roger Dixon and Thomas Dixon.

Dixon, Roger, son of John Dixon, Esq., of Bristol, and brother of Rev. John Dixon; went from King and Queen county to Spottsylvania county; admitted to practice as an attorney in Spottsylvania court, February 7, 1748. He lived in Fredericksburg, where he purchased a large tract of land at the lower end of the town, which he later divided into smaller tracts and sold. He owned large tracts of land in various counties. He engaged largely in merchandizing. He was vestryman of St. George's parish; justice of the peace for Spottsylvania county 1760-1770; first clerk for Culpeper county, 1749-1772; trustee of the town of Falmouth; member of the house of burgesses for Spottsylvania county, 1769-1771. He married Lucy, daughter of Major Philip Rootes, of Rosewall, King and Queen county, Virginia, and Mildred, his wife, daughter of Thomas Reade, of Gloucester county, his first cousin.

Doak, Robert, burgess for Fincastle county, in 1772-1774, but unseated May 9, 1774, because at the time of his election he held the office of deputy surveyor.

Doe, Thomas, was burgess from Archer's Hope, in the assembly of 1629.

Doggett, Rev. Benjamin, appears to have come from Ipswich, England, to Virginia. He was minister in Lancaster county for quite a number of years. He died in 1682 leaving descendants.

Donelson, John, was a burgess from Pittsylvania county in the assemblies of May, 1769, 1769-1771, 1772-1774.

Doran, was a burgess for New Kent county in the assembly of 1734-1740.

Dormer, Sir Fleetwood, formerly of Arle-Court, Gloucestershire, son of Sir Fleetwood Dormer, of Lee Grange and Purton, Bucks, was in Virginia in 1649, probably a royalist refugee. In 1684, John Dormer, of James

Braxton, George, Jr., son of Col. George Braxton, was a member of the house of burgesses for King and Queen county in 1758-1761, in which latter year he died. He married Mary, daughter of Col. Robert Carter, and was the father of George Braxton and Carter Braxton, the last a signer of the Declaration of Independence.

Bray, James, son of James Bray, Esq., of the council, was justice of the peace from James City county, and member of the house of burgesses in 1688 and 1702. He married about 1697 Mourning, widow of Thomas Pettus, of "Little Town," James City county. He died Nov. 25, 1725, leaving issue Thomas, James and Elizabeth.

Bray, Robert, justice of the peace for Lower Norfolk county, and lieutenant colonel of the militia. He was son of Edward Bray of Biggleswade, Bedfordshire. He died in 1681. He had a brother Plomer Bray, also resident of Lower Norfolk county.

Breman, Thomas, was a burgess of Gloucester county in 1654.

Brent, George, a royalist, son of George Brent, of Gloucestershire, England, and Marianna Peyton, daughter of Sir John Peyton of Dodington, Cambridgeshire, came to Virginia about the year 1650, settled in Stafford county, and secured large grants of land, including the estates of Woodstock and Brenton. He was a Roman Catholic, and James II. granted him and his associates the free exercise of their religion. He was captain of the militia in 1675, agent for Lord Fairfax, a member of the house of burgesses for Stafford county in 1688, and a partner in the practice of the law with William Fitzhugh. On May 2, 1683, he was appointed receiver general north of the Rappahannock. In 1688-89, when there was a wild rumor of Catholics inciting Indian uprisings, Capt. Brent, incurred many dangers on account of his religion, but was protected by William Fitzhugh. He died about 1694. He married (first) a daughter of William Greene and niece of Sir William Layton, and (second) a daughter of Col. Henry Sewell, of Maryland, whose widow married Lord Baltimore.

Brent, Giles, son of Richard Brent, Esq., of Gloucestershire, England, emigrated to Maryland in 1637 and was followed by his brother Fulke and sisters Margaret and Mary. In Maryland he filled the highest offices, was a burgess in 1639, commander of Kent Island in 1640, member of the council in 1642, and in 1643 he was appointed by Gov. Calvert as governor, lieutenant general and admiral, in his absence to England. He was a strong royalist. In 1645 he removed to Virginia where he patented large tracts of land in Stafford county, including the estates of "Peace" and "Richland." He married (first) Mary ———; and (second) Frances Whitgreaves, widow of Dr. Jeremiah Harrison, and daughter of Thomas Whitgreaves who saved the life of Charles II. at the battle of Worcester. Giles Brent died in 1671.

Brent, Giles, son of Col. Giles Brent, of Maryland and Virginia, and his wife Mary, was born in Virginia about 1652. Under a commission from Nathaniel Bacon Jr., created general by the assembly in 1676, he raised a body of troops to march against the Indians, but on learning that Bacon had been denounced as a rebel by Gov. Berke-

VIR—13

ley marched, instead, against his general. His troops, however, would not follow him and disbanded. He married a daughter of George Brent and Marianna Peyton, died in Middlesex county, Sept. 2, 1679.

Brent, Margaret, daughter of Richard Brent, Esq., of Gloucestershire, England, came to Maryland in 1638. Gov. Leonard Calvert relied greatly upon her, and made her his attorney and at his death in 1648 his administratrix; keenly alive to her rights, she claimed the right to vote in the assembly "for herself and also as his Lordship's attorney." Some years later she went with her sister Mary to "Peace," her brother Col. Giles Brent's estate in Westmoreland county (now Stafford) Virginia. She made her will in 1663.

Brent, William, of "Richland" Stafford county, was son of Giles Brent of Stafford and grandson of Col. Giles Brent, first of Maryland and then of Virginia. In 1708 he went to England to recover an inheritance, and married May 12, 1709, Sarah Gibbons of Box parish, Middlesex county, England, daughter of William Gibbons and sister of Sir John Gibbons, M. P., for Middlesex. William Brent died in England Dec. 20, 1709. His widow married (secondly) in Virginia, Rev. Alexander Scott of Overwharton parish, Stafford county. William and Sarah Brent had one child, William Brent of "Richland."

Brereton, Thomas, was clerk of the council in 1661, one of the justices of Northumberland county and lieutenant-colonel; he married Jane Claiborne, daughter of Colonel William Claiborne, and died about 1688, leaving issue. The records refer to his ring, with his coat-of-arms upon it; and he appears to have come from the county of Chester, as in 1736 Thomas Brereton, of Shotwick Park, Chester, who seems to have been a descendant, made a deed for land in Northumberland county, Virginia.

Brewer, John, son of John Brewer, Esq., of the council of state, was a member of the house of burgesses for Isle of Wight county in 1657-58. The name has continued in Nansemond to the present day.

Brewster, Edward, son of William Brewster, who is supposed to have been the same as the Pilgrim Father, was a member of the Virginia Company of London in 1609, and came to Virginia with Lord Delaware in 1610, when the latter arrived at Point Comfort, he dispatched Brewster in command of the pinnace *Virginia* to Jamestown, June 8, 1610; he met the settlers at Mulberry Island on their way to England and turned them back. He performed a useful part against the Indians, and in 1618 had charge of Lord Delaware's estate in Virginia. Having complained of Gov. Samuel Argall's unlawful use of Lord Delaware's servants; he was arrested and sentenced to death. On petition, however, of the ministers of the colony his life was spared and he was banished. The company in London set the order aside. He remained in London and in 1635 he and Henry Seile were booksellers near the north door of St. Paul's Cathedral.

Brewster, Richard, was living in Virginia before 1624, and in 1629 was a burgess for Neck of Land in James City corporation.

Brewster (Brewer), Thomas, "alias Sackferd, of Sackferd Hall in the county of Suffolk, gent.," was married to Elizabeth Wat-

BURGESSES AND OTHER PROMINENT PERSONS

kins, widow of John Watkins, of Surry county, Virginia, in 1655. He has descendants in Virginia.

Bridger, James, son of Col. William Bridger, of "White Marsh," was burgess for Isle of Wight in 1758-1761, 1761-1765, 1766-1768; coroner of the county in 1768; then burgess in 1769, 1770, 1772, 1773, 1774.

Bridger, Col. Joseph, of "White Marsh," son of William Bridger, son of Col. William Bridger, of "White Marsh," Isle of Wight county, was burgess for the county in 1756, 1758-1761, 1762, 1763, sheriff in 1764. He married Mary Pierce, a sister of Thomas Pierce, member of the convention of 1788. He died in 1769 when his widow married Col. Josiah Parker of "Macclesfield." Col. Bridger left a daughter Judith, who married Richard Baker, clerk of Isle of Wight county 1754 to 1770.

Bridger, Samuel, son of Col. Joseph Bridger of the council, was justice and lieutenant colonel of the militia of Isle of Wight county and burgess in 1705-1706.

Bridger, Colonel William, of "White Marsh," son of Colonel Joseph Bridger, of the council, was born in Isle of Wight county, in 1678, married Elizabeth Allen, daughter of Major Arthur Allen, of Surry, was a burgess for Isle of Wight county, 1714, 1718 and 1720-22. His will was proved in Isle of Wight county November 23, 1730. He left a son William, whose son Joseph, was a burgess, and a son James, who was also a burgess (q. v.).

Bridges, Charles, was an artist who came to Virginia before 1735, and painted portraits. In many families some of these portraits are extant, and almost always, in case of women, may be known by a lock of hair resting on the front of the shoulder. He painted for the Byrds and Pages, and an order in Caroline county shows that he painted the King's arms to hang in the county court.

Briggs, Gray, was a son of Howell Briggs, of Surry county, and a descendant of Henry Briggs, who came to Virginia before 1668. Gray Briggs represented Sussex county in the house of burgesses in 1756-1758. John Howell Briggs, who represented Surry in the convention of 1788, was his son and Elizabeth Briggs, who married Colonel William Heth, of the Revolution, was his daughter.

Bristow, Robert, son of Robert Bristow, Esq., of Ayot, St. Lawrence, Hertfordshire, England, was born in 1643 and settled in Virginia about 1660. In 1663 and the following years he purchased various estates in the counties of Lancaster, Gloucester and Prince William. He resided in Gloucester and as major of the militia took sides with Governor Berkeley in Bacon's rebellion. He incurred great losses from the rebels, and returning to England in 1677 became a merchant in London, and acquired a large fortune. He died in the parish of Fenchurch, London, between 1700 and 1707. By his wife Avarilla, daughter of Major Thomas Curtis, of Gloucester county, Virginia, he left an only son Robert Bristow, who was associated with him in business and was M. P. for Winchelsea in the parliament of 1698 and 1700. Robert Bristow, of Braxmore Park, the great-grandson of Robert, first named, heired all the Virginia estates, but they were confiscated in 1776 by an act of the Virginia legislature.

Broadwater, Charles, was a Scotchman, who located in Fairfax county, and named his estate "Cameron," after the clan to which he belonged. He was a burgess in the assembly in 1775 and member of the conventions of March 20, 1775, July 17, 1775, and of December 1, 1775.

Brockenbrough, Colonel Austin, born November 3, 1738, son of William Brockenbrough, of Richmond county, was a lieutenant in Washington's First Virginia Regiment during the French and Indian war. At the beginning of the revolution he was a Tory, and went to England, where he remained till the end of the war. He was a man of large means. He married in 1761, Lucy, daughter of Colonel John Champe, of Lamb's Creek, King George county. He was a brother of Dr. John Brockenbrough of Tappahannock.

Brockenbrough, Dr. John, an eminent physician, son of William Brockenbrough, of Richmond county. He resided at Tappahannock, Virginia, was justice of Essex county, surgeon in the Virginia navy in the revolution, married Sarah, daughter of William Roane, of Essex, and was father of Dr. John Brockenbrough, president of the bank of Virginia.

Brodhurst, Walter, was the son of William Brodhurst, of Lilleshall in county Shallop, England. He settled in Northumberland county and was a burgess for the county in 1653. He died in 1659, leaving children Gerrard, Walter and Elizabeth, and widow Anne, who became the wife successively of Henry Brett, of Plymouth, England, and of John Washington, of Westmoreland county, Virginia.

Brodnax, Edward, son of William Brodnax, of Jamestown, was one of the justices of Charles City county in 1745. In 1748 he was elected a burgess, but died before taking his seat, and Benjamin Harrison succeeded him. He was grandfather of General William Henry Brodnax (1786-1834).

Brodnax, Major John, of Godmersham, in Kent county, England, was a cavalier officer who came to Virginia and died in 1657. He was great-uncle of William Brodnax (q. v.).

Brodnax, William, son of Robert Brodnax, a goldsmith of London and a descendant of the Brodnaxes of Godmersham in Kent county, England, was born February 28, 1675, and married, soon after his arrival in Virginia, Rebecca, widow of Edward Travis, of Jamestown. He represented Jamestown in the house of burgesses from 1722 to 1726, when he died leaving issue.

Bronaugh, William, son of Colonel Jeremiah Bronaugh and Simpha Rosa Enfield Mason, widow of John Dinwiddie (brother of Governor Dinwiddie) and sister of the statesman, George Mason. He lived in Loudoun county, signed the Westmoreland county protest against the Stamp Act in 1765, and died in Loudoun county, where his will dated March 24, 1796 was recorded April 14, 1800. He left issue.

Brooke, George, of "Pampatike," King and Queen county, was a son of Humphrey Brooke and Elizabeth Braxton, daughter of George Braxton, Sr. He was lieutenant-colonel of the King and Queen county militia, and burgess from 1765 to 1775 and member of the state conventions of 1774,

1775 and 1776. His will dated in 1781 was proved May 13, 1782. He married Hannah, daughter of Colonel Richard Tunstall.

Brown, Charles, doctor of physic, resided in Williamsburg, where he died in 1738. He had the finest library of books in physic and natural philosophy ever offered to sale in the colony.

Brown, Dr. John, of Coldstream, North Britain, came to Williamsburg, Virginia, in the early part of the eighteenth century. He first married Margaret, who died in 1720; second Mildred Washington, who married (secondly) Colonel Henry Willis, of Fredericksburg. He died September 24, 1726.

Browne, Devereaux, was one of the first justices of Accomac county as created anew in 1663, and was burgess in September, 1663.

Browne, Henry, who was son of Henry Browne, and grandson of Captain William Browne of "Four Mile Tree," Surry county. Married Hannah Edwards, daughter of Colonel Benjamin Edwards. He was a burgess from Surry county in 1761 and 1762, and died the latter year.

Browne, John, was a burgess for Shirley Hundred in 1629.

Browne, William, married Mary, daughter of Colonel Henry Browne, of "Four Mile Tree," Surry county; justice of Surry county, 1668-1705; major of militia, 1672, and lieutenant-colonel, 1679, 1687; presiding justice, 1687; sheriff 1674 and 1687; and member of the house of burgesses, 1676-1677, 1679, 1681 and 1682. He married (second) Elizabeth Meriwether, widow of Nicholas Meriwether.

Browne, Captain William, was son of Lieutenant-Colonel William Brown, of "Four Mile Tree," Surry county, and was born in 1671. He married Jane Meriwether, daughter of Nicholas Meriwether; justice in 1693 and for many years later, becoming in 1710 presiding justice of Surry county. His will dated July 3, 1746, was proved in Surry, January 19, 1747.

Browne, William, of "Four Mile Tree," Surry county, son of Captain William Browne, was born March 5, 1739; member of the county committee of safety, February, 1776; member of the house of delegates, 1777, 1780. His will was dated June 19, 1786 and proved June 27, 1786.

Browne, William Burnett, was son of William Browne of Salem, Massachusetts, by Mary Burnett, his wife, only daughter of William Burnett, governor of Massachusetts, son of the celebrated bishop, Gilbert Burnett. He married Judith, daughter of Charles Carter, of "Cleve," in King George county, Virginia. He died at "Elsing Green," King William county, May 6, 1784, leaving three daughters: Elizabeth Carter, who married John Bassett; Judith Carter, who married Robert Lewis; Mary, who married Herbert Claiborne of "Sweet Hall," King William county.

Browning, John, was a burgess for Elizabeth City in 1629, and 1629-30.

Bruce, George, immigrant, was born in 1640, and settled in Rappahannock county, Virginia, before 1668. His will was proved in 1715, and names children George, Charles,

William, John, Hensfield and Jane. The son of Charles Bruce was Charles Bruce of "Soldiers' Rest." For Bruce Genealogy see "Virginia Magazine of History and Biography," xi., 107, 328, 441; xii., 446.

Bryan, Dr. Richard, was son of Richard Bryan, of King George county; in 1753 he received £250 for discovering a cure for the "dry gripes," dysentery. His wife was Frances Batteley, daughter of Moseley Batteley, of Spottsylvania, a descendant of Governor Samuel Mathews, of Virginia.

Buck, Rev. Richard, came to Virginia with Sir Thomas Gates in 1610. He is said to have been a graduate of Oxford. He was minister of Jamestown from 1610 to his death between 1621 and 1624. He acted as chaplain of the general assembly which convened in the church at Jamestown July 30, 1619, the first law making body to meet on the American continent. His widow Bridget married (secondly) John Burrows, of "Burrows Hill" and (thirdly) John Bromfield. He had four, probably five, children: Sarah, Benoni, Gershom, Peleg and Elizabeth, wife of Sergeant Thomas Crump.

Buckner, John, of St. Sepulchre's, citizen and salter of London, was born in 1630, married Deborah Ferrers, of West Wickham, Bucks in 1661, came to Virginia with his brother Philip, and settled in Gloucester county. He was the first man to use a printing press in Virginia and employed one John Nuthead to print the laws of the general assembly of 1680. He was forbidden to print further without license. He left issue William (q. v.); Thomas (q. v.); John (q. v.), and Richard (q. v.).

Buckner, John, son of John Buckner, of Gloucester county, was burgess for Gloucester in 1715. He removed to Essex county and died before 1727, leaving sons John and William.

Buckner, John, son of Major William Buckner, of Yorktown, was captain of the militia, and burgess for York county, in 1734-1740. He died without issue, leaving his lands to his nephew, Griffin Stith.

Buckner, Richard, son of John Buckner, of Gloucester county, was clerk of Essex county in 1703, and clerk of the house of burgesses in 1713.

Buckner, Richard, was a burgess for Cardin county, in the assembly of 1727-1734. He died at the opening of the session in 1734. He was probably a son of Richard Buckner, clerk of Essex county in 1703 (q. v.).

Buckner, Samuel, son of Thomas Buckner, resided in Gloucester county, which he represented in the house of burgesses in 1744-1747. He was lieutenant-colonel of the militia and made his will November 5, 1763. He left three children: 1. Dorothy, who married Baldwin Mathews Buckner. 2. Mary, who married Charles Mynn Thruston. 3. Elizabeth, who married Colonel William Finnie.

Buckner, Thomas, son of John Buckner, of Gloucester county, was burgess for Gloucester county in 1698, 1715, 1718. He married Sarah, daughter of Captain Francis Morgan, and left issue.

Buckner, William, son of John Buckner, appointed justice of York county 1694; sheriff 1695, 1696, and member of the house of burgesses 1698, 1699, 1714; by appointment of William and Mary College surveyor general of the colony 1708-1716. He was major of the militia and a prominent merchant with extensive business in Virginia and England. He died in 1716 and was father of John Buckner, of York and Stafford counties.

Bugg, Samuel, immigrant ancestor of a widely scattered family in the south, died in New Kent county, Virginia, September 13, 1710.

Bulloch, William, author of a well known tract on Virginia, was a resident of London, but his father Captain Hugh Bullock, of London, patented 2,550 acres of land here, on which he had a corn-mill and sawmill. Robert Bullock, son and heir of William Bullock, came to Virginia and brought suit in the general court about a tract of 5,500 acres situated in Warwick county. This last probably left descendants in Virginia.

Burgess, Thomas, was a burgess for Warrosqueake in 1629-30, for Martin's Hundred in 1632 and 1633.

Burnham, John, son of Rowland Burnham, was justice and lieutenant-colonel of Middlesex county, Virginia, militia in 1680, and died unmarried before July, 1681; burgess in 1675-76.

Burnham, Rowland, was a justice of York county, and a burgess in 1644, 1645 and 1649. He moved to Lancaster where his will, dated 1655, is recorded.

Burnley, Zachariah, son of John Burnley, of Albemarle county, was a burgess for Bedford county in 1758-17— and for Orange county in 1765 and 1766-1768.

Burrows, Benoni, son of Christopher Burrows, was burgess for Norfolk county in 1697. He was grandson of John Burrows, who married the widow of Rev. Richard Buck.

Burrows (Burroughs), Christopher, patented land in 1635 in what is now Princess Anne county, and was a burgess for Lower Norfolk county 1645, 1646, 1652, and was a justice in 1652. He was born in 1612 and died before 1671, leaving two sons William and Benoni. He was probably a son of John Burrows, of "Burrows' Hill" in Surry county.

Burrows, John, patented about 1624 150 acres on the south side of the James river above Jamestown and called his place "Burrows Hill." He married Bridget, the widow of Rev. Richard Buck, and was probably the father of Christopher Burrows by an earlier marriage.

Burton, John, burgess for Northampton county in the assemblies of 1769-1771, 1772-1774 and the convention of 1775.

Burwell, Armistead, son of Colonel Lewis Burwell, of "Kingsmill," was burgess for Williamsburg in the assembly of 1752-1755, but died in 1754 and was succeeded by George Wythe. He married Christian Blair, daughter of President John Blair, of the council.

Burwell, James, was a son of Major Lewis Burwell, of "Carter's Creek," Gloucester county, and Abigail Smith his wife. He was born February 4, 1680, and died in

1718. He resided at "King's Creek" plantation in York county, where his tomb still stands. He was one of the justices for the county and a burgess for 1715 and 1718.

Burwell, Lewis, son of Major Lewis Burwell, of "Carter's Creek," Gloucester county, and Martha Lear, his second wife, was a student at William and Mary College in 1718. He resided at "Kingsmill" in James City county, and was a colonel of the militia and burgess in 1742-1747.

He laid out great sums of money in building a mansion house and gardens on James river. He died about 1744, leaving issue Lewis (q. v.) and Armistead (q. v.).

Burwell, Lewis, immigrant, was son of Edward Burwell, of Bedfordshire, England, and Dorothy Bedell, his wife. He was born March 5, 1621, and died November 4, 1653. He settled in Virginia about 1640, and resided at Carter's Creek in Gloucester county, where his tomb long remained. He married Lucy, daughter of Captain Robert Higginson, and was "sergeant major" of the militia.

Burwell, Lewis, son of President Lewis Burwell, studied law at the Inner Temple, sheriff of Gloucester county in 1767; burgess 1769-1774; member of the conventions of 1775, and 1776, died in 1779. He married Judith Page, daughter of Mann Page, and had Alice Grymes, who married William C. Williams; Judith, who married George Miles; Nathaniel, sheriff of Gloucester in 1808 and Lewis, who married Judith Kennon.

Burwell, Lewis, of "Kingsmill," was son of Lewis Burwell, who was son of Major Lewis Burwell of Carter's Creek, who died in 1710. He married Frances Thacker, widow of James Bray in 1745. He was member of the house of burgesses for James City county from 1758 to 1775, and died in 1784.

Burwell, Nathaniel, of "Carter's Creek," Gloucester county, baptized October 14, 1680, was the eldest son of Major Lewis Burwell and Abigail Smith, his wife, niece of Hon. Nathaniel Bacon. He was a member of the house of burgesses for Gloucester county in 1710, and major of the county militia. He married Elizabeth Carter, daughter of Colonel Robert Carter, and died in 1721. His widow married (secondly) Dr. George Nicholas.

Bush, John, gentleman, came at his own charge in 1618; and his wife Elizabeth, and two children, Elizabeth and Mary came in 1619; settled at Kecoughtan, where he patented land in 1624; died in 1625.

Bushrod, John, son of John Bushrod, and grandson of Richard Bushrod, the immigrant to Virginia. He resided at "Bushfield," in Westmoreland county, and was justice, colonel of the militia and burgess for that county from 1746 to 1756. His daughter Hannah married John Augustine Washington, brother of General George Washington and father of Judge Bushrod Washington of the United States Supreme Court.

Bushrod, Thomas, born 1604, was one of the justices of York county and a burgess in 1658 and 1659. He was a Quaker and in his will dated December 18, 1676, he forbids "common prayers to be read at his grave." He was a brother of Richard Bushrod, ancestor of Judge Bushrod Washington.

Butler, Captain Nathaniel, eldest son of John Butler Esq., of Toîte in Sharnbrooke, Bedfordshire, was a member of the council in England for Virginia, governor of the Bermuda Islands from 1619 to 1622, was in Virginia during the winter of 1622-23, when he conducted an expedition against the Indians. He went to England in the spring and published his "Unmasking of Virginia." He was on the Virginia commission of 1624, was at Cadiz in 1625, the Isle of Rhé in 1627; a captain in the Royal navy; governor of the Bahamas 1638-1641; committed to Newgate by the council of state of the commonwealth for dispersing treasonable books in June, 1649.

Butler, Rev. Thomas, was pastor of the parish of Denbigh. He married Mary Brewer, widow of John Brewer Esq., of the council of state, and in 1635 he was given a patent for 1,000 acres in Isle of Wight county on account of the persons imported by Mr. Brewer. The land is still known as Brewer's Neck and lies between Brewer's and Chuckatuck creeks.

Butler, William, was a burgess for James City county in 1641 and 1642, and for Surry county in 1653 and 1658. He was major of the militia of Surry. He was probably a son of Rev. Thomas Butler (q. v.).

Butt, Thomas, was son of Robert Butt, of the "Southern Branch of the Elizabeth River," Norfolk county, who made his will in 1675 which was proved in 1676. He was burgess for Lower Norfolk county in 1700-1702.

Cabell, John, son of Dr. William Cabell, the immigrant, resided at "Green Hill," Buckingham county. He was chairman of the county committee of safety in 1775; was a member of the convention of May, 1776; was county lieutenant of Buckingham; member of the house of delegates from 1777 to 1788. He married (first) Paulina, daughter of Colonel Samuel Jordan, (second) Elizabeth Brereton Jones. His will, dated April 22, was proved June 12, 1815.

Cabell, Joseph, son of Dr. William Cabell, the immigrant, lived at "Sion Hill," Buckingham county, Virginia. He was born September 19, 1732; was justice of Albemarle in 1760; major in 1762; burgess for Buckingham county from 1761 to 1771, and for Amherst county from 1772 to 1775, and member of all revolutionary conventions except that of May 6, 1776, when he was paymaster of the troops on the frontier. He was afterwards a member of the house of delegates, 1776 to 1779; county lieutenant of Amherst, 1778 and other years; state senator, 1781-1785; member of the house of delegates, 1788-1790. He married Mary, daughter of Dr. Arthur Hopkins, and died March 1, 1798, leaving issue.

Cabell, Dr. William, was the son of Nicholas Cabell, of Warminster, England, and was born March 9, 1699; emigrated to Virginia about 1724, and died April 12, 1774. He held a great variety of offices; was county surveyor, sheriff, justice of the peace and county lieutenant. His life is identified with the counties of Henrico, Goochland, Albemarle, Amherst and Nelson. In 1756-1758 he was burgess for Albemarle. He married (first) Elizabeth Burks, (second)

Mrs. Margaret Meredith, widow of Samuel Meredith Sr., of Hanover.

Cabell, William, Jr., son of Dr. William Cabell, the immigrant, was born March 13, 1730; received a good education and held many offices; he was sub-sheriff of Albemarle county in 1751; captain of a company in the French and Indian war, and in 1760 was colonel of the militia of Albemarle. He was also a burgess for Albemarle county in 1758-1761. When Amherst county was formed, in 1761, he held all the leading offices. He was president of the county court, coroner, surveyor, vestryman, county lieutenant, and from 1761 to 1775 was a burgess. He also represented Amherst in the conventions of 1775 and 1776. He was, moreover, a member of the public committee of safety. During the revolution he was state senator; after it was over, a member of the constitutional convention of 1788. His residence was known as "Union Hill." He died March 23, 1798.

Callaway, James, son of Colonel William Callaway, was colonel and afterwards county lieutenant of Bedford county during the revolution; served in the French and Indian war; operated iron works and lead mines; burgess for Bedford at the assembly of 1766-1768. He died near New London, Campbell county, November 1, 1809.

Callaway, William, founder of New London, in Campbell county; county lieutenant of Bedford county during the French and Indian war, and burgess from Bedford county from 1754 to 1765. He married Elizabeth Tilley, and was father of James Callaway (q. v.).

Callicut, William, a silversmith, who in 1608 accompanied Christopher Newport in his expedition to the Monacan country and was the first to discover the veins of gold and silver that traverse Fluvanna county.

Caithorpe, Colonel Christopher, came to Virginia in 1622, and was the second son of Christopher Calthorpe, Esq., of Blakeney, Norfolk county, England, and Maud, his wife, daughter and co-heir of John Thurston, Esq., of Brome, county Norfolk, and grandson of Sir James Calthorpe, of Stirston, in Suffolk, and Barbara Bacon, his wife. He settled in York county, of which in 1658 he was colonel commanding the militia and justice of the peace. He was burgess for York county in 1644, 1645, 1653 and 1660. May 23, 1661, a commission of administration of his estate was granted to his relict Anne. He has many descendants in Virginia and the south (see "William and Mary Quarterly," ii. 106-112; 166-168 for Calthorpe family).

Calvert, Cornelius, came from Lancaster county, England. He was justice of Norfolk county, July 18, 1729, to January 17, 1730; for many years member of the common council of Norfolk borough. He married Mary Saunders, July 29, 1718, in Princess Anne county, and died in 1748, leaving among other children Cornelius Calvert Jr.

Calvert, Cornelius, was son of Cornelius Calvert and Mary Saunders; was a prominent merchant of Norfolk. He was born March 13, 1723; married, June 19, 1749, Elizabeth Thoroughgood, daughter of John Thoroughgood. In 1776 he was member of the association called "The Sons of Liberty." He had issue—Saunders T. Calvert; Ann, wife of James Tucker, and Mary, wife of William Walke.

Campbell, Andrew, a resident of Frederick county, is believed to have been the "Mr. Campbell" who was a burgess from Frederick county in 1745-1747. He was one of the first justices of Frederick county.

Campbell, Archibald, came to Virginia in 1745. He was son of Archibald Campbell, of Kernair, Argyleshire, Scotland, and his wife, Anna Stewart, of Ascog. He was minister of Washington parish from 1754 to 1774. He had a brother, Alexander Campbell, who was a merchant at Falmouth, Virginia, but returned to Scotland. This brother was father of Thomas Campbell, the poet.

Campbell, Colin, was major and adjutant for the eastern district of Virginia in 1775. He died in Surry county in 1780, leaving sons, Archibald, M. D., and Colin.

Campbell, Hugh, a native of Scotland, was an attorney-at-law, Norfolk county. By his deed in 1691 he gave 200 acres of land in each of the counties of Norfolk, Isle of Wight and Nansemond for free schools.

Cant, Major David, was a resident of Gloucester county, which he represented in the house of burgesses in 1659-60. He married a daughter of Colonel Augustine Warner, and had sons—Augustine, David, Walter, and probably John (q. v.).

Cant, John, probably a son of Major David Cant; member of the house of burgesses from Middlesex in 1692.

Cargill, John, son of Rev. John Cargill, who went from England to the Leeward Island in 1708 and thence to Virginia. John Cargill Jr. married, in Virginia, Elizabeth Harrison, daughter of Nathaniel Harrison,

of "Wakefield," Surry county. He was burgess for Surry county in the assembly of 1742-1747, but died in 1744 before the assembly ended, leaving a son John, who married (first) Sarah Avery, (second) Anne Jones.

Carlyle, John, was a scion of an ancient and influential family of Dumfriesshire, Scotland. He was a son of William Carlyle, a surgeon of Carlisle, England, and Rachel Murray, his wife. He was born February 6, 1720, came to Virginia about 1740, and settled first at Dumfries, Prince William county, but as early as 1744 he was a merchant at Belhaven, afterwards Alexandria. He was one of the incorporators and a member of the first board of trustees of Alexandria, where he built in 1752 the historic "Carlyle House," which was the headquarters of General Edward Braddock in 1755. In 1754 he was appointed major and commissary of the Virginia forces; in 1758 he was collector of the customs of South Potomac, and in 1775 member of the county committee of safety. With Mr. John Dalton he was engaged for twenty-five years in a mercantile and shipping business. He married (first) in 1748, Sarah Fairfax, second daughter of Hon. William Fairfax, (second) Sybil West, daughter of Hugh and Sybil (Harrison) West. He died in October, 1780.

Carpenter, Nathaniel, a Devonshire gentleman, brother of Coryndon Carpenter, Esq., of Launceston, Cornwall, England; was a physician and a collector of the customs; resident in King and Queen county, Virginia, in 1768. He married Nancy Fauntleroy, daughter of Bushrod Fauntleroy, of Northumberland county, and left issue.

Carr, Thomas, was the son of Thomas Carr, "gentleman," who patented lands in King William county in 1701; justice of the peace for King William from 1714; sheriff in 1722-1723; major of militia and burgess for King William in 1727-1734. He patented large tracts of land, and died in Caroline county, May 29, 1737. He married Mary Dabney.

Carrington, George, son of Paul Carrington, merchant, was born in St. Philip's parish, Barbadoes, in 1711, and came to Virginia in 1723. He married, before 1732, Anne, daughter of Major William Mayo. He lived at "Boston Hill," Cumberland county. He was justice of peace for Goochland in 1740; major in 1743, and afterwards lieutenant-colonel and colonel of Goochland county. He was first county lieutenant and presiding justice of Cumberland. He was burgess (in place of William Randolph, deceased) from Goochland in the sessions of February 20, 1745, and March 30, 1747, and in the assembly of 1748-1749; and from Cumberland in the assemblies of 1752-1755, 1756-1758, 1758-1761, and in the sessions of November 3, 1761, January 14, 1762, March 30, 1762, November 2, 1762, May 19, 1763, January 14, 1764. In the session of October 30, 1764, Thomas Prosser represented Cumberland in place of George Carrington, who had accepted the office of sheriff. He was the chairman of the Cumberland county committee of 1774-1776. He died on February 7, 1785.

Carrington, Paul, settled in Barbadoes about 1700 and afterwards came to Virginia. He was a large shipping merchant. His son George was ancestor of the famous Virginia family of that name.

Carter, Colonel Charles, of "Cleve," King George county, was born in 1707. He was the son of Robert Carter, of "Corotoman," and his wife Judith, daughter of John Armistead, of "Hesse." He was burgess from King George county in the assemblies of 1736-1740, 1742-1747, 1748-1749, 1752-1755, 1756-1758, 1758-1761, and in the sessions of November 3, 1761, January 17, 1762, March 30, 1762, November 2, 1762, May 19, 1763, and January 12, 1764. In the session of October 30, 1764, William Champe was burgess from King George in place of Charles Carter, deceased. Colonel Carter married (first) Mary Walker, (second) Anne, daughter of William Byrd, of "Westover," (third) Lucy Taliaferro.

Carter, Charles, of "Corotoman" and "Shirley," born 1732, the son of John and Elizabeth Hill Carter; was burgess from Lancaster county in 1758-1761, 1761-1765, October, 1765, 1766-1768, May, 1769, 1769-1771, 1772-1774, 1775-1776; member of the conventions of 1775, and of the first state council, 1776. He married (first) Mary W., daughter of Colonel Charles Carter, of "Cleve," (second) Ann Butler, daughter of Bernard Moore, of "Chelsea," King William county. He died in 1806.

Carter, Charles, of "Ludlow," son of Colonel Charles Carter, of "Cleve," and his first wife, Mary Walker, daughter of Joseph Walker, Esq., of York county, married Elizabeth, daughter of Colonel John Chiswell. He was burgess from King George county in the assemblies of 1756-1758, 1758-1761, 1761-1765, October, 1765, 1766-1768 and 1769-1771.

Carter, Edward, of "Blenheim," Albemarle county, son of John Carter, of "Corotoman" and "Shirley," was born about 1726, and was a burgess from 1765 to 1769. He married Sarah Champe, daughter of John and Anne (Carter) Champe, of King George county.

Carter, Robert Wormeley, son of Colonel Landon Carter, of "Sabine Hall," was burgess for Richmond county in the last assembly, 1775-1776, and member of the conventions of 1774 and 1775. He married Winifred Travers Beale, daughter of Captain William Beale, of Richmond county.

Carter, Thomas, ancestor of a numerous family of the name in Virginia and the south. He settled first in Nansemond county, and afterwards removed to Lancaster. He was a justice, captain of the militia, etc., and married Katherine Dale, eldest daughter of Major Edward Dale and Diana Skipwith, his wife. He died October 22, 1700, aged about seventy years. He was probably a near kinsman of Colonel John Carter, of Corotoman.

Carver, Captain William, was a prominent merchant of Lower Norfolk county; was a justice in 1663 and other years; sheriff in 1670; member of the house of burgesses in 1665 and June 15, 1669, and April 16, 1672; while temporarily insane he killed a man in 1672. When the civil war broke out in 1676, Carver sided with Bacon and was dispatched by him to Accomac to seize Berkeley, but his ship was surprised by Colonel Philip Ludwell, and Carver was captured and hanged.

Cary, Major Francis, a cavalier officer who came to Virginia in 1649; returned to England.

Cary, Henry, son of Miles Cary, the immigrant, lived at "The Forest," Warwick county. Born about 1650 and died in 1720. He was a builder and contractor, and had charge of the erection of the capitol and governor's house at Williamsburg, when the government was removed from Jamestown. He later also superintended the building of the church in Williamsburg and the restoration of the college after the fire of 1705. He married Judith Lockey, and had issue, among others Henry Cary Jr. (q. v.).

Cary, Henry, Jr., was a son of Henry Cary and Judith Lockey, his wife. Born about 1680. He was like his father, a builder and contractor. He removed to Williamsburg, and in 1721 was vestryman of Bruton church. Among the buildings erected by him were the president's house at the college, the chapel constituting the south wing of the college, the church at Hampton, and probably the Brafferton building at the college. About 1733 he removed to "Ampthill," Chesterfield county. He married Anne Edwards, and died in 1749. He was father of Colonel Archibald Cary, of the revolution.

Cary, John, was a merchant of London, who came to Virginia; married Jane Flood, daughter of Colonel John Flood (q. v.). He presented a piece of plate to Brandon church, which is still preserved. In 1670 he was living in London, where he had the care and tuition of his wife's brother Walter Flood (born in 1656).

Cary, Miles, son of Colonel Miles Cary, the immigrant, was born about 1655; educated in England; clerk of the general court, 1691; burgess for Warwick county in 1688, for James City 1692-93, and for Warwick county from 1698 to 1706; register of the vice-admiralty court, 1697; naval officer of York river; trustee of William and Mary College, 1693, and afterwards rector; surveyor-general, 1692 to 1708. He married (first) Mary Milner; no issue. He married (second) Mary, daughter of Colonel William Wilson, and left issue. He died February 27, 1709.

Cary, Oswald, was son of James Cary, merchant of London, who was engaged in the Virginia trade. He was sheriff of Middlesex county, Virginia, in 1690, and captain of the militia. He died in 1690 and his widow Ann married (second) Randolph Seager, and (third) Rev. Samuel Gray. His daughter Anne married James Smith ("William and Mary Quarterly," ix, 45, 46).

Cary, Captain William, born about 1657, was a son of Colonel Miles Cary, of the council. He resided in Warwick county, which he represented in the house of burgesses in 1693, 1702 and 1710. He married Martha, daughter of Colonel John Scarsbrook, of York county, and died in 1713, leaving issue.

Cary, Colonel Wilson, son of Colonel Miles Cary (q. v.) and Mary Wilson, his wife, was born in 1702; studied in the grammar school of William and Mary College, and on June 30, 1721, was admitted a student at Trinity College, Cambridge University; appointed collector and naval officer of Lower James river; presiding magistrate and county lieutenant of Elizabeth county. He lived at "Ceeleys," in Elizabeth City county. He died in 1772.

Cary, Wilson Miles, only son of Colonel Wilson Cary, of "Ceeleys" (son of Miles Cary and Mary Wilson), was born in 1723; educated at William and Mary College; burgess for Elizabeth City county from 1760 to 1772; member of the convention of 1776, and afterwards of the house of delegates; married Sarah, daughter of John Blair, of Williamsburg, president of the council; died at "Carysbrook," Fluvanna county, about December 1, 1817, leaving issue.

Catchmaie, George, was a burgess from Upper Norfolk in the assembly of 1659-60.

Catlett, Colonel John, was born in the parish of Sittingbourne, county Kent, England, and was long one of the leading men in Rappahannock county, Virginia, where the parish of Sittingbourne was named for his original residence in England; presiding justice in 1665, and died about 1670, killed, it is said, while defending a frontier fort against the Indians. He left a son of the same name (q. v.).

Catlett, John, Jr., was the son of John Catlett (q. v.). John Catlett Jr. married Elizabeth Gaines; was a member of the house of burgesses from Essex in 1693, 1696, 1700-1702; justice of the county court, 1680, and colonel of the Essex militia. He died in 1724, leaving issue surviving.

Cave, Benjamin, was a burgess from Orange county in the assemblies of 1752-1755, 1756-1758, 1758-1761. His will, dated June 26, 1762, was proved in Orange county, November 25, 1762.

Caufield, Robert, was a burgess from Surry county in the assembly of 1676. He was a son of Major William Caufield (q. v.) and died in 1691.

Caufield (Cofield, Cowfield), William, was a burgess from Surry county in 1657-58,

1658-59, 1659-60. He was probably a son of Gresham Caufield, who patented land in Isle of Wight county in 1640. He was captain and major of the Surry militia. He was father of Captain Robert Caufield (q. v.).

Cawsey, Nathaniel, was an old soldier that arrived in the *First Supply*, January, 1608, and in 1625 he and his wife Thomasine, who came in 1609, were living with five servants at Charles City (City Point). In 1620 he patented 200 acres on Kimages creek, in the present Charles City county, which he named "Cawsey's Care." He was a burgess in 1624. He died before 1634, when John Cawsey, supposed to be his son, sold this land to Lieutenant-Colonel Walter Aston.

Ceely, Thomas, came to Virginia at an early date, and was burgess for Warwick river in 1629 and 1639. He owned land at the mouth of Salford's creek, which afterwards, under the name of "Ceeleys," was made the residence of Colonel Wilson Miles Cary.

Chamberlayn, Thomas, was burgess for Charles City in 1695-1696.

Chamberlayne, William, "descended from an ancient and worthy family in the county of Hereford" (tombstone); settled in New Kent county, where he was a successful merchant. His son Thomas married Wilhelmina, daughter of William Byrd, of Westover. William Chamberlayn died August 2, 1736.

Chanco, a converted Indian who informed his master, Richard Pace, of "Pace's Paines," of the impending massacre of 1622, and enabled him to notify the authorities at Jamestown, whereby that settlement and the ones adjoining were saved.

Chandler, John, was member of the house of burgesses from Elizabeth City in November, 1645, and 1647, and a justice of that county in 1652. In 1636 he obtained a grant for 1,000 acres in Elizabeth City county for importing his wife and nineteen other persons. About 1639 he purchased Newport News from the Gookins. In 1639 there is a joint bond from him and Samuel Chandler, merchant of London. Subsequently he sold Newport News to Captain Benedict Stafford, from whom it came to William Digges.

Chaplin, Isaac, came to Virginia with Sir Thomas Gates in 1610, and Mary, his wife, arrived in 1622. He patented "Chaplin's Choice," on James river, near Jordan's Point, in 1619. The patent called for 200 acres. In 1629 he represented Chaplin's in the general assembly. Later "Chaplin's Choice" was owned by Captain Anthony Wyatt.

Charleton, Stephen, burgess for Northampton county in the assemblies of 1645 and 1652. When Colonel Henry Norwood and his friends in 1649 were stranded on the eastern shore of Virginia, Charleton received them at his house most hospitably. He married (first) Bridget Pott, sister of Governor John Pott, (second) Anne West, widow of Anthony West. By his first wife he had two daughters, but both died issueless. His estate, consisting of 1,500 acres, went to the parish, according to the provisions of his will.

Chesley, Philip, emigrated from Wellford, in Gloucestershire, about 1650, and was captain of militia for the county of York, and church warden in 1674 of Bruton parish.

He married Margaret, sister of Daniel Wild. His will, proved in York county, May 10, 1675, names many nephews and cousins, who made their home with him in Virginia.

Chester, Captain Anthony, was commander of the ship *Margaret and John*, which traded to Virginia. In March, 1621, on his way with passengers to Virginia, he was attacked by two large Spanish armed ships in the West Indies, and after a heroic fight beat them off. This was exploited greatly in England.

Chew, John, said to have been from Somersetshire, England, came to Virginia in 1620, and was one of the leading merchants. In 1625 he had a lot in Jamestown. He was burgess for Hog Island in 1623, 1624 and 1629. Afterwards he removed to York county, and was burgess for that county in 1642, 1643 and 1644. About 1649 removed to Maryland and settled in Anne Arundell county. Ancestor of Chief Justice Benjamin Chew, of Germantown, Pennsylvania.

Chew, Larkin, son of Joseph Chew, of Maryland, and grandson of John Chew, the immigrant to Virginia, settled in Spottsylvania county, Virginia, and was a justice of that county in 1722; sheriff in 1727, and burgess for Spottsylvania from 1723 to 1726. He married Hannah Roy, and left issue.

Chichester, Richard, immigrant ancestor; of an ancient and distinguished family, was second son of John Chichester, of Widworthy, and Margaret Ware, his wife. He came to Virginia in 1702, bringing with him his son John. He lived in Lancaster county, where his will, dated April 14, 1734, is duly recorded. His son John married Elizabeth Symes, of Dorset, England, and had Richard Chichester, who lived at "Fairwethers," Lancaster county, Virginia, but is buried at Powerstock, Dorset, England.

Chiles, John, was a son of Walter Chiles Jr., and resided in King William county. He was messenger of the council in 1693; justice of King William in 1714, and in 1723 was a member of the house of burgesses from that county. He died the latter year. He married (first) Mary ———, (second) Eleanor Webber, daughter of Henry Webber, of King William, and had a daughter Susannah, who married Joseph Martin, of Albemarle, father of General Joseph Martin, a distinguished pioneer of Southwestern Virginia.

Chiles, Walter, Jr., son of Colonel Walter Chiles, of the council, came to Virginia with his father before 1638, lived at Jamestown, and was burgess for James City county in 1658-59 and 1660. He married Mary Page, daughter of Colonel John Page, the councillor, and had by her one son John and a daughter Elizabeth, who married Henry Tyler, of Middle Plantation, ancestor of President John Tyler.

Chilton, Edward, was a barrister of the Middle Temple, who came to Virginia some time before 1682, when he was clerk of the council and of the general court. In 1697 he had a part in the compilation of a pamphlet called "The Present State of Virginia," his co-laborers being Henry Hartwell, Esq., and Dr. James Blair. He was attorney-general of Virginia from 1692 to 1698. In 1699 he became attorney-general of Barbadoes. He married Hannah, daughter of Colonel Edward Hill, of Shirley, but she died issueless.

City county, Virginia, was a vestryman of Bruton parish church, at Middle Plantation (now Williamsburg).

Douglas, Edward, was an early resident of Northampton county, where he was a justice, captain of the militia and at the time of his death in 1657 lieutenant-colonel. He was burgess for the county in 1644 and 1646. He left descendants.

Douglas, George, a native of Accomac county, and burgess in 1742-1747, and 1752-1755. He was a descendant of Lieutenant-Colonel Edward Douglas (q. v.).

Douglas, William, was the son of Hugh Douglas, of Gavalland in the parish of Old Cumnock, Scotland. In 1770 he was one of the justices of Loudoun county, Virginia, and in 1780 high sheriff. His will dated June 3, 1780, was proved at March term of the Loudoun county court.

Doughty, Francis, was the son of a Bristol alderman and had been vicar of Sodbury, Gloucester. He first settled in New England, then moved to Manhattan and getting in trouble in both places, he went in 1656 to Northampton county, Virginia, where he lived with his brother-in-law, William Stone, afterwards governor of Maryland. He became minister of Hungar's parish, and in 1657 married Ann Eaton, widow of Nathaniel Eaton. He did not remain long but moved to Essex county, where he was minister of Sittingbourn parish. In 1659 he is next found in Maryland living with his daughter. He is generally regarded as of Puritan sympathies.

Downing, Mr. John, was a burgess from Northumberland county in the assembly of 1692-93. Richard Rogers and Richard Flint were first elected representatives from Northumberland in that assembly; their seats were, however, contested, and the sheriff of Northumberland was required to amend his return in favor of Mr. John Downing and Captain William Jones.

Downman, John, was born in 1592, came to Virginia in 1614; one of the commissioners of the peace for Elizabeth City, March, 1629, and burgess for the same October, 1629; Elizabeth Downman, doubtless his wife was born in 1599, came in the *Warwick*, 1621.

Downes, George, member of the house of burgesses for "the lower parish of Elizabeth City," February, 1631-1632, and September, 1632.

Downs, Henry, was a burgess from Orange county in the session of May 6, 1742. He was expelled during that session for "stealing a white sheep," in Maryland, before he settled in Virginia. He was at one time a King's justice. In 1751 he is mentioned in an Orange county court order as "a runaway."

Dowse, Thomas, was a burgess from the city of Henricus in the assembly of 1619. He came to Virginia in 1608, and was one of the few early settlers that survived.

Doyley, Cope, son of Charles Doyley, of Southrop, county Gloucester, England, matriculated at Wadham College, Oxford, March 10, 1675-1676, aged 16; B. A. from Merton College, 1680. Came to Virginia about 1697 and was minister of Bruton parish till his death in 1704. He had two sons, Charles and Cope, and a brother Rev. Robert Doyley, B. A. and M. A. of Wadham College, and rector of several parishes in England.

Drew, Dolphin, was a burgess for Isle of Wight county in the assembly of 1766-1768, and justice of the peace in 1772.

Drummond, Richard, son of John Drummond, of Accomac county, born 1636, who married the daughter of Richard Hill, was burgess for Accomac in the sessions of 1712-14 and 1715.

Drummond, Sarah, wife of Colonel William Drummond, one of the heroines of Bacon's rebellion. When others doubted she picked up from the ground a small stick and broke it, and said: "I fear the power of England no more than a broken straw." She was probably a daughter of Edward Prescott, who in his will left her a lot at Jamestown. After the execution of her husband, she complained to the British government of the cruelty of Sir William Berkeley to her husband and five children

Drummond, William, a native of Scotland, came to Virginia about 1660, and in 1665-1667 served under Berkeley as first governor of North Carolina, afterwards resided at Jamestown; was sheriff of James City county in 1660; was burgess in 1676; took sides with Bacon in Bacon's rebellion, and was executed January 20, 1676, at Middle plantation. The English authorities condemned his execution and his property was restored to his widow, Sarah. He left a son William, and a daughter married Samuel Swann, of North Carolina.

Dudley, Ambrose, was a burgess from Gloucester county in the assembly of 1710-1712. Son of Richard Dudley, of Middlesex county, and brother of Major Robert Dudley (q. v.).

Dudley, Robert, son of Richard Dudley, was major of the militia in Middlesex county and one of the justices. From 1685 to 1697 he was one of the burgesses for the county. He had property both in England and Virginia. His will dated October 14, 1701, was proved November 3, 1701. He left a brother Ambrose Dudley, two sons, Robert and George, and two daughters, Avarilla and Elizabeth.

Dunn, Nicholas, chief clerk to the kitchen of Charles I., came to Virginia about 1649. He died there.

Dunston, John, was burgess for James City in 1649.

Dunlap, Rev. William, came to Virginia from Pennsylvania, and in 1774 was minister of Stratton Major parish, King and Queen county. He had a library of "several thousand volumes in most arts and sciences." He was afterwards rector of St. Paul's parish, Hanover county. He died in September, 1779. His daughter, Deborah, married John Robinson, of "Green Branch," Middlesex county, Virginia.

Dunlop, William, merchant of Dumfries, Prince William county, was born in 1707 and died December 21, 1739. He was son of Alexander Dunlop, Greek professor in the University of Glasgow, and grandson of William Dunlop, president of that University, who died in Glasgow in March, 1700. Both his father and grandfather had lived in South Carolina.

Durand, William, was an elder in the Puritan congregations, in Nansemond and

Elizabeth City counties. Because he would not conform to the established church of the colony, he was banished in 1648, and went to Maryland with many other banished Virginia Puritans. He became secretary of the province in 1654, and was one of Governor William Fuller's councillors in 1655. His will was proved in 1672.

Duvall, Samuel, a merchant of Henrico county, was burgess for the county from about March 10, 1772 to 1776, and member of the convention of August, 1774, and March 20, 1775; member of the county committee of Henrico; in 1780 one of the committee to locate the capitol square in Richmond; his will was proved in Henrico, March 1, 1784. His daughter, Lucy married Major Andrew Dunscomb, of New York, who settled in Richmond and was mayor of the city in 1780.

Dykes, James, was son of John Dykes, of Waterford, Scotland. He was born November 3, 1769, and married Sarah, daughter of William Roane, of Essex county, brother of Judge Spencer Roane.

Each, Captain Samuel, of Limehouse, in Middlesex county. England, mariner, contracted in 1622 with the Virginia Company of London to build a blockhouse on the Oyster banks at Blunt Point, James river. He was to be given 60,000 pounds of tobacco for the work, but in his voyage over in his ship the *Abigail,* a distemper broke out of which he and most of his men died. Captain Each owned land in Martin's Brandon. His will was proved April 21, 1623.

Earle, Samuel, was a burgess from Frederick county, in the assembly of 1742-1747.

Eaton, John, son of John Eaton, of York county, who died in 1717, was burgess for James City county in the assemblies of 1727-1734 and of 1734-1740. He was captain of militia. Died in 1739 and William Marable took his place in the house of burgesses.

Eaton, Nathaniel, was the first principal of Harvard College, and brother of the governor of New Haven. For his unchristian methods he was debarred from teaching in Massachusetts, and in 1639 came to Accomac. His wife and children were drowned at sea, but after his arrival he married Anne Graves, daughter of Thomas Graves, a member of the Dorchester church, who immigrated to Virginia. Eaton became one of the assistants of Rev. John Rozier. In 1646 he left the colony for England, where he lived privately till the revolution of Charles II. He conformed and preached at Biddiford, where, it is said, he persecuted the Puritans. He fell into debt in some way, was cast in prison, and died while a prisoner.

Eaton, Thomas, founder of the second free school, patented lands at the head of Back river in Elizabeth City county in 1634. In 1638, he patented in the same quarters 650 acres, and in 1659 "being at present weak but whole and perfect in memory," deeded 500 acres of this land and all the housing, together with two negroes, twelve cows and two bulls, twenty hogs, young and old, one bedstead, a table, a cheese press, twelve milk trays, a twelve gallon iron kettle, potracks and pot hooks, milk pails, water tubs and powdering tubs for the support of an able schoolmaster to teach the children born in Elizabeth City county." In 1805 "Eaton's School" was incorporated with Syms' school as Hampton Academy. It is now known as the Syms-Eaton Academy. The joint fund amounts at present to $10,000.

Edlow (Edloe), Matthew, came to Virginia in 1618, and in 1629 was a member of the house of burgesses for "the plantation at the College." He married Alice, the widow of Luke Boys. He was dead in 1637, leaving a son Matthew (q. v.).

Edlow (Edloe), Matthew, son of Matthew Edlow (q. v.), had a grant of 1,200 acres in James City county, over against Chippokes Creek in 1637. As captain, he was burgess for James City in 1659. He was later lieutenant-colonel of the militia. He married Tabitha (probably Minge) and died in 1668, leaving a son John.

Edmunds, John, probably son of Thomas Edmunds, of Surry, was burgess for Sussex county in the assemblies of 1752-1755, 1756-1758, 1758-1761, 1761-1765, October, 1765, 1766, 1768, May, 1769 and 1769-1771. He died before the last assembly was out. His will dated February 13, 1770, was proved April 10, 1770.

Edmunds, Thomas, was burgess for Surry county in the assembly of 1736-1740. He died in 1738, before his term was out.

Edmundson, James, son of Thomas Edmundson, and Dorothy, daughter of Colonel William Todd, was burgess for Essex county in the assemblies of 1769-1771, 1772-1774, 1775-1776 and the conventions of 1774, 1775 and 1776. He married Miss Throckmorton, and died about 1791, leaving his property to his Throckmorton nephews and nieces.

Edmondson, Thomas, was a burgess from Essex county in the assemblies of 1693, and 1696-97; and in the sessions of December 5, 1700, and May 13, and June 18, 1702. He died in 1715 leaving eight sons: James, Joseph, William, Bryant, Thomas, Samuel, Benjamin, and John, and two daughters, Sarah Baughan and Anne Haynie.

Edwards, Nathaniel, son of John Edwards, settled in Brunswick county, where he was one of the first members of the county court. He was a justice of the peace and major of the militia. He married Jane Eaton, widow of Anthony Haynes, and died in 1771, leaving issue, several children, one of whom was Nathaniel, Jr., who represented Brunswick in the house of burgesses from 1769 to 1771.

Edwards, William, merchant, was probably son of William Edwards, mentioned among the dead in 1624; patented lands on the south side of James river opposite to Jamestown about 1648, was a burgess for Surry in 1652 and 1653, and clerk from 1653 till his death in 1673. He was born in 1615 and had by his wife Dorothy, three sons, William (q. v.), John and Thomas.

Edwards, William, son of William Edwards, and Dorothy, his wife, was clerk of the general court in 1688, from 1673 till 1698 was clerk of Surry county court, and in 1694 was clerk of the council for the colony. He married Ann Manfield, daughter of George Manfield, and died in 1698. He resided, for the most part, in Jamestown, where he had a lot near the church tower, and another near Orchard Run. He left issue a son William (q. v.).

Edwards, William, son of William Edwards, and Ann Manfield, his wife, had lots at Jamestown and plantations in Surry. He represented Surry county in the house of burgesses, 1703-1705, 1706, and his will dated January 9, 1722, was proved in Surry county, February 25, 1722. He married (first) Elizabeth, daughter of Colonel Benjamin Harrison; (second) a daughter of Micajah Lowe merchant, of Charles City, and nephew of Micajah Perry, of London.

Eggleston, Joseph, was a burgess for James City county in the assembly of 1727-1734, but he died in 1732. He was ancestor of the Egglestons of Amelia county.

Eldridge, Thomas, son of Thomas Eldridge, an attorney-at-law, and Judith Kennon, his wife. He married (first) Martha Bolling, a descendant of Pocahontas; (second) Elizabeth Jones, daughter of James and Sarah (Howell) Jones, of Surry county. By his first marriage he had Rolfe Eldridge, clerk of Buckingham county from 1770 to 1806.

Elligood, Jacob, probably descended from Elias La Guard, one of the French Vigneron planters at Buck Roe, Elizabeth City county, in 1620; justice of Princess Anne county in 1730 and other years; burgess in the assemblies of 1736-1740, 1742-1747, 1748-1749 probably father of Colonel Jacob Elligood, who sided with Dunmore in 1775, and left the colony.

Ellyson (Ellison), Robert, came to Maryland as "Barber Chirurgeon" before 1643, and after holding the office of high sheriff of St. Mary's county, emigrated to Jamestown, where he was high sheriff of James City county, and sergeant-at-arms of the house of burgesses in 1657-1658, and a leading burgess in 1656, 1660, 1661, 1663, with the rank of captain. He left a daughter Hannah, who married Anthony Armistead, and a son Gerard Robert Ellyson

Embry, Henry, was in 1727 captain of the Surry county militia. In 1732 he was a justice of the first court of Brunswick. He represented that county in the assembly in the sessions of 1736-1740 and in 1748-1749. In 1746 he was commander of the Lunenburg militia. Died about 1758, and his widow Priscilla married William Hill.

Embry, William, son of Henry Embry, was a burgess from Lunenburg county in the assemblies of 1754, 1755 and 1756-1758. He was an early vestryman of Cumberland parish, Lunenburg county. His will, dated in 1760, names sons William and Henry.

Emerson, William, was a burgess from Weyanoke in the assembly of 1632-33.

Emerson, Rev. Arthur, was a son of John Emerson, of New Castle-on-Tyne; B. A. of Oxford University, 1733; went to Antigua in 1736, and in 1755 was member of Accomac. He left a son, Arthur, who was also a minister (q. v.).

Emerson, Rev. Arthur, son of Rev. Arthur Emerson, educated at William and Mary College, where he was assistant usher and usher to the grammar school (1762-1765); was ordained a minister in England and returned in 1768; rector of Meherrin parish, Greensville county, 1773-1776; afterwards rector in Nansemond county, where in 1785 he had a classical school; rector of Portsmouth parish, Norfolk county, from 1785 to 1801, when he died.

Emperor, Francis, probably son of Francis

Emperor, of Norwich, England, who was born in 1584. He appears to have come to Virginia about 1650, and settled in Lynhaven parish, Norfolk county. He was a commissioner, high sheriff and surveyor and collector of the customs. He had his own ships and traded with New Amsterdam, New England and the West Indies. He was a Puritan in sympathy. He married Mary Tully and died in 1676, leaving sons Francis, William and Tully Emperor, and daughter Elizabeth Philips. The original name appears to have been De Keyser, and its first members in England were Dutchmen.

English, Captain John, of Isle of Wight county, burgess in 1658-59; will proved October 9, 1678.

English, William, justice for York county in 1633, member of the house of burgesses for Elizabeth City county in 1629, 1632, and 1633. As sheriff of Charles river, or York county, in 1635, he was present at the meeting at William Warren's house near the present Yorktown, which was held to protest against the tyranny of Sir John Harvey. He was arrested by Harvey, but released by the assembly. He died in 1646, leaving issue by his wife Susannah, Elizabeth, William and Dennis English.

Ennails, Bartholomew, emigrated to Virginia about 1660, and in 1661 married Mary, niece of Francis Heyward, deceased. He afterwards removed to Maryland where in 1674 he patented "Bartholomew's Range." He died in 1688, leaving issue.

Eppes, Francis, son of Captain Francis Eppes, of the council, was born about 1628 and died in 1678. He was a justice of Henrico county, lieutenant-colonel of militia, married, and left issue, Francis, William, Littlebury, Mary, married John Hardiman, and Anne.

Eppes, Colonel Francis, of Henrico, born 1659, died about January, 1718-1719, was the son of Lieutenant-Colonel Francis Eppes, and grandson of Captain Francis Eppes, of the council. He was justice of Henrico county in 1683 and for many other years; sheriff; burgess, 1691, 1693, and 1703-1705, 1705-1706. He married Ann, daughter of Henry and Katherine Isham, of Bermuda Hundred, and his will was proved in June, 1720.

Eppes, Colonel Francis, son of Colonel Francis Eppes, and Anne Isham, his wife, was made a justice of Henrico county in 1710; and in March, 1719-1720, was appointed a trustee of Bermuda Hundred, in the place of his deceased father. He was a member of the house of burgesses in 1712-1714, and died in 1734.

Eppes, Francis, was a burgess for Prince George county in 1736, 1738, 1740, 1742, 1744, 1745, 1746, 1747, 1748, 1749.

Eppes, John, was a burgess for Prince George county in 1755.

Eppes, Richard, son of Colonel Francis Eppes, of Henrico, who died in 1734, resided in Chesterfield county, and was burgess for that county in the assemblies of 1752-1755, 1756-1758, 1759-1761, 1761-1765. He died in 1764. Married Martha, daughter of Robert Bolling. His will is recorded in Chesterfield county, and disposes of a large estate.

Epps, Captain William, came to Virginia in 1619, and resided on the eastern shore of

Virginia in 1624 with Mrs. Epps, and Peter and William Epps. Not long after his arrival, he had a duel with Captain Edward Stalling, whom he killed. In 1633, he appears to have been resident in the Island of St. Christopher's.

Eppes, Littlebury, was a son of Colonel Francis Eppes, of Henrico, and grandson of Captain Francis Eppes, of the council. He resided in Charles City county, was justice of the peace in 1699 and many other years, burgess for Charles City in 1710-1712 and 1712-1714, and county clerk in 1714.

Eskridge, Colonel George, came to Virginia about 1690, was a lawyer, attorney for the King in Westmoreland county, member of the house of burgesses in 1705-1706, 1710-1712, 1712-1714, 1718, 1720-1722, 1723-1726 and 1727-1734. From 1702 to 1729, he was granted several thousand acres of land in the eastern part of Virginia. He died about 1730. He married Hannah Ashton and left issue; portraits of himself and his wife are still preserved.

Eskridge, Samuel, son of Colonel George Eskridge, was a burgess for Northumberland county in the assemblies of 1769-1771 and 1772-1774, but died before the last session, and Peter Presley Thornton took his place. He married Jane Steptoe.

Everard, Thomas, was clerk of Elizabeth City county from 1743 to 1745, then clerk of York county from 1745 to 1784. He served also as clerk of the committee of courts of the house of burgesses, and as commissioner of accounts. His daughter, Martha, married Dr. Isaac Hall, of Petersburg. He was probably a near relative of Sir Richard Everard, governor of North Carolina.

Ewell, Solomon, was a burgess from Accomac county in the assemblies of 1718 and 1720-1722. He was probably a brother of Charles Ewell, of Northumberland county.

Eyre, Littleton, was burgess from Northampton county from 1742 to 1761. Descended from Thomas Eyre, who died in 1657.

Eyre, Severn, probably a son of Littleton Eyre (q. v.), was burgess in the assemblies of 1766-1768, 1769, 1769-1771 and 1772-1774, but he died in 1773. He visited New England for his health and John Adams commented upon his ability and general intelligence.

Eyres (Eyre) Robert, was a burgess from Lower Norfolk county in the assemblies of 1646 and 1648. Thomas Eyre, a Quaker, lived about the same time in Accomac county and died in 1657. His widow, Susanna (Baker) Eyres, married (second) Captain Francis Pott, and (third) Lieutenant-Colonel William Kendall. Robert Eyres, or Eyre, died before 1647, when John Custis married his widow, Elizabeth. Robert and Thomas Eyre may have been sons of Thomas Ayres or Eyres, who was one of the company to settle near Warascoyack in Isle of Wight county in 1622.

Fairfax, Bryan, eldest son of Hon. William Fairfax (q. v.), of the council of state, and Deborah Clarke, his second wife. He served in the French and Indian war, went to England in 1765, and while there the troubles began in Virginia relative to the Stamp Act. He condemned the Stamp

Act and although he disapproved of the later revenue act, he disapproved of forcible resistance. In the year 1789 he became a minister of the Protestant Episcopal Church, and on the death of Rev. David Griffith, he became minister of Fairfax parish. He served from 1789 to 1792, when he resigned. In 1800 the house of lords admitted his title as Lord Fairfax of Cameron, and his right to a seat in their body. He died in 1802 at Mount Eagle, near Alexandria, Virginia.

Fairfax, Ferdinando, was a Virginia merchant of London, and resided in Virginia in 1659 and other years. He was son of Colonel Charles Fairfax, of Menston, Yorkshire, and grandson of Thomas, first Lord Fairfax. He was born in 1636, and died in 1664.

Fairfax, Lord Thomas, of Leeds Castle, Kent, England, sixth baron of Cameron in Scotland, was the son of Lord Thomas Fairfax, fifth baron, matriculated at Oriel College, Oxford, January 24, 1709-1710. Was heir through his mother Catherine, only daughter and heiress of Lord Thomas Culpeper, to the northern neck of Virginia, came to Virginia in 1739 and again in 1745, when he remained until his death, December 9, 1781, aged ninety years. He lived at "Greenway Court," near Winchester, and was a friend of George Washington. He never married, and he was succeeded as seventh baron by his brother Robert in Scotland, and he in turn by his cousin, Rev. Bryan Fairfax as eighth baron.

Farley, Thomas, of Worcestershire, gentleman, came in the *Ann* in 1623, and the same year was living at Archer's Hope with his wife, Jane and daughter Ann. He was a burgess for the plantations between Harrop and Archer's Hope and Martin's Hundred at the session of March, 1629-30, and for Archer's Hope, February, 1631-32.

Farlow, George, was one of Cromwell's soldiers, and an expert mathematician. He came to Virginia probably about 1660 and took part with Bacon in 1676. He was captured and hanged. His niece Lydia married Major Edmund Chisman, another of Bacon's officers.

Farmer, Lodowick, was a burgess for Lunenburg county in the assembly of 1769-1771. He died in 1780, and left issue.

Farmer, Thomas, was burgess from The Plantations of the college and neck of land, in the assembly of 1629-30.

Farnefold, John, son of Sir Thomas Farnefold, of Gatwickes in Staynning, Sussex county, England, came to Virginia before 1672, and was minister of Fairfield parish Northumberland county. In 1680 he was minister of St. Stephen's parish, and remained so till his death in 1702. By his will he provided for a free school in Northumberland county. He married Elizabeth, widow of Captain William Nutt, but left no issue.

Farrar, Lieutenant-Colonel John, was son of Captain William Farrar of the Virginia council, who was a kinsman of Nicholas Farrar (Ferrer), deputy treasurer of the Virginia Company of London. He was justice of Henrico county, 1677-1684, sheriff, 1683; burgess, 1680, 1682, 1684, and died unmarried about March, 1685.

Farrar, Colonel William, was son of Captain William Farrar, of the council, a kinsman of Nicholas Farrar (or Ferrer), deputy treasurer of the London Company. He lived at Farrar's Neck in Henrico county, and was burgess, 1662, 1663, 1666. He married Mary ———, and died about January, 1678.

Farrar, Major William, son of Colonel William Farrar and Mary, his wife, was born 1657, died 1715; justice of Henrico county, 1685-1715; sheriff, 1690 and other years; burgess in 1700-1702. He married (first) Priscilla, daughter of William Baugh Jr., and (second) Mary, widow of William Ligon. He probably died in 1721, as in May of that year, his widow Mary presented an inventory of his estate in Henrico county curt.

Farrell, Major Hubert, was one of Berkeley's officers during Bacon's rebellion, was wounded in defence of Jamestown, and killed in a fight at Colonel Nathaniel Bacon's house at King's Creek in August, 1676. He married Dorothy, daughter of Colonel Thomas Drew, of Charles City county. Her tomb which was removed a few years ago from Weyanoke, Charles City county, to St. Paul's Church, Norfolk, states that she died January 18, 1673.

Faulcon, Nicholas, was a burgess for Surry county in the assembly of 1772-1774, in the place of Hartwell Cocke, who died about August, 1772.

Fawdoin (Fawdown), George, resided in Isle of Wight county where he was major of the militia in 1653, and burgess in 1646 and 1652. He married Ann Smith, who was daughter of the first wife of Colonel Nathaniel Bacon, Ann Bassett.

Fauntleroy, Moore, was a member of an ancient English family and was son of John Fauntleroy, gentleman, and Phoebe Wilkinson, his wife, of Crondall, Hampshire. He settled, first at Nansemond, and afterwards removed to the northern neck of Virginia. He was major and colonel of the militia, and burgess for Upper Norfolk, Nansemond county, in 1645 and 1647; for Lancaster county, in 1651, 1653 and 1656; and for Rappahannock county in 1659 and 1660. He was a man of great influence in the colony. He married (first) in England, Dorothy, daughter of Thomas Colle; (second) in Virginia, Mary Hill. He died before 1665, leaving issue.

Fauntleroy, William, grandson of Colonel Moore Fauntleroy (q. v.), and son of William Fauntleroy, of Rappahannock county, by Katherine Griffin, his wife, was born in 1684; was lieutenant-colonel of the Richmond county militia and burgess for that county in 1736-1740, 1742, 1747 and 1749. He married Apphia, daughter of John Bushrod, of Westmoreland county, and died in 1757, leaving issue.

Fawcett (Fossett), Thomas, was a burgess from Martin's Hundred in the assemblies of 1629 and 1629-1630.

Feild, John, son of Abraham Feild, of Culpeper county, served as captain in the French and Indian war, was burgess for Culpeper in the assemblies of 1761-1765, 1766-1768, and was killed while colonel of a regiment at the battle of Point Pleasant, October 10, 1774.

Feild, Henry, Jr., son of Henry Feild, succeeded his father as vestryman of St. Mark's parish, Culpeper county, and was burgess for the county in the assemblies of

1769, 1769-1771, 1772-1774 and 1775, and in the conventions of August, 1774, March, 1775, July, 1775, December, 1775, and May, 1776. He died in 1785, leaving six sons.

Feild, Peter, born about 1647, was major of the militia of Henrico and burgess in 1688 and 1693. He died in New Kent county, July 24, 1707. He married twice, (first) Judith Soane, daughter of Henry Soane, speaker of the house of burgesses, by whom he had Mary, who married Thomas Jefferson, grandfather of President Thomas Jefferson; (second) Alice ———, who survived him.

Felgate, Captain Robert, was in Virginia before 1626, was a justice of the peace, and a burgess for the "Plantations on the other side of the Water," in 1629 and 1630, patented land on Fellgate's Creek, York county, and died there about 1655. He married twice (first) Margaret ———; (second) Sibella Atkins, widow of ——— Atkins. His brother Tobias was a well known ship captain and another brother, William, was a skinner in London, who settled in Virginia and died 1660.

Felgate, Captain Tobias, mariner, patented in 1632, lands adjoining his brother Captain Robert Felgate's. As early as 1632 he had made five voyages to Virginia as mate and master. Felgate's Creek in York county gets its name from him.

Fielding, Ambrose, was a son of Rev. Roger Fielding, an Episcopal clergyman of Horton, Gloucestershire, England, and settled in Northumberland county, Virginia, in 1667. He was a justice of the county court from 1669 to his death in 1675. His inventory mentions plate with the Fielding arms. He left issue Richard, Edward and Anne. His brother, Dr. Robert Fielding, was ejected in 1648 from his fellowship in Baliol College, Oxford, by the parliamentary party. His brother Richard lived for a time in Virginia and had a large estate in both England and Virginia. His brother Edward was one of the aldermen of the city of Bristol, and had a plantation in Northumberland county, Virginia.

Filmer, Henry, was a burgess from James City county in the assembly of 1642-1643. He resided in James City and Warwick counties; he was son of Sir Edward Filmer, of East Sutton, Kent, and his wife, Elizabeth, daughter of Richard Argall and sister of Samuel Argall, governor of Virginia. Henry Filmer's brother, Sir Robert, was a strong cavalier and suffered much for his loyalty to the King. Henry Filmer left descendants and his name appears in several of the present Warwick county families.

Fishback, John, son of Philip Fishback and Elizabeth Heimbach, his wife, of Truppbach, near Siegen, Nassau, Germany, was born July 12, 1691, and came to Virginia as a member of the colony of miners settled by Spotswood at Germanna, Virginia, in 1714. He moved with the other German settlers to Germantown in Fauquier county about 1721. He married Agnes Haeger, daughter of the pastor, Henry Haeger. His will was probated in Prince William county, March 19, 1734.

Fitzhugh, George, son of William Fitzhugh, of "Bedford," was a member of the house of burgesses for Stafford county in 1718. He married Mary, daughter of Colonel George Mason, of Stafford, and died intestate about 1722, leaving issue George and William.

Fitzhugh, Henry, son of William Fitzhugh, of "Bedford," King George county, was born January 15, 1686-87, and died December 12, 1758. He was high sheriff of Stafford county in 1715, and burgess in 1712-1714. He married February 24, 1718, Susanna, daughter of Mordecai Cooke, of Gloucester county. He was a man of large estate in lands and slaves. His portrait by John Heselius is still preserved.

Fitzhugh, Henry, of "Bedford," son of Henry Fitzhugh, was born September 10, 1723, and died in February, 1783. He married, October 23. 1746, Sarah Battaile, of Caroline county. He was colonel of the Stafford county militia. He had issue Henry, John Battaile, William, George, Thomas, Nicholas, Richard, Mordecai Cooke, Battaile, Giles, Sarah, Susan, Mary.

Fitzhugh, Henry, only son of William Fitzhugh, Esq., of "Eagle's Nest." Stafford county, (now King George), was born in 1706 and died December 6, 1742. He matriculated at Christ Church, Oxford, October 20, 1722, and on his return to Virginia settled on his paternal estate in Stafford county (now King George). He was member of the house of burgesses in 1736-1740 and 1742-1747, and was once an unsuccessful candidate for speakership. He was also lieutenant-colonel of the Stafford militia. He married Lucy, daughter of Hon. Robert Carter, of "Corotoman." He left a large and valuable estate.

Fitzhugh, Major John, son of William Fitzhugh, of "Bedford," was a member of the house of burgesses for Stafford county from 1727 to his death, January 21, 1733. He married on or before 1719, Anna Barbara, daughter of Daniel McCarthy, speaker of the house of burgesses. He left issue William, Daniel, Sarah, Barbara, John.

Fitzhugh, Colonel William, of "Marmion" Stafford county, (now King George), son of Major John Fitzhugh, was born April 13, 1725, and died in 1791; major of the Stafford militia in 1752, and burgess from 1761 to 1765. He married twice, (first) Ursula, daughter of Colonel William Beverley, of Blandfield, Essex county, and (second) Hannah ———.

Fitzhugh, William, son of Henry Fitzhugh, of the town of Bedford, England, was baptized at St. Paul's Church, Bedford, January 10, 1651. He acquired a good education and came to Virginia about 1670 and settled at Bedford in Stafford county (but now King George). William Fitzhugh practiced law and was also a large planter and dealer in tobacco. He was burgess for Stafford from 1676 to 1686, and lieutenant-colonel commanding the Stafford militia. At his death in 1700, he left an estate of 54,000 acres of land. He married Mary, daughter of John Tucker, of Westmoreland county. He had issue, four sons. William, Henry, Thomas, George and John.

Fitzhugh, William, son of George Fitzhugh, born 1721, died February 11, 1798. resided first in Stafford county, Virginia. In 1740 he was captain in Vernon's Carthaginian expedition, under Sir William Gooch. He was member of the house of burgesses for Stafford from 1748 to 1758. In 1759 he removed to Maryland and was soon appointed a member of the colonial council there. An active friend of the revolution, he was a member of the Maryland convention of August, 1776, and was afterwards of the council of state. During the revolution his house, "Rousby Hall," was burnt by the British. He married (first) March 28, 1744, Martha, daughter of Richard Lee, widow of George Turberville. He married (second) Anne, daughter of Peregrin Frisby, of Cecil county, Maryland.

Fleming, John, Jr., son of Colonel John Fleming, was a lawyer, and represented Cumberland county in the house of burgesses in the assemblies of 1755, 1756-1758, 1759-1761, 1761-1765 and 1765-1768. The "Virginia Gazette" recorded the death of this "eminent practitioner of the law," January 21, 1767. He left a son John.

Fleming, John, was son of Charles Fleming and Susannah Tarleton, his wife. He was colonel commanding the militia of Goochland, and burgess for Goochland in 1732. He married Mary Bolling, and his will recorded in Cumberland, December 27, 1756, names sons John, Charles, Thomas, Richard and William, and daughters Mary, married William Bernard, and Caroline. His sons Charles and Thomas were prominent officers in the American revolution and his son William was judge of the superior court of Virginia.

Fleming, Robert, was a burgess from Caroline county in the session of August 5, 1736. In the session of November 1, 1738, John Martin represented Caroline county in place of Robert Fleming, deceased.

Fletcher, George, brother of James Fletcher, gentleman, of Eltham, Kent, England. In 1647, George Fletcher is called of London, merchant. He was burgess in 1652 for Northumberland county, Virginia, and lieutenant-colonel of the militia.

Fleet, Henry, was son of William Fleet, gentleman, of Chartham in Kent, England, by his wife Deborah Scott, daughter of Charles Scott, of Egerton, Kent, and Jane Wyatt, his wife. He had three brothers Edward, Reynold and John, who were members of the Maryland legislature. Henry Fleet, born probably 1595-1600 came to Virginia about 1623, and was one of the expedition of twenty-six men, who under Henry Spelman went to trade with the Anacostan Indians and other Indian bands between Potomac Creek and the falls of the Potomac. Spelman was killed; Fleet was taken prisoner, and remained with the Indians about four years, during which time he acquired a familiar knowledge of the Indian language. He was ransomed in 1627, and went to England and became a partner and agent for several London merchants in the Indian trade. He was an interpreter, trader and legislator in Maryland. He acted as guide to Leonard Calvert and his settlers to St. Mary's in 1634. After the civil war began in England, Fleet identified himself with the Virginia colony, and settled at Fleet's Bay, Northumberland county. He traded with the Indians, and in 1646 was authorized to build a fort on the Rappahannock river. In December, 1652, he was burgess for Lancaster county. About this time he and William Claiborne were authorized to hunt out new places for Indian trade. In 1654 he was made interpreter of the expedition then planned against the Indians. He was a justice of Lancaster county in 1656 and lieutenant-colonel of the militia. He died about 1661, leaving a widow Sarah, who had previously married Colonel John Walker.

Flint, Richard, burgess for Northumberland county, 1693, but his seat was contested, and he was unseated.

Flint, Lieutenant Thomas, came to Virginia in 1618, burgess for Warwick River, 1629, 1629-1630; for Keith's Creek, 1631; for Stanley Hundred, 1632; for Denbigh, 1632-1633; for Warwick county, 1642-1643, 1647; commissioner for Warwick River, 1631. He married Mary ———. In 1628 he received 1,000 acres on Warwick river for importing twenty persons into the colony.

Flinton, Pharoah, gentleman, came to Virginia in 1612, settled in Elizabeth City, where he patented land between Newport News and Blunt Point in 1624.

Flood, John, came to Virginia in 1610, his wife Margaret in 1620; in 1616 was one of Rev. Alexander Whitaker's men at Charles City, living at Jordan's Journey in 1625; burgess for Flower Dewe Hundred in 1630 and for Westover, Flower Dewe Hundred and Weyanoke in 1632; settled about 1638 on the south side of James river in Surry county, near "Four Mile Tree"; burgess for James City county in 1642, 1645. Indian interpreter, 1646; burgess for James City county, 1652, 1656. Captain in 1642, lieutenant-colonel, 1652. He died in Surry county, 1661. His son Captain Thomas Flood succeeded him as interpreter. He married Fortune Jordan, sister of Colonel George Jordan.

Flournoy, Jacob, son of Jaques Flournoy, of Geneva, Switzerland, was born January 5, 1663. He was a Huguenot, who came to Virginia in 1700, and settled with other persons of same religious views at Manakintown, above Richmond. He had a nephew John James Flournoy, who also settled in Virginia.

Flournoy, John James, born November 17, 1686, was son of Jaques Flournoy, of Geneva, and Julia Eyraud, his wife, came to Virginia about 1717, and settled at Williamsburg, where he married Elizabeth, daughter of James Williams, and widow of Orlando Jones. He was nephew of Jacob Flournoy, immigrant.

Floyd, Charles, was a burgess from Northampton in the session of November 16, 1714, and in the assembly of 1718.

Folliott, Rev. Edward, son of Sir John Folliott and Elizabeth Aylmer, daughter of John Aylmer, Bishop of London, was born in 1610, matriculated at Hart Hall, Oxford, April 13, 1632, and was rector of Alderton, Northamptonshire, in 1634 and until it was sequestered by parliament. He came to Virginia before 1652. In 1660 he was minister of Marston parish in York county, and afterwards of York parish. He left two daughters: 1. Elizabeth Folliott who married (first) Josias Moody, and (secondly) Captain Charles Hansford. 2. Mary, who married (first) Dr. Henry Power, and (secondly) John Seal.

Follis, "Mr. Thomas," was a burgess from James City in the assembly of 1641.

Fontaine, Francis, a French Huguenot, son of Rev. James Fontaine, who was born at Jenouelle, France, and grandson of James Fontaine, pastor of Vaux and Royan. He was born September 16, 1697, was minister of the French settlement at Manakintown,

Virginia, from 1720-1722, professor of Oriental languages in William and Mary College in 1729, rector of Yorkhampton parish, 1722-1749. Died the latter year. He married (first) Mary Glaneson; (second) Susanna Brush. He left issue.

Fontaine, James Maury, son of Rev. Francis Fontaine, by Susanna Brush, his wife, was born in 1738, educated at William and Mary College, where he was described as "knowing more than any other boy in the country of his age"; was ordained in England in 1763; on his return was rector of Petsworth and Ware parishes in Gloucester county.

Fontaine, John, brother of Rev. Francis Fontaine (q. v.), was born in 1693, ensign in the British army and served in Spain, visited Virginia in 1714 and went with Governor Spotswood on the "Ultra Montane Expedition" of which he kept a diary. He returned to England.

Fontaine, Peter, brother of Francis Fontaine (q. v.), was born in 1691; ordained a minister by the Bishop of London, came to Virginia in 1716, rector of Manakintown and Westover parishes, chaplain to the Virginia commission which ran the boundary line between Virginia and North Carolina in 1728-1729. He died July, 1757. He married (first) Elizabeth Fourreau; (second) Elizabeth Wade.

Foote, Richard, was the emigrant ancestor of the Foote family in Virginia and the south. He was son of John Foote, gentleman, and was born at Cardenham, county Cornwall, England, August 10, 1632. The Footes were an old family in Cornwall. He married Hester, daughter of Nicholas Hayward, of London, merchant, who dealt extensively with Virginia. He came to Virginia about 1655, and was carrying on the business of a merchant in London in 1689. He left a son Richard Foote, born June 31, 1666, who came to Virginia about the end of the seventeenth century, settled in Stafford county, where he died March 21, 1719. He was ancestor of Hon. H. S. Foote, of Mississippi.

Ford, Richard, was a burgess from James City in the assembly of 1659-1660.

Fossaker, Captain Richard, was a burgess for Stafford county in 1702, 1704, 1705. He married the daughter and executrix of Captain John Withers, and had a grandson, John Fossaker, living in Stafford in 1756.

Foster, Joseph, nephew of Captain William Bassett, first of that name in Virginia, came from Newport, Southampton county, England, and was a justice of New Kent county, and burgess in 1688, 1696, and 1700-1702; vestryman of St. Peter's parish, New Kent, and lieutenant-colonel of the militia. He died about 1715, leaving issue.

Foster, Captain Richard, a burgess from Lower Norfolk county in 1656.

Fouace, Stephen, came to Virginia in 1688, was minister of Hampton parish, York county, one of the original trustees of William and Mary College, 1693. He returned to England in 1702, when he resided in Chelsea, Middlesex county. In 1729 he joined with Dr. James Blair, as the only other surviving trustee under the college charter, in executing a deed of transfer to the faculty.

Fowke (Foulke), Gerard, a royalist, son

of Roger Fowke, of Gunston Hall, Staffordshire, England, came to Virginia about 1650 and in 1655 was a justice of Westmoreland county; lieutenant-colonel in 1661, and a burgess in 1663. In 1664 he removed to Maryland, where he was a burgess for Charles City county in 1665, and became justice for the same October 22, 1667. He died in 1669. He married Ann, widow of Colonel Job Chandler, of Port Tobago, Maryland. His daughter Mary was grandmother of Colonel George Mason, author of the "Virginia Declaration of Rights."

Fowke (Foulke), Thomas, brother of Colonel Gerard Fowke (q. v.), was born in England and came to Virginia about 1650; captain of militia and burgess for James City county in 1659, and afterwards on his removal to Westmoreland county was burgess in 1660. He died in 1663 without issue.

Fowler, Bartholomew, was commissioned attorney general of Virginia, June 22, 1699. He resided in Henrico county, and died about 1703, when his widow Sarah (Archer) married Dr. Archibald Blair.

Fowler, Francis, born 1601, was a burgess in 1641 and 1642, for James City county. In 1635 he patented 900 acres of land in James City county, opposite Jouring Point.

Fox, David, son of Captain David Fox, a prominent merchant and officer of Lancaster county, who died in 1669, was born March 12, 1650. He married Hannah Ball, daughter of Colonel William Ball. He was one of the justices with the rank of captain, and served as burgess for Lancaster in the assemblies of 1677, 1680, 1685-86, 1692-93. He died in 1702, and was father of William Fox (q. v.).

Fox, Henry, was son of John Fox, a ship captain, who traded extensively with Virginia from 1655 to his death in 1683. Henry Fox was a vestryman of St. John's parish, King and Queen county in 1695, and justice of the court in 1699. When King William county was formed from King and Queen county, Henry Fox's estate was in that county. He was a member of the house of burgesses in 1710, 1712, 1714, and died in 1714. By his wife, Anne, daughter of Colonel John West, he had several sons, John, Thomas and Henry Fox.

Fox, Henry, son of Henry Fox, of King William county, was sheriff of King William in 1724 and 1725, and about 1730 he removed to Brunswick county, of which he was one of the first justices and one of the two first representatives in the house of burgesses in 1732.

Fox, Rev. John, was usher in the grammar school of William and Mary College in 1729, master of the Indian school 1730-1737, and afterwards served as rector of Ware parish, Gloucester county. He married Isabella, daughter of Thomas Booth, of Gloucester county.

Fox, Major Richard, a royalist officer, came to Virginia in 1649. He afterwards returned, was at once arrested by order of the council of state, but released on promising "to leave town in four days and be of good behavior."

Fox, William, son of Captain David Fox (q. v.), was a justice of the peace and burgess for Lancaster county in 1700-1702. He was also a captain of militia. He married Ann Chinn, but died without issue in 1718.

His widow married (secondly) Richard Chichester, Esq.

Francis, Thomas, was a burgess from Upper Norfolk in the assembly of 1657-1658.

Franklin, "Mr. Ferdinand," was a burgess from James City in the assembly of 1641, and a burgess (county unknown) in the assembly of 1642.

Fry, John, son of Colonel Joshua Fry and his wife, Mary Micou, was born November 7, 1737. He was vestryman of St. Anne's parish, Albemarle county, and burgess for the county from 1761 to 1764, when his seat was vacated by his accepting the office of coroner. He was colonel of the Albemarle militia. He married Sarah, daughter of Ebenezer Adams, of New Kent, by whom he left issue.

Fry, Joshua, son of Joseph Fry, of Crewkerne, Somersetshire, England, yeoman, was born in 1700; matriculated at Wadham College, Oxford, March 31, 1718. He came to Virginia about 1720, was vestryman and magistrate in Essex county. In 1729 he was appointed master of the grammar school at William and Mary College and in 1732 was made professor of natural philosophy and mathematics and continued as such till 1737, when he was succeeded by John Graeme. He removed to Albemarle county, which he represented in the house of burgesses from 1744 to 1754. In 1732 Joshua Fry, Robert Brooke, and William Mayo petitioned the house of burgesses for aid in making a map of the colony of Virginia, but the petition was rejected. He was a justice and surveyor for Albemarle county and in 1745 was appointed county lieutenant. The same year he acted as commissioner to mark the western line of the northern neck, granted to Lord Culpeper. In 1749 Joshua Fry and Peter Jefferson completed their map of Virginia, and the same year he was one of the commissioners to continue the line between Virginia and North Carolina, which in 1728 had been run from the Atlantic ocean to Peter's Creek by William Byrd and others. This line was completed to the Tennessee river by Thomas Walker and David Smith, on the part of Virginia as commissioners. In 1752 he was one of the commissioners to negotiate the treaty of Logstown in the Ohio, by which the "Six Nations" surrendered their claim to the territory south of the Ohio river. When the French and Indian war began, Fry was made colonel of the regiment to defend the Ohio river, and Washington was lieutenant-colonel. Soon after, while on the march, he died at Wills' Creek, May 31, 1754. He married Mary Micou, widow of Colonel Hill, and daughter of Paul Micou, who was an exile from France to Essex county.

French, Daniel, lived in Culpeper county where he was one of the justices. He was son of Hugh French, of St. Mary's parish, Richmond county, who died about 1701, and father of Margaret French, who married James Strother.

Fulford, "Mr. Francis," was burgess from Henrico in the assembly of 1641.

Gaines, Harry, was burgess for King William county in 1766 and 1767, and major of the militia. He died in July, 1767.

Gaddes (Gadis), John, burgess for James City county in 1705-1706.

Gale, Thomas, was a burgess from Isle of Wight in the assembly of 1752-1755.

Galt, Dr. John M., was son of Samuel Galt, a covenanter, of Londonderry, Ireland, who came to Virginia about 1735, and married Lucy Servant. He was born in 1744, was educated at William and Mary College and studied medicine at Edinburgh and Paris, 1765-66-67. He was for a time a surgeon with the Hudson Bay Company, settled in Williamsburg, Virginia, and was vestryman of Bruten parish church. In 1774 he was one of the committee of safety for Williamsburg. During the American war he had charge of the sick soldiers in the hospitals in and around Williamsburg. He married Judith Craig, daughter of Alexander Craig and Mary Manpin, his wife. He died in 1808.

Galthorpe, Stephen, sailed with the first settlers to Virginia in 1606. In the West Indies he attempted to raise a mutiny among the passengers. He died during the summer at Jamestown, August 15, 1607.

Gany, William, came to Virginia in 1616, and his wife Ann came in 1620. In 1624, aged thirty-three, he was living at Elizabeth City. In 1635 he obtained a patent for land in Accomac, due him on account of the personal adventure of his wife Ann, son William, daughter Ann, brother Henry Gany, and the importation of twenty-one servants.

Gardner, Captain Thomas, had command in 1673 of his majesty's hired ship *The Barnaby*. In 1676 he was in command of *The Adam and Eve* stationed in James river and captured Bacon when he came to take part in the assembly after his first march against the Indians. This caused his arrest during Bacon's assembly and his being imprisoned and fined.

Garnett, James, son of John Garnett, of Essex county, was a burgess from Essex county in 1741 and in the assembly of 1742-1747. He married Elizabeth Muscoe, daughter of Salvator Muscoe, a lawyer and burgess, and his will was proved in Essex county, July 15, 1765. He was father of Muscoe Garnett, who married Grace Fenton Mercer, daughter of John Mercer, the celebrated lawyer.

Gaskins, Thomas, son of Thomas Gaskins and Mary Conway, daughter of Colonel Edwin Conway, was burgess for Northumberland county in 1766-1768; lieutenant-colonel, justice, etc. He married Sarah Eustace, and was father of Thomas Gaskins, lieutenant-colonel of the Fourth Virginia Regiment in the revolution. His will was proved April 12, 1785.

Glasscock, Thomas, member of an influential family of Richmond county, was burgess for that county in the assembly of May, 1769.

George, John, patented, in 1635, 900 acres on Bayley's Creek in Prince George county, due for the importation of his wife Jane and seventeen other persons. He was afterwards a prominent citizen of Isle of Wight county, for which he was burgess in 1647 and 1652; lieutenant-colonel of militia, etc. He died in 1678.

Gerrard, Dr. Thomas, an early emigrant to Maryland, where he was for a long time member of the council. His first wife was Susanna, daughter of Justinian Snow,

Lord Baltimore's factor in the tobacco trade. Gerrard was banished from Maryland for taking part in the rebellion of Josias Fendall. He settled at Machodick, Westmoreland county, and his will dated February 1, 1672, was proved November 19, 1673.

Gibbes, Lieutenant, was a burgess from Captain Ward's plantation in the assembly of 1619.

Gibson, Jonathan, was burgess from Caroline county in the assembly of 1736-1740.

Giles (Gyles), John, was burgess from Isle of Wight county in the assembly of 1696-97, 1698, 1699.

Giles (Gyles) Thomas, was a burgess from Isle of Wight county in the sessions of May 13, and June 18, 1702. In 1694 he was one of the justices of Isle of Wight county.

Gill, Captain Stephen, a chirurgeon, patented in 1636 100 acres in Charles River county (York) on account of the personal adventure of his now wife, Ann Gill, and her late husband, Henry Toppin. He was a justice of York in 1652 and burgess in 1653. His will was proved August 2, 1653.

Glassell, Andrew, son of Robert Glassell, of Rucan, in Dumfriesshire, Scotland, who lived "near Torthorwald, the castle of the Douglass," was born in Galloway, Scotland, October 8, 1738, emigrated to Madison county, Virginia, in 1756. He built a splendid mansion upon the Upper Robinson river and called it "Torthorwald." He married Elizabeth Taylor, daughter of Erasmus Taylor, great-uncle of President Zachary Taylor. He died in Virginia, July 24, 1827, leaving issue. His brother, John Glassell, was a merchant in Fredericksburg, who acquired a large fortune. On the breaking out of the American revolution he returned to Scotland and resided on his estate, Long Nidry, sixteen miles from Edinburgh. His only daughter and heiress, Joanna, married April 17, 1820, John, seventh Duke of Argyle

Godfrey, Matthew, was a burgess from Norfolk in the sessions of December 5, 1700, May 13, and June 18, 1702. He was son of John Godfrey, whose will was proved in Norfolk county, May 15, 1710.

Godwin, Joseph, burgess for Isle of Wight county in 1710-1712, 1712-1714, 1723-1726, 1727-1734. He was son of Colonel Thomas Godwin and Martha Bridger, his wife.

Godwin, Rev. Morgan, entered Oxford in 1661 and March 16, 1665, received the Bachelor of Arts degree. He came to Virginia soon after and took charge of Marston parish, York county. He resided for a short time at Jamestown, and after visiting the West Indies returned to England. In 1680 he published a pamphlet against slavery called "The Negroes' and Indians' Advocate" and five years later preached a sermon in Westminster Abbey against the evils of the slave trade, thus preceding Wilberforce and Clarkson by more than a century. His father, Rev. Morgan Godwin, was archdeacon of Shropshire, his grandfather bishop of Hereford, and his great-grandfather, Thomas Godwin, was bishop of Bath and Wells.

Godwin, Thomas, first of the family in Virginia, was burgess for Nansemond county in 1654 and 1655. In 1674 "Capt. Thomas Godwin is referred to as an 'antient'

inhabitant of Nanzemond Countie Court." In March, 1676, he is referred to as "colonel," and as "Col. Thomas Godwin" he was speaker of the house of burgesses in June, 1676, which passed "Bacon's Laws." His will was dated March 24, 1677, and names sons, Thomas (q. v.) and Edmund, and daughter Elizabeth.

Godwin, Thomas, son of Colonel Thomas Godwin, was member of the Nansemond county court in 1680, with title of captain. He was later colonel, commanding the militia of Nansemond, and presiding justice of the county. He married Martha Bridger, daughter of Colonel Joseph Bridger, of the council. His will, dated May 3, 1712, was proved in Nansemond, May 27, 1714. He had issue—Thomas, Joseph, Edmund, Samuel, William, Martha, Mary and James.

Godwin, Thomas, Jr., son of Colonel Thomas Godwin and Martha Bridger, his wife, was returned by the sheriff as elected to a seat in the assembly of 1699, but the assembly set aside the return in favor of Thomas Milner. He was a member in 1710-1712, 1712-1714 and 1723-1726, and sheriff, 1731, 1732 and 1734. He married Mary Fitt, and left issue.

Gooch (Gouge, Gough), Henry, was probably a brother of Major William Gooch, of the council, who died in York county, October 29, 1655. He was a justice and lieutenant-colonel of the York county militia. He took sides with Bacon in 1676, and after the surrender of West Point, January 16, 1677, Lawrence and the other rebels held their last meeting at Colonel Gooch's home in what is now King William county, on the Pamunkey river. While Lawrence, Whaley and Forth took to the wilderness, Gooch surrendered to Sir William Berkeley. He was sentenced to pay a fine of 6,000 pounds of tobacco and to beg mercy on his bended knees in court. He married Jane Jones, daughter of Rev. Rowland Jones, of Bruton parish, York county (see "William and Mary College Quarterly," vol. v, 110-112).

Goodrich, Charles, was a burgess from Charles City county in the assembly of 1696-97. He was son of John Goodrich, who made his will in Isle of Wight county in 1698.

Goodrich, Edward, son of Edward Goodrich, of Prince George county (q. v.), was a burgess from Brunswick county in 1755-1758, 1758-1761. He was sheriff of Brunswick in 1759.

Goodrich, Edward, was a burgess from Prince George county in 1711, 1712-1714, 1715, 1718, 1720. He died the latter year, and in his will names children—Mary, Elizabeth, Benjamin and Edward.

Goodrich, John, was burgess for Isle of Wight county in 1695-1696, but died before the opening of the second session. He was born in 1652 and left issue—George and John, and four daughters.

Goode, Bennett, was son of John Goode, of Fall's Plantation, Chesterfield county, and grandson of John Goode, the immigrant. He married Martha Jefferson, daughter of Thomas Jefferson, grandfather of President Jefferson. He died in Goochland county in 1771, and his will named his son Bennett, who was a member of the revolutionary conventions of 1775 and 1776 from Mecklenburg county, and of the state convention of 1788.

Goode, John, immigrant, resided in Henrico county, Virginia, before 1676. He took sides with Nathaniel Bacon until the latter avowed his intentions of resisting the King's soldiers. He settled at "Whitby," on the James river. He died in 1709, leaving issue. His brother, Rev. Marmaduke Goode, was of Ufton, Berkshire, England.

Goodwin, James, was the youngest son of Peter Goodwin, salter, of Tower street ward, London, and Sarah, daughter of John Hilliard, or Highlord. His pedigree is published in the "Visitation of London," 1633. James, who was probably a royalist refugee, was justice of York county from 1657 to 1662, and in 1658 he represented York county in the house of burgesses. He had the rank of major in the militia and died in 1679, leaving issue.

Gookin, Daniel, was of an ancient family of Kent, in England, son of Sir Vincent Gookin. He removed to Cariggaline, a few miles south of Cork, in Ireland, on the shores of Cork harbor. He came to Virginia in 1622 from Newce's Town, in Cork county, founded by Sir William Newce. He received from the London Company 2,500 acres, which was located at Newport News. Shortly after his arrival the first Indian massacre occurred, but Daniel Gookin, with his servants and company, at Newport News successfully repelled the attack. A few weeks later he sailed to England in the ship which first brought the news of the massacre of more than 300 English. It is probable that he never returned to Virginia, but carried on his plantation at Newport News through his son, Daniel Gookin Jr.

Gookin, Daniel, Jr., son of Daniel Gookin and Mary Bird, his wife, was born about 1612. He was agent for his father at Newport News and was residing there in March, 1633, when Captain Peter de Vries anchored his ship before the place. He was burgess for Upper Norfolk county in 1641 and commander of that county. In 1642 he joined in a petition to the general court of Massachusetts for three able ministers to occupy the parishes in his neighborhood. In answer John Knowles, William Thompson and Thomas James were sent. But Governor Berkeley and his assembly came down so hard upon them that the Puritan ministers soon returned to Massachusetts and Daniel Gookin went with them. He became one of the leading men in Massachusetts, a major-general, etc. He died March 19, 1687, and was buried at Cambridge, where his tombstone may still be seen.

Gookin, John, was probably a son of Daniel Gookin, Sr., as he joined in a deed with Daniel Gookin, Jr., to convey Newport News to John Chandler. He was a burgess for Upper Norfolk county (Nansemond) in 1639 and 1641. He was also presiding magistrate for Lower Norfolk county. He married Sarah Offley, widow of Captain Adam Thoroughgood, and had a daughter Mary, who married (first) William Moseley, (second) Lieutenant-Colonel Anthony Lawson. He died November 2, 1643. His widow married (third) Colonel Francis Yardley and deceased August, 1657.

Gordon, James, born 1714, came with his brother John to Virginia in 1738 from Newry, county Down, Ireland. He was a son of James Gordon, of Sheepsbridge and Lisdaff, in that county, a Presbyterian, whose ancestor came from Scotland to Ireland probably at the time of the Ulster

Plantation. He settled in Lancaster county, was a justice of the peace, colonel of the militia and a prominent planter and merchant. He was one of the pioneers of Presbyterianism in Eastern Virginia, and was intimate with Samuel Davies and James Waddell, "the Blind Preacher," who married his daughter Mary. He married (first) Milicent Conway, (second) Mary, daughter of Colonel Nathaniel Harrison, of Surry county, and dying June 2, 1708, left issue. James Gordon kept an interesting diary which has been published in the "William and Mary Quarterly Magazine."

Gordon, Rev. John, son of Patrick Gordon, regent of King's College, Aberdeen, was minister of Wilmington parish, James City county, Virginia, and died *circa* 1705. He was brother of Alexander Gordon, professor of humanity in King's College, Aberdeen, and of George Gordon, professor of Oriental languages in said college.

Gordon, Samuel, son of David Gordon, of Craig, in the Stewartry of Kirkcudbright, Scotland; an eminent merchant of Petersburg. He was born in 1727 and died April 14, 1771. His tombstone, with coat-of-arms, lies in Blandford churchyard.

Gorsuch, Rev. John, a royalist minister, rector of Walkhorn, Herefordshire, 1633, came to Virginia and died in Lancaster county in 1657. He married Anne Lovelace, sister of Colonel Francis Lovelace and Richard Lovelace, the poet. They had several sons, and three daughters—Katherine, who married ——— Whitty; Ruth, who married William Whitby, of Warwick county, and Anne, who married Thomas Todd, of Mobjack Bay.

Gosnold, Anthony, brother of Captain Bartholomew Gosnold (q. v.), came to Virginia among the first settlers in 1607. He was a brave soldier, and very serviceable, but lost his life with Matthew Scrivener and Nathaniel Waldoe in a storm when attempting by boat to reach Hog Island in 1609.

Gosnold, Anthony, son of Anthony Gosnold (q. v.), came to Virginia in 1607 with his father and uncle. In 1621 the Virginia Company granted him three shares of land in Virginia for his subscriptions.

Gough, Matthew, was a burgess for Henrico in 1642-43.

Gough, Nathaniel, was a burgess (county unassigned) in the assembly of 1642.

Couldman, Francis, was burgess from Essex county in the sessions of April 24, 1706, October 22, 1712, and November 16, 1714.

Gough, William, son of Mr. John Gough, patented in 1694, 1,225 acres on Pepettico swamp, formerly the land granted his father. He was burgess for King and Queen at the assembly of 1700-1702, but died before the opening of the third session in 1702.

Gourgainy (Gurgany, Gourgaing), Edward, was granted in 1617 by the Virginia Company of London 400 acres afterwards known as "Longfield" and still later as "Curles." In 1619 he represented Argall's Gift in the first general assembly at Jamestown. He died the same year, leaving a widow Anne, who bequeathed "Longfield" to Captain Thomas Harris. It was afterwards the residence of Nathaniel Bacon Jr.

Gower, Abell, was a justice of Henrico county, Virginia, from 1679 till his death in 1689; sheriff in 1681, and member of the house of burgesses in 1679. He married Jane, daughter of Edward Hatcher, of Henrico. He appears to have left one daughter Tabitha. He appears to have been a son of Abell Gower, of Boulton, county Gloucester, England, esquire.

Graffenreidt, Christopher de, son of Baron Christopher de Graffenreidt, of Berne, in Switzerland, founder of Newberne, North Carolina. He married in Charleston, South Carolina, February 22, 1714, Barbara Tempest Needham, born in Hertfordshire, England. He moved to Williamsburg, Virginia, where they kept an ordinary. In 1734 he patented land in Brunswick county. Mrs. Barbara de Graffenreidt survived her husband, and in 1739 the "Virginia Gazette" has notices of "dancing assemblies" given by her. He left issue.

Graham, John, son of John Graham, of Wakenston, Perthshire, Scotland, was born April 30, 1718; was a merchant in Dumfries, Prince William county. He married Elizabeth Catesby Cocke, daughter of William Cocke, secretary of state, and died in August, 1787, leaving issue.

Graham, Richard, son of Richard Graham, of Brampton, Cumberland; matriculated at Queen's College, Oxford, March 14, 1737, aged seventeen; Bachelor of Arts, 1742, and Master of Arts, February 18, 1746; qualified as professor of natural philosophy and mathematics in William and Mary College, 1749; removed by the board in 1758; appointed to the chair of moral philosophy, June 26, 1761, and reinstated by the privy council to his former position in January, 1764. In 1764 he was defeated for the presidency by James Horrocks, and in 1766 returned to Oxford University, of which he was a fellow.

Grantham, Captain Thomas, was in 1676 commander of an English ship which arrived in Virginia during Bacon's rebellion. He rendered material assistance in suppressing the disturbances and left an account of the transactions he was engaged in. He was afterward knighted.

Graves, Captain Thomas, an ancient planter, subscribed twenty-five pounds to the Virginia Company of London, went to Virginia in 1608, was captured by the savages and rescued by Thomas Savage; a member of the first house of burgesses in 1619 for Smythe's Hundred; living on the eastern shore in 1620; a burgess for Accomac in 1629-32; a commissioner in 1621-1632. In 1628 he received a grant for 200 acres on account of his subscription to the stock of the London county.

Gray, Colonel Edwin, son of Colonel Joseph Gray, of Southampton county, was burgess for that county from 1769 to 1776 and member of the conventions of 1774, 1775 and 1776, and of the house of delegates and state senate, and member of congress from 1799 to 1813.

Gray, Francis, son of Thomas Gray, the immigrant, was burgess for Surry county in 1663. He died about 1679.

Gray, Francis, went at an early day from England to Maryland. In 1637 he was living in St. George's Hundred, Maryland, which he represented that year in the general assembly. By trade a carpenter. He was a Protestant and was compelled on account of his opposition to Lord Baltimore to emigrate in 1647 across the Potomac to Machodoc, in Westmoreland county. He died in 1677. He was ancestor of the Grays of Caroline and Culpeper counties.

Gray, Colonel Joseph, was born in Surry county, and was the son of either Gilbert or William Gray Jr., his brother. He was burgess for Isle of Wight from 1736 to 1749, and for Southampton county from 1754 to 1758, 1762 to 1769. He is believed to have been the father of Colonel Edwin Grey, of Southampton county (q. v.).

Gray, Rev. Samuel, came to Virginia before 1693; one of the first trustees of William and Mary College; minister of Christ Church, Middlesex county, till 1699, when he was removed because of his whipping a negro slave to death, for which he was tried for his life and barely escaped condemnation. He was afterwards minister of St. Peter's Church from 1707 to 1709, and died on the 25th of December, the latter year.

Gray, Thomas, immigrant, patented land in Surry in 1635, 1639 and 1642. He was born in 1593 and died after 1653. He left four sons—William, Thomas, John and Francis (q. v.). Gray's creek, opposite to Jamestown Island, formerly Rolfe's creek, gets its name from him.

Gray, William, probably a son of William Gray, son of Thomas, the immigrant, was justice for Sussex county in 1710; sheriff in 1718, 1719, and burgess for Surry, 1710, 1712, 1713, 1714 and 1715. His will, dated June 3, was proved November 18, 1719. He left a son, William Gray Jr. (q. v.).

Gray, William, Jr., son of William Gray, was burgess for Surry county, 1723-1726. In 1736 he married Elizabeth, widow of William Chamberlayne, of New Kent, and removed to that county, of which he was appointed justice in 1742. In 1739 he patented 5,800 acres in Goochland county, in which neighborhood still resides a prominent family of the name.

Green, John son of Colonel William Green, was burgess for Culpeper in 1769-1771; colonel in the revolution, distinguished at Brandywine. He married Susanna Blackwell, and they were parents of William Green, and grandparents of John William Green, judge of the supreme court of appeals of Virginia, who was father of William Green, LL. D.

Green, Robert, son of William Green, of England, who served in the body guard of William, Prince of Orange, came to Virginia in 1712 with his uncle, William Duff, a Quaker. He inherited much property from Duff. He was vestryman of St. Mark's Parish, Orange county, and in 1736 and in 1738 represented the county in the house of burgesses. He married Eleanor Dunn, and his will, dated February 22, 1747-48, was proved in Orange county, July 28, 1748. He had six sons—William, Robert, John, Nicholas, James and Moses—from whom are descended many men of distinction.

Green, Roger, was minister in Nansemond county in 1653, and in 1656 was minister at Jamestown. In 1661 he published in England a pamphlet called "Virginia's Cure." He was alive in 1671.

Green, William, son of Robert Green, of Orange county, was vestryman of St. Mark's Parish and burgess for Culpeper county from 1752 to 1760. He married Miss Coleman, of Caroline county, and died in 1770.

Greenhill, David, son of Paschal Greenhill, was burgess for Amelia county in 1761-1765. He married Catherine Claiborne, sister of William Claiborne, of "Romancoke," who died in 1746. He died in Amelia in 1772, leaving among other children Paschal Greenhill (q. v.). His Uncle Joseph left him lands in Great Britain.

Greenhill, Paschal, was a son of David Greenhill, and was burgess from Prince Edward county in the assemblies of 1769-1771 and 1772-1774. He died in Amelia county in 1812.

Gregory, Richard, was burgess for King and Queen county in 1698. His will was proved in Essex county, February 17, 1701, and names sons, Richard and John, and daughters, Sarah and Elizabeth.

Gregson, Thomas, was a burgess for Essex county in 1698. His will, dated December 20, 1704, was proved January 10, 1705-06. He names his brother, William Gregson, of London; his sister Rachel, wife of George Arthur, of Bristol, and nephews, Henry and Samuel Lloyd, sons of Henry Lloyd, late of Bristol; wife Ann.

Grendon (Grindon, Grindall), Edward, came to Virginia before 1616, and in 1620 patented 150 acres on the south side of James river, over against Jamestown. This land, called "Grindall's Hill," was the same as the "Old Fort" land which Captain John Smith fortified for a retreat. It was a mile up Gray's creek, and went to Thomas Grendon, his heir, and he in 1649 sold it to Mountjoy Evelyn. In 1625 Edward Grendon was burgess.

Grendon, Sarah, wife of Lieutenant-Colonel Thomas Grendon, was a sympathizer with Nathaniel Bacon. In 1677 she was excepted from the general pardon. She afterward married Mr. Brain, a merchant of London. Evidently a woman of strong mind and purpose.

Grendon, Thomas, son of Thomas Grendon, was a London merchant, who resided frequently in Virginia. He represented "Smyth's Mount, The Other Side of the Water, and Hogg Island" (now in Surry county) in the assembly in 1633. In 1649 he sold Grindall's Hill, patented by Edward Grindon, to Mountjoy Evelyn. He married Elizabeth, widow of Thomas Stegge Sr., merchant of Virginia and London, who died at sea in 1651. He was succeeded by his son, Thomas Grendon Jr.

Grendon, Thomas, Jr., son of Thomas Grendon, merchant, settled in the parish of Westover, Charles City county, and had large estates in Virginia and England. He was lieutenant-colonel of the Charles City militia in 1680, commanding the cavalry. He married Sarah, widow of Thomas Stegge Jr., and died in 1684, when his will disposes of a great estate in Virginia, Staffordshire, England, etc.

Griffin, Lady Christina, wife of Judge Cyrus Griffin, and daughter of John Stuart, sixth Earl of Traquair, in Scotland. She died in Williamsburg, 1807.

Griffin, Corbin, of Yorktown, Virginia, son of Leroy Griffin and Mary Anne Bertrand, his wife, graduated Doctor of Medicine; member York county committee of safety, 1775-76; surgeon in the state line during the revolution; state senator, 1780; died 1813. Married Mary Berkeley, daughter of Colonel Edmund Berkeley, of "Barn Elms," Middlesex county, Virginia.

Criffin, Samuel, of Northumberland county; justice of the peace in 1702; died in 1703. Katherine, his only daughter, married (first) William Fauntleroy, of Richmond county, (second) David Gwyn, of Richmond county.

Griffin, Thomas, son of Colonel Leroy Griffin, of Richmond county; burgess, 1718-1723; married Elizabeth Lee, and his will was proved in Richmond county in 1733. Leroy Griffin, high sheriff of Richmond county, who married Mary Anne Bertrand, only daughter and heiress of Rev. John Bertrand, was his son. One of his daughters, Winifred, married Captain Samuel Peachy.

Griffin, William, of King and Queen county; sheriff of that county, and colonel commanding the militia, 1781; married, 1771, Susanna, daughter of Colonel John Chiswell, and widow of Speaker John Robinson. He was son of Leroy Griffin and Mary Anne Bertrand, his wife.

Griffith, Edward, was major of the militia and burgess for Warwick county in 1660 and 1663.

Grymes, Benjamin, was a son of Hon. John Grymes, of "Brandon," Middlesex county. He was a burgess from Spottsylvania county in the assemblies of 1761-1765 and 1766-1768, 1769-1771. He married (first) Elizabeth L. Fitzhugh, (second) Miss Rootes. He left issue.

Grymes, Charles, of "Moratico," Richmond county, was a grandson of Rev. Charles Grymes, who came from England to Virginia and was minister of Hampton parish, York county, in 1645. He was son of John Grymes and Alice Townley, his wife, and brother of Hon. John Grymes, of "Brandon." He was justice from 1721; sheriff, 1724, 1725, and member of the house of burgesses. He was educated at William and Mary College, married Frances, daughter of Hon. Edmund Jenings, and died in 1743.

Grymes, Philip Ludwell, eldest son of Philip Grymes, of "Brandon" on the Rappahannock river, was burgess for Middlesex county in the assemblies of May, 1769, 1769-1771; member of the house of delegates, 1778, and of the state council, 1803. He died May 18, 1805.

Grymes, William, son of Sir Thomas Grymes, of Peckham, England, was living in Virginia in 1694.

Gwyn, David, was burgess from Richmond in the session of March 19, 1702-03. He died in 1704. He had a sister, Elizabeth, wife of Mr. Benjamin Gwyn, of Bristol, and a brother, Edward Gwyn, clerk, in Wales. Left to his sister Mary all of his real estate in Wales lying in and about Harford West.

Gwyn, Hugh, was an early settler in Charles River county, subsequently York county. He was a justice from 1641, and a burgess for York in 1639 and 1646. He patented lands at the mouth of the Pyanketank river in 1642 and removed to that region, and in 1652 was one of the two first burgesses for the new county of Gloucester. He died about 1654, and Gwyn's Island perpetuates his name. He left issue.

Gwyn, Rev. John, was a cavalier minister, who came to Virginia during Cromwell's time. In 1672 he was rector of Ware parish, Gloucester county, and of Abington in 1674 and 1680. His son, Edmund Gwyn, of Gloucester county, who an old record says was "a regular Doctor of Physics," married Lucy Bernard, daughter of Colonel William Bernard, of the council ("Virginia Magazine," iv, 204; "William and Mary Quarterly," xviii, 60-62).

Hack, Peter, son of Dr. George Hack, of Cologne, Germany, and Anne Herman, sister of Augustine Herman, of Amsterdam, and afterwards of Delaware, resided in Northumberland county, was ranger general of the Northern Neck, 1690; justice of the county court; colonel of the Northumberland militia; burgess in 1705-1706, 1720-1722. He was living in 1727.

Hacker, Henry, a wealthy merchant, came from Devonshire, England to Williamsburg, Virginia, about 1720. Born 1689, died in Williamsburg, August 5, 1742. His widow Mary married (second) Thomas Hornsby, also a prominent merchant.

Hackett, Captain Thomas, was burgess from Lancaster county in the assembly of 1653.

Haeger, John Henry, born at Antzhausen, in Nassau-Siegen, Germany, September 25, 1644. Held various positions as teacher and rector at Siegen. In 1714 emigrated to America and settled at Germanna, Virginia, where he organized the first German Reformed congregation in America, organized at St. George's Parish. Removed with his parishioners to Germantown, in Fauquier county, in 1721. Lived there till his death in 1733. After his death the schoolmaster, Holtzclaw, conducted the religious exercises.

Hairston, Samuel, was a burgess from Bedford county in the assembly of 1758-1761. Ancestor of the Hairston family of Henry county.

Hall, Robert, was a burgess from Prince George county in the assembly of 1718.

Hall, Thomas, clerk of New Kent county, in 1676. He took sides with Nathaniel Bacon, and was executed by Sir William Berkeley, who said that his pen was worth to Bacon "forty armed men."

Ham, Jeremy (Jerom), was a burgess from York county in the assembly of 1657-58. He died in 1660, when his widow Sibella married Matthew Huberd.

Hamerton, Edward, was a burgess for Middlesex county in 1715.

Hamilton, James, burgess for Loudoun county in 1758-1761, 1761-1765, 1766-1768, 1769-1771, but he resigned in 1770 to accept the office of coroner.

Hamlin, John, was a burgess from Prince George county in the session of November 16, 1714, and in the assembly of 1720-22. He was probably a grandson of Stephen Hamlin, the immigrant (q. v.). He was captain of the militia and lived at "Maycocks," on James river, conveyed to him by Roger Drayton in 1696.

Hamlin, Stephen, patented land at Middle Plantation, York county, in 1637. He afterward patented lands in that part of Charles City county now known as Prince George. He was burgess for Charles City county in 1654. He was dead before 1666, leaving a son Stephen.

Hamilton, Andrew, an eminent lawyer, was doubtless a native of Scotland and settled in the latter part of the seventeenth century in Northampton county, Virginia. In 1706 he married Anne, widow of Joseph Preeson, and daughter of Thomas Browne, of Northampton county. In 1713, having removed to Philadelphia, he sold his estate on Hungar's creek. After that his public life belongs entirely to Pennsylvania. He died August 4, 1741.

Hamilton, James, represented Loudoun county in the house of burgesses from 1758 to 1770. He accepted the office of coroner and vacated his seat in the assembly.

Hammond, John, came to Virginia in 1635, and settled in Isle of Wight county. After Virginia succumbed to the rule of parliament in 1652, he was expelled from the house of burgesses because of his strong royalist sympathies. In 1654 he left Virginia to reside under the government of Lord Baltimore, in Maryland. He took sides against Bennett and Claiborne, and after the battle of the Severn in 1655, he fled to England. While there he wrote his excellent treatise on the two colonies, Virginia and Maryland, which he entitled "Leah and Rachel," dedicating it to his friends, Captain William Stone, of Maryland, and Dr. James Williamson, of Rappahannock. He later returned to Maryland, in which state he has been represented by prominent descendants.

Hamor, Thomas, brother of Captain Ralph Hamor, of the council, was at George Harrison's house, near Warrascoyack, at the time of the massacre of 1622. He defended himself and escaped. But on January 24, 1623, Harrison wrote that Thomas Hamor was very sick. He probably died soon after.

Hardiman, Francis, son of Colonel John Hardiman (q. v.), was burgess for Charles City county in 1718; justice of Charles City county, and died about 1741 when his will was admitted to probate. He married (first) Henrietta Maria, daughter of Captain John Taylor, clerk in 1699 of Charles City, and who died in 1707. He married (second) Jane Cross, widow of John Cross.

Hardiman, John, came from Bristol to Virginia, and was a justice of Charles City county in 1699 and 1702; burgess for Prince George county in 1710; lieutenant-colonel of the militia, and died before 1711. He married Mary, daughter of Colonel Francis Eppes, of Henrico county, and left issue— John, Francis, James, Littleberry and William.

Hardwick (Hardinge, Hardidge, Hardage), William, was son of William Hardwick, a tailor, prominent with his father-in-law, Thomas Sturman, in the disturbances of Maryland. The son was a justice and lieutenant-colonel of militia in Westmoreland county and was a burgess in the assemblies of 1686, 1688 and 1692-93. His daughter and heiress, Elizabeth, was wife of Colonel Henry Ashton.

Hardy, George, came from Bristol, England to Virginia before 1636, when he is called "shipwright." In 1644 he patented 300 acres of land on Lawne's creek. He had a noted mill on Lawne's creek, and its successor is still used. He was burgess for Isle of Wight in 1641, 1644, 1645, 1649 and 1652 His will, dated March 16, 1654, was proved April 14, 1655, and by it he left his estate mainly to his "kinsman," George Hardy Jr., ancestor of Samuel Hardy, president of the continental congress, who died in 1785.

Harlowe, John, was a burgess from Warwick county in the assembly of 1658-59.

Harmanson, George, son of Thomas Harmanson (q. v.), was burgess for Northampton county in 1720-1722, 1723-1726.

Harmanson, John, was a burgess from Northampton county in the assemblies of 1761-1765, 1766-1768, and May, 1769. A descendant of Thomas Harmanson, immigrant from Germany.

Harmanson, Matthew, a descendant of Thomas Harmanson (q. v.), was a burgess for Northampton county in 1736-1740, 1742-1747 and 1748-1749.

Harmanson, Thomas, son of Thomas Harmanson (q. v.), was a burgess in 1723-1726.

Harmanson, Thomas, a German Protestant, born in Brandenburgh, settled in Northampton county, Virginia, about 1680, and was naturalized by act of assembly, October 24, 1684. In 1688 he was a burgess in the assembly.

Harmer, Charles, son of John Harmer, warden of Winchester College in England, came to Virginia in 1622, aged twenty-four; was a commissioner or justice for Accomac; burgess in 1632 and died before 1644. He married Anne Southey, daughter of Henry Southey, Esq., of Rimpton, in Somerset, England, and she married (second) Colonel Nathaniel Littleton, of the council. He died issueless, and his property was heired by his brother, John Harmer, Greek reader at Oxford, who sent his son, Thomas Harmer, to Virginia about 1652.

Harmer, John, was burgess from Williamsburg in the assembly, 1742-1747. A justice of the York county court.

Harris, John, of an ancient Devonshire family, settled at an early date in St. Stephen's parish, Northumberland county, Virginia. His father was Joseph Harris, and his uncle, William Harris, of Hayne, member of parliament for St. Ives and Oakhampton in several parliaments in the reign of William and Mary. He was burgess for Northumberland in 1703-1704, and his will, dated September 20, 1718, was proved May 20, 1719. He married Hannah Kenner, daughter of Captain Richard Kenner, of Northumberland county.

Harris, John, several years in Virginia; burgess for Shirley Hundred Island, in Charles City Corporation in 1629 and 1630.

Harris, Richard, was a burgess from Hanover county in the assembly of 1723-26.

Harris, Robert, was a burgess from Hanover county in the assembly of 1736-1740, and in the session of May 6, 1742. In the session of September 4, 1744, William Meriwether represented Hanover in place of Robert Harris, who had accepted the place of surveyor of a county (Louisa).

Harris, Captain Thomas, born 1586, came to Virginia during the government of Sir Thomas Dale, and settled at the Neck of Land, in Henrico; member of the house of burgesses in 1623-24, 1639 and 1647. He married (first) Adria ———, (second) Joane ———, and had a son, Major William Harris (q. v.).

Harris, William, son of Captain Thomas Harris, was burgess for Henrico in 1653, 1656 and 1658; captain and major in the militia. He married Lucy ———, and his will was proved in Henrico, June, 1678. He left issue.

Harris, William Samuel, was a burgess from Halifax county from 1753 to 1758.

Harrison, Benjamin, patented lands in Virginia in 1635. He was clerk of the council, 1634, and burgess in 1642. He acquired a large estate in the present Surry and Prince George counties. He died in 1649. Ancestor of the Harrison family which has furnished two presidents to the United States.

Harrison, Benjamin, son of Benjamin Harrison, of "Berkeley," Charles City county, was sheriff of Charles City county, 1728. He was burgess in 1736-1740, 1742, 1744, and died while he was a member the last year named. He married, *circa* 1722, Anne, daughter of Colonel Robert Carter, of "Corotoman," and was father of Benjamin Harrison, the signer (q. v.).

Harrison, Benjamin, of "Berkeley," was the oldest son of Colonel Benjamin Harrison, of the council of state. He was born in 1673; was attorney-general, 1699, and burgess in 1705-1706, during which session he was speaker; treasurer of the colony. He married Elizabeth, daughter of Major Lewis Burwell. He died April 10, 1730, leaving issue—Benjamin (q. v.) and Elizabeth.

Harrison, Burr, was son of Cuthbert Harrison, of Acaster, Caton and Flaxby, in York county, England, and was baptized in the parish of St. Margaret's, Westminster, December 28, 1637. He settled in Stafford county, Virginia, and was ancestor of the Harrisons of Northern Virginia.

Harrison, Lieutenant George, son of William Harrison, of Aldcliffe, Lancashire. He came to Virginia in 1618. In the spring of 1624 he was mortally wounded in a dual fought with Colonel Richard Stephens, of the council. Sir John Harrison, his brother, was a member of the Virginia Company of London. Sir John owned Aldcliffe Hall; was member of parliament; was knighted, and died September 28, 1669.

Harrison, Dr. Jeremiah, came to Virginia about 1649 and patented lands near Williamsburg. His wife was Frances Whitgreaves, sister of Thomas Whitgreaves, of county Stafford, England, who saved the life of Charles II. at the battle of Worcester. He died without issue and his widow married Colonel Giles Brent, of "Peace," in Stafford county.

Harrison, Thomas, born in 1616, qualified as minister of Elizabeth River parish in 1640, and used his influence against the Puritans, who were numerous on the south side of James river. After the Indian massacre in 1644 he turned Puritan. He refused to read the book of common prayer and was banished from the colony. He visited Boston and then went to England, where he was chaplain to Henry Cromwell, and in Christ Church preached a sermon on the death of Oliver Cromwell.

Harrison, Thomas, Jr., sheriff of Prince William county, 1732; burgess for that county at the assembly of 1742-1747, 1748-1749, 1752-1755; burgess for Fauquier county, 1761-1765, 1766-1769, when he was succeeded by Colonel Thomas Marshall.

Harrison, William, burgess for Prince George county in 1703-1705.

Hartwell, William, brother of Henry Hartwell, Esq., of the council, was a justice of the peace for James City county, and during Bacon's rebellion was captain of Sir William Berkeley's body guard. He had a son William, whose only daughter married Colonel William Macon; a daughter Mary, who married George Marable, and a son John, whose daughter Elizabeth married Richard Cocke.

Harwood, Colonel Edward, son of Colonel William Harwood (q. v.), was a justice for Warwick county in 1770; member of the house of delegates, 1780; county lieutenant of Warwick in 1788, etc.

Harwood, Humphrey, son of Captain Thomas Harwood, was captain and major; burgess for Warwick county in 1685 and 1692; father of William Harwood (q. v.).

Harwood, Joseph, was a burgess for Charles City county in 1715, probably a son of Joseph Harwood, who patented land in the county in 1665.

Harwood, Samuel, son of Joseph Harwood, who patented lands in Charles City county in 1665; was burgess for Charles City county in 1710-1712. He married Temperance Cocke, daughter of Captain Thomas Cocke Sr., of Henrico, and was father of Samuel Harwood (q. v.).

Harwood, Samuel, Jr., son of Samuel Harwood and Temperance Cocke, his wife, was burgess for Charles City county in 1720-1723. His will was proved by his widow, Agnes, in 1745, father of Major Samuel Harwood (q. v.).

Harwood, Major Samuel, of Weyanoke, son of Samuel Harwood Jr., was a member of the convention of 1776; died in 1778. Married Margaret Woddrop, daughter of John Woddrop, of Nansemond, a prominent merchant.

Harwood, William, son of Humphrey Harwood, and grandson of Captain Thomas Harwood, of the council of state, resided in Warwick county; was major of the Warwick militia and burgess for the county in the assemblies of 1712-1714 and 1727-1734; died by a fall from his horse June 2, 1737; father of William Harwood, of Warwick county (q. v.).

Harwood, William, son of William Harwood, of Warwick county, was colonel of the Warwick militia and represented that county in the general assembly from 1742 to 1775, and in the famous convention of 1776 that declared for state independence. He was father of Colonel Edward Harwood, long a member of the house of delegates.

Hatcher, William, was born in 1614, and was a member of the house of burgesses for Henrico county in 1644, 1645, 1646, 1649, 1652, 1654 and 1659. For speaking disrespectfully of the speaker of the house, he was censured by the house in 1654. His temper got him into trouble again during Bacon's rebellion, with which he was doubtless a sympathizer. He was heavily fined. He died not long after.

Haviland, Anthony, an active promoter of the rebellion of Nathaniel Bacon, Jr. He resided in that part of Charles City county now known as Prince George county. He was the author of the first proclamation issued by Bacon. His wife, "an excellent divulger of news," went up and down the country carrying Bacon's manifestoes. Haviland was fined for his part in the rebellion

5,000 pounds of tobacco, about one-tenth of his estate. He died in 1679.

Hawkins, John, doubtless a brother of Major Thomas Hawkins, was a member of the house of burgesses for Essex in 1711, 1714, 1718, 1720-1722. His will, dated February, 1725-26, was proved in Essex, June, 1726. He left two sons, Thomas and William, besides daughters, Mary and Elizabeth Rennolds.

Hawkins, Captain Thomas, represented Denbigh, on James river, in the house of burgesses in 1632, removed to Rappahannock, where he was vestryman of Sittingbourn parish in 1665 and a justice of Rappahannock county in November, 1670, or earlier. His will, dated February 8, 1675, was proved November, 1677. His legatees were his wife Francis and sons, Thomas and John.

Hawkins, Major Thomas, son of Captain Thomas Hawkins, commanded a force which protected the frontiers of Essex county after Bacon's rebellion. During the rebellion he sided with Sir William Berkeley, but was captured and imprisoned by Bacon. He died before 1696. He probably left no children.

Hay, Anthony, was a cabinetmaker of Williamsburg, and in 1767 purchased the famous Raleigh Tavern, which was the favorite meeting place of the patriots before the revolution. He was the father of George Hay, who prosecuted Aaron Burr for treason. Anthony Hay died in 1772.

Hay, Dr. Peter, a prominent physician of Williamsburg. He died in 1766, leaving a brother, David Hay, of New York; a widow, Grissell Hay, and children, David, Robert, Lydia, Helen and Mary Hay.

Hay, William, John and Peter, were sons of James Hay and Helena Rankin, his wife, of Kilsythe parish and shire of Sterling in Scotland. William Hay was educated at the University of Glasgow and came to Virginia in 1768. He studied law under John Tazewell of Williamsburg, and practiced his profession till the revolutionary war shut up the courts; afterwards he never resumed it. He married (first) Ann Cary; (second) Elizabeth Tompkins, and left issue. He was father of William Hay, the lawyer, whose name figures in Randolph's "Reports," and Hening and Munford's "Reports." Hon. James Hay, now United States Congressman from Virginia, is a great-grandson of William Hay, the immigrant.

Hay, William, was born in 1613, and settled in York county, where he was one of the justices of the county court, and burgess in 1658 and 1659. He died January 23, 1668-69. He married several times, but left only one daughter, Elizabeth, who married Samuel Snignell, and she leaving no children, his property descended to Robert Hay, son of John Hay, his brother.

Haynes, Thomas, was a burgess from Warwick county in the assembly of 1736-1740.

Haynie (Haney), John, was a burgess from Northumberland county in the assembly of 1657-1658. He was father of Richard Haynie (q. v.).

Haynie, Richard, was a burgess from Northumberland county in 1695, 1696, 1697.

1698 and 1702-1705. He married Elizabeth Bridgar, and died about 1724. In his will, he names sons Bridgar, Richard, McMillon, Ormesby, Charles and Samuel.

Hayrick, Thomas, was a burgess from the upper part of Elizabeth City in the assembly of 1629-30.

Heyrick, Henry, was a burgess from Warwick county in the assembly of 1644.

Hayward, Samuel, came to Virginia about 1675. His father, Nicholas Hayward, had extensive business with Virginia and was a well known notary public in London. Samuel was clerk of Stafford county and in 1685 was a member of the house of burgesses for the county. He married Martha, sister of John and Lawrence Washington, the immigrant ancestors of the Washington family of the Northern Neck. His sister married Richard Foote, of London, who came to Virginia and was ancestor of the Foote family. His son Samuel was English consul at Venice in 1741.

Heale, George, son of Nicholas Heale or Haile, of York county, planter, was justice of Lancaster court from 1684 and was a burgess for Lancaster county in 1695 and 1697. He died the latter year, leaving issue, Nicholas, George, John, Joseph, Ellen, Elizabeth, Sarah and William.

Heale, George, grandson of George Heale (q. v.), was a burgess for Lancaster county from 1759 to 1761 inclusive. He married Sarah Smith, daughter of Philip Smith, of Northumberland county, and had issue, William, who married Susannah Payne, daughter of Josias Payne, the elder, of Goochland county.

Hedgman, Peter, was a burgess from Prince William county in 1736-1740, and for Stafford county in 1742-1747, 1748-1749, 1752-1755 and 1756-1758. He was a justice of Stafford in 1745 and other years. He made his will November 29, 1764, which was proved August 12, 1765. He left issue.

Heley, Willis, was pastor of Mulberry Island, and in 1635 he received a grant for 250 acres in Mulberry Island on account of his pious and godly conduct.

Henley, Rev. Samuel, born in 1740, came to Virginia in 1770, and qualified as professor of moral philosophy in William and Mary College. He was secretary of the "Virginia Society for the Promotion of Useful Knowledge," in 1772. In 1775 he returned to England and was assistant master at Harrow school. In 1778 he was elected a fellow of the Society of Antiquaries and four years later was made rector of Rendlesham in Suffolk. Finally in 1805 he was appointed principal of the newly established East India College at Hertford. He resigned this post in January, 1815, and died December 29, of the same year. He engaged largely in literary work, and had an extensive correspondence. But the most important of his works was the translation of Beckford's romance "Vathek," which made him famous.

Herbert, John, of Prince George county, Virginia, was a son of John Herbert, apothecary of London, and grandson of Richard Herbert, citizen and grocer of London. He was born in 1659, and died March 17, 1704, leaving issue Buller and Richard Herbert. This family had the same arms and crest as the poet George Herbert. He left a large estate and a handsome library.

Herrick, Henry, was a burgess for Warwick county in 1644 and 1644-1645. In a note in the Richmond "Standard," he is said to have been a nephew of Thomas Herrick, of Elizabeth City county.

Herrick, Thomas, was a burgess for Elizabeth City county in 1629-1630.

Hethersall, Thomas, came to Virginia in 1621 in the *Margaret and John*, which had a famous fight with two Spanish ships which she beat off. Hethersall wrote an account of the fight (still in manuscript) in which he describes himself as "late Citysone and Grocer of London." In 1623, as of Pashbehay, gentleman, he patented 200 acres at Blunt Point. The headrights included himself, his wife Mary, and his children, Richard and Mary. A John Hethersall died in York county in 1679.

Heyman, Peter, grandson to Sir Peter Heyman, of Summerfield, in county Kent, England, was collector of customs for lower James river in 1699, and in 1692 was one of the deputy postmaster generals for the colonies. He was killed on board the *Shoreham* in a fight with a pirate ship near Cape Henry, April 29, 1700. Buried at Hampton, where his tombstone was lately seen.

Heyward (pronounced Howard), **John,** ancestor of the Howard family of York county patented lands in James City county in 1635, on account of the adventure of his brother, Francis, and others into the colony. He was a member of the house of burgesses in 1654, and died in 1661, leaving issue Henry, William and Elizabeth.

Hickman, Richard, clerk of the council, was son of Thomas Hickman, and Martha, his wife, daughter of Captain Henry Thacker. His will was proved in York county in 1731, and names brothers and sisters. He was a descendant of Nathaniel Hickman, who patented lands in Northumberland county in 1653.

Higginson, Captain Robert, "citizen and printer-stainer of London," was a son of Thomas Higginson and Anne, his wife, of Berkeswell, county Warwick, England. About 1625 he married Joanna Torkesy, and in 1643 removed to Virginia, where in 1645 he commanded at Middle Plantation (then a palisaded settlement). He died in 1649, leaving an only daughter Lucy, who married successively three prominent men, (first) Sergeant Major Lewis Burwell; (second) Colonel William Bernard, of the council, and (third) Colonel Philip Ludwell, by each of whom she had children.

Hill, Edward, came to Virginia before 1622, when he was living at Elizabeth City; he fought off the Indians and escaped the massacre of 1622, was buried May 15, 1622. He left a daughter, Elizabeth; brother of John Hill, mercer of London in 1620.

Hill, Humphrey, was an extensive merchant of King and Queen county. He was vestryman of St. Stephen's parish, and colonel of the county militia. His will, dated February 8, 1774, was proved March 13, 1775. He married Frances Baylor, and had issue Humphrey, Robert, William, Baylor, John, Edward, Ann and Elizabeth.

Hill, John, was a son of Stephen Hill of Oxford, England, fletcher. He was a bookbinder before his immigration to Virginia, in 1621. He was one of the justices, and was a burgess in 1642, for Lower Norfolk county.

Hill, Nicholas, was a justice of the county court of Isle of Wight, major of the militia and burgess in 1660, 1663, 1666. He married Silvestra Bennett, one of the two daughters of Edward Bennett, a wealthy merchant of London, who was greatly interested in the settlement of Virginia. He died in 1675, leaving issue.

Hill, "Mr. Thomas," was a burgess from James City in the assembly of 1641. He afterwards settled in York county, where his place was named "Essex Lodge," which was the headquarters of Washington at the siege of Yorktown in 1781. His widow married Thomas Bushrod (q. v.).

Hite, Abraham, son of Jost Hite, was a leading man of affairs in Hampshire county, Virginia, and represented it in the house of burgesses in 1769, 1770, and in the convention of May 6, 1776.

Hite, Isaac, son of Jost Hite, was born May 12, 1723, married Eleanor Eltinge, April 12, 1745; prominent in affairs in the Shenandoah. He died September 18, 1795, leaving issue Anne, who married James Buchanan, of Falmouth; Mary, married Dr. John McDonald; Eleanor, married John Williams; Rebecca, married General William Aylett Booth; Isaac; Sarah, married Jonathan Clark.

Hite, John, son of Thomas Hite, was a burgess for Berkeley county in the assembly of 1775-1776.

Hite, Jost, a native of Strasburg, in Alsace, emigrated to Pennsylvania, and in 1732 came with his three sons-in-law, George Bowman, Jacob Chrisman, Paul Froman, and others to the valley of Virginia. In 1734 he was appointed one of the first magistrates to administer justice in the valley. He greatly aided in stimulating the rapid settlement of that part of Virginia.

Hite, Thomas, son of Jost Hite, was burgess for Berkeley county in the assembly of 1772-1774.

Hobbs, Francis, born in 1624, was burgess for Isle of Wight county in 1654, captain of militia and justice in 1666.

Hobson, Thomas, born in 1666, son of Thomas Hobson, was clerk of Northumberland county from about 1710 to 1716. His father, who was born about 1635, was clerk from about 1664 to about 1710. Thomas Hobson, Jr., was burgess in 1700-1702. In consequence of the long terms of the clerkship in the family he named one of his daughters "Clerk" Hobson.

Hockaday, William, came to Virginia about 1640, was a merchant and lawyer, and in 1635 was a burgess for York county. When New Kent was separated from York in 1654, his residence fell into that county.

Hockaday, William, was a resident of New Kent county, and a burgess for that county in the assembly from 1748-1749. He was a descendant of William Hockaday, merchant, who came to Virginia about 1640.

Hoddin (Hodin), John, was a burgess from Elizabeth City in the assemblies of 1642-1643 and 1644.

Hodges, Thomas, was a burgess from Norfolk county in the assemblies of 1696 and 1696-1697.

Hoggard, Nathaniel, was selected in 1722 to the vacancy in the house of burgesses from Warwick county caused by the death of James Roscow. Anthony Hoggart died in Albemarle county in 1754. His will names son, Nathaniel Hoggart, and grandson Anthony Hoggart.

Holecroft, Captain Thomas, son of Sir Thomas Holecroft, of Vale Royal, Cheshire, England, came to Virginia with Lord Delaware in 1610, commanded one of the forts at Kecoughtan, and died there. He married the celebrated Mary, daughter of Hon. Henry Talbot, son of George, Earl of Shrewsbury.

Holiday, Anthony, was a burgess from Isle of Wight county in the assembly of 1692-93, and 1705-06 and one of the justices.

Holladay, Anthony, was burgess from Nansemond county in the assembly of 1752-1755. Doubtless a descendant from Anthony Holiday of Isle of Wight (q. v.).

Holland, Gabriel, yeoman, one of the first settlers at Berkeley Hundred in 1620; burgess in 1623, when he was a signer of "The Tragical Relation of the General Assembly," married twice, (first) Mary ———; (second) Rebecca ———.

Hollier, Simon, burgess for Elizabeth City county in 1727-1734; son of Simon Hollier, who died about 1697; justice of the peace, and captain of militia. He died in 1747, when his inventory shows that he owned forty-seven negroes.

Holloway, John, a prominent lawyer, came to Virginia from England about 1700, and was first a resident of King and Queen county, for which he was a burgess in 1710-1712, and 1712-1714. Removed to Williamsburg and was first mayor of the city under the charter of 1722. Burgess for York county in the assemblies of 1720-1722, 1727-1734, and for Williamsburg, in that of 1723-1726. He was elected speaker November 2 1720, and continued to hold that office in connection with that of treasurer till his death in 1734. He married Elizabeth Cocke, widow of Dr. William Cocke, secretary of state, and sister of Mark Catesby, the naturalist, but he left no issue.

Hollows, John, was one of the first justices of the court for Westmoreland county, being in 1655 major of the militia. In 1654 he was a burgess for the county.

Holman, James, burgess from Goochland county in the assembly of 1736-1740. He left issue a son James, who in 1769 married Sarah Miller, daughter of William Miller.

Holmwood, John, was an emigrant from England to Charles City county. He was a burgess in 1656 and a justice in 1658. He married Jane, daughter of Gregory Bland, son of John Bland, an eminent merchant of London. She had been previously the wife of her cousin, Edward Bland, of "Kimages," in Charles City county.

Holt, James, son of Thomas Holt, formerly of Hog Island in the county of Surry, was a successful lawyer of Norfolk, and was burgess for Norfolk county in the assembly of 1772-1774 and 1775-1776, and in the conventions of 1774, 1775 and 1776. He died in 1779, and left his law library to the court of the county of Norfolk, and most of his property to the children of his brother

Henry, whom he names Claremond, Leander, Sarah and Thomas.

Holt, John, was brother-in-law of William Hunter, editor of the "Virginia Gazette." He was born in 1720, received a good education, was a merchant of Williamsburg, mayor, and on his removal to New York was editor of the "New York Gazette and Post Boy." He was printer to the state of New York. He died January 30, 1784, and there is a tombstone to his memory in St. Paul's churchyard, New York City.

Holt, Robert, was a burgess from James City in the assembly of 1655-1656.

Holt, Thomas, was a burgess from Surry county in the assembly of 1699 and in 1700. He was a son of Randall Holt, of Hog Island, who married Elizabeth Hansford, sister of Major Thomas Hansford.

Holtzclaw, Jacob, was a prominent member of the first German colony of miners, who were from, or from near, Nassau-Siegen, Germany. He was the schoolmaster of this colony. His will was admitted to probate February 29, 1760, and his descendants are numerous in Virginia and the south.

Hone, Major Theophilus, was the son of Thomas Hone, of Farnham, Essex county, England, who married Judith Aylmer, daughter of Theophilus Aylmer, archdeacon of London; justice of Warwick county in 1652; burgess for James City county in 1666, and sheriff in 1676. He died before 1689, when his widow Katherine Armistead, sister of Colonel John Armistead of "Hesse" married Major Robert Berkeley (his second wife).

Honeywood, Philip, served as colonel in the royal army during the civil wars. But in 1649 he came to Virginia. He obtained a large grant of land in New Kent, and probably remained in the colony till the restoration in 1660. He was knighted for his services and loyalty by the King. In 1662 he was in command of the garrison of Plymouth and soon after he was its governor. He died at Charing, county Kent, England, in 1684.

Hooe, Rice, was born about 1599 and came to Virginia in 1635; was burgess for Shirley Hundred Island 1632, and for Charles City county 1644, 1645, and 1646. He had a son Rice Hooe, who was doubtless father of Rice Hooe, of Stafford county, (q. v.).

Hooe, Rice, probably a grandson of Rice Hooe, the original settler of the name, was burgess for Stafford county in 1702-1703; he was also lieutenant-colonel of the county militia.

Hope, George, of Hampton, Virginia, was born in Cumberland county, England, March 28, 1749. He came to Virginia from White Haven about 1771. During the American revolution he superintended the construction of gunboats for the American navy. He married Rebecca Meredith. His son, Wilton, married Jane, daughter of Commodore James Barron, and was father of the poet, James Barron Hope, of Norfolk.

Hornby, Daniel, son of Daniel Hornby, merchant tailor, of Richmond county. He was burgess for that county in 1732-1734, succeeding John Tayloe, who was promoted to the council. He married Winifred Travers, daughter of Captain Samuel Travers.

Horsey, Stephen, was a burgess from Northampton county in the assembly of 1653.

Hoskins, Anthony, was a burgess from Northampton county in the assembly of 1652.

Hoskins, Bartholomew, was born in 1600, received a grant in 1620 for in the corporation of Elizabeth City; vestryman of Lynhaven parish in 1640; burgess for Lower Norfolk county in 1649, 1652, 1654; living in 1655.

Hough, Francis, came to Virginia in 1620 and in 1624 lived at Elizabeth City. He finally settled in Nansemond county, when he had various grants of land. He was a burgess for Nutmeg Quarter in February, 1633; and in 1645, during the Indian war, was a member of the council of war for the counties of Isle of Wight and Upper and Lower Norfolk. He died in the parish of St. Peter's, the Poor, London, but left descendants in Virginia.

Howard, Allen, was a burgess from Albemarle county in the assemblies of 1752-1755 and 1758-1761. His will was proved in Goochland county, July 21, 1761, and names issue Benjamin, William, John, Anne, Rebecca and Elizabeth.

Howard, Benjamin, son of Allen Howard, of Goochland county, whose will was proved July 21, 1761; was burgess for Buckingham county in 1769-1771. He was elected to the assembly of 1772-1774, but died before the assembly began.

Howe, John, of Accomac, gentleman, was born in 1593, was a justice for Accomac in 1631, a burgess in 1632-1633, and commander-in-chief of the county from July, 1637, to January 2, 1647, about which time he died.

Hubbard, Robert, was a burgess from Warwick county in the assembly of 1696-1697.

Huddleston, John, was commander of the ship *Bona Nova* of 200 tons, and performed many voyages to Virginia carrying servants and passengers. He patented land in Virginia. After the Indian massacre in 1622, he was sent on a fishing voyage to Newfoundland, and stopped at Plymouth. He found the settlers there starving, and shared his provisions with them, thus saving the colony.

Hull, Peter, was a burgess from Isle of Wight county in the assembly of 1644.

Hull, Richard, son of Richard Hull, and a descendant of John Hull, immigrant, who died in Northumberland county in 1668. He was colonel of the Northumberland militia, and a burgess for Northumberland county in the assembly of 1762-1765, succeeding Presley Thornton, promoted to the council. He married Elizabeth Gaskins, and died in 1777.

Hume, George, son of Lord George Hume of the barony of Wedderburn, Berwickshire, Scotland, and Margaret, his wife, daughter of Sir Patrick Hume of Lumsden, was born at Wedderburn Castle May 30, 1697, and came to Orange county, Virginia, in 1721, and engaged in land surveying. He made the first survey of Fredericksburg. He married Elizabeth Proctor, of Spottsylvania county, in 1728, and died in Culpeper county in 1760, leaving issue. The titles and honors of the family as Earl of Dunbar and Marchmont, are dormant, but really belong to the descendants of George Hume. He had an uncle Francis, who took sides with the pretender and was captured at the battle of Preston in 1715, and sent to Virginia in 1716, where he was factor to Governor Spotswood and died in 1723.

Hunt, William, was "a principal aider and abettor" of Nathaniel Bacon, Jr., in his rebellion, was taken prisoner and died in prison before the rebels were reduced to their allegiance. He resided at Bachelor's Point, Charles City county, where his tombstone records his death as of November 11, 1676. His descendants have been numerous and respectable.

Hunter, William, born at Yorktown, was the son of William Hunter, of Hampton. He was deputy postmaster general to Benjamin Franklin. After the death of William Parks in 1750, he was editor of the "Virginia Gazette," published in Williamsburg. He died in August, 1761.

Hunter, William, a burgess for Nansemond county in the assembly of 1748-1749.

Hutchings, John, son of Daniel Hutchings, mariner, of Norfolk county, and grandson of John Hutchings, of "Pembroke Tribe," Bermuda, was born in 1691 and died in April, 1768. He was an eminent merchant of Norfolk; was mayor of the borough in 1737, 1743 and 1755; and burgess from 1738 to 1756. He married Amey, daughter of John Godfrey, of Norfolk, and had issue John, Jr. (q. v.), Joseph (q. v.), Elizabeth married Richard Kelsick, Mary married Dr. John Ramsay, Frances married Charles Thomas, and Susanna married Edward Champion Travis.

Hutchings, John, Jr., son of Colonel John Hutchings (q. v.), was member of the house of burgesses from 1756 to 1758.

Hutchings, Joseph, son of Colonel John Hutchings (q. v.), was a burgess from Norfolk borough in the assemblies of 1761-1765, October, 1765, 1766-1768, May, 1769, 1769-1771, 1772-1774, and 1775-1776. He represented Norfolk borough in the conventions of March and July, 1775; colonel of the Virginia militia in the skirmish at Kempsville, where he was captured.

Hutchinson, Captain Robert, was a burgess from James City in the assemblies of 1641, 1642-1643, of 1644-1645 and of 1647.

Hutchison (Hutchinson), William, was a burgess from Warrosqueake in the assembly of 1632.

Hutt, Daniel, merchant of London, and master of the ship *May Flower* came to Virginia in 1668. He settled at Nomini Bay, Westmoreland county. He had a plantation of 1,505 acres, twenty-seven servants, and 100 head of cattle. He married Temperance, daughter of Dr. Thomas Gerrard, in 1669, and his will was proved in 1674. He left issue Anne Hutt and Gerrard Hutt. His widow Temperance married (secondly) John Crabb, merchant.

Hyde, Robert, a lawyer of York county, Virginia. He married Jane, daughter of Captain John Underhill, Jr., of Felgate's Creek, York county, and formerly of the city of Worcester, England. He has descendants in the Saunders, Hansford, etc., families. By tradition he was closely related to Edward Hyde, Lord Clarendon. He died in 1718, leaving a son Samuel, and a daughter, who married John Saunders.

Ingles, Mungo, a native of Scotland, born in 1657, died in 1719; master of arts of the University of Edinburgh and brought over to Virginia as master of the grammar school of the college of William and Mary by President Blair, when he returned with the charter in 1693. He served till 1705 when he resigned because of difficulty with Dr. Blair; but in 1716 he was reelected and served till his death in 1719. He was one of the first feoffees of Williamsburg and a justice of James City county. He married in Virginia, Ann, daughter of Colonel James Bray, of the council. His son James was clerk of Isle of Wight from 1729 to 1732.

Ingram, Joseph, came to Virginia in 1675 with Sir Thomas Grantham. He was a young man of standing in England, and had the title of "Esquire." After Bacon's death he was elected general of the rebels, and met with much success in defeating Sir William Berkeley's forces. Grantham persuaded him to make terms by surrendering West Point, a Bacon stronghold, and from that moment, January 16, 1676, the rebellion collapsed.

Innes, Hugh, was a burgess for Pittsylvania county in May, 1769, 1769-1771, 1772-1774. He was one of the justices of that county.

Innis, Henry, was the son of Rev. Robert Innis, and was born in Caroline county, Virginia, January 4, 1752. He studied law, and on coming of age removed to Bedford county, Virginia. Here he served as escheator (1779) and in 1781 was commissioner of the specific tax and commissary of the Bedford militia. In 1782 he was appointed commissioner for the district composed of the counties of Bedford, Campbell, Charlotte, Halifax, Henry and Pittsylvania. In November, 1784, Mr. Innis was elected by the legislature, attorney general for the western district of Virginia, but early in the year 1785 he removed to Kentucky, where he served as attorney general. He died September 20, 1826. He was brother of Captain James Innis, attorney general of Virginia.

Irvine, Alexander, qualified as professor of natural philosophy and mathematics in William and Mary College in 1729. In 1728 he ran the dividing line between Virginia and North Carolina.

Isham, Henry, son of William Isham, of Bedfordshire, England, and his wife Mary, sister of Sir Edward Brett, of Blendenhall, county Kent, England, came to Virginia about 1656, where he had a grant of land. Settled at Bermuda Hundred, where he married Katherine, widow of Joseph Royall of Henrico county, and had: 1. Henry, who died unmarried. 2. Mary, who married William Randolph. 3. Elizabeth, who married Colonel Francis Eppes of Henrico. A fine impression of the Isham arms, on a red wax seal, is attached to a paper at Henrico court house.

Iverson, Abraham, was a burgess from Gloucester county in the assembly of 1653.

Jackson, Rev. Andrew, was minister in Lancaster county, succeeding John Bertrand. He came from Belfast, Ireland, and had probably been a Presbyterian minister. He died in 1710.

Jackson, John, was a burgess from Martin's Hundred in the assembly of 1619, and from James City Island in the assembly of 1632.

Jackson, Mr. Joseph, was a burgess from Charles City in the assembly of 1641.

Jackson, Robert, was a son of Joseph Jackson, of Carlisle, Cumberland, England. He resided at Yorktown, Virginia, where he married in 1731-32 a Miss Brett, of that place. He was grandfather of Sir John Jackson, of Kingston, Jamaica.

Jarrell, Thomas, was a burgess from Southampton in the session of February 1, 1752. In the session of November 1, 1753, Robert James represented Southampton in place of Thomas Jarrell, deceased.

Jaquelin, Edward, son of John Jaquelin, of county Kent, England, and Elizabeth Craddock, his wife, came to Virginia in 1697; settled at Jamestown, where he married Rachel Sherwood, widow of William Sherwood. When she died, he married in 1706, Martha, daughter of William Cary, of Warwick county. He was born in 1668 and died in 1739. His eldest daughter Elizabeth married Richard Ambler, a merchant of Yorktown, and his daughter Mary married John Smith, of "Shooter's Hill," Middlesex county.

Jefferson, John, was a burgess from Flowerdieu Hundred in the first assembly of 1619. He is believed to have been ancestor of Thomas Jefferson.

Jefferson, Peter, son of Thomas Jefferson, of Henrico, was a justice of the peace, and a vestryman of his parish. He was a burgess from Albemarle county (in the place of Joshua Fry, deceased), and in the sessions of August 22, 1754, October 17, 1754, May 1, 1755, August 5, 1755, October 27, 1755. He was a man physically strong, a good mathematician, skilled in surveying, fond of standard literature, and in politics a British Whig. He and Fry were the compilers of a map of Virginia, known as Fry and Jefferson's map. He married in 1738 Jane, daughter of Isham Randolph, of Goochland county. He was the father of President Thomas Jefferson. He died in 1757.

Jenkins, Henry, came probably from the city of Dublin, where he states his brother Daniel Jenkins lived. He was 1695 "justice of the Quorum and commander-in-chief for the county of Elizabeth City." In 1676 he had supported Nathaniel Bacon, Jr. He was burgess from Elizabeth City in 1685, and for York in the assembly of 1696-1697. His will was proved in Elizabeth City county September 24, 1698. He had issue Henry Jenkins, Jr.

Jenings, Edmund, son of Edmund Jenings, Esq., of Virginia, was admitted attorney in the Baltimore county court March, 1724; burgess for Annapolis in the Maryland assembly; took his seat in the Maryland council, October 21, 1732, and was an active member till 1752; was commissioned secretary of the province, March 20, 1732-1733, and resigned that office in 1755. He married Ariana, widow of Thomas Bordley and daughter of Matthias Vanderheyden, July 2, 1728, and died in Yorkshire, England, in March, 1756. His daughter Ariana married John Randolph, attorney general of Virginia.

Jenings, Edmund, son of Edmund Jenings, Esq., of Maryland, was a lawyer of Lincoln's Inn, London. In 1769 he presented to "the Gentlemen of Westmoreland county," a portrait of the Earl of Chatham, which hangs in the court house at Montross.

He had estates in Yorkshire, and was living in 1778.

Jenings, Peter, was born in 1631 and died in 1671. He is spoken of as one "who faithfully served" King Charles I. He settled in Gloucester county, where he was King's attorney and in 1663 a member of the house of burgesses. September 16, 1670, he received a grant for the attorney general's office. He died in 1672, and his widow Catherine, daughter of Sir Thomas Lunsford, married Ralph Wormeley, Esq.

Jennings, John, clerk of Isle of Wight county, 1662-1677, was an adherent of Nathaniel Bacon during Bacon's rebellion of 1676. He was sentenced to banishment, but died before the time set for leaving the county. He married Martha, daughter of Robert Harris, and left descendants.

Jerdone, Francis, son of John Jerdone, magistrate of Jedburgh, Scotland, was born January 30, 1721, came to Virginia in 1745, and settled at Yorktown. Later he moved to Louisa county, where he died in 1771. He was an eminent merchant. He married Sarah Macon, daughter of Colonel William Macon, of New Kent county, Virginia.

Johnson, Jacob, born about 1639, probably in Holland, patented land in Virginia in 1673, was naturalized in 1679, was a member of the house of burgesses in 1693, and died in 1710. He was a brick merchant and lawyer. He had a Presbyterian church on his land, and the minister, Josiah Mackie, lived with him. His son, Jacob Johnson, Jr., married Margaret Langley, daughter of Captain William Langley, of Norfolk county.

Johnson, John, "yeoman and ancient planter" was living at Jamestown in 1624, with his wife Anne, son John and daughter Anne, who married Edward Travis, ancestor of a family long resident on the island.

Johnson, Joseph, was a burgess from Charles City in the assembly of 1639.

Johnson, Rev. Josiah, probably a native of England, came as minister to Virginia in 1766, when he was admitted master of the grammar school of the college of William and Mary. In 1771 he married Mildred Moody, of Williamsburg, and died in 1773. His widow married (secondly) Thomas Evans, afterwards a member of congress.

Johnson, Philip, was a burgess from King and Queen county in the assemblies of 1752-1755 and 1756-1758. He was son of William Johnson, of King William county, who died before 1738. He married Elizabeth Bray, daughter of Colonel Thomas Bray, of "Littletown," James City county, Virginia. He had a son James Bray Johnson, whose only daughter Elizabeth married Samuel Tyler, chancellor of the eastern district of Virginia; and by a second wife he had James Johnson, of Isle of Wight county, who was a member of congress.

Johnson, Richard, was a burgess from King and Queen county in the assemblies of 1722 and 1723-1726. He was a son of Colonel Richard Johnson of the council, and made his will in 1733, leaving his property to his two nephews Thomas and Richard.

Johnson, Thomas, son of Colonel Richard Johnson, of the council, was a burgess from King William county in the assemblies of 1715, 1718, and 1720-1722. He lived at "Chericoke" in King William county, on Pamunkey river. He married Ann, daughter of Colonel Nicholas Meriwether, of New Kent. He died and was buried at "Chericoke" in 1734.

Johnson, Thomas, was a burgess from Northampton county in the assemblies of 1645, 1646, 1652, 1653 and 1654. He was one of the justices of the county court and lieutenant-colonel of the militia in 1656. His will, dated November 25, 1658, was proved December 28, 1658, and names sons Obedience and Richard Johnson and probably Thomas Johnson.

Johnson, Thomas, son of Thomas Johnson of "Chericoke," (q. v.), was known as Thomas Johnson "major" to distinguish him from his nephew of the same name. He was member of the assembly from Louisa county from 1758 to 1775, of the county committee of safety, and of the conventions of 1775 and 1776. He was also one of the signers of the association in 1769.

Johnson, William, was a burgess from Spottsylvania county in the assembly of 1736-1740.

Johnson, William, son of Thomas Johnson of "Chericoke," was a member of the house of burgesses for Louisa in 1761-1765. At the last session, May 1, 1765, his place was taken by Patrick Henry, Johnson having accepted the office of coroner. He married Elizabeth Hutchinson. His son Thomas, was father of the celebrated lawyer, Chapman Johnson.

Johnston, Andrew, a native of Glasgow, in Scotland, was born in 1742; came to Petersburg, Virginia, where he acquired a large fortune as a merchant. He died May 5, 1785.

Johnston, George, an eminent lawyer of Fairfax county, burgess in the assemblies of 1758-1761 and 1761-1765. He seconded in a powerful and logical speech Patrick Henry's resolutions of May 30, 1765, against the Stamp Act. He lived in Alexandria. He was reelected to a seat in the assembly which convened November 4, 1766, but died in the summer of 1766. He married Sarah McCarty, daughter of Major Dennis McCarty, of Westmoreland county, Virginia. His will dated February 23, 1766, was proved January 19, 1767, and names wife, Sarah, and children, Mary Massey, George and William Johnston. George Johnston, one of these was lieutenant-colonel and aide-de-camp to Washington, and his confidential military secretary from December, 1776, until his death at Morristown, June, 1777.

Johnston, Peter, was born at Annan, in Scotland in 1710, come from Edinburgh to Osborne's on James river, where he was a prominent merchant; he moved to Prince Edward county for which he was a burgess at the assembly of May, 1769. He gave the land on which Hampden Sidney College was established, and his will, which was proved December 18, 1786, shows that he was a man of culture. He married Martha Rogers, a widow, daughter of John Butler, and had Peter, born 1763, judge of the general court, and father of General Joseph E. Johnston.

Johnston, William, was a burgess from Spottsylvania county in the sessions of May 19, 1763, January 12, 1764, October 30, 1764, and May 1, 1765.

Jones, Anthony, was born in 1598 and came to Virginia in 1620; burgess for Isle of Wight, 1639, and March, 1642-1643. He made his will in Isle of Wight county, August 16, 1649.

Jones, Cadwallader, son of Richard Jones, merchant of London, was lieutenant-colonel in the Stafford militia in 1680. He carried on a trade with the Indians and was living in 1699. He wrote an essay on the Indian trade, with a MS. map or plat of Louisiana.

Jones, Rev. Emmanuel, was licensed for Virginia May 28, 1700. He was son of John Jones, of Anglesea, Wales. He was born in 1688, matriculated at Oriel College, Oxford, April 26, 1687, and took his B. A. degree March 3, 1692. He was minister of Petsworth parish, Gloucester county, Virginia from 1700 till his death January 29, 1739, leaving sons Emmanuel Jones, Jr., and Richard Jones.

Jones, Emmanuel, Jr., son of Rev. Emmanuel Jones, was a student of William and Mary College and usher of the grammar school. In 1755 he was made master of the Indian school at the college and held that position till 1777, when he resigned. He appears to have been afterwards minister of St. Bride's parish, Norfolk county. He married Miss Macon, of New Kent, and had Emmanuel Macon Jones, of Essex.

Jones, Gabriel, was the son of John and Elizabeth Jones, emigrants to Virginia from Montgomery county, North Wales. He was born May 17, 1724, near Williamsburg. In April, 1732, his family being at that time in England, he was admitted as a scholar of the "Blue Coat School," Christ's Hospital, London, where he remained seven years. He was then apprenticed for six years to Mr. John Houghton, solicitor in the high court of chancery. Returning to Virginia, he lived for a time near Kernstown, Frederick county. In 1746, when only twenty-two, he was appointed prosecuting attorney for August county. On October 16, 1749, he married Margaret, widow of George Morton, and daughter of William Strother of King George. He was burgess from Frederick county in the assembly of 1748-1749, from Augusta county in the assembly of 1756-1758, from Hampshire in the assembly of 1758-1761, and from Augusta again in the assemblies of May, 1769, and 1769-1771. When Rockingham county was constituted in 1777, he became a citizen of that county and its prosecuting attorney. He was a member of the state convention of 1788, and died in October, 1806.

Jones, Rev. Hugh, came to Virginia from England in 1716, and was appointed mathematical professor in William and Mary College. He preached at Jamestown and served as chaplain of the general assembly and lecturer in Bruton church, Williamsburg. He left the province for England in 1722, and in 1724 brought out his "Present State of Virginia." He returned to Virginia and resumed his work in St. Stephen's parish, King and Queen county. Not long afterwards he went to Maryland where he served in various parishes. He died September 8, 1760. In his will he expressed his desire to be buried with his feet to the westward, contrary to the usual mode of burial. "He wanted," he said, "to be facing his people as they rose from their graves. He was not ashamed of them."

Jones, John, son of Peter Jones, founder of Petersburg, was a member of the county court of Brunswick, and in 1772 a member of the house of burgesses. In 1788 he represented Brunswick in the state convention. In after years he was in the state senate and was president of that body. He married Elizabeth Binns, daughter of Charles Binns, in July, 1758.

Jones, Orlando, son of Rev. Rowland Jones, first minister of Bruton parish, Williamsburg, was burgess from King William in 1712-1714, 1715, 1718. He married (first) Martha Macon, daughter of Gideon Macon, and (second) Mary Williams, daughter of James Williams, of King and Queen county. He was born December 31, 1681, was a scholar at William and Mary College in 1699, and died June 12, 1719, leaving by his first wife, one son, Lane Janes, and a daughter, Frances, who married Colonel John Dandridge.

Jones, Rev. Owen, was licensed for Virginia August 17, 1703, and came to Virginia soon after, where he was made rector of St. Mary's parish, Essex county, and still held the charge twenty years later.

Jones, Peter, was in 1674 major in command of a fort near the falls of Appomattox river. He had a son Peter, who died in 1721. A grandson, Peter Jones, son of Peter Jones, was the founder of Petersburg. The last was captain and then major of the Prince George county militia, and died in Amelia county in 1754. (William and Mary College Quarterly, xix., 287).

Jones, Rice, came from Canada in 1623; settled in Warwick county and patented land in Warrosqueake, on the south side of the James river in 1628.

Jones, Richard, was a burgess from Amelia county in the assembly of 1736-1740. He was probably the Richard Jones who died in Amelia county in 1759, and names sons Richard, Peter, Daniel and Llewellyn Jones, and daughter Amy Watson, Prudence Ward, Rebecca Ward and Martha Jones.

Jones, Robert, a royalist, who received many wounds in the civil war, emigrated to Virginia about 1650. In 1676 he took sides with Bacon, was condemned to death, but was spared because of his former loyalty to the King. Major Thomas Hansford, prominent in the rebellion had in his family a tutor, a Robert Jones, who may have been this man.

Jones, Robert, was a burgess for Surry county in the assembly of 1752-1755.

Jones, Robert, represented Southampton county in 1753 in place of Thomas Jarrell, deceased.

Jones, Robert, was a burgess from Essex county in the assembly of 1723-1726.

Jones, Roger, ancestor of a distinguished family of the United States, came to Virginia in 1680 with Lord Culpeper, and had charge of a sloop-of-war in Chesapeake Bay, for the collection of customs and the suppression of piracy. He married Dorothy Walker, daughter of John Walker, of Mansfield, in Nottinghamshire, England, and died in 1701, leaving sons Frederick and Thomas (q. v.).

Jones, Rev. Rowland, was a son of Rev. Rowland Jones, vicar of Wendover, in county Bucks, England. He was born at Swinbrook, near Burford in Oxfordshire, educated at Merton College, Oxford, was first pastor of Bruton parish, Williamsburg, Virginia, in 1674, and after a service of fourteen years died April 23, 1688, and was buried in Williamsburg.

Jones, Thomas, son of Captain Roger Jones, was a man of large estate and had extensive commercial transactions. He patented large bodies of land, and was a colonel of the militia in King William county. He married February 14, 1725, Elizabeth Pratt, widow of William Pratt, and eldest daughter of Dr. William Cocke, formerly secretary of state.

Jones, William, member of a prominent family in Northumberland county, was burgess for that county in 1692-1693. He was a son of Mr. Robert Jones, of "Fleet's Bay," who died in 1675, leaving sons Samuel, Robert, Maurice and William, and a brother John Jones.

Jones, William, was a burgess for Northampton county in 1659; a prominent justice of the peace.

Jones, Wood, brother of Peter Jones, the founder of Petersburg, was a member of the house of burgesses for Amelia county in 1752.

Jordan, Colonel George, came to Virginia in 1635 and resided in Surry county, near "Four Mile Tree," on James river. He was a justice of Surry in 1652, and for many years later; burgess in 1659, 1674 and 1676; attorney general of the colony from 1670 to 1678, when he died. In 1673, Surry court gave him a certificate for the importation of thirty-eight persons into the colony, among whom were Mr. William Jordan, Mrs. Ann Jordan, his wife, Mr. John Cary, Mr. Robert Lee, etc. He left no issue, but his brother, Arthur Jordan, is numerously represented through descendants.

Jordan, John, was burgess for Westmoreland county in 1695-1696. He came from Maryland and married Dorcas, widow of Patrick Spence. His stepdaughter, Elinor Spence, married Andrew Monroe, ancestor of President James Monroe.

Jordan, Richard, was burgess for Isle of Wight county in 1676. He left a son John, whose son John of Newport parish, Isle of Wight county, made a deed about 1730. The family were Quakers.

Jordan, Samuel, settled on James river at an early date and called his place "Jordan's Jorney." He represented the plantation in the first assembly 1619. In the massacre of 1622 he successfully fought off the Indians. He died in 1623, and his widow Cecilly married William Ferrar, of the council of state, after a flirtation with the minister of the parish, Greville Pooley, that was taken notice of by the council in a solemn proclamation.

Jordan, Samuel, was justice of the peace for Albemarle county, 1746-1761; captain 1753; sheriff, 1753-1775; county lieutenant of the new county of Buckingham in 1761, and burgess of Buckingham, 1766-1769. During the revolution he served as colonel of the county militia and was commissioner for the carting of cannon in Buckingham. He married Ruth Meredith, daughter of Colonel Samuel Meredith, of Hanover. His daughter Margaret married Colonel William Cabell.

Jordan, Thomas, was born in 1600 and was living in Virginia in 1624; burgess for Warrosqueake, Isle of Wight, 1629, 1631, and September, 1632, and a commissioner in 1629. His descendants have been numerous in Isle of Wight county. Richard Jordan, a burgess for Isle of Wight in 1676 was probably a son.

Julian, William, was living at Elizabeth City in 1625. He patented 600 acres on the eastern branch of Elizabeth river July 4, 1636. He was a justice of Lower Norfolk county in 1637. In 1646 the governor and council relieved him from all his offices on account of his great age. His wife was named Sarah.

Justice, Ralph, burgess for Accomac county in 1753-1755, succeeding Edmund Allen, who accepted the office of sheriff.

Kecatough (Catataugh), brother of Powhatan, a chief of the Pamunkey Indians in 1607.

Keeling, William, a burgess for Princess Anne county in 1756-1758. He was a descendant of Ensign Thomas Keeling, of Lower Norfolk county, 1639, first of his family in Virginia.

Keeton, John, was a burgess for Nansemond county. He was a Dutchman and was naturalized by act of assembly in 1679.

Keith, George, is styled by John Smith as "a Scotchman who professed scholarship," was for a time minister at Bermuda, but came to Virginia in 1617. He was born in 1581. In 1624 he was minister of Elizabeth City and in 1635 he was pastor of Chiskiak, one of the new settlements in the York. He was probably ancestor of the celebrated George Keith, who figured in Pennsylvania at the close of the century. Keith's or Skiffes creek in James City county, Virginia, perpetuates his name.

Keith, James, was a burgess from Hampshire in the sessions of November 3, 1761, January 14, 1762, and March 30, 1762. In the session of November 2, 1762, James Mercer represented Hampshire "in place of James Keith, who had accepted a clerkship."

Keith, James, was a native of Scotland, and on March 4, 1728-29, received the King's bounty of twenty pounds to go as minister to Virginia. He probably settled at first in Henrico county, where he married Mary Isham Randolph, daughter of Thomas Randolph and Judith Fleming, a daughter of Colonel Charles Fleming. He then lived in Hamilton parish, Fauquier county, for many years. His daughter, Mary Randolph Keith, married Colonel Thomas Marshall, father of John Marshall, chief justice of the United States.

Kemp, Edmund, was nephew of Richard Kemp, secretary of state; justice for Lancaster county in 1655; his widow married Sir Gray Skipwith, and his son Matthew was member of the council.

Kemp, Matthew, son of Colonel Matthew Kemp, member of the council, was burgess for Middlesex county in 1685, and 1692; justice from 1698 and sheriff 1706. His will was dated May 4, 1715 and proved in Middlesex, January 2, 1716. He left a son Matthew (q. v.).

Kemp, Matthew, son of Matthew Kemp, of Middlesex county, was born in 1695 and died in December, 1739; was burgess for Middlesex county in 1723-1726 and 1727-

1734; sheriff of Middlesex in 1729, afterward in 1732 clerk of the general court and the secretary's office, as well as James City county. His daughter Elizabeth married Robert Elliott, clerk of Middlesex county, 1762-1767.

Kempe, William, of Howes in Leicestershire, England, gentleman, emigrated to Virginia in 1618. He was a justice in 1628 and in 1629-30 he represented "the upper parts of Elizabeth City" in the house of burgesses.

Kemper, John, son of John George Kemper, elder of the German Reformed Church at Meusen, near Siegen in Germany, and Agnes Kleb, his wife. He was one of the original colonists at Germanna, who were brought over by Governor Spotswood to operate his iron works in Spottsylvania county. He married in 1715 or 1716 Elisbeth (Alice) Utterbach, daughter of Harman Utterbach.

Kendall, John, was a member of the house of burgesses for Northampton from 1752 to 1761 inclusive. He was probably the John Kendall who was a member of the Northampton committee of safety, 1774-1776.

Kendall, William, was burgess for Northampton county at the sessions of March, 1657-1658, September, 1663, when he is styled lieutenant-colonel, October, 1666, and doubtless all the sessions of the "Long Assembly" until 1676, November, 1683, when he is styled colonel, April, 1684, and November, 1685, when he is styled speaker. His will dated December 29, 1685, was proved July 28, 1686, and names son-in-law Hancock Lee and Mary, his wife, and son William Kendall.

Kendall, William, son of Colonel William Kendall (q. v.), was a member of the house of burgesses for Northampton county in 1688 and 1692-1693. He made his will January 29, 1695, which was proved July 28, 1696. He left two sons William and John, and three daughters.

Kenner, Richard, was a burgess from Northumberland county in the assembly of 1688 and in the session of April 16, 1691. He was captain in the militia and a justice of the peace. He married Elizabeth, daughter of Matthew Rodham, in 1664, and was father of Captain Rodham Kenner (q. v.).

Kenner, Rodham, son of Captain Richard Kenner, was born in St. Stephen's parish, Northumberland county, March 23, 1671. He was a captain, justice of the peace, and burgess from Northumberland in 1695, 1699 and 1700-1702. He married Hannah Fox, daughter of Captain David Fox and Hannah Ball, his wife, and left issue.

Kenner, Rodham, son of Richard Kenner, who descended from Richard Kenner, the emigrant from England to Virginia about 1660. He attended William and Mary College in 1769, and was burgess for Northumberland county from 1773 to 1775, and member of the conventions of 1774, 1775 and 1776. He was a signer of the Westmoreland address against the Stamp Act in 1769 and county lieutenant in 1785. He married in 1763, Elizabeth Plater, daughter of George Plater, Esq., of Maryland.

Kennon, Richard, founder of the family in Virginia, was a prominent merchant living at Bermuda Hundred, on James river. In 1685 he was factor for Mr. William Paggen, a London merchant. He was a constant visitor to London; justice of the peace for Henrico county in 1680 and other years; burgess in 1686. He married Elizabeth Worsham, daughter of William Worsham and Elizabeth, his wife. He died in 1696 and in his will names his children Richard, William, Martha, married Robert Munford, Mary married Major John Bolling, of "Cobbs," Elizabeth married Joseph Royall, Sr., Sarah, and Judith, married Thomas Eldridge.

Kennon, Richard, son of Colonel William Kennon, of "Conjuror's Neck," near Bermuda Hundred, and grandson of Richard Kennon (q. v.). He was born April 15, 1712, and settled on James river in Charles City county, at a place still called "Kennon's" opposite to Brandon in Prince George county. He was justice of Charles City county, colonel of the militia, and burgess from 1738 to 1755. He married Anne Hunt, daughter of William Hunt, of Charles City county; died in 1761, and left issue.

Kennon, William, son of Colonel Richard Kennon, of Charles City county, was a justice of the peace and colonel of the militia. He was burgess for Charles City county during the assemblies of 1758-1761, and 1761-1765, after which time he removed to North Carolina. In 1774 he was chairman of the county committee of Rowan county, North Carolina, and in 1775 chairman of that of Micklenburg county. He married Priscilla Willis, daughter of Colonel Francis Willis, of Gloucester county, Virginia, and left issue.

Key, Thomas, "an ancient planter," had land on Warwicksqueake river, opposite Basse's Choice; in 1626 was member of the house of burgesses for Denbigh, 1829-1830. His wife was named Martha.

King, Henry, descended from Michael King, who lived in Nansemond county, about 1690; was a justice of Elizabeth City county from 1769; burgess in 1772, 1773 and 1774, and member of the conventions of 1774, 1775 and 1776. He married Rachel Westwood, daughter of William Westwood.

Kingsmill, Richard, came to Virginia before 1625, when with his wife Jane, son Nathaniel and daughter Susan, he was living at "Neck of Land," which he represented in the house of burgesses in 1624. He afterwards lived on Jamestown Island and had also a patent for 850 acres on the east side of Archer's Hope Creek, still known as Kingsmill. He was survived by an only daughter who married (first) Colonel William Tayloe; (second) Colonel Nathaniel Bacon. He used the same arms as Sir William Kingsmill, of Hampshire, England.

Kingston, Thomas, a burgess for Martin's Hundred in 1629. He was agent for Thomas Covell, of London, merchant. He died about 1639 when his widow married Thomas Loving.

Kingswell, Edward, born about 1593, came to Virginia in 1633 from St. Sepulchre's parish, London. He died about 1636. His wife, Jane, was the widow of Sir William Clifton, of Little Giddings, Huntingdonshire, England.

Kippax, Rev. Peter, son of John Kippax, of Colne, county Lancashire, England. He matriculated at Brazenose College, Oxford.

BURGESSES AND OTHER PROMINENT PERSONS

January 18, 1689, aged eighteen, and was B. A. in 1693. He was licensed for Virginia November 1, 1699, and was present at the convention of the clergy in Williamsburg in February, 1705. He lived in Richmond county.

Klug, George Samuel, was born in Elbing, Prussia, and was student under the celebrated Mosheim, who wrote "The Ecclesiastical History." He was ordained at Danzig, August 30, 1738, and soon after came to Virginia and was second minister of the German Lutheran settlers in Madison county. He died in 1761.

Klug, Samuel, a native of Gloucester county, Virginia, was a student of William and Mary College, and in 1765 became sub-usher of the grammar school. He visited England for ordination as a minister, returning in 1768. He then became minister of Christ Church, Middlesex county. In 1775 he was chairman of the county committee of safety for Gloucester county. He married Elizabeth Yates and continued minister of Christ Church till his death in 1795.

Knight, Nathaniel, son of Mr. Samuel Knight, of Strodwater, in Gloucestershire, England, was a chirurgeon in Surry county, and died in 1678 without issue. In his will he leaves numerous legacies to his friends.

Knight, Captain Peter, was a burgess for Gloucester county in 1658 and 1660, and for Northumberland county in 1684 and 1685.

Knott, James, was living in 1632-1635 in Accomac county, and in 1632 was given fifty acres at the mouth of Hampton river, together with "the house called the great house," to keep a house of entertainment for strangers.

LaGuarde, Elias, one of the vignerons from Languedoc, France, sent over in 1620 to Buckroe in Elizabeth City county. He was living in 1633. The name was probably anglicised into "Elligood," a prominent family in Princess Anne county in later times.

Lamb, Anthony, an early resident of Poquoson parish, York county. He died December 29, 1700. He was ancestor of the Lamb family, represented by Hon. John Lamb, late a member of congress.

Lambert, Thomas, was the first person to introduce the method of drying tobacco on lines or sticks, instead of in heaps; sheriff of Lower Norfolk county, 1643; burgess in 1649, 1652, 1661; lieutenant-colonel of the militia. Lambert's Point, near Norfolk, is named for him.

Landon, Thomas, son of Thomas Landon, gentleman, of Credenhill, Herefordshire, England, settled in Middlesex county, about 1688. He had been "eldest groom of his majesty's buttery" before coming. His brother Silvanus was president of the English company at Baudjarmassingh, India. Thomas Landon died in 1709. His daughter Betty was one of the wives of Colonel Robert Carter, of Corotoman, and was mother of Colonel Landon Carter, of "Sabine Hall," Richmond county.

Lane, Captain John, was a burgess for King and Queen county in 1692-93, but his seat was vacated by order of the house. His daughter Jane married (first) Willis Wilson; (second) Colonel Gawin Corbin.

Langbourn, William, was son of Robert Langbourn and Mary Dandridge, his wife, of Fetter Lane, London. He was born October 21, 1723, came to Virginia and settled in King William county. He married Susanna Smith of "Shooter's Hill," Middlesex county. He died March 19, 1766. He left son William, who was lieutenant-colonel in the American revolution.

Langhorne, John, probably a grandson of Captain John Langhorne living in 1689, was a burgess for Warwick county in 1748-1749. He was father of William Langhorne, who was a burgess for Warwick county in 1772-1774, and 1775, the last session; and member of the conventions of 1774 and 1775.

Langley, Ralph, a member of the family of Langleys of Yorkshire, England, resided at York plantation, York county, Virginia, was justice, captain, burgess in 1657, and sheriff in 1667. He married Mary, widow of Robert Lewis, and died issueless in 1683.

Langley, William, son of William Langley, who patented land in Lower Norfolk county in 1656. He lived on Tanner's Creek, was a justice of the peace in 1691, captain in 1708, and a member of the house of burgesses in 1715. He married Margaret Thelaball, daughter of James Thelaball and Elizabeth Mason, daughter of Francis Mason. He died about 1718, and left issue.

Lanier, John, came from England to Virginia about 1670 and settled in Prince George county. He took sides with Bacon in the rebellion of 1676. He was ancestor of the poet Sidney Lanier. He made his will June 5, 1717, which is recorded in Prince George county and names children Nicholas, Sampson, John, Robert and Sarah married Brewer.

Langston, Anthony, formerly ensign in Prince Maurice's regiment during the civil war. He spent fourteen years in Virginia, and on his return to England was a captain in the naval service. John Langston, who took part with Bacon in 1676, and left descendants in Virginia was probably a near relative.

Lankford, Benjamin, was a burgess for Pittsylvania county in the assembly of 1775-1776 and a member of the conventions of July, 1775, and May, 1776.

Latané, Rev. Lewis, a Huguenot, fled from France to England in 1685, after the revocation of the Edict of Nantes and came to Virginia in 1700, where he at once became minister of South Farnham parish, Essex county. He was a man of education and high character. He died in 1733, leaving children John, Charlotte, Phebe, Henrietta and Marian.

Lawne, Captain Christopher, arrived in Virginia April 17, 1609, with 100 settlers, sent out by a private company in which Richard Wiseman, Nathaniel Basse and others were joined with him as associates. He settled on or near what is still known as Lawne's Creek, dividing Isle of Wight and Surry counties. Captain Lawne represented his plantation in the first assembly July 30, 1619. He died before November 4, 1620. This was the first plantation in Isle of Wight county, Virginia.

Lawrence, Rev. John, was the eldest son of John and Dorothy Lawrence of Wormleyberry House, parish of Wormeley, Herefordshire, England. He was associated with the early history of Presbyterianism in America. He had a sister in Virginia where he resided, and then went to Maryland where he preached three years. After that he went to Carolina and, returning to Virginia, died in Lower Norfolk county in 1684.

Lawson, Anthony, merchant of Londonderry, Ireland, came to Virginia about 1668 as agent for certain persons of that city. He married (first) Ann Okeham, relict of Mr. John Okeham; and (second) Mary Gookin, daughter of Colonel John Gookin, and widow of William Moseley. He was justice of Lower Norfolk county from 1673 to 1693 and of Princess Anne from 1696 to 1701. Burgess for Lower Norfolk in 1688. He died in 1701, leaving son Thomas and other children.

Lawson, Anthony, son of Thomas Lawson, and grandson of Anthony Lawson, who came to Virginia from Londonderry, was born in 1729, practised law, was a justice of Princess Anne county, 1760-1775; sheriff, 1768-1770; lieutenant-colonel of the militia of Princess Anne; was captured by the British and sent to East Florida, but was exchanged. Died in 1785.

Lawson, Rowland, came to Virginia about 1637 with his wife Lettice, and his brothers Richard and Epaphroditus. He was a justice of Lancaster 1652-1655, and died about 1661, leaving children Rowland, Jr., Elizabeth, John and Henry. The will (1706) of Rowland Lawson, Jr., bears a seal showing arms—a chevron between three martlets, identical with the arms of the Lawsons, of Yorkshire and Northumberland, England.

Laydon, John, born in 1581, came to Virginia in 1607, among the first settlers, in the ship Sarah Constant. His marriage to Ann Burras, a maid of Mrs. Forest who came in the second supply (October, 1608) was the first Christian marriage in the English settlements. She was fourteen years younger than her husband. They passed safely through the starving time, as the census of 1625 shows that they were both living at Elizabeth City with their four children—Virginia, Alice, Katherine and Margaret.

Laydon, Virginia, daughter of John Laydon, and Anne Burras, his wife, was the first child of English parents born in Virginia. She was born about 1609, and was living with her parents at Elizabeth City in 1625.

Lear, John, son of Thomas Lear and Elizabeth Bridger, his wife, and grandson of Colonel John Lear of the council, was a member of the house of burgesses for Nansemond county in 1715-1720 and 1727-1734, and in 1723 he was sheriff.

Lederer, John, German explorer. In 1669 he made an exploration from the headwaters of York river, towards the mountains. In May, 1670, in company with Major Harris, he made a second voyage from the falls of James river to the Monacan village, thence 100 miles westward to the south branch of the James river and from thence southwest to the Chowan and the Roanoke rivers, and visited the Tuscaroras. Later he went to Maryland, and Sir

William Talbot translated his journal from the Latin and published it.

Lee, George, only son of Richard Lee, (who was grandson of Richard Lee, the immigrant), and Martha Silk, his wife, was born in London August 18, 1714, settled at "Mt. Pleasant," Westmoreland county. On the death of Colonel Daniel McCarty, he represented his county in the house of burgesses, and was a delegate in 1744-1747, 1748-1749; deputy clerk under his brother-in-law, George Turrberville, from 1740 to 1742, clerk 1742-1761; vestryman of Cople parish 1755, and justice of the peace. His will, dated September 15, 1761, was proved January 26, 1762.

Lee, Hancock, son of Richard Lee, Esq., was born in 1653, was justice for Northampton county in 1677, later removed to Northumberland county, where he was justice in 1687 and burgess in 1688 and 1698. His military rank was that of captain. He married (first) Mary, only daughter of Colonel William Kendall; (second) Sarah, daughter of Isaac Allerton, Esq. He died May 25, 1709, leaving issue.

Lee, Dr. Henry, was an early resident of York county; was justice of the peace and burgess in 1652. He died in 1657. He married Marah Atkins, daughter of Thomas Atkins, and was the ancestor of the Lees of the Peninsula of Virginia. He is supposed to have been a brother of Richard Lee, of Westmoreland, ancestor of General Robert E. Lee.

Lee, Henry, of "Leesylvania," Prince William county, third son of Henry Lee and Mary Bland, his wife, was born in 1729, probably at "Lee Hall," Westmoreland. He was justice of the peace of Prince William and county lieutenant. He was burgess in the assemblies of May, 1769, 1769-1771, 1772-1774, and 1775-1776, and member of the conventions of 1774, 1775, 1776. Henry Lee married Lucy Grymes, the "Lowland Beauty." He died in 1787. He was father of Light Horse Harry Lee, and grandfather of General Robert E. Lee.

Lee, John, was the son of Hancock Lee and Mary Kendall, his wife, was clerk of Essex county from 1745 to 1761, and burgess from 1761 to 1767. He died August 11, 1789, at the home of his nephew, John Lee, Jr., son of his brother Hancock Lee.

Lee, Richard, the second son of Henry Lee and Mary Bland, his wife, was born about 1726, and was generally known as "Squire Richard Lee." He was a justice of the peace of Westmoreland county, one of the vestry of Cople parish, naval officer of the port of South Potomack; burgess from 1756 to 1775, member of the conventions of 1774, 1775, 1776; and of the house of delegates from 1777 to 1793. He married his first cousin, Sally, daughter of Peter Poythress. His will, dated February 6, 1790, was proved in Westmoreland county, March 23, 1795.

Lee, William, was a practicing physician in York county in 1660. He had a brother George Lee, "citizen and grocer of London," who dealt largely with Virginia. Among the servants shipped over by him were his two nephews, John Jones and John Symonds. In 1660 George Lee sent his "brother" George Underwood to collect his dues in hands of his brother William and others, resident in Virginia.

BURGESSES AND OTHER PROMINENT PERSONS

Le Grand, Peter, came to Virginia with his wife and five children in 1700 and settled at "Manakintown," Goochland county. His will is recorded at the court house and bears date February 12, 1736-1737. His son Peter was a burgess for Goochland county in 1758-1761, and for Prince Edward county in 1761-1765, 1766-1768, 1772-1774 and 1775. He married Lucy Nash, daughter of Colonel John Nash, and was father of Nash Le Grand.

Leigh, William, probably a son of Francis Leigh of the council, was burgess for King and Queen county in 1696, 1697, 1698, 1699, 1700-1702, 1703-1704, and died the last year (1704). He was in 1702 colonel commanding the militia of King and Queen county, as well as judge of the vice-admiralty court of the colony.

Lewis, Andrew, son of John Lewis (q. v.), and Margaret Lynn, his wife, was born in Ulster, Ireland, 1720; served in the French and Indian war as major, and in the unfortunate expedition of Major Grant, in 1758, was taken prisoner and carried to Montreal; in 1774 he was made a brigadier general; and defeated the Indians at Point Pleasant in October, of that year; a representative of Botetourt county in the house of burgesses in 1772, 1773, 1774 and 1775, and in the conventions of 1774 and 1775; commissioned colonel and promoted brigadier general in the continental army. He drove Lord Dunmore from Norfolk and Gwyn's Island in 1776 and was on duty in the lower part of the state when he contracted a fever of which he died September 25, 1781.

Lewis, Charles, son of John Lewis (q. v.), and Margaret Lynn, his wife, was born in 1736; killed October 10, 1774 at the battle of Point Pleasant, where he was a major of the Virginia troops.

Lewis, Fielding, son of Colonel John Lewis of "Warner Hall" and Frances Fielding, his wife, was born July 7, 1725, and resided in Spottsylvania county, which he represented in the house of burgesses in 1760-1761, 1761-1765, 1765-1768. He was vestryman, justice, and colonel of the militia. He lived at "Kenmore" in Fredericksburg. He married (first) Catherine Washington; (second) Elizabeth or Betty Washington, sister of General Washington. Fielding Lewis made his will in 1781.

Lewis, John, son of Charles Lewis of "The Byrd," Goochland county; descended from John Lewis who came to Virginia in 1653 and settled on Poropotank Creek, Gloucester county; was burgess for Halifax county in the assembly of May, 1769. He married his cousin, Jane Lewis, daughter of his uncle, Robert Lewis, of Albemarle. His will dated October 26, 1790, was proved in Pittsylvania county, August 21, 1794.

Lewis, John, immigrant, first settler in present limits of Augusta county. He was born in France in 1673, of Scotch-Irish parents, but went to Scotland after the revocation of the Edict of Nantes. While there he married Margaret Lynn, a daughter of the laird of Loch Lynn. He removed to county Donegal, province of Ulster, Ireland, but there slaying his landlord in a quarrel, he came to Pennsylvania where he spent the winter of 1731-1732. In the summer of the latter year he emigrated with his sons to the valley of Virginia and reared his cabin one mile east of Staunton. In 1745, when Augusta was formed into a county, he was made one of the first justices. He employed much of his time in surveying lands, and in one of his trips to the country west of the Alleghanies he gave the Greenbriar river its name. He died leaving five sons, all distinguished in the history of Virginia—Thomas, Andrew, William, Charles, and Samuel.

Lewis, Robert, son of Colonel John Lewis and Elizabeth Warner, his wife, was born at "Warner Hall," Gloucester county, and baptized May 4, 1704. He removed to Louisa county, and was vestryman of Fredericksville parish, justice, and colonel of the militia, and in 1745 and 1746 was burgess in the general assembly. His will dated September 1, 1751, was proved September 11, 1766. He married (first) Jane Meriwether, daughter of Colonel Nicholas Meriwether, by whom he had issue. He married (second) Elizabeth Thornton, by whom no issue.

Lewis, Thomas, son of John Lewis (q. v.) and Margaret Lynn, his wife, was born in Donegal, Ireland, April 27, 1718, came to Virginia with his father, was surveyor of Augusta county in 1746; was a member of the conventions of 1775 and 1776, commissioner in 1778 to treat with the Indians and member of the convention of 1788 from Rockingham county. He died January 31, 1790.

Lewis, William, son of John Lewis (q. v.) and Margaret Lynn, his wife, was born about 1724, taught by Rev. James Waddell, studied medicine in Philadelphia, severely wounded in Braddock's defeat, practiced medicine in Augusta county; colonel in the continental line during the American revolution. He died in 1812.

Lewis, Zachary, son of Zachary Lewis, of Brecon, Brecknock, Wales, was born in Spottsylvania county, June 1, 1702. He was a lawyer of large wealth and practice. He served in the house of burgesses in 1757-1758 and 1758-1761. He married, in 1729, Mary Walker, daughter of Colonel John Walker. He was a vestryman of St. George's parish, Spottsylvania county. He died January 20, 1765, leaving issue.

Lightfoot, William, son of Colonel Philip Lightfoot, resided at Yorktown and at "Tedington," Charles City county. He was a burgess for Charles City county in 1756, 1757 and 1758, and died before 1771, leaving issue by his wife Mildred Howell, William Philip, Mary married William Allen, of Surry, Mildred married Walter Coles.

Lindsay, David, son of Sir Hierome Lindsay, knight of the mount, Lord Lyon-king-at-arms of Scotland, was born at South Leith, Scotland, January 2, 1603, and was rector of Yeocomico parish, Northumberland county, Virginia. He died April 3, 1667, leaving an only daughter Helen, who married Captain Thomas Opie, who has descendants in Virginia.

Lister, Thomas, fifth son of James Lister, of Shibden Hall, Yorkshire, baptized December 9, 1708, died August 15, 1740, in Virginia; married Ann, daughter of John Lewis of Virginia, 1733. He had a son William who returned to England, and several daughters, who married Virginians.

Lister, William, burgess for Lancaster county in 1705-1706; he was justice and major of the militia.

Littlepage, Colonel James, was son of Richard Littlepage (q. v.), and was born

July 14, 1714; first clerk of Louisa county, 1742-1760; burgess for Hanover county in 1764 to succeed Nathaniel West Dandridge, whose election he contested and who employed Patrick Henry to defend his cause; was reelected to the assembly of 1766-1768, but died in 1766. By his second wife Elizabeth Lewis, daughter of Zachary Lewis, he had General Lewis Littlepage, who was chamberlain and confidential secretary to the King of Poland.

Littlepage, Richard, was son of Mr. Richard Littlepage, who patented land in New Kent, Virginia, 1660. He was vestryman of St. Peter's church, justice, and burgess for New Kent in 1685. He died March 20, 1717, and was father of James Littlepage (q. v.).

Livingston, William, was a merchant of New Kent county. He contracted in 1716 with Charles Stagg, dancing master and theatrical manager, to operate the first theatre in America at Williamsburg. The theatre was built, and comedies and tragedies represented.

Llewellyn, Daniel, of Chelmsford, Essex, England, came to Virginia in or before 1642 and settled near Shirley in Charles City county. He received various grants of land, was justice of the peace for Charles City county, a captain of militia and a member of the house of burgesses for Henrico county in 1643 and 1644 and for Charles City county in 1646, 1652, 1655, 1656. He married Anne, widow of Robert Hallam and died at Chelmsford, in 1664, leaving a son Daniel in Virginia, born 1647.

Lloyd, Cornelius, was a London merchant who came to Virginia and was member of the house of burgesses for Lower Norfolk county 1642-43 and 1644, for Isle of Wight 1645, and again for Lower Norfolk county, 1647, 1652, when he received the rank of lieutenant-colonel, and 1653 when he held the rank of colonel. He was born about 1608 and died before December 20, 1654.

Lloyd, Edward, was a brother of Colonel Cornelius Lloyd, and was a burgess for Lower Norfolk county 1644-1646, was a Puritan and removed to Maryland in 1648, and was ancestor of the family of the Lloyd name there.

Lloyd, John, son of Colonel William Lloyd, of Rappahannock, was justice for Richmond county in 1693, and was recommended to the English government as a suitable man in estate and standing for appointment to the council. He married, about 1693, Elizabeth, only child and heiress of Colonel John Carter, Jr. He removed to England about 1700 and resided in the city of Chester.

Lloyd, Thomas, son of Colonel William Lloyd, of Rappahannock county, was burgess for Richmond county in 1699.

Lloyd, William, came to Virginia before 1667 and patented extensive tracts of land. In 1686, he was a justice of Rappahannock and lieutenant-colonel of the militia. He married (first) Mary, widow of Moore Fauntleroy; and (second) Elizabeth, widow of John Hull. He was burgess for Rappahannock in 1685. He had two sons John and Thomas (q. v.).

Lobb, George, was a burgess in 1656; one of the principal silk-raisers in Virginia.

Lockey, Edward, was a merchant of

London, who came to York county, Virginia, about 1650. He married in 1661 Elizabeth, widow of Mr. John Hansford, father of Colonel Thomas Hansford, of Bacon's rebellion. He died in 1667 in the parish of St. Catherine Creechurch, London, leaving his property to his nephew Isaac Collier, and other relatives in Virginia. His brother John Lockey was a London ship captain and merchant.

Lomax, Lunsford, of "Portobago," Caroline county, son of John Lomax, and grandson of Rev. John Lomax, M. A., of Emmanuel College, Cambridge, a Puritan divine, was born November 5, 1705, and represented Caroline county in the house of burgesses from 1742 to 1756. He married twice (first) Mary Edwards; (second) Judith Micou, and died June 10, 1772, leaving issue.

Lord, John, son of Thomas Lord, one of the original proprietors of Hartford, Connecticut, removed to Virginia, and was living in Westmoreland county 1668; justice and militia captain for that county, November 5, 1677. He had issue Elizabeth, who married James Neale, of Maryland, and William Lord, sheriff of Westmoreland county in 1729.

Loving, Thomas, was a merchant who resided at Martin's Hundred, James City county. He was member of the house of burgesses for James City county in 1644, 1646 and in March, 1657-1658. He was also surveyor general of Virginia until his death in 1665. He married before 1639 the widow of Thomas Kingston. His daughter and heiress Anne married October 28, 1666, Dr. Edward Thruston, son of John Thruston, chamberlain of Bristol, England, who has descendants in Virginia.

Lovelace, Colonel Francis, son of Sir William Lovelace, and brother of Richard Lovelace, the poet, served Charles I. in Wales, and commanded Caermathen from 1644 until it was captured by Langhorne in October, 1645. His estate was sequestered by the parliamentarians and in 1650 he came to Virginia. At the surrender of Virginia to the parliamentary commissioners in 1652 he was allowed to repair to Charles II. with the news. After the restoration he was made governor of New York from 1667 to 1673. His sister Anne married Rev. John Gorsuch, of England and Virginia.

Lucas, Thomas, gentleman, patented 600 acres in Lancaster county in 1652 and was burgess for that county in 1657-1658, and died in 1673. He had had two wives, the last being Margaret, widow of Captain John Upton, whom he married in 1657. His son Thomas by the first marriage died without issue, and administration on his estate in England was granted to his cousin and next of kin John Lucas.

Luddington, William, burgess for York county in 1646.

Ludlow, Thomas, son of Gabriel and Phillis Ludlow, of an ancient family in Wiltshire, England, and nephew of Colonel George Ludlow (q. v.). He was baptized at Warminster November 1, 1624, came to Virginia and became lieutenant-colonel of the militia of York county. His brother John qualified on his estate December 20, 1660. He left a son George, who died without issue and a daughter Elizabeth, who married John Wiles of Culford parish, county Suffolk, England, and a daughter Mary. His widow Mary married Rev. Peter Temple, of York county, Virginia.

Luke, George, was the son of Oliver Luke Esq., of Woodend, Bedfordshire, England, and grandson of Sir Samuel Luke, who is supposed to be the hero of Hudibras. He was born July 29, 1659, came to Virginia about 1690, and in 1722 was collector of the customs for the lower district of James river. He married Mary Fitzhugh, the widow of Dr. Ralph Smith, and died 1724. His wife survived him and kept ordinary in Williamsburg.

Lupo, Lieutenant Albino, gentleman, born in 1584, came to Virginia in 1610; his wife Elizabeth born 1597, came to Virginia in 1616; both patented lands in Kecoughtan parish, Elizabeth City corporation.

Lyddall, Captain John, son of Colonel George Lyddall, was a burgess for New Kent county in 1692-1693. George Lyddall was a son of Sir Thomas Lyddall and Bridget, his wife. In 1679 he had command of a fort on the Mattapony river, and died in New Kent January 19, 1705.

Lyde, Cornelius, son of Lionel Lyde, who was "an eminent merchant in Bristol," lived in King William county, which he served as major of the militia and representative in the house of burgesses in 1736-1738. He died the latter year.

Lynch, Charles, emigrant, was a justice for Albemarle county in 1745, captain in 1747, burgess for Albemarle in 1748-1749. He married Sarah, daughter of Christopher Clark, Sr., and his will was proved May 10, 1753. He had issue Charles Lynch, who originated "Lynch Law" in Virginia against predatory Tories—John, the founder of Lynchburg, Christopher, Edward and Mary.

Lyne, George, burgess for King and Queen county at the last assembly 1775-1776, and a member of the conventions of 1774, 1775 and 1776. Brother of William Lyne (q. v.).

Lyne, William, was burgess from King and Queen county May 1, 1769 and 1769-1771; member of the committee of safety of King and Queen county; afterwards was a colonel in the revolution. He was son of William Lyne, who came from Bristol, England. He married his first cousin Lucy, daughter of Henry Lyne.

Mackie, Josias, son of Patrick Mackie, of St. Johnstone, county Donegal, Ireland, was an early Presbyterian minister, who came to Virginia about 1700 and died in 1716. He resided, at the time of his death, at the house of Jacob Johnson, on whose land in Princess Anne county, there was a Presbyterian church. By his will he left his Latin, Greek and Hebrew books to three non-conforming ministers on Potomac river—Mr. Henry, Mr. Hampton and Mr. Makemie.

Macklin, Frederick, was son of Colonel John Macklin, and grandson of William Macklin, who came from Scotland to Virginia about 1725. He was justice, county lieutenant, burgess for Brunswick county in 1765-1769, and member of the conventions of 1775 and 1776. He married Lucy Rollins and his will was probated in Brunswick December 26, 1808.

Macon, Gideon, who is believed to have been a Huguenot, or of Huguenot descent, was living in New Kent county as early as

1682 and was a member of the house of burgesses for that county. He died before 1703, when his widow Martha married Nathaniel West and afterwards a Mr. Bigger. His daughter Martha married Orlando Jones, and their daughter Frances Jones married Colonel John Dandridge and was the mother of Mrs. Martha Washington.

Macon, William, son of Gideon Macon, was born November 11, 1694, and was burgess for New Kent county in 1736-1740. He married Mary Hartwell September 24, 1719, and had two sons William and Henry, and six daughters Ann, Martha, Mary, Elizabeth, Sarah, Judy.

Macon, William, son of William Macon, and grandson of Gideon Macon, the emigrant, was born January 4, 1725; was burgess for Hanover county in May, 1769, and 1769-1771. He married Lucy Scott, and died before November 24, 1813, leaving issue.

Madison, James, son of Ambrose Madison, was born March 27, 1723. He resided in Orange county and was lieutenant-colonel of the militia. He died February 29, 1801. He was father of James Madison, president of the United States.

Madison, John, son of Captain John Madison, of King and Queen county, and Isabella Todd, his wife, was first clerk for Augusta county, and member of the house of burgesses in 1748, 1749, 1752, 1753, 1754. He was father of James Madison, president of William and Mary College, and of George Madison, governor of Kentucky.

Major, Edward, patented land in 1637, 450 acres in the upper county of New Norfolk (Nansemond), and in 1645, 1646, 1652 and 1653 he was a member of the house of burgesses for Nansemond. He was speaker of the house in 1652 and lieutenant-colonel of the militia in 1653. He married Susanna Aston, daughter of Lieutenant-Colonel Walter Aston, of Charles City county, and was dead in 1655.

Makemie, Francis, was born near the town of Ramelton, county Donegal, in 1658. He was student of ministry at Glasgow University in 1676; licensed to preach in 1681 and went as missionary to America. He travelled in Maryland, Virginia and Barbadoes trading as well as preaching. In 1690 he became a resident of Accomac county, where he married Naomi, eldest daughter of William Anderson (q. v.). In the spring of 1706, he formed at Philadelphia the first Presbytery ever organized in America. The next year he was arrested at Newtown, Long Island, for preaching without a license. He was released but fined heavily. In 1708 he died at his residence in Accomac, Virginia.

Mallory, Philip, came of an ancient and distinguished family in Yorkshire. He was son of Thomas Mallory, dean of Chester, was baptized April 29, 1618, and was matriculated May 28, 1634, at Corpus Christi College. B. A. from St. Mary's Hall, April 27, 1637; M. A. January 16, 1639-1640 and was rector of Norton, county Durham, from 1641 to 1644 when he was ejected by the parliamentary authorities. He is said to have gone with Prince Rupert's fleet to the West Indies. The date of Mr. Mallory's arrival in Virginia is not known but in 1656 he was appointed together with Mr. John Green to examine all ministerial candidates for parishes. In September, 1660, he officiated as a minister in York county at the celebration of the restoration of Charles II. In March, 1661, he was sent to England by the general assembly in regard to church affairs, and died in London soon after his arrival. He left all his Virginia estate to his nephew, Roger Mallory, from whom the Virginia family descends, and among his legacies was £20 to "erecting and building a college in Virginia." He married Catherine, daughter of Robert Batte, vice-master of University College, Oxford, but had no issue.

Mallory, Roger, was son of Thomas Mallory, D. D., rector of Eccleston, in county Lancaster, England, a royalist minister and brother of Rev. Philip Mallory. Roger Mallory came to Virginia before 1660, settled in New Kent county, was justice of King and Queen in 1690. His son William was ancestor of the Mallorys of Elizabeth City county. He probably had a son, Roger, ancestor of the Mallorys of Louisa county.

Mallory, Thomas, was son of Thomas Mallory, D. D., a royalist minister, brother of Rev. Philip Mallory. He settled in that part of Charles City county afterwards known as Prince George county and was ancestor of the Mallorys resident in Prince George, Brunswick, etc. He was born in 1636. (See Virginia Magazine, xii, 402).

Mann, John, merchant, emigrated to Virginia from England and died in Gloucester county January 7, 1694. He married Mary, widow of Edmund Berkeley. He left a daughter, Mary, who was wife of Colonel Matthew Page, of the council, and a daughter, Sarah, who married (first) Joseph Ring; (second) Joseph Walker, Esq.

Mansell (Mansfield), David, came to Virginia in 1619, and was one of the hired men of George Sandys, treasurer. He lived on the south side of the James river, opposite to Jamestown. Later in 1631-1632, he represented Martin's Hundred in the house of burgesses.

Marable, George, was son of George Marable of Jamestown. He resided at Jamestown, was captain of the militia and member of the house of burgesses from James City county in 1714-1718, taking a leading part. He married Mary Hartwell, daughter of Captain William Hartwell, brother of Henry Hartwell of the council of state. He had George Marable, Jr., and Henry Hartwell Marable. The former died in Charles City county in 1770, leaving issue Edward, William, Benjamin, Hartwell, George and Abraham, and daughters Amy Drinkard, Agnes Collier and Martha Major.

Marable, Matthew, represented Brunswick county in the house of burgesses from 1769 to 1775.

Marable, William, was a burgess for James City county in 1736-1740.

Marot, Jean, came to Virginia in the Huguenot emigration in 1700. He was in 1704 secretary of Colonel William Byrd at Westover, and was then twenty-seven years old. The next year he opened an ordinary in Williamsburg. He died in 1717, and by his wife Anne had issue Edith, who married Samuel Cobbs, Rachel who married Richard Booker, and Anne who married (first) James Ingles; (second) James Shields, of York county.

Marshall, John, one of Bacon's supporters in 1676. When the royal commissioners opened their office in 1677 at Swann's Point, Marshall and others lodged complaints against Sir William Berkeley which they recanted; Marshall begged pardon on his bended knees. His will was proved June 9, 1688, and mentions son Humphrey, daughter Mary, "a younger son" unnamed, and brothers Humphrey Marshall and Peter Best.

Marshall, Captain Roger, born in 1611, was in the military service of the colony, and in 1646 was in command of Fort Royall alias Rickahock Fort on the Mattapony river.

Marshall, Thomas, son of John Marshall, of Westmoreland county and Elizabeth Markham, his wife, was born in Washington parish, Westmoreland county, April 2, 1730; was a lieutenant in the French and Indian war; burgess for Fauquier county in the assemblies of 1761-1765, 1766-1769, 1769-1771, 1772-1774, 1775, and a member of the conventions of 1774, 1775, 1776; colonel of the Third Virginia Regiment in the Continental army; in 1780 surveyor-general of the lands in Kentucky appropriated to the officers and soldiers of the Virginia Continental line; removed to Kentucky and died there June 22, 1802. He married Mary Randolph Keith, and was father of Chief Justice John Marshall.

Marshall, Thomas, was burgess for Northampton county at the last session of the assembly of 1723-1726, in the place of Thomas Harmanson, who died. He was burgess in the assembly of 1727-1734, but in 1732 vacated his seat by accepting the office of sheriff.

Marshall, Captain William, came from Barbadoes to Virginia. He was burgess for Elizabeth City county in 1692 and died the same year, being murdered by some sailors at Hampton, Virginia. He married Hannah Hand and left one son, William Marshall. His widow married (second) Captain Richard Booker, of Gloucester county, and left issue by him. The name Marshall has descended in the Booker family.

Marshart, Michael, was a London merchant who settled in Virginia about 1640 and furnished the colony with supplies at different times. He had ships trading as far as Canada.

Martian (Martue), Nicholas, was a French Walloon, who obtained his denization in England before coming to Virginia; born in 1591; arrived before 1620; first burgess for the first settlement on the York river, 1632; took a leading part in 1635 at the meeting at William Warren's house, near the present Yorktown, in protesting against Sir John Harvey's tyranny. His will, dated March 1, 1656, was proved April 24, 1657, and in it he names his three daughters—Elizabeth, wife of Colonel George Reade; Mary, wife of Lieutenant-Colonel John Scasbrook, and Sarah, wife of Captain William Fuller, sometime governor of Maryland.

Martin, Colonel John, came to Virginia about 1730. In 1738 he advertised for a stolen silver pint cup with his arms engraved thereon, "a chevron between three half moons." He was a member of the house of burgesses for Caroline county, where he resided in 1738-1740 and 1752-1756, in which last year he died. He married Martha Burwell (1703-1738), and left three sons—George, John and Samuel—and four daughters, one of whom, Lucia, married (first) Henry Boyle, youngest son of the Earl of Shannon, (second) James Agar, of county Kilkenny, Ireland, Lord Clifden; another daughter, Elizabeth (born July 16, 1721), married Patrick Barclay, merchant of Louisa county Virginia; and another, Patty, married, in 1756, Edmund Sexton Perry, speaker of the Irish house of commons (1771-1785). Colonel John Martin's sons were doubtless Tories, and went to England at the time of the revolution. He had three brothers—George Martin, of Dublin, Esq., Doctor of Physic; Sparkes Martin, Esq., of Bush House, county Pembroke, England, and Henry Martin, who went to Virginia.

Martin, John, was a burgess for Lower Norfolk county in 1651.

Martin, Thomas Bryan, was the nephew of Lord Thomas Fairfax, being a son of his sister Frances. He came to Virginia in 1751 and succeeded George William Fairfax as the Lord's land agent. He was a burgess for Hampshire county in the assembly of 1756-1758, and for Frederick county in the assembly of 1758-1761; colonel of the militia. When Lord Fairfax died in 1781, "Greenway Court" was willed to Colonel Martin.

Marye, Rev. James, a native of Rouen, Normandy, France, came to England in 1726, and was ordained in the English church. He married, in London, Letitia Maria Anne Staige, sister of Rev. Theodosius Staige. He came to Virginia in 1729 and was for a short time minister of the Parish of St. James, Northam, Goochland county. In October, 1735, he became minister of St. George's Parish, Spottsylvania, and continued till his death in 1767. He was succeeded by his son, Rev. James Marye, Jr.

Marye, Peter, was a son of Rev. James Marye, a native of Rouen, France, who came in 1729, by way of England to Virginia as a minister of the Church of England. He was born February 20, 1737; studied at William and Mary College; was burgess for Spottsylvania county in May, 1769. He married, December 6, 1773, Eleanor, daughter of Colonel William and Anne (Coleman) Green, of Culpeper county.

Mason, David, son of John Mason Jr., who was one of the first justices of Sussex county (1754) and grandson of Captain John Mason, who died September 3, 1755; was burgess for Sussex county in the assemblies of 1761-1765, 1766-1768, 1769-1771, 1772-1774, 1775, and a member of the conventions of 1774, 1775 and 1776. His will was proved in Sussex, June 16, 1785, and shows that he left sons—William, John, James, Henry, David, Benjamin, Peyton and Joseph Mason—and daughters—Rebecca, wife of Timothy Rives; Elizabeth Rives, and Mary Jeffries.

Mason, Lieutenant Francis, born in 1585, came to Virginia in 1613 with his wife Anne and daughter Anne. He married (second) in 1623-1625, Alice ———. He was justice of Lower Norfolk county from 1637 to 1648; sheriff in 1646. He died in 1648, leaving a daughter Elizabeth, who married James Thelaball (a Huguenot immigrant), and sons, Lemuel and James (q. v.).

Mason, Francis, son of James Mason, was born in Surry county, Virginia, in 1647; was a justice, major of militia and burgess in 1692. He married, in 1673, Elizabeth Binns, daughter of Lieutenant-Colonel Walter Aston, of Westover, and widow of Thomas Binns. By a former marriage he had a son James.

Mason, George, immigrant, born 1630, came to Virginia about 1651, a strong royalist, settled in Stafford county; was a member of the Northern Neck committee in 1667; sheriff of Stafford, 1669; member of the house of burgesses for Stafford in 1676, and county lieutenant commanding the militia. He died in 1686.

Mason, Colonel George, son of Colonel George Mason, the immigrant, was like his father county lieutenant of Stafford and was a burgess for the county April, 1688, April, 1691, October, 1693, April, 1695, September, 1696, April and October, 1697; September, 1698; April, 1699; August, 1701, and May and June, 1702. He married three times and died in 1716. He was grandfather of George Mason, of the American revolution.

Mason, James, a son of Francis Mason, of Lower Norfolk county, was a burgess for Surry county in 1654; he died about 1670, leaving a son Francis, born in 1647, who married Elizabeth Aston, widow of Thomas Binns, and daughter of Lieutenant-Colonel Walter Aston, of Westover.

Mason, Colonel Lemuel, son of Lieutenant Francis Mason, was born in Virginia about 1628; was justice of Lower Norfolk county from 1649; sheriff, 1664 and 1668; member of the house of burgesses, 1654, 1657, 1658, 1659, 1660, 1663, 1666, 1675, 1685, 1692; colonel of the militia in 1680, and presiding justice. His will, dated June 17, 1695, was proved September 15, 1702. He married Anne, daughter of Henry Seawell, of Seawell's Point (Sewell's Point).

Mason, Thomas, burgess for Norfolk county in 1696-1697.

Massie, Thomas, son of Peter Massie, who emigrated from England and patented lands in New Kent county, Virginia, in 1698; was vestryman of St. Peter's Church, New Kent, in 1708, and burgess in the assembly of 1723-1726. He married Mary Walker, March 23, 1699, and had issue. He was father of William Massie (q. v.).

Massie, William, son of Thomas Massie (q. v.), was born in New Kent county, May 28, 1718. He was burgess for the county in 1748 and 1749, in which latter year he died. He married Martha Macon, daughter of Colonel William Macon, and after his death she married Theodorick Bland. He was father of Major Thomas Massie, of Amherst, aide to Washington.

Mathew, Thomas, was a merchant, who acquired lands in Stafford and Northumberland counties. In 1676 he represented Stafford in the house of burgesses. He removed to England at a later date and lived in the parish of St. Margaret, Westminster. He is celebrated as the author of a narrative of Bacon's rebellion, published in Force's Tracts, signed "T. M." In his will dated May 6, 1703, and recorded February 8, 1706, in the probate court of Canterbury, he refers to himself as "formerly of Cherry Point, in the parish of Bowtracy, Northumberland county., Va.," and asks to be buried by the side of his son William in the "Church of St. Dunstan's in the East." He gave all his estate in England and Virginia to his three children—John, Thomas and Anna—and in 1712 the will was presented in Northumberland county court by his "brother-in-law," Captain John Crallé. Robert Walton, in his will proved in Northumberland, July 19, 1671, mentions his sister, Frissie Mathew, and brother-in-law, Thomas Mathew, and there is a power of attorney dated January 3, 1737, and on record in Northumberland, from Thomas Mathew, of Sherbon Lane, London, gent., and Mr. John Mathew, of London, merchant, and Anna, his wife, which Thomas and Anna were the surviving children of Thomas Mathew, formerly of Cherry Point, in Virginia, to Thomas Crompton, of Maryland, to sell his lands in Virginia.

Matthews, George, son of John Matthews, who came to Virginia about 1737 and was one of the first settlers on the great tract of land granted to Benjamin Borden, was born in 1739; was first a merchant in Staunton; in 1774 a captain of a company in the battle of Point Pleasant; in June, 1775, a burgess for Augusta in the assembly; soon after appointed lieutenant-colonel of the Ninth Virginia Regiment; captured with his regiment at Germantown; exchanged in 1781 and commanded the Third Virginia Regiment under General Green in the south; removed to Georgia in 1785, where he was elected to the first congress, 1789-1791, and made governor, 1793-1796; brigadier general in the expedition for the capture of West Florida in 1811. He died in Augusta, Georgia, August 30, 1812.

Maury, James, son of Matthew Maury and Mary Anne Fontaine, was born April 8, 1718; was educated at William and Mary College; ordained a minister in 1742; then was a minister one year in King William county, and afterwards was minister of Fredericksville parish, Hanover and Louisa counties; plaintiff in the famous parson's cause, 1763; and died June 9, 1769. He married Mary Walker, daughter of James Walker, and was father of Rev. Matthew Maury, who succeeded him in the parish, and of Rev. Walker Maury (q. v.).

Maury, Matthew, was of Castle Mauran, Gascony, France, came to Virginia in 1708. He married, in 1716, Mary Anne Fontaine, sister of Revs. Francis and Peter Fontaine (q. v.). He was ancestor of the Maurys of Virginia.

Maury, Walker, son of Rev. James and Mary (Walker) Maury, was born July 21, 1752; educated at William and Mary College, 1770-1774, where in the latter year he obtained the Botetourt gold prize for classical learning; had a grammar school in Williamsburg, and in 1786 was made principal of the Norfolk Academy. He died of the yellow fever, October 11, 1788. He married Mary Grymes.

Mayo, John, son of Major William Mayo and Anne Perratt, his wife, was born in Virginia about 1737; was burgess from Cumberland county in the place of John Fleming, deceased, at the session of March 31, 1768, till the close of the assembly, 1769; then burgess for Cumberland in 1769-1771, 1772-1774, 1775-1776; member of the conventions of 1774, 1775, 1776; he was colonel of militia; died at his seat "Powhatan," in Henrico county, June 17, 1780. He married Mary Tabb, of Gloucester county and left issue.

Mayo, William, a noted surveyor, was son

of Joseph Mayo and Elizabeth Hooper, his wife, of Poulshot, county Wilts, England, and was baptized at Poulshot, November 4, 1684; he first emigrated to Barbadoes, of which he made a survey. He married here Frances Gould and went with her to Virginia in 1723; qualified in 1728 as one of the first justices for Goochland; in 1730 appointed major of militia; in 1729 one of the surveyors to run the dividing line between Virginia and North Carolina; made in 1737 a map of the Northern Neck; surveyed Richmond in 1737; in 1740 colonel of the Goochland militia. He married (second) Anne Perratt, about the year 1732. He died October 20, 1744.

McCarty, Charles, a descendant of Dennis McCarty, who came to Virginia about 1670; was a member of the convention of May, 1776. He married Winifred Tarpley, daughter of Travers Tarpley, of Richmond county, and his will, dated 1784 and proved 1788, names children—Bartholomew, Charles Travers, Fanny, Winney, Elizabeth, Tarpley, Presley and John.

McCarty, Daniel, son of Dennis McCarty, who died in Richmond county in 1694, was born in 1679; was burgess for Westmoreland county in 1705-06, 1715, 1718, 1720-1722, 1723. He was speaker of the house of burgesses in 1715 and 1718. He was a man of great estate and his massive silver table service, still preserved, bears the date of 1620, and the arms of the Earls of Clancarty. He died May 4, 1624, leaving issue, among others Daniel McCarty Jr. (q. v.).

McCarty, Daniel, Jr., son of Daniel McCarty (q. v.), was collector of Potomac river, colonel of the militia, and burgess for Westmoreland county from 1734 to 1744, when he died. He married Penelope Higgins, and had issue.

McDowell, Samuel, son of John McDowell, a surveyor for Benjamin Borden (q. v.), and grandson of Ephraim McDowell, who emigrated from Ireland to Pennsylvania and thence to Virginia about 1735. He was burgess for Augusta county, 1772-1774, 1775-1776, and member of the conventions of 1774, 1775 and 1776. He was father of the celebrated surgeon, Ephraim McDowell, who married a daughter of General Evan Shelby.

McKenzie, Dr. Kenneth, born in Scotland, resided in Williamsburg; married Joanna Tyler, daughter of John Tyler, of James City county. His will was proved March 17, 1755. Portraits of Dr. McKenzie and his wife are still extant.

Mead, William, born in Bucks county, Pennsylvania, October 10, 1727, moved to Loudoun county, Virginia, in 1746, and thence to Bedford county, about 1754. He was one of the incorporators of New London, Bedford county; sheriff of the county, justice of the peace and deputy surveyor under Richard Stith. He served as lieutenant of militia in the French and Indian war, and as ensign in the American revolution. He married (first) Anne Haile, (second) Martha Cowles.

Meade, Andrew, was the son of David Meade (q. v.), of Nansemond county. He married Susanna, daughter of Buckner Stith, of Brunswick county. He represented Nansemond county in the conventions of July 17, 1775, and December 1, 1775.

Meade, David, was the son of Andrew Meade (born in the county of Kerry, Ireland) and Mary Latham, his wife. David Meade, in 1729 or 1730, married Susanna, daughter of Sir Richard Everard, governor of North Carolina, and Susannah Kidder, his wife, eldest daughter of Dr. Richard Kidder, bishop of Bath and Wells. He resided in Nansemond county, and died there in 1757, in his forty-seventh year.

Meade, David, son of David Meade and Susanna Everard, his wife, was born July 29, 1744. He was a burgess for Nansemond county in 1769, but in 1774 removed to "Maycox," on James River in Prince George county. In 1796 he removed to Jessamine county, Kentucky, where at a very old age he died at his beautiful residence "Chaumière des Prairies." He married Sarah Waters, daughter of William Waters, of Williamsburg, and left issue.

Meade, Richard Kidder, son of David Meade (q. v.) and Susanna Everard, his wife, was born in 1750, in Nansemond county. During the American revolution he was first captain of a company in the Second Virginia Regiment commanded by Colonel William Woodford, and afterwards was aide-de-camp to General Washington. He married (first) Jane Randolph, aunt of John Randolph, of Roanoke, and (second) Mary Grymes, daughter of Benjamin Grymes. He was father of Bishop William Meade.

Meares, Thomas, patented 300 acres in the Upper county of New Norfolk in 1637; was burgess for Lower Norfolk in February, 1645, October, 1646, and November, 1647. He was a Puritan and removed to Maryland in 1649, and in 1654 was a resident at Providence or Annapolis. He was born in 1602.

Melling, William, came from England to Virginia before 1636, when he obtained a grant for 100 acres in Accomac. He was a member of the house of burgesses from Northampton, July, 1653, and March, 1657-58. There is a notice June 28, 1661, in the Northampton records of "William Mellings, late of Virginia, now resident in London, gentleman."

Mercer, George, eldest son of John Mercer, of "Marlborough," was born June 23, 1733, was educated at William and Mary College; was lieutenant and captain in Washington's First Virginia Regiment in the French and Indian war, and later lieutenant-colonel of Colonel Byrd's Second Virginia Regiment; aide-de-camp to Washington, and was wounded at Fort Necessity, July 3, 1754. In 1761-63 he was burgess for Frederick county, and in 1763 went to England as agent for the Ohio Company. While there he was appointed stamp distributor and was given charge of the stamps for Maryland and Virginia. When he reached Virginia and learned of the feeling among the people, he resigned his office and, entrusting the stamps to Captain Sterling, commander of his majesty's ship, *Rainbow*, he returned to England. He married, on August 18, 1767, at Scarboro, England, Mary Neville, daughter of Christopher Neville, of Lincoln. He was later appointed lieutenant-governor of North Carolina, but he did not ever act as governor. He died in London, April, 1784.

Mercer, James, younger brother of John

Mercer, of "Marlborough," was born February 19, 1716; was a resident of Virginia before 1745. He was captain in the Carthagena expedition in 1740. He returned to Virginia in 1755 as captain of the Eighteenth Regiment of Foot, commanded by Colonel Dunbar, in the expedition against Fort Duquesne, and continued in the military service till his death, when he had attained the rank of lieutenant-colonel. He died unmarried at Albany, New York, September 27, 1757.

Mercer, John, of "Marlborough," an eminent lawyer, was son of John Mercer, of Dublin, Ireland, and his wife, Grace Fenton, and grandson of Robert Mercer and his wife, Elinor Reynolds, and great-grandson of Noel Mercer, of Chester, England, and his wife, Ann Smith; born in Dublin, February 6, 1740, and emigrated to Virginia in 1720, at the age of sixteen. He studied law, and entered on the practice in 1728. He acquired large landed possessions in Virginia and Ireland, and improved his great natural abilities by extensive study in polite literature. He left a library of 1500 volumes, one-third of which were law books. He was secretary of the Ohio Company and vestryman of Acquia church. He was the author of an "Abridgement of the Laws of Virginia," published at Williamsburg in 1737, with a continuation in 1739, no copy of which last is known; and of a second edition published in Glasgow, Scotland, in 1759. He was also the author of a tract against the Stamp Act, said to be the first published in Virginia. He married (first) Catherine Mason, aunt of George Mason, the statesman of the revolution; married (second) Anne Roy, of Essex county. He died at his seat, "Marlborough," in Stafford county, Virginia, October 14, 1768.

Mercer, John Fenton, son of John Mercer, of "Marlborough," was ensign in 1754 in Fry's regiment in the French and Indian war, lieutenant in Robert Stewart's company on the Fort Duquesne expedition, and captain in Washington's regiment; was killed in action and scalped by the Indians, April 18, 1756, at Edwards' Fort, on the Warm Springs mountains, while in command of a scouting party of 100 men.

Meredith, Samuel, son of Samuel Meredith (died April 14, 1762), was born in Hanover county in 1732; captain of a company in the French and Indian war, 1758; captain of an independent company of Hanover in 1775; burgess for Hanover county in 1766-1769, and member of the convention of December, 1775 appointed colonel of the first battalion of minute men in May, 1776; moved from Hanover to Amherst county about 1780; was lieutenant-colonel of the Amherst militia, justice of the peace and sheriff. He died December 22, 1808. His second wife was Jane Henry, a sister of Patrick Henry.

Meriwether, Francis, son of Nicholas Meriwether, a native of Wales, was a large landholder in Essex county; clerk of Essex county from 1692 to 1702; senior justice of Essex in 1711; and burgess for the county in 1705-1706. He married Mary Bathurst, daughter of Lancelot Bathurst, and died in 1712 or 1713.

Meriwether, Nicholas, son of Nicholas Meriwether, of Wales, was born October 26, 1667; resided first in James City county, then in New Kent, and latterly in Hanover.

He was a justice, coroner, sheriff and lieutenant-colonel; burgess for New Kent in the assemblies of 1705-1706, 1710-1712, 1712-1714, 1715, 1718, 1720-1722; burgess for Hanover, 1723-1726 and 1727-1734. He was a large landowner in New Kent, Hanover and Albemarle counties. He married Elizabeth Crafford, and his will was proved in Goochland county, November 20, 1744.

Meriwether, Nicholas, a native of Wales, born in 1631; was clerk of Surry county, Virginia, in 1655, and in 1656 purchased from Nathaniel Bacon the "Island house," on Jamestown Island; appointed justice of Surry county in 1672 and died December 19, 1678. He was a large patentee of land and founder of an influential Virginia family.

Meriwether, William, son of Colonel Nicholas Meriwether, of Hanover county, was a burgess in 1734-1740. He married Elizabeth, daughter of John Bushrod, of Westmoreland county and had issue.

Metcalfe, Richard, son of Gilbert Metcalfe, merchant of London, descended from an ancient family in Yorkshire; settled in Richmond county, Virginia. He died before 1712, leaving Gilbert Metcalfe and other children.

Metcalfe, Thomas, son of Samuel Metcalfe, grocer of Northwich, Cheshire, Englanl, was born August 10, 1734. He came to Virginia in 1751 with his uncle, John Metcalfe, and settled in King William county. He married, in 1756, Elizabeth, eldest daughter of Dr. John Strachey, formerly of Sutton Court, England, but then of King and Queen county, Virginia. Left issue.

Meux, John, immigrant, resided in New Kent county, Virginia. He died March 19, 1727, and his wife, Elizabeth, died August 7, 1713. They left issue—John, Ann, Richard.

Milner, Francis, son of Colonel Thomas Milner, was a burgess for Nansemond county in 1699. His daughter Anne married Major Thomas Cary.

Milner, George, an officer under Bacon, who made terms for his life at the surrender of West Point, January 16, 1677.

Milner, Thomas, lived in Nansemond county in 1675; was clerk of the house of burgesses, 1681-84; burgess in 1688 and 1691-93, and speaker during 1692 and 1693. He was lieutenant-colonel of the militia of Nansemond in 1680. His daughter Mary married Colonel Miles Cary, of "Rich Neck," Warwick county, and died October 27, 1700. He used the same coat-of-arms as the Milners of Yorkshire and Lincolnshire, England. He died in 1694.

Milner, Thomas, son of Colonel Thomas Milner, was a burgess for Nansemond county in 1698, 1699, 1700-1702. It was doubtless his son Thomas, third of the name in Virginia, that married, in 1719-20, Mary Selden, daughter of Samuel Selden and Rebecca, his wife, of Elizabeth City county. They had a son, Samuel Milner, who died without issue in 1788.

Minge, James, was the first of the family of Minge in Virginia. He lived in Charles City county, Virginia; was well educated, and in 1671 is called a surveyor. He took sides with National Bacon, Jr., and was clerk of the house of burgesses which assembled in June, 1676 under Bacon's authority. He was also clerk of the assembly called by General Ingram, shortly after Bacon's death, in October, 1676. He was very useful to Bacon in drawing up his laws and papers.

Minor Doodes, was a Dutch ship captain who came to Virginia about 1650, and settled first in Nansemond county. In 1665 he was living in Lancaster county. In 1673 the general assembly naturalized Minor Doodes and his son Doodes Minor. His will, dated December 13, 1677, was proved in Lancaster county. It is sealed with the wax impression of a ship. He was ancestor of the Minor family of Spottsylvania county.

Miller (Müller), Adam, was a native of "Shresoin," Germany, and was the first settler, or one of the first settlers, in the valley of Virginia. In 1726 or 1727 he located land at Massanutting, on the Shenandoah river. This tract, now in the southwestern part of Page county, near the Rockingham line, he sold; and in 1741 settled near Elkton, at Bear Lithia Springs. He served in the French and Indian war, and died about the close of the revolution. In religion he was a Lutheran.

Mitchell, John, was an eminent physician and botanist. He was born in London, and his Virginia home was at Urbanna, Middlesex county. He was a fellow of the Royal Society and gave to Linnaeus much valuable information on American flora. Among his researches in this science are "Dissertio brevis de Principio Botanicorum et Zoologorum," dedicated to Sir Hans Sloane, and dated Virginia, 1738, and "Nova Plantarum Genera," dedicated to Peter Collinson (1741). They were published at Nuremberg, 1769. He contributed several articles to the "Philosophical Transactions." He wrote an article on the "Yellow Fever in Virginia in 1737-42," which was published by Benjamin Rush in the "American Medical and Philosophical Register" (1755). He is also credited with "A Map of the British and French Dominions in North America," London, 1755; "The Contest in America between Great Britain and France" (anonymous about 1757), and "The Present State of Great Britain and North America." Linnaeus bestowed Mitchell's name on the "Mitchella Repens." He died in London in March, 1768.

Mitchell, Richard, was burgess for Lancaster county in the assemblies of 1761-1765, October, 1765, 1766-1768, 1769-1771, 1772-1774. He was son of Robert Mitchell (q. v.). He was living in 1789.

Mitchell, Robert, was burgess for Lancaster county in the assembly of 1742-1747; living in 1755; father of Richard Mitchell (q. v.).

Mitchell (Michell), William, came to Northampton county from Maryland, where he had in 1650 served as councillor; was burgess for Northampton in 1658; captain, etc. He appears to have been an early example of an atheist (see Neill, "Virginia Carolorum").

Molesworth, Colonel Guy, was son of Anthony Molesworth, Esq., of Fotherington, in county Northampton, England. During the civil wars (1642-1649) he was colonel of a regiment of horse and received twenty-five wounds battling for the King. In 1650 he was banished to Barbadoes, and afterwards came to Virginia. In 1660 he aided

Berkeley in drawing an address to Charles II. for pardon, and soon thereafter returned to England. His nephew, Robert Molesworth, was created Viscount Molesworth in 1716.

Monroe, Andrew, uncle of President James Monroe, represented Westmoreland county in the house of burgesses from 1742-1746.

Monroe, Andrew, ancestor of President Monroe, was an early resident of Maryland, where he commanded a pinnace in the service of Cuthbert Fenwick, general agent of Lord Baltimore. He was a Protestant, and when Richard Ingle declared for parliament in 1645, Monroe took sides against Lord Baltimore's government and eventually settled like other refugee Marylanders at Mattox Creek, in Westmoreland county, under the Virginia authority. He died there in 1668.

Monroe, Andrew, grandfather of President James Monroe, was a burgess for Westmoreland county in 1742-1747.

Montague, James, son of William Montague, a descendant of Peter Montague (q. v.), was born in Middlesex county, February 18, 1741. He was one of the magistrates of the county and a burgess in the assemblies of 1772-1774 and 1775. He was a captain of militia. He married Mary Eliza Chinn, daughter of Joseph Chinn, and died in 1781 or 1782, leaving issue.

Montague, Peter, was born in 1600, and was the son of Peter and Eleanor Montague, of Boveny parish, Burnham, Buckinghamshire, England. He came to Virginia in 1621 and was employed by Captain Samuel Mathews on his plantation on James river. He afterwards removed to Upper Norfolk (Nansemond) county, which he represented in the house of burgesses in 1652 and 1653. About 1654 he removed to Lancaster county, then including Middlesex, and represented that county from 1651 to 1658. He was a large landholder and leading citizen. His will was recorded in Lancaster, May 27, 1659. He has numerous descendants in Virginia.

Moody, Sir Henry, baronet, was son of Sir Henry Moody, baronet, of Garsden, Wiltshire, and Deborah Dunche, his wife. After her husband's death, in 1632, Lady Deborah, with her young son, sailed for America, and after living at Lynn, Massachusetts, from 1639 to 1643 sought religious freedom among the Dutch at Gravesend, Long Island. Her son, Sir Henry, served in the army of King Charles I., and in 1650, after due submission to the parliamentary authorities, he sailed to Long Island in order to join his mother. Later he came to Virginia, and in 1660 was sent by the assembly to New York to make a treaty with the Dutch, but Governor Berkeley would not confirm the articles. He returned to Virginia and died at the house of Colonel Francis Moryson, at Elizabeth City, about 1662.

Moon, Captain John, born at Berry, near Gosport, in the parish of Stoke, Hampshire, England. He represented Isle of Wight county in the house of burgesses in 1639, 1652, 1654, and perhaps other years. His will was recorded August 12, 1655, in Isle of Wight county, and mentions a wife Prudence and three daughters, Sarah, Susanna and Mary Moon.

Moore, Augustine, came from England to Virginia about 1705, and acquired a great fortune in the tobacco trade. He was born about 1685 and died July 28, 1743. He erected a large brick building on his plantation in King William county, which he called "Chelsea," after the more famous seat of his ancestors in England. He was a descendant of Sir Thomas Moore. He married twice, (first) Mary Gage, (second) Elizabeth Todd, daughter of Thomas Todd and Elizabeth Bernard, his wife, daughter of Colonel William Bernard, of the council.

Moore, Augustine, was son of Bernard Moore (q. v.) and was burgess from King William county, succeeding his father in the assemblies of 1772-1774 and 1775-1776. He married Sarah Rind, and left issue.

Moore, Bernard, was son of Colonel Augustine Moore, of "Chelsea," King William county, and Elizabeth Todd, his wife. He was a justice and colonel of the militia in King William county, and was burgess for the county from 1744 to 1758 and from 1761 to 1772. He married Anna Katherine Spotswood, daughter of Governor Alexander Spotswood, and was father of Augustine Moore (q. v.).

Morgan, Francis, was a justice of York county in 1648; captain of militia, and burgess for York in 1647, 1652 and 1653. He died in 1657, leaving one son Francis, who was heir to his large estate. This last left two daughters, co-heiresses, living in 1698 —Sarah, wife of Thomas Buckner, and Anne, wife of Dr. David Alexander.

Morgan, Morgan, a Welshman, removed from Pennsylvania to Virginia; settled within the present boundaries of Berkeley county, West Virginia, and erected, about 1726 or 1727, at the site of the village of Bunker Hill, within the present county of Berkeley, West Virginia, what is said to have been, and probably was, the first cabin on the Virginia side of the Potomac, between the Blue Ridge and North mountains. He died in 1779.

Morlatt (Morlet), Thomas, was a burgess in 1624 and signed "The Tragicall Relation."

Morley, William, was a burgess for James City county in 1660.

Moryson, Colonel Charles, son of Major Richard Moryson, succeeded his uncle, Major Francis Moryson, as captain of the fort at Point Comfort. In 1680 he was colonel of the militia of Elizabeth City county and presiding justice. He died about 1692 at Plymouth, in England, when about to return to Virginia. His widow, Rebecca, who had previously been the widow of Leonard Leo, married (third) Colonel John Lear.

Moryson, Lieutenant Robert, son of Sir Richard Moryson, of Leicestershire, lieutenant-general of the ordnance, was lieutenant of the fort at Point Comfort in 1641, in the absence of his brother, Captain Richard Moryson. In York county the court permitted his widow, Jane, to qualify as an administratrix on his estate October 25, 1647.

Moseley, Arthur, son of William Moseley, an English merchant of Rotterdam, Holland, who came to Virginia in 1649 and received grants of land in Lower Norfolk county, was burgess in 1676, and one of the justices of his county. He died in 1705.

Moseley, Edward Hack, son of Hillary

and Hannah (Hack) Moseley, was a burgess for Princess Anne county in 1752, 1753, 1754, 1755; 1755, surveyor and searcher of Elizabeth and Nansemond rivers; burgess for Princess Anne from 1762 to 1769. He was also sheriff and colonel of the county; a Loyalist in the revolution and friend of Benedict Arnold. He married Mary Bassett, daughter of Colonel William Bassett, of "Eltham," New Kent county, who died in her thirty-eighth year, August 23, 1755, and is buried at "Greenwich," Princess Anne county, one of the Moseley seats. He married (second) Frances Wylie, who survived him. His will was dated May 24, 1782, and was proved April 10, 1783. He left a son Edward Hack Moseley, Jr. His residence in Princess Anne was called "Rolleston."

Moseley, Edward, son of William Moseley and Mary Gookin, his wife, daughter of Captain John and Sarah Gookin, was born in 1661, and was county lieutenant of Princess Anne county, justice of the peace and high sheriff, and burgess in 1700-1702, 1703-1705, 1706. He died in 1736. He married several times, his first wife being Frances, daughter of Colonel John Stringer, of Northampton county. His father, William Moseley, was second son of William Moseley, merchant of Rotterdam.

Moseley, Edward Hack, Jr., son of Colonel Edward Hacke Moseley and Mary Bassett, his wife, was burgess for Princess Anne county from 1769 to 1775. He was born in 1743, and died February 4, 1814. He married Martha Westwood.

Moseley, William, lived in Essex county, was burgess for that county in 1695. His will, proved April 10, 1700, names sons, William and John, daughter Martha, and three brothers, Edward, Robert and Benjamin Moseley.

Mossom, Rev. David, son of Thomas Mossom, chandler, was born at Greenwich, Kent, England, March 25, 1690, schooled at Lewisham, admitted sizar at St. John's College, Cambridge, June 5, 1705. He became rector of St. Peter's Church, New Kent county, Virginia, in 1727, and continued forty years. On January 6, 1759, he performed the marriage of George Washington to Martha Custis, widow of Colonel Daniel Parke Custis, and daughter of Colonel John Landridge. He died January 4, 1767, leaving issue.

Mottrom, John, resided in 1644 at York, in York county, Virginia. He was a successful merchant and shipper. About 1645 he removed to Chicacone—the first settlement on the Virginia side of the Potomac river—where his house became a resort for Protestants who fled from Maryland. When Northumberland county was formed in 1645, he represented it in the house of burgesses. He was burgess again in 1652, and was justice of the peace and colonel of the militia. He had issue, among others Major John Mottrom (q. v.).

Mottrom, John, son of Colonel John Mottrom, was a justice of Northumberland county court, and a major in the county militia. In 1675 he was a burgess. He left issue, Captain Spencer Mottrom.

Moyses, Theodore, was living in Virginia in 1625. Burgess for Archer's Hope in James City corporation in 1629.

Munford, Robert, son of James Munford,

who in 1689 patented lands in Prince George county. He was a vestryman of Bristol parish, Prince George county; a member of the house of burgesses, 1720-1722; justice of the county court, and colonel in the militia. He married, in 1701, Martha Kennon, daughter of Colonel Richard Kennon, of "Conjuror's Neck," Henrico (now Chesterfield county). He died about 1735, leaving issue: 1. Major James Munford. 2. Colonel Robert Munford (q. v.). 3. Edward.

Munford, Robert, son of Colonel Robert Munford and Martha Kennon, his wife, was a member of the house of burgesses for Prince George county in 1736-1740. He married Anna Bland and died in 1744, leaving children, Robert, Theodorick and Elizabeth. His widow married (second) George Currie, by whom she had two daughters.

Munford, Robert, son of Robert Munford and his wife, Anna Bland, was educated at Wakefield, England. He was in the French and Indian war under Colonel William Byrd, last of that name. When Brunswick county was formed in 1765 he was made county lieutenant and was one of the first two members of the house of burgesses. He was burgess from 1765 to 1775. During the American revolution he saw much service of different kinds. He was a scholar, and in 1798 published a volume of prose and poetry. He married Elizabeth, daughter of William Beverley, of Essex, his cousin, and had issue.

Nantaquas, brother of Pocahontas, whom John Smith compliments as "the manliest, comeliest, boldest spirit I ever saw in a savage."

Nash, Abner, son of Colonel John Nash, was burgess for Prince Edward county in the assemblies of 1761-1765; he moved to North Carolina, where he was elected first speaker of the senate, second governor of North Carolina, member of the assembly and member of the continental congress (1782-1786). His brother, General Francis Nash fell in the battle of Germantown.

Nash, John, was a burgess for Prince Edward county in the assemblies of 1752-1755 and 1756-1758; one of the first justices of Prince Edward county (1754); colonel of the militia. He died in 1776 and names in his will sons, John, Abner and Francis; daughters, Anne Haskins, Lucy Le Grand, Mary Read and Betty Read, and grandson, Nash Le Grand.

Nash, John, Jr., son of Colonel John Nash, was member of the convention of March 20, 1775. He married, in 1768, Anna Tabb, daughter of Thomas Tabb, of Lunenburg.

Nash, Thomas, a burgess for Lunenburg county in 1756-1758.

Neale, Christopher, son of Christopher Neale and Hannah Rodham, his wife, daughter of Matthew Rodham, was born June 23, 1671, and was burgess for Northumberland county in 1705-1706 and 1710-1712. He died in 1721.

Neale, John, merchant, leased fifty acres at Strawberry Banks, in Elizabeth City, in 1632, removed to Accomac, and did a large business between 1632 and 1639; vestryman, 1636; sheriff, 1636, and burgess for Accomac in 1639, and was justice the same year. His daughter, Henrietta Maria, married the second Richard Bennett.

Neale, Richard, son of Christopher Neale and Hannah Rodham, his wife, was born August 28, 1682; was burgess for Northumberland county in 1712-1714.

Necottowance, chief of the Pamunkey Indians and the last who held authority over the Powhatan confederacy. He made a treaty of peace with the English in 1646, in which he consented to many restrictions of his power.

Needler, Benjamin, son of Culverwell Needler, clerk assistant of the house of commons, and grandson of Rev. Benjamin Needler, a non-conformist minister, was bred to the bar in England. He came to Virginia and became distinguished as a lawyer. He was vestryman of Stratton Major parish, King and Queen county; clerk of the council, 1739, and died before 1741. He married Alice, daughter of Gawin Corbin, of Virginia, and had at least one daughter, who married Rev. William Robinson, commissary to the bishop of London ("Virginia Magazine," xiv, 26).

Nelson, Captain Francis, probably third son of Thomas Nelson, of Cheddleworth, Berkshire, England. He commanded the Phoenix, which brought a part of the First Supply, but did not arrive till April 20, 1608. He made several voyages to Virginia and in 1612 sailed with Captain Thomas Button to Hudson's Bay, and died there in the winter of 1612-13, at "Port Nelson," named for him.

Nelson, Thomas, an eminent merchant of Yorktown, son of Hugh Nelson, of Penrith, county Cumberland, England, was born February 20, 1677, and came to Virginia about 1700, where he amassed a large fortune. He married (first) Margaret Reade, daughter of Robert Reade, eldest son of Colonel George Reade, secretary of state, and (second) Mrs. Frances Tucker (née Courtenay). He was father of William Nelson, president of the Virginia council.

Nemattenow, or "Jack-o'-the-Feather," an influential chief and a great favorite with Opechancanough. He killed a white man and was killed in turn by the white man's friend. It is believed that his death was the immediate cause of the Indian massacre of 1622.

Neville, Joseph, a burgess for Hampshire county from 1773 to 1776, and a member of the conventions of December 1, 1775, and May 6, 1776, which last declared independence.

Newman, Alexander, burgess for Richmond county in 1696-1697.

Newton, George, was born 1678, and went to school in Lancaster, England. He was son of George Newton, one of the justices of Lower Norfolk county, Virginia, as early as 1645. He was a burgess for Norfolk county at the assembly of 1723-26. He married Apphia Wilson, daughter of Colonel James Wilson, and left issue—Thomas Newton, who was father of Thomas Newton, burgess (q. v.).

Newton, John, eldest son of Thomas Newton, of Hull, Yorkshire, was a ship captain, and settled in Westmoreland county about 1670. He married Rose Tucker, daughter of John Tucker, of that county, and died in 1695-1697. He was founder of a distinguished family in that section of Virginia.

Newton, Thomas, son of Thomas Newton

and Amey Hutchings, daughter of John Hutchings, of Norfolk, was burgess for Norfolk county from 1765 to 1775, and member of the conventions of 1775 and 1776. He married Martha Tucker, daughter of Colonel Robert Tucker, of Norfolk, and was father of Colonel Thomas Newton, member of Congress from 1801 to 1831.

Nicholas, Major Abraham, was appointed adjutant-general of the militia of the colony in 1733 and was mayor of Williamsburg in 1736. He died in September, 1738. He was father of Abraham Nicholas Jr., attorney-at-law, who died December 18, 1751.

Nicholas, Dr. George, an eminent physician, had a grant for land in Virginia in 1729. He married Elizabeth Carter, daughter of Colonel Robert Carter, of "Corotoman," and widow of Nathaniel Burwell, of "Carter's Creek," Gloucester county. He was father of Robert Carter Nicholas, the distinguished treasurer of Virginia at the time of the revolution.

Nicholas, John, son of Dr. George Nicholas and Elizabeth Carter, his wife, served as clerk for Albemarle county from 1749 to 1815; as burgess from 1756 to 1768; and as member of conventions of 1774 and 1775 for Buckingham county. He married Martha, daughter of Colonel Joshua Fry.

Nimmo, James, came to Virginia from Linlithgow county, Scotland, about 1720, and settled in Princess Anne county, where he married Mary, daughter of Jacob Johnson. For several years he taught school, but in 1728 he was appointed King's attorney and continued in that office till November 10, 1752. He also acted as surveyor of the county. He died in 1753, leaving issue.

Nimmo, William, came from Linlithgow county, Scotland, to Virginia, where he qualified as an attorney-at-law in the general court in 1743. He had a large practice. His will was proved in the general court September 12, 1748. He was nephew of James Nimmo, of Princess Anne county, Virginia (q. v.).

Norsworthy, Tristram, patented 150 acres in 1643 in Isle of Wight county. He was burgess for Upper Norfolk county (Nansemond) in January, 1639-40. In 1656 he is referred to as "Lt. Col. Tristram Norsworthy of ye Ragged Islands, gent." In 1654 he was one of the justices of Nansemond. In 1699 George Norsworthy, eldest son of Major George Norsworthy, which last was eldest son of Tristram Norsworthy above named, was appointed by the council lieutenant-colonel and commander-in-chief of Nansemond county.

Norton, John, a merchant of London, came to Virginia and settled at Yorktown; burgess for York county in 1752-1755. He married Courtenay Walker, daughter of Jacob Walker, of Elizabeth City county, and had issue—Frances, who married her first cousin, John Baylor, and John Hatley, George and Daniel Norton, who all came from London and settled in Virginia.

Norton, Captain William, contracted with some private merchants in London to come to Virginia in 1621 to conduct the glass factory near Jamestown. Norton took four Italians and two servants with him, and made all manner of glass, especially glass beads for trade with the Indians. He died in 1623, and George Sandys succeeded him in charge of the glass works.

Norvell, William, a descendant of Hugh Norvell, an early immigrant, was burgess at the last assembly under the royal government, 1775-1776, and member of the conventions of 1775 and 1776. He died in 1802, leaving his property to his great-nephews and nieces, children of William Lightfoot, of James City county.

Norwood, Captain Charles, was a near kinsman, perhaps a brother, of Colonel Henry Norwood, and served in the army of King Charles I. From 1654 to 1657 he was clerk of the general assembly of Virginia. He was afterwards a captain under Colonel Henry Norwood at Tangier in 1667.

Norwood, Colonel Henry, was an officer in the royal army during the civil wars; emigrated to Virginia in 1649, and afterwards wrote an account of his voyage; was sent by Governor William Berkeley to King Charles II. in 1650, and in 1653 went to England, where he was arrested and confined for several years in the Tower of London; at the restoration was made treasurer of Virginia and captain of Sundown Castle, lieutenant-colonel of Lord Rutherford's regiment, and lieutenant-governor of Tangier. He was living as late as 1682.

Nottingham, Benjamin, was a burgess for Northampton county, 1703-1705 and 1710-1712. He left issue, and the family is still prominent on the "Eastern Shore."

Ogle, Cuthbert, a musician, residing in Williamsburg. He died in 1735, leaving an interesting collection of songs and other musical literature.

Oldis, Thomas, settled in Elizabeth City county and was burgess in January, 1640. His grandson Thomas was living in Elizabeth City in 1691. William Oldis, merchant, and his wife Jane, were living in Isle of Wight county in 1665. William Oldis had a brother Valentine, an apothecary of London.

Opechancanough, chief of the Pamunkey Indians; he planned the massacres of 1622 and 1644. He was captured by Sir William Berkeley and was killed while a captive at Jamestown in 1646 by a soldier out of revenge. He was also known as Apachisco. He was able, resourceful and unforgiving.

Opitchapam, brother of Powhatan, who was succeeded by him in 1618 as chief of the Powhatan confederacy. He was also known as Taughaiten, Itopatin, Istan, Sassapen, etc. He was succeeded by Opechanough.

Opie, Thomas, was a ship captain from Bristol, England. He married, about 1672, Helen Lindsay, daughter of Rev. David Lindsay, of Northumberland county, who was son of Sir Hierome Lindsay, of Scotland. He died in 1702, leaving issue in Virginia.

Opussoquionuske, Queen of the Appomattox Indians. In 1610 she surprised some of the members of the company sent by Lord Delaware to find gold mines and killed fourteen of them at a feast. Captain Yardley then landed and burnt her town. When Dale founded Bermuda Hundred in 1613, he drove the Indians away entirely.

Osborne, Edward, Jr., was a son of Edward Osborne, of Chesterfield county. He was a justice in 1749 and member of the house of burgesses in 1769 and 1770.

Osborne, Jenkin, was born in 1600, came to Virginia in 1617, and was living at Shirley Hundred in 1624. In 1635 he patented 400 acres in Charles City county on the south side of James river, between the lands of Captain John Woodlief and William Bailey.

Osborne, Richard, was a delegate to the house of burgesses for Fairfax county in 1748-1749.

Osborne, Captain Thomas, came to Virginia in November, 1616, and settled at Coxendale, in the present Chesterfield county, about 1625. He also patented land on Proctor's creek, Henrico county (now Chesterfield); was a commissioner (justice) for the "upper parts" in 1631, and member of the house of burgesses, 1629, 1629-30, 1631-32, 1632-33.

Osborn, Thomas, was born in Chesterfield county, and removed to Prince William county, of which he was a burgess in 1736. He died before 1750, leaving a daughter Anne, who married John Randolph, and a daughter Mary, who married William Henley, of Henrico.

Owen, Goronwy (Gronow), son of Owen Goronwy, was born at Llanfair, Mathafarn Eithaf, in the shire of Anglesea, Wales. He attended the grammar school at Bangor, and was afterwards at Jesus College, Oxford, from 1741 to 1745. After this time he was curate of several parishes in Wales and England and taught school. In 1757 he was appointed master of the grammar school of the College of William and Mary, and came to Virginia. He held this place till about September, 1760, when he was compelled to resign because of his drinking habits. He was soon after appointed minister of St. Andrew's Parish, Brunswick county. He died in 1770. Mr. Owen was not only celebrated for his classical attainments, but also for his poetic genius, which ranks him as the greatest poet of Wales. He married three times (first) Ellen Hughes, (second) Anne Dawson, widow of James Clayton, (third) Joan Simmons. He has descendants living in Alabama and Louisiana. His most famous poems are "The Last Day of Judgment" and an "Elegy" on his friend Lewis Morris.

Ousley, Captain Thomas, was burgess for Stafford county in 1692-93.

Pace, Richard, came to Virginia before 1620, when he received a grant for 400 acres on the south side of James river, four miles above Jamestown, which grant he called "Pace's Paines." In 1622 he saved Jamestown and other settlements by informing the authorities of the impending massacre which had been revealed to him by one of his servants, a converted Indian named Chanco. His widow, Isabella, married (second) Captain William Perry, of the council. His son and heir, George Pace, married Sarah, daughter of Captain Samuel Maycox.

Page, Francis, eldest son of Colonel John Page, of the Middle Plantation, was first clerk of the house of burgesses commissioned by the governor, which he held till his death. He died May 10, 1692, aged thirty-five. He married Mary Digges, daughter of Governor Edward Digges, and had an only daughter Elizabeth, who married her cousin, John Page.

Pagett, Anthony, came in 1623 as a servant; burgess for Flowerdieu Hundred in 1629.

Palmer, John, was a clerk in the office of the attorney-general, and in 1740 was admitted as an attorney to practice in the county courts. He was bursar of the College of William and Mary and died in 1759. He married Elizabeth Low Tyler, daughter of John Tyler, and left daughters.

Palmer, Thomas, came to Virginia with his wife and daughter in 1621, burgess for Shirley Hundred Island in Charles City corporation in 1629.

Panton (Penton), Anthony, first rector of the first settlements on York river—Chiskiack and York; he came to Virginia about 1630, and after several years incurred the displeasure of Governor Harvey and Richard Kemp, his secretary of state, and on October 8, 1638, he was heavily fined and banished from the colony, on pain of death if he returned. He appealed his cause to the King, who upon the recall of Harvey referred the complaint to his successor, Sir Francis Wyatt and his council. They suspended Harvey's order and required that Panton should be indemnified for his losses out of Harvey's estate which was done. His York plantation and his lots at Jamestown were sold to reimburse Panton and his other creditors.

Paradise, John, was son of Peter Paradise, of Greek extraction, who in 1753 was English consul at Salonica, where John Paradise was born. He was educated at the University of Padua, but resided the greater part of his life in London, where he was an intimate of Dr. Samuel Johnson. He married Lucy Ludwell, youngest daughter of Hon. Philip Ludwell, of "Greenspring," Virginia, removed to Virginia but about 1788 returned to London and died there December 12, 1795. A table at which Dr. Johnson and other members of the Essex Street Club played, and formerly the property of Paradise, is still preserved in Williamsburg. His daughter Lucy, born in England about 1770 married in 1787 Count Barziza, a Venetian subject, and one of their sons came to Virginia and made Williamsburg his home.

Farahunt, a son of Powhatan, sometimes called "Tanx Powhatan," the little Powhatan. He was chief of the Indians at the falls of James river in 1607.

Parker, George, of Accomac was son of Thomas Parker, 1633-1685, of Isle of Wight county. He was sheriff of Accomac, for many years justice of the peace and major of the militia. He bought lands in Accomac county called "Poplar Grove." He died in 1674, leaving a son, Major George Parker, who married Anne Scarborough.

Parker, Richard, son of Dr. Alexander Parker, a prominent physician of Essex county, Virginia, was born in 1729, and died in 1813. He studied law and settled at "Lawfield," Westmoreland county. In 1775, he was member of the Westmoreland county committee of safety, and in 1788 was elected judge of the general court, in which office he continued till his death. He married Elizabeth, daughter of William Beale, of Richmond county.

Parker, Richard, son of James Parker, of Trangoe, Cornwall, England, emigrated to Nansemond county, Virginia, about 1654. He had three sons, Thomas, Richard and

Francis Parker, who were living in 1681. From Richard was descended Dr. Richard Henry Parker, who died at Portsmouth in 1855.

Parker, Sacker, was a burgess for Accomac county in 1736-1738, and died in July, 1738.

Parkes, William, born in England, and emigrating to Maryland, he established in 1729 at Annapolis "The Maryland Gazette." Soon after he established a printing press at Williamsburg, Virginia, and was employed by both governments to print their laws. He issued in Williamsburg, on Friday, August 6, 1736, the first number of a weekly called "The Virginia Gazette." In 1742 he opened a book store in Williamsburg. He died at sea on a trip to England, April 1, 1750. His daughter Sarah married John Shelton, and their daughter Sarah was first wife of Patrick Henry.

Parramore, Thomas, was a burgess for Accomac county in 1748-1749, 1758-1761, 1761-1765, 1766-1768, 1769, 1769-1771.

Pasteur, Dr. John, a native of Geneva, came to Virginia in 1700 in the French Huguenot colony. He settled at Williamsburg and practiced his profession as surgeon, barber and wigmaker. He married and had several children, among them: 1. James, rector of St. Bride's parish, Norfolk. 2 John James "peruke maker." 3. Dr. William, mayor of Williamsburg.

Pasteur, Dr. William, was son of Dr. Jean Pasteur, and was partner with Dr. George Gilmer, as surgeon and apothecary; justice of the peace of York county, and mayor of Williamsburg in 1775, when the powder was removed from the magazine by Lord Dunmore. He married Elizabeth, daughter of William Stith, president of William and Mary College.

Pate, Richard, was a member of the house of burgesses for Gloucester county in July, 1653. He died in 1657, when his nephew, John Pate, afterwards member of the council, qualified as administrator.

Patton, James, was born in 1692 at Newton Limmavady, Ireland, and was for many years master of a merchant vessel, engaged in bringing immigrants from Ireland to Virginia. He was largely interested with William Beverley in investments in Virginia lands. He settled finally in Augusta county, and on May 27, 1742, was commissioned county lieutenant, and was burgess for Augusta in the assembly of 1752-1755. While still a member he was killed by some Indians at Draper's Meadow in Montgomery county. He left issue Mary, wife of William Thompson and Margaret, wife of Colonel John Buchanan. His sister Elizabeth was wife of John Preston, of Donegal, Ireland, who also came to Virginia.

Payne, Florentine, was a burgess for Elizabeth City county in 1641 and 1658-1659.

Payne, John, son of George Payne and Mary Woodson, his wife, was born December 4, 1713, in Goochland county. He served in the house of burgesses from 1752 to 1768, and was lieutenant-colonel commanding the militia. He married twice, but the name of his first wife is not known. His second wife was Jane Smith, daughter of Philip Smith, of Northumberland county, and widow of John Chichester. He died July 28, 1784.

Payne, Josias, son of George Payne and Mary Woodson, his wife, was born October 30, 1705. He married Anna Fleming, and was burgess for Goochland in 1761-1765, and 1766-1769. He removed to Pittsylvania county, and died there in 1785.

Feachey, Samuel, son of Robert Peachey and Ann Hodgskin, his wife, of Milden Hall, Suffolk, England. He came to Virginia in 1659, was justice of Richmond county, and in 1704 lieutenant-colonel of the militia. He died about 1712. He was great-grandfather of William Peachey, colonel of the 5th Virginia Regiment in the war of the revolution.

Fead, Rev. Duell, came from England in 1683 and was minister of Christ Church, Middlesex county, and held the charge seven years. He then returned to England, and became minister, it is believed, of Newland St. Lawrence, county Essex, England.

Pecke, Thomas, a merchant at Skiffe's Creek, Warwick county, in 1659. He was son of Mr. H. Pecke, of London, England.

Peeine, William, was a burgess in March, 1624.

Peirse, Thomas, sergeant-at-arms of the first general assembly at Jamestown, July 30, 1619.

Pelham, Peter, son of Peter Pelham, an early New England artist, committee clerk of the house of burgesses, organist for Bruton Church, living in 1776, father of Peter Pelham, Jr., clerk of Brunswick county.

Pendleton, Henry, son of James Pendleton, descendant from Philip Pendleton, who was born in Norwich, England, in 1650, and came to Virginia in 1674. He was burgess for Culpeper county in 1769-1771, 1772-1774, and 1775-1776, and member of all the conventions of 1774 and 1775. He was nephew of the famous statesman of the revolution, Edmund Pendleton.

Pepiscumah, or **Pipsico**, a chief of the Quiyoughcohannocks on James river in 1608. His name is still preserved in that of a place in Surry county, called "Pipsico."

Peppet, Lieutenant Gilbert, was living at Flower de Hundred in 1624; in 1627 had 250 acres at the mouth of Warwick, adjoining Stanley Hundred; burgess in 1625.

Ferkins, Peter, was a burgess for Pittsylvania county in 1775-1776, and a member of the conventions of March and December, 1775.

Ferrin, Thomas, son of Edward Perrin, merchant of Bristol, was living in Gloucester county, Virginia, in 1686. He married Elizabeth ———, and was father of Captain John Perrin, of Sarah's Creek, who died November 2, 1752.

Ferrott, Richard, was a resident of York county in 1647. In 1657 he was appointed sheriff of Lancaster, and in 1670 sheriff of Middlesex county. He was presiding magistrate of the latter county, and burgess in the assemblies of October 10, 1676, and October 10, 1677. He died November 11, 1686, leaving sons Richard (q. v.) and Henry Perrott, who was the first American to enter Gray's Inn, 1674. Seals of the Perrotts at Middlesex courthouse bear three pears for arms.

Perrott, Richard, son of Richard Perrott, Sr., (q. v.), was born February 24, 1650, being the first male child of English parents born on the Rappahannock river. He was justice of Middlesex county in 1673, and other years. He married Sarah Curtis (born in Gloucester county, August 16, 1657) daughter of Major Thomas Curtis, and widow of William Halfhide. He left issue.

Perry, Peter, brother of Micajah Perry, merchant of St. Catherine, London, came to Virginia about 1685 as agent for his brother's great firm. Located first in York county and then in Charles City county, of which he was burgess in 1688. He left descendants in Charles City.

Peter, John, son of Thomas Peter, and brother of Alexander Peter, of Glasgow, Scotland, settled with his brother Walter Peter in Surry county, and died in 1763.

Pettus, Thomas, was a burgess from Lunenburg in the assemblies of 1769-1771, 1772-1774 and 1775-1776. Descended from Colonel Thomas Pettus of the council, who lived at "Littletown," James City county in 1660. He died in 1780.

Peyronie, William Chevalier de, was a French Protestant, settled in Virginia and highly esteemed; at Fort Necessity he was ensign and was severely wounded; he received the thanks of the house of burgesses and was given a captain's commmission, August 25, 1754. He was killed July 9, 1755, at the defeat of General Braddock.

Peyton, Francis, son of Valentine Peyton, and brother of Colonel Henry Peyton (q. v.), was born in Prince William county, and was burgess for Loudoun county in the assemblies of 1769, 1769-1771, 1772-1774, 1775, and the conventions of 1775 and 1776. He was vestryman, justice, county lieutenant, 1781 and other years, member of the house of delegates 1780 and of the state senate, 1798-1803. He died in 1808-1810. Married Frances Dade.

Peyton, Henry, son of Valentine Peyton (q. v.), was burgess for Prince William county in the assemblies of 1756-1758 and 1758-1761; sheriff 1751; justice, 1754-1761; county lieutenant in 1755. His will was proved in Prince William county, August 6, 1781. He left issue.

Peyton, Henry, brother of Colonel Valentine Peyton (q. v.), was born in London, 1630-1631, was a citizen and merchant tailor of that city, came to Westmoreland county, Virginia, about 1656, and died there in 1659. He married Ellen Partington, daughter of Richard Partington, of London, and left issue.

Peyton, Robert, son of Thomas and Elizabeth Yelverton Peyton, and grandson of Sir Edward Peyton, Bart, of Isleham, Cambridgeshire. He came to Virginia before 1679, was a lawyer and in 1680 was a major of the Gloucester county militia. His grandson, John Peyton, succeeded to the title of knight baronet by failure of title in England.

Peyton, Valentine, son of Henry Peyton of Lincoln's Inn, Middlesex county, England, a royalist, was baptized in St. Dunstan's Church, West End, London, July 31, 1627, and came to Virginia about 1650. He was lieutenant-colonel of the Westmoreland county militia and one of the justices of the court. He died in 1665. His wife who was Frances Gerard, daughter of Thomas Gerard, married (first) Colonel Thomas Speke; (second) Valentine Peyton; (third) Captain John Appleton; (fourth) Colonel John Washington.

Peyton, Valentine, son of Henry Peyton, and grandson of Henry Peyton, the emigrant (q. v.), was born in Hamilton parish, Prince William county, *circa* 1686-1688, was burgess for the county in the assembly of 1736-1740; was justice in 1743 and sheriff in 1749; and died 1751. He left issue Henry Peyton (q. v.).

Phelps, John, a burgess for Bedford county in 1752-1755.

Phettiplace, William, was a member of the Virginia Company of London, came to Virginia in 1607, was a valuable soldier. Probably returned to England.

Phettiplace, Michael, was a member of the Virginia Company, came to Virginia in 1607. Probably returned to England.

Pilkington, William, came to Virginia in 1620, at his own expense; his wife Margaret came at her own expense. He patented 300 acres in 1635 on the east side of Lawne's Creek, which separates Surry and Isle of Wight counties.

Pinkard, Captain John, was a resident of Lancaster county, Virginia, and in 1688 was a burgess in the assembly. He died in 1690. He left sons John, Thomas, and James, daughters, and wife, Elizabeth.

Pleasants, John, son of John Pleasants, of St. Savior's, Norwich, England, worsted weaver, was baptized February 27, 1644- 1645, and emigrated to Virginia about 1665. He acquired a large property, but, having adopted the religious tenets of the Quakers, was not allowed to take his seat in the house of burgesses to which he was elected from Henrico in 1692-1693. He married Jane Larcom, widow of Samuel Tucker, of Bristol. He died in 1698, leaving three children John, Joseph and Elizabeth.

Proby, Peter, believed to have been the Peter Proby, who was son of Emmanuel Proby, lord mayor of London, was a justice of the county court of Elizabeth City. He married Jane, daughter of Bertrand Servant, a Frenchman naturalized, and died in 1692, leaving sons Peter, Bertrand, Thomas and John.

Pocahontas, the celebrated daughter of Powhatan, head warchief or werowance of the Powhatan confederacy of eastern Virginia. In December, 1608, she saved the life of John Smith, and at various times afterwards brought supplies to the famished colonists. In April, 1613, while on a visit to the Potomac Indians, she was captured by Captain Samuel Argall and brought to Jamestown, where a year later she married John Rolfe. She is believed to have lived afterwards at Varina with her husband till she accompanied him to England in 1616. Here she was made much of, wined and dined and taken to the play. Lord and Lady Delaware introduced her at court. Her portrait was engraved by the celebrated artist, Simon de Passe. When about to return to Virginia, with her husband, she died at Gravesend, and was buried there March 21, 1617. She left an only son Thomas Rolfe, who was reared in England by his uncle, Henry Rolfe, and afterwards came to Virginia, where he was captain, etc. His daughter Jane married Robert Bolling.

Pochins, a son of Powhatan, and chief of the Kecoughtan Indians in 1607. In 1610, because of the murder of Humphrey Blunt by some of his tribe, Gates drove him and all his tribe away from the neighborhood of Hampton.

Pole, David, one of the vine dressers sent in 1620 to Buckroe to teach the colonists how to plant mulberry trees and vines, raise silkworms and make wine. In 1627 he leased sixty acres at Buckroe for ten years.

Pollard, Joseph, born in 1687, in King and Queen county, and moved to Goochland in 1754. He married Priscilla Hoomes, and had nine children—two sons and seven daughters. Sarah, one of his daughters, married Judge Edmund Pendleton, the great Revolutionary patriot. The present attorney-general of the State, John G. Pollard, is a descendant.

Pollington, John, came to Virginia before 1619, where he was a member of the first general assembly from Henrico. After the massacre of 1622 he removed to Warwicksqueake plantation, in the present Isle of Wight county, and represented it in the general assembly of 1624.

Poole, Henry, member of the house of burgesses from Elizabeth City in 1647.

Poole, Robert, probably the minister "Mr. Poole," who preached at Jamestown on the afternoon of the arrival of Sir Thomas Dale, May 19, 1611. He had two sons Robert and John. The former in 1619 was an interpreter, and in 1627, as heir of his father and brother John he received a patent for 300 acres east of the church in Mulberry Island.

Fope, Nathaniel, immigrant, settled in Maryland as early as 1637 and was a member of the Maryland general assembly. About 1648, he removed over to Virginia, to escape the turmoils of Maryland, and lived in Westmoreland county till his death in 1660. He was one of the magistrates, and a lieutenant-colonel of militia. He had several children, one of whom, Ann, married Colonel John Washington, ancestor of President George Washington.

Fopeley, Lieutenant Richard, patented in 1637 700 acres in the lower county of New Norfolk, due in right of his marriage with Elizabeth, widow of Henry Sothell, and for the transportation of fourteen persons. He was born in 1598 in the parish of Wooley, Yorkshire, England, and in 1620 came to Virginia, where in 1624 he was living in Elizabeth City. In 1631 he accompanied William Claiborne to Kent Island. In 1639 he was captain at middle plantation, where he patented 1,250 acres west of the palisades. He died about 1643.

Fopleton (Fopkton), William, came in 1622 as a servant of John Davies; burgess for "Jordan's Jorney" in Charles City corporation in 1629.

Fortlock, William, a burgess for Norfolk county in 1748-1749.

Pott, Captain Francis, brother of Governor John Pott (q. v.), came to Virginia before 1628, captain of Point Comfort in 1630; removed from office in 1634, when Captain Francis Hooke was put in command; took part in a meeting at York in

1635 to protest against the tyranny of Sir John Harvey; went to England on the same ship with the deposed governor as one of the agents of the assembly; arrested on arrival there and confined in Fleet prison; released and patented 2,000 acres in Northampton county. Burgess in 1635; died about 1658 in Northampton county, Virginia.

Powell, John, came to Virginia in the *Swallow* in 1609, and in 1624 John Powell, of Newport News, "an ancient planter" received a patent there for 150 acres. In September, 1632, he was a burgess for the district from "Waters' Creek to Marie's Mount." He was probably father of John Powell (q. v.).

Powell, John, probably son of John Powell, "ancient planter," (q. v.), was a member of the house of burgesses for Elizabeth City county in 1657-1658, 1659-1660, 1663, 1666-1676.

Fowell, John, was a burgess for Northampton county in 1700-1702.

Powell, Captain William, came to Virginia with Sir Thomas Gates in 1610, was the commander of the fort at Jamestown, one of the two first members for James City corporation in the general assembly, 1619, repelled the Indians when they attacked Jamestown in March, 1622. He afterwards led an expedition against the Chickahominy Indians and was probably killed by them between January 20 and January 24, 1623. His widow married Edward Blaney. He left a son George Powell, who died in Virginia about 1650. The family seems to have come from Surrey county, England, and in 1656 William Powell of Southwarke in the county of Surrey, England, baker, as heir of George Powell, sold certain lands in Surrey county, Virginia, patented originally by Captain William Powell, brother of the said William Powell. Two brothers were often given the same name.

Power, James, an eminent lawyer, who came to Virginia from Ireland, was a member of the house of burgesses for King William county in 1742-1747, and for New Kent in 1752-1755 and 1756-1758. His daughter married Peter Lyons, the counsel for the parsons in the famous case in Hanover in 1763. His armorial book-plate is well known to collectors.

Fower, Dr. John, was son of John Power, a Spanish merchant, of England, of ancient family. He settled in York county, where he married Mary, daughter of Rev. Edward Folliott, of Hampton parish, York county. He died about 1692, and left issue, Major Henry Power, of New Kent county, who died in 1739, John Power who died in 1720, and Elizabeth Power who married Colonel Cole Digges.

Powhatan, head warchief, or emperor, of the Powhatan confederacy, numbering about thirty-four tribes. He is said to have been the son of an Indian, who was driven by the Spaniards from the West Indies. He was born at the falls of Richmond, lived at Werrowocomoco, Purton Bay, York river, till about three years after the arrival of the English, when he took up his residence at "Orapakes," at the head of White Oak Swamp. He died in April, 1618. He was also called Wahunsenacawh, Ottaniack, and Manatowick.

Poythress, Francis, came to Virginia

about 1633, and patented lands on James river, in that part of Charles City county now known as Prince George. He was burgess for Charles City county in 1645 and 1647, and for Northumberland county in 1649. He had the rank of captain. He married, and had a daughter who married Thomas Rolfe and a son Francis.

Poythress, John, was son of Major Francis Poythress, of Charles City county, and grandson of the immigrant, Captain Francis Poythress. He was burgess for Prince George county in 1723 and 1726.

Poythress, Peter, of "Flower de Hundred," Prince George county, was son of John Poythress, and was member of the house of burgesses from Prince George from 1768 to 1775, and also member of the revolutionary conventions of 1774, 1775 and 1776. He was also a member of the house of delegates. His only daughter and heiress Anne, born December 13, 1712, died April 9, 1758, married Richard Bland, of Jordan's Point, Prince George county.

Prentis, William, was a prominent merchant of Williamsburg. He married Mary Brooke, daughter of John Brooke. He died about 1769, leaving among other sons Joseph Prentis, a prominent patriot of the revolution, and for many years judge of the general court.

Presley, Peter, son of Peter Presley (q. v.), lived at "Northumberland House," Northumberland county. He was a justice of the peace and lieutenant-colonel of the militia, and a burgess for Northumberland from 1711 to 1748, about which time he was murdered by two of his white servants. His will was proved September 10, 1750. He married Winifred Griffin, daughter of Colonel Leroy Griffin, and left an only daughter, Winifred, who married Anthony Thornton. His grandson Colonel Presley Thornton (q. v.), inherited all the Presley estates and was member of the council 1760-1769.

Presley, Peter, son of William Presley (q. v.), was burgess for Northumberland county in 1677, 1684, 1691, also one of the justices of the county. He was father of Peter Presley, of "Northumberland House."

Presley, William, son of William Presley (q. v.), was burgess in the long assembly 1661-1675, but was returned to Bacon's assembly in June, 1676. After the restoration of Berkeley, he was again a representative and is remembered for his saying that "he believed that the governor would have hanged half the country, if they had let him alone."

Presley, William, was an early inhabitant of Northumberland county and was burgess in 1647, 1648. He died in 1657, leaving two sons, William (q. v.), and Peter (q. v.).

Preston, William, was son of Rev. William Preston, of Brougham, Westmoreland county, England. He was master of arts of Queen's College, Oxford. In 1752 he came to Virginia and became professor of moral philosophy in William and Mary College. In 1755 he was minister of James City parish. In 1757 he resigned and went back to England where he was rector of Ormside and died in 1778. He married Mary Tyler, daughter of John Tyler, of James City county, Virginia.

Preston, William, son of John Preston, a

ship carpenter from Newton. Limmavady, in the north of Ireland, and Elizabeth Patton, his wife, was born December 26, 1729, and came with his father to Virginia in 1735. He was a man of marked energy and decision, and served as surveyor and county lieutenant of Fincastle, and Montgomery counties, and was a burgess for Augusta county in 1765, and 1766-1768, and for Botetourt county in 1769-1771. He married Susanna Smith, daughter of Francis Smith, of Hanover, and was progenitor of a very distinguished Virginia family. He died June 28, 1783.

Price, Arthur, was a burgess for Elizabeth City county in February, 1645, and for York county in November, 1645.

Frice, Thomas, was burgess for Middlesex county in 1734-1740. He vacated his position the latter year by becoming clerk of the county, in which office he continued till 1762. He was burgess again in 1758-1761.

Frice, Walter, came in 1618, burgess for Chaplain's Choice in Charles City corporation in 1629, and for Jordan's Jorney and Chaplain's Choice in 1630.

Prince, Edward, was a burgess for Charles City county in 1645.

Proctor, John, was brother of Thomas Proctor, "citizen and haberdasher of London." On July 5, 1623, he engaged with the London Company, of which he was a member, to carry over 100 settlers. He came to Virginia and resided on his lands on Proctor's Creek in the present Chesterfield county. When the massacre occurred in 1622 he was probably in England, for his wife, Mrs. Alice Proctor, is mentioned as holding the plantation successfully against the Indians. In 1625 he resided with his wife in the present Surry county.

Pryor, Captain William, was one of the first settlers on York river. He was a justice of York county from 1633 till his death in 1647. His will shows that he was a man of very large estate. He left two daughters Mary and Margaret—the latter of whom married Thomas Edwards, of the Inner Temple, London.

Pugh, Daniel, burgess for Nansemond county in the house of burgesses 1734-1740.

Furdie, Alexander, born in Scotland and was employed by Joseph Royle in the office of "The Virginia Gazette." He succeeded him as editor on his death in 1766, and soon formed a partnership with John Dixon, who married the widow of Joseph Royle. In 1774 the partnership was terminated and Purdie ran an independent "Gazette." This "Gazette" appeared every Friday. He died at Williamsburg in 1779.

Pyland, James, was a resident of Isle of Wight county, and for his strong royalist sympathies was expelled from the house of burgesses in 1652. He left a son Edward, and there was a James Pyland living in Isle of Wight in 1724. Robert Pyland was burgess for Warwick county in 1647.

Quiney, Richard, citizen and grocer of London, was son of Richard Quiney, of Stratford-on-Avon, and brother of Thomas Quiney, who married, February 10, 1615-1616, Shakespeare's daughter Judith. He married Ellen, daughter of John Sadler, of Stratford, and niece to Anne Sadler, the wife of John Harvard, founder of Harvard College. He and his father-in-law, John Sadler, purchased Brandon on James river from Robert Bargrave, grandson of Captain John Martin. They also owned Powell Brooke, or Merchant's Hope. These estates became vested about 1720 in Nathaniel Harrison. His will was proved in England, January 3, 1656.

Ramsey, Captain Edward, probably son of Thomas Ramsey, was burgess for James City county 1663, 1665, and possibly other years.

Ramsay, Patrick, son of Andrew Ramsay, provost of Glasgow, Scotland, 1734-1735, was a merchant at Blandford, Virginia, married November 26, 1760, Elizabeth Poythress and left issue in Virginia; grandfather of General George D. Ramsay, brigadier-general United States army.

Ramsey, (sometimes spelt Ramshawe), Thomas, was a member of the house of burgesses for Warwick river in 1631-1632, for Gloucester in 1655, 1656, 1658.

Randolph, Beverley, son of William Randolph, of "Turkey Island," and Elizabeth Beverley, his wife, was justice of Henrico for 1741; succeeded Edward Barradall as burgess for the college in 1744-1747 and was burgess for it again in 1748-1749. He married Elizabeth, daughter of Francis Lightfoot, but left no issue.

Randolph, John, son of Sir John Randolph, was born in Williamsburg in 1728; educated at William and Mary College; studied law at the Middle Temple, London, in 1745; returned to Virginia and became eminent as a lawyer; succeeded Peter Randolph as clerk of the house of burgesses, 1752-1766; burgess for Lunenburg county in 1769, and for William and Mary College in 1774 and 1775. He was a Tory in his sympathies, and went to England at the beginning of the American revolution, and died there January 31, 1784. He married Arianna, daughter of Edmund Jenings, attorney general of Maryland. His body was brought back to Virginia and buried in the College Chapel.

Randolph, Henry, half-brother to the poet Thomas Randolph, and uncle of William Randolph of Turkey Island, came to Virginia in 1642. He was clerk of Henrico county from about 1656 and of the house of burgesses from 1660 to his death in 1672. He married Judith, daughter of Henry Soane, speaker of the house of burgesses. She married (secondly) Major Peter Field, and had a son Captain Henry Randolph, of Swift's Creek, Henrico, now Chesterfield county.

Randolph, Isham, son of William Randolph, of "Turkey Island," lived at "Dungeness," Goochland county. He succeeded Abraham Nicholas as adjutant general of the militia in 1738, and was burgess for Goochland in 1736-1740. He died in November, 1742, and was buried at Turkey Island, Henrico county. His daughter Jane married Colonel Peter Jefferson, father of Thomas Jefferson.

Randolph, Sir John, was son of Colonel William Randolph of "Turkey Island," Henrico county; born 1693, died March 9, 1737. He was educated at William and Mary College, Gray's Inn, and the Temple in London and on his return engaged in the practice of law in Virginia; was clerk of the council, treasurer, agent of the assembly in England, president of the county court of Gloucester, lieutenant-colonel of the militia for that county; burgess and speaker. He was the only native resident. who ever received the honors of knighthood. He was also first recorder, in 1736, of the borough of Norfolk. He seems to have been considered as head of the Virginia bar in his day. He was interred in the chapel of William and Mary College, which he represented in the legislature. He was a great nephew of Thomas Randolph, the poet. He was father of John Randolph, attorney general of Virginia, and of Peyton Randolph, first president of the continental congress. In his latter years he resided in Williamsburg.

Randolph, Richard, son of William Randolph and Mary Isham, his wife, of Turkey Island, resided at "Curls Neck," Henrico county; justice of Henrico and colonel of the county; burgess at the assemblies of 1727-1734, 1734-1740, 1742-1747 and 1748-1749; treasurer of Virginia 1736-1738; married Jane, daughter of Major John Bolling, of Cobbs. He died in 1749.

Randolph, Richard, son of Richard Randolph of "Curls Neck," Henrico county, was justice of the peace, and burgess for Henrico in 1766-1769, 1770-1772, and signer of the associations of 1769 and 1772. He married Anne, daughter of David Meade, of Nansemond. He left issue. He was brother of John Randolph, father of John Randolph, of "Roanoke."

Randolph, Thomas, son of William Randolph and Mary Isham, of "Turkey Island," was born about 1683, justice of Henrico in 1713, burgess in 1720-1722. He married Judith Fleming of New Kent county. He settled at "Tuckahoe," in Goochland county set off from Henrico in 1727.

Randolph, William, born in 1651, died April 11, 1711; was son of Richard Randolph, a royalist, and Elizabeth Ryland, his wife. His family was an ancient one in Northamptonshire, England. He came to Virginia about 1673, succeeded his uncle Henry Randolph as clerk of Henrico county in 1673, and held the office until 1683; burgess 1685 to 1699, and in 1703, 1704-1705 and 1710; attorney general 1696; speaker of the house of burgesses 1698. He married Mary, daughter of Henry Isham, of Bermuda Hundred, on James river, and had issue: William, the councillor, who married Elizabeth Beverley; Thomas, of "Tuckahoe;" Isham, of "Dungeness;" Sir John; Richard, of "Curls;" Elizabeth, who married Richard Bland; Mary, married William Stith; Edward, a sea captain; Henry, died unmarried.

Randolph, William, son of Thomas Randolph, of "Tuckahoe," was born in 1712, burgess for Goochland in the assembly of 1742-1747, but died in 1745 and was succeeded by George Carrington. He married Maria Judith, daughter of Mann Page, of "Rosewell" Gloucester county.

Randolph, William, of "Wilton," Henrico county, was son of William and Elizabeth (Beverley) Randolph of "Turkey Island," was burgess for Henrico in 1758-1761; married Anne, daughter of Benjamin Harrison, of Berkeley, and died in 1761.

Ransone, Captain James, son of Peter Ransone, resided on the North river, and represented Gloucester county (now Mathews) in the house of burgesses from 1692 to 1700. He left three sons George, Robert and Peter.

Ransone, Peter, father of Captain James Ransone, settled in Elizabeth City county, which he represented in the house of burgesses in 1652. The same year he patented lands on Mobjack Bay in the present Mathews county. He had issue three sons James (q. v.), George and William.

Ravenscroft, Samuel, came to Boston from England in 1679, and served in the military of Massachusetts with the title of captain. He was a member of the church of England, and on June 15, 1686, took steps, with others, to found King's Chapel in Boston and was later one of its wardens. He owned a sloop, which traded to Virginia. He was a friend of Governor Andros and when that official was seized and imprisoned by the Boston authorities, the same fate befell Captain Ravenscroft. He was released, and came to Virginia about the time (1692) when Andros became governor of that colony. He married Dyonisia, daughter of Captain Thomas Savage, and died about 1695. His widow married (secondly) Thomas Hadley, superintendent of the building of the capitol in Williamsburg (1705).

Ravenscroft, Thomas, son of Captain Samuel Ravenscroft, was born in Boston June 29, 1688; came to Virginia with his father in 1692. He was sheriff of James City county in 1722, but in 1723 removed to Prince George county, where he purchased a tract of land on James river originally patented by Captain Samuel Maycox, killed by the Indians in the massacre of 1622. He was a burgess for Prince George in the assembly of 1727-1734, and in that of 1734-1740, dying in the year 1736. He was father of John Ravenscroft, a justice of Prince George county. John Stark Ravenscroft, first bishop of North Carolina, was his great-grandson.

Read, Clement, was born in King and Queen county in 1707, was educated to the law, qualified as an attorney in Goochland and Brunswick in 1733. In February, 1746, he became the first clerk of the new county of Lunenburg, which position he held for seventeen years; burgess for that county in the assemblies of 1748-1749, 1752-1755, 1758-1761 and 1761-1763; also county lieutenant, presiding magistrate, member of the vestry. He died January 2, 1763, and was buried at his seat called "Bushy Forest" in the present county of Charlotte.

Read, Clement, Jr., son of Colonel Clement Read (q. v.), succeeded his father as burgess for Lunenburg in 1763 and continued a burgess till the session of May, 1765, when he accepted the office of coroner. He was, however, burgess for the new county of Charlotte in October, 1765, and in 1766-1768.

Read, Isaac, son of Clement Read (q. v.), was burgess for Charlotte county, succeeding his brother Clement in the assemblies of May, 1769 and 1769-1771, and later was a member of the conventions of August, 1774, and March and July, 1775, by which last body he was appointed lieutenant-colonel of the Fourth Virginia Regiment. During the war he died from exposure, and was buried in Philadelphia.

Reynolds, Charles, is said to have lived in Isle of Wight, for which he was a burgess in 1652. But the name was more likely Christopher Reynolds who came in 1622 and died in Isle of Wight county in 1654, leaving wife Elizabeth, and children Christopher, John, Richard, Abbasha, Elizabeth and Jane.

Revell, Randall, a wine cooper, was a member of the Maryland general assembly in 1638, and in 1658 was a burgess for Northampton county, Virginia. His descendants were prominent on the eastern shore.

Richards, Richard, was a burgess for "Captain Perry's downward to Hogg Island" in February and September. 1632, and for James City county in 1641.

Richardson, John, was a burgess for Princess Anne county in 1692-1693.

Richardson, Richard, was burgess for New Kent county in 1727-1734, but in 1732 he accepted the office of sheriff and resigned. He was father of John Richardson, of New Kent.

Ricketts, James, one of the justices of Elizabeth City county in 1712 and other years, was burgess for the county in 1720-1722, and in 1723. He died about 1726. He married Jane Wilson, daughter of Colonel William Wilson, and widow of Nicholas Curle. She married (thirdly) Meritt Sweeney.

Riddick (Reddick), James, a burgess for Nansemond county in 1715, 1718, 1720-1722. Probably father of Lemuel Riddick (q. v.).

Riddick (Reddick), Lemuel, burgess for Nansemond county from 1736 to 1775 and member of the convention of March 20, 1775. He was probably father of Willis Riddick.

Riddick (Reddick), Willis, burgess for Nansemond county from 1756 to 1775 and member of the convention of March 20, 1775.

Ridley, Peter, was burgess for James City county in February, 1645, and November, 1645.

Ring, Joseph, lived at "Ringfield" formerly patented by Captain Robert Felgate in York county on Felgate's Creek. He was a prominent justice of York county, and in 1691, one of the feoffees of Yorktown. He was recommended to the authorities in England by the governor as a suitable man for membership in the council. He died February 26, 1703, aged fifty-seven, and the house in which he lived is still standing. In the garden is his tombstone, bearing his coat-of-arms.

Rind, William, was an apprentice of Jonas Green of Annapolis. He was invited in 1766 to Williamsburg by the leading Virginia patriots to set up an opposition paper, the "Gazette" then published in Williamsburg being too much under government control. On November 7, 1766, he was elected public printer. He died August 19, 1773, and his paper was continued two years by his widow Clementina. In 1775, John Pinckney was editor of the paper.

Roane, Charles, immigrant, was son of Robert Roane, gentleman, of Chaldon, Surrey county, England, who died about 1676. He came to Virginia before 1672 and had numerous grants of land in Petsworth parish, Gloucester county, and other places in Virginia. During Bacon's rebellion he suffered much from the rebels on account of his sympathy with Governor Berkeley.

Roane, William, son of William Roane, of Essex county, by his wife Sarah Upshaw, was a descendant of Charles Roane and was burgess for Essex in 1769, 1770-1772, 1772-1774, and qualified as King's deputy attorney in 1768. He was a member of the Essex county committee in 1774, and was colonel of the Essex militia in 1777. He married Elizabeth Ball, daughter of Colonel Spencer Ball, and was father of Judge Spencer Roane, of the Supreme Court of Appeals.

Robertson, Archibald, son of William Robertson, merchant and baillie of Edinburgh and brother of Arthur Robertson, chamberlain of Glasgow, 1760, migrated to Virginia in 1746 and settled in Prince George county. He married Elizabeth daughter of John Fitzgerald and Elizabeth Poythress, his wife. One of his sons was John Robertson, deputy commissary general of Virginia in 1781, and another was William Robertson, clerk of the council and father of Lieutenant-Governor Wyndham Robertson.

Robertson, Moses, a minister of the Established Church, who came to Virginia in 1729, and had charge of a parish in Lower Norfolk county. He married Susanna Thruston, daughter of Dr. Edward Thruston. From 1743 till his death in 1752 he was minister of St. Stephen's parish, Northumberland county. He left three sons Moses, Francis and John Willoughby Robertson.

Robertson, William, came to Virginia about 1700. He was a lawyer and served for many years as clerk of the council of Virginia. He died in 1739, leaving an only daughter Elizabeth, who married John Lidderdale, a merchant of Williamsburg.

Robins, John, son of John Robins, who died on his voyage to Virginia, settled about 1630 in Elizabeth City county, with his servants. He patented several tracts of land —one of them in 1642 being for 2,000 acres, in Gloucester county, on which he resided the last years of his life, and which is still known as Robins' Neck; burgess for Elizabeth City in 1646 and 1649, and a justice for that county in 1652.

Robinson, Colonel Beverley, son of John Robinson, president of the Virginia council, was born in Virginia in 1723, and is stated to have gone to New York in 1745 as captain of an independent company from Virginia. He is also stated to have served under Wolfe at the capture of Quebec, in 1759. He married an heiress, Susanna, daughter of Frederick Phillipse, of Phillipse Manor, New York. At the time of the revolution he raised the Royal American Regiment of Tories, and was appointed its colonel. At the conclusion of the war he went to New Brunswick and thence to England, where he resided at Thornsbury, near Bath. He died there in 1793.

Robinson, Christopher, son of Colonel Christopher Robinson, of Middlesex county, Virginia, and nephew of Bishop John Robinson of London, was born in 1681; matriculated at William and Mary College, and was member of the house of burgesses in 1705-1706, 1710-1712, 1712-1714, and died February 20, 1727. He married, in 1703, Judith, daughter of Colonel Christopher Wormeley, and widow of William Beverley.

Robinson, Henry, son of John Robinson, president of the council, was born in Middlesex county April 7, 1718. He settled in

Hanover county and represented that county in the house of burgesses in 1752-1755 and 1756-1758. He married Molly, daughter of Colonel Thomas Waring, of "Goldsberry," Essex county, Virginia. He died before September 21, 1756.

Robinson, John, son of John Robinson, president of the council, was born February 3, 1704. He studied at William and Mary College, and after graduation was probably for many years the most influential man in Virginia. He resided in King and Queen county upon the Mattaponi river where his residence was known as "Mt. Pleasant." He was a member of the house of burgesses for King and Queen county from 1736 to 1765 and speaker of the house from 1738 to 1765, and treasurer during the same period. As a presiding officer he was compared to Richard Onslow, speaker of the house of commons. As treasurer he ably administered the financial affairs of the colony, but was too free in lending out the colony's money. On his death in 1765, it was found that he owed the public £100,761 7s. 5d. It seems certain, however, that he expected to return this sum from the payments of the creditors or from his own estate. In the end this was indeed done, and the public suffered no loss. He died May 11, 1766. He married three times (first) Mary Storey, (second) Lucy Moore and (third) Susanna Chilton, daughter of Colonel John Chilton, of Williamsburg. His only known descendants are those by his daughter Susan of the last marriage, who married Robert Nelson, of "Malvern Hill."

Robinson, Mrs. Mary, daughter of William Ramsey, of London, grocer, and niece of Sir Thomas Ramsey, lord mayor of London, married (first) John Wanton, of London, gentleman, and (second) John Robinson, chief searcher of the customs in London. Through her will dated February 13, 1617, and proved September 26, 1618, she gave money to many friends and charities. Among her benefactions was one of £200 to found a church in Smythe's Hundred in Virginia. Smythe's Hundred (afterward Southampton Hundred) was a great tract of land extending from Weyanoke on James river to the Chickahominy river. In 1619 a person unknown gave to the Virginia Company a communion service for this church. This cup and paten bearing the date of 1617-1618 are now in the custody of St. John's Church, Hampton. They are the oldest pieces of church silver which have come down from the colonial period in the United States.

Robinson, Peter, son of Christopher Robinson, brother of Commissary William Robinson lived in King William county, was born March 1, 1718, studied at Oriel College, Oxford, was a member of the house of burgesses for King William from 1758 to 1761. His wife was Sarah Lister, whom he married in 1750. He died in 1765, leaving issue Christopher, Peter, Judith, Lucy, Sarah which last married Benjamin Grymes, of Orange.

Robinson, Colonel Tully, son of Captain William Robinson, a magistrate of Lower Norfolk county. He was born August 31, 1658, was magistrate and colonel of militia in Accomac county and died November 12, 1683. His tombstone describes him as loyal to his prince, and a firm believer in the church of England. His daughter Scarburgh married John Wise, ancestor of Henry A. Wise.

Robinson, William, was a nephew of Maximilian Robinson, of Redcriff, mariner, (who had formerly lived and owned considerable land in Virginia), came to Virginia about 1695 and settled on an estate later known as "Bunker Hill." He was high sheriff of Richmond county, 1708, county lieutenant 1718, and was a burgess for the county from 1704 to 1730. He married Frances, only daughter of Captain Samuel Bloomfield. He died September 20, 1742, leaving issue Maximilian Robinson, of King George county.

Robinson, William, was a burgess for Norfolk county at the assembly of 1695-1696, but died before the opening of the second session (1696).

Robinson, William, son of Maximilian Robinson, was burgess for King George county in the assemblies of 1766-1768, 1769, 1769-1772.

Rogers, John, was a burgess for James City in 1645.

Rogers, Richard, son of Captain John Rogers, was burgess for Northumberland county in 1692-1693, but his seat was contested and vacated by order of the house. He left several daughters, one of whom Elizabeth Middleton, wife of Benedict Middleton, of Cople parish, Westmoreland county, as coheiress, made a deed in 1723 to her son Robert Middleton for some land patented by her grandfather, Captain John Rogers in 1662.

Rookins, William, born in 1598, came to Virginia in 1619 in the *Bona Nova*. He married Jane Baxter and in 1625 was servant at Elizabeth City in Sergeant Barry's muster. He was living in 1641. He was father of William Rookins, of Surry county, one of Bacon's majors, who was condemned to death at a court marshal held at Green Spring January 24, 1677, but died in prison. He was a brother-in-law of Captain Nicholas Wyatt, and left children William, Elizabeth and Jane.

Roscow, James, of Hampton, son of William Roscow, of Blunt Point, Warwick county, was appointed receiver-general of Virginia January 22, 1716, and was member of the house of burgesses for Warwick county in 1720 and 1722, in which latter year he died, and was succeeded in the general assembly by his brother William.

Roscow, William, gentleman, born at Chorley, Lancashire, November 30, 1664; lived at "Blunt Point," Warwick county, Virginia; one of the Warwick justices of the peace, married Mary, daughter of Colonel William Wilson of Elizabeth City county; died November 2, 1700; his tombstone shows his coat-of-arms. He left issue: 1. William, who married Euphan Dandridge, and died before 1717. 2. James, appointed receiver-general of Virginia January 22, 1716; died without issue. 3. William (q. v.). 4. Willis, born about 1701, died under age, without issue.

Roscow, William, son of William Roscow of "Blunt Point," Warwick county, Virginia, sheriff of Warwick, lieutenant-colonel, and burgess in 1734-1740; died before 1768, leaving issue by his wife, Lucy, daughter of Colonel William Bassett, of

"Eltham," New Kent county, James Roscow, of "Blunt Point," justice for Warwick in 1769, and other years.

Rootes, Colonel George, was a son of Major Philip Rootes, of "Rosewall," King and Queen county. He removed to western Virginia, and was a member of the house of burgesses for Augusta county in 1775-1776 and a member of the convention of July, 1775.

Rootes, John, a son of Colonel Philip Rootes, of "Rosewall," was a captain in Byrd's Second Virginia Regiment in the French and Indian war and died in 1798, leaving an only son Philip then alive, who appears to have been the Philip Rootes appointed lieutenant United States army in 1800.

Rootes, Colonel Philip, of "Rosewall" King and Queen county, eldest son of Major Philip Rootes married December 2, 1756, Frances Wilcox. He was sheriff of his county in 1765, and died before 1787.

Rootes, Major Philip, was the earliest known ancestor of the Rootes family in Virginia. He lived at "Rosewall," King and Queen county, immediately opposite to West Point, Virginia; justice of King and Queen in 1739; vestryman of Stratton Major parish. He married Mildred, daughter of Thomas Reade. His will was dated August 3, 1756, and he left issue Colonel Philip Rootes, of "Rosewall."

Rootes, Thomas Reade, son of Colonel Philip Rootes, of "Rosewall," was a prominent man in King and Queen county. He married Maria, daughter of John Smith of "Shooter's Hill," Middlesex county, and had at least one son, Thomas Reade Rootes, of "Federal Hill," near Fredericksburg, Virginia, and afterwards of White Marsh, Gloucester county, Virginia.

Roper, William, was a prominent citizen of the eastern shore, who was burgess in 1636 and a justice in 1637. In the former year he had a grant for 150 acres in Accomac for his own personal adventure and the importation of two servants.

Rossingham, Ensign Edmund, was a nephew of Sir George Yardley, and was burgess in the first assembly (1619) from Flower dieu Hundred, one of Yardley's plantations.

Rozier, Rev. John, came to Virginia about 1638, when he was made by Harvey minister of the parishes of Chiskiack and York, to supply the vacancy caused by the banishment of Rev. Anthony Panton. After the return of Panton he became, on the death of Rev. Wiliam Cotton, minister of Accomac in 1640. After seven years he removed to Westmoreland county, where he was minister till his death. He married Jane Hillier, and left a son John.

Rowlston, Lyonell (Coulston, Goulston), lived about 1627 at Elizabeth City, and was burgess in 1629; was in 1630 one of the first settlers at Kiskyacke, on York river, was burgess for York in 1632 and 1632-1633, and one of the first justices.

Royle, Joseph, was bred to printing in England, and was foreman in Hunter's printing establishment in Williamsburg. After Hunter's death, he succeeded him as editor of the "Virginia Gazette." He married Hunter's sister, Rosanna Hunter. He died in 1766.

Ruffin, John, was a great-grandson of William Ruffin, who appears in the records of Isle of Wight county in 1651. He was burgess for Surry county from 1738 to 1747, and from 1754 to 1756. He was also colonel of the Surry militia, and died in Mecklenburg county in 1775. He married Pattey Hamlin and had issue, Robert, of "Mayfield," Dinwiddie county, (q. v.), and other children.

Ruffin, John, son of Robert Ruffin of "Mayfield," Dinwiddie county, represented Dinwiddie in the state conventions of 1775.

Ruffin, Robert, of "Mayfield," Dinwiddie county, son of Colonel John Ruffin of Surry and Brunswick, was burgess from Dinwiddie county in the assembly of 1758-1761. He married Mary Clack, daughter of John and Mary Clack of Brunswick county, and widow of Colonel John Lightfoot. In his later days he moved to King William, where he resided at the Clayborne mansion called "Sweet Hall." He left issue.

Russell, Richard, a physician, resided in Norfolk county, engaged in silk culture and in his will proved December 16, 1667, gave a part of his estate for a school to educate poor children, twelve at a time.

Russell, Dr. Walter, came to Virginia in the First Supply which arrived at Jamestown in January, 1608. He was an expert physician, accompanied John Smith in his explorations of Chesapeake Bay, and it was due to his medical skill that Smith escaped death from a wound caused by a sting-ray at the mouth of Rappahannock river. Russell died previous to September, 1609.

Rutherford, Robert, was a burgess for Frederick county in 1766-1768, 1769, 1769-1771, 1772-1774, but he resigned in 1773 to accept the office of coroner; afterwards was burgess for Berkeley county in the conventions of 1775 and 1776.

Rutherford, Thomas, burgess for Hampshire county in the assemblies of 1761-1765, 1766-1768. During the French and Indian war (1754-1763) he was agent for Dr. Thomas Walker in supplying the troops with provisions.

Sadler, John, was born at Stratford-on-Avon, England, and, with his son-in-law, Richard Quiney, was the owner of Martin's Brandon and Merchant's Hope, on James river. His sister, Anne Sadler, married John Harvard, founder of Harvard College. His will dated December 11, 1658, was proved January 3, 1659.

Sadler, Rowland, was a burgess for James City county in 1642-1643.

Salford, John, son of Robert Salford (q. v.), came in 1616 settled at Kecoughtan, patented land between Newport News and Blunt Point in 1624.

Salford, Robert, yeoman, was born in 1569, came to Virginia in 1611, settled at Kecoughtan, patented land in 1620 on Salford's Creek (Salter's Creek); wife Joane, an ancient planter.

Salmon, Joseph, was a burgess for Isle of Wight county in 1641.

Sandys, David, minister of Jamestown, came in the **Bona Ventura** in 1620.

Sanford, Samuel, of Gloucestershire, came to Virginia and settled in Accomac county. He was a member of the house of burgesses in March, 1692-1693. He left 3,420 acres for a free school in Accomac county. He died in 1710. His brother John Sanford was a large landholder in Princess Anne county, and a justice of the peace. He died in 1693.

Saunders, John Hyde, was a great-grandson of John Saunders, who died in York county, Virginia in 1700. He was a student at William and Mary College in 1762, went to England and on his return in 1772, was made minister of St. James parish, Southam, Cumberland county. In 1775 he was a member of the county committee, espousing the American side of the revolution. (For descendants, see Saunders' "Early Settlers in Alabama").

Saunders, Jonathan, was minister of Lynhaven parish, Princess Anne county. He died in 1702. His widow Mary married Maximilian Calvert. Jonathan Saunders left issue a son Captain John Saunders, mariner, who died in 1734 leaving three children Jonathan, Margaret and Mary.

Saunders, Roger, was a burgess for Accomac in 1632-1633.

Savage, Captain John, of Savage's Neck, Northampton county, born in 1624, was son of Ensign Thomas Savage; burgess for Northampton 1666 to 1676; married (first) Anne Elkington; (second) Mary, daughter of Colonel Obedience Robins.

Savage, Colonel Littleton, probably son of Thomas Savage and Esther Littleton, his wife, was born in 1740, member Northampton committee of safety 1774-1776 and justice 1792; colonel of the militia; born in 1741, died January 9, 1805.

Savage, Nathaniel Littleton, son of Thomas Savage and Esther, daughter of Nathaniel Littleton, great-great-grandson of Ensign Thomas Savage, was member of the Northampton committee of safety 1774-1776, of the convention of 1776 and of the first house of delegates 1776.

Savage, Thomas, came to Virginia with the first settlers in 1608 when thirteen years old, and soon after was given to Powhatan by Newport in exchange for an Indian, Namontack. He remained with Powhatan about three years, and afterwards performed a useful part as interpreter of the Indian language; was ensign and had an arrow shot through his body. About 1619 he went to the eastern shore, where he received from the "Laughing King" a tract of land called Savage's Neck. He died about 1635. He left an only son John Savage.

Savin, Robert, a burgess for Warrosquoyack in 1629.

Sayer, Francis, was in 1672 a justice and major of militia in Lower Norfolk county; he was a burgess for Norfolk county in 1692-1693. His son Charles Sayer, was a vestryman of Lynhaven parish, Princess Anne county in 1723, and clerk of the court.

Scarburgh, Colonel Edmund, was a member of the house of burgesses from Accomac 1723, 1726, 1738, 1740; sheriff in 1721; naval officer in 1731; removed to York county where he married Anna Maria Jones. He died in York county in 1753, leaving a son William, a grandson Edmund Scarburgh, and daughters Elizabeth Hall and Priscilla Johnson.

Scarburgh, Colonel Edmund, son of Captain Edmund Scarburgh, patented in 1635 200 acres in Accomac, on Maggoty Bay, due for the personal adventure of his late father, his mother Hannah, himself and a servant. He was member of the house of burgesses for Accomac or Northampton counties from 1642 to 1671, speaker of the house in 1645; sheriff of Northampton 1660, 1661; was surveyor-general of Virginia 1655-1670; he erected salt works and carried on a large business. He died in 1670 or 1671. He had issue by his wife Mary: 1. Charles. 2. Edmund. 3. Littleton. 4. Matilda married John West of Accomac. 5. Tabitha.

Scarburgh, Captain Edmund, was justice of Accomac in 1631, and member of the house of burgesses for that region in 1629, 1631, 1632. He married Hannah ———, and died in 1634-1635, leaving issue: 1. Sir Charles Scarburgh, member of parliament, etc., (q. v.). 2. Edmund (q. v.). He was ancestor of the Scarburgh or Scarborough family.

Scarburgh, Henry Jr., was a justice of Accomac in 1731 and was a member of the house of burgesses from Accomac in 1726, 1736, 1742, 1744 and died in the last year.

Scarlett, Captain Martin, was burgess for Stafford county in 1692-1693, a justice in 1680, and his tombstone at the mouth of Occoquan Creek records his death in 1698.

Sclater, Rev. James, succeeded in 1686 Rev. Thomas Finney as minister of Charles parish (formerly called New Pocoson) York county, Virginia. He continued minister till his death November 19, 1723. He had issue several sons and daughters, and was founder of the family of his name in Elizabeth City county.

Scotchmore, Robert, was a burgess for Martin's Hundred in 1629-1630.

Scott, Alexander, son of Rev. John Scott, of Dipple parish, Elgin, Morayshire, Scotland. He was born at Dipple July 20, 1686, was minister of Overwharton parish, Stafford county, Virginia, in 1711, where he ministered nearly twenty-eight years.

Scott, Edward, of "Manakintown," was a burgess for Goochland in the assembly of 1734-1740, but died in 1738; and his will names his sons Daniel and John, both under sixteen, and daughter Frances.

Scott, James, son of Rev. John Scott, and brother of Rev. Alexander Scott (q. v.), was born at Dipple, Morayshire, Scotland. He came to Virginia about 1739, and succeeded his brother as rector of Overwharton parish, Stafford county. He married Sarah Brown, daughter of Dr. Gustavius Brown. He made his will in 1782, and died, leaving issue.

Scott, James, son of Rev. James Scott, of "Dipple," Virginia, was born January 8, 1742, was burgess for Fauquier county in the assemblies May, 1769, 1769-1771, 1772-1774, 1775-1776 and the conventions of 1774, 1775, 1776; captain of a militia company at the battle of Great Bridge, died of exposure in service in the continental army in 1779. He married Elizabeth Harrison, daughter of Cuthbert Harrison.

Scott, John, was a burgess for Westmoreland county in 1698.

Scott, Samuel, son of Edward Scott of

Goochland county, burgess for Cumberland county at the assembly of 1752-1755. He died sometime before May 1, 1755.

Scott, Thomas, burgess for Prince Edward county in the assemblies of May, 1769, and 1769-1771.

Seawell, Henry, merchant, was burgess for Elizabeth City in 1632, and in 1639 was burgess for Lower Norfolk county. He died about 1644. Seawell's Point on the Elizabeth river is named for him. He left a son Henry, who died intestate and without issue, and a daughter Anne, who married Colonel Lemuel Mason (q. v.).

Sedgwick, William, came from Burlen Hall, Lancashire, and was clerk of York county, Virginia, from 1690 till his death in 1705. He had two brothers Isaac Sedgwick, bachelor, a lawyer of York county, and deputy clerk in 1688, who died in the parish of St. Catherine Creechurch, London, and Thomas Sedgwick, of London.

Selden, James, son of Richard Selden (q. v.), represented Lancaster county in the last house of burgesses 1775; was member of the Lancaster county revolutionary committee and member of the state conventions 1775, 1776.

Selden, Richard, son of John Selden, was deputy King's attorney for Elizabeth City county in 1752, and grandson of the immigrant, Samuel Selden (q. v.), was one of the justices of Lancaster county, and burgess for the same in 1756-1758. He married Mary Ball, daughter of Major James Ball, of "Bewdley," and had besides other sons, James Selden (q. v.).

Selden, Samuel, a lawyer who came to Virginia in 1699 and settled in Elizabeth City. He married Rebecca ———, cousin and heir of Rebecca, who was wife successively of Colonel Leonard Yeo, Colonel Charles Moryson, and Colonel John Lear. He died in 1720. He left a son John Selden and other issue.

Selden, Rev. William, son of John Selden, and grandson to Samuel Selden, the immigrant, was born in 1741, was educated at William and Mary College 1753, afterwards studied law and practiced, but abandoned the profession for the ministry, and was ordained a minister in London March 10, 1771. He was rector of the church at Hampton from 1771 till his death June 25, 1783. He married May 29, 1767, Mary Ann Hancock, of Princess Anne county, Virginia.

Semple, James, was brother of John Semple (q. v.), was born May 18, 1730, came to Virginia in 1755, was minister of St. Peter's parish, New Kent county in 1767. He married in 1763, Rebecca Allen, of New Kent, and died about 1787. He was father of Judge James Semple, professor of law in William and Mary College.

Semple, John, was a son of Rev. James Semple, minister of Long Dreghorn, Ayrshire, Scotland. He was born October 17, 1727, emigrated to King and Queen county, Virginia, in 1752, was a lawyer. He married in 1761 Elizabeth Walker, and was father of John Walker Semple, an eminent lawyer of Kentucky, who married (first) Miss Laurie of Caroline county, Virginia; and (second) Lucy, daughter of Donald Robertson.

Semple, Robert Baylor, was son of John

Semple (brother of Rev. James Semple), who emigrated to New Kent county in 1755. John Semple was a lawyer who married Elizabeth Walker in 1761. R. B. Semple, their youngest son, was born at "Rose Mount," King and Queen county, January 20, 1769; went to school under Rev. Peter Nelson; studied law; but becoming converted to the tenets of the Baptists, he became an eminent preacher in that sect. He married Ann Lowry, daughter of Colonel Thomas Lowry, of Caroline county. He died December 25, 1831.

Servant, Bertram (or Bertrand), "a natural born subject of the kingdom of France," was born in 1632, came to Elizabeth City county in 1650, and was naturalized in 1698. He was a justice of the peace and prominent citizen. He had issue, Jane, who married Peter Probey, Rebecca, who married Jacob Walker, Frances, who married John George, Mary, who married Francis Ballard, and James, who died in 1735, leaving issue. He died in November, 1707.

Seward, John, immigrant, came to Virginia from Bristol, England, before 1635. He was a merchant and had grants of land in Isle of Wight county, one of which was called "New Hemington." He was burgess for Isle of Wight in 1645, and his will dated November 30, 1650, was proved February 9, 1650-1651, in the general court and afterwards recorded in Isle of Wight county in 1705. He left two sons John and James Seward.

Sharpe, Samuel, came to Virginia in the *Seaventure* in 1609 with Sir Thomas Gates, and his wife came in the *Margaret and John* in 1620. He was burgess for Charles City in the assembly of 1619, and for the neck of land in October, 1625. He was then styled Sergeant Sharpe.

Sharpe, Rev. Thomas, came to Virginia in 1699 and was minister first of St. Paul's parish, New Kent county, afterwards Hanover. On April 23, 1620, he became minister of St. Peter's Church, but died September 3 of the same year; ancestor of the Sharpe family of Henrico and Norfolk.

Sharples, Edward, was clerk of the council, and acting secretary of state on the death of Christopher Davison in 1624. Contrary to the orders of the council, he delivered to the commissioners sent over from England by the King certain papers entrusted to his care. As a consequence, he was removed and lost a part of one of his ears. This order was entered May 10, 1624.

Sheild, Robert, was an early settler in York county and married Elizabeth Bray, sister of Arthur Bray, wine cooper of London. He died about 1661, leaving a son Robert from whom descends the Sheild family still prominent in Virginia.

Sheild, Rev. Samuel, son of Major Robert Sheild, of York county and Rebecca Hyde, his wife, entered the grammar school of William and Mary College in 1769, entered the philosophy schools in 1771, and in 1773 received the Botetourt medal for classical learning. In 1774 he went to England to be ordained, and on his return in 1775 was made minister of Drysdale parish, Caroline county. In 1779 he became minister of York Hampton parish, to which he added in 1792 the duties of the adjoining Charles parish. He died in 1803.

Shelley, Walter, was a burgess for Smythe's Hundred in the first assembly,

1619. He died on the third day of the meeting.

Sherman, Michael, was burgess for James City county in 1696-1697. He was ancestor of the Sherman family of New Kent county.

Shields, James, son of James Shields, who kept ordinary in Williamsburg and Anne Marot, daughter of Jean Marot, a French Huguenot. He was born October 27, 1739, married Susannah Page, daughter of John and Mary Page and died in 1795, leaving issue. He was captain of the York county militia and surveyor and escheator for the county.

Shephard (Shepherd), Robert, was living on his plantation over against James City (in the present Surry county) in 1625. He was member of the house of burgesses for James City county in October, 1646, and November, 1647, and was also captain of the militia. He died before 1654 when his widow Elizabeth married Mr. Thomas Warren. Captain Shepheard left issue, sons John, Robert and William and daughters Anne, Priscilla and Susanna.

Shepherd, John, was a burgess for James City county in 1644.

Sheppard, John, was burgess for Elizabeth City in 1652 and 1653. His son John had a daughter, Anne, who married Thomas Wythe, grandfather of George Wythe, statesman of the American revolution.

Sheppard, Thomas, was a burgess for the upper part of Elizabeth City county in 1632-1633.

Sherwood, Grace, known as "the Virginia witch," was the wife of James Sherwood of Princess Anne county, who died in 1701. In 1706, she was charged with witchcraft, but after imprisonment was released. She lived till about 1740, when her will was proved. She gave her estate to her three sons John, James and Richard Sherwood.

Sherwood, William, was born in the parish of White Chapel, London, was bred to the law, and served in the office of Sir Joseph Williamson. As the result of some youthful indiscretion committed against his patron, he came to Virginia in 1668, and for five years served as deputy sheriff of Surry county. He demeanored himself in such a way as to win the praise of the court. In 1674 he removed to Jamestown, where he practiced law in the general court, and married Rachel James, widow of Richard James, who owned a large part of Jamestown Island and kept an ordinary. He was present in Jamestown in 1676, when Nathaniel Bacon forced a commission from Governor Berkeley, and wrote to Williamson, his former patron, an interesting account of the affair. In March, 1678, he was appointed attorney general of the colony and served about two years. He was coroner and justice of James City county in 1684, and again in 1696 represented Jamestown in the house of burgesses. He died in 1697, when the widow Rachel married (thirdly) Edward Jaquelin. At the time of his death, Sherwood owned about 378 acres at the west end of the island, and this property came by marriage and purchase to Edward Jaquelin.

Sidney, John, was a burgess for Lower Norfolk county in 1644, 1647, 1656, 1658, 1659, 1660. He was colonel of the militia and one of the justices.

Simmons, John, son of William Simmons,

of Southwark parish, Surry county, was burgess for Surry in 1710-1712 and 1727-1734. He died about 1737, leaving a wife Rebecca and children William, John and Mary Simmons. A John Simmons was burgess for Isle of Wight county in 1734-1740, 1742-1747 and 1748-1749. He was probably father of Benjamin Simmons, who was burgess for Southampton county in 1758-1761, 1761-1765 and 1766-1768.

Simpson, Southey, was a burgess for Accomac in 1761-1765, 1766-1768, 1769-1771, 1772-1774, and a member of the convention of May, 1776.

Skaife, Rev. John, son of John Skaife, husbandman, was born at Ledburgh, Yorkshire, schooled at Ledburgh, alumnus of St. John's College, Cambridge, came to Virginia about 1708, and was rector of the parish of Stratton Major, King and Queen county, till his death November 3, 1736. He married Susanna Peachy Walker, widow of Thomas Walker, of King and Queen.

Skelton, Reuben, was son of James Skelton of Essex county, Virginia, who contracted to rebuild the capitol in Williamsburgh and died in 1754. Reuben Skelton was clerk of St. Paul's parish, Hanover county, and member of the house of burgesses in 1758, 1759. He died before 1760. He married Elizabeth Lomax, who married (secondly) John Wayles, of Charles City county, father-in-law of Thomas Jefferson.

Skipwith, Sir Grey, was the son of Sir Henry Skipwith, of "Prestwould," in Leicestershire, and being a royalist came to Virginia about 1650. He settled in Middlesex county, Virginia, of which he was one of the justices. He was father of Sir William Skipwith, who married Sarah, daughter of John Peyton, of Gloucester county. A sister, Diana, married Major Edward Dale, of Lancaster county.

Skyren, Henry, was born in Whitehaven, England, in 1729, came to Virginia in 1763, and was minister of St. John's parish, King William county. In 1790 he removed to Hampton, and died there in 1795. He married Lucy Moore, daughter of Colonel Bernard Moore and his wife Anne Catherine Spotswood. He was father of Colonel John Spotswood Skyren, of King William county.

Slaughter, Francis, son of Colonel Robert Slaughter (q. v.), was born in Culpeper, about 1730. Served in the French and Indian wars as lieutenant-colonel of militia, and represented Dunmore county in the house of burgesses in 1772, 1773, 1774, 1775. He married Miss Suggett.

Slaughter, Robert, son of Robert Slaughter, born in Essex county 1702. Died in Culpeper county in 1768; commissioned captain of militia on September 2, 1729; later colonel of militia. He was vestryman and churchwarden of St. Marks parish, 1730, member of the house of burgesses 1742; presiding justice for Orange county 1745. He was well known for his fine imported horses. He married, about 1723, Mary Smith, daughter of Augustine Smith, of Essex.

Slaughter, Thomas, son of Robert Slaughter (q. v.), was commissioned in 1756 as lieutenant-colonel of the forces for Culpeper county against the Indians above Winchester. He was burgess for Culpeper in 1756-1758, and though elected to the assembly of

1759-1761 vacated his seat by accepting the office of sheriff in November, 1759. He was burgess again in 1766-1768. He married Miss Robinson and had issue.

Small, Dr. William, a native of Scotland, and probably a graduate of the University of Edinburgh, qualified as professor of natural philosophy and mathematics in the college of William and Mary, October 18, 1758; after the removal of Mr. Rowe in August, 1760, Dr. Small filled the chair of moral philosophy also till June 26, 1761, and was the first who ever gave in that college—and doubtless the first who ever gave in any colonial college—"regular lectures in ethics, rhetoric and Belles Lettres." In September, 1764, he returned to Europe and took up his residence at Birmingham, England. In 1767 he purchased for the college an elaborate physical apparatus costing upwards of £332 sterling. He was intimate with Erasmus Darwin and with James Watt, the inventor of the steam engine, and it was on his advice that Watt left Glasgow and came to Birmingham. Small introduced him to Matthew Bolton, the founder of the Soho engineering works with whom Watt formed a partnership in making steam engines. Dr. Small died at Birmingham in 1775. John Page, one of his students at William and Mary, referred to him as the "illustrious Dr. Small," and Thomas Jefferson, another student who fell under his instructions, declared that Dr. Small "fixed the destinies of his life."

Smith, Arthur, gentleman, was born in 1597 and came to Virginia in 1622 in the company of Farrar Flinton; burgess for Isle of Wight county in 1644-1645. By his will dated October 1, 1645, he left sons Thomas, Arthur, Richard and George Smith.

Smith, Colonel Arthur, son of Arthur Smith (q. v.), was born in 1638, resided on Pagan Creek, Isle of Wight county, was justice in 1675 and 1680; colonel of the militia the latter year; and burgess in 1685. His will dated December 2, 1696, was proved in Isle of Wight county June 10, 1697.

Smith, Arthur, son of Colonel Arthur Smith, of Isle of Wight county, who died in 1696-1697, was born in 1670; was burgess for Isle of Wight county in 1703-1705, 1710-1712, 1715, 1718, 1720-1722. He had a son Arthur who was the founder of Smithfield, Virginia.

Smith, Rev. Charles Jeffrey, A. M., was a Presbyterian minister of Long Island, New York. He formed a partnership with another Presbyterian, William Holt, of Virginia, and in 1765 held 500 acres in James City county, and a mill called "Kennon's Mill." He founded a settlement in New Kent county which he called "Providence" (now Providence Forge), and built thereon iron, grist and saw mills. He died in 1771. After his death the forge at New Kent was conducted by Francis Jerdone and William Holt.

Smith, Francis, son of Captain Nicholas Smith, Jr., was vestryman and justice of Essex county, 1740; major of horse, 1753, and afterwards colonel; member of the house of burgesses for Essex, 1752-1758. His will dated March, 1760, and proved March 15, 1762, disposes of a large estate; father of Meriwether Smith, prominent in the American revolution.

Smith, Rev. Guy, came to Virginia before 1700 and was minister of Abingdon Church, Gloucester county. He was a member of the convention of the clergy that assembled at William and Mary College in 1719. He died about 1720, leaving issue at least four sons, John, Guy, Constantine and Lawrence.

Smith, John, came to Virginia about 1652, married Anna Bernard, daughter of Richard Bernard, of "Purton," in Gloucester county. He was major in 1665, lieutenant-colonel before 1674, and sided with Sir William Berkeley in 1676 against Bacon. His son, John Smith, of Purton, married Mary Warner, daughter of Colonel Augustine Warner.

Smith, Major John, came to Virginia about 1650, and resided first in Warwick county; was speaker of the house of burgesses in 1658; removed to Westmoreland county, where he was known as Major Francis Dade. He died in 1662. Ancestor of the Dade family of Virginia.

Smith, John, son of Augustine Smith, of "Shooter's Hill," Middlesex county and Sarah Carver, his wife, was born November 13, 1715. He was burgess for Middlesex in the assemblies of 1761-1765, October, 1765, 1766-1768. He was a wealthy planter, married Mary Jaquelin, daughter of Edward Jaquelin, of Jamestown, and died near Winchester, November 19, 1771. He was father of General John Smith, of "Hackwood," Frederick county.

Smith, John, burgess for Goochland county in 1756-1758. He was son of Guy Smith, of Gloucester county, was born September 23, 1725, and married in 1751, Elizabeth Hopkins, daughter of Arthur Hopkins, of Goochland.

Smith, Joseph, came from Ireland to Virginia about 1710, was justice of the peace of Essex and colonel of the Essex militia. He died 1727. He was a wealthy merchant and mentions in his will his brothers John Smith, late of Biddeford, merchant, Benjamin Smith, of the kingdom of Ireland, and James Smith of Rosse in Ireland.

Smith, Lawrence, was a resident of Gloucester county, Virginia, and in March, 1675-1676, he commanded a fort at the head of Rappahannock river. In Bacon's rebellion he sided with Governor Berkeley, and after Bacon's death led the Gloucester "trained hands" against Ingram, but they deserted him. He was surveyor for the counties of Gloucester and York in 1686, and in 1691 laid out Yorktown. In 1699 the governor recommended him as suitable for appointment to the council. He died in 1700. From his coat-of-arms Major Smith appears to have belonged to the Smiths of Totne, county Devon, England. He was father of Colonel John Smith, of the Virginia council.

Smith, Lawrence, son of Major Lawrence Smith, of Gloucester county, settled in York county, where he was lieutenant-colonel of the militia, justice of the peace, sheriff, and one of the feoffees of Yorktown. In 1720 and several succeeding years he represented York county in the house of burgesses. He married (first) Mildred, daughter of Captain Thomas Chisman, and (second) Mildred, daughter of Robert Reade. He died in 1739, at his house near Yorktown.

Smith, Lawrence, son of Colonel John Smith, Esq., of Gloucester county, was born about 1700, and represented Gloucester county in the house of burgesses in 1734-1740. He died the latter year (1740).

Smith, Nicholas, son of Nicholas Smith, and Efsobah, his wife, of the city of London, was born at London, September 4, 1666; a justice and coroner of Richmond county, one of the first justices of the new county of King George, member of the house of burgesses 1723, 1726, 1732-1734; lieutenant-colonel of the King George militia; he died possessed of a very large estate, March 18, 1734, and is buried at his manor plantation "Smith's Mount" in Westmoreland county. His daughter and heiress Elizabeth married Major Harry Turner.

Smith, Nicholas, of Petsworth parish, Gloucester county, Virginia, was a vestryman October 13, 1697, churchwarden in 1700. He left a son Captain Nicholas Smith, who was father of Colonel Francis Smith of South Farnham parish, Essex county, (q. v.).

Smith, Nicholas, was a justice and member of the house of burgesses for Isle of Wight county in 1659-1660. His will, dated November 19, 1695, and recorded there, shows that the two daughters of Thomas Powell in Maryland were his only descendants.

Smith, Rev. Thomas, son of Gregory Smith of King and Queen county, Virginia, was born in 1741, attended the school at Wakefield in Yorkshire, England, and took his A. B. degree at Trinity College, Cambridge, England, in 1763. He was ordained by Bishop Porteus in 1765. On his return to America he became rector of Yocomoco and Nomini Churches in Westmoreland county, Virginia, and died May 20, 1789. His son John Augustine Smith became president of William and Mary College.

Smith, Toby, was a burgess for Warwick River county in March, 1643; for Nansemond October, 1649. He removed to Lancaster county where he was justice in 1652 and 1653. When Rappahannock county was formed, he was appointed December 11, 1656, one of the justices, and colonel of the militia. He married Phebe Fauntleroy, sister of Moore Fauntleroy. His will dated December 29, 1677, was recorded in Rappahannock county. He left a son Henry and other children.

Smyth, John, came to Virginia in 1611, purchased "Burrows Hill," patented by John Burrows, and called it "Smyth's Mount." It lay next to Pace's Paines. Smyth was a burgess for Pace's Paines in 1629, for Pace's Paynes and Smyth's Mount in 1630.

Soane, Henry, came to Virginia about 1651 where he obtained land for importing six persons, viz: Henry Soane, Sr., Henry Soane, Jr., Judith Soane, Sr., Judith Soane, Jr., John Soane and Elizabeth Soane. He was a burgess for James City county in 1652, 1653, 1654, 1658, 1660 and 1661, and was speaker the last session. He died about this time, leaving issue.

Soane, Henry, Jr., son of William Soane, of Henrico county, was burgess for James City county in 1714. He made his will May 21, 1722.

Soane, William, son of Henry Soane, speaker of the house of burgesses, was born in 1651, was burgess for Henrico in 1695-1696. He died in 1714, leaving among other children Henry Soane, Jr., (q. v.).

Somerville, James, merchant, born at Glasgow, Scotland, February 23, 1742, located at Fredericksburg and acquired a large fortune. He died at Port Royal, Virginia, April 25, 1798. He left his large estates to his nephew, James Somerville, who came to Virginia, and died there leaving issue.

Southcoat, Captain "Thomas," was burgess for Charles City county October, 1666. He was probably Captain Otho Southcoat, gentleman, of Westover, who was agent in 1665 for Sir John, Lord Pawlett, when he sold Westover to Theodoric Bland.

Southern, John, of Jamestown, gentleman, came to Virginia in 1621; burgess for James City in 1623 and 1629-1630. In 1627 he patented twenty-four acres on the island of Jamestown. After Edward Sharpless was removed, Southern was appointed acting secretary of the colony.

Span, Cuthbert, was burgess for Northumberland county in 1693. He was son of Richard Span, and left sons Richard and John Span, living in 1712.

Sparrow, Charles, was a burgess for Charles City county in 1645, 1649, 1652 and 1660. He was major, one of the justices of Charles City, and was buried September 11, 1660.

Speed, James, son of John Speed, of Mecklenburg county who died in 1785, was burgess for Charlotte county in 1772-1774, 1775-1776.

Speke, Thomas, born 1623, patented 1,000 acres in Northumberland county, Virginia, in 1650 and in 1651 was a burgess; afterwards in 1655 justice of Westmoreland county, and lieutenant-colonel. He married Frances, daughter of Dr. Thomas Gerrard, and died in 1659. His widow married successively, between that time and 1676, Valentine Peyton, John Appleton and John Washington. He left a son Thomas, and a brother John living in Bath, Somersetshire, England. The son died without issue and his property in Virginia descended to Hugh Speke, Esq., of Bath, who disposed of it. The Spekes were an old Somersetshire family.

Spelman (Spilman), Henry, third son of Sir Henry Spelman, the famous antiquary. He was baptized 1595, came to Virginia in August, 1609; was taken by Captain Smith to the falls of James river and given to Powhatan in return for the site of the Indian town; escaped and returned to Jamestown; sent back to Powhatan in October, 1609, with whom he remained till March, 1610, when he ran away to the King of Potomac. With this chief he remained till September, 1610, when he was ransomed by Captain Argall; served afterwards as interpreter and rose to the rank of captain, but in 1619 was degraded from his rank by the assembly for speaking disrespectfully of Governor Yardley. In 1623 he went up the Potomac river to trade, and was betrayed and killed by the Anacostan Indians.

Spence, Alexander, son of Patrick Spence, of Westmoreland county, Virginia. He was captain of the militia and burgess from 1696 to 1702 for Westmoreland county.

Spencer, Captain Robert, was born in 1630, was justice of Surry, and made his will March 5, 1678. He is believed to have been a brother of Nicholas Spencer, president of the council, who had a brother Robert of about the same age.

Spencer (Spence), William, "yeoman and ancient planter" came to Virginia in the First Supply, 1608; was "an honest, valiant and industrious laborer," was "a farmer" at Jamestown in 1614, and the first to choose his land; promoted ensign and was burgess for Jamestown in the first assembly in 1619; burgess for Mulberry Island in 1624; patented twelve acres on Jamestown Island in 1624, at which time he had a wife Alice, and daughter Alice, born in 1620. In 1632-1633 he was a burgess for Mulberry Island.

Spicer, Arthur, was a lawyer and prominent merchant, burgess for Richmond county in 1691. His will, dated September 18, 1688, was proved April 3, 1700. His legatees were his son John, whom he desired to be sent to England and schooled at the Charter House, Lydia, daughter of his brother, John Spicer, of London, and Frances Robinson, wife of William Robinson and daughter of Samuel Bloomfield.

Spilman, Thomas, gentleman, came to Virginia at his own cost in 1617, born in 1601, patented land at Kecoughtan; his wife Hannah was born 1602 and came in 1620. Died at Truro in Cornwall in England about 1627.

Spotswood, John, son of Governor Alexander Spotswood, was burgess for Orange county in 1748-1749; for Culpeper in 1752-1755 and for Spottsylvania in 1756-1758. He was a colonel of the militia. He married Mary Dandridge, daughter of Colonel William Dandridge, and died May 6, 1756, leaving two sons, General Alexander Spotswood and Colonel John Spotswood, who served with distinction during the American revolution.

Spratt, Henry, was son of Henry Spratt and Isabella, his wife, of Lower Norfolk county. He was a major in the militia and justice of the peace for Princess Anne county in 1705; member of the house of burgesses for Princess Anne in 1723-1726.

Squire, Rev. Richard, was licensed for Virginia October 2, 1702, and was elected rector of St. Peter's Church, New Kent county, April 23, 1703. He was present in Williamsburg at the convention of the clergy in 1705. He died in New Kent county December 12, 1707.

Stacy, Robert, was a burgess for Martin's Brandon in the assembly of 1619, but he was not permitted to take his seat because of the too independent authority of John Martin's patent.

Stagg, Charles, dancing master and Mary his wife, were employed by William Livingston, of New Kent, merchant, to conduct a peripatetic dancing business. In 1716 they were engaged by him to open a theatre in Williamsburg, and the agreement was carried out, the theatre built, and plays conducted till Stagg's death in 1735. Afterwards, Mrs. Stagg had for some years dancing assemblies in Williamsburg.

Stalnaker, Samuel, a sturdy frontiersman, was a German emigrant from Pennsylvania, who settled in 1750 on the middle fork of the Holston river, where he was still living in 1768 or 1769 when visited by J. F. D. Smythe, the English traveller. In 1757 he was a captain of militia.

Stanard, William, born February 15, 1682, was son of William Stanard, of Middlesex county, and Eltonhead, widow of Henry Thacker, and daughter of Edwin

Conway and Martha Eltonhead, his wife. He was clerk of Middlesex county from 1716 till his death December 3, 1732. He married Elizabeth Beverley, daughter of Major Harry Beverley.

Stanup, John, son of Captain John Stanup, of York county, who died in 1694; was a burgess for New Kent county in 1710-1712, 1715 and 1718.

Starke, Bolling, son of William Stark, and Mary Bolling, his wife, was born September 20, 1733; burgess for Dinwiddie county in the assemblies of May, 1769 and 1769-1771 and of the convention of May, 1776, which declared independence. He was afterwards a member of the house of delegates, of the governor's council; and state auditor. He died in Richmond in January, 1788.

Starke, John, merchant, of New Kent county, Virginia, was son of Thomas Starke, a rich London merchant. He patented land in King William and King and Queen counties in 1688, and was probably ancestor of the Starkes of Hanover county, Virginia, formerly a part of New Kent.

Starke, Richard, son of William and Mary Bolling Starke, was bred a lawyer. He compiled Starke's "Justice of the Peace," and was committee clerk of the house of burgesses. He died in 1772, leaving "a numerous and distressed family."

Starke, William, son of Dr. Richard Starke and Rebecca, his wife, lived in York county, Virginia, where he was one of the justices of the county court. In 1711 he joined with others in establishing a school house, and gave a quarter of an acre of land for the site. He married Mary Bolling.

Stephens, George, was a burgess for James City county in 1645, 1652.

Stephens, Major Philip, a cavalier officer, who came with Major Henry Norwood to Virginia in 1649, and in 1650 received from the council of state of England fifty pounds for his sufferings in Virginia. He died in York county, Virginia, in 1658, where his estate was outcried.

Stith, Drury, son of Lieutenant-Colonel Drury Stith and Elizabeth Buckner, was born about 1718 and died in 1770. He was surveyor of Brunswick county (1740, 1751), sheriff 1757, justice (1747, 1756, etc.), major of horse 1746, colonel of foot 1753, and colonel of the county militia 1759. He was a burgess for his county in 1748-1756. He died in 1770. He married (first) Martha ———, (second) Elizabeth Jones, widow of Thomas Eldridge.

Stith, Drury, son of Lieutenant-Colonel Drury Stith and Susanna Bathurst, his wife, was born about 1695, lived for some time in Prince George county, and later in Brunswick county. In 1726 he was a justice of Prince George county and in 1727 a captain in the militia, but he was lieutenant-colonel before 1735. He qualified as clerk of Brunswick county, May 11, 1732, and he was also county surveyor. He was interested in a copper mine. He married Elizabeth Buckner, and died in 1740, leaving issue Drury Stith (see above).

Stith, Drury, was son of Major John Stith, of Charles City county, and patented land in 1703. He was one of the justices of the county (1714), sheriff 1719, 1714-1725, and county surveyor 1720. He was lieutenant-colonel of the militia and in 1704-05 burgess for Charles City county. He married Susanna Bathurst, daughter of Lancelot Bathurst, of New Kent county. His will was presented in court in 1741. He left issue.

Stith, John, came to Virginia before 1656 and settled in Charles City county. In 1656 he was a lieutenant of militia, in 1676 a captain, and in 1680 a major. He was also a merchant, a lawyer and a justice of the peace. He was a prominent supporter of Sir William Berkeley during Bacon's rebellion in 1676. In 1680 he was a burgess for Charles City county. He left issue—John Stith, Drury Stith, Anne, married Colonel Robert Bolling.

Stith, John, son of Major John Stith (q. v.), had in 1692 a patent for land on the south side of Chickahominy river, in James City county. He was captain of the militia in 1692, sheriff in 1691, and burgess for Charles City county in 1692-93. He married Mary Randolph, daughter of William Randolph, of Turkey Island, and Mary Isham, his wife. He died before 1724, leaving issue: 1. Rev. William Stith, president of William and Mary (q. v.). 2. John Stith. 3 Mary Stith, married William Dawson, president of William and Mary College.

Stith, John, son of John Stith and Mary Randolph, had large tracts of land in Charles City and Prince George counties. He was burgess for Charles City county, 1718, 1723, 1726, and in May, 1737, took the oath as lieutenant-colonel of the militia. He married Elizabeth Anderson, a daughter of Rev. Charles Anderson, of Westover, and died about 1758.

Stith, Richard, surveyor of Bedford county, was a justice of the peace in 1758 and a burgess for Bedford in 1756 and 1757. He was probably a son of lieutenant-colonel John Stith, of Charles City county and Elizabeth Anderson, his wife. In 1772 he was still living in Bedford.

Stith, Thomas, son of Lieutenant-Colonel Drury Stith and Elizabeth Buckner, his wife, was born December 29, 1729, and died in 1801. He was a burgess for Brunswick from 1769 to 1774; was one of the justices of the county (1765-1784), and was county surveyor in 1783. He qualified April 27, 1772, as major of the county militia.

Stith, William, son of Captain John Stith, of Charles City county, and Mary Randolph, his wife, daughter of Colonel William Randolph. His father died before 1724, when his mother was matron at William and Mary College. He was educated at William and Mary College and at Queen's College, Oxford, where he took Bachelor of Arts and Master of Arts; master of the grammar school at William and Mary (1731); rector of Henrico parish (1738); president of William and Mary College (1752-1755); chaplain to the house of burgesses (1753), and rector of York-Hampton parish (1752-1755); author of a history of Virginia, of a sermon preached before the house of burgesses on "The Sinfulness of Gaming," etc. He married Judith Randolph, daughter of Thomas Randolph, of Tuckahoe. He died September 19, 1755.

Stobo, Robert, was born in Glasgow in 1727 of respectable parentage; settled in Virginia about 1742 as merchant; appointed captain, and surrendered July 3, 1754, with Van Braam at Fort Necessity as hostages for the fulfillment of the articles of capitulation. He escaped and joined the English at Louisburg. Afterwards he served in the West Indies in 1762. He left the army in 1770, and died not long after.

Stockden (Stockton), Rev. Jonas, born 1584, was son of Rev. William Stockden, parson of Barkeswell, county Warwick, England. He came to Virginia in 1620, settled at Elizabeth City, and in May, 1621, he wrote a letter, several times printed, regarding the treacherous character of the Indians, and the futility of any attempt to convert them "till their priests and ancients were put to death." The massacre took place the next year. In 1627 he leased fifty acres on Hampton river.

Stoever, John Casper, was born at Frankenberg, Hesse, about 1685, and in 1728 came with his son of the same name to Philadelphia. He was pastor of the German miners who came to Germanna, in Virginia, in 1717 and 1719, and afterwards removed to the present Madison county about 1727 and founded a Lutheran congregation. He was ordained minister in 1733 and that year took charge of the church in Madison county. In 1734 he went to Germany with two of his congregation to collect money for his congregation. He was quite successful and after staying abroad four years started to return with about £3,000 and a good supply of books, but died and was buried at sea. His will was proved at Philadelphia, March 20, 1739. With the money, the fruit of his labors, the congregation after his death built in 1742 a church and bought lands and slaves. His son, Rev. John Casper Stoever, Jr., was born December 2, 1707, in the duchy of Berg; was ordained in 1733 and organized many Lutheran congregations in the eastern counties of Pennsylvania.

Stokes, Christopher, ancestor of the Stokes family in Virginia and the south; was burgess for Warwick river, 1629, and for Denbigh in 1629-30. He afterwards lived in New Poquoson parish, York county, and he died there, leaving four sons, mentioned in an order of court in 1648—Christopher, William, Francis and Thomas.

Stone, Captain William, of Hungar's creek, on the eastern shore of Virginia, was born in Northamptonshire, England, in 1603, and came to Virginia in or before 1633. He was nephew of Thomas Stone, a wealthy haberdasher of London; justice of Accomac in 1633; vestryman and sheriff in 1635; removed with other non-conformists to Maryland in 1648, and in the same year was made governor of Maryland by Lord Baltimore. He was removed from office in 1653 by the parliamentary commissioners, Claiborne and Bennett, and in 1655 headed the royalist element, which on March 25 was defeated at the Severn by the adherents of parliament, under the command of Captain William Fuller. Stone was captured and sentenced to death, but was pardoned. He died about 1695, at his manor of Avon, in Charles county, Maryland. Among his descendants was Thomas Stone, signer of the Declaration of Independence. Governor Stone married Verlinda, sister of Rev. William Cotton, minister of Accomac.

Story, Joshua, a burgess for King and Queen county in 1695-96 and 1696-1697. The last year (1697) he was made sheriff of his county.

Stoughton, Samuel, was burgess for Nansemond county in 1646.

Stover, Jacob, a native of Switzerland, obtained on June 17, 1730, for himself and divers German and Swiss families from the Virginia council a grant of 10,000 acres in Page and Rockingham counties. He was the founder of Strasburg, of which the original citizens were all Germans. He died about 1741, leaving a son of the same name.

Strachey, Dr. John, son of John Strachey. Esq., of Sutton Court, in England, a descendant of William Strachey, secretary to Lord Delaware; born in 1700, came to Virginia and settled in King and Queen county. He married Elizabeth Vernon, and had among other children, Elizabeth, who married Thomas Metcalfe, of King William county. He died in 1759.

Strafferton, Mr., was a burgess for Elizabeth City in 1639.

Stratton, Joseph, was burgess for Nutmeg Quarter (now in Warwick county), and for "from Waters' Creek to Marie's Mount," 1632. In 1635 he patented a tract of land in Nutmeg Quarter which was bounded on the southwest by a tract of land "that did formerly belong to Captain John Smith."

Streeter, Captain Edward, was a burgess for Nansemond county in 1656.

Stretchley, John, born in 1648, was clerk of Lancaster county from 1674 to 1698; burgess in 1692-93; he died December 8, 1698.

Stringer, John, was a burgess for Northampton county in 1659 and 1660. He was then colonel and a leading justice.

Strother, French, was a member of the convention which met in Williamsburg, May 6, 1776. He was son of James Strother and Margaret French, and great-grandson of William Strother, who made his will in Richmond county in 1700.

Strother, William, son of William Strother and Margaret Thornton, his wife, was burgess for King George county in the assembly of 1727-1734, though he died before the close (about 1732). He had issue: 1. Elizabeth, married John Frogg. 2. Alice, married Henry Tyler, clerk of Stafford county. 3. Anne, married Francis Tyler, brother of Henry. 4. Agatha, married John Madison, clerk of Augusta county. 5. Jane, married Thomas Lewis, of Augusta county. 6. Margaret, married Gabriel Jones, a prominent lawyer.

Stuart, John, a native of Glasgow, in Scotland, was born in 1754, came to Virginia and settled in Petersburg, where he engaged in merchandizing and acquired a large fortune. He died February 1, 1814.

Stubblefield, George, son of George Stubblefield, who died in 1751-1752, was burgess for Spottsylvania in the assemblies of 1772-1774 and 1775-1776, and member of the conventions of 1775.

Studley, Thomas, first cape merchant or keeper of the public stores at Jamestown. He died August 28, 1607.

Sullivan, Daniel, was clerk of Nansemond county in 1702 and other years. He owned the land on which Suffolk was afterwards built. His son, Daniel Jr., had a daughter Margaret who married Jethroe Sumner and they were parents, it is believed, of General Jethroe Sumner, of the American revolution.

Sully, Thomas, "yeoman and ancient planter," patented six acres of land near the blockhouse on Jamestown Island in 1624, and in 1628 ninety-four acres additional at the head of Hampton river. He was aged thirty-six in 1625, and had come in the *Sarah* in 1611. His wife, Maudlyn, aged thirty, had come in the *London Merchant* in 1620.

Swann, Alexander, was one of the justices and a captain of militia in the county of Middlesex. He married Mary Landon, daughter of Thomas Landon, of Credenhill, Herefordshire, and died in 1710.

Swann, Colonel Samuel, was son of Colonel Thomas Swann, of Swann's Point, Surry county. He was born May 11, 1653, succeeded his father at Swann's Point and was for many years a prominent man in Virginia and North Carolina; justice of Surry county, 1674; major of militia, 1687; sheriff, 1676 and 1678; member of the house of burgesses for Surry in 1677, 1680, 1682, 1684, 1686, 1692, 1693. He soon after moved to North Carolina and was speaker of the assembly there prior to 1715.

Swann, Captain Thomas, was son of Colonel Thomas Swann, of Swann's Point; member of the Virginia house of burgesses, 1693, 1695, 1696, 1698, and sheriff of Surry in 1697. He married Elizabeth, daughter of William Thompson, of Nansemond county, and died in 1705, leaving an eldest son, Major Thomas Swann, sheriff of Nansemond 1740, whose eldest son, Thompson Swann, was clerk of Cumberland county from 1754 to 1781.

Swann, William, patented in 1635 1,200 acres in the county of James City, on the south side of James river, "bounded west from Smith's Mount to the half way neck." His patent was renewed in the name of Thomas Swann, his son, who became a member of the council of state. The point of land on the south side of James river, opposite to Jamestown, still bears his name, "Swann Point."

Swearingen, Thomas, burgess for Frederick county in the assembly of 1756-1758; vestryman for Frederick parish in 1769.

Sweeney (Swinney), Meritt, was son Edmund Sweeney, a justice of the peace for Elizabeth City county in 1687 and other years. Meritt Sweeney was also a justice, and was a burgess for Elizabeth City county in the assemblies of 1736-1740 and 1742-1747. He married Jane Wilson, daughter of Colonel William Wilson, and widow of Nicholas Curle and James Ricketts, and left issue—Roscoe Sweeney and others.

Sykes, Bernard, was an active friend of Nathaniel Bacon Jr.; resided in Charles City county and was a member of the assembly called by General Ingram after Bacon's death in October, 1676.

Syme, John, was a resident of Hanover county. He was burgess in 1722 and colonel of the Hanover militia. He died in 1731, while engaging in laying out the boundaries of Hanover and Louisa counties. His widow, who was Sarah, daughter of Isaac and Mary Dabney Winston, married (second) Colonel John Henry, of Hanover, and had Patrick Henry, the orator.

Syme, John, son of John Syme, who died in 1731, was born in 1730. He was burgess for Hanover county in 1756-1758, 1758-1761,

1761-1765, 1766-1768, 1773-1775, and he was a member of all the conventions, 1774, 1775, 1776. He was frequently a member of the legislature during the American revolution.

Syms, Benjamin, founder of the first free school in English America, was born in 1580, and in 1623 was living at "Basse's Choice," in what was subsequently known as Isle of Wight county. He afterwards settled in Elizabeth City county, and by his will made February 12, 1634-1635, he gave 200 acres on Poquosin river, Elizabeth City county, with the milk and increase of eight cows, to erect a school house and support the poor scholars of the parishes of Elizabeth City and Kiquotan. In 1648 there was a fine school house and the kine had increased to forty. In 1805 the school was united with "Eaton's School" to form Hampton Academy, which is now known as the "Syms-Eaton Academy." It is probably the only instance of a school in America carried on, either in whole or part, by the original funds.

Tabb, Edward, son of Thomas Tabb, and grandson of Humphrey Tabb, the immigrant, served as captain, justice of York county and burgess in 1723-1726. He died December 5, 1731. He married Margaret Howard, daughter of Colonel Henry Howard, of York county, and left issue.

Tabb, Humphrey, son of Thomas Tabb, emigrated to Virginia about 1637 and patented land in Elizabeth City county. He died before 1659, when the fragment of a record shows that Anne Tabb, widow of Humphrey Tabb, made a deed to Richard Hull, guardian of Thomas Tabb, son of Humphrey Tabb, deceased.

Tabb, John, son of Thomas Tabb, was captain, colonel, justice and sheriff of Elizabeth City county; burgess in the assemblies of 1756-1758, 1758-1761. He married (first) Mary, daughter of Rev. James Selater, (second) Martha Wallace.

Tabb, Thomas, was a son of John Tabb, of Elizabeth City county, and Martha Hand, his wife. He resided at "Clay Hill," in Amelia county. He was one of the leading merchants in Virginia and represented Amelia county in the house of delegates from 1749 to 1759 and from 1761 to 1769. He was colonel of the militia. He died at his residence "Clay Hill," Amelia county, November 23, 1769. He left issue, Colonel John Tabb, a member of the committee of safety (1775).

Taberer, Thomas, son of William Taberer, of Derbyshire, England, was heir to his brother, Joshua Taberer, who died in Isle of Wight county, Virginia, in 1654. He was burgess for that county in 1658, and for a long time one of the justices and major of the militia. He sympathized with the Quakers. His will was proved in Isle of Wight county, February 9, 1694-95. He had issue, Ruth, who married John Numan; Mary, married William Webb; Christian, married Robert Jordan; Elizabeth, married ——— Copeland.

Talbot, John, was a burgess for Bedford county from 1761 to 1775, and member of the conventions of 1774, 1775, 1776. He was a son of Matthew Talbot, one of the first justices of Bedford county (1754), who died in 1758. John Talbot married (first) Sarah Anthony, of Bedford, and (second) Phebe Mosby, of Henrico. He moved to Wilks county, Georgia, in 1784. Issue: Phebe, Thomas, Matthew and Mary.

Taliaferro, John, son of Robert Taliaferro, immigrant, was lieutenant of rangers against the Indians, justice of Essex, sheriff, and in 1699 member of the house of burgesses. He married Sarah, daughter of Major Lawrence Smith, of Gloucester county. His will, dated June 1, 1715, was proved in Essex county, June 21, 1720, and mentions issue.

Taliaferro, Walker, was a son of Captain William Taliaferro, a justice of Essex county, who was grandson of Robert Taliaferro, the emigrant from England. He lived in Caroline county and was burgess in 1765, 1766-1768, 1769-1772, 1772-1774, 1775, and member of the conventions of 1774, 1775, 1776.

Taliaferro, William, was a burgess for Orange county in the assembly of 1758-1761, but resigned in 1760 and accepted the office of coroner.

Talman, Captain Henry, son of William Talman, of Felmingham Hall, Norfolk county, England (an architect and collector of prints and drawings), resided in St. Peter's Parish, New Kent county, Virginia, but spent much of his time at sea as captain and owner of the ship *Vigo*. He married Anne Elizabeth Ballard, daughter of Thomas Ballard. He died in London in 1775, leaving issue in Virginia.

Tarleton, Stephen, settled in New Kent county, and was probably a Quaker. He begged the council for pardon in taking the oath Bacon imposed upon the people. He had a daughter Judith, who married John Woodson, and probably another Susanna, who married Charles Fleming, of New Kent.

Tarpley, James, a prominent merchant of Williamsburg, who in 1761 donated to Bruton church the historic bell which still swings in the steeple of the church. He was son of John Tarpley, of Williamsburg, and Elizabeth Ripping, daughter of Captain Edward Ripping, of York county, and grandson of Colonel John Tarpley, of Richmond county, and Anne Glasscock, his wife.

Tatem, John, burgess for Norfolk county in 1758-1761.

Tayloe, William, was nephew of Colonel William Tayloe, of the Virginia council. He emigrated to Virginia and in 1687 settled in Richmond county, then part of Rappahannock county. He was one of the first justices of Richmond county, and in 1704, as colonel and commander-in-chief of the county militia, subdued an attempted uprising of the Indians. He was burgess for Richmond county in 1700, 1701, 1702 and 1706, and died in 1710. He married Anne, daughter of Henry Corbin, of "Buckingham House," and had issue: 1. John, of "Mt. Airy," member of the council. 2. William, of Lancaster county. Colonel William Tayloe had at least two brothers—Joseph, clerk of Lancaster county, and Robert, a ship captain, who died in 1705.

Taylor, Rev. Daniel, came to Virginia about 1703, when he was appointed minister of Blissland parish, New Kent county. He continued minister till after 1724. He left a son of the same name who was also a minister (q. v.).

Taylor, Rev. Daniel, son of Rev. Daniel Taylor, of Blissland parish, New Kent county, Virginia, studied in the grammar school of William and Mary College, entered

St. John's College, Cambridge, 1723, and took Bachelor of Arts at Trinity College in 1727; received holy orders and on his return to Virginia in 1727 was elected rector of St. John's Parish, King William county, Virginia. He married Alice, daughter of Richard Littlepage, gent. He died September 9, 1742.

Taylor, Ethelred, was son of Henry Taylor, of Charles City county (who died in 1743), and Charlotte Anderson, daughter of Rev. Charles Anderson, of Westover. He was burgess for Southampton county in the assembly of 1752-1755, and died the latter year, leaving by his will sons, Henry, William, Kinchen, Ethelred, John, James and Richard; daughters, Mary, and Elizabeth, wife of Miles Cary.

Taylor, George, was a justice of the peace of Richmond county in 1692 and other years; captain and colonel of the militia; burgess in the assembly of 1700-1702. His will was proved August 7, 1706, and his legatees were his wife Susannah; his daughter, Martha Gaines, wife of Bernard Gaines, and her eldest son, Daniel Gaines.

Taylor, George, son of James Taylor and Martha Thompson, his wife, and grandson of James Taylor, who came from Carlisle, England, to Virginia, was burgess for Orange county in 1748-1749, 1752-1755, 1756-1756-1758; member of Orange county committee, 1774; born 1711 and died January 17, 1784. He had thirteen sons, all of whom are said to have served in the American revolution.

Taylor, Henry, son of Henry Taylor, of Charles City county, was burgess for Southampton county in the assemblies of May, 1769, 1769-1771, 1772-1774, 1775-1776, and member of the conventions of 1774, 1775 and 1776. His will is dated June 14, 1781, and was proved in Southampton county. He left issue—sons, Ethelred, John and Henry, and daughters, Charlotte, Mary and Martha.

Taylor, James, a burgess for King and Queen county in 1702 to supply the place of William Gough, who died before the opening of the session. He was probably James Taylor, son of James Taylor, of Carlisle, England, who afterwards located in Orange county; married Martha Thompson, and died in 1729.

Taylor, John, resided in that part of Charles City county afterwards known as Prince George; burgess for Charles City county in 1696-1697, 1698, 1699, 1700-1702; clerk of the county court in 1699, and doubtless other years; captain of the militia; died in 1707. He left two daughters—Sarah, who married John Hardiman, and Henrietta Maria, who married his brother, Francis Hardiman, both of Charles City county.

Taylor, Philip, was a burgess for Northampton county in 1644.

Taylor, Thomas, burgess for Warwick county in 1646. His daughter Ann married Miles Cary, the first of that family in Virginia.

Taylor, William, son of Rev. Daniel Taylor Jr., of St. John's Parish, King William county, was born in 1732; was clerk of Lunenburg county, 1763-1814, and member of the house of burgesses for Lunenburg county in 1765-1769. He died September 11, 1820.

Taylor, William, son of Henry Taylor, of Charles City county, and brother of Ethelred Taylor, was burgess for Southampton county in the assemblies of 1756-1758 and 1758-1761. He married Lucy Mason and died in 1772, leaving issue: Ann, wife of William Brown; Mary Mason Taylor, Martha Taylor, William Taylor and Robert Taylor.

Taylor, William, burgess for Lunenburg county in the assembly of 1766-1768.

Teackle, John, was son of Rev. Thomas Teackle, of Northampton county, and was born September 2, 1693. He was lieutenant-colonel of the militia and burgess in 1720 until his death the following year. He married Susanna Upshur, daughter of Arthur Upshur and Sarah Brown, his wife.

Teackle, Rev. Thomas, was son of Thomas Teackle, of Gloucester, England, and was born in 1624, and died in 1695. He was a warm royalist and came to Virginia about 1653, and was minister in Northampton county. He married (first) Isabella, widow of Lieutenant-Colonel Edward Douglass, (second) Margaret Nelson, daughter of Robert Nelson, of London, merchant. He left descendants.

Tebbs, Foushee, was a burgess for Prince William county in the assemblies of 1776-1768, May, 1769, 1769-1771, 1772-1774.

Temple, Joseph, was in 1722 attorney of certain Bristol merchants at their iron works in Virginia. He settled in King William county and carried on a large mercantile business and patented much wild land. He married Ann, daughter of Benjamin Arnold, and had ten children. He died before 1760. Joseph Temple was a son or grandson of William Temple, gentleman, of Bishopstone House, near Warminster, Wiltshire, England.

Temple, Peter, minister of York parish, York county, Virginia, received a grant of land December 24, 1665. He married, in 1669, Mary, widow of Lieutenant-Colonel Thomas Ludlow, of York county, and was the nominal head of the clergy in the colony. Before 1686 he returned to England and lived at Sible-Heningham, in Surry county, and later at Lambeth, Surrey. He had a son, Captain Peter Temple, of York county, Virginia, who married Anne, daughter of Colonel James Bray.

Tennant, Dr. John, of Port Royal, Caroline county, came to Virginia in 1723 and became prominent as a physician. In 1735 he visited England, where he secured the friendship of such distinguished physicians as Sir Richard Mead and James Monro. In 1736 he published what was probably the first work on medicine printed in Virginia, "An Essay on the Pleurisy." He gained considerable note by his advocacy of the virtues of the Seneca rattlesnake root as a specific for many diseases, especially pleurisy, and was awarded £100 by the general assembly in 1738. He married Dorothy Paul in 1731 and left issue—a son of the same name who was distinguished during and after the revolution.

Terrell, Richmond, founder of the family of that name in Virginia, was brother of Robert Terrell, of the city of London, merchant. He had a brother, William Terrell, who also settled in Virginia (see "Virginia Mag. Hist. and Biog.," xvi, p. 190).

Terrell, Robert, citizen and fishmonger of

London, was a resident of Virginia in 1647. He was a brother of Richmond Terrell and of William Terrell, who also came to Virginia. He died in 1677.

Terry, Nathaniel, was burgess for Halifax county in 1758-1761, 1761-1765, 1766-1768, 1769-1771, 1772-1774, 1775, and was a member of the conventions of 1774, 1775 and 1776.

Thacker, Edwin, son of Henry Thacker, and Eltonhead Conway, was born August 19, 1663; was burgess for Middlesex county at the assemblies of 1700-1702 and 1703-1705, but died in 1704.

Thelaball, James, a French Protestant, came to Virginia about 1648; was a member of the court of Lower Norfolk county; a vestryman, church warden and sheriff, and was naturalized by the council in 1683. He married Elizabeth, daughter of Francis Mason, and his will, dated April 9, 1693, was proved September 15, 1693.

Thomas, Cornelius, was burgess for Amherst county in the assemblies of 1761-1765, 1766-1768, 1769, 1769-1771; a justice of the peace, captain of militia, church warden. He married and had John, who went to Albemarle county; Cornelius; Elizabeth, married John Wood; Lucy, married James Lewis; Sally, married Thomas Moon.

Thomas, William, was a burgess for Surry county in 1652 and 1656.

Thomson, Stevens, was son of Sir William Thomson, sergeant-at-law; was admitted to the Middle Temple in 1688, and in 1704 was appointed in England attorney-general for Virginia, succeeding Benjamin Harrison. He arrived in Virginia not long after. A memorial of his opinions has come down to us with the famous case of Grace Sherwood, of Princess Anne county, who was tried for witchcraft. He died about 1714, leaving a daughter Anne, who married Colonel George Mason, father of George Mason, the famous statesman of the American revolution.

Thompson, Andrew, born at Stoneblue, in Scotland, in 1674, came to Virginia in 1712, and was minister of Elizabeth City parish till his death, September 1, 1719, in the forty-sixth year of his age. Administration was granted in England on his estate April 9, 1724, to his brother, Dr. Alexander Thompson.

Thompson, George, son of Ralph Thomson, of Chestnut, in Hertfordshire, born in 1603; came to Virginia, 1625; burgess for Elizabeth City county, 1629; lieutenant against the Indians, 1629; one of the justices of Elizabeth City county, 1629; living in London in 1639, when with his brother Maurice and other merchants he patented Berkeley Hundred, purchased of the original proprietors. His sister Mary married Captain William Tucker, of Elizabeth City, Virginia.

Thompson, John, was son of Rev. William Thompson, of Surry and Westmoreland counties, Virginia, who came to Virginia in, or shortly before, 1662. He was a member of the house of burgesses for Surry in 1692, 1695 and 1696. He married Elizabeth, widow first of John Salway, of Surry, and second of Joseph Malden, of Surry. He died in 1699, without issue.

Thompson, Maurice, came to Virginia in 1620; son of Ralph Thomson, of Chestnut,

Hertfordshire, England; patented 150 acres near Newport News in 1624; returned to England, where he was a prominent merchant; in 1636 patented with partners Berkeley Hundred in Virginia; took sides with parliament against the king, and was intimate with Cromwell. His eldest son, Sir John Thompson, was a prominent member of parliament, and was created, May 4, 1696, Baron Haversham.

Thompson, Samuel, was son of Rev. William Thompson, of Surry and Westmoreland, and brother of John Thompson. He was member of the house of burgesses for Surry in 1700-1702, 1715 and 1718. He married, before 1682, Mary, daughter of Major William Marriott, of Surry. He died in 1720 or 1721, without issue.

Thompson, Rev. William, appears to have come from New London, Connecticut, and was probably a son of Rev. William Thompson, who was sent about 1642 from New England to minister to the Virginia dissenters in Lower Norfolk county. He was minister of Southwark parish, Surry county from 1662 to about 1690, when he was minister of Washington parish, Westmoreland county. He had issue: 1. John. 2. Samuel. 3. William. 4. Katherine, wife of Robert Payne, of Essex county. 5. Elizabeth, who married (first) William Catlett and (second) —— Moseley.

Thompson, William, son of Ralph Thompson, of Chestnut, in Hertfordshire, born in 1614; living at Elizabeth City, Virginia, in 1624; returned to England; was knighted; in the reign of Charles II. was a governor of the East India Company. He was a brother of George and Maurice Thompson (q. v.).

Thornbury, Thomas, born 1604, came to Virginia in 1616; lived a few years in Maryland, where he was member of the assembly in 1649; returned to Virginia and was burgess for Elizabeth City in July, 1653.

Thornton, Sir Charles Wade, son of Colonel Presley Thornton, was taken to England just before the revolution, settled there and became a lieutenant-general in the English army. He died in 1854. He was half-brother of Colonel Peter Presley Thornton (q. v.).

Thornton, Francis, son of Francis Thornton, of "Fall Hill," was born about 1704 and died in 1749. He was a member of the house of burgesses from Spottsylvania in 1744, 1745, 1752, 1754; was a justice of Spottsylvania and appointed colonel of the militia in 1742. He married shortly after November 3, 1736, Frances, daughter of Roger Gregory, deceased, and his wife, Mildred Washington, aunt to President Washington.

Thornton, George, son of Francis Thornton, of "Fall Hill," near Fredericksburg, was a member of the state convention of May, 1776, and the house of delegates in 1777 and perhaps other years. He is said to have been a major in the Continental line. He married Mary, daughter of John Alexander.

Thornton, Colonel John, was son of Francis Thornton, of "Fall Hill," Spottsylvania county. He lived first in Spottsylvania and afterwards in Caroline. In 1742 he was justice of the peace of Spottsylvania in 1751; was sheriff, and December 6, 1753, was elected a member of the house of burgesses for Spottsylvania to supply the place of William Waller, who became coroner; senior colonel of the Spottsylvania militia in 1756. He died before 1778.

Thornton, John, was vestryman of Blissland parish, New Kent, and burgess in 1720-1722, 1723-1726. He was also major of the militia. He died in 1730.

Thornton, Peter Presley, son of Colonel Presley Thornton, of "Northumberland House," was born August 10, 1750. He was a member of the house of burgesses in 1772-1774, and of the conventions of July and December, 1775. Was appointed colonel of a regiment of minute-men in 1775, but afterwards resigned to accept a position as aide-de-camp to Washington. He married Sally, daughter of Robert Throckmorton, of Gloucester county, and died in or before 1781.

Thornton, William, son of Francis Thornton, of Stafford county, and grandson of the immigrant, William Thornton (descended from the Thorntons of Yorkshire), was born December 14, 1680; settled in that part of Richmond county afterward known as King George county; sheriff of Richmond in 1709 and 1711; burgess for Richmond in 1712-1714, and one of the two first burgesses for King George county in 1720-1722. He married Frances ———, and died in 1743, leaving a son William. Probably he was the Thornton who represented Stafford county in 1727-1734.

Thornton, William, son of Francis Thornton, of Gloucester county, was born December 20, 1717, and removed to Brunswick county. He was a member of the house of burgesses from Brunswick from 1756 to 1768, inclusive. He married, June 25, 1738, Jane Clack, born January 9, 1721, daughter of James Clack, of Brunswick county. His will was proved in Brunswick county, November 23, 1790.

Thorowgood, Adam, son of Captain Adam Thorowgood, of the council, and Sarah Offley, his wife, resided in Lower Norfolk county, for which he was burgess in 1666; justice and sheriff in 1669, and lieutenant-colonel. He married the daughter of Colonel Argall Yeardley, and had issue with other children, John and Adam Thorowgood, of Princess Anne county.

Thorowgood, Adam, son of Lieutenant-Colonel Adam Thorowgood, of Lower Norfolk county, succeeded his brother John as burgess for Princess Anne county in 1702, and was a member also of the assemblies of 1703-1705 and 1705-1706. He was lieutenant-colonel, justice, etc. He married Mary Moseley, and died issueless.

Thorowgood, John, son of Lieutenant-Colonel Adam Thorowgood, of Lower Norfolk county; was sheriff, justice and lieutenant-colonel of Princess Anne county, and burgess in the assemblies of 1695-1696, 1696-1697, 1698, 1699 and 1700-1702. He died in 1702, and was succeeded by his brother, Colonel Adam Thorowgood.

Thorowgood, John, was a member of the convention of May, 1776, that declared independence and of the house of delegates from 1777 to 1786. He represented Princess Anne county and was a great-great grandson of Colonel John Thorowgood, who died in 1702. He died in 1804.

Thorpe, Major Otho, was a resident of Middle Plantation, Virginia (Williamsburg), and in 1660 married Elizabeth, widow of Richard Thorpe, of the same place. He was a kinsman of George Thorpe, superintendent of the college lands at Henrico, and who was massacred by the Indians in 1622. He was a justice of York county in 1674 and major of the militia in 1680. He died in the parish of All-Hallows—the Wall, London, in 1686-87, and left his property in Virginia to his nephew, Captain Thomas Thorpe, his niece, Hannah Thorpe, and his cousin, John Grice.

Throckmorton, Gabriel, immigrant, born 1655, died in Ware parish, Gloucester county, January, 1737; was son of John Throckmorton, of Ellington, in the county of Huntingdon, Great Britain, a highly respectable family of ancient lineage. He was for many years presiding magistrate of Gloucester county. He married, in 1690, Frances Cooke, daughter of Mordecai Cooke, and left descendants in Virginia.

Throckmorton, Robert, immigrant, was the eldest son of Gabriel Throckmorton and his wife, Alice, daughter and heir of William Bedles, and was born at Ellington, Huntingdonshire, England, about 1608. He came to Virginia about 1637, when he patented 300 acres in York county. He returned to England and died there in September, 1657, leaving sons, Albion, Robert and John—the last of whom left descendants in Virginia.

Thruston, Charles Mynn, son of Colonel John Thruston, of Gloucester county, by his wife, Sarah Mynn, was born November 6, 1738, and attended the College of William and Mary in 1754. He was a captain of the Gloucester militia and a vestryman of Petsworth parish, Gloucester county. In 1764 he took orders and was minister of Petsworth parish till 1768, when he resigned and removed to Frederick county. Here he was the minister of Frederick parish and represented the county in the conventions of 1775 and 1776. On the breaking out of the revolution he raised a company of troops and was wounded at the battle of Trenton. He was known as the "Warrior" or "Fighting Parson," and was promoted on his recovery to lieutenant-colonel. He was afterwards a prominent member of the Virginia legislature. In 1808 he removed to Louisiana and died there in 1812. He married (first) Mary Buckner, (second) Anne Alexander. By the first marriage he had Judge Buckner Thruston, of Louisiana.

Thruston, Dr. Edward, son of John Thruston, chamberlain of Bristol, England, was born January, 1638-39, and came to Virginia before 1666. He settled at Martin's Hundred, where he married Anne Loving, daughter of Thomas Loving, surveyor-general of Virginia. About 1671 he removed to Long Ashton, in Somersetshire, England, and married (second) Susanna Perry, daughter of Nicholas Perry, a lawyer. In 1717 he came from Boston to reside with his son Edward, in Norfolk county, Virginia.

Thruston, Malachy, son of John Thruston, chamberlain of Bristol, England, was born January 19, 1637-38, and emigrated to Virginia about 1666. He was for many years a justice and clerk of Norfolk county from 1666 till his death in 1699. His will mentions sons John, Malachy and James, and daughters Sarah, Jane and Martha, wife Martha.

Tillyard, Rev. Arthur, was born in 1673 and matriculated at All Souls' College, Oxford, October 15, 1689. He was licensed for

Virginia June 23, 1702, and was minister of York parish in York county till his death in 1712. He gave his library to Colonel Cole Digges, who lived in his parish.

Timson, Samuel, merchant of London, who came to Virginia in 1677 as attorney of William Fellows, woodmonger of London. He was a justice of York county in 1683 and subsequent years and died January 23, 1693. He married Mary Juxon and left issue.

Tindall (Tyndall), Robert, was gunner to Prince Henry; came to Virginia with the first settlers. He went on the trip with Newport up James river from May 21 to June 21, 1607, and kept a journal of the voyage and made a chart of the river, neither of which is preserved. The next year (1608) he went with Newport to Werowocomoco, York river, and made a chart of James and York rivers. At this time Gloucester Point was named after him, Tindall's Point, and it went by that name for a hundred years. In 1609 he went from England as master under Captain Samuel Argall to fish for sturgeon in James river. Afterwards employed by Lord Delaware, in June, 1609, in fishing, and doubtless afterward sailed constantly with Captain Argall.

Todd, Thomas, founder of an influential family in Virginia, patented land in Elizabeth City county in 1647 and in Gloucester county in 1664. He removed to Maryland where he was burgess for Baltimore county. He died at sea in 1676, leaving issue, among others Thomas Todd of "Toddsbury," Gloucester county, Virginia. His wife was Ann Gorsuch, daughter of Rev. John Gorsuch, a cavalier minister.

Todkill, Anas, came with the first settlers to Virginia in 1607. In 1609 he went on a search for Sir Walter Raleigh's lost colony, under the conduct of Pipisco, chief of the Warrascoyacks. He reported that he could learn nothing of them. He wrote an account of his stay in Virginia, which Smith used in his history.

Tomkies, Dr. Charles, practitioner of physic, died in Gloucester county in May, 1737.

Tompkins, Christopher, born on North river, Gloucester county, October 17, 1705, married Joyce Reade, on Gwyn's Island, probably the daughter of Benjamin Reade. He died in Caroline county, August 8, 1771, leaving issue ("Virginia Magazine," xix, p. 196).

Tompkins, Humphrey, immigrant ancestor, was an early resident of New Pocoson parish, York county. He married about 1661 Hannah Bennett, daughter of Samuel Bennett, and widow of Abraham Turner. He had issue Mary, Edith, Samuel, William, Humphrey, Hannah, Elizabeth, Ann and John.

Tonge, John, captain in the Cold Stream Foot-guards, and muster-master of the militia in Cumberland, Westmoreland counties, England; was quartermaster in the regiment sent over in October, 1676, to subdue Bacon's rebellion.

Tooke, Henry, eldest son of Henry Tooke, of Winton, Southamptonshire, England, settled in Surry county about 1690, was sheriff and captain of the militia. He died October 20, 1710.

Totopotomoy, chief of the Pamunkey Indians and husband of Queen Anne, of that tribe. He was killed in 1656, while fighting as an ally of the whites, under Captain Edward Hill, against the Richahecrians. The battle, which was disastrous to the whites, took place on a creek in Hanover county, which bears Totopotomoy's name.

Towles, Henry, immigrant ancestor, came from Liverpool to Virginia about the middle of the seventeenth century. He married Ann Stokeley, of Accomac county, and had issue Henry and Stokeley Towles, who have many descendants.

Trahorne, John, was a burgess for Weyanoke in 1629-1630.

Travers, Raleigh, patented land on Rappahannock river in 1653; justice of the peace for Lancaster county in 1656; burgess for Lancaster in 1651, 1661, 1665, 1666 and 1669. He was lieutenant-colonel of the Lancaster militia. He died before 1674, as in that year his widow Elizabeth married Robert Beckingham. He was brother of Colonel William Travers, of Richmond county.

Travers, Samuel, son of Colonel William Travers (q. v.), was justice of the peace for Rappahannock county in 1686 and 1687, and burgess for Richmond county in 1696-1697 and sheriff in 1697. He married Frances Allerton, daughter of Colonel Isaac Allerton. He had three daughters, Elizabeth who died unmarried; Winifred who married Daniel Hornby, and Rebecca who married Captain Charles Colston.

Travers, Colonel William, an early resident of Rappahannock county, was speaker of the house of burgesses in 1677. He died in 1679, leaving by his wife Rebecca, Samuel, Raleigh and William Travers. His wife married (secondly) John Rice.

Travis, Champion, son of Colonel Edward Champion Travis, was a member of the conventions of 1775 and 1776, colonel of the state regiment in 1775, naval commissioner in 1776, justice and sheriff of James City county. He married Elizabeth Boush, of Norfolk.

Travis, Edward, came to Virginia before 1637 and in that year patented land at Chippokes Creek in Surry county. He soon located at Jamestown and married the "daughter and heiress" of John Johnson, who owned land on the island. In 1644-1645 he represented the island in the house of burgesses. He died before 1663, leaving a son Edward.

Travis, Edward Champion, was a descendant of Edward Travis (q. v.). He owned a large part of Jamestown Island, and was burgess for the same from 1752 to 1765 as well as colonel of the James City militia. He married Susanna Hutchings, daughter of Colonel Joseph Hutchings, of Norfolk county. He was born in 1721 and died in August, 1770; father of Colonel Champion Travis.

Tree, Richard, came to Virginia in 1619 with Captain Abraham Piersey, cape-merchant; had fifty acres of land at Blunt Point, James river and fifty acres at James City Island, burgess for Hog Island in 1627 and 1629; by trade a carpenter; had a son John, aged thirteen in 1625.

Trent, Alexander, was son of Alexander Trent, one of the first justices of the new county of Cumberland (1749), and was burgess for Cumberland from 1765 to 1771. He married in 1753, Elizabeth Woodson, daughter of Stephen Woodson. He had a brother Peterfield Trent.

BURGESSES AND OTHER PROMINENT PERSONS 345

Trigg, Stephen, descended from Abraham Trigg who emigrated from Cornwall, England, about 1710, was a burgess for Fincastle county at the last assembly under the regal government 1775-1776, and member of the convention of July, 1775; went to Kentucky as member of a land commission and was killed in the battle of Blue Licks at the head of his regiment. Trigg county was named in his honor. He was brother of Colonel Abraham Trigg, a member of congress.

Trussell, John, born 1605, came to Virginia in 1622, was a burgess for Northumberland 1649, 1651, 1654 and 1655, and justice of that county in 1683; lieutenant-colonel in 1655, and in 1659 he was presiding justice of the county. He died about 1660, leaving a widow Mary and children: Elizabeth, who married Matthew Rodham; Anna and John.

Tucker, Robert, was a wealthy merchant of Norfolk, who came from Barbadoes. He was justice of Norfolk county from 1711 to his death in 1722. He left a son Robert Tucker (q. v.). His wife was Frances Courtenay, who married (second) Thomas Nelson, of Yorktown.

Tucker, Colonel Robert, was the son of Robert Tucker and Francis Courtenay, his wife, who were originally from Barbadoes. He was a prominent merchant of Norfolk, was alderman and mayor, and burgess for Norfolk county from 1753 to 1755, when he resigned to accept the office of sheriff. He married Joanna Corbin, daughter of Gawin and Martha Corbin, and died July 1, 1767, leaving among other children Robert Tucker (q. v.).

Tucker, Robert, son of Colonel Robert Tucker and Joanna Corbin, his wife, was born September 24, 1741, and was burgess for Norfolk county from 1765 to 1769. He died in 1780, without issue.

Tuke (Took), James, was a burgess for Isle of Wight in 1639. He left descendants in that county.

Tunstall, Edward, patented lands in Henrico county, and was burgess for Henrico in 1639; ancestor of a prominent Virginia family.

Tunstall, Colonel Richard, a descendant of Edward Tunstall (q. v.), was clerk of King and Queen in 1739 and 1742; burgess for King and Queen in the assembly of 1766-1768; chairman of the committee of safety for that county 1774, and clerk 1777. He married Anne Hill, daughter of Leonard Hill, of Essex, and died previous to 1782. His daughter Hannah married George Brooke of "Pampatike," King and Queen county.

Turberville, John, immigrant, descended from the Tubervilles of Bere Regis, Dorset, England, was a justice of Lancaster county in 1699, burgess in 1703-1704, sheriff in 1705-1707 and died in 1728, leaving issue George Turberville, of "Hickory Hill," Westmoreland county, clerk of that county from 1726 to 1742. The book-plate, showing the Turberville arms, of George Turberville's son, George Lee Turberville, is well known.

Turner, Harry, son of Colonel Thomas Turner, and Martha Taliaferro, his wife, was a vestryman of Hanover parish, King George county, major of militia, clerk of the county from 1742 to 1751, and member of the house of burgesses from 1742 to 1749.

He married Elizabeth, daughter and heiress of Colonel Nicholas Smith, of "Smith's Mount," Westmoreland county. He died in 1751.

Turner, Thomas, resided, first, about 1714 in Essex county, and afterwards was clerk of King George from 1723 to 1742. He was justice of King George and vestryman of Hanover parish in that county. In 1736-1740 and 1752-1755, he served as a member of the house of burgesses for King George county. His residence on the Rappahannock was called "Walsingham." He married Martha Taliaferro in 1715 and died in 1758. Father of Major Harry Turner.

Twine, John, clerk of the first general assembly 1619.

Tyler, Charles, was the apparent founder of the family of Tylers which beginning in Westmoreland county spread through Prince William, Fauquier and Loudoun counties. He had four sons Charles, Benjamin, Joseph and William. He died in 1723, leaving a widow Jane who married (secondly) William Woffendall. He was ancestor of John Webb Tyler, judge of the Virginia Supreme Court and who died in 1862.

Tyler, Henry, immigrant, born in 1604, came to Virginia before 1645, and in 1652-1653 patented 254 acres at Middle Plantation, subsequently Williamsburg. He was justice of the peace of York county in 1653. He subsequently, in 1666, received a certificate from York county for 1,800 acres. He married (first) Mary, and (second) Ann, widow of John Orchard. He died in 1672, and left three sons Henry, John and Daniel. His widow Anne married (secondly) Martin Gardner, justice and sheriff of York county, and previously grocer of London.

Tyler, Henry, son of Henry Tyler, lived at Middle Plantation, Virginia, was born about 1664, and was justice, coroner and sheriff of York county. In 1699 he was appointed one of the directors for building Williamsburg, the new capital city. As senior warden of the Bruton Church in Williamsburg, he headed the petition of the vestry in 1710 to the general assembly for a new brick building. This was finished in 1715 and is still standing. Henry Tyler married Elizabeth Chiles, a granddaughter of Colonel Walter Chiles, member of the council in 1651. He was ancestor of John Tyler, president of the United States in 1841-1845.

Tyler, John, son of John Tyler, of James City county, and grandson of Henry Tyler, of York county, was born in James City county about 1715, and died in Williamsburg in August, 1773. He was long marshal of the vice-admiralty court of the colony. He married Anne, daughter of Dr. Lewis Contesse, a French Huguenot physician, and had issue: 1. Mary, who married John Irby, of Charles City county. 2. Elizabeth, who married John Greenhow. 3. Rachel, married (first) William Drummond, (second) Stith Hardyman. 4. Anne, who married Dr. Anthony Tucker Dixon. 5. Louis. 6. John, governor of Virginia from 1808-1811. 7. Joanna, married Major Wood Bouldin, of Charlotte county.

Tyler, Richard, was son of Richard Tyler of Essex, the immigrant. He was a justice of the peace in Essex and major of the militia. He married (first) Catherine, widow of Thomas Montague, and (second) Anne

———. He died in 1701, issueless. Richard Tyler, the father, is believed to have been Richard Tyler, of London, who in 1674 had interests in Gloucester county, Virginia.

Tyler, William, was son of Richard Tyler of Essex county, the immigrant, and was clerk of Caroline county. He died in 1767. He was ancestor of the present J. Hoge Tyler, late governor of the state.

Underwood, Major William, was son of William Underwood, who in 1650 patented land in Rappahannock county. He was burgess for Rappahannock in 1652 and justice in 1656. His mother Margaret Underwood married (secondly) Captain John Upton, and (thirdly) Thomas Lucas, Sr., of Rappahannock county.

Upshaw, John, son of James Upshaw (1730-1806), was burgess for Essex county in 1758-1761, and 1761-1765. His sister Sarah married William Roane.

Upshur, Arthur, was born in county Essex, England, in 1625, settled at Occahamock in Northampton county, and died January 26, 1709, in the eighty-fifth year of his age. He was ancestor of Abel P. Upshur, secretary of state under Tyler.

Upton, Captain John, came to Virginia in 1622, aged twenty-six, went with Captain Madison up Potomac river, the same year; settled in Warwicksqueak, Isle of Wight county, which he represented in the assembly in 1629-1630, 1632-1633, 1641, 1642, 1645, 1647; justice for many years. At the session of 1645, the assembly provided for a mint, and Captain Upton was made mint master general. His will was proved in Isle of Wight county December 16, 1652.

Uttamatomakkin, an Indian who accompanied Pocahontas to England in 1615. He was instructed to number the people in that country, and at first made a notch in a stick for every man he saw, but soon grew tired of the task.

Van Metre, John and Isaac, were sons of John Van Metre, an Indian trader of New Jersey whose father Jan Jooster Van Meteren, the founder of the family in America, came to New Amsterdam in 1662, with his wife and five children. John and Isaac Van Metre after a sojourn in New Jersey, migrated to Maryland and Virginia. They obtained a grant in 1730 for 40,000 acres of land in the forks of the Shenandoah. Their descendants have been prominent.

Vaulx, Robert, burgess for Westmoreland county 1752-1755, was son of Robert Vaulx of the same county, who was grandson of Robert Vaulx, merchant of London who came to Virginia with brothers Humphrey, Thomas and James. Robert Vaulx, burgess, died about 1755, when his will was proved.

Veale, George, was a burgess for Norfolk county in the assembly of 1756-1758.

Venable, Abraham, son of Abraham Venable, who emigrated from England to Virginia about 1685 where he married about 1700 Elizabeth, daughter of Hugh Lewis, of James City county, and widow of Henry Nicks. He was born March 12, 1700, married about 1723 Martha (or Hannah Davis), daughter of Nathaniel Davis, a Quaker from Devonshire, England. He owned much land in Hanover, Louisa and Goochland counties. He was justice of the peace for Hanover county and one of the first justices of the peace for Louisa from December 13, 1742, vestryman of Fredericksville parish, county lieutenant of Louisa, and member of the house of burgesses from 1742 to 1756. He was the friend, legal client and political supporter of Patrick Henry. He died December 16, 1768, and was father of Nathaniel Venable (q. v.).

Venable, Nathaniel, son of Abraham Venable and Martha Davis, his wife, of Louisa county, was born November 1, 1733, and resided first in Buckingham county and then in Prince Edward county, was vestryman of St. Patrick's parish, became a Presbyterian, and organized the first Presbyterian church in Prince Edward county; was justice of the peace and burgess for Prince Edward, in the assembly of 1766-1768, and afterward a member of the Virginia house of delegates. He was one of the earliest promoters and one of the first trustees (in 1775) of Hampden Sydney Academy and (in 1783) of Hampden Sydney College. He died December 27, 1804. He married Elizabeth Woodson, of Prince Edward.

Wadding, Rev. James, was minister at Jamestown in 1672, and afterwards served in Gloucester county in 1676. He was the minister whom Nathaniel Bacon so sharply reproved, because of some unpleasant advice. He married Susanna, widow of Walter Chiles, Jr., of Jamestown.

Wade, Armiger, believed to have been descended from Armingall Wade, of Bellsize, near Hampstead, England, who was father of Sir William Wade, frequently mentioned in the progress of James I., and of whom there is a curious and interesting history in "Parke's History of Hampstead." He was a justice of York county and burgess in 1656. His will was proved April 24, 1677. Issue: 1. Armiger. 2. Mary married Captain John Hay. 3. Dorothy married John Lilly.

Wade, Robert, was a burgess for Halifax county in 1758-1761 and 1761-1765. He died about 1770, and mentions in his will sons Robert, John, Stephen, Edward and Charles, daughters Sarah Stokes, Mary Hunt; grandson Hampton Wade, son of Robert Wade, Robert Wade, son of Charles, Robert Wade, son of son Robert.

Waddell, James, was born in Ulster, Ireland, July, 1739, of Scotch parentage. Shortly after his birth, his parents emigrated to Pennsylvania. He was schooled under Dr. Finley of Nottingham and was a tutor in the school at fifteen. At nineteen years he came to Hanover county, Virginia, where he met Rev. Samuel Davies, and was licensed to preach by the Hanover Presbytery in 1761. He had charge of a church in Lancaster county till 1778; then removed to his estate of "Spring Hill" near Waynesborough, where he remained for seven years, acting continuously as minister of Tinkling Spring and sometimes at Staunton. In 1785 he moved to Louisa county where he resided till his death in 1805. Besides preaching in various churches in the neighborhood, he taught school. William Wirt immortalized him as "The Blind Preacher," in the essays of the "Old Bachelor."

Wagener, Rev. Peter, was licensed by the Bishop of London for Maryland August 9, 1703, but soon came to Virginia, where he was a minister of a parish in 1705. He returned to England and was living there in Essex county in 1739.

Wagener, Peter, attorney-at-law, was the only son of Rev. Peter Wagener, of county Essex, England, and was born April 5, 1717. He came to Virginia and settled in Essex county, where he married Catherine Robinson, daughter of John Robinson, of the council. There are numerous descendants of this marriage.

Wager, William, was clerk of Elizabeth City county from 1746 to 1791, and burgess in 1758-1761, 1761-1765.

Walke, Anthony, born in 1692, was a son of Thomas Walke, who came from Barbadoes to Lower Norfolk county in 1662, by Mary, his wife, daughter of Lieutenant-Colonel Anthony Lawson. He lived at "Fairfield," in Princess Anne county. He was justice for Princess Anne, and a member of the house of burgesses from 1720 to 1765. He married three times, (first) Mary Sanford; (second) Elizabeth Newton; (third) Anna Lee Armistead. He died November 8, 1768.

Walke, Anthony, the second son of Colonel Anthony Walke and Anna Lee Armistead, was born January 3, 1726. He was a rich merchant of Norfolk, and was lieutenant-colonel of the militia. He gave the land, and built at his own expense a church edifice known as "Old Donation," about twelve miles from Norfolk. He married (first) Jane, daughter of Richard and Jane Bolling Randolph; (second) Mary Moseley, daughter of Colonel Edward Hack Moseley. His will was proved March 14, 1782.

Walke, Thomas, son of Thomas Walke, who came from Barbadoes, by Mary, his wife, daughter of Lieutenant-Colonel Anthony Lawson, was a member of the house of burgesses for Princess Anne in 1712-1714. He was brother of Anthony Walke.

Walker, George, was son of George Walker, who lived on Mill Creek, Elizabeth City county, and was pilot for James river in 1697. George Walker, the younger, was a gunner and storekeeper of the fort at Point Comfort. He married Anne, daughter of the celebrated George Keith, and was a Quaker. He was grandfather of George Wythe, signer of the Declaration of Independence.

Walker, James, burgess for Orange county in the assemblies of 1761-1765, 1766-1768, 1769, 1769-1771.

Walker, John, was burgess for King and Queen county at the third session of the assembly of 1703-1705. He married Rachel Croshaw, daughter of Captain Richard Croshaw, and was probably a son of Lieutenant-Colonel Thomas Walker, of King and Queen (q. v.).

Walker, John, son of John Walker of Ashborne-in-the-Peak, Devonshire, settled in Middlesex county. He married Catherine Yates, daughter of Rev. Bartholomew Yates, and Sarah Stanard, his wife, and had issue Sarah who married John Robinson, of "Hewick," and Clara who married John Allen. He died in 1745. His uncle, Richard Walker, was a merchant of Urbanna, Virginia.

Walker, Peter, was burgess for Northampton county in 1654, captain of militia, and one of the justices.

Walker, Dr. Thomas, son of Thomas Walker, of King and Queen county, and

Susanna Peachey, his wife, and great-grandson of Thomas Walker of Gloucester county, (q. v.), was born January 25, 1715. Educated at William and Mary College, and afterwards studied medicine. He was also an active merchant and surveyor of land, engaging in many enterprises. In 1748 he went on an expedition to Kentucky and kept a diary of his trip. In 1753 Colonel Joshua Fry recommended the discovery of a route to the Pacific coast, and Dr. Walker was to be the chief conductor of the enterprise. From 1752 to 1754 he was a representative in the house of burgesses for Louisa county, but resigned when appointed county surveyor. In 1754 he was appointed by Governor Dinwiddie commissary of stores for the troops on the frontier. He was at the surprise of Braddock, and was active throughout the war with France. From 1757 to 1761 he represented Hampshire county in the house of burgesses, after which time he changed his residence to the east, and represented Albemarle in the house of burgesses from 1761 to 1772. In 1768 he was commissioned to attend, with General Andrew Lewis, the conference with the Six Nations at Fort Stanwix, New York; and in 1774 he was commissioner to treat with the Indians after their defeat at Point Pleasant. Again in 1775 he presided over the conference held with the Indians at Pittsburgh. He represented Louisa county in the last house of burgesses, 1775-1776, and in the revolutionary conventions of 1775 and 1776, and was made a member of the committee of safety for the colony in 1775. In 1777 he was a member of the council of state, and in 1779 was chief of the commissioners on the part of Virginia to meet the commissioners from North Carolina to run the boundary line between the two states. During the war and for some years after it, he was a member of the house of delegates of Virginia. He was an intimate friend of Thomas Jefferson. He died at his residence "Castle Hill," in Albemarle county, November 9, 1794. He married twice, first in 1741, Mildred Thornton, widow of Nicholas Meriwether, and second Elizabeth Thornton. His son John was a senator of the United States and his son Francis, a member of the house of representatives.

Walker, Thomas, represented Gloucester in the house of burgesses in 1663 and 1666. He was captain of militia in 1663, and major in 1666. In 1683 he was lieutenant-colonel residing in King and Queen county. He was probably father of John Walker, of King and Queen county, and grandfather of Thomas Walker, father of the distinguished Dr. Thomas Walker (q. v.).

Walklett, Gregory, one of the commanders under Bacon, at West Point. By the terms of his surrender in 1677, his life was spared, but he was prohibited from holding any office in Virginia.

Wall, John, a burgess for Brunswick county in 1734-1740.

Wallace, Rev. James, of Erroll, Scotland, was born in 1668, and came to Virginia about 1690, where he was minister of Elizabeth City parish, twenty-nine years. He also practiced medicine, and was the founder of a well known family. He married in 1695 Anne, daughter of John Sheppard, of Elizabeth City county, and widow of Thomas Wythe, and died November 3, 1712. He was father of Captain James Wallace, of

BURGESSES AND OTHER PROMINENT PERSONS 351

Elizabeth City county, who married Martha ———.

Wallace, James, son of Captain James Wallace, of Elizabeth City county, and Martha, his wife, was a student of William and Mary College in 1757, burgess for Elizabeth City county 1769, 1772, justice of the county and member of the county committee of safety (1775). He also served in the militia with the rank of captain. He married Elizabeth Westwood. Grandson of Rev. James Wallace (q. v.).

Wallace, Dr. Michael, son of William Wallace, of Galrigs, Scotland, merchant, who was of the same family as Sir William Wallace, the heroic defender of Scottish independence, was born at Galrigs, May 11, 1719, learned medicine and surgery as an apprentice to Dr. Gustavius Brown, of Maryland, settled at Fredericksburg, in Virginia, before 1747, had a very large practice and died in January, 1767. He married Elizabeth Brown, daughter of Dr. Gustavius Brown.

Waller, Benjamin, was son of Colonel John Waller, of "Newport," Spottsylvania county, and was born October 1, 1710. He was a lawyer of distinction, removed when a young man to Williamsburg, was clerk of the council, burgess for James City county 1744-1761, and a judge of the state admiralty and the state general courts, 1776-1785. He died May 1, 1786. He married Martha Hall (1728-1780).

Waller, John, was third son of John Waller, M. D., of Newport Pagnel, Buckinghamshire, England, which last is believed to have been a son of Edmund Waller, the poet. He located in King and Queen county, Virginia, and was sheriff of the county in 1702, a justice of King William county in 1705, and a member of the house of burgesses for King William in 1710-1712, 1712-1714, 1720-1722. When Spottsylvania county was organized out of King William in 1722, he was first clerk of the new county. He was lieutenant-colonel of the militia of Spottsylvania county. He married Dorothy King, and had issue six children. His will was proved in Spottsylvania county October 1, 1754.

Waller, William, son of Colonel John Waller (q. v.), was born in Spottsylvania county in 1714, and represented his county in the house of burgesses in 1742, 1744, 1745, 1746, 1748, 1749, 1752, 1753, when he resigned to accept the place of coroner. He died January 10, 1760.

Wallings, George, was a burgess for Nansemond county in 1663.

Walthoe, Nathaniel, came to Virginia before 1744, when he was clerk of the general assembly. He continued in that office till his death in 1772. He left his property in Virginia to his sister, Henrietta Marmillard, and his nieces Mary and Martha Hart, of Great Britain. There is a portrait of Nathaniel Walthoe at Lower Brandon, in the collection of William Byrd.

Walton, Isaac Row, was burgess for Brunswick in 1761-1765. He was son of George Walton, whose will dated July 7, 1764, was proved in Brunswick January 26, 1767. Isaac Row Walton's will, dated June 19, 1770, was proved in Brunswick, October 22, 1770.

Ward, Seth, lieutenant-colonel and great-grandson of Seth Ward, the immigrant to

Virginia, of "Sheffield" and "Winterpock" in the present Chesterfield county; was justice of Henrico in 1745, sheriff of Chesterfield, member of the house of burgesses in 1764, 1765, 1766-1768. He married Mary Goode.

Ward, Seth, of Varina, ancestor of the Ward family of Virginia, patented in 1634 fifty acres near "Powhatan Tree" in Henrico county.

Ware, Rev. Jacob, was minister of St. Peter's parish, New Kent, from 1690 to 1695 and afterwards was minister of Henrico parish, till his death in 1709.

Wareham, Thomas, was a burgess for Mounts Bay in 1632 and 1632-1633.

Waring, Francis, son of Colonel Thomas Waring, was colonel of the Essex county militia, and burgess for Essex in 1758-1761, 1761-1765 and 1766-1768; was one of the signers of the Northern Neck protest against the Stamp Act. He died in 1771.

Waring, Thomas, emigrated from England and settled at "Goldsberry," St. Anne's parish, Essex county, Virginia, in the latter part of the seventeenth century. He was vestryman, justice of the peace, and member of the house of burgesses in 1736. He died at his family seat, January, 1754, leaving two sons Francis and Thomas, and three daughters, Elizabeth who married Thomas Todd of King and Queen county, Mary who married Henry Robinson, of Hanover, and Anne who married Rev. James Smith, of Essex. He married Lucy Cocke, daughter of William Cocke.

Warne, Thomas, was a burgess for James City county in 1645.

Warnet, Thomas, of Southwark, London, son of John Warnet, of Hempstead, Sussex, was the principal merchant at Jamestown in 1628. He died in February, 1630, and the legacies given in his will show the style of living in his day. His wife was Thomasine, daughter of William Hall, of Woodalling, county Norfolk, England.

Warren, Thomas, born in 1621, patented lands in Charles City county in 1635, due by reason of the personal adventure of his wife Susan Greenleafe, and of Robert Greenleafe, "an ancient planter," her former husband. He was member of the house of burgesses for James City county in 1644, 1645, and for Surry county in 1658-1659 and 1666. He died about 1670, leaving a widow Jane and son William. His sister Alice was wife of Major William Marriott, of Surry county.

Washbourn, John, was a burgess for Accomac county in 1703-1705.

Washer, Ensign, was a burgess for Flower dieu Hundred in the first assembly 1619.

Washington, Augustine, youngest son of Augustine Washington and Jane Butler, his wife, was born in 1720 and was given by his father, Augustine, the family estate in Westmoreland county, known as "Wakefield." He was a burgess for Westmoreland county from 1754 to 1758, and a member of the Ohio Company. He married Anne Aylett, daughter and coheiress of William Aylett, of Westmoreland county. Half-brother of General George Washington.

Washington, Colonel John, son of Rev. Lawrence Washington, royalist clergyman, of Purleigh in county Essex, England, was born about 1631, came to Virginia as a master's mate under Edward Prescott about 1657; chosen vestryman of Appomattox parish, Westmoreland, July 3, 1661; justice of the peace June 24, 1662; lieutenant-colonel in 1670, and member of the house of burgesses 1666, 1676. He commanded against the Indians in 1675, and was friendly to Sir William Berkeley in 1676. He died in 1677. He was ancestor of General George Washington.

Washington, John, settled in Surry county before 1658, was justice of the peace and major of the militia. Issue a son Richard, who sold land in 1678 and died in 1725. He was ancestor of Sidney Lanier, but no known relative to the Washingtons of Westmoreland county.

Washington, Lawrence, merchant, son of a royalist clergyman, Rev. Lawrence Washington, of Purleigh, county Essex, England, came to Virginia about 1656. He married Mary Jones, of Luton, county Bedford, England; died in Virginia. He was brother of Colonel John Washington (q. v.).

Washington, Lawrence, second child and oldest surviving son of Augustine Washington and Jane Butler, his first wife, was born at Pope's Creek, Westmoreland county, Virginia, in 1718. He was a half brother of General George Washington. He was educated in England and settled upon the "Hunting Creek Plantation," devised him by his father in Fairfax county. He was burgess for Fairfax from 1742 to 1749 and was one of the originators of the Ohio Company (1749). He was also interested in the manufacture of iron, both in Virginia and in Maryland. He was a captain in the British army, and in 1740-1742 served under Admiral Vernon in the expedition against Carthagena. Later he was commissioned a major in the Virginia service. On account of sickness he resigned and in 1751 went to Barbadoes for his health in company with his brother George. He died July 26, 1752, at his residence "Mt. Vernon" named in honor of his old commander, Admiral Vernon. He married on July 19, 1743, Anne, eldest daughter of Hon. William Fairfax of "Belvoir," but left no surviving issue.

Waters, Edward, born 1584, and left England for Virginia in the same ship, the *Seaventure*, which brought Sir Thomas Gates, as first governor of Virginia under the second charter (1609); wrecked on the Bermudas; went with the other castaways to Jamestown in 1610; in the same year returned with Sir George Somers to Bermuda; when Matthew Somers sailed for England he was one of the three who remained to hold the island for England and found an immense piece of ambergris; member of the council of Bermuda; left Bermuda for Virginia in 1618 or 1619; married, probably about 1620, Grace O'Niel; taken prisoner with his wife by the Indians of Nansemond at the great massacre in 1622; escaped, and in January, 1625, was living at Blunt Point, James river, with his wife and two children, William and Margaret. He had the rank of captain, and in 1628 was appointed commander of the plantations in Elizabeth City county; burgess in 1625. He is sometimes confounded with Robert Waters, left behind by Gates in the Bermudas, when he sailed in 1610 for Jamestown, and who killed a man.

Waters, William, son of Edward Waters, of Elizabeth City county, was high sheriff of Northampton county in 1652, major of militia in March, 1652, and a justice of the quorum; burgess for Northampton in 1654 and 1659-1660. He married the widow of George Clarke, and his will probated in 1685 names sons William, Richard, Thomas, John, Obedience and Edward.

Waters, William, son of Major William Waters, was sheriff for Northampton county in 1696, and burgess in 1696, 1705 1714, 1718 and 1720. He died before 1722.

Watkins, Benjamin, son of Stephen Watkins, whose will is recorded in Chesterfield county (1758), was clerk of the county from 1749 to 1779 and burgess for Chesterfield in the assembly of 1772-1774 and 1775-1776 and member of the conventions of 1774, 1775 and 1776.

Watkins, Henry, was a burgess in 1624 and signed "The Tragical Relation." He was then living on the eastern shore.

Watkins, Micajah, son of John Watkins, of Prince Edward county, whose will dated April 20, 1762, is on record. He was burgess for Halifax county in the assembly 1775-1776, and served in the conventions of 1775 and 1776.

Watson, Abraham, was a burgess for James City county in 1652, 1653, 1654.

Watson, Joseph, was a burgess for Dunmore county (Shenandoah) in 1772 and 1773. He died before May 5, 1774.

Watts, Matthew, was a burgess for Elizabeth City county at the April session, 1696, of the house of burgesses.

Waugh, James, succeeded Henry Fitzhugh, who died, as burgess for Stafford county in 1744 and served till 1747. He was a captain of militia, etc., and was a grandson of Rev. John Waugh (q. v.).

Waugh, Rev. John, was a minister of the church of England in a parish in Stafford county, Virginia, where he was living as early as 1666. During the reign of James II., Virginia, like England, was very much agitated with rumors of Popish plots, and John Waugh greatly inflamed the people by his harangues against the Catholics. In 1699, he was elected to the general assembly, but declared ineligible as a minister. He died in 1706, leaving a wife Christian and sons Joseph, John, Alexander and David.

Waugh, John, son of Rev. John Waugh, was burgess for Stafford county in 1710-1712.

Wayles, John, an eminent lawyer, born at Lancaster, England, in 1715. He resided in Charles City county, Virginia, where his residence was called "The Forest." He married at least twice, (first) Martha, widow of Lewellyn Eppes, who was herself an Eppes before marriage, and (second) Elizabeth Lomax, widow of Reuben Skelton. Martha, his child, by Martha Eppes, married Thomas Jefferson. He died in 1773.

Webb, George, son of Conrad Webb, of London, merchant, resided in New Kent county, Virginia, *circa* 1728, father of Lewis Webb (q. v.).

Webb, Giles, was a burgess for Nansemond county in 1658, 1659, 1660. He was probably father of Giles Webb, of Henrico county, who died in 1713, and of Thomas Webb, of the city of Gloucestershire, England, gentleman, who was alive in 1718.

Webb, Lewis, son of George Webb and Lucy, his wife, of New Kent county, was born April 19, 1731, and was a burgess for New Kent county in the assembly of 1758-1761.

Webb, Stephen, born at Breshley, Worcestershire, and baptized there September 1, 1598, son of Stephen and Ann Webb. He was a burgess for James City county, then including Surry, in March, 1643, and October, 1644. He had two sons who died without issue, and his property in Virginia went to his brother William Webb, of Tewkesbury, Gloucestershire, England.

Webb, Wingfield, was a burgess for Gloucester county in 1654.

Webster, Richard, probably son of Roger Webster; he resided at Jamestown where he purchased from the colony the "Country House"; was major of the militia, and burgess for James City county, March, 1657-1658.

Webster, Roger, and Joanna, his wife, was living at Hog Island in 1625, member of the house of burgesses for "Glebe Land and Archer's Hope" September, 1632; probably father of Major Richard Webster, of Jamestown.

Weekes, Abraham, was chosen as vestryman of Lancaster county in 1657, and justice in 1666. He was afterwards a justice of Middlesex and burgess at the assemblies October 10, 1676, and October 10, 1677. He died in 1692. The Middlesex county records show that in 1738 the oldest descendant bearing the name was Thomas Hobbes Weekes, Esq., of Southampton, England.

Weir (Weyer), Major John, settled in Old Rappahannock county. In 1666 he had three grants of land, aggregating 6,570 acres. He was burgess for Rappahannock March, 1658-1659. In 1697 Elizabeth Gardner, of St. Mary's county, Maryland, daughter and heiress of John Weire, late of Rappahannock county, deceased, conveyed 2,502 acres in Richmond county, patented by him June 6, 1666.

Welbourn, Thomas, burgess for Accomac county in 1700-1702.

Weldon, Poynes, a lawyer, burgess for James City county in 1695-96. He was probably son of Major Samuel Weldon, of London, who came to Virginia in 1675 and died in James City about 1693. The latter in turn was doubtless a son of Rev. John Weldon, minister in 1666 of the parish of St. Mary Newington, Surry county, England. The city of Weldon, in North Carolina, was named for this family (see "William and Mary Quarterly," vi, p. 121).

Wellford, Dr. Robert, was born in England, April 12, 1753; he came to America in 1775, and in 1776 was surgeon in the British army. After the war, having rendered himself popular with the American prisoners by his tender attentions, he settled in Fredericksburg and acquired a large practice. He married, January 1, 1781, Mrs. Catherine Thornton, widow of John Thornton, Esq., of Stafford county, and daughter of Bartholomew Yates, of Gloucester county. Died April 24, 1823.

Wells, Richard, was a burgess for Upper Norfolk county in 1645.

West, Anthony, came to Virginia in 1622; in 1624 resided at James City, and in 1625 at the plantations opposite on the south side; settled in Northampton county, where he was one of the justices and lieutenant-colonel of the militia. He died in 1651, leaving a son, John West. He was some relation to Lord Delaware, as the arms of his family were the same as those of his lordship. Anne, his widow, married (second) Stephen Charleton.

West, Francis, burgess for King William county in 1748-1749, 1756-1758, was a son of Captain Thomas West, who was a grandson of Captain John West, brother to Lord Delaware. He was justice of the peace and colonel of the militia. He married Jane Cole, widow, first, of Ferdinand Leigh, and afterward of Stephen Bingham. He had a daughter Agnes, who married William Dandridge.

West, Henry, patented 900 acres on the Blackwater, in Isle of Wight county, 1673. He took part in Bacon's rebellion, and by court-martial, held January 24, 1677, was found guilty of treason and rebellion and banished from Virginia for seven years, and all of his estate except five pounds confiscated.

West, Hugh, was descended from John West, who came from Muston, in Yorkshire, it is believed, about the latter part of the seventeenth century. He was a burgess for Fairfax county, Virginia, 1752, 1753, 1754. He died the latter year and was succeeded by his son, Hugh West (q. v.).

West, Hugh, Jr., attorney-at-law, was son of Hugh West (q. v.), and succeeded him as the representative for Fairfax county in 1754. He continued to sit for Fairfax until 1755, when he removed to Frederick county and represented that county in 1756, 1757, 1758. His will was proved in Fairfax county, June 18, 1767, and names issue.

West, Lieutenant-Colonel John, of Northampton county, was son of Anthony West. He was a contemporary of Colonel John West, of West Point, but unlike him took sides with Bacon in 1676. He was pardoned by Sir William Berkeley on due submission and acknowledgment of his guilt. He married Matilda Scarburgh and had issue—Anthony, Alexander, John the eldest, Jonathan, and John the younger.

West, Colonel John, son of Captain John West, governor, etc., was born at "Bellfield," York river, in 1632, being the first child of English parents born on York river; lived at West Point; sat on the courts-martial that tried the rebels in Bacon's time; senior justice and colonel of the New Kent county militia; married Unity, daughter of Major Joseph Croshaw; burgess for New Kent county in 1685 and 1686. He had three sons—John, Nathaniel and Thomas, and one daughter—Unity, who married Henry Fox, of King William county.

West, John, known as "Capt. John West, Jr.," was son of Hugh West (q. v.), and represented Fairfax in the house of burgesses from 1755 till his death in 1775. He married Catherine, daughter of Major Thomas Colville, and left issue.

West, John, of King William county, son of Colonel John West and Unity Croshaw, his wife, was a member of the house of burgesses in 1702-1706. He married, in October, 1698, Judith, daughter of Major Anthony Armistead, of Elizabeth City county, and had one son Charles, who, dying without issue, left the West Point estate (4,000 acres) to his cousin, Thomas West.

West, Captain Thomas, of King William county, son of Colonel John West and Unity Croshaw, his wife, was burgess for King William in 1702-1706. He married Agnes ———, and had a son Thomas, who was given the West Point estate (4,000 acres) by his cousin, Charles West.

West, Thomas, son of Captain Thomas West, of King William county, was a burgess for that county in 1742-1747. He died in 1743, before the assembly ended. Charles West, his cousin, left him the West Point estate. He married Elizabeth Seaton, daughter of George Seaton, of King and Queen county, and left issue, of whom the eldest son was John West.

West, William, nephew of Lord Delaware, killed by the Indians at the falls of James river, Virginia, in 1611.

Westcomb, James, was clerk of Westmoreland county from January 24, 1690, to July, 1709, and burgess for the county in the assembly of 1700-1702.

Westhrope, John, was a London merchant, who in 1650 patented 1,500 acres on Ward's creek, in Charles City county (now Prince George). He was major of militia, and in 1644 represented Charles City county in the house of burgesses. His will, dated September 24, 1655, was proved in London, June 12, 1658. He married a daughter of John Sadler, of London, but had no surviving issue. He gave his estate to his five sisters.

Westwood, William, was son of Worlich Westwood, of Elizabeth City county, and was a member of the house of burgesses in 1736-40, 1742-47, 1748-49, 1752-55, 1756-58. His will was proved in May, 1770.

Westwood, Worlich, son of William Westwood, of Elizabeth City county, was a member of the house of burgesses in 1772-1774 and 1775-1776, and of the conventions of 1775, 1776 and 1788, and member of the house of delegates in 1785, 1790 and 1802-03.

Wetherall, Robert, was burgess for James City county in 1645, 1652.

Wetherburn, Henry, keeper of the Raleigh Tavern, in Williamsburg. He married Anne Marot, widow of James Shields, also keeper of an ordinary. He died in 1752.

Whaley, James, son of Major Thomas Whaley, was born in 1652. He was a prominent merchant of York county, Virginia. He died May 16, 1701. He married, April, 1695, Mary Page, niece of Colonel John Page, and left an only son Matthew, who died at the age of nine years.

Whaley, Mary, daughter of Matthew Page, and widow of James Whaley, of York county, Virginia. Upon the death of her son Matthew, at the age of nine years, she established in 1706 a free school near Williamsburg in his honor. She removed some years afterwards to England, where she died in St. Mary Bedfont parish, January 31, 1743. The school still continues under the supervision of the College of William and Mary.

Whaley, Thomas, was an early resident of York county, Virginia. In Bacon's rebellion he was a major and commanded at Colonel Nathaniel Bacon's house on King's creek, where he repulsed an attack of Sir William Berkeley's men and killed their commander, Captain Hubert Farrell. At the collapse of the rebellion he rode away into the forest with Richard Lawrence and two others. He left a son, James Whaley, who married Mary Page.

Whateley (Wheatley), Rev. Solomon, came to Virginia from Maryland in 1700; was minister of Bruton church from 1702 to 1710. He died in Williamsburg the latter year. In the same year his brother, Thomas Whateley, of Bromeley St. Leonard's, in the county of Middlesex (England), gentleman, made a power of attorney concerning his estate, which was recorded in York county, Virginia.

Whitaker, Alexander, "the Apostle to Virginia," son of Dr. William Whitaker, a celebrated Puritan divine and head of St. John's College, Cambridge, was born at Cambridge in 1585; was Master of Arts of that University about 1604; had a good parish in the northern part of England, but gave it up to come to Virginia in 1611; was preacher to the colony at Henrico in 1612 and after; living at "Rock Hall," his parsonage, opposite Henrico, in 1614; minister at Bermuda Nether Hundred in the spring of 1616; drowned before June, 1617. He was author of "Good News from Virginia," published in 1613.

Whitaker, Dr. Walter, resided in Middlesex county; was justice, 1673; burgess in 1676; high sheriff, 1685. He died July 27, 1692. He married Sibella ———, and a deed calls him "Walter Andrewes als. Whitaker."

Whitaker, William, probably a son of William Whitaker, Esq., of the council, was burgess for James City county in 1658-59, and captain of the militia. In 1681 William Whitaker and Agnes, his wife, kept the "French Ordinary," halfway between Middle Plantation and York. In 1706 William Whitaker, of Warwick, and Sarah, his wife, daughter of Isaac Collier, joined in a deed.

Whittaker, Richard, was a member of the house of burgesses for Warwick county in 1685, 1688 and 1697, and the last year he was sheriff of Warwick.

Whitby, William, lived in Warwick county, which he represented in the house of burgesses in 1641, 1652, 1653, 1654; presiding as speaker in 1653. He received two considerable tracts of land, one in Warwick, where he lived, and the other on Potomac creek. He married Ruth Gorsuch, daughter of Rev. John Gorsuch, and Anne Lovelace, sister of Colonel Francis Lovelace, and had a son William, who lived in Middlesex county, Virginia, and died about 1676 issueless.

White, John, was burgess for James City county in 1641. He had a lot at Jamestown in 1644, between the state house and the church. He was probably son of William White, haberdasher of London ("Virginia Magazine," xv, 64). His will was proved in Surry county in 1679 and he left his property to his two sisters, Lucy Corker and Mary White.

White, Rev. William, minister, died in Lancaster county in 1658. He was probably father of Rev. Jeremiah White, Cromwell's well-known chaplain.

Whitehead, Philip, son of Richard Whitehead, living in Gloucester county in 1671; was burgess for King William county in the assemblies of 1723-1726 and 1727-1734. He used arms very nearly the same as the arms of Whitehead of Uplands, Lancaster county, England. His sister Mary married Philip Ryan, of King and Queen county, and a daughter married William Claiborne, of "Romancoke," King William county.

Whiting, Beverley, son of Henry Whiting and Anne Beverley, daughter of Peter Beverley, Esq., was burgess for Gloucester county from 1740 to 1755, when he died, and was succeeded by Thomas Whiting (q. v.).

Whiting, Thomas, of "Gloucestertown" and "Elmington," was burgess for Gloucester from 1755 to 1776, inclusive, and member of the conventions of 1775 and 1776. He was chairman of the Virginia naval board during the revolution. In his will, dated October 15, 1780, he names his children, Thomas (who was ancestor of the Whitings of Hampton), Henry, Horatio, Sarah, Catherine, Eliza L., Susanna, who married (first) in 1786, Gibson Cluverins and (second) John Lowry; Jane, who married Charles Grymes, and Anne, who married (first) Major John Pryor and (second) Charles Frémont, father of General John C. Frémont.

Wickliffe, David, first child of Protestant parents born in the state of Maryland, was the son of David Wickliffe, of Maryland, who died in 1642. After his father's death his mother emigrated to Mattox creek, Westmoreland county, where he married Mary Nicholas, and had a son David. The Wickliffe family has been conspicuously represented in Kentucky, to which state members of the family immigrated.

Wilford, Thomas, was the second son of a knight who had been killed while fighting for King Charles. He was burgess for Northumberland county in 1651, acquired the Indian language and served as interpreter. In 1676 he joined with Bacon and was captured and executed. He is described "as a small man with a great heart."

Wilkins, John, was a burgess for Accomac county in 1641, and died in 1651. The Wilkins family is still prominent on the eastern shore, and has had frequent representatives in the assembly of Virginia.

Wilkinson, John, was a burgess for Accomac in 1632-33.

Wilkinson, William, a surgeon, who came with the first settlers in 1607.

Wilkinson, Rev. William, patented 700 acres near Ensign Thomas Keeling, on Lynhaven river, due for the importation of his wife Naomi and other persons, and by assignment from Robert Newkirk. In 1644 he was minister at Elizabeth City, and, removing to Maryland, was the second Protestant minister in that colony.

Willcox, Captain John, came to Virginia in 1620, and in 1621 made a settlement on "Old Plantation Creek," in Northampton county. In 1624 he was a burgess, being one of the signers of the "Tragical Relation." After the massacre of 1622 he commanded expeditions against the Indians. He died sometime before 1628, when his will, dated in 1622, was proved in England. He mentions no children, but he had doubtless sons born after the date of his will and before its proof.

Willcox, Captain John, was a burgess for Nansemond county in 1656, and for Northampton county in 1658. He was doubtless a son of Captain John Willcox, the burgess of 1624, and was born after the date of his will (1622). He died in 1662, leaving his property to his wife for life, with reversion to his unborn child. In case the child died he devised the estate to his wife's children, Edmund and Henry Yardley; mentions his brother, Henry Willcox, and the Yardley children's uncle, John Custis.

Williams, Dr. Robert, was burgess for Isle of Wight county in 1666. The same year he patented 3,854 acres on the waters of the Black Swamp. He died in Isle of Wight in 1669, leaving a wife Jane, who married Mr. Robert Burnell, and sons, Robert, George, Arthur and Francis.

Williamson, Dr. James, married Ann Underwood, daughter of William Underwood, of Isle of Wight county. John Hammond dedicated to him his tract, "Leah and Rachel." He afterwards moved to Lancaster county, where he was one of the justices in 1652, but died before 1656, leaving two daughters, Margaret, who married William Ball, Jr., and Mary, who married John Rosier, Jr.

Willis, Colonel Francis, of Gloucester county, Virginia, was son of Francis Willis, of Oxfordshire, England, which last was nephew of Colonel Francis Willis, of the Virginia council. He was a justice of the peace and lieutenant-colonel of the militia for Gloucester county and burgess from 1727 to 1740 and from 1745 to 1749. He married (first) Anne Rich, niece of Elias Rich, Esq., of St. Paul Covent Garden, London, and (second) Elizabeth, widow of Henry Harrison, and daughter of John Smith, of "Purton," Gloucester county, Virginia.

Willis, Colonel Henry, son of Francis Willis, of Oxfordshire, and brother of Francis Willis (q. v.), represented Gloucester county in the house of burgesses in 1718 and 1723. He was the founder of Fredericksburg in 1727, and represented Spottsylvania county in the house of burgesses in 1740, and died the same year. He married three times and had issue by each marriage.

Willis, John, son of Colonel Francis Willis, of Gloucester county (q. v.), moved to Brunswick county, which he represented in the house of burgesses from 1752 to 1755. His will, in which he calls himself John Willis, of "Bedingfield Hall," was dated November 7, 1764, and proved January 26, 1769. He married, January 26, 1743, Mildred Smith, daughter of Augustine Smith, of "Shooters Hill," Middlesex county, Virginia, and left numerous issue.

Willoughby, John, of Willoughby Point, Norfolk county, great-great-grandson of Captain Thomas Willoughby, the immigrant to Virginia, was member of the house of burgesses from Norfolk county in 1754 and 1755; chairman of the Norfolk county committee of safety, 1774-75, and county lieutenant, 1774-75; in 1776 compelled by Lord Dunmore to take the oath of allegiance to the king; examined by the convention of Virginia and excused, but shortly afterwards rejoined Lord Dunmore. He died the same year (1776).

Willoughby, Thomas, only son of Captain Thomas Willoughby, of the council, born in Virginia, December 25, 1632; educated at the Merchant Tailors' School, London; married Sarah, daughter of Richard Thompson, November 18, 1652. He was lieutenant-colonel of the militia and had large grants of land in Lower Norfolk county. He left an only son, Thomas Willoughby.

Wills, John Scasbrook, a descendant of Emmanuel Wills, immigrant, and son of John Wills, was a burgess for Isle of Wight county in the last assembly under the royal government, and member of the conventions of 1775 and 1776. He was, during the revolution, a major of militia and afterwards brigadier-general. He died in 1794.

Wills, Miles, son of Emmanuel Wills and Elizabeth Cary, sister of Miles Cary, the immigrant, was burgess for Warwick county in 1714 to succeed William Cary, who died the latter year.

Wilson, James, was an eminent merchant of Norfolk county. He was brother of Colonel William Wilson, of Elizabeth City county. He was a justice of the peace and lieutenant-colonel. He was burgess for Norfolk county in 1698, 1703-05, 1710-12, and his will was proved December 19, 1712, and mentions son Willis (q. v.) and others.

Wilson, Rev. John, was minister of Elizabeth river parish in 1637.

Wilson, John, burgess for Norfolk county in 1769-1772. He was a descendant of James Wilson, lieutenant-colonel, sheriff and burgess of Norfolk county.

Wilson, John, of Augusta county, was one of the early Scotch-Irish settlers in the valley of Virginia. He was born in 1702; settled on Middle river, and was colonel of the militia and burgess for Augusta from 1748 till his death in 1773. He left many descendants.

Wilson, William, was for many years presiding justice of Elizabeth City county and naval officer of the Lower James river. He was burgess for Elizabeth City in 1685, 1688, 1702 and other years. He lived at "Ceeleys," at the mouth of Saltford's creek, and died in 1713. He left one son, Willis Wilson, and two daughters, Mary, who married (first) William Roscow, and (second) Colonel Miles Cary, of "Rich Neck," and Jane, who married successively Nicholas Curle, James Ricketts and Merrit Sweeney

Wilson, Willis, son of Colonel James Wilson, of Norfolk county, was burgess for Norfolk county in 1718, 1734, 1748-49. He died in 1758, leaving children, Lemuel, Thomas and Euphan, wife of Joseph Alston.

Wilson, Willis, was son of Colonel William Wilson, of Elizabeth City county. He was captain in the militia and represented Elizabeth City in the house of burgesses in 1696, 1697 and other years, and died without issue in 1701.

Windham, Edward, was a burgess in 1642 and 1643 for Lower Norfolk county and a lieutenant-colonel of militia.

Windmill, Christopher, came to Virginia before 1625, lived at the "Indian Thicket," in Elizabeth City, where he had several leases of the public lands.

Winn, John, burgess for Amelia county in the assemblies of 1769-1771, 1772-1774,

1775-1776, and of the conventions of 1774, 1775 and 1776.

Winston, Anthony, was a burgess for Buckingham county in 1775-1776, and member of the convention of March, 1775.

Wise, John, emigrated to Virginia in 1635, aged eighteen years, and settled on the eastern shore. He married Hannah Scarburgh, daughter of Captain Edmund Scarburgh. He was one of the justices and died in 1695. His son, "John Wise, Jr.," to distinguish him from an older brother of the same name, was burgess for Accomac county in 1705-1706, and died in 1717, leaving issue, John Wise and others. This last John Wise married Scarburgh, daughter of Colonel Tully Robinson, and had issue, with others, Colonel John Wise, who married Margaret Douglas, and was father of John Wise, speaker of the senate of Virginia, who was father of Governor Henry A. Wise.

Withers, Captain John, was one of the justices of Stafford county and burgess in 1696-97. It appears from an act in Hening's Statutes at Large that his family came from Lancaster county, England. He married Frances, widow of Francis Dade, and daughter of Colonel Robert Townsend, of Stafford county. After the death of Captain Withers, his wife married Mr. Rice Hooe, of Stafford, conveying negroes and other property to her sons, Robert, Francis and Cadwallader Dade. He died before 1699, leaving two daughters, Sarah, who married Christopher Conway, and Elizabeth, who married Captain Richard Fossaker.

Wood, Henry, was born in London in 1696, arrived at Yorktown 1713, after which he lived for two years as an apprentice with Christopher Robinson, a wealthy merchant on the Rappahannock river and secretary of state in 1703. He married Martha Cocke, at "Bremo," in 1723. He practiced law and was clerk of Goochland for thirty years (1728-1757). He died in 1757 and was buried at his seat, "Woodville," in Goochland county. He left issue.

Wood, James, was surveyor of Orange county in 1738; clerk of Frederick county from 1743 to 1760, and was founder of Winchester. He was a member of the house of burgesses from 1766 to 1776, and a member of the convention of May, 1776. He was father of Colonel James Wood, who was later governor of Virginia.

Wood, Percival, a burgess for Archer's Hope in 1631-32.

Wood, Valentine, born September 2, 1724, married, January 3, 1764, Lucy Henry, sister of Patrick Henry (born in Hanover county, March 29, 1743). He was son of Henry Wood (q. v.), and in 1757 succeeded his father as clerk of Goochland county. He was colonel of the county militia and one of the first justices appointed to Albemarle county. His daughter Mary married Judge Peter Johnston, father of General Joseph E. Johnston.

Woodbridge, William, burgess for Richmond county in 1715, 1718, 1720-1722; justice in 1710; captain of militia; died in 1726, naming in his will cousin, George Woodbridge, daughter Elizabeth and son John, who was burgess for Richmond county in 1734-1740, 1742-1747, 1748-1749.

Woodhouse, Henry, son of Sir Henry Woodhouse and Anne, daughter of Sir Nicholas Bacon, lord keeper, was governor of

Bermuda from October, 1623, to January 13, 1626; served in the expedition to the Isle of Rhé and Rochelle, 1627-28; was master of the muster of Suffolk county, England; in 1631 was promised by King Charles the governorship of Virginia. He owned six shares of land in Hamilton Tribe, Bermuda, which he gave to his son Henry, who settled in Virginia.

Woodhouse, Henry, son of Captain Henry Woodhouse, governor of Bermuda. He was born in 1607, came to Virginia in 1637 and settled in Lower Norfolk county (now Princess Anne). He was justice of the county 1642-43; member of the house of burgesses 1647 and 1652, and died in 1655, leaving several daughters and four sons, Henry, Horatio, John and William, who have numerous descendants.

Woodhouse, Horatio, son of Henry Woodhouse, of Princess Anne county, who died in 1688; was captain of the militia and burgess for Princess Anne in 1715. He was grandson of Henry Woodhouse, the immigrant to Virginia.

Woodlief, Captain John, first went to Virginia in 1608 and remained eleven years; interested with Richard Berkeley, John Smyth, of Nibley, George Thorpe and William Tracy and other Gloucestershire men in the settlement of Berkeley Hundred, in Virginia. On December 4, 1619, the *Margaret* arrived from Bristol at Jamestown, bringing about thirty-eight passengers, under the command of Woodlief as governor, but his authority was soon rescinded. In 1626 he owned 550 acres below Jordan's Point, on the south side of James river. The Woodliefs who appear in the records of that region are doubtless his descendants.

Woodson, Colonel John, a descendant of Dr. John Woodson, who came from Dorsetshire, England, to Virginia in 1619 with Sir George Yardley, and lived in Henrico county. He was vestryman of the parish of St. James Northam, and lieutenant-colonel of the Goochland militia. From 1769 to 1775, inclusive, he represented the county in the house of burgesses and was member of the conventions of 1775, 1776. He married Dorothea Randolph, aunt of President Jefferson. He died December 2, 1789, leaving issue.

Woodward, Christopher, a burgess for Westover in 1629.

Woodward, Christopher, born 1594, came to Virginia in 1620, and was burgess for Westover, 1629. Probably he was ancestor of Samuel Woodward, of Charles City county, who married Sarah, daughter of Robert Hallam, and died in 1680, having a son Samuel Woodward, who settled in Massachusetts.

Woodward, Thomas, assayer of the mint in London and a royalist, was dismissed by the parliamentary authorities in 1649, and came to Virginia. At the restoration he and his son John were appointed assay masters, but Thomas remained in Virginia, and was appointed first surveyor-general of Carolina. He patented large tracts of land in Isle of Wight county, Virginia. He had two sons, John, above named, and Thomas, who left descendants in the south.

Woory, Joseph, nephew of Sir John Yeamans, baronet, was a merchant in Isle of Wight county, and died there in 1694.

Worleigh, George, was a burgess for Charles River county (York) in 1641.

Worlich (Worledge, Woolritch), William, came to Virginia in 1622, aged fifteen, and in 1625 was a servant of Francis Chamberlin, in Elizabeth City. He was a member of the house of burgesses for Elizabeth City county in 1644, 1649, 1654 and 1659; lieutenant-colonel of the militia.

Wormeley, Ralph, of "Rosegill," Middlesex county, was born October 5, 1715, and served as a member of the house of burgesses for Middlesex from 1742 to 1764, when he accepted the place of coroner. He was twice married, (first) to Sally, daughter of Colonel Edmund Berkeley, of "Barn Elms," Middlesex county, and (second) to Jane, daughter of James Bolles. He was a son of John Wormeley, of "Rosegill," and a descendant of Sir John de Wormeley, of Hadfield, county York, England. He died August 19, 1790; father of Ralph Wormeley, of the council (1771).

Wotton, Thomas, a surgeon who came with the first settlers in 1607.

Wowinchopunka, chief of the Paspahegh Indians in 1607. Jamestown was in his territory. He was a mortal enemy of the white settlers. He was killed by Ensign William Powell in 1610. His chief town was at the present Sandy Point.

Wright, Christopher, was a burgess for Princess Anne county at the assemblies of 1772-1774 and 1775-1776 and a member of the convention of March, 1775, and December, 1775.

Wright, John, a burgess for Nansemond county in 1695-1696.

Wright, Robert, born in 1680, came in 1608, and with his wife Joan and two children was living at Elizabeth City in 1625. He was included in the muster of Anthony Bonall. In 1626 he patented twelve acres eastward of James City. He was probably ancestor of the Wrights of Nansemond county.

Wright, William, burgess for Nansemond county in 1712-1714.

Wyatt, Anthony, born in 1604, came to Virginia in 1624, and was a member of the house of burgesses for Charles City county in 1645, 1653 and 1656. He lived at "Chaplin's Choice," formerly patented by Captain Isaac Chaplin. It lay on James river, near Jordan's Point, in that part of Charles City county now called Prince George county. He was living in 1664. He left a son Nicholas.

Wyatt, Sir Dudley, was a royalist officer who fought for King Charles I. He was one of the grantees of the Northern Neck of Virginia from Charles I., September 18, 1650, and he came to Virginia and died soon after. His will, dated March 29, 1650, was recorded at Jamestown, September 25, 1651 ("William and Mary College Quarterly," iii, p. 37).

Wyatt (Wiatt), Rev. Hawte, brother of Governor Sir Francis Wyatt, was born at Boxley, Kent, in 1594; matriculated at Queen's College, Oxford, October 25, 1611, and was a student at Gray's Inn. He came to Virginia with his brother in October, 1621, and was minister of Jamestown till 1628, when he returned to England with his brother, Sir Francis. He was inducted rector of Boxley, in Kent, October 3, 1632, and died July 31, 1638. He left two sons, who lived at Middle Plantation, Virginia—

George and Edward Wyatt—and from them descend many of the Wiatt name in the south.

Wyche, Henry, ancestor of the Wyche family of Virginia, was son of Rev. Henry Wyche, rector of Sutton church, Surrey county, England. His father was a royalist and he was born January 27, 1648-49. His name appears first in the records of Surry county, Virginia, September 2, 1679. In 1687 he is mentioned among the foot soldiers of the county. His will, dated August 1, 1712, was proved March 18, 1714. He left issue, Cyril and other children.

Wynne (Winn), Joshua, son of Colonel Robert Wynne, was burgess for Charles City county in 1702 and 1703-1705. When Prince George county was set off from Charles City in 1705, he was a justice for that county and major of militia.

Wynne, Captain Robert, came from Kent, England, where he had several houses in Canterbury, and was burgess for Charles City county from 1658 to 1675, being, during the entire existence of Virginia's "Long Parliament," 1661-1675, speaker of the house of burgesses. He married a widow, Mary Poythress, and had sons, Thomas and Joshua, and a daughter who married Woodlief (see "Virginia Magazine of History and Biography," xiv, 173).

Wythe, Thomas, was the son of Thomas Wythe, of Elizabeth City county, and Anne Shephard, his wife, daughter of John Shephard. He was a justice of the peace and was a burgess for Elizabeth City county from 1718 to 1726. He married Margaret Walker, daughter of George Walker, in 1720, and was father of the celebrated George Wythe, one of the patriots of the revolution.

Yancey, Robert, was born in Virginia and ordained a minister in England in 1768. He was rector of Trinity parish, Louisa county. He was father of Major Charles Yancey, a prominent member of the Virginia legislature in 1820.

Yardley, Francis, son of Sir George Yardley, first of Northampton county, was appointed a member of the Maryland council in 1652, but soon returned to Virginia and was burgess for Lower Norfolk county, 1653. In 1654 he wrote a long letter to John Ferrar, of Little Giddings, Huntingdonshire, England, describing his recent exploration of the country to the south of Virginia. He married Sarah Offley, widow of Captain Adam Thorowgood, and before that of Captain John Gookin. He died before 1657, without issue.

Yates, Rev. Bartholomew, son of William and Katherine Yates, of Shackley, Donnington parish, England, was baptized August 24, 1676, and graduated at Brazenose College, Oxford, about October 12, 1698. He came to Virginia, February 2, 1700, and served first as minister of Sittenbourne and Kingston parishes. After three years he became minister of Christ Church, Middlesex county, and continued minister till his death. In 1723 he was a member of the board of visitors of William and Mary College, and in 1729 was elected professor of divinity. He married Sarah, widow of Tobias Mickleborough. He died July 26, 1734, leaving three sons, Bartholomew, William and Robert, distinguished like himself for their piety and beneficence as ministers.

Yates, Rev. Batholomew, son of Rev. Bartholomew Yates (q. v.), was born February 9, 1713; matriculated at Oriell College, Oxford, February 29, 1732; Bachelor of Arts, 1735; served Christ Church, Middlesex county, Virginia, from 1735 to 1767; visitor of William and Mary College in 1766. He married Elizabeth Stanard in 1741, and had issue (see Hayden, "Virginia Genealogies," p. 122).

Yates, Rev. Robert, son of Bartholomew Yates, was born in 1715; matriculated at Oriell College, Oxford, July 12, 1733, and graduated Bachelor of Arts, 1735. He was minister of Petsworth parish, Gloucester county, Virginia, from 1741 to 1761. He married Mary Randolph, daughter of Edward Randolph, and died in 1761.

Yates, Rev. Robert, son of William Yates, of Shackley, in the parish of Donnington, England, was baptized October 30, 1673, and came to Virginia in 1699, where he was rector of Christ church parish, Middlesex county, until ill health caused his return to England in 1703. His vestry so highly esteemed him that they continued his salary for some time in hopes of his return. When he did not return, they elected his brother, Rev. Bartholomew Yates, as minister.

Yates, Rev. William, son of Rev. Bartholomew Yates, was born December 10, 1720; educated at William and Mary College, at which he was elected usher of the grammar school, April 10, 1744; qualified as president of the college, March 10, 1761; rector of James City parish from 1745 to 1755; married Elizabeth, daughter of Edward Randolph, and died between March and November, 1764.

Yeo, Hugh, son of Justinian Yeo, of Hartland, Devonshire, England, was a burgess in 1663 and died before 1680. His lands passed to his eldest son Richard, who sold them in 1680 to his brother, Hugh Yeo.

Yeo, Leonard, settled in Elizabeth City county about 1637. He was evidently of the family of the Yeos of Devonshire. Burgess for Elizabeth City county, February, 1644-45, September, 1663, and June and October, 1666. In 1666 he was commander-in-chief of Elizabeth City county, with the title of colonel. He died in or before 1670, and his widow Rebecca married subsequently Colonel Charles Moryson, commander of Elizabeth City county, and next Colonel John Lear, of the Virginia council. He had a brother, Robert Yeo; and Hugh Yeo, of Accomac, brother of Justinian Yeo, of Hartland, Devonshire, was doubtless a kinsman.

Young, Captain Thomas, son of Gregory Young, a grocer of London, was born about 1583. In 1633 he obtained special permission to fit out ships and make explorations in America. He explored Delaware Bay, and in 1636 went up the Kennebec river, and by carrying canvass with him, crossed over to the St. Lawrence river, where he was captured by the French. He purchased a farm in James City county, Virginia, and left a son known as "Capt. Thomas Young, of Chickahominy."

Young, Thomas, was son of Captain Thomas Young, who was uncle of George Evelyn, commander of Kent Island, Maryland. He served in the parliamentary wars under General Monk, and afterwards came to Virginia, where his father had a farm on the Chickahominy, in James City county.

He sided with Nathaniel Bacon Jr. in 1676, and being captured by Berkeley was executed January 12, 1677. He was known as "Captain Young of Chickahominy."

Young, William, burgess for Essex county in 1715. He married Catherine Montague, who married, after William Young's death, Richard Tyler, Jr., of Essex. He had a son, Henry Young.

Yowell (Youell), Captain Thomas, born in 1615; married Anne, daughter of Thomas Sturman, cooper, who came to Virginia from Maryland. He had: 1. Thomas (born 1644), married Anne daughter of Colonel Richard Lee. He was a justice and burgess for Westmoreland county in 1688. 2. Richard. 3. Anne. 4. Winifred. 5. Penelope. His son Thomas' will was proved in 1694-1695.

Zane, Isaac, son of William Zane, who came from Pennsylvania about 1735; was burgess for Frederick county in 1773-1744 and 1775-1776, and served for that county in the conventions of 1775 and 1776. Zanesville, Ohio, obtains its name from this family.

Zouch, Sir John, of Codnor, Derbyshire, and his son, John Zouch, Esq., were long engaged in colonial enterprises. The former was in 1631 appointed by the King one of the commissioners to devise a new plan of government in Virginia. He went to Virginia in 1634 with his son John and a daughter. In addition to a plantation the father and son attempted to set up iron works, but failed for lack of support. Sir John was an intimate friend of Samuel Mathews and others of the party in Virginia opposed to Governor Harvey, and on his return to England in April, 1635, seems to have carried the statement of the grievances of the popular party. He owned land at "Roxdale," in Chesterfield county. His son in 1623 was a member of the Virginia Company of London. Sir John died in 1639. His grandfather, who was named also Sir John Zouch, was a companion in arms of Sir Walter Raleigh, in Ireland, in 1581-82.

OMITTED BURGESSES

In order to make the list of the members of the House of Burgesses of Virginia as complete as possible, the following names are added, with the counties represented and the years of service. Sketches of many of them are found in Volume II. under the head of the "Fathers of the Revolution." It is also to be noted that most of the Councillors have been Burgesses.

Allonby, Thomas, Elizabeth City county, 1684, 1688.
Anderson, John (county unknown), 1685-1686.
Andrews, William, Accomac, 1727-1734.
Armistead, Henry (q. v., 173), Gloucester, 1727-1734.
Bailey, William, Surry, 1763, 1764, 1765.
Baker, Benjamin (q. v., 175), Nansemond, 1768, 1769.
Baker, William, Nansemond, 1742-1747.
Banister, John, Dinwiddie, 1766-1768, 1769-1776.
Barradall, Edward (q. v., 180), Williamsburg, 1742-1747.
Bisse, James, Charles City county, 1680-1682.
Blair, John, Jr., William and Mary College, October, 1765, 1766-1768, 1769-1772.
Bland, Richard, Prince George, 1742-1776.
Blunt, Richard, Surry, 1772, 1773.
Booker, Edward, Jr., Halifax, 1766-1769.
Bowdoin, John, Northampton, 1773-1776.
Braxton, Carter, King William, 1761-1765, 1766-1769, 1775-1776.
Buckner, Richard, Caroline, 1727-1732.
Burgess, Charles, Lancaster, 1727-1734.
Burwell, Carter, James City county, 1742-1747, 1748-1749, 1752-1755.
Carter, Landon, Richmond county, 1748-1765.
Cary, Archibald, Chesterfield, 1756-1776.
Champe, John, King George, 1734.
Champe, William, King George, 1764.
Clement, Jeremy, James City county, 1641.
Cocke, Richard, Henrico, 1715.
Crawford, David, New Kent, 1692.
Cunningham, Mr. (county unknown), 1745.
Custis, William, Accomac, 1676, 1677.
Dacker, William (county unknown), 1642.
Digges, Dudley, York, 1752-1776.
Edwards, Mr. (county unknown), 1745.
Eppes, Isham, Dinwiddie, 1752-1755.
Ewell, Samuel, Accomac, 1732-1734.
Fallowes, Thomas (county unknown), 1642.
Faulcon, Nicholas, Jr., Surry, 1773-1776.

Fitzhugh, William, King George, 1772-1774, 1775-1776.
Fleming, William, Cumberland, 1772-1774, 1775-1776.
Fry, Henry, Albemarle, 1764.
Fry, John, Albemarle, 1761-1764.
Gouldman, Thomas, Rappahannock, 1680-1682.
Gray, Francis, Charles City county, 1661-1676.
Hardy, Richard, Isle of Wight, 1772, 1773-1776.
Harrison, Benjamin, Charles City county, 1749-1776.
Henry, James, Accomac, 1772, 1773-1776.
Henry, Patrick, Louisa, 1765-1769; Hanover, May, 1769, 1769-1776.
Jarrell, Thomas, Southampton, 1752-1753.
Jarvis, Thomas, Elizabeth City county, 1680-1682, 1684, 1683-1686, 1695.
Jefferson, Mr., Flower dieu Hundred, 1619.
Jefferson, Thomas, Albemarle, May, 1769, 1769-1776.
Jenifer, Captain Daniel, Accomac, 1720-1722.
Jones, John, Dinwiddie, 1752-1755.
Jones, John, Brunswick, 1771, 1772.
Jones, Joseph, King George, 1772-1776.
Jones, Thomas, William and Mary College, 1720-1722.
Jordan, Thomas, Nansemond, 1696-1697.
Kearne, Barnaby, Nansemond, 1684.
King, Joseph (county unknown), April, 1691.
Land, Mr., Princess Anne, 1734.
Langhorne, John, Warwick, 1680-1682.
Langley, Ralph, York, 1655-1656.
Langley, William, Norfolk, 1715.
Lankford, Benjamin, Pittsylvania, June, 1775.
Lawne, Christopher, Lawne's Plantation, 1619.
Lee, Francis Lightfoot, Loudoun, 1758-1761; Richmond, 1765-1769.
Lee, Richard Henry, Westmoreland, 1758-1776.
Lee, Thomas Ludwell, Stafford, 1758-1765.

OMITTED BURGESSES

Lee, William, Northumberland, 1693.
Lewis, William, James City county, 1691-1692.
Liggon (Lyggon), Thomas, Henrico, 1655-1656.
Littleton, Nathaniel, Northampton, 1698, 1699.
Littleton, Southey, Accomac, 1676-1677.
Marshall, James, Fauquier, 1775.
Marshall, William, Elizabeth City county, 1691-1692.
Mason, George, Fairfax, 1758-1761.
Mason, Thompson, Stafford, 1758-1761, 1765-1768, 1770-1772.
Matthews, George, Augusta, 1775.
Meade, David, Nansemond, 1727-1734.
Mercer, James, Hampshire, 1762-1776.
Mihill, Edwards, Elizabeth City county, 1680-1682.
Milby, Adiel, Northampton, 1775.
Mills, Henry (county unknown), 1680-1682..
Minge, Valentine, Charles City county, 1715.
Morris, George, New Kent, 1680-1682
Morton, Joseph, James City county, 1756-1758.
Moss, James, New Kent, 1703-1705.
Muscoe Salvator (q. v., 298), Essex, 1727-1734, 1736-1740.
Nelson, Thomas, York county, 1761-1775.
Nicholas, George, William and Mary College, 1727-1732.
Nicholas, Robert Carter, James City county, 1765-1776.
Page, John, William and Mary College, 1770, 1772-1774.
Parker, Mr., Hampshire, 1752-1755.
Parker, Thomas, Charles City county, 1710.
Pate, Thomas, Gloucester, 1684.
Pendleton, Edmund, Caroline, 1752-1776.
Pendleton, John, King and Queen, 1762-1763.
Perkins, Mr., Frederick, 1753-1755.
Peyton, John, Stafford, 1734-1740.
Peyton, Yelverton, Stafford, 1772.
Pierce, William, Westmoreland, 1680-1682.
Pitt, Thomas, Isle of Wight, 1680-1682.
Power, Mr. (county unknown), 1732-1734.
Prosser, Thomas, Cumberland, 1764.
Randolph, Peyton, Williamsburg, 1761-1774.

Randolph, Thomas Mann, Goochland, 1769-1776.
Reade, Robert, York, 1688.
Richinson, John, Princes Anne, 1693 (see John Richardson, p. 313).
Ring, Joseph (q. v., 313), York, 1693.
Sandiford, John, Lower Norfolk, 1692-1693.
Scarburgh, Charles, Accomac, 1680-1682, 1684, 1685-1686, 1688, 1691-1692.
Sherman, Michael, James City county, 1692-1693.
Smith, Augustine, Spotsylvania, 1727-1734.
Smith, Charles, Louisa, 1758-1761.
Smith, Isaac, Accomac, 1775.
Smith, John, Gloucester, 1685-1686, 1688, 1691, 1692.
Smith, Lawrence, Gloucester, 1691-1692.
Smith, Meriwether, Essex, 1772-1776.
Stone, Captain John, Rappahannock, 1691-1692.
Spier, John (county unknown), 1680-1682.
Swann, Alexander, Lancaster, 1699.
Tabb, John, Amelia, 1772-1776.
Tarpley, John, Richmond, 1711-1712.
Taylor, James, Orange, 1758-1761, 1761-1765.
Tazewell, Henry, Brunswick, 1775-1776.
Thomas, Edward, Essex, 1692, 1693.
Thorpe, Otho, York, 1680-1682.
Todd, Robert, Norfolk, 1748-1749.
Veal, Thomas, Norfolk, 1762-1765.
Walker, John, Albemarle, 1773-1776.
Ward, John, Ward's Plantation, 1619.
Washington, George, Frederick county, 1758-1765; Fairfax, 1766-1776.
Washington, Lawrence, Westmoreland, 1684, 1691-1692.
West, Nathaniel, New Kent, 1703-1705.
White, Alexander, Hampshire, 1774.
White, William, James City county, 1680-1682.
Whittington, William, Northampton, 1680-1682.
Williamson, Robert, Isle of Wight, 1661-1676.
Winston, Anthony, Buckingham, 1775.
Withers, John, Stafford, 1691-1692.
Woory, Joseph, Isle of Wight, 1684.
Wythe, George, Williamsburg, 1754-1756; William and Mary College, 1758-1761; Elizabeth City county, 1761-1769.

ERRATA—ADDENDA—INDEX

ERRATA AND ADDENDA

Page 8. Hawkins, William, for "Lancaster," read "Launceston."
Page 26, Rich, Sir Nathaniel, col. 1, line 2, for "Hutton," read "Hatton."
Page 38, line 4, West, Thomas, for "Annie," read "Anne."
Page 42, Powell, Nathaniel, col. 2, line 16, for "March 12," read "March 22."
Page 44. Pott, John, for "governor," read "deputy governor."
Page 47. Bennett, Richard, was governor until March 31, instead of March 2 and March 30, 1655.
Page 47. Digges, Edward, governor from March 31, 1655.
Page 49. Moryson, Francis, was deputy governor, instead of governor.
Page 50. Chicheley, Sir Henry, was lieutenant-governor, instead of deputy governor.
Page 60, line 9. Carter, Robert, for "nephew" of Gen. Edmund Ludlow, read "cousin."
Page 79. West, Francis, deputy governor, instead of governor.
Page 84, for "Yeardley," read "Yardley."
Page 96, col. 2, line 16, for "assembling," read "asserting."
Page 102, col. 2, line 8. Bullock, Hugh, for "Bollock," read "Bullock;" line 9, for "Jennings," read "Jenings."
Page 108, Sibsey, John, line 3, for "Kichoughtan," read "Kicchoughtan."
Page 110. Wormeley, Ralph, line 17, ignore last sentence, date of death.
Page 118. Morrison, Francis, deputy governor instead of governor.
Page 122. Carter, John, Sr., for "Cromwell," read "Richard Cromwell."
Page 124. Elliott, Anthony, line 2, for 1654-55, read 1645-46.
Page 170. Ambler, John, for 1765 read 1735.
Page 186, for "Blackheard," read "Blackbeard."
Page 360, Williams, Robert, for "Williams," read "Williamson."

INDEX

NOTE—An asterisk (*) against a name refers the reader to note in Addenda and Errata.

Abbott, Jeffrey, 169
Abraham, Robert, 169
Ackiss, John, 169
Acrill, William, 169
    William, Jr., 169
Adams, Richard, 169
    Robert, 169
Aitchison, William, 169
Alexander, Gerard, 169
    John, 169
Allen, Maj. Arthur, 170
    Edmund, 170
    Edward, 170
    William, 170
Allerton, Isaac, 140
    Willoughby, 170
Allington, Lieut. Giles, 170
Ambler, Edward, 170

John, 170
    Richard, 171
Amherst, Jeffrey, 68
Amidas, Philip, 15
Anderson, Charles, 171
    Rev. Charles, 171
    David, 171
    George, 171
    Matthew, 171
    Richard, 171
    Robert, 171
    William, 171
Andrews, Rev. Robert, 171
    William, 172
    William, Jr., 172
Andros, Sir Edmund, 56
Anne, Queen of Pamunskey Islands, 172

Appleton, John, 172
Applewhaite, Henry, 172
    Capt. Henry, 172
Archer, Gabriel, 78
    James, 172
Argall, Samuel, 41
    Sir Samuel, 81
Armistead, Anthony, 172
    Gill, 173
    Col. Henry, 173
    John, 140
    Robert, 173
    William, 173
Arundell (Erondelle), John, 173
    Peter, 174
Ashton, Charles, 174
    Henry, 174

374 INDEX

James, 174
Peter, 174
Aston, Walter, 174
Atkins, John, 174
Atkinson, Roger, 174
Aubrey, Henry, 174
Aylett (Aylet), William, 174
    William, 175
    William, 175
Aylmer, Justinian, 175
Bacon, Edmund, 175
    John, 175
    Nathaniel, 132
    Nathaniel, Sr., 54
    Nathaniel, Sr., 121
Bagnall, James, 175
    Roger, 175
Bagnell, Henry, 175
Bagwell, Thomas, 175
Bailey, Thomas, 175
Baker, Benjamin, 175
    Henry, 176
    Capt. Lawrence, 176
    Richard, 176
    Thomas, 176
Baldridge, Thomas, 176
Baldry, Robert, 176
Ball, George, 176
    George, 176
    Henry, 176
    Col. James, Jr., 176
    Maj. James, 177
    Col. Joseph, 177
    Col. Spencer, 177
    Spencer M., 177
    Capt. William, Jr., 178
    Col. William, 178
    William, 178
Ballard, Francis, 178
    Robert, 178
    Thomas, 130
    Thomas, 178
Banister, John, 179
Bankhead, James, 179
Banks, Thomas, 179
Barber, Charles, 179
    Thomas, 179
    William, 179
    William, Jr., 179
Barbour, James, 180
    Thomas, 180
Bargrave, George, 180
    Capt. John, 180

Rev. Thomas, 180
Barham, Anthony, 180
Barker, William, 180
Barlow, Arthur, 15
Barnes, Lancelot, 180
Barradall, Edward, 180
Barret, Charles, 180
    Rev. Robert, 181
    Thomas, 181
Barrett, William, 181
Barrington, Robert, 181
Barron, Samuel, 181
Baskervyle, John, 181
Basse, Nathaniel, 100
Bassett, Burwell, 181
    William, 181
    William, 181
Bates, John, 182
Bathurst, Lancelot, 182
Battaile, Capt. John, 182
Batte, Capt. Henry, 182
    John, 182
    Thomas, 182
    William, 182
Baugh, John, 182
Baughan, Capt. James, 182
Bayley, Arthur, 183
    Richard, 183
    William, 183
Baylis, John, 183
Baylor, John, 183
    John, 183
Baynham, Alexander, 183
Baytop, Thomas, 183
Beale, Thomas, 127
Beazley, Robert, 184
Beckwith, Sir Marmaduke, 184
Bell, Henry, 184
    John, 184
    Rev. John, 184
Benn, Capt. James, 184
Bennett, Philip, 184
    *Richard, 47
    Richard, 111
    Thomas, 184
Benskin, Henry, 184
Bentley, Matthew, 184
    William, 184
Berkeley, Edmund, 150
    Edmund, 184
    John, 98
    Norborne, 69

Capt. William, 184
Sir William, 46
Bernard, Richard, 184
    Capt. Thomas, 185
    William, 117
    William, 185
Berry, Sir John, 185
Bertrand, Rev. John, 186
Beverley, Capt. Harry, 185
    Peter, 152
    Robert, 136
    Robert, 185
    William, 159
    William, 186
Beverly, William, 186
Bibb, William, 186
Bickley, Sir William, 186
Bigge, Richard, 186
Bill, John, 186
Bird, Abraham, 186
    William, 186
Bishop, Henry, 186
    John, 186
Blackbeard, 186
Blackburn, Richard, 187
    Thomas, 187
    Capt. William, 187
Blacke, William, 187
Blackwell, Joseph, 187
    Samuel, 187
Blacky, William, 187
Blagrave, Henry, 187
Blair, Dr. Archibald, 187
    James, 154
    James, D. D., 62
    John, 66
    John, 157
Blake, Capt. John, 188
Blakiston, Nathaniel, 188
Bland, Edward, 188
    Giles, 188
    Peregrine, 188
    Richard, 188
    Theodorick, 129
    Theodorick, Sr., 188
Blaney, Edward, 94
Blayton, Thomas, 188
Blewitt, Mr., 87
Blow, Michael, 189
Bohun, Laurence, 88
Bolling, Alexander, 189
    John, 189
    Robert, 189

INDEX

375

Robert, 190
Robert, Jr., 190
Bonall, James, 190
Bond, Maj. John, 190
Booker, Edmund, 190
  Edward, 190
  Richard, 190
Booth, Robert, 190
  Thomas, 191
Borden (Burden), Benjamin, 191
Boucher, Daniel, 191
Bouldin, Thomas, 191
Bourne (Borne), Capt. Robert, 191
Boush, Maximillian, 191
  Samuel, 191
  Samuel, Jr., 191
Bowden, William, 191
Bowdoin, Peter, 191
Bowker, Rev. James, 192
  Rev. Ralph, 192
Bowler, Thomas, 133
Bowyer, John, 191
Boyse, Cheney, 191
  John, 192
  Luke, 192
Bradley, Thomas, 192
  William, 192
Branch, Christopher, 192
  John, 192
Brasseur, John, 192
Braxton, George, 192
Bray, David, 155
  James, 131
  James, 193
  Robert, 193
Breman, Thomas, 193
Brent, George, 193
  Giles, 193
  Giles, 193
  Margaret, 194
  William, 194
Brereton, Thomas, 194
Brewer, John, 102
  John, 194
Brewster, Edward, 194
  Richard, 194
Brewster (Brewer), Thomas, 194
Bridger, James, 195
  Joseph, 130
  Col. Joseph, 195

Samuel, 195
Col. William, 195
Bridges, Charles, 195
Briggs, Gray, 195
Bristow, Robert, 195
Broadwater, Charles, 196
Brocas, William, 105
Brockenbrough, Col Austin, 196
  Dr. John, 196
Brodhurst, Walter, 196
Brodnax, Edward, 196
  Maj. John, 196
  William, 196
Bronaugh, William, 196
Brooke, George, 196
Brown, Charles, 197
  Dr. John, 197
Browne, Devereaux, 197
  Henry, 104
  Henry, 197
  John, 197
  William, 197
  William B., 197
  Capt. William, 197
Browning, John, 197
Bruce, George, 197
Bryan, Dr. Richard, 198
Buck, Rev. Richard, 198
Buckner, John, 198
  John, 198
  John, 198
  Richard, 198
  Richard, 198
  Samuel, 198
  Thomas, 198
  William, 198
Bugg, Samuel, 199
*Bullock, Hugh, 102
  William, 199
Burgess, Thomas, 199
Burnham, John, 199
  Rowland, 199
Burnley, Zachariah, 199
Burrows, Benoni, 199
  John, 199
Burrows (Burroughs), Christopher, 199
Burwell, Armistead, 199
  James, 199
  Lewis, 64
  Lewis, 147
  Lewis, 157

Lewis, 200
Nathaniel, 200
Robert C., 164
Bush, John, 200
Bushrod, John, 200
  Thomas, 200
Butler, Capt. Nathaniel, 201
  Rev. Thomas, 201
  William, 201
Butt, Thomas, 201
Byrd, William, 151
  William, Sr., 138
  William (3rd), 161
Cabell, John, 201
  Joseph, 201
  Dr. William, 201
  William, Jr., 202
Cabot, John, 7
  Sebastian, 7
Callaway, James, 202
  William, 202
Callicut, William, 202
Calthorpe, Col. Christopher, 202
Calvert, Cornelius, 202
  Cornelius, 202
Camm, John, 165
Campbell, Andrew, 203
  Archibald, 203
  Colin, 203
  Hugh, 203
  John, 67
Cant, Maj. David, 203
  John, 203
Capps, William, 98
Cargill, John, 203
Carlyle, John, 203
Carpenter, Nathaniel, 203
Carr, Thomas, 204
Carrington, George, 204
  Paul, 204
Carter, Charles, 204
  Col. Charles, 204
  Edward, 125
  Edward, 204
  John, 153
  *John, Sr., 122
  *Robert, 60
  Robert, 147
  Robert, Jr., 160
  Robert W., 205
  Thomas, 205
Carver, Capt. William, 205

INDEX

Cary, Maj. Francis, 205
  Henry, 205
  Henry, Jr., 205
  John, 205
  Miles, 130
  Miles, 205
  Oswald, 206
  Capt. William, 206
  Col. Wilson, 206
  Wilson M., 206
Catchmaie, George, 206
Catlett, Col. John, 206
  John, Jr., 206
Cave, Benjamin, 206
Cavendish, Sir Thomas, 16
Caufield, Robert, 206
  William, 206
Cawsey, Nathaniel, 207
Cecil, Sir Robert, 207
  William, 8
Ceely, Thomas, 207
Chamberlayn, Thomas, 207
Chamberlayne, William, 207
Chanco (Indian), 207
Chandler, John, 207
Chaplin, Isaac, 207
Charleton, Stephen, 207
Cheesman (Chisman), John, 115
Chesley, Philip, 207
Chester, Capt. Anthony, 208
Chew, John, 208
  Larkin, 208
*Chicheley, Sir Henry, 50
  Sir Henry, 131
Chichester, Richard, 208
Chiles, John, 208
  Walter, 114
  Walter, Jr., 208
Chilton, Edward, 208
Chinn, Joseph, 209
Chisman, Edmund, 209
  Lydia, 209
  Thomas, 209
Chiswell, Charles, 209
  Col. John, 209
Christian, Israel, 209
  Thomas, 210
  William, 210
Christmas, Doctoris, 210
Church, Richard, 210
Churchill, William, 150
Clack, Rev. James, 210

John, 210
  Sterling, 210
Claiborne, Col. Augustine, 210
  Maj. Buller, 210
  Herbert, 210
  Leonard, 211
  Leonard, Jr., 211
  Col. Nathaniel, 211
  Philip W., 211
  Richard, 211
  Thomas, 211
  Lt. Col. Thomas, 211
  Capt. Thomas, 211
  *William, 96
  William, 211
Clapham, Josias, 212
Clarke, John, 212
Clause (Close), Phettiplace, 212
Clay, John, 212
Clayton, Jasper, 212
  Rev. John, 212
  John, Gloucester Co., 212
  John, James City Co., 212
  Thomas, 213
  Thomas, M. D., 213
  Col. William, 213
Clements, Francis, 213
Clinch, William, 213
Clopton, William, 213
Cobbs, Samuel, 213
Cocke, Col. Allen, 213
  Benjamin, 213
  Bowler, 214
  Bowler, Jr., 214
  Hartwell, 214
  James, 214
  Richard, 214
  Richard (emigrant), 214
  Thomas, 214
  Capt. Thomas, 214
  William, 215
  Dr. William, 150
Cockeram, Capt. William, 215
Codd, Col. St. Leger, 215
Coke, John, 215
Cole, Rev. Samuel, 215
  William (Nutmeg Quarters), 215
  William, Warwick Co., 215

Coleman, Francis, 215
  Henry, 215
Coles, John, 216
  Walter, 216
Collclough, George, 215
Collier, Isaac, 216
  Samuel, 216
  William, 216
Colston, William, 216
Colville, John, 215
Comrie, Dr. William, 216
Coney, Henry, 216
Conway, Edwin, 216
  Maj. Peter, 216
Cooke, Giles, 216
  John, 217
  Mordecai, 217
  Mordecai, Jr., 217
Cooper, George, 217
  Sampson, 217
Copeland, John, 217
  Rev. Patrick, 28
Corbin, Gawin, Middlesex Co., 217
  Gawin, Jr., 165
  Gawin ("Pekatone"), 217
  Henry, 128
  John T., 218
  Richard, 158
Corker, John, 218
  William, 218
Corprew, Joshua, 218
Cotton, Anne, 218
  Rev. William, 218
Covington, Richard, 218
Cowles, Thomas, 218
Cowlinge, Christopher, 99
Coxe, Richard, 218
Crabb, John, 218
Craddock, Lieut. William, 218
Cranfield, Lionel, 27
Crashaw, Raleigh, 218
  Rev. William, 20
Crawford, William, 219
Crawley, Thomas, 219
Crew, Randall, 219
Crews, Capt. James, 219
Cripps, Zachariah, 219
Croshaw, Joseph, 219
Crump, Sergt. Thomas, 219
Culpeper, Capt. Alexander, 219

INDEX

Lord Thomas, 51
Curle, Nicholas, 219
Currie, David, 219
Curtis, John, 220
    Rice, 220
Custis, Hancock, 220
    John, 135
    John, 147
    John (3d), 155
Dade, Francis, 220
Daingerfield, William, 220
    William, Jr., 220
Dalby, Thomas, 220
Dale, Edward, 220
    Sir Thomas, 37
    Sir Thomas, 81
Dandridge, Bartholomew, 220
    Col. John, 220
    Martha, 221
    Nathaniel W., 221
    William, 154
Danvers, Sir John, 26
Davenant, Sir William, 113
Davenport, Joseph, 221
Davies, Samuel, 221
Davis, James, 221
    John, 9
    Thomas, 221
    Thomas, Warwick Co., 221
    William, 221
Davison, Christopher, 95
Dawkes, Henry, 221
Dawson, Rev. Musgrave, 221
    Rev. Thomas, 161
    Rev. William, 156
Day, John, 222
Death, Richard, 222
Debedeavon, 222
DeButts, Lawrence, 222
Delany, Henry, 222
Delaware, Lord, 38
Delke, Capt. Clement, 222
    Roger, 222
Denson, William, 222
DeRichebourg, Claude P., 222
Dew, Thomas, 120
Dewey, Stephen, 222
Dick, Charles, 223
    Cole, 152
    Dudley, 146

Digges, Dudley, 224
    Sir Dudley, 28
    Edward, 47
    Edward, 111
    Edward, 223
    William, 223
Dinwiddie, Robert, 64
    Robert, 156
Dipnall, Thomas, 223
Dixon, Adam, 223
    Rev. John, 223
    John (printer), 224
    John (merchant), 224
    Roger, 224
Doak, Robert, 224
Doe, Thomas, 224
Doggett, Rev. Benjamin, 224
Donelson, John, 224
Donne (Dunn), George, 105
Doran, John, 224
Dormer, Sir Fleetwood, 224
Doughty, Francis, 225
Douglas, Edward, 225
    George, 225
    William, 225
Downing, Mr. John, 225
Downman, John, 225
Downes, George, 225
Downs, Henry, 225
Dowse, Thomas, 225
Doyley, Cope, 225
Drake, Sir Francis, 10
Drew, Dolphin, 226
Drummond, Richard, 226
    Sarah, 226
    William, 226
Drysdale, Hugh, 59
Dudley, Ambrose, 226
    Robert, 226
Duke, Henry, 148
Dunn, Nicholas, 226
Dunston, John, 226
Dunlap, Rev. William, 226
Dunlop, William, 226
Durand, William, 226
Duvall, Samuel, 227
Dykes, James, 227
Each, Capt. Samuel, 227
Earle, Samuel, 227
Eaton, John, 227
    Nathaniel, 227
    Thomas, 227
Edlow, Matthew, 228

Edmondson, Thomas, 228
Edmunds, Jennings, 57
    John, 228
    Thomas, 228
Edmundson, James, 228
Edwards, Nathaniel, 228
    William, (merchant), 228
    William, 228
    William, (of Jamestown), 228
Eggleston, Joseph, 229
Eldridge, Thomas, 229
Elizabeth, Queen, 8
Elligood, Jacob, 229
Elliott, Anthony, 124
Ellyson, Robert, 229
Embry, Henry, 229
    William, 229
Emerson, William, 229
    Rev. Arthur, 229
    Rev. Arthur, (W. and M. Coll.), 229
Emperor, Francis, 229
English, Capt. John, 230
    William, 230
Ennalls, Bartholomew, 230
Epes (Eppes), Francis, 115
Eppes, Francis, 230
    Col. Francis, 230
    John, 230
    Richard, 230
    Capt. William, 230
    Littlebury, 231
Eskridge, Col. George, 231
    Samuel, 231
Evelyn, Robert, 107
Everard, Thomas, 231
Ewell, Solomon, 231
Eyre, Littleton, 231
    Severn, 231
Eyres, Robert, 231
Fairfax, Bryan, 231
    Ferdinando, 232
    George W., 163
    Lord Thomas, 232
    William, 156
Farley, Thomas, 232
Farlow, George, 232
Farmer, Lodowick, 232
    Thomas, 232
Farnefold, John, 232
Farrar, Lt. Col. John, 232

INDEX

Col. William, 232
Maj. William, 233
Farrar (Ferrar), William, 93
Farrell, Maj. Hubert, 233
Faulcon, Nicholas, 233
Fawdoin, George, 233
Fauntleroy, Moore, 233
William, 233
Fauquier, Francis, 67
Fawcett, Thomas, 233
Feild, John, 233
Henry, Jr., 233
Peter, 234
Felgate, Capt. Robert, 234
Capt. Tobias, 234
Ferdinands, Simon, 13
Ferrar, John, 24
Nicholas, Jr., 24
Nicholas, Sr., 23
Fielding, Ambrose, 234
Filmer, Henry, 234
Finch, Henry, 99
Fishback, John, 234
Fitzhugh, George, 234
Henry, 235
Henry (of "Bedford"), 235
Lt. Col. Henry, 235
Maj. John, 235
William, 162
Capt. William, 235
Col. William, 235
Lt. Col. William, 235
Fitzwilliams, Richard, 154
Fleming, John, 236
John, Jr., 236
Robert, 236
Fletcher, George, 236
Fleet, Henry, 236
Flint, Richard, 237
Lieut. Thomas, 237
Flinton, Pharaoh, 237
Flood, John, 237
Flournoy, Jacob, 237
John J., 237
Floyd, Charles, 237
Folliott, Rev. Edward, 237
Follis, Mr. Thomas, 237
Fontaine, Francis, 237
James M., 238
John, 238
Peter, 238

Foote, Richard, 238
Richard (emigrant), 238
Ford, Richard, 238
Fossaker, Capt. Richard, 238
Foster, Joseph, 238
Capt. Richard, 238
Fouace, Stephen, 238
Fowke (Foulke), Gerard, 238
Thomas, 239
Fowler, Bartholomew, 239
Francis, 239
Fox, David, 239
Henry, 239
Henry (sheriff), 239
Rev. John, 239
Maj. Richard, 239
William, 239
Francis, Thomas, 240
Franklin, Mr. Ferdinand, 240
Freeman, Bridges, 113
French, Daniel, 240
Frobisher, Sir Martin, 9
Fry, John, 240
Joshua, 240
Fulford, Mr. Francis, 240
Gaddes, John, 240
Gaines, Harry, 240
Gale, Thomas, 241
Galt, Dr. John M., 241
Galthorpe, Stephen, 241
Gany, William, 241
Gardner, Capt. Thomas, 241
Garnett, James, 241
Gaskins, Thomas, 241
Gates, Sir Thomas, 36
Sir Thomas, 80
George, John, 241
Gerrard, Dr. Thomas, 241
Gibbes, Lieut., 242
Gibson, Jonathan, 242
Gilbert, Adrian, 13
Bartholomew, 18
Sir Humphrey, 12
Sir John, 13
Raleigh, 18
Giles, John, 242
Thomas, 242
Gill, Capt. Stephen, 242
Glasscock, Thomas, 241
Glassell, Andrew, 242

Godfrey, Matthew, 242
Godwin, Joseph, 242
Rev. Morgan, 242
Thomas (first in Va.), 242
Thomas, 243
Thomas, Jr., 243
Gooch, Henry, 243
William, 60
William, 121
Goode, Bennett, 243
John, 244
Goodrich, Charles, 243
Edward, 243
Edward (sheriff), 243
John, 243
Goodwin, James, 244
Gookin, Daniel, 244
Daniel, Jr., 244
John, 244
Gordon, James, 244
Rev. John, 245
Samuel, 245
Gorsuch, Rev. John, 245
Gosnold, Anthony, 245
Bartholomew, 76
Gough, Matthew, 245
Nathaniel, 245
William, 245
Gouldman, Francis, 245
Gourgainy, Edward, 245
Gower, Abell, 245
Graffenreidt, Christopher de, 246
Graham, John, 246
Richard, 246
Grantham, Capt. Thomas, 246
Graves, Capt. Thomas, 246
Gray, Col. Edwin, 246
Francis (emigrant), 246
Francis, 246
Col. Joseph, 247
Rev. Samuel, 247
Thomas, 247
William, 247
William, Jr., 247
Green, John, 247
Robert, 247
Roger, 247
William, 247
Greenhill, David, 248
Paschal, 248

INDEX

Gregory, Richard, 248
Gregson, Thomas, 248
Grendon, Edward, 248
    Sarah, 248
    Thomas, 248
    Thomas, Jr., 248
Grenville, Sir Richard, 15
Griffin, Lady Christina, 248
    Corbin, 248
    Samuel, 249
    Thomas, 249
    William, 249
Griffith, Edward, 249
Grymes, Benjamin, 249
    Charles, 249
    John, 154
    Philip, 159
    Philip L., 249
    William, 249
Gwyn, David, 249
    Hugh, 249
    Rev. John, 249
Hack, Peter, 250
Hacker, Henry, 250
Hackett, Capt. Thomas, 250
Haeger, John H., 250
Hairston, Samuel, 250
Hakluyt, Rev. Richard, 12
Hall, Robert, 250
    Thomas, 250
Ham, Jeremy, 250
Hamerton, Edward, 250
Hamilton, Andrew, 250
    George, 56
    James, 250
    James, 251
Hamlin, John, 250
    Stephen, 250
Hammond, John, 251
    Mainwaring, 126
Hamor, Thomas, 251
    Ralph, 81
Hardiman, Francis, 251
    John, 251
Hardwick, William, 251
Hardy, George, 251
Hariot, Thomas, 16
Harlowe, John, 252
Harmanson, George, 252
    John, 252
    Matthew, 252
    Thomas, 252

Thomas (emigrant), 252
Harmer, Ambrose, 110
    Charles, 252
    John, 252
Harris, John, 252
    John (emigrant), 252
    Richard, 252
    Robert, 252
    Capt. Thomas, 252
    William, 252
    William S., 253
Harrison, Benjamin, 146
    Benjamin (1635), 253
    Benjamin (Charles City Co.), 253
    Benjamin (1673), 253
    Burr, 253
    Lieut. George, 253
    Henry, 155
    Dr. Jeremiah, 253
    Nathaniel, 152
    Thomas, 253
    Thomas, Jr., 253
    William, 253
Hartwell, Henry, 144
    William, 253
Harvey, Sir John, 45
    Sir John, 102
Harwood, Col. Edward, 254
    Humphrey, 254
    Joseph, 254
    Samuel, 254
    Samuel, Jr., 254
    Maj. Samuel, 254
    Thomas, 118
    William, 87
    William (1712), 254
    William (1742), 254
Hatcher, William, 254
Haviland, Anthony, 254
Hawkins, John, 255
    Sir John, 8
    Capt. Thomas, 255
    Maj. Thomas, 255
    *William, 8
Hawley, Jerome, 107
Hay, Anthony, 255
    Dr. Peter, 255
    John, 255
    Peter, 255
    William (emigrant), 255
    William, York Co., 255

Haynes, Thomas, 255
Haynie, John, 255
    Richard, 255
Hayrick, Thomas, 256
Hayward, Samuel, 256
Heale, George, York Co., 256
    George, Lancaster Co., 256
Hedgman, Peter, 256
Heley, Willis, 256
Henley, Rev. Samuel, 256
Henry VII., 7
Herbert, John, 256
Herrick, Henry, 257
    Thomas, 257
Hethersall, Thomas, 257
Heyman, Peter, 257
Heyrick, Henry, 256
Heyward, John, 257
Hickman, Richard, 257
Higginson, Humphrey, 112
    Capt. Robert, 257
Hill, Edward, 257
    Edward, Jr., 141
    Edward, Sr., 119
    Humphrey, 257
    John, 257
    Nicholas, 258
    Thomas, 258
Hinton, Thomas, 103
Hite, Abraham, 258
    Isaac, 258
    John, 258
    Jost, 258
    Thomas, 258
Hobbs, Francis, 258
Hobson, John, 108
    Thomas, 258
Hockaday, William, New Kent Co., 258
    William, York Co., 258
Hoddin (Hodin), John, 258
Hodges, Thomas, 258
Hoggard, Nathaniel, 259
Holecroft, Thomas, Capt., 259
Holiday, Anthony, 259
Holladay, Anthony, 259
Holland, Gabriel, 259
Hollier, Simon, 259
Holloway, John, 259
Hollows, John, 259
Holman, James, 259

INDEX

Holmwood, John, 259
Holt, James, 259
   John, 260
   Robert, 260
   Thomas, 260
Holtzclaw, Jacob, 260
Hone, Maj. Theophilus, 260
Honeywood, Philip, 260
Hooe, Rice, Charles City Co., 260
   Rice, Stafford Co., 260
Hooke, Francis, 105
Hope, George, 260
Hornby, Daniel, 260
Horrocks, Rev. James, 163
Horsey, Stephen, 261
Horsmanden, Warham, 122
Hoskins, Anthony, 261
   Bartholomew, 261
Hough, Francis, 261
Howard, Allen, 261
   Benjamin, 261
   Francis, 53
Howe, John, 261
Hubbard, Robert, 261
Huddleston, John, 261
Hull, Peter, 261
   Richard, 261
Hume, George, 261
Hunt, William, 262
Hunter, Col. Robert, 50
   William, Editor, 262
   William, Nansemond Co., 262
Hutchings, John, 262
   John, Jr., 262
   Joseph, 262
Hutchinson, Capt. Robert, 262
Hutchison, William, 262
Hutt, Daniel, 262
Hyde, Robert, 262
Ingles, Mungo, 263
Ingram, Joseph, 263
Innes, Hugh, 263
Innis, Henry, 263
Irvine, Alexander, 263
Isham, Henry, 263
Iverson, Abraham, 263
Jackson, Rev. Andrew, 263
   John, 263
   Joseph, 264
   Robert, 264

James VI., 17
Jaquelin, Edward, 264
Jarrell, Thomas, 264
Jefferson, John, 264
   Peter, 264
Jeffreys, Herbert, 49
Jenings, Edmund, 46
   Edmund, Prov. Sec., 264
   Edmund, 264
   Peter, 131
   Peter, 265
Jenkins, Henry, 264
Jennings, John, 265
Jerdone, Francis, 265
Johnson, Jacob, 265
   John, 265
   Joseph, 265
   Rev. Josiah, 265
   Philip, 265
   Richard, 146
   Richard, 265
   Thomas, King William Co., 265
   Thomas, Louisa Co., 266
   Thomas, Northampton Co., 266
   William, Spottsylvania Co., 266
   William, Coroner, 266
Johnston, Andrew, 266
   George, 266
   Peter, 266
   William, 266
Jones, Anthony, 266
   Cadwallader, 267
   Rev. Emmanuel, 267
   Emmanuel, Jr., 267
   Gabriel, 267
   Hugh, Rev., 267
   John, 267
   Orlando, 268
   Rev. Owen, 268
   Peter, 268
   Rice, 268
   Richard, 268
   Robert, Royalist, 268
   Robert, Surry Co., 268
   Robert, Southampton Co., 268
   Robert, Essex Co., 268
   Roger, 268
   Rev. Rowland, 268

   Thomas, 269
   William, Northampton Co., 269
   William, Northumberland Co., 269
   Wood, 269
Jordan, Col. George, 269
   John, 269
   Richard, 269
   Samuel, Buckingham Co., 269
   Samuel, (Jordan's Jorney), 269
   Thomas, 269
Julian, William, 270
Justice, Ralph, 270
Kecatough (Catataugh), 270
Keeling, William, 270
Keeton, John, 270
Keith, George, 270
   James, Hampshire, 270
   James, Fauquier Co., 270
Kemp, Edmund, 270
   Matthew, 138
   Matthew, Middlesex Co., 270
   Matthew, Jr., 270
   Richard, 47
Kempe, William, 271
Kemper, John, 271
Kendall, John, 271
   George, 77
   William, Northampton Co., 271
   William, Jr., 271
Kenner, Richard, 271
   Rodham, Northumberland Co., 271
   Rodham, Signer, 271
Kennon, Richard, Henrico Co., 271
   Richard, Charles City Co., 272
   William, 272
Keppel, William A., 61
Key, Thomas, 272
King, Henry, 272
Kingsmill, Richard, 272
Kingston, Thomas, 272
Kingswell, Edward, 272
Kippax, Rev. Peter, 272
Klug, George S., 273
   Samuel, 273

INDEX

Knight, Nathaniel, 273
    Capt. Peter, 273
Knott, James, 273
La Guarde, Elias, 273
Lamb, Anthony, 273
Lambert, Thomas, 273
Landon, Thomas, 273
Lane, Capt. John, 273
    Capt. Ralph, 16
Langbourne, William, 274
Langhorne, John, 274
Langley, Ralph, 274
    William, 274
Lanier, John, 274
Langston, Anthony, 274
Lankford, Benjamin, 274
Lapworth, Michael, 92
Latane, Rev. Lewis, 274
Lawne, Capt. Christopher, 274
Lawrence, Rev. John, 274
Lawson, Anthony, Lower Norfolk Co., 275
    Anthony, Princess Anne Co., 275
    Rowland, 275
Laydon, John, 275
    Virginia, 275
Lear, John, 139
    John, 275
Lederer, John, 275
Lee, George, 276
    Hancock, 276
    Henry, 276
    Dr. Henry, 276
    John, 276
    Philip L., 162
    Richard, 116
    Richard, 276
    Richard, Jr., 134
    Thomas, 63
    Thomas, 156
    William, 276
Leech, Mr., 95
LeGrand, Peter, 277
Leigh, Francis, 135
    William, 277
Lewis, Andrew, 277
    Charles, 277
    Fielding, 277
    John, Jr., 157
    John, Sr., 149
    John, Augusta Co., 277

John, Halifax Co., 277
    Robert, 278
    Thomas, 278
    William, 278
    Zachary, 278
Lightfoot, John, 144
    Philip, 156
    William, 278
Lindsay, David, 278
Lister, Thomas, 278
    William, 278
Littlepage, Col. James, 278
    Richard, 279
Littleton, Nathaniel, 110
Livingston, William, 279
Llewellyn, Daniel, 279
Lloyd, Cornelius, 279
    Edward, 279
    John, 279
    Thomas, 279
    William, 279
Lobb, George, 279
Lockey, Edward, 279
Lomax, Lunsford, 280
Lord, John, 280
Loving, Thomas, 280
Lovelace, Col. Francis, 280
Lucas, Thomas, 280
Luddington, William, 280
Ludlow, George, 113
    Thomas, 280
Ludwell, Philip, 145
    Philip, Jr., 147
    Philip (3d), 160
    Thomas, 126
Luke, George, 281
Lunsford, Sir Thomas, 115
Lupo, Lieut. Albino, 281
Lyddall, Capt. John, 281
Lyde, Cornelius, 281
Lynch, Charles, 281
Lyne, George, 281
    William, 281
Mace, Samuel, 17
Mackie, Josias, 281
Macklin, Frederick, 281
Macock, Samuel, 94
Macon, Gideon, 281
    William, New Kent Co., 282
    William, Hanover Co., 282
Madison, Isaac, 92

James, 282
John, 282
Major, Edward, 282
Makemie, Francis, 282
Mallory, Philip, 282
    Roger, 283
    Thomas, 283
Mann, John, 283
Mansell (Mansfield), David, 283
Marable, George, 283
    Matthew, 283
    William, 283
Marot, Jean, 283
Marshall, John, 283
    Capt. Roger, 284
    Thomas, Fauquier Co., 284
    Capt. William, 284
Marshart, Michael, 284
Martian (Martue), Nicholas, 284
Martin, John, 77
    Col. John, 284
    John, 285
    Richard, 27
    Thomas B., 285
Marye, Rev. James, 285
    Peter, 285
Mason, David, 285
    Lieut. Francis, 285
    Francis, 285
    George, Stafford Co., 286
    Col. George, 286
    James, 286
    Col. Lemuel, 286
    Thomas, 286
Massie, Thomas, 286
    William, 286
Mathew, Thomas, 286
Mathews, Samuel, 48
    Samuel, Jr., 119
Matthews, George, 287
Maury, James, 287
    Matthew, 287
    Walker, 287
Mayo, John, 287
    William, 287
McCarty, Charles, 288
    Daniel, 288
    Daniel, Jr., 288
McDowell, Samuel, 288
McKenzie, Dr. Kenneth, 288

382

INDEX

Mead, William, 288
Meade, Andrew, 288
    David, Nansemond Co., 289
    David, "Chaumiere des Prairies," 289
    Richard K., 289
Meares, Thomas, 289
Meese, Henry, 136
Melling, William, 289
Menifie, George, 104
Mercer, George, 289
    James, 289
    John, 290
    John F., 290
Meredith, Samuel, 290
Meriwether, Francis, 290
    Nicholas, New Kent Co., 290
    Nicholas, Island House, 291
    William, 291
Metcalfe, Thomas, 291
    Richard, 291
Meux, John, 291
Middleton, David, 87
Milner, Francis, 291
    George, 291
    Col. Thomas, 291
    Thomas, Nansemond Co., 291
Minge, James, 291
Minor, Doodes, 292
Miller (Muller) Adam, 292
Mitchell, John, 292
    Richard, 292
    Robert, 292
Mitchell (Michell), William, 292
Molesworth, Col. Guy, 292
Monroe, Andrew, 293
    Andrew, 293
    Andrew, 293
Montague, James, 293
    Peter, 293
Moody, Sir Henry, 293
Moon, Capt. John, 293
Moore, Augustine, "Chelsea," 294
    Augustine, King William Co., 294
    Bernard, 294
Morgan, Francis, 294

Morgan, 294
Morlatt (Morlet), Thomas, 294
Morley, William, 294
*Morrison, Francis, 118
Morrison (Moryson), Richard, 111
*Moryson, Francis, 49
    Charles, 294
    Lieut. Robert, 294
Moseley, Arthur, 294
    Edward H., 294
    Edward, 295
    Edward H., Jr., 295
    William, 295
Mossom, Rev. David, 295
Mottrom, Col. John, 295
    John, Northumberland Co., 295
Moyses, Theodore, 295
Munford, Col. Robert, 295
    Robert, Jr., 296
    Robert, Brunswick Co., 296
Murray, John, 70
Nantaquas, 296
Nash, Abner, 296
    John, Prince Edward Co., 296
    John, Jr., 296
    Thomas, 296
Neale, Christopher, 296
    John, 296
    Richard, 297
Necottowance, 297
Needler, Benjamin, 297
Nelson, Capt. Francis, 297
    Thomas, 157
    Thomas, 297
    William, 70
    William, 157
Nemattenow, 297
Neville, Joseph, 297
Newce, Thomas, 85
    Sir William, 91
Newman, Alexander, 297
Newport, Christopher, 75
Newton, George, 297
    John, 297
    Thomas, 297
Nicholas, Maj. Abraham, 298
    Dr. George, 298

    John, 298
Nicholson, Sir Francis, 54
    Sir Francis, 142
Nimmo, James, 298
    William, 298
Norsworthy, Tristram, 298
Norton, John, 298
    Capt. William, 298
Norvell, William, 299
Norwood, Capt. Charles, 299
    Col. Henry, 299
Nott, Edward, 57
Nottingham, Benjamin, 299
Ogle, Cuthbert, 299
Oldis, Thomas, 299
Opechancanough, 299
Opie, Thomas, 299
Opitchapam, 299
Opussoquionuske, 299
Osborne, Edward, Jr., 299
    Jenkin, 300
    Richard, 300
    Capt. Thomas, 300
    Thomas, Prince William Co., 300
Ouldsworth, Mr., 94
Ousley, Capt. Thomas, 300
Owen, Goronwy, 300
Pace, Richard, 300
    Francis, 300
Page, John, 136
    John (North End), 164
    Mann, 152
    Matthew, 147
Pagett, Anthony, 300
Palmer, John, 301
    Thomas, 301
Panton (Penton), Anthony, 301
Paradise, John, 301
Parahunt, 301
Parke, Daniel, Jr., 143
    Daniel, Sr., 132
Parker, George, 301
    Richard, "Lawfield," 301
    Richard, Nansemond Co., 301
    Sacker, 302
Parkes, William, 302
Parramore, Thomas, 302
Pasteur, John, Dr., 302
    William, Dr., 302

INDEX

Pate, John, 131
　Richard, 302
Patton, James, 302
Paulett, Robert, 90
Pawlett (Paulett), Thomas, 112
Payne, Florentine, 302
　John, 302
　Josias, 303
Peachey, Samuel, 303
Pead, Rev. Duell, 303
Pecke, Thomas, 303
Peeine, William, 303
Peirce, William, 101
Peirse, Thomas, 303
Pelham, Peter, 303
Pendleton, Henry, 303
Pepiscumah, 303
Peppet, Lieut. Gilbert, 303
Percy, George, 35
Percy (Piercy), Abraham, 92
Perkins, Peter, 303
Perrin, Thomas, 303
Perrott, Richard, Middlesex Co., 303
　Richard, Jr., 304
Perry, Henry, 119
　Peter, 304
　William, 102
Peter, John, 304
Pettus, Thomas, 111
　Thomas, 304
Peyronie, William C., 304
Peyton, Francis, 304
　Henry, Prince William Co., 304
　Henry, Westmoreland Co., 304
　Robert, 304
　Valentine, Westmoreland Co., 304
　Valentine, Prince William Co., 305
Phelps, John, 305
Phenny, George, 155
Phettiplace, William, 305
　Michael, 305
Pilkington, William, 305
Pinkard, Capt. John, 305
Pitt, Robert, 143
Place, Rowland, 133
Pleasants, John, 305

Pocahontas, 305
Pochins, 306
Pole, David, 306
Pollard, Joseph, 306
Pollington, John, 306
Poole, Henry, 306
　Robert, 306
Pope, Nathaniel, 306
Popeley, Lieut. Richard, 306
Popleton (Popkton), William, 306
Porteus, Robert, 151
Portlock, William, 306
Pory, John, 84
Pott, Capt. Francis, 306
　*John, 44
　John, 92
Pountis, John, 87
Powell, John, Ancient Planter, 307
　John, Elizabeth City Co., 307
　John, Northampton Co., 307
　*Nathaniel, 42
　Nathaniel, 84
　Capt. William, 307
Power, James, 307
　Dr. John, 307
Powhatan, 307
Poythress, Francis, 307
　John, 308
　Peter, 308
Prentis, William, 308
Presley, Col. Peter, 308
　Peter, Northumberland Co., 308
　William, 308
　William, Northumberland Co., 308
Preston, William, Minister, 308
　William, Augusta Co., 308
Price, Arthur, 309
　Thomas, 309
　Walter, 309
Prince, Edward, 309
Pring, Martin, 18
Proctor, John, 309
Pryor, Capt. William, 309
Pugh, Daniel, 309
Purchas, Rev. Samuel, 29

Purdie, Alexander, 309
Purefoy, Thomas, 100
Pyland, James, 309
Quarry, Robert, 148
Quiney, Richard, 309
Raleigh, Sir Walter, 14
Ramsay, Patrick, 310
Ramsey, Capt. Edward, 310
　Thomas, 310
Randolph, Beverley, 310
　John, 310
　Henry, 310
　Isham, 310
　Sir John, 310
　Peter, 160
　Richard, Curls Neck, 311
　Richard, Henrico Co., 311
　Thomas, 311
　William, 155
　William, Henrico Co., 311
　William, Goochland Co., 311
　William, "Wilton,", 311
Ransone, Capt. James, 311
　Peter, 312
Ratcliffe, John, 33
Ravenscroft, Samuel, 312
　Thomas, 312
Read, Clement, 312
　Clement, Jr., 312
　Isaac, 312
Reade, George, 123
Revell, Randall, 313
Reynolds, Charles, 312
*Rich, Sir Nathaniel, 25
　Sir Robert, 25
Richards, Richard, 313
Richardson, James, 313
　Richard, 313
Ricketts, James, 313
Riddick (Reddick), James, 313
　Lemuel, 313
　Willis, 313
Ridley, Peter, 313
Rind, William, 313
Ring, Joseph, 313
Roane, Charles, 313
　William, 314
Robertson, Archibald, 314

INDEX

Moses, 314
William, 314
Robins, John, 314
Obedience, 121
Robinson, Col. Beverley, 314
Christopher, 142
Christopher, 314
Henry, 314
John, 63
John, 153
John, 315
Mary, Mrs., 315
Peter, 315
Col. Tully, 315
William, "Bunker Hill," 316
William, King George Co., 316
William, Norfolk Co., 316
Rev. William, 162
Rogers, John, 316
Richard, 316
Rolfe, John, 82
Rookins, William, 316
Rootes, Col. George, 317
John, 317
Col. Philip, 317
Maj. Philip, 317
Thomas R., 317
Roper, William, 317
Roscow, James, 316
William, "Blunt Point," 316
William, Warwick Co., 316
Rossingham, Edmund, Ensign, 317
Rowleston, Lyonell, 317
Royle, Joseph, 317
Rozier, John, Rev., 317
Ruffin, John, "Mayfield," 318
John, Surry Co., 318
Robert, 318
Russell, Richard, 318
Dr. Walter, 318
Rutherford, Robert, 318
Thomas, 318
Sackville, Sir Edward, 29
Sadler, John, 318
Rowland, 318
Salford, John, 318
Robert, 318
Salmon, Joseph, 318

Sandys, David, 318
Sir Edwin, 20
George, 89
Sanford, Samuel, 318
Saunders, John H., 319
Jonathan, 319
Roger, 319
Savage, Capt. John, 319
Col. Littleton, 319
Nathaniel L., 319
Thomas, 319
Savin, Robert, 319
Sayer, Francis, 319
Scarborough, Charles, 142
Scarburgh, Col. Edmund, 319
Capt. Edmund, Accomac Co., 320
Col. Edmund, Northampton Co., 320
Henry, Jr., 320
Scarlett, Capt. Martin, 320
Sclater, Rev. James, 320
Scotchmore, Robert, 320
Scott, Alexander, 320
Edward, 320
James, Stafford Co., 320
Scrivener, Mathew, 34
Matthew, 79
James, Fauquier Co., 320
John, 320
Samuel, 320
Thomas, 321
Seawell, Henry, 321
Sedgwick, William, 321
Selden, James, 321
Richard, 321
Samuel, 321
Rev. William, 321
Semple, James, 321
John, 321
Robert B., 321
Servant, Bertram (Bertrand), 322
Seward, John, 322
Sharpe, Samuel, 322
Rev. Thomas, 322
Sharples, Edward, 322
Sheild, Robert, 322
Rev. Samuel, 322
Shelley, Walter, 322
Shephard (Shepherd), Robert, 323
Shepherd, John, 323

Sheppard, John, 323
Thomas, 323
Sherman, Michael, 323
Sherwood, Grace, 323
William, 323
Shields, James, 323
*Sibsey (Sipsey), John, 108
Sidney, John, 323
Simmons, John, 323
Simpson, Southey, 324
Skaife, Rev. John, 324
Skelton, Reuben, 324
Skipwith, Sir Grey, 324
Skyren, Henry, 324
Slaughter, Francis, 324
Robert, 324
Thomas, 324
Small, Dr. William, 325
Smith, Arthur, Isle of Wight Co., 325
Col. Arthur, 325
Arthur, Jr., 325
Rev. Charles J., 325
Francis, 325
Rev. Guy, 326
John, 76
John, 149
John (4th Prest.), 34
Lieut. Col. John, 326
Maj. John, 326
John, Goochland Co., 326
John, Middlesex Co., 326
Joseph, 326
Lawrence, Gloucester Co., 326
Lawrence, York Co., 326
Lawrence, Yorktown, 326
Nicholas, Isle of Wight Co., 327
Nicholas, King George Co., 327
Nicholas, vestryman, 327
Robert, 128
Rev. Thomas, 327
Toby, 327
*Smith (Smyth), John (antiquary), 27
Sir Thomas, 19
Smyth, John, 327
Soane, Henry, 327
Henry, Jr., 327
William, 327

INDEX

Somers, Sir George, 79
Somerville, James, 327
Southcoat, Capt. Thomas, 328
Southern, John, 328
Span, Cuthbert, 328
Sparrow, Charles, 328
Speed, James, 328
Speke, Thomas, 328
Spelman (Spilman), Henry, 328
Spence, Alexander, 328
Spencer, Nicholas, 53
 Nicholas, 131
 Capt. Robert, 328
Spencer (Spence), William, 329
Spicer, Arthur, 329
Spilman, Thomas, 329
Spotswood, Alexander, 58
 John, 329
Spratt, Henry, 329
Squire, Rev. Richard, 329
Stacy, Robert, 329
Stagg, Charles, 329
Stalnaker, Samuel, 329
Stanard, William, 329
Stanup, John, 330
Starke, Bolling, 330
 John, 330
 Richard, 330
 William, 330
Stegg (Stagg), Thomas, 114
Stegg, Thomas, Jr., 129
Stephens, George, 330
 Maj. Philip, 330
 Richard, 99
Stith, Drury, Brunswick Co., 330
 Drury, Charles City Co., 330
 Drury, surveyor, 330
 John, 331
 John, 331
 John, Charles City Co., 331
 Richard, 331
 Thomas, 331
 William, 331
Stobo, Robert, 331
Stockden (Stockton), Rev. Jonas, 332
Stoever, John C., 332
Stokes, Christopher, 332

Stone, Capt. William, 332
Stoner, John, 104
Story, Joshua, 332
Stoughton, Samuel, 333
Stover, Jacob, 333
Strachey, Dr. John, 333
 William, 81
Strafferton, Mr., 333
Stratton, Joseph, 333
Streeter, Capt. Edward, 333
Stretchley, John, 333
Stringer, John, 333
Strother, French, 333
 William, 333
Stuart, John, 333
Stubblefield, George, 333
Studley, Thomas, 333
Sullivan, Daniel, 333
Sully, Thomas, 334
Swann, Alexander, 334
 Col. Samuel, 334
 Thomas, 125
 Capt. Thomas, 334
 William, 334
Swearingen, Thomas, 334
Sweeney (Swinney), Meritt, 334
Sykes, Bernard, 334
Syme, John, Hanover Co., 334
 John, Jr., 334
Symonds, Rev. William, 20
Syms, Benjamin, 335
Tabb, Edward, 335
 Humphrey, 335
 John, 335
 Thomas, 335
Taberer, Thomas, 335
Talbot, John, 335
Taliaferro, John, 336
 Walker, 336
 William, 336
Talman, Capt. Henry, 336
Tarleton, Stephen, 336
Tarpley, James, 336
Tatem, John, 336
Tayloe, John, 156
 John, Jr., 164
 William, 336
Taylor (Tayloe), William, 117
Taylor, Rev. Daniel, 336
 Rev. Daniel, Jr., 336

 Ethelred, 337
 George, Orange Co., 337
 George, Richmond Co., 337
 Henry, 337
 James, 337
 John, 337
 Philip, 337
 Thomas, 337
 William, 338
 William, Lunenburg Co., 337
 William, Southampton Co., 338
Teach, Edward, 186
Teackle, John, 338
 Rev. Thomas, 338
Tebbs, Foushee, 338
Temple, Joseph, 338
 Peter, 338
Tennant, Dr. John, 338
Terrell, Richmond, 338
 Robert, 338
Terry, Nathaniel, 339
Thacker, Edwin, 339
Thelaball, James, 339
Thomas, Cornelius, 339
 William, 339
Thompson, Andrew, 339
 George, 339
 John, 339
 Maurice, 339
 Samuel, 340
 Rev. William, 340
 William, 340
Thomson, Stevens, 339
Thornbury, Thomas, 340
Thornton, Sir Charles W., 340
 Francis, 340
 George, 340
 Col. John; 340
 John, New Kent Co., 341
 Peter P., 341
 Presley, 162
 William, King George Co., 341
 William, Brunswick Co., 341
Thorowgood, Adam, 105
 Adam, 341
 Adam, 341
 John, 341

INDEX

John, 341
Thorpe, George, 86
  Maj. Otho, 341
Throckmorton, Gabriel, 342
  Robert, 342
Thruston, Charles M., 342
  Edward, Dr., 342
  Malachy, 342
Tillyard, Rev. Arthur, 342
Timson, Samuel, 343
Tindall (Tyndall), Robert, 343
Todd, Thomas, 343
Todkill, Anas, 343
Tomkies, Charles, Dr., 343
Tompkins, Christopher, 343
  Humphrey, 343
Tonge, John, 343
Tooke, Henry, 343
Totopotomoy, 343
Towles, Henry, 344
Townsend, Richard, 106
Tracy, William, 87
Trahorne, John, 344
Travers, Raleigh, 344
  Samuel, 344
  Col. William, 344
Travis, Champion, 344
  Edward, 344
  Edward C., 344
Tree, Richard, 344
Trent, Alexander, 344
Trigg, Stephen, 345
Trussell, John, 345
  Daniel, 85
Tucker, Robert, 345
  Robert, 345
  Col. Robert, 345
  William, 93
Tuke (Took), James, 345
Tunstall, Edward, 345
  Col. Richard, 345
Turberville, John, 345
Turner, Harry, 345
  Thomas, 346
Twine, John, 346
Tyler, Charles, 346
  Henry, 346
  Henry, Jr., 346
  John, 346
  Richard, 346
  William, 347

Underwood, Maj. William, 347
Upshaw, John, 347
Upshur, Arthur, 347
Upton, Capt. John, 347
Utie, John, 93
Uttamatomakkin, 347
Van Metre, John, 347
  Isaac, 347
Vaulx, Robert, 347
Veale, George, 347
Venable, Abraham, 347
  Nathaniel, 348
Waddell, James, 348
Wadding, Rev. James, 348
Wade, Armiger, 348
  Robert, 348
Wagener, Rev. Peter, 348
  Peter, Jr., 349
Waher, William, 349
Waldo, Richard, 79
Walke, Col. Anthony, 349
  Anthony, Jr., 349
  Thomas, 349
Walker, George, 349
  James, 349
  John, 14
  John, 124
  John, King and Queen Co., 349
  John, Middlesex Co., 349
  Peter, 349
  Thomas, Dr., 349
  Thomas, King and Queen Co., 350
Walklett, Gregory, 350
Wall, John, 350
Wallace, Rev. James, 350
  James, Elizabeth City Co., 351
  Dr. Michael, 351
Waller, Benjamin, 351
  John, 351
  William, 351
Wallings, George, 351
Walsingham, Sir Francis, 8
Walthoe, Nathaniel, 351
Walton, Isaac R., 351
Ward, Seth, Henrico Co., 351
  Seth, "Powhatan Tree," 352
Ware, Rev. Jacob, 352
Wareham, Thomas, 352

Waring, Francis, 352
  Thomas, 352
Warne, Thomas, 352
Warner, Augustine, 124
  Augustine, Jr., 135
Warnet, Thomas, 352
Warren, Thomas, 352
Washbourn, John, 352
Washer, Ensign, 352
Washington, Augustine, 352
  Col. John, 352
  John, Surry Co., 353
  Lawrence, Fairfax Co., 353
  Lawrence, merchant, 353
Waters, Edward, 353
  William, Jr., 354
  William, Northampton Co., 354
Watkins, Benjamin, 354
  Henry, 354
  Micajah, 354
Watson, Abraham, 354
  Joseph, 354
Watts, Matthew, 354
Waugh, James, 354
  Rev. John, 354
  John, 354
Wayles, John, 354
Webb, George, 354
  Giles, 354
  Lewis, 355
  Stephen, 355
  Wingfield, 355
Webster, Richard, 355
  Roger, 355
Weekes, Abraham, 355
Weir (Weyer), Maj. John, 355
Welbourn, Thomas, 355
Weldon, Poynes, 355
Wellford, Dr. Robert, 355
Wells, Richard, 356
West, Anthony, 356
  Francis, 44
  *Francis (dep. gov.), 79
  Francis, 356
  Henry, 356
  Hugh, 356
  Hugh, Jr., 356
  John, 102
  John, 356
  Capt. John, 45

INDEX

Col. John, 356
Lieut. Col. John, 356
Thomas (Lord Delaware), 38
*Thomas, 38
Thomas, 357
Capt. Thomas, 357
William, 357
Westcomb, James, 357
Westhrope, John, 357
Westwood, William, 357
Worlich, 357
Wetherall, Robert, 357
Wetherburn, Henry, 357
Weyman, Sir Ferdinando, 80
Weymouth, George, 18
Whaley, James, 357
Mary, 357
Thomas, 358
Whateley (Wheatley), Rev. Solomon, 358
Whitaker, Alexander, 358
Jabez, 95
Dr. Walter, 358
William, 125
William, 358
Whitby, William, 358
White, John, 358
Capt. John, 17
Rev. William, 358
Whitehead, Philip, 359
Whiting, Beverley, 359
Henry, 141
Thomas, 359
Whittaker, Richard, 358
Wickham, William, 95
Wickliffe, David, 359
Wilford, Thomas, 359
Wilkins, John, 359
Wilkinson, John, 359
William, 359
Rev. William, 359
Willcox, Capt. John, 359
Capt. John, Nansemond Co., 360
Williams, Dr. Robert, 360
Williamson, Dr. James, 360
Willis, Francis, 124

Col. Francis, 360
Col. Henry, 360
John, 360
Willoughby, John, 360
Thomas, 109
Thomas, 360
Wills, John S., 361
Miles, 361
Wilson, James, 361
Rev. John, 361
John, Augusta Co., 361
John, Norfolk Co., 361
William, 361
Willis, Elizabeth City Co., 361
Willis, Norfolk Co., 361
Windham, Edward, 361
Windmill, Christopher, 361
Wingate, Roger, 111
Wingfield, Edward M., 33
Edward M., 76
Winn, John, 361
Winston, Anthony, 362
Wise, John, 362
Withers, Capt. John, 362
Wolstenholme, Sir John, 26
Wood, Abraham, 122
Henry, 362
James, 362
Percival, 362
Valentine, 362
Woodbridge, William, 362
Woodhouse, Henry, Gov. of Bermuda, 362
Henry, Lower Norfolk Co., 363
Horatio, 363
Woodlief, Capt. John, 363
Woodson, Col. John, 363
Woodward, Christopher, 363
Christopher, 363
Thomas, 363
Woory, Joseph, 363
Worleigh, George, 363
Worlich (Worledge, Woolritch), William, 364
Wormeley, Christopher, 106
Christopher, 139

*Ralph, 110
Ralph (2d), 142
Ralph, 143
Ralph (3d), 164
Ralph, 364
Wotton, Thomas, 364
Wowinchopunka, 364
Wright, Christopher, 364
John, 364
Robert, 364
William, 364
Wriothesley, Henry, 22
Wroth, Sir Thomas, 26
Wyatt, Anthony, 364
Dudley, Sir, 364
Sir Francis, 42
Sir Francis, 113
Wyatt (Wiatt), Rev. Hawte, 364
Wyche, Henry, 365
Wynne (Winn), Joshua, 365
Peter, 79
Capt. Robert, 365
Wythe, Thomas, 365
Yancey, Robert, 365
Yardley, Francis, 365
George, 39
Yates, Rev. Bartholomew, 365
Rev. Bartholomew, Jr., 366
Rev. Robert, Gloucester Co., 366
Rev. Robert, Middlesex Co., 366
Rev. William, 366
Yeardley, Argall, 111
*Sir George, 84
Yeo, Hugh, 366
Leonard, 366
Young, Capt. Thomas, 366
Thomas, James City Co., 366
William, 367
Yowell (Youell), Capt. Thomas, 367
Zane, Isaac, 367
Zouch, Sir John, 367

Printed in U. S. A.

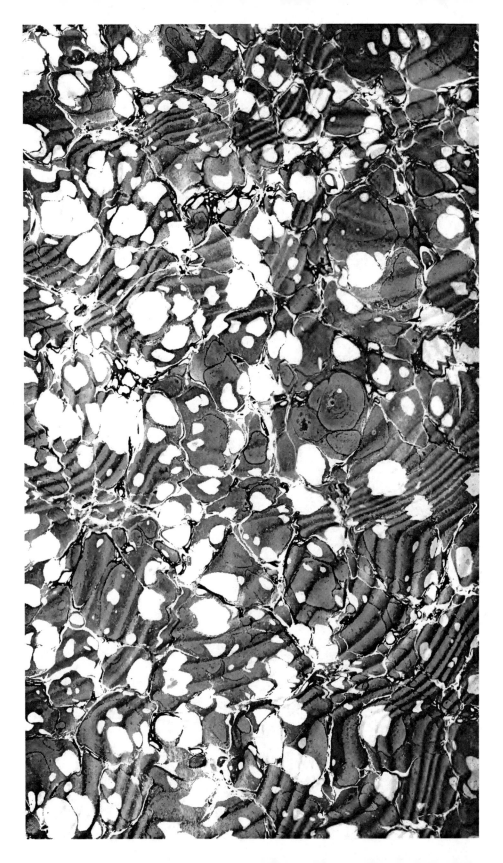

ImTheStory.com

Personalized Classic Books in many genre's
Unique gift for kids, partners, friends, colleagues
Customize:
- Character Names
- Upload your own front/back cover images (optional)
- Inscribe a personal message/dedication on the inside page (optional)

Customize many titles Including
- Alice in Wonderland
- Romeo and Juliet
- The Wizard of Oz
- A Christmas Carol
- Dracula
- Dr. Jekyll & Mr. Hyde
- And more...